Contents

8   STATUTORY EMPLOYMENT PROTECTIONS   209

9   PROTECTION FROM DISCRIMINATION: INTRODUCTION (THE EQUALITY ACT 2010)   247

CONTENTS

13 PROTECTION FROM DISCRIMINATION (4) DISABILITY DISCRIMINATION — 343

14 PROTECTION FROM DISCRIMINATION (5) RECENT DEVELOPMENTS IN DISCRIMINATION LAW — 365

CONTENTS

CONTENTS

Guide to the book

Unlocking the Law books bring together all the essential elements for today's law students in a clearly defined and memorable way. Each book is enhanced with learning features to reinforce understanding of key topics and test your knowledge along the way. Follow this guide to make sure you get the most from reading this book.

AIMS AND OBJECTIVES

Defines what you will learn in each chapter.

definition

Find key legal terminology at a glance

SECTION

Highlights sections from Acts.

ARTICLE

Defines Articles of the EC Treaty or of the European Convention on Human Rights or other Treaty.

tutor tip

Provides key ideas from lecturers on how to get ahead

CLAUSE

Shows a Bill going through Parliament or a draft Bill proposed by the Law Commission.

REGULATION

Defines a provision in a statutory instrument.

CASE EXAMPLE

 Illustrates the law in action.

JUDGMENT

Provides extracts from judgments on cases.

QUOTATION

Encourages you to engage with primary sources.

ACTIVITY

Enables you to test yourself as you progress through the chapter.

student mentor tip

Offers advice from law graduates on the best way to achieve the results you want

SAMPLE ESSAY QUESTIONS

Provide you with real-life sample essays and show you the best way to plan your answer.

SUMMARY

Concludes each chapter to reinforce learning.

Acknowledgements

The books in the Unlocking the Law series are a departure from traditional law texts and represent one view of a type of learning resource that the editors always felt is particularly useful to students. The success of the series and the fact that many of its features have been subsequently emulated in other publications must surely vindicate that view. The series editors would therefore like to thank the original publishers, Hodder Education, for their support in making the original project a successful reality. In particular we would like to thank Alexia Chan for showing great faith in the project and for her help in getting the series off the ground. We would also like to thank the current publisher, Routledge, for the warm enthusiasm it has shown in taking over the series. In this respect we must also thank Fiona Briden, Senior Publisher, for her commitment and enthusiasm towards the series and for her support.

This book is dedicated to James Arthur Turner (Jim), 12 April 1909 to 16 September 1976, and Peter Arthur Turner (Pete), 8 December 1940 to 4 January 1973.

Preface

The 'Unlocking the Law' series on its creation was hailed as an entirely new style of undergraduate law textbooks and many of its groundbreaking features have subsequently been emulated in other publications. However, many student texts are still very prose dense and have little in the way of interactive materials to help a student feel his or her way through the course of study on a given module.

The purpose of the series has always been to try to make learning each subject area more accessible by focusing on actual learning needs, and by providing a range of different supporting materials and features.

All topic areas are broken up into manageable sections with a logical progression and extensive use of headings and numerous sub-headings as well as an extensive contents list and index. Each book in the series also contains a variety of flow charts, diagrams, key facts charts and summaries to reinforce the information in the body of the text. Diagrams and flow charts are particularly useful because they can provide a quick and easy understanding of the key points, especially when revising for examinations. Key facts charts not only provide a quick visual guide through the subject but are also useful for revision.

Many cases are separated out for easy access and all cases have full citation in the text as well as the table of cases for easy reference. The emphasis of the series is on depth of understanding much more than breadth of detail. For this reason each text also includes key extracts from judgments where appropriate. Quotations from academic comment in journal articles and leading texts are also included to give some insight into the academic debate on complex or controversial areas. In both cases these are highlighted and removed from the body of the text.

Finally the books also include much formative 'self-testing', with a variety of activities ranging through subject specific comprehension, application of the law and a range of other activities to help the student gain a good idea of his or her progress in the course. Appendices with guides on completing essay style questions and legal problem solving supplement and support this interactivity. Besides this a sample essay plan is added at the end of most chapters.

A feature of the most recent editions is the inclusion of some case extracts from the actual law reports which not only provide more detail on some of the important cases but also help to support students in their use of law reports by providing a simple commentary and also activities to cement understanding.

Employment law is a massive area and relevant to a much larger readership than many areas of law. Many students on vocational courses such as HND/HNC and professional courses such as CIPD are called on to study discrete areas of employment law. Besides this of course the law is important to all those who are themselves employed, those who employ and all those who advise either employers or employees. Employment law is also an exciting area because it constantly changes and is a mix of common law and statutory principles as well as being heavily influenced by EU law. It is also a contentious area since there is continuous political input in statute which reflects the attitudes of the government of the day.

The book is designed to cover all of the main topic areas on undergraduate and professional employment law syllabuses and to help provide a full understanding of each.

I hope that you will gain as much enjoyment in reading about employment law, and testing your understanding with the various activities in the book as I have had in writing it, and that you gain much enjoyment and interest from your study of the law.

The law is stated as I believe it to be on 1 April 2013.

List of figures

Table of cases

European Court of Human Rights

INTERNATIONAL
United States

Table of statutes and other instruments

TABLE OF STATUTES AND OTHER INSTRUMENTS

Table of legislation

TABLE OF LEGISLATION

xlviii

TABLE OF LEGISLATION

Table of EU Treaty Articles and legislation

Secondary legislation

Directives listed in numerical order

1

The origins of modern employment law

AIMS AND OBJECTIVES

After reading this chapter you should be able to:

▮ Understand where regulation of employment practices originated

▮ Understand the very different patterns of work that emerged with the growth of industrialism

▮ Understand how and why as a result more specific regulation developed in the wake of the Industrial Revolution both by statute and through the common law

▮ Understand how and why employment protection through legislation emerged in the twentieth century

▮ Understand the reasons for advances and reductions in employment rights in the modern employment context

▮ Be able to critically appreciate the historical development of laws on employment

1.1 The origins of the regulation of employment

It would be easy to imagine that employment law is a very modern development in the legal system of the UK, perhaps a development out of the welfare reforms of the 1940s or resulting from the strength of the trade unions in the 1960s and 1970s and the additional protections given to a range of groups including consumers during that time as well as employees.

This would be a reasonable mistake to make but nevertheless it is to ignore the historical development of regulation of employment.

Legal regulation of employment in fact goes back as far as the so-called Statute of Labourers in 1349. Obviously the medieval guilds (in some ways the forerunners of the modern trade unions) had a major impact on the regulation of employment practices also. However, these were internal regulation of specific trades, concerned apprenticeships, methods of work and trading and were often protectionist in nature but not specifically reinforced by law.

The major regulation of employment or work prior to the onset of industrialism in the eighteenth century was the Statute of Artificers and Apprentices 1562.

1.1.1 The Statute of Artificers and Apprentices 1562

The statute (subtitled 'An Act touching divers Orders for Artificers, Labourers, Servants of Husbandry and Apprentices' – itself a comprehensive description) was a comprehensive piece of legislation which in section 1 repeals all previous law on the subject. S1 also identifies the aim of the legislation:

SECTION

'S1 [it will] banish idleness, advance husbandry and yield unto the hired person both in the Time of Scarcity and in the Time of Plenty, a convenient Proportion of wages.'

Section 3 demonstrates just how comprehensive the legislation was in terms of whom it affected when considered in the context of the available areas of work at the time.

SECTION

'S3 Clothiers, Woollen Cloth Weavers, Tuckers, Fullers, Clothworkers, Sheremen, Dyers, Hosiers, Taylors, Shoemakers, Tanners, Cappers, Hatmakers, Pewterers, Bakers, Brewers, Glovers, Cutlers, Smiths, Farriers, Curriers, Saddlers, Spurriers, Turners, Feltmakers, Bowyers, Fletchers, Arrow-head makers, Butchers, Cooks or Millers.'

Although we may not recognise many of these trades today, the list does cover most of the trades that would have been operating at that time. Several trades at the start of the list represent the sixteenth century woollen and clothing industry which was the main export income of the time.

Even then the Act goes on to state that it should be used as the 'standard means of regulating all forms of employment' at the time, so it was a truly comprehensive piece of legislation.

Section 4 goes on to state that all people capable of working and not sustained by independent means, in other words having no private wealth or income, could be compelled to work by an independent order of two Justices of the Peace (the forerunner of the modern magistrates). In this way it was a massively different attitude to work compared to our present day welfare state.

Further provisions found in sections 5–8 bind servants to their masters so that no master could 'put away' his servant and nor could a servant leave his work until it was completed. (Master and servant were the words used to describe employers and employees right up to the early twentieth century.) Besides this a servant who left his master could be imprisoned and a servant fleeing to another area could be caught and returned under a writ known as *capias*.

An interesting contrast with modern employment conditions is found in section 12. This specifies working hours, particularly in the case of agricultural labourers who would have accounted for a large portion of the working population at that time. The section required that labourers should be present at their work during the months from March through to September between 5.00 a.m. and 8.00 p.m. This provision covered all workers between the ages of twelve and sixty.

Section 13 required that all of the work should be finished before a workman could 'quit' his work. Much later, in the nineteenth century, this provision was frequently used as a means of checking trade union activity. Manchester has argued in fact in *Modern Legal History* that the use of this section of the old Act had a more profound effect than the hated Combination Laws.

Another significant purpose of the legislation was to provide a standard means for regulating wages. This is found in section 15 which gives Justices of the Peace the authority to 'limit, rate, and appoint' wages. In setting a wage the justices were required to take account of the 'plenty or scarcity of the time and other circumstances necessarily to be considered'. In other words wages were determined according to the current economic circumstances. This is obviously massively different to the way that wages are determined in the modern economy. Besides this, under section 18, a master who failed to pay the wage that the justices had decided could be fined, again an enormous difference from the market forces led system that we work under today.

It is an interesting illustration of the imbalance in the employment relationship and the laws regulating it that a master in breach of his contractual obligations to his servant could be fined while a servant in breach of his contractual obligations to his master could be imprisoned.

The second half of the Act deals specifically with apprentices (workers learning their trade) and journeymen (those who had successfully completed an apprenticeship). Apprenticeships were of a fixed seven years and there was a restriction on the number of apprentices that could enter a trade at one time.

The statute, subject to a few later amendments, remained the basis of the law governing employment until well into the eighteenth century when the demands of the Industrial Revolution began to limit its effectiveness. Nevertheless, it shows that, while we commonly emphasise that employment is based on a contractual relationship it has for centuries also been subject to statutory intervention.

1.1.2 The application of the Statute of Artificers and Apprentices 1562 in the eighteenth century

As we have seen above one of the stated aims of the statute was the 'preservation of a reasonable livelihood'. As a result of this many workers in many different trades had grown to rely on its provisions. Even so it is questionable whether it actually enforced or achieved this stated aim and there is evidence of this in the frequency of petitioning for enforcement of its provisions and in case law.

In 1719 the Broad and Narrow Loom Weavers of Stroud petitioned the House of Commons to enforce a 1555 statute regulating weaving. In 1726 members of the Wiltshire and Somerset weaving community petitioned the King over worsening conditions of work. In 1728 Gloucester Weavers petitioned local justices to 'fix a liberal scale of wages for weavers'. Many petitions were unsuccessful.

Besides this, combining (in other words the equivalent of trade unions) to increase wages had always been considered illegal. In *R v The Journeymen Taylors of Cambridge* (1726) 8 Mod 10, 11. 88 ER 9–10 the court clarified this position:

JUDGMENT

'A conspiracy of any kind is illegal, although the matter about which they conspired might have been lawful for them, or any of them, to do, if they had not conspired to do it.'

The conspiracy involved was in fact a petition by the journeymen's trade association to have the rate of pay set as required under s15 of the statute. It is hard to see how one individual worker would be more able to petition successfully for an enforcement of the law when a petition by the whole group of workers amounted to an unlawful combination.

It is true that petitioning for enforcement of the statute gained some limited success. In 1748 weavers, traditionally the best paid section of the workforce, obtained from

Parliament a special prohibition of 'truck' in their trade. 'Truck' was an increasing practice of the time by which employers paid wages in goods, usually in the form of vouchers or tallies that could only be spent in the employers' shops, rather than in money which obviously could be used anywhere. The clear implication and purpose of truck was that it gave the employer another means of regulating or limiting wages by charging higher prices for goods in their shops. A Woollen Cloth Weavers Act in 1756 also allowed justices to fix piecework rates, which the weavers hoped would stop the current practice of cutting down rates and then underselling. In fact the table of wage rates that resulted only created greater conflict, further petitions and cross-petitions from the employers. They were eager to argue the greater benefits to the economy of freedom of contract and unrestrained competition in the industry.

Interestingly following a petition in 1776 by weavers, spinners, scribblers and other woollen trades in Somerset against the introduction of the 'Spinning Jenny', Parliament, which only two centuries before had prohibited the introduction of the 'Gig Mill' would not even accept or read the petition.

The weavers were not the only workers who expressed grievances over worsening conditions and changing methods. There was a Parliamentary enquiry into the stocking making industry. Hatters, a formerly privileged section of the workforce had previously enjoyed protection under the Act through the limiting of the numbers of apprentices. They lost this protection in an amending statute in 1777. It is the removal of the controls on apprentice numbers at a time of increasing population and unemployment that is often blamed by historians such as the Hammonds and the Webbs for the massive increases of unskilled labour.

Increasingly petitioning for enforcement of provisions within the 1562 statute became ineffective or only worked against the interests of the workers of the time, and it is doubtful whether the wage setting and apprenticeship clauses of the statute were in operation at all by the end of the eighteenth century. Despite this, regulations were still introduced in the late eighteenth century where enormous public pressure or even riots made it expedient, as in the 'Spitalfield Acts' of 1765 and 1773. These were passed following mass demonstrations by the London mob when drastic levels of unemployment amongst silk weavers had been blamed on a refusal by employers to follow past regulation in the industry and with an increasing shift towards the import of cheap foreign material.

There is argument between historians over whether there were real and sustained reductions in living standards at the time. E P Thompson in *The Making of the English Working Class* (Penguin, 1980), in examining the complexity of average circumstances provided in reports of the time, suggests that well-being, or at least feelings of relative well-being, is as important in deciding the consequences of social change as statistics which may not take account of particular events or particular circumstances. While account has to be taken of the effects of the massive increase in population at the time, and of the general increase in the wealth of the nation as a whole as a result of industrialisation, the introduction of the so-called 'Speenhamland system', means-tested sliding-scale of wage supplements used to mitigate the worst effects of rural poverty, as well as general increases in the Poor Relief Rate, are evidence of a general reduction in the living standards of the traditional workforce.

A piece of writing that emerged during this time was to have a profound effect on economic thinking and the course that industrialisation would follow. *The Wealth of Nations* by Adam Smith was published in 1776 and committed itself to the concept of laissez-faire economics, leave it to the market. Smith's philosophy had already in effect been anticipated within the legal system. A request by Oldham check weavers in 1759 for the enforcement of the apprenticeship restrictions of the Statute of Artificers was met with open hostility by the judge in Assizes:

JUDGMENT

'In the infancy of Trade, the Acts of Queen Elizabeth might be well calculated for the public Weal [good], but now, when it is grown to that perfection we see it, it might perhaps be of Utility to have those laws repealed, as tending to cramp and tye down that knowledge it was at first necessary to obtain by rule.'

The philosophy put forward by Smith of unregulated trade, freedom of contract and individual liberty, was so in keeping with the economic demands of the contemporary capitalists that the abandonment of those aspects of the statute which were seen as beneficial to working people became almost a foregone conclusion.

The regulations for setting wage rates were abolished by Act in 1813 and the apprenticeship regulations were abolished by Act in 1814. In fact by this stage attitudes had moved so far from the provisions of the Statute of Artificers that in 1808, when hand-loom weavers were able to show that their actual remuneration had reduced by two-thirds in ten years, that they were considered to have no action in law. The House of Commons Committee reported that the weavers' proposal to fix a minimum wage was:

QUOTATION

'wholly inadmissible in principle, incapable of being reduced to practice by any means which can be devised and if practicable, would be productive of the most fatal consequences'.

Their proposal to limit the numbers of apprentices was identified in the Report as:

QUOTATION

'entirely inadmissible, and would if adopted by the House, be attended with the greatest injustice to the manufacturer as well as to the labourer'.

Similarly Lord Ellenborough's judgment in *R v Justices of Kent* [1811] 14 East 395 on the question of whether the Justices were required to set a rate under the Statute of Artificers states:

JUDGMENT

'It rests with them to act upon it or not as they see fit.'

As a result the Justices refused to set a rate.

1.1.3 Developments in the common law in the eighteenth century

At the beginning of the nineteenth century workers in all trades would have found that those provisions in the Statute of Artificers that were aimed at securing 'a convenient livelihood' were more or less ineffective by this time. At the same time the common law was restating the relationship of master and servant. In *Limland v Stephens* [1801] 3 Esp 269 Lord Kenyon identified that there were 'reciprocal duties between Master and Servant. From the Servant is due obedience and respect; from the Master protection and good treatment'.

It has been questioned whether the duties of the master, which may have been appropriate in the closed knit agricultural communities of the Tudor period could ever be effectively integrated into the complex industrial relations of the nineteenth century.

With working practices changing from relative independence and semi-independence to direct employment, workers gradually became governed more by the rules of contract:

- An assumption had developed that where a servant was hired with no mention as to the duration of the contract, then that employment should continue for one year *R v St Peter's Dorchester* [1763] 34 Digest 52, 265.

- Any inducement to breach a contract already attracted liability *Keane v Boycott* [1795] 34 Digest 167, 1299.

- A master also had an action where a servant, who was contractually bound to him, became employed by another, even where he was not enticed away, if the other continued to employ the servant once he was aware of the master's rights *Blake v Lanyon* [1759] 34 Digest 170, 1331.

- Because normal rules of contract applied to the relationship, consideration was an essential element. This normally took the form of work in return for wages. However, in *R v Worfield (Inhabitants)* [1794] 34 Digest 52, 269 a grant of food and lodging by the master was accepted as good consideration.

- At one stage an apprentice could be bound by his obligation to perform even though illness prevented him from doing so *R v Hales-Owen (Inhabitants)* [1718] 34 Digest 517, 4332 (although this was later overruled).

- Moral issues also figured in the employment contract so that the harsh measure of summary dismissal could be justified where an unmarried maidservant became pregnant *R v Brampton (Inhabitants)* [1777] 34 Digest 77, 536, and where a manservant fathered an illegitimate child *R v Walford (Inhabitants)* [1778] 34 Digest 77, 537.

These certainly seem to suggest an imbalance in a so-called free contractual relationship.

Tortious liability and remedies were also appropriate:

- As such a master's liability for his servant's acts had already been established in *Michael v Alstree* [1677] 2 Lev 172.

- Even earlier a master had been extended the right to moderately chastise an apprentice who misbehaved *Gylbert v Fletcher* [1629] 34 Digest 505, 4193.

- It was possible for a servant to be held legally responsible for a wrong that he had committed even though he had done so under the express orders of his master *Perkins v Smith* [1752] 1 Wils 325.

- In the torts of assault and battery the servant could bring a defence to either where the wrongs occurred in the defence of his master, but no such defence applied where the master acted in defence of his servant *Leeward v Basilee* [1695] 1 Salk 407. 1 which seems to suggest that a servant merited fewer rights than the master.

1.2 Changes in conditions of employment in the Industrial Revolution

The early nineteenth century charts a change from domestic cottage industry to large scale factory production. Cotton consumption rose from five million pounds weight in 1781 to 164 million pounds in 1818. Cotton overtook wool, which itself rose from fifty-eight million pounds in 1780 to eighty million pounds in 1820. Iron production increased from 70,000 tons in 1790 to 400,000 tons in 1820 (G D H Cole and R Postgate, *The Common People 1746–1946*, Methuen, 1965). These changes had profound consequences for traditional patterns of employment.

Undoubtedly the demands of the Napoleonic wars together with the rise of population (a population that appears to have been relatively stable at around six million in the mid-eighteenth century rose to nine million in the first ever census in 1801 and by the census of 1821 was in excess of twelve million) left the country dependent on imported grain, and this kept food prices high. The wars also left the country with a national debt of £860 million. The effect was also increased in real terms by falling prices for important war commodities as the war ended. The combined effect of all these factors was unemployment and wage cutting.

1.2.1 Reduction in status of traditional work

Increased competition led to a reduction in the status of the traditional established artisan trades, particularly in the woollen industry. The history of each trade does differ, but it was common in most trades at the turn of the century for a 'dishonourable' trade (not bound by traditional working practices), comprising unskilled and semi-skilled workers, to set up alongside the regular trade.

Shoe and boot makers, who had commonly petitioned for enforcement of the apprenticeship regulations, were severely hampered by a 'dishonourable' trade throughout the war years. By the time of the Trade Union crisis of 1834, they had lost their artisan status entirely. In tailoring there was a lengthy competition between the traditional trade, the 'flints', and the 'dishonourable' unskilled workers, the 'dungs'.

Artisan craftsmen had always relied on their trade associations and on the protection of the traditional regulation under the Statute of Artificers for their independence and security. The illegalisation of the associations on the one hand and the repeal of the statute on the other left them at the mercy of both the wealthy masters and the huge increase in unskilled labour.

The growth of the 'dishonourable' trade was one factor that enabled the larger masters and the merchants to drive down piecework rates, wages and even wholesale prices. The state of an individual trade, the costs of raw materials and tools, the levels of skill attached to particular work and the relative availability of markets were all influences on varying rates of decline amongst the traditional workforce.

An ordinary woodworker might only require very basic and affordable tools to complete his work. In poor times he could set up as a 'garret master', and involve his whole family in the trade and 'hawk' his own products. A high class joiner, carpenter or cabinet maker, on the other hand, needed a much more substantial capital outlay to set up in business. Unemployed journeymen from these trades could be forced into the so-called 'strapping shops'. Closer in character to the new factories, harsh working conditions were the norm and summary dismissal was common for those unable to match the pace of work expected. Many small master craftsmen, unable to cope with the competition of the wealthier enterprises were forced into the same conditions.

Building workers also suffered from competition from the 'dishonourable' trade. In earlier times they had enjoyed some of the strongest trade associations and the protection this offered. The repeal of the wage fixing and apprenticeship controls from the Statute of Artificers weakened their position. They were neither in a position to buy the raw materials of their trade nor, because of the nature of their work, to peddle wares in the way that producers of goods could do. They became totally subjected to the control of the large contractors and rarely had work during the winter months.

There were, of course, industries in which the workers enjoyed improved conditions. This was particularly true of shipwrights and engineers, which were both emerging industries. In neither case were workers in a position of independence, as had been the traditional trades, but, because of the scarcity of skilled workers they were able to enjoy good wages. In some of the traditional crafts where high status remained, workers also maintained a relatively high standard of living. Coach building is an example.

Of all the traditional crafts, the weavers suffered the worst reductions in their circumstances. The massively increased supply of machine spun yarn as well as the exaggerated demand for cloth during the war years led to a huge increase of unskilled and unapprenticed labour in the trade. The repeal of the apprenticeship and wage fixing controls meant that they were powerless to defend against it.

Wage cutting had been sanctioned throughout the early years of the Industrial Revolution. This in itself was justified by the argument that poverty was an essential spur to industrious behaviour. J Smith in *Memoirs of Wool* describes it as follows:

QUOTATION

'[It] is a well known fact that scarcity, to a degree, promotes industry, and that the manufacturer who can subsist on 3 days work will be idle and drunk the remainder of the week.... We can fairly [state] that a reduction in wages in the woollen manufacture would be a national blessing and advantage, and no real injury to the poor.'

It was not uncommon, when markets were poor, for employers in manufacturing to use the situation to their advantage. Work would be given to unemployed weavers, desperate for work, at very low pay rates. Then, when the market recovered, these cheaply produced goods could be sold not only increasing profits but restricting the ability of the weavers to gain a good rate for their work even in good times.

Weavers had to work longer and longer hours to earn less and less money. Working longer hours also only served to increase each other's chances of unemployment. Cobbett, in the Political Register of 1832 described their situation as follows:

QUOTATION

'It is truly lamentable to behold so many thousands of men who formerly earned 20 shillings to 30 shillings per week now compelled to live upon 5 shillings, 4 shillings or even less.... It is the more sorrowful to behold the men in their state, as they still retain the frank and bold character they formed in the days of their independence.'

The weavers are seen by some historians as a casualty in an otherwise beneficial technological advance. Having been for centuries the single largest section of the adult workforce, their fall represents the most dramatic consequence of industrialism and a laissez-faire economy. As E P Thompson says in *The Making of the English Working Class* (Penguin, 1980):

QUOTATION

'[if] we are to assess the living standards in these years, not in "futuristic" terms, but in the terms of the living generations who experienced them, then we must see the weavers as a group who not only did not share in the benefits of economic progress but who suffered a dramatic decline. Since textiles were the staple diet of the Industrial Revolution, and since there were far more adults involved in the weaving than in the spinning branches, this would seem as valid a way of describing these years as any.'

1.2.2 Unemployment and casual employment

A further insecurity of working people of the period was the irregularity of work available. Agricultural workers had suffered semi-employment for many years. The factory system, child employment, the increase in population, and fluctuating markets made it a reality for many journeymen and small masters.

Certainly many tradesmen remained in regular employment, possibly in the same craft, for the whole of their lives. Indeed laissez-faire economics meant that fortunes could be made by men from quite humble beginnings. This was particularly true of the railway building boom in the nineteenth century. Sir Edward Banks, one successful contractor, was said to have left home as a boy with only 'two shillings [equivalent to 10p] and two shirts' having begun his working life as an agricultural labourer. Joseph Firbank 'at the age of seven joined his father down the mine' and after being a successful railway contractor 'died a rich man'. Even George Stephenson started as a colliery engine boy.

Many, however, suffered from the changed conditions of the time and could not maintain regular employment. B Wilson in *The Struggles of an Old Chartist* (Halifax, 1857) (cited by E P Thompson in *The Making of the English Working Class*, Penguin, 1980) demonstrates this:

QUOTATION

'Labour was bad to get then and wages were very low. I have been a woollen weaver, a comber, a navvy on the railway and a bearer in the delph [a quarryman] that I claim to know some little of the state of the working classes.'

Estimates made in the nineteenth century also show dire levels of unemployment.

QUOTATION

'Estimating the working classes as being between four and five million in number, I think we may safely assert – considering how many depend for their particular employment on particular times, seasons, fashions, and the vast quantity of overwork and scamp-work in the cheap trades ... the number of women and children who are being continually drafted into the different handicrafts with the view of reducing the earnings of the men, the displacement of human labour in some cases by machinery ... all these things being considered I say I believe we may safely conclude that ... there is barely sufficient work for the REGULAR employment of half our labourers, so that only 1,500,000 are fully and constantly employed, while 1,500,000 more are employed only half their time, and the remaining 1,500,000 are wholly unemployed, obtaining a day's work OCCASIONALLY by the displacement of some of the others.'

Henry Mayhew *London Labour and the London Poor, 1862*, Constable, 1968

The degradation of the workhouse system following the New Poor Law of 1834, with its less eligibility test (that the condition of those in the workhouse should be less than the poorest workers outside) are well documented. The extent of poverty created by the lack of stable employment is shown by the consistent rise of numbers of inmates of these institutions.

1.2.3 Child labour

Industrialisation led to imbalances not only between skilled and unskilled labour but also between men on the one hand and women and children on the other. In the early

1830s between one-third and one-half of the estimated labour force in the cotton mills was under the age of twenty-one. In the worsted trade, this ratio was even higher. Amongst adult workers, over half were women. The Reports of the Factory Inspectors led Ure to estimate an adult labour force in textiles mills of 191,671, 102,812 being women and only 88,859 being men.

Children were used extensively in the factory based textiles industry. They were also widely used in the mines, where their size was advantageous in the narrower tunnels, although they were also used as 'hurryers' (taking ore to the surface). In the sweat shops and the 'dishonourable' trade they were a means of cheapening the costs of the manufacturer.

The consequence for adult males was often degradation, forced into dependence on their wives and children for their subsistence. Of course conditions for child workers were also often grave.

Children had traditionally been used to help their families in domestic based cottage industries, sometimes also in quite harsh circumstances. The conditions in the mines and the factories were different. In the home they might have found some variety in the chores that they were given and might even have the chance of some play and relaxation in the fresh air. They also enjoyed whatever security family life offered. In the mines and mills they were subjected to long hours, monotonous and arduous work and the repression of overseers.

The Reports of the Children's Employment Committee in 1842 show pauper boys as young as six being apprenticed to colliers. Evidence before these commissions helps to illustrate working conditions of the time, as in that of a young girl, Patience Kershaw, below:

QUOTATION

'[The] bald place on my head is made by thrusting the corves [coal trucks]; my legs have never swelled but sister's did when they went to mill; I hurry the corves a mile and more underground and back; they weigh 3 cwt [hundredweight] … the getters I work for are naked except for their caps. Sometimes they beat me if I am not quick enough … I would rather work in mill than in coal pit.'

Children's Employment Commission. First Report of the Commissioners. Mines. Parliamentary Papers (1842) Vol. XV p. 43

The situation of the 'climbing boys' (chimney sweeps) shows some of the harshest conditions of child labour. Despite the possibility of brush sweeping, sweeps continued to use little boys to clean chimneys until Lord Shaftesbury's reforms in 1875. Not only did they risk burning and suffocation but the nature of the work put them at risk of a variety of diseases and deformity. They dislodged kneecaps from the constant pressure on them in climbing the chimneys. They contracted disease from soot getting into cuts and grazes. They often had deformed spines from the weight of the sacks of soot. They were also often victims of a scrotal infection known at the time as 'chimney sweep's cancer', the only available remedy at the time being castration.

1.2.4 Conclusions

The consequence of industrialisation for working people was a dramatic change in the character of their employment. From being often self-employed, from usually being craftsmen with pride in their abilities, they often became reduced to the level of mere machine minders. The factory system introduced new problems of long hours, of insecure wage levels, and of insecurity of employment itself. The new machinery brought with it issues of health and safety and of the systematic abuse of child labour. In *The Making of the English Working Class* E P Thompson recognises the consequences of change in a further respect:

QUOTATION

'when we follow through the history of particular industries, and see the new skills arise as old ones decline, it is possible to forget that the old skill and the new almost always were the prerequisite of different people. Manufacturers in the first half of the nineteenth century pressed forward each innovation which enabled them to dispense with adult male craftsmen and to replace them with women or juvenile labour. Even where an old skill was replaced by a new process requiring equal or greater skill, we rarely find the same workers transferred from one to the other, or from domestic to factory production. Insecurity and hostility in the face of machinery and innovation, was not the consequence of mere prejudice and (as authorities then implied) of insufficient knowledge of "political economy". The cropper or woolcomber knew well enough that, while the new machinery might offer skilled employment for his son, or for someone else's son, it would offer none for him. The rewards of the "march of progress" always seemed to be gathered by someone else.'

Many adult males lost their jobs following industrialisation and traditional crafts disappeared. The new factories employed many child workers and long hours of work were required. Unlicensed competition meant that wages could be easily reduced. Obviously the conditions experienced during the period led to calls for reforms and for improvements.

1.3 Legislation and the development of industrial law in the nineteenth century

A V Dicey (in *Lectures on the Relationship Between Law and Public Opinion in England in the Nineteenth Century*, Liberty Fund, 2008) characterises the legislation of the nineteenth century in three periods. The first, up to 1830, he calls 'Old Toryism' or legislative quiescence. The second, from 1825 to 1870 he identifies as a period of Benthamism. The third, from 1865, he classifies as collectivist or socialist.

The terminology is open to question but the rough division is useful because it comes close to splitting the century by the dates of the two reform acts which extended the franchise, 1832 and 1867.

1.3.1 Legislation on employment prior to 1832

The governments of this period were clearly shaken by the revolution in France and were repressive in their treatment of opposition or dissent. However, there were some Acts, dealing mostly with the worst abuses of the industrial system.

The earliest attempt to regulate industry was the Health and Morals of Apprentices and Others Act 1802 introduced by Robert Peel senior. The Act applied to cotton and wool mills and other factories where there were either three or more apprentices or more than twenty other people employed.

Premises were to be lime washed twice a year and the number of windows should be adequate for proper ventilation. Apprentices were to be supplied with clothing and were not to work for more than twelve hours a day. Some period of the day was to be set aside for instruction in reading, writing and arithmetic during the first four years of apprenticeship. Boys and girls were to have separate dormitories, and there were to be no more than two children sharing a bed. Religious instruction on Sundays was mandatory. Inspectors, usually clergymen, could be appointed.

The Act was limited in its application and did nothing to improve the conditions of any except the pauper apprentices. W D Evans, a stipendiary magistrate from Manchester giving evidence before a Commons Select Committee (Parliamentary Papers 1816) identified that the Act was ineffective, had never been put into practice in Lancashire and Cheshire, and that he had only read it himself the day before giving evidence to the Commission.

Peel introduced another Act, the Cotton Mills Regulation Act 1819, influenced by, but not really following, evidence given by Robert Owen to the Royal Commission. It applied only to cotton mills, prohibited the employment of children under the age of nine and limited the hours of work of children under the age of sixteen to twelve hours per day. However, mills based on water power were allowed to exceed these limits according to how the current in the stream or river affected them.

The Combination Acts (making trade associations illegal) were repealed in the Combination of Workmen Act 1824 largely through the compelling argument made by Francis Place that illegal combinations posed a greater threat of revolution than would legal ones. The Combination of Workmen Act 1825, however, while maintaining the legality of trade unions made illegal every conceivable form of industrial action.

Outworkers and pieceworkers at the time had a serious problem in trying to understand the way that their wages were worked out by their masters or the merchants. The Master and Workmen Arbitration Act 1824 created the so-called 'particulars' clause. Under this there was a requirement that workers should be given the necessary particulars to be able to work out what their wages should be. It was, however, of limited use since ss18 and 19 made this a voluntary undertaking on the part of the master.

Probably the most important Act of the period was the Truck Act 1831. The paying of wages in goods had occurred in earlier times but was incongruous within the framework of industrial society and often led to abuses. With the stated aim of ending these abuses the Act at s1 provides that it is an offence for an employer to contract that the wage payable to his servant be paid other than in current 'coin of the realm' (proper currency). Such a contractual term would be illegal and void. Under s13 the entire amount should be paid in currency, and under s14 workmen could recover for sums paid in another form. Another important provision within the Act prohibited the employer from dictating the place where the workmen spent their wages. This was aimed at reducing the effect of the so-called 'Tommy shops'. These were shops owned by the employer where workers were bound to exchange their tallies for goods often at inflated prices and often selling food that was bulked out with impurities. A major problem of the Act arose over the exact meaning of 'workman' which led to definition of the term in later Acts. The Act was passed when the reform bill was before Parliament and the government was under pressure.

Another Act passed before the political reforms of 1832 was the Labour in Cotton Mills Act 1831 which included minor regulation of the working hours of young people. Of course the actual value of all of the factory legislation was limited because there was no mechanism for monitoring or enforcing it.

1.3.2 Legislation on employment between the two Reform Acts of 1832 and 1867

The so-called 'Great Reform Act' of 1832 did little to alter the franchise; the electorate increased by about 217,000 to about 670,000 in a population of over fourteen million.

Nevertheless, it advanced power into different hands. The monopoly of the landed gentry was limited. Redistribution of seats, the removal of 'rotten boroughs' and extending representation to previously unrepresented industrial boroughs limited the influence of both Crown and Lords. The property qualification of £10 enfranchised large numbers of middle class, including new industrialists. Those that agitated most for the reforms, working people, did not get the vote.

The factory legislation during this second period is significant because, in following the principles of Bentham and the Utilitarians, it attempted to solve problems by the creation of administrative mechanisms.

The Factory Act 1833, framed by Edwin Chadwick, was the first Act to introduce a professional service of government inspectors. While it did not produce the same level of opposition as the Poor Law, also introduced by Chadwick, there was still opposition, particularly to the reductions in working hours. There were only four inspectors nationally, but at least the process had been introduced. The inspectors were authorised to create such regulations as they felt were necessary to enforce the provisions in the Act.

Regulating hours of work in the textiles industry, the Act in ss7 and 8 prohibited the employment of children under the age of nine, and s11 restricted the hours of work of those under the age of thirteen to nine hours per day. Where mechanical power was used, young people between thirteen and eighteen could only work between the hours of 8.30 a.m. and 5.30 p.m., but this did not apply in lace making or in the processes of fulling, roughing and boiling woollens. S10 attempted to prevent abuses of previous legislation by insisting that a child under thirteen could only work a total of nine hours per day no matter how many places he was employed in.

The Act made far greater provision for schooling and indeed each child was required to present a voucher signed by a teacher confirming attendance before starting work. A Certifying Surgeon was also introduced with the task of reporting on the strength and appearance of working children.

Both reformers and industrialists were critical of the Act. The former doubted the reliability or independence of the inspectors, the latter resented what they saw as bureaucratic interference.

In the 1840s legislation was introduced in other areas of industry. The first was the Mines and Collieries Act 1842. Women were not to be employed in mines and indentures of apprenticeship offered to females became void. Children were protected to the extent that boys under ten were not to be employed or apprenticed. A colliery inspectorate was also created and there were also many penal provisions.

The legislation so far appeared to be mainly concerned with creating administrative controls. The Factory Act 1844 actually limited this control by removing the magisterial powers given to the inspectors in the 1833 Act. Powers of entry were increased and a central office was set up in London to keep records of inspections. Anyone opening a factory had to report this to the inspectors.

The Act for the first time addressed some of the dangers of industry. Against fierce opposition a requirement for fencing of moving machinery was included. All accidents were to be reported to the surgeon, whose duty it was to enquire into the cause and report to the inspectors. An inspector might initiate actions for compensation for injured workers.

Mechanical processes introduced more danger into the workplace than existed in traditional industry. The common law was harsh in this respect. The rule in *Baker v Bolton* [1808] 34 Digest 181, 1478 meant that where a worker died from an accident his right of action died with him. The rules of common employment also made it difficult for a worker injured by a workmate to claim against his employer. Some relief came in the Fatal Accidents Act 1846. S1 provided that a person, who would be liable for an injury if death had not occurred, would still be deemed liable for damages. S4 allowed that the action could be for the benefit of the wife, husband, parent or child of the deceased.

Another approach to improving conditions came in an attempt to reduce hours in the so-called 'Ten Hour Bill', one of the most contentious campaigns of the time. The Factories Act 1847 which resulted made no specific provision for reducing the hours of adult males. Women and children under eighteen were prohibited from working for more than eleven hours per day or sixty-three hours in a week. From May 1848 this was to be reduced to ten hours per day and fifty-eight hours per week.

The Act, together with the Factory Act 1850, however, was insignificant to men. The latter Act prohibited women and children from working between the hours of 6.00 p.m. and 6.00 a.m. and after 2.00 p.m. on Saturdays, and it repealed the earlier provision which allowed the use of overtime to make up for time lost during the permitted hours of work. Since it often proved uneconomical to open factories without the full workforce, the hours worked by men actually began to fall.

The Print Works Act 1845, the Bleaching and Dyeing Works Act 1860, the Lace Factories Act 1861 and the Factory Act Extension Act 1864, which applied to the manufacture of earthenware, percussion caps and cartridges, paper staining and fustian cutting, all extended factory regulation further.

While the legislation of this period represents a gradual emergence of administrative systems to deal with employment questions it does not signify a universal shift in attitudes towards the plight of people affected by changed working conditions. Most legislation was the subject of controversy and many reforms took years to achieve. The Liberal statesman George Cornwell Lewis expressed it as follows:

QUOTATION

'with respect to legislation for the working classes there is a thorough anarchy of opinion'.
Edinburgh Review, Vol. LXXXIII, January 1846

One provision in the Offences Against the Person Act 1861 possibly illustrates the real regard held for working people at the time. Under s26 a master who was legally liable to provide food, clothing or lodging for a servant who wilfully and without lawful excuse neglects this duty or causes to be done any bodily harm to the servant so that the life or health of a servant or apprentice is endangered commits a misdemeanour. 'Misdemeanour' would surely understate the significance of wilfully endangering someone's life.

1.3.3 Legislation on employment from 1867

The second reform Act extended the franchise and gave votes to nearly all adult males. A combination of increased representation and a new pragmatism were partly responsible for a series of trade union reforms. The Trade Union Act 1871, the Trade Union Act 1876 and the Conspiracy and Protection of Property Act 1875 meant that trade union activities were not automatically unlawful merely because they were in restraint of trade, and immunities were granted to unions and their members, and s13 of the Statute of Artificers was repealed.

Of course these provisions were not always favourably interpreted by the judges, giving rise to the complaint that what Parliament gave on the one hand the judiciary took away with the other.

Two other Acts in the year of the reform Act were also important. The Factory Acts Extension Act 1867 extended the application of previous Acts to many more industries. Blast furnaces, copper mills, iron mills, foundries, premises manufacturing metal products, India rubber and gutta parcha by machine, manufacturing paper, glass and tobacco, or book binding and printing, all became subject to regulation. Any factory employing more than fifty workers was also covered by the Act.

Sunday working for women and young people was prohibited. No boy under the age of twelve and no female was to work on Sunday. No female was to work in a factory where glassmaking or annealing took place. No children under the age of eleven could be used in the metal grinding trades. Attention was also placed on health and, as well as compulsory meal breaks, the Act prohibited these from being taken in working areas of the factory premises. Inspectors were given power to enforce the installation of fans to re-direct noxious fumes.

The second Act, the Workshop Regulation Act 1867, brought much smaller establishments within the scope of the regulations. Workshop was at last defined as any room or place, covered or in the open air, in which any manual labour was exercised by way of trade, and for the purposes of gain, by any child, young person or woman and to which the employer had the right of access and control. Hours for children and young people were again reduced and further provision for education was included.

Conditions in mining had been criticised in Royal Commissions and became the subject of legislation in the Metalifferous Mines Regulations Act 1872. Colliers who used boys underground were required to report that fact to the owner or his agent. Adequate ventilation in the shafts, the safe use of explosives, guarding against spillage from tubs and wagons being hauled up the shafts, and the prevention of escaping gases were all provided for. Payment of wages in public houses, a common practice at the time, was also prohibited. The Metalifferous Mines Regulations Act 1875, the Coal Mines Act 1877 and the Quarries Act 1894 extended regulations and included quarrying. The 1877 Act also dealt with the problem of the effect that weighing ore could have in depressing wages.

Factory legislation was by now extensive both in content and in the number of industries to which it applied, limiting the hours worked by women and children being a constant theme. The Factory Act 1874 prohibited the employment of children under ten at all, workers under fourteen became classed as child workers, and women, children and young people were only allowed to work between either 6.00 a.m. and 6.00 p.m. or 7.00 a.m. and 7.00 p.m. There was to be no continuous work for more than four-and-a-half hours without a meal break and all work had to cease during such breaks. More emphasis was placed on the education of young workers and the sections of the 1833 and 1856 Acts allowing an employer to recover for lost time were repealed.

The Factory and Workshop Act 1878 was clearly the most important of the period for employment. Containing 107 sections and six schedules, it consolidated much of the earlier law and influenced legislation to come. Provisions relating to sanitation and safety were drawn with relative precision. The requirement of fencing machinery was made absolute for the first time. S9 prohibited children from cleaning machinery when this would place them in danger. There was even mention of holiday entitlement. Part 2 of the Act listed extensive regulations on particular classes of workshop or factory.

Despite its thoroughness, amending legislation was passed in the Factory and Workshop Act 1891 and the Factory and Workshop Act 1895. The powers of inspectors were increased in the first. The age below which children were allowed to work was raised to eleven, and women were not to work within four weeks of giving birth. Both Acts made the provisions of former Acts more precise. Safety was emphasised once again. The second Act highlighted overcrowding and a requirement for a working area of 250 cubic feet for every worker was introduced. Courts were given powers to shut factories considered to be dangerous by the inspectors and to shut down dangerous machinery. They could also order the installation of fire escapes. The Acts also covered laundries, docks and warehouses for the first time.

Workman was a commonly used term in nineteenth century Acts and, ambiguously interpreted had been a means of employers avoiding liability. The Employers and Workmen Act 1875 defined the term. Under s1 a workman was:

SECTION

'any person who being a labourer, servant of husbandry, journeyman, artificer, handicrafts-man, miner or otherwise engaged in manual labour has entered into or works under a contract with an employer whether it be a contract of service or a contract personally to execute any work or labour'.

The Act allowed for proceedings between employer and workman in both the courts of summary jurisdiction and the County Courts. S4 provided for an action for breach of contract together with limited powers to order performance in s3. The apprenticeship laws were also reviewed in ss5–10.

There were also reforms in civil liability. The Employer's Liability Act 1880 attempted to limit the common law defence of 'common employment' (where the employer could avoid liability for injuries caused by a fellow worker). The doctrine was not, however, fully repealed until the Law Reform (Personal Injuries) Act 1948. The problem of proving negligence in accidents causing death or injury was dealt with in the Workmen's Compensation Act 1897 which created statutory rights of action for workmen.

There was further legislation on wages also. The Truck Act was reviewed and made more flexible in the Truck Amendment Act 1887 and the Truck Act 1896 and the restraint on truck was supplemented in the Payment of Wages in Public Houses Act 1883. By s1 of this Act no wages should be paid to any workman at or within a public house, beer shop or similar place, or in any office, garden or place belonging to such premises, except where the wages are paid by the resident owner or occupier to a workman employed by him. S3 prevented an employer from using the defence that the practice had been carried out by his agent and he would be liable unless he could show that he had taken all reasonable steps to prevent it.

Two further industries were brought under legislation by the end of the century. Shop workers worked some of the longest hours in employment. Indeed even after the Shop Hours Regulation Act 1886 young shop workers were only limited to a seventy-four-hour week. The statute was only temporary and not made permanent until the Shop Hours Act 1892. The Merchant Shipping Act 1894 implemented some reform in an industry where one seaman in sixty met a violent death, as against one worker in 315 in the mines.

1.3.4 Comment

Many of the provisions in these statutes, particularly reductions in working hours, applied only to women, children and young workers. Statutory protection for adult male workers was always argued against as being unnecessary since they were in a free contractual relationship with the employer. Animals used in industry were often granted greater protection on the same argument.

While rights to certain legal action by working people was granted during the period, this was often of little effect without the support of effective trade union representation.

There was a variety of Acts making a variety of provisions for a variety of industries but there was no simple and universal statement of law. Indeed this prevailed until the latter end of the twentieth century. The legislation of most significance of workers in industry, that concerning industrial health and safety, was only addressed in a cursory manner. While provisions were included in certain Acts for fencing of machinery or installation of fire escapes, no concerted effort was made to investigate the whole area of industrial disease and industrial injury. With only four inspectors little success could be anticipated in enforcing the provisions in the Acts. The degree of power enjoyed by the inspectors also varied from Act to Act and from time to time.

Nothing in the legislation replaced the former protections such as the restrictions on entry into different trades which might have been achieved prior to the repeals in 1813 and 1814. Neither did the legislation attempt to check the imbalances in the employment contract, nor to reverse the unemployment and casual employment that industrialisation had led to.

Finally all legislation was still subject to the interpretation of a judiciary which showed itself to be supportive of laissez-faire economics and which trade unionists would have argued was hostile to the aspirations of ordinary working people.

1.4 The common law approach to employment in the nineteenth century

1.4.1 The 'master servant' relationship

While legislation attempted to tackle some of the moral and physical problems that industrialisation created, the common law showed a much greater interest in the contractual relationship between employer and employee. Since case law is generally more restricted to individual points of law than statute, it is easier to view developments by topic rather than purely chronologically.

The common law view of the employment was mainly contractual. In the words of an old textbook on industrial law:

QUOTATION

'The relationship of employer and employed, of master and servant, is, according to the common law, a voluntary relationship into which the parties may enter on terms laid down by themselves within limitations imposed only by the general law of contract.'

W Mansfield Cooper, *Outlines of Industrial Law*, Butterworths, 1954

Such a free contractual view of the relationship was entirely incompatible with the economic demands of the period and it was this side of the relationship which was developed and enforced.

QUOTATION

'Every person has a right under the law, as between him and his fellow subjects, to full freedom in disposing of his own labour or his own capital, according to his own will. It follows that every other person is subject to the correlative duty arising therefrom and is prohibited from any obstruction to the fullest exercise of this right which can be made compatible with the exercise of similar rights by others.'

Sir William Earle, Memorandum on the Law Relating to Trade Unions, Eleventh and final Report of the Royal Commissioners, No. 4123. Parliamentary Papers (1869) Vol. XXX

As the nineteenth century progressed, the growth of industry led to increasingly complex and increasingly specialised patterns of employment. With the distinctions of the Statute of Artificers removed, and new legislation concerning working people in place, clear definitions of the relationship were needed. The courts had to examine many relationships similar to master and servant to decide what law applied. In *R v Marshall* [1870] 15 Digest 924, 10,182 it was held that, where one worker agreed to fetch and distribute the wages of fellow workmen, that this was an act of agency, not in the course of his employment. In *Walker v Hirsch* [1884] 27 Ch D 460 it was held that where a workman was in a position to receive profits as well as be liable for losses he was a partner, not a servant. Lord Bramwell framed the definition of servant in *Yewens v Noakes* [1880] 6 QBD 530:

QUOTATION

'A servant is a person subject to the command of his master as to the manner in which he shall do his work.'

This remained the accepted test well into the twentieth century. Inevitably, with complex work patterns, flexibility in the definition was needed. In *Reedie v London and North Western Railway Co* [1849] 4 Exch 244 the court accepted the need for delegation so that someone other than the master might have the power to dismiss the servant. Indeed, in *R v Faulkes* [1875] 34 Digest 20, 6 it was held possible even for someone who received no wages to be classed as a servant, as in family enterprises.

1.4.2 Employment and the basic rules of contract
Formation of contract
The courts adopted the normal rules of contract: an agreement supported by consideration and with an intention to be legally bound.

The agreement would be the offer of employment to a specific worker followed by their unconditional acceptance of the offer of work *Hudspeth v Yarnold* [1850] 12 Digest (Repl.) 68, 381.

The value of the consideration was not something that the courts felt the need to examine providing there was some value. In *Hitchcock v Coker* [1837] 6 Ad & El 438 Tindall CJ stated:

JUDGMENT

'It is enough that there actually is a consideration for the bargain; and that such consideration is a legal consideration of some value.' In *Pilkington v Scott* [1846] 12 Digest (Repl.) 232, 1747 the court felt that it was not its role to make bargains for the parties.

While the principle of law cannot be argued with, on the facts the sailors in *Stilk v Myrick* [1809] 2 Camp 317 may have legitimately felt to have been harshly treated.

In *Taylor v Brewer* [1813] 12 Digest (Repl.) 467, 3490 it was held that the relationship must have been intentionally a legal one rather than one based on honour.

Capacity and 'infant' workers
With so much of the workforce being children and young people, their legal capacity was clearly important to the enforcement of employment contracts.

The courts evolved the opinion that employment contracts were enforceable where they were substantially for the benefit of the infant. In *De Francesco v Barnum* [1890] 45 Ch D 430 Fry LJ suggested that the question should be:

JUDGMENT

'is the contract for the benefit of the infant … the court must look at the whole contract having regard to the circumstances of the case'.

The position was further clarified by Lord Esher in *Corn v Matthews* [1893] 1 QB 310:

JUDGMENT

'It is impossible to frame a deed as between master and apprentice in which some of the stipulations are not in favour of one and some in favour of the other. But if we find a stipulation in the deed which is of such a kind that it makes the whole contract an unfair one, then that makes the whole contract void.'

Duration and termination

Prior to the main onslaught of industrialisation, where a servant was hired for an indefinite period, it was deemed to be a general hiring and said to last one year *R v St. Peter's Dorchester* [1763] 34 Digest 52, 265. Lord Mansfield here recognised that the principle could be rebutted but only in circumstances which made the presumption unlikely.

In the nineteenth century relationships were less personal and economic considerations had a greater significance. To industrialists a general hiring was inflexible and unsatisfactory. *Baxter v Nurse* [1844] 34 Digest 57, 326 and *Fairman v Oakford* [1860] 34 Digest 57, 327 show that decisions on the period for which an employment contract should run were based much more on economic need than on the apparent intentions of the parties.

Courts also had to consider the ending of contracts of employment. As early as 1831 in *Callo v Brouncker* [1831] 34 Digest 76, 533 they had laid down criteria for justified dismissal, which included moral misconduct, pecuniary misconduct, wilful disobedience and wilful neglect. In *Edwards v Levy* [1860] 34 Digest 78, 553 it was held that an isolated act of insubordination would only justify dismissal where the act was such that it made it impossible for the master and servant to continue on the same terms.

While the moral misconduct of the servant might justify dismissal, in *Latter v Braddell* [1881] 34 Digest 80, 558 Lord Lindley established that a mistress of a household could not order an internal examination of a maidservant to establish if she had acted immorally. Nevertheless, while the court accepted that the girl had only reluctantly agreed to the examination, in a tearful and distraught condition, she was deemed to have consented so that her action for assault failed. It seems strange that the court should feel that a menial servant, constrained by her duty of obedience to her mistress, should feel capable of refusing to comply with her mistress's demands.

Another question for the courts was what reasonable notice was where no provisions existed in the contract. In *Johnson v Blenkinsopp* [1841] 34 Digest 37, 134 the court made a distinction between menial servants and other types of worker. A menial servant was generally allowed no more than one month's notice. In *Nichols v Greaves* [1864] 34 Digest 37, 137 it was suggested that in close relationships it was in the interests of both parties for termination to be effected in the shortest possible time. *Green v Wright* [1876] 34 Digest 64, 396 suggested that other employees might expect periods of notice to be reasonable and based on the circumstances of their employment. In *Nowlan v Abbott* [1835] 34 Digest 36, 131 a head gardener was considered a menial servant, where in *Lawler v Linden* [1876] 34 Digest 36 d. the housekeeper of a large hotel was not.

Illness and death

Illness and the consequent inability to work, or failure to perform, was obviously important to workers in the nineteenth century. Illness by itself did not terminate the contract, nor the obligations under it, but of course the failure to perform meant that the master was free to end the engagement. The principle was explained by Baron Bramwell in *Jackson v Union Marine Insurance Co* [1874] 34 Digest 71, 484:

JUDGMENT

'A enters the service of B and is ill and cannot perform his work. No action will lie against him; but B may hire a fresh servant and not wait for his recovery, if his illness would put an end in the business sense to their business engagement and would frustrate the object of that engagement.'

This is not to say that short illnesses would necessarily be an appropriate reason to end the contract. Campbell CJ in *Cuckson v Stones* [1858] 12 Digest (Repl.) 425, 3270 stated:

JUDGMENT

'We think that want of ability to serve for a week would not of necessity be an answer to a claim for a week's wages if in truth the plaintiff was ready and willing to serve had he been able to do so and was only prevented from serving by the visitation of God.'

But if the servant was unable to serve and the work could not be delegated to someone else, then the contract was frustrated and all liability ended, *Robinson v Davison* [1871] LR 6 Exch 269.

Death of either master or servant brought the contract to an end. In *Farrow v Wilson* [1869] 12 Digest (Repl.) 666, 5155 it was held that the personal representatives of a deceased master were under no obligation to continue with the employment. In *Stubbs v Hollywell Railway Co.* [1867] 12 Digest (Repl.) 666, 5154 the death of the servant brought the contract to an end.

Remedies for breach of contract

The two available remedies were damages and injunctions. If the payment of damages satisfied the breach then they would be awarded. If the breach might continue and the award of damages would not compensate the claimant then an injunction might be allowed *Doherty v Allman* [1878] 3 App Cas 709. In some cases a servant might recover on a *quantum meruit* (for the work done).

Following *Hadley v Baxendale* [1854] 9 Exch 341 damages for breach of contract were based on losses that were a foreseeable consequence of the breach, or those in the contemplation of the parties when the contract was formed.

Fry LJ in *De Francesco v Barnum* [1890] 45 Ch D 430 explained when injunctions would be granted:

JUDGMENT

'[to] extend decisions the effect of which is to compel persons who are not desirous of maintaining continuous personal relations with one another to continue these personal relations, I think the courts are bound to be zealous lest they turn contracts of service into contracts of slavery; and … I should lean against the extension of the doctrine of specific performance and injunction in such a manner.'

Nevertheless, workers might still feel harshly treated by the strict application of common law principles. For example in *Cutter v Powell* [1795] 12 Digest (Repl.) 130, 809 a widow of a seaman was denied recovery on a *quantum meruit* for the work that he had done on a voyage. He had signed on for the whole voyage but had died with less than a quarter of the voyage remaining. Because the contract was 'entire', and to 'preserve certainty for mercantile contracts' there was no wage and no remedy.

Restraint of trade

In the advancing technology and highly competitive atmosphere of the nineteenth century, employers were eager to protect their trade secrets and processes. Covenants to achieve this were drafted into individual contracts of employment. These were generally well received by the courts and enforced provided their inclusion was reasonable. As Tindall CJ stated in *Rannie v Irvine* [1884] 43 Digest 36, 321 it was not the business of the court to:

JUDGMENT

'look out for improbable and extravagant contingencies to make it void'.

The right of an employer to protect his trade secrets and processes was clearly recognised. In *Haynes v Doman* [1899] 2 Ch 13 a covenant by the employee not to serve a person or firm engaged in a similar business, within a twenty-five-mile radius, after leaving the employment, without the express permission of the employer, was upheld. As Lord Lindley MR noted:

JUDGMENT

'The prohibition against disclosing trade secrets may well be worthless without the restriction against entering the service of rivals.'

1.4.3 The implied duties of master and servant
The duties of the master

Protection of the servant was a traditional obligation of the master. Originally the master had been 'obliged to provide for his servant in sickness and in health', *Scarman v Castell* [1795] 1 Esp 270 with a consequent liability to pay for medicines. This obligation was removed early in the nineteenth century in *Sellen v Norman* [1829] 34 Digest 115, 861, and in *Cooper v Phillips* [1831] 34 Digest 115, 866 it was decided that a master was under no obligation to pay for the services of a doctor attending a servant who had been injured in an accident while in his service. However, while there was no obligation to meet medical costs, the master might be required to seek medical assistance for his sick or injured servant. So, in *Jeffrey v Donald* [1901] 9 SLT 199 it was considered to be negligent of a master to fail to call a doctor to attend to a seriously injured servant.

In *Adamson v Jarvis* [1827] 4 Bing 66 it was held that a master had a duty to reimburse a servant for all expenses which the servant had properly incurred in the course of his employment whenever the master appeared to have authorised the servant's acts.

It was accepted in *Carol v Bird* [1800] 3 Esp 201 that masters were not under a duty to provide servants with testimonials (references). However, in *Foster v Charles* [1830] 7 Bing 105 it was held that, where such a testimonial was supplied to a third party, and contained information the master knew to be false, even though he had acted without malice or hope of gain, there could be an action in deceit by the third party and the master could be liable for damage for any misconduct of the servant. However, under *Weatherson v Hawkins* [1786] 1 Term Rep 110 the master would incur no liability to a servant for making adverse statements about him, whether oral or written, unless the servant could prove malice (this was the position until *Spring v Guardian Assurance plc* [1994] IRLR 460 HL). This was because communications between masters had qualified privilege and only malice would count as an abuse of that privilege, *Stuart v Bell* [1891] 32 Digest 122, 1545.

The duties of the servant

The common law sought to control the employment relationship by implying terms into the contract, imposing duties on the parties. It has to be said that the duties owed by masters seem minimal by contrast to those imposed on servants.

Paramount was the duty of faithful service. While the character of the duty varied with the employment, certain conduct constituting a breach of contract was common to all. As was said in *Lomax v Arding* [1855] 10 Exch 734:

JUDGMENT

'suppose the plaintiff has conducted himself on all occasions in a negligent and lazy spirit, there may be insuperable difficulty in a legal definition of the plaintiff's conduct and yet the defendant would be justified in discharging him'.

In this way any act inconsistent with the express or implied terms of the contract which was harmful to the master's interests amounted to a breach of the duty of faithful service. The servant could never place himself in a position where his own interests conflicted with his duty to the master. Thus in *Pearce v Foster* [1886] 17 QBD 536 a clerk who was required to provide his master with impartial advice, was rightly dismissed when it was found that he was speculating on the stock market.

In *Lamb v Evans* [1893] 1 Ch 218 it was held that the use of the master's tools or materials for the service of another was a breach of duty justifying dismissal. Similarly, in *Robb v Green* [1895] 2 QB 315 Lord Esher suggested that there was a term implied into all contracts, where the servant had access to confidential information, not to communicate it.

The duty extended to taking reasonable care of the master's property and demonstrating reasonable levels of skill in performance of the work. Thus, in accepting employment, the servant was deemed to have guaranteed that he possessed the necessary skill for the work. As Willes J commented in *Harmer v Cornelius* [1858] 5 CBNS 236:

JUDGMENT

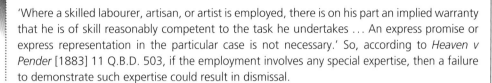

'Where a skilled labourer, artisan, or artist is employed, there is on his part an implied warranty that he is of skill reasonably competent to the task he undertakes ... An express promise or express representation in the particular case is not necessary.' So, according to *Heaven v Pender* [1883] 11 Q.B.D. 503, if the employment involves any special expertise, then a failure to demonstrate such expertise could result in dismissal.

The second major duty was that identified in *Spain v Arnott* [1817] 2 Stark. 256 to obey all lawful and reasonable commands of the master. What was reasonable was a question of fact in each case. For instance, in *Hallward v Snell* [1886] 2 TLR 836 a regulation in a boarding school forbidding smoking in the dining room was considered reasonable and the refusal by one teacher to obey the regulation justified his dismissal. However, in *Jacquot v Bowru* [1839] 34 Digest 70, 478 a defence to a claim for wages on the grounds that the servant had obstinately refused to work was denied where the judge commented:

JUDGMENT

'if the plaintiff's wife had been requested to work during church time and had obstinately refused that would have been to her credit'.

Certainly a servant was bound to disobey commands which were in conflict with his legal duties. As a result in *Wilson v Stewart* [1863] 9 Cox CC 354 a servant who, acting under his master's orders, harboured prostitutes, was convicted of aiding and abetting. On the other hand, observance of a moral duty did not necessarily justify disobedience. In *Turner v Mason* [1845] 34 Digest 69. 463 a servant whose mother had suffered a seizure and was believed likely to die, was refused permission to visit her by her employer. She went anyway and the court concluded that:

JUDGMENT

'It is very questionable whether any service to be rendered to any other person than the master would suffice as an excuse; she might go, but it would be at the peril of being told that she could not return.'

1.4.4 The legal relationship of master and servant and third parties

Since servants were essentially 'men of straw', without the means to compensate, the common law developed rules to impose liability on masters for wrongs committed by their servants, but only where they occurred within the course of employment. In *Quarman v Burnett* [1840] 34 Digest 23, 29 Baron Parke explained:

JUDGMENT

'Upon the principle <u>qui facit per alium facit per se</u> the master is responsible for the acts of his servant and that person is undoubtedly liable, who stood in the relation of the master to the wrongdoer – he who had selected him as his servant, from the knowledge of a belief belief in his skill and care, and who could remove him for his misconduct, and whose orders he was bound to receive and obey.'

Where the master gave the servant discretion how to act, he had to accept the consequences of that discretion being used inadvisably. In *Bayley v Manchester, Sheffield and Lincolnshire Railway Co.* [1872] 7 CP 415 where a porter, believing a passenger was on the wrong train, ejected him so forcibly that he was injured, Willes J observed:

JUDGMENT

'A person who puts another in his place to do a class of acts in his absence, necessarily leaves him to determine, according to the circumstances, when an act of that class is to be done; and consequently he is held answerable for the wrong of the person so entrusted either in the manner of doing such an act or in doing such an act under circumstances in which it ought not to have been done, provided that what was done was done, not from any caprice of the servant, but in the course of employment.'

However, in *Williams v Jones* [1865] 34 Digest 138, 1077 it was stated that the servant doing what he was employed to do in a negligent fashion was not within the scope of employment. Nevertheless, providing the act was deemed to be in the course of employment, it could make the master liable even where he had forbidden the act. This included leaving a house unattended despite express instructions so that a third party was injured *Whatman v Pearson* [1868] 34 Digest 130, 1,000, and causing injury to a third party while racing with a competitor's vehicle despite an express prohibition *Limpus v General Omnibus Co.* [1862] 34 Digest 129, 989.

Since every tortfeasor is ultimately liable for his own wrongdoing, the servant was not able to plead his contract of employment as a defence in actions against him, so that his own liability might remain *Dixon v Fawcus* [1861] 34 Digest 187, 1544. In *Stephens v Elwall* [1815] 34 Digest 186, 1525 it was considered that the servant's ignorance and the fact that the act was solely for the benefit of the master was no justification or defence for the wrong.

1.4.5 The liability of the master for injury to his servant
The master's duties
One of the most important considerations of workers in the new industrial environment was the consequence of injury or illness caused through work. It is reasonable to suggest that in the changed working conditions they were more likely to suffer either.

Before the introduction of statutory safety provisions there was little obligation on an employer to compensate or help an injured worker. Cairns LC in *Wilson v Merry* [1868] 34 Digest 211, 1747 explained:

JUDGMENT

'The master is not and cannot be liable to his servant unless there be negligence ... in that in which he ... has contracted with his servant to do. What the master is bound to his servant to do, in the event of his not personally superintending and directing the work, is to select proper and competent persons to do so.'

So the master would only have to compensate a worker if there was evidence of negligence and, provided that he could show that he had engaged reasonably competent servants, he bore no liability for injuries to his workers.

By the end of the nineteenth century, and even after much statutory reform, the common law position had only changed to the extent that, in the case of premises which contained an element of danger, there should be, as the judge stated in *Thomas v Quartermaine* [1887] 18 QBD 685 an obligation to take 'such precautions as are reasonable in each instance to prevent mischief'.

The defence of Volenti non fit injuria

Employers were able to avoid liability at common law for injury to their workers if they could show that they were aware of any risks and accepted them as part of their employment. In *Thomas v Quartermaine* (above) an employee worked in a narrow alley between two vats, one a boiling vat and the other a cooling vat. In trying to remove a board, he pulled hard and fell into the boiling vat. Although he worked in a narrow space, making his work difficult, he was held to have consented to the risk.

Whether or not the servant did accept the risk of harm was considered to be a question of fact, not law, although the burden of proof was on the master *Williams v Birmingham Battery & Metal Co.* [1899] 2 QB 338. The master had to show that the servant willingly undertook the risk, not that he was merely aware of it. In *Smith v Baker* [1891] AC 325 evidence was given that the claimant avoided walking under the hoppers of stone which caused his injury whenever possible. The evidence removed any doubt that he had consented.

Contributory negligence

Contributory negligence was another defence enabling an employer to avoid liability or reduce levels of compensation to an injured servant. Lord Ellenborough defined the basis of the rule in *Butterfield v Forrester* [1809] 11 East 60:

JUDGMENT

'One person's being in fault will not dispense with another's using ordinary care for himself.'

So, where a master might be liable for injury to his servant, but the servant had done or omitted to do some act which made the injury more likely, then he might lose his claim altogether, or lose a proportion of compensation based on the degree to which the court felt that he had contributed to his own harm.

The scope of the defence was later limited (ultimately in the Law Reform (Contributory Negligence) Act 1945). In *Bridge v The Grand Junction Railway Co.* [1838] 3 M & W 244 Baron Parke stated:

JUDGMENT

'Although there may have been negligence on the part of the plaintiff, yet, unless he might, by the exercise of ordinary care, have avoided the consequences of the defendant's negligence, he is entitled to recover: if by ordinary care he might have avoided them, he is the author of his own wrong.'

Res ipsa loquitur

When a claimant was required to prove the negligence of the defendant, the courts sometimes extended the assistance of the doctrine of *res ipsa loquitur* (literally 'the thing speaks for itself'). This was explained by Erle CJ in *Scott v The London and St. Katherine Docks Co.* [1865] 3 H & C 596:

JUDGMENT

'There must be reasonable evidence of negligence, but where the thing is shown to be under the management of the defendant or his servants, and the accident is such as in the ordinary course of things does not happen if those who have the management use proper care, it affords reasonable evidence, in the absence of explanation by the defendants, that the accident arose from want of care.'

Common employment

Probably the legal doctrine which most adversely affected working people at the time was 'common employment', known also as the 'fellow servant' rule, framed by Lord Abinger in *Priestly v Fowler* [1837] 3 M & W 1. In brief, once a servant accepted work, he undertook to run all risks that were consequent of the employment, and these risks included the wrongs of fellow servants. In assessing whether a master should be liable in respect of his servant's negligence, he stressed that the inconvenience, not to say the absurdities, of these consequences afforded a sufficient argument against the application of the principle in the actual case.

The rule was really established in *Hutchinson v The York, Newcastle and Berwick Railway Co.* [1850] 5 Exch 351 where Baron Alderson held that the negligence of the fellow servant:

JUDGMENT

'was a risk which Hutchinson must be taken to have agreed to run when he entered into the defendant's service, and for the consequences of which, therefore, they are not responsible'.

In *Skip v Eastern Counties Railway Co.* [1851] 9 Exch 223 the judge similarly held that the engagement of an insufficient number of workers by the employer was also a normal risk to be accepted as part of the injured servant's contract.

Again in *Wilson v Merry* [1868] 34 Digest 211, 1747 the court confirmed that all the employer needed to do was to demonstrate that he had engaged competent staff, and equipped them with adequate resources, to escape liability for industrial injuries.

The rule meant that workers, particularly in the mines and on the railways, were left without adequate compensation when injured at work, so that the rule was inevitably criticised by representatives of workers.

QUOTATION

'In common fairness and equity, I think that if the individual employer is responsible for his own act, so the owner who delegates his authority for the carrying out of the work to the one or the many, ought to be responsible for the acts of all those that do what he himself would do, if he did not delegate his power.'

William Crawford Secretary of the Durham Miners, Report of the Select Committee on Employer's Liability for Injury to their Servants

The establishment response in the same Report was intransigent:

QUOTATION

> 'There can be no doubt that the effect of abolishing the defence of "common employment", would effect a serious disturbance in the industrial arrangements of the country.'

In fact the rule was not abolished until 1948.

1.4.6 Comment

The sections above indicate that the common law was interested in clarifying the complexities of the new employment relationship, which it viewed as being based on a free contractual relationship. In that respect the rules seem fair and impartial.

However, to workers like the weavers and artisans, whose former trades and independence was under threat, direct employment was a new way of life, and only then for those who could secure it. Formerly they might have expected to dictate some of the terms of their employment and to have received the reward for their finished work. Following industrialisation they were subjected to the unlicensed competition of unskilled labour and were forced into wage labour themselves. To them entering into direct employment must have seemed anything but the result of free contractual negotiations. The courts, as a result, ignored these very imbalances in the relationship in developing contractual laws.

On the question of the conditions in the factories, the courts appear to have played no role at all in achieving improvements, and in fairness this is probably more the role of Parliament. Nevertheless, when the implications of the fellow servant rule are realised, then the common law can be seen to have had a detrimental effect on the conditions of industrial workers. In short the common law in the nineteenth century appears to have done little if anything for realising the aspirations of or improving the conditions of working people.

1.5 Advancements and reductions in modern employment rights

The experiences of the nineteenth century and changing working conditions gave rise to a committed and coordinated trade union movement. It also led to the development of a political party which also had a stated aim of representing the interests of working people. With improvement in working conditions being a stated aim of both the push for employment protections became a political as well as an industrial campaign. Since the twentieth century threw up governments representing both employers' and employees' interests, regulation of employment and working conditions has inevitably varied according to the party in power. Some of these developments are charted below as advances and consequent reductions in employment protection.

1.5.1 Advances in employment rights and protections

1. Early in the twentieth century protective rights were supplemented by measures to curb exploitation e.g. the Wages Councils.

2. In the 1950s conditions were generally settled by free collective bargaining – 'collective *laissez faire*' Otto Kahn-Freund.

3. A move towards a basic 'floor of rights' emerged in the 1960s:
   - the Contracts of Employment Act 1963 – introduced minimum notice periods and written statements of terms;

- the Redundancy Payments Act 1965 – the idea that employer should consider alternatives to dismissal;
- the Trade Disputes Act 1965 reversed *Rookes v Barnard*.

4. The Donovan Commission 1968 suggested pay bargaining at local level to improve productivity and resolve differences quickly.

5. Labour followed this with the White Paper 'In place of strife' – but industrial unrest defeated it.

6. The Industrial Relations Act 1971 tried to create a framework for industrial relations – it failed but it did introduce the idea of unfair dismissal.

7. Labour between 1974 and 1979 introduced a consolidation package with:
   - the Employment Protection Act 1975, the Employment Protection Consolidation Act 1978 – on employment rights;
   - the Sex Discrimination Act 1975 and the Race Relations Act 1976.

8. The EU (formerly the EC) has also been a major source of increased employee rights:
   - though the effect was much reduced by hostility of Conservative governments between 1979 to 1997 to European employment law;
   - using the reasoning that [EC] employment law and social policy were just 'socialism entering by the back door';
   - but certain law was forced on the government during the period often as a result of infringement proceedings in the European Court of Justice (ECJ) e.g. the Equal Pay Directive 75/117 in the Equal Pay (Amendment) Regulations 1983; and the Acquired Rights Directive 77/187 in the Transfer of Undertakings (Protection of Employment) Regulations 1981;
   - and EU case law had similar effect *Marshall v Southampton and South West Hampshire AHA (No 1)* [1986].

9. The Labour government 1997–2010 was committed to employee protection.

10. It signed the Social Chapter so the EU could introduce social legislation that built up in Protocol process but was not introduced.

11. A number of measures were introduced:
    - the Working Time Regulations 1998 – which introduced minimum conditions for working time, rest periods, holidays, night work etc. from the Working Time Directive;
    - the National Minimum Wage Act 1998 – reintroduced minimum wage rates, but not restricted to particular industries;
    - the Public Interest Disclosure Act 1998 – for whistle-blowing;
    - the Data Protection Act 1998 – regulation on protected data;
    - the Unfair Dismissal Order 1999 – qualifying period to one year;
    - the Employment Relations Act 1999 – including rules on union recognition, representation on disciplinary and grievance procedures, and family friendly policies such as parental leave, dependant relative leave, etc.;
    - the EC Part Time Workers Directive and the Fixed Term Contract Directive, and movement on Works Councils.

1.5.2 Reductions of employee rights and protections

1. Legislation of 1980s–1990s restricted rights and protections enjoyed by employees in a number of ways:
   - right to return after pregnancy limited by Employment Act 1980;

- unfair dismissal qualifying period increased;
- deposits required for employment tribunals by Employment Act 1989;
- rights to particulars of disciplinary procedures for small firms (fewer than twenty employees) in Employment Act 1989;
- Wages Councils abolished in Trade Union Reform and Employment Rights Act 1993;
- criminal sanctions for unauthorised deductions from pay abolished in the Wages Act 1986;
- restrictions on heavy work and night work in factories for women removed in the Employment Act 1989;
- time off for trade union activities was restricted;
- trade union immunities curtailed by Employment Act 1980 and 1982, and Trade Union Act 1984;
- government of 1980s and 1990s resisted employment protection measures required under EC law;
- although mass of legislation built up led to introduction of consolidating Act – Employment Rights Act 1996.

2. The current government has changed the unfair dismissal qualifying period back to two years.

Over the last forty years Britain has again undergone a dramatic transformation in the character of employment. The benefits of computer technology and the development of machinery to exploit it have made labour intensive industry often unnecessary or uneconomic. Traditional skills have been again made redundant, similar to the handloom weavers in the nineteenth century. A more recent dependence on the financial services market and the subsequent crash have posed even greater problems. Great emphasis has been placed on retraining for new skills and more inclusive education, but the effectiveness of each in producing actual employment could be questioned.

There appear to be great parallels with the experiences of the nineteenth century. Suggestions for lowering wages and removing minimum wage levels, even the suggested threat of withdrawing from the EU in some quarters, are deemed to be essentials for making industry profitable but at the same time echo the so-called 'last hour' argument constantly used in the nineteenth century debate against lowering hours of work. Lack of investment, increasing unemployment, a lowering of wages in real terms and an increased cost of living all pose problems not just for working people but for the economy itself which depends, in terms of public services at least, on the taxes of ordinary employees.

SUMMARY

- Comprehensive regulation of employment dates back as far as the Statute of Artificers and Apprentices 1562.
- The statute covered every type of employment of the time.
- Important provisions included wage fixing clauses and clauses fixing the numbers that could be apprenticed to different trades.
- This was still the law as the Industrial Revolution developed in the mid eighteenth century.
- But increasingly the courts would not enforce its provisions because of the development of laissez-faire economics and the needs of capitalist enterprises.

- Between 1750 and 1850 the character of work changed dramatically – people became more dependent on wage labour, unskilled labour increased, women and children were the largest part of the workforce and there was high unemployment amongst adult males.

- In the nineteenth century Parliament tried to improve working conditions, mainly through industrial safety law and regulating hours of work, but most provisions only applied to women and child workers.

- The judiciary developed the 'master and servant' relationship, applied strict rule of contract and considered that the employment relationship was a free contractual one, even though this failed to recognise the imbalances in the relationship.

- The courts also developed the duties of master and servant.

- Masters also had defences of *Volenti non fit injuria*, contributory negligence (at that time a complete defence), and the 'fellow servant' rule which made it hard for workers to gain compensation for injuries that they suffered at work

Further reading

Cole, G D H and Postgate, R, *The Common People 1746–1946*. Methuen, 1963.

Dicey, A V, *Lectures on the Relation between Law and Public Opinion During the Nineteenth Century*. Macmillan, 1905.

Gaskell, P, *The Manufacturing Population in England 1833*. Reprinted in the Cass Library of Industrial Classics, 1968.

Hammond, J L and Hammond, B, *The Skilled Labourer*. Longmans, 1919.

Hammond, J L and Hammond, B, *The Town Labourer*. Longmans, 1978.

Hammond, J L and Hammond, B, *The Village Labourer*. Longmans, 1924.

Hobsbawn, E, *The Age of Revolution 1789–1848*. New American Library, 1962.

Manchester, A H, *Modern Legal History 1750–1950*. Butterworths, 1980.

Mansfield Cooper, W, *Outlines of Industrial Law*. Butterworths, 1954.

Thompson, E P, *The Making of the English Working Class*. Penguin, 1980.

2

The effects of EU membership on UK employment law

AIMS AND OBJECTIVES

After reading this chapter you should be able to:

- Understand the background to UK membership of the EU
- Understand what is meant by the supranational order
- Understand the concepts of supremacy, direct effect, indirect effect and state liability and how they operate
- Understand how EU labour has developed and how it impacts on UK employment law
- Critically analyse the area
- Apply the law to factual situations and reach conclusions

2.1 UK membership of the European Union

2.1.1 Introduction

Many areas of English Law have now developed beyond recognition as a result of the UK joining what originally was the European Economic Community (EEC), later the European Community (EC), which following the Treaty on European Union (TEU) became a central pillar of the European Union (EU), and now following the Treaty of Lisbon is the European Union.

The UK was in fact invited to take part in the framing of the original three Treaties with a view to becoming a member of an economic community that in effect began with six nations, France, Italy, Germany, Belgium, the Netherlands and Luxembourg, in 1957. However, for various reasons, both economic and political, the UK declined to become involved either in the drafting of the Treaties or founding membership. Later abortive attempts to join were made but it was not until sixteen years later that the UK eventually became a Member State on 1 January 1973. Membership of the EU has had a significant impact on the UK in most economic areas and this is certainly the case with the law governing employment, particularly those providing employment protections.

2.1.2 The basis of UK membership

The UK government having signed the treaty of accession was also required then to pass an Act of Parliament to incorporate membership and the Treaties into English law. This is because the UK has a *dualist* constitution: this means that international treaties do not automatically become part of the constitution and gain force merely on signing, they need to be incorporated. Other Member States have dualist constitutions, including Germany, Italy and Belgium. In *monist* constitutions, on the other hand, the treaty is automatically incorporated into the national legal system at the point of ratification. Member States with monist constitutions include France and the Netherlands.

Other than the power to implement EU legislation through delegated legislation granted in section 2(2) there are two other critical sections. Section 2(2) states:

SECTION

'2

(2) Subject to Schedule 2 to this Act, at any time after its passing Her Majesty may by Order in Council, and any designated Minister or department may by regulations, make provision –

(a) for the purpose of implementing any Community obligation of the United Kingdom, or enabling any such obligation to be implemented, or of enabling any rights enjoyed or to be enjoyed by the United Kingdom under or by virtue of the Treaties to be exercised; or

(b) for the purpose of dealing with matters arising out of or related to any such obligation or rights or the coming into force, or the operation from time to time, of subsection (1) above.'

This section was of course vital, not only for the purpose of implementing EU legislation as required under the Treaties but for being able to repeal inconsistent national law without the constant need for Act of Parliament.

The section actually incorporating the Treaties, and in consequence EU (at that time EC) law, is section 2(1). This section states:

SECTION

'2

(1) All such rights, powers, liabilities, obligations and restrictions from time to time created or arising by or under the Treaties, as in accordance with the Treaties, are without further enactment to be given legal effect or used in the UK and shall be recognised and available in law, and be enforced, allowed and followed accordingly, and the expression "enforceable Community right" and similar expressions shall be read as referring to one to which the subsection applies.'

This is a quite straightforward enactment and is a simple statement of intent. The UK by the enactment automatically incorporated all existing EU law including the Treaties and all existing secondary legislation. Also all future EU legislative provisions would become law and be recognised as enforceable.

In the case of future EU legislative measures such as Regulations this would be automatic because they are described in Article 288 TFEU as 'directly applicable', meaning that they automatically become law in Member States with no need for further enactment, except possibly to repeal inconsistent domestic legislation. In the case of directives these are defined in Article 288 as 'binding as to the result to be achieved'. Member

States are obliged to implement by a set date but can do so in the manner they choose. In the case of directives then section 2(1) identifies that this will happen.

One other clear consequence of section 2(1) is that the case law of the Court of Justice becomes a part of English law and because of the doctrine of precedent will exist as precedent for English courts to follow.

Section 2(1) is also supplemented and reinforced by section 2(4), which states:

SECTION

'2

(4) The provision that may be made under subsection (2) above includes, subject to schedule 2 to this Act, any such provision (of any such extent) as might be made by Act of Parliament, and any enactment passed or to be passed, other than one contained in this part of this Act, shall be construed and have effect subject to the foregoing provisions of this section.'

Following the enactment of the Act the existence of previous English law that might conflict with the broad aims of the Treaties presented no real problem; it was in effect automatically repealed by the Act. The major problem concerns either the possibility of English law made after the passing of the Act which is inconsistent with provisions of EU law, or a failure by the UK government to implement or give effect to EU law as required. The problem seems to hinge on the extent to which the above sections are in fact entrenched or whether they are merely aids to construction.

2.2 The supranational legal order of the EU

One of the major problems facing a union of nations subjecting themselves to a common legal order is that there is likely to be a wide variance in how the Treaties are then interpreted and applied in the individual Member States. In fact the whole history of the EU (and the former EC) demonstrates a constant tension between the commitment of the EU institutions, particularly the Court of Justice, striving to achieve the objectives of the Treaties and national self-interest acting as a break on progress.

In consequence it was envisaged even before the Treaties were drafted that for the legal order to have any effect the institutions must be 'supranational' in character and in effect. Supranational simply means in areas involving Treaty obligations or those created under subsidiary legislation, the EU institutions and obligations are superior to national law and institutions. In pursuing supranationalism and seeking to give full effect to the EU legal order and the attainment of Treaty objectives the Court of Justice has undeniably been the most significant institution both in administering and defining EU law. In many ways it has created the principle of 'supranationalism' through developing the principles of supremacy, direct effect, indirect effect and state liability.

QUOTATION

'ECJ has uniformly and consistently been the most effective integration institution in the Community [now EU]. . . . From its very inception in the Treaty, the ECJ set about establishing its hierarchical authority as the ultimate court of constitutional review. In this area two areas in particular are important. First there is the role of the ECJ in controlling Member State courts, and, second, there is the role of the Court in managing the incessant inter-institutional struggles.'

Ian Ward *A Critical Introduction to European Law*, Butterworths, 1996

2.2.1 EU legal instruments

The Treaties, now principally the Treaty on the Functioning of the European Union (TFEU) and the Treaty on European Union (TEU) are obviously the most significant source of EU law and they are the primary source of law. Apart from anything else they include the broad objectives of the EU as well as outlining a variety of substantive rights. Inevitably, however, legislation is needed to provide greater detail.

EU subsidiary legislation is given force in Article 288 of the TFEU (originally Article 189 EC Treaty). This identifies that:

ARTICLE

'288
To exercise the Union's competences, the institutions shall adopt regulations, directives, decisions, recommendations and opinions.'

Besides identifying the power of the institutions to introduce legislation, Article 288 also goes on to define the different forms of secondary legislation. There are in fact five but two are of particular significance; regulations and directives.

ARTICLE

'288
A regulation shall have general application. It shall be binding in its entirety and directly applicable in all Member States.
   A directive shall be binding, as to the result to be achieved, upon each Member State to which it is addressed, but shall leave to the national authorities the choice of form and methods.'

Regulations

Regulations are relatively straightforward legislative instruments often used for development of broad principles. Looking at the terminology used in the Article:

- 'General application' means that a regulation applies generally to the whole of the EU, to all Member States.
- 'Binding in its entirety' is also straightforward; it means that Member States have to give effect to the whole regulation with no exception.
- 'Directly applicable' is probably has the least obvious meaning but is hugely significant in terms of supranationalism meaning that a regulation automatically becomes law in each Member State on the date specified without any need for implementation of any kind – the consequence being that it is superior law to inconsistent national law, if not before, certainly after the creation of the doctrine of supremacy of EU law (see Chapter 2.2.2).

Regulations are also obviously capable of creating rights and obligations which are then directly enforceable in the national courts through the principle of direct effect (see Chapter 2.2.3).

Directives

Directives are a more complex and potentially more problematic legislative measure. Looking at the terminology in Article 288 there are two significant aspects to directives:

- 'Binding as to the object to be achieved' means that, while directives are binding on Member States, unlike regulations which are directly applicable and demand absolute uniformity, they are used instead for harmonisation of law, to ensure that Member States adapt their own laws for the application of common standards in order to achieve the objectives laid out in the directive.

- 'Shall leave to the national authorities the choice of form and methods' means again that, unlike with regulations that automatically become law in Member States, directives give an element of discretion to the Member States and allow them to choose the most appropriate method of implementation to achieve the objectives set out in the directive.

A third key aspect of directives is that Member States are given an implementation period so that the directive must be implemented into domestic law within a set deadline.

Because directives are harmonising measures they are mainly used in areas where the diversity of national laws could prevent the effective functioning of the single market. There are many examples in the field of employment which can be found in the following chapters including:

- the Pregnant Workers Directive 92/85 in Chapter 8;

- the Agency Workers Directive 2008/104 in Chapter 4;

- the Equal Pay Directive 75/117, Equal Treatment Directive 76/207 and the Recast Directive 2006/54 that replaced them in Chapters 10 and 11;

- the Working Time Directive 93/104, the Young Workers Directive 94/33 and the Working Time Directive 2003/88 in Chapter 16;

- the Acquired Rights Directive 77/187 in Chapter 18.

There are references to EU directives in most chapters indicating the influence of EU membership on UK employment law.

One problem associated with directives is whether they are enforceable if Member States fail to implement or fail to implement properly. An example of the former can be found in Chapter 16 with the then UK Conservative government failing to implement at all the Working Time Directive 93/104. This was only implemented in the UK after a change of government in 1997. Examples of the second can be found in Chapter 10 where the UK government was the subject of infringement proceedings in the ECJ for its failure to fully implement Directive 75/117, the Equal Pay Directive by providing an action for equal pay for work of equal value. The problems caused by the definition of directives under Article 288 led to the ECJ developing the concepts of direct effect, indirect effect and state liability in order to ensure that EU citizens were able to benefit from the rights given in directives (see Chapter 2.2.3) and the seminal case of *Marshall v Southampton and South West Hampshire AHA (Teaching) (No 1)* 152/84 [1986] QB 401 provides another classic example of an incompletely or improperly implemented directive, and also of the determination of the ECJ to ensure that the enforceability of rights emanating from it.

2.2.2 Supremacy

Supremacy is probably the most entrenched and yet surprisingly the least contested of EU principles. This of course is fairly surprising in the UK considering the almost institutionalised scepticism towards the EU and the fact that membership is still a hotly debated issue, even in political circles, nearly forty years after the UK joined and almost as many since a Yes vote in a referendum on membership.

The Treaties in fact make no reference to supremacy of EU law over national law. Article 4(3) TEU does state what has often been referred to as the oath of allegiance (formerly in Article 10 EC Treaty).

ARTICLE

'4

(3) Pursuant to the principle of sincere cooperation, the Union and the Member States shall, in full mutual respect, assist each other in carrying out tasks which flow from the Treaties.

The Member States shall take any appropriate measure, general or particular, to ensure fulfilment of the obligations arising out of the Treaties or resulting from the acts of the institutions of the Union.

The Member States shall facilitate the achievement of the Union's tasks and refrain from any measure which could jeopardise the attainment of the Union's objectives.'

It is obvious that it is essential that EU law should be uniformly applied throughout all Member States. Without supremacy the institutions would not be supranational and would have no effective power and the full economic integration necessary to achieve the single market would have been impossible if Member States were able to ignore or even deliberately defy the supranational powers of the institutions of the EU. The single market depends upon harmonisation of laws between Member States, which in turn depends on uniform application of EU law within the Member States. In fact the whole structure of the EU was based on the idea of supranationalism.

The ECJ has been proactive in developing a doctrine of supremacy of EU law without which the institutions would have been deprived of any supranational character and effect and uniformity would inevitably have been sacrificed to national self-interest.

In consequence there are two real justifications for the ECJ having developed the doctrine:

- First it prevents any possibility of a questioning of the validity of EU law within the Member States themselves.

- Second it fulfils what has sometimes been referred to as the 'doctrine of pre-emption'. It achieves this in two principal ways:

  - first supremacy of EU law over inconsistent national law means that the courts in the Member States are prevented from producing alternative interpretations of EU law which may then result in lack of harmony and a disruption to the effective running of the single market;

  - second the doctrine has the other critical consequence that the legislative bodies of the individual Member States are prevented from enacting legislation that would conflict with EU law.

The first statement suggesting the supremacy of EU law over national law came in *Van Gend en Loos v Nederlandse Administratie der Belastingen* [1963] 26/62 ECR 1, [1963] CMLR 105 (the case principally concerns the issue of direct effect and is therefore more fully discussed in 2.2.3 below). A Dutch citizen suffered financial loss as a result of a breach of EU (at the time EC) law. In a reference to the ECJ the question was whether or not the treaty created rights on behalf of individuals that were then enforceable in national courts.

In the reasoned opinion the Advocate General declared that this was not the case and that the appropriate means of resolution in such circumstances was in an action against the Member State under Article 258 TFEU (at the time Article 169 EC treaty). The Judges in the ECJ disagreed.

JUDGMENT

In their judgment the judges made the following significant comment: 'The community [now EU] constitutes a new legal order in international law for whose benefits the states have limited their sovereign rights, albeit within limited fields.'

The major explanation of the doctrine and its implications was provided by the court only two years later.

CASE EXAMPLE

Costa v ENEL 6/64 [1964] ECR 585

ENEL (more formally known as *Ente Nazionale per l'Energia Elettrica*) was a state electric company under which the Italian government had nationalised (put under state ownership) both the production and distribution of electricity. Costa owned shares in the company and argued that the law privatising the industry breached EU (then EC) competition law. Following a judgment in the Italian constitutional court, a reference was made to the ECJ. The Italian government argued that those proceedings were unlawful as the court should have followed the Italian law which came after that ratifying the Treaty. The ECJ expanded on the principle that it had first stated in *Van Gend en Loos* and expanded with some significant statements.

JUDGMENT

First the court stated: 'By contrast with ordinary international treaties, the EC Treaty [now TFEU] has created its own legal system which on entry into force … became an integral part of the legal systems of the member states and which their courts are bound to apply. By creating a Community of limited duration having … powers stemming from a limitation of the sovereignty, or a transfer of powers from the states to the community, the member states have limited their sovereign rights, albeit within limited fields, and have thus created a body of law which binds both their nationals and themselves.'

It also added: 'The transfer, by member states from their national orders in favour of the [EU] order of its rights and obligations arising from the Treaty, carries with it a clear limitation of their sovereign right upon which a subsequent unilateral law, incompatible with the aims of the community cannot prevail.'

Concluding: 'It follows from all these observations that the law stemming from the Treaty, an independent source of law, could not, because of its special and original nature, be overridden by domestic legal provisions, however framed, without being deprived of its character as [EU] law and without the legal basis of the [EU] itself being called into question.'

This was the first clear definition and explanation of the consequences of the doctrine of supremacy. It was followed by *International Handelsgesellschaft GmbH v EVGF* 11/70 [1970] ECR 1125, [1972] CMLR 255 which extended the principle supremacy to include national constitutional principles over which EU law would still be supreme. In *Simmenthal SpA v Amministrazione delle Finanze dello Stato* 70/77 [1978] ECR 1453, [1978] 3 CMLR 670 the ECJ also identified that supremacy applies whether the national rule comes before or after the EC (now EU) rule. In *Commission v France (The Merchant Sailor's case)* 167/63 the court also identified that supremacy applies not just to directly conflicting national law but to any contradictory law which encroaches on an area of Community (now the EU) competence.

There are some obvious consequences of the doctrine:

- Member States have given up certain of their sovereign powers to make law – in fact sovereignty is pooled rather than lost.
- The Member States as well as their citizens are bound by EU law (and may gain rights from EU law – see 2.2.3 below).
- The legislature of Member States cannot unilaterally introduce law that conflicts with their EU obligations.

The clearest example of this last point and also the most dramatic statement of supremacy interestingly involves legislation of the UK Parliament.

CASE EXAMPLE

R v Secretary of State for Transport ex p Factortame Ltd C-213/89 [1990] ECR 1–2433

UK registered companies involved in trawling were mostly owned by Spanish nationals. The Merchant Shipping Act 1988 and the Merchant Shipping (Registration of Fishing Vessels) Regulations 1988 required that a certain percentage of ownership should be in the hands of UK nationals. In the English court the applicants argued that the requirement was in breach of Article 18 as it discriminated on nationality, as a result of which they were denied fishing rights otherwise guaranteed by EU (then EC) law. The problem for the then House of Lords was that the Act enacted after accession to the Treaties in 1972 specifically contradicted EU law. Because the applicants had sought an interim injunction pending a final decision on the issue if the court granted it this would involve suspending operation of an Act of Parliament until the inconsistency issue could be settled on reference to the ECJ. The Divisional Court had decided that a reference should be made and had granted an injunction and had ordered the Secretary of State to stop applying the parts of the Act in question until a preliminary ruling was given by the ECJ. The Secretary of State appealed and the Court of Appeal granted the appeal setting aside the order of the Divisional Court resulting in an appeal to the House of Lords. The problem facing the House of Lords was that there was no rule of English constitutional law that would allow the injunction and it was unsure whether EU law overrode the supremacy of Parliament to the extent of allowing a national court to suspend operation of a provision within an Act. It made a reference to the ECJ posing the question whether in order to protect EU rights a national court must grant the interim suspension of an Act of Parliament.

JUDGMENT

The ECJ stated: 'it is for the national courts in application of the principle of co-operation laid down in [article 4(3) TEU] ... to ensure the legal protection which persons derive from the direct effect of provisions of [EU] law ... any provision of a national legal system and any legislative, administrative, or judicial practice which might impair the effectiveness of [EU] law by withholding from the national court having jurisdiction to apply such law the power to do everything necessary ... to set aside national legislative provisions which might prevent, even temporarily, [EU] rules from having full force and effect are incompatible with those requirements which are the very essence of [EU] law ... the full effectiveness of [EU] law would be just as much impaired if a rule of national law could prevent a court seized of a dispute governed by [EU] law from granting interim relief in order to ensure the full effectiveness of the judgment to be given on the existence of the rights claimed under [EU] law. It therefore follows that a court which in those circumstances would grant interim relief, if it were not for a rule of national law, is obliged to set aside that law.'

Is there English law on an area covered by EU law?
- Parliament passes new legislation on an area covered by EU Law
- an English court delivers a judgment on an area governed by EU law

YES

Is the English law inconsistent with EU law?
- Parliament introduces English law that ignores or contravenes EU law (an example is the Merchant Shipping Act and the case of Factortame)
- an English court gives a ruling which is incompatible with EU law principles (an example is *Macarthys Ltd v Smith* [1980] ICR 672)
- Parliament fails to implement a directive at all (an example is the failure of the UK government to implement the Working Time Directive 93/104) or Parliament fails to fully or properly implement a directive (an example is directive 76/207, the Equal Treatment Directive and the case of *Marshall v Southampton and South West Hampshire AHA* (Teaching) (No 1) 152/84 [1986] QB 401)

YES

EU LAW TAKES PRECEDENCE OVER INCONSISTENT DOMESTIC LAW – THE NATIONAL LAW IS INVALID – INFRINGEMENT PROCEEDINGS UNDER ARTICLE 258 IF THE SITUATION IS NOT REMEDIED

Figure 2.1 Flow chart illustrating how supremacy of EU law works

2.2.3 Direct effect, indirect effect and state liability

The basic requirements for direct effect

As with supremacy (see 2.2.2 above) direct effect was the creation of the ECJ. It created both concepts in the same case. Direct effect simply means the ability of a citizen of the EU to enforce principles of EU law in a national court. Both concepts are essential if the objectives of the treaties are to be achieved and the principle of supranationalism on which the single market is based. In this case the citizen would have had no protection if he had been unable to rely on EU law in the case.

CASE EXAMPLE

Van Gend en Loos v Nederlands Administratie der Belastingen 26/62

In *Van Gend en Loos* (as we have seen in 2.2.2 above), the claimant had objected to paying an increased duty which he argued contravened the then Article 12 EC Treaty (now Article 30 TFEU). In the reference to the ECJ the Dutch court questioned whether the Article was capable of creating rights in favour of individuals which a national court was then bound to protect. The Advocate General in his reasoned opinion suggested that, since the Article contained no explicit mention of individual rights, that it could not be construed as granting individual rights and that the appropriate action was infringement proceedings (now under Article 258 TFEU). The *judges* in the ECJ held that, since the treaty was clearly intended to affect individuals, even though it made no specific mention of rights, it must clearly be capable of creating rights that would be enforceable by individuals in national courts.

JUDGMENT

The court identified: 'Independently of the legislation of the member states [EU] law ... not only imposes obligations on individuals but is also intended to confer upon them rights which become part of their legal heritage. These rights are granted not only where they are expressly granted by the Treaty, but also by reason of obligations which the Treaty imposes in a clearly defined way upon individuals as well as upon member states and the institutions of the [EU]' and that the Article was: 'ideally adapted to produce direct effects between member states and their subjects'.

As indicated by the Advocate General the original method for ensuring that EU law was enforced in Member States was by infringement proceedings under Article 258. The ECJ established the process of direct effect because it was a much more effective means of ensuring that citizens of Member States could enforce the rights given to them by the Treaties. The uncompromising nature of the court led to it also developing the principles of indirect effect and state liability to ensure that citizens benefit from the rights granted them in the Treaties. However, this has been dependent on reference procedure and the national courts.

QUOTATION

F Mancini in 'The making of a constitution for Europe' (1989) 26 *CML Rev* 595 (Kluwer Academic Publishers) identifies the significance of this. 'The national courts ... by referring to Luxembourg sensitive questions of interpretation of [EU] law ... have been indirectly responsible for the boldest judgments the Court has made. Moreover, by adhering to these judgments in deciding the cases before them, and therefore by lending them the credibility which national judges usually enjoy in their own countries, they have rendered the case-law of the Court both effective and respected throughout the [EU].'

The court also identified the criteria for direct effect.

- The provision must be sufficiently clear and precisely stated – the ECJ in *Defrenne v SABENA* 43/75 was satisfied that the principle that 'men and women shall receive equal pay for equal work' was sufficiently precise to create direct effect even though the exact meaning of 'equal pay and equal work' would inevitably require further definition by the courts.
- The provision must be unconditional or 'non-dependent' – in the sense that it should not depend on the intervention of another body or require further legislative action either by the [EU] institutions or Member States.

Besides these for individuals to be able to enforce a provision of EU law there must be an identifiable right granted by the Treaty or subsidiary legislation.

Direct effect in application

In *Van Gend en Loos* the action was against the state. The next significant issue was whether a citizen could rely on the principle of direct effect to enforce a provision against another citizen as the case had confirmed they could against the state. In *Defrenne v SABENA* involving a claim for equal pay made against an employer under what is now Article 157 TFEU (see Chapter 10), the ECJ rejected the argument that direct effect was a means only of enforcing substantive EU laws against the Member States. The court clarified that there were in fact two types of direct effect, vertical direct effect (against the state) and horizontal direct effect (against other citizens and private bodies. This was necessary because otherwise citizens would be denied effective remedies where they were granted rights under EU law.

JUDGMENT

'the reference to "Member States" in [Article 157 TFEU] cannot be interpreted as excluding the intervention of the courts in the direct application of the Treaty.... Since [Article 157 TFEU] is mandatory in nature, the prohibition on discrimination between men and women applies not only to the action of public authorities, but also extends to all agreements which are intended to regulate paid labour collectively, as well as to contracts between individuals.'

The court has also developed the principle of direct effect so that it applies generally to most types of EU law, both primary and secondary. It has generally followed its own criteria in *Van Gend en Loos*. However, the test from the case was originally strictly applied but the court has also gradually taken a more relaxed approach to ensure that citizens can take advantage of the rights given to them in the Treaties.

In the case of Treaty Articles there is no problem in conforming to the criteria in *Van Gend en Loos* since Treaty Articles automatically become part of national law by signing the Treaty or also by ratifying in a duellist constitution such as the UK which did so through Act of Parliament. Neither are there any problems in enforcing Regulations since, as identified in Article 288, they are directly applicable, meaning they automatically become law in Member States without need for implementation. This was established in *Leonesio v Ministero dell'Agricoltora & delle Foreste* 93/71 *(The widow Leonesio)*.

Direct effect and directives

In the case of directives there was a potential problem because of how they are defined in Article 288. They create obligations on Member States to pass national laws within a set time to achieve the objectives in the directive but this means that they fail one part of the test in *Van Gend en Loos*. They are conditional. They are not non-dependent. They are entirely dependent on implementation by the Member States.

The ECJ identified this problem at an early stage in *Van Duyn v Home Office* 41/74 which involved enforcement of what was then Directive 64/221 (now Directive 2004/38) and derogations against the free movement of workers under what was then Article 48 EC Treaty (now Article 45TFEU). The ECJ considered the problem of the direct effect of directives and reached an important conclusion.

JUDGMENT

The court identified: 'it would be incompatible with the binding effect attributed to a Directive by [Art 288] to exclude, in principle, the possibility that the obligation which it imposes may be invoked by those concerned'.

The judges foresaw that directives could be made ineffective without allowing direct effect and was prepared to overlook the potential limitation involved in their definition in Article 288.

JUDGMENT

As the court also observed: 'where the [EU] authorities have, by directive, imposed on Member States the obligation to pursue a particular course of conduct, the useful effect of such an act would be weakened if individuals were prevented from relying on it before their national courts and if the latter were prevented from taking it into consideration'.

On this basis, while the court gave little other reasoning it identified that a directive can indeed be enforced by the means of direct effect provided that the remaining criteria from *Van Gend en Loos* are met. During the implementation period the rights produced by directives are not enforceable because Member States have a time limit within which to implement. As a result, for directives the court added an extra criterion to the *Van Gend en Loos* test in *Pubblico Ministero v Ratti* 148/78 that direct effect of a directive is not in question until such time as the implementation period has expired.

The Court of Justice can only deal with problems as they arise in references to it. The next limitation to be identified was that directives have only vertical direct effect. They can never be horizontally directly effective and so can only be relied upon and enforced against the state.

CASE EXAMPLE

Marshall v Southampton and South West Hampshire AHA (Teaching) (No 1) 152/84

A reference was made to the Court of Justice on the issue of whether having different retirement ages for men and women in the UK was discrimination under the then Equal Treatment Directive (now replaced by the Recast Directive 2006/54 – see Chapter 11). The ECJ confirmed that it was. It also identified that the applicant was able to use the directive against her employer but only because her employer was in fact the health service, an organ of the state.

JUDGMENT

The ECJ stated: 'According to [Article 288 TFEU] ... the binding nature of a directive ... exists only in relation to 'each Member State to which it is addressed'. It follows that a directive may not of itself impose obligations on an individual and that a provision of a directive may not be relied upon as such against such a person.'

This left an anomalous and unjust situation that showed up in *Duke v GEC Reliance* [1988] 2 WLR 359 which involved the same issue as *Marshall*, but the employer was a private company. The House of Lords held that it was not bound to apply Directive 76/207 because the directive could not be effective horizontally. Even though the UK was at fault for failing to fully implement the directive the availability of a remedy then was entirely dependent on the identity of the employer.

The ECJ was subsequently able to extend the scope of vertical direct effect to include bodies that could be described as an 'emanation of the state' (or 'arm of the state'). The court devised a test in *Foster v British Gas plc* C-188/89 another case involving the issue in *Marshall*:

- is the body one that provides a public service, and

- is the body under the control of the state, and

- is the body able to exercise special powers that would not be available to a private body?

The ECJ made progress in making the rights arising from directives enforceable but the absence of horizontal effect meant that there were still problems.

QUOTATION

As Sionaidh Douglas-Scott identifies in *Constitutional Law of the European Union*, Longman, 2002, p. 296: 'In *Marshall* the Court held that an individual may rely upon a directive against the State, regardless of whether the State is acting as a public authority or employer. The consequence of this ruling is that, for example, a private employee may not rely on a directive but a state employee may. The ruling has been attacked as provoking unjust and anomalous situations, particularly in the field of labour law, where the scope of the Equal Treatment Directive has been reduced. The decision also led to the necessity for an impossibly rigorous definition of the state which proved very difficult to apply in case law.'

Indirect effect

In yet another case involving the Equal Treatment Directive and its improper or incomplete implementation in Member States the ECJ was able to develop a further process to avoid the problem that unimplemented directives cannot be enforced through horizontal direct effect. This was the process of indirect effect which was explained by the court in two cases referred to it by the German Labour Court.

CASE EXAMPLE

Von Colson and Kamann v Land Nordrhein-Westfalen 14/83; *Harz v Deutsche Tradax GmbH* 79/83

The German government failed to properly implement the Equal Treatment Directive 76/207 by having inadequate compensation by contrast to that required by the directive. Von Colson applied to work for the prison service, a state body, while Harz applied to work for a private company. The ECJ identified that the failure was improper or incomplete implementation. However, while Von Colson would have had a remedy through vertical direct effect, Harz would have been denied a remedy because of the anomaly resulting from lack of horizontal direct effect. The ECJ resolved the problem in a novel way by using the obligation on Member States (now in Article 4(3) TEU) to introduce the principle of indirect effect. The German Court was bound to give full effect to the directive and so must order full compensation in both cases.

JUDGMENT

As the court said: 'Since the duty under [Article 4(3) TEU] to ensure fulfillment of [an] obligation was binding on all national courts ... it follows that ... courts are required to interpret their national law in the light of the wording and purpose of the Directive.'

Article 4(3) TEU is phrased as follows:

ARTICLE

'4.
(3). Pursuant to the principle of sincere cooperation, the Union and the Member States shall, in full mutual respect, assist each other in carrying out tasks which flow from the Treaties. The Member States shall take any appropriate measure, general or particular, to ensure fulfilment of the obligations arising out of the Treaties or resulting from the acts of the institutions of the Union The Member States shall facilitate the achievement of the Union's tasks and refrain from any measure which could jeopardise the attainment of the Union's objectives.'

Indirect effect is a process of sympathetic interpretation by a national court seeking to give effect to the objectives in a directive and is a way of avoiding the problem of there being no horizontal direct effect of directives. The judgment was not clear on which national law the process of indirect effect could actually apply to. This was resolved in *Marleasing SA v La Commercial Internacional de Alimentacion* C-106/89.

JUDGMENT

The ECJ explained: 'in applying national law, whether the provisions concerned pre-date or post-date the directive, the national court asked to interpret national law is bound to do so in every way possible in the light of the text and the aims of the directive to achieve the results envisaged by it'.

However, there are limitations to the process the most significant being that the process is entirely dependent on the willingness of the national courts to use it. As has been seen in *Duke* the national courts are not always so willing so that there is the possibility of lack of uniformity throughout the EU.

QUOTATION

As Josephine Steiner identifies in *Textbook on EC Law 8th edition* (Oxford University Press, 2003, p. 109): 'the indirect application of EC directives by national courts cannot be guaranteed. This reluctance on the part of the national courts to comply with the Von Colson principle, particularly as applied in Marleasing, is hardly surprising. It may be argued that in extending the principle of indirect effect in this way the ECJ is attempting to give horizontal effect to directives by the back door, and impose obligations, addressed to Member States, on private parties, contrary to their understanding of domestic law. Where such is the case, as the House of Lords remarked in Duke ... this could be most unfair.'

The other limitation is that it would be unlikely that a national court could give indirect effect to a directive which had not been implemented at all. This would first mean that the court was legislating and second would be unfair on a citizen who was only complying with national law.

State liability
Despite the efforts of the ECJ to ensure that citizens were able to enforce the provisions of improperly implemented directives first through vertical direct effect against the state and emanations of the state and second by introducing the process of indirect effect

there were still situations where a party could be without a remedy because of the failure of a Member State to implement at all or fully implement a directive. As a result, when it got the opportunity the ECJ developed a third way of ensuring that citizens did not lose rights given in directives. This is the process of state liability. If a citizen lacks a remedy and suffers loss or damage because of the failure of a Member State to implement EU law then that Member State should be made liable for the damage suffered.

CASE EXAMPLE

Francovich and Bonifaci v Republic of Italy C-6/90 and C-9/90

Italy had failed to implement directive 80/987 which required a scheme to provide a minimum compensation for workers whose employers went into insolvency. The claimants who had been made unemployed were left without a remedy. The ECJ found that Italy was in breach of its obligations and was liable to compensate the workers for the loss resulting from that breach. It justified this state liability on Article 340 TFEU which is an action for citizens who have suffered loss or damage because of a wrong of one of the EU institutions.

JUDGMENT

The ECJ identified: 'the full effectiveness of [EU] rules would be impaired and the rights they recognise would be undermined if individuals were unable to recover damages where their rights were infringed by a breach of [EU] law attributable to a member state'.

The court set three conditions for state liability to apply:

- The directive must confer rights on individuals.
- The contents of those rights must be identifiable in the wording of the measure.
- There must be a causal link between the damage suffered and the failure to implement the directive.

In *Brasserie du Pecheur SA v Federal Republic of Germany; R v Secretary of State for Transport, ex parte Factortame Ltd* C-46 and C-48/93 the court then modified the conditions from *Francovich*, ignoring the original second condition and replacing it with a new one:

- The rule of Community law infringed must be intended to confer rights on individuals.
- The breach must be sufficiently serious to justify imposing state liability.
- There must be a direct causal link between the breach of the obligation imposed on the state and the damage actually suffered by the applicant.

The definition of state has widened to include acts and omissions of any organ of the state and the scope of liability has been extended beyond directives to include any breach of EU law, regardless of whether or not it has direct effect.

One issue is what will amount to a sufficiently serious breach of EU law. *Dillenkofer and others v Federal Republic of Germany* C-178, 179, 188, 189 and 190/94 identified that there are situations where the seriousness of the breach is obvious and the imposition of state liability is then almost a form of strict liability. An example is where there is a failure to implement a directive at all. *R v Ministry of Agriculture, Fisheries and Food, ex parte Hedley Lomas (Ireland) Ltd* C-5/94 identifies that in all other cases the seriousness of the breach must be established.

State liability conflicts with national rules on non-implementation but the need to show direct effect is removed as is the strained construction of national law through indirect effect. Instead it focuses on the duty of the Member State to implement EU law while in effect attaching rigorous sanctions for failure to implement. As a result it has the effect of removing any advantage that Member States might gain from non-implementation. State liability is the most far reaching principle of all and it has several implications:

ACTIVITY

Self-assessment questions

1. In what ways does the European Communities Act 1972 actually define the relationship between the UK and the EU?
2. What is the importance of s2(4) of the European Communities Act 1972?
3. To what extent have the English courts willingly accepted a doctrine of supremacy of EU law?
4. Why is a doctrine of supremacy of EU law necessary?
5. What precisely is the 'doctrine of pre-emption' and how does it affect the Member States?
6. In *Van Gend en Loos* the ECJ identified that 'the [EU] constitutes a new legal order in international law'. What exactly does this mean?
7. What is the significance of the definition of supremacy given by the ECJ in *Costa v ENEL*?
8. What effect does the doctrine of supremacy of EU law have upon the sovereignty of the Member States?
9. Why is *Factortame* such an important case?
10. What were the original problems of allowing direct effect of directives?
11. Why did the ECJ feel in *Van Duyn* that directives should be enforceable?
12. How did the ECJ overcome the problem?
13. What are the major effects of the decision in *Marshall (No 1)*?
14. What impact does the test in *Foster v British Gas* have on the principle of direct effect?
15. What shortcomings are there in using vertical direct effect as a means of enforcing directives?
16. How does the principle in *Von Colson* assist individuals to enforce rights that are granted them by EU law?
17. How effective is the *Von Colson* principle?
18. In what ways does the case of *Marleasing* extend the principle in *Von Colson*?
19. How does the principle in *Francovich* add to the rules on direct effect?
20. In what significant way does the test in *Brasserie De Pecheur* add to or alter the *Francovich* test?
21. How did the cases of *Dillenkofer* and *Hedley Lomas* develop the test further?

2.3 The importance of EU membership to UK employment law

2.3.1 UK implementation of EU law

As we have seen in 2.1.2 above initially the most significant implementation of EU law was the European Communities Act 1972. This incorporated into English law all existing EU law and identified that all future law would also become English law. At the time there was actually a limited amount of law in the Treaty specifically on employment. However, since that time an enormous amount of employment law has been affected by

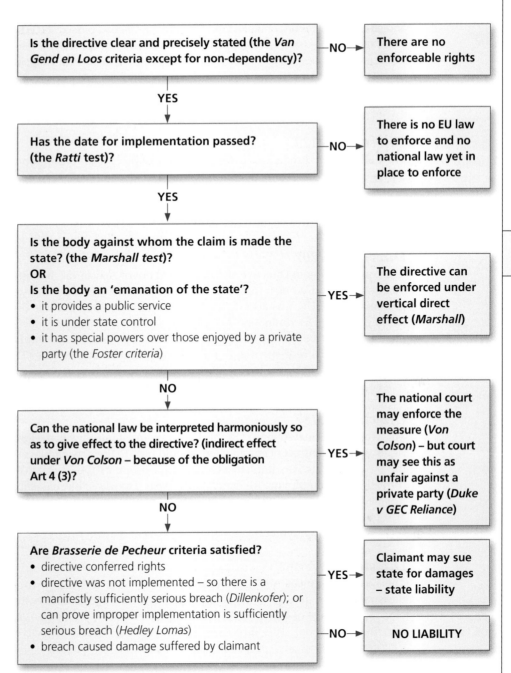

Figure 2.2 Diagram illustrating the possible means of enforcing rights contained in directives

EU law. This has particularly arisen through the passing of numerous directives which have been introduced under different Treaty Articles and which have had a major impact on UK employment law.

Directive 75/117

The equal pay directive was one of the first significant directives to gain force after the UK joined the EU. It expanded on Article 157 (at the time Article 119) on equal pay for men and women and identified the two types of equal pay, equal pay for equal work and equal pay for work of equal value. While the UK had passed the Equal Pay Act 1970 in advance of its successful application for membership, it was also the subject of infringement proceedings under Article 258 (at the time Article 169) since it had failed to properly implement the directive. This resulted in the passing of the Equal Pay (Amendment) Regulations 1983. It has now been replaced by the Recast Directive 2006/54 (see Chapter 10).

Directive 75/129

The Collective Redundancies Directive requires a process of consultation with employee representatives on large scale redundancies and also notification to appropriate public bodies. The Directive is now provides the significant rules on redundancy in the Trade Union and Labour Relations (Consolidation) Act 1992. It has also been replaced by a more recent Directive 98/59 (see Chapter 23).

Directive 76/207

The Equal Treatment Directive also developed out of Article 157. It required equal treatment of men and women in other conditions of work including transfer, training and promotion. The UK was also deficient in its implementation of this directive. Despite passing the Sex Discrimination Act 1975 the UK government had failed to fully implement this directive also because it had not taken into account the implications of there being differential retirement ages for men and women at that time. The directive has now been replaced by the Recast Directive 2006/54. Sex is now also a protected characteristic under the Equality Act 2010 (see Chapter 11).

Directive 77/187

This was the original Acquired Rights Directive and it introduced the idea that employee rights under a contract of employment should pass to the new employer on a transfer of the business. This was implemented in English law as the Transfer of Undertakings (Protection of Employment) Regulations 1981. The directive has subsequently been updated and the law on the area is now in Directive 2001/23. The UK regulations have also been modified and updated and now the law is in the Transfer of Undertakings (Protection of Employment) Regulations 2006 (see Chapter 18).

Directive 79/7

The Equal Treatment in Social Security Matters was introduced to ensure that the measures in the Equal Treatment Directive extended to social security matters including obviously a range of benefits. This was implemented by amendment to various social security legislation. The directive is now in the Recast Directive 2006/54 (see Chapter 11).

Directive 89/391

The Framework Directive on Health and Safety develops earlier EU health and safety provisions. EU health and safety law has been responsible for the introduction of the so-called 'six pack of regulations'. These were first in fact introduced in 1992 but most have subsequently been modified. They are the Management of HASAW Regulations 1999 (amended 2006), the Workplace (Health, Safety and Welfare) Regulations 1992, the Provision and Use of Work Equipment Regulations 1998, the Personal Protective Equipment at Work Regulations 1992, the Manual Handling Operations Regulations 1992 and the Health and Safety (Display Screen Equipment) Regulations 1992 (see Chapter 16.4.2).

Directive 93/104

This was the original Working Time Directive. It was in fact a health and safety directive introduced under the then Article 139. The UK government at the time tried hard to resist it claiming that it was in fact part of social policy from which it had an opt out following the TEU. However, this was disproved in an action in the ECJ. The Working Time Regulations were then introduced in 1998 after a change of government. The directive has now been replaced and updated in the Working Time Directive 2003/88 (see Chapter 16).

Directive 94/33

The Protection of Young People at Work Directive is self-explanatory in seeking to regulate the work of young people for health and safety purposes. It has been implemented as part of the range of regulations known as the 'six pack' particularly in the Management of Health and Safety at Work Regulations 1999 and amended in 2006 and also in the Working Time Regulations (see Chapter 16).

Directive 96/34

The Parental Leave Directive introduced the idea of parental leave and dependant care leave. It introduced a minimum floor of basic rights on such leave. The directive has subsequently been replaced and modified in the Parental Leave Directive 2010/18. The directive has been implemented into English law in a variety of regulations. These include the Maternity and Parental Leave (Amendment) Regulations 2001, the Paternity and Adoption Leave Regulations 2002, the Additional Paternity Leave Regulations 2010 as well as insertions in the Employment Rights Act 1996 (see Chapter 8).

Directive 97/81

The Part-Time Workers Directive was introduced to ensure that part-time workers would not be discriminated against by contrast with full-time employees. This reflects many findings of the Court of Justice more related to sex discrimination but, since part-timers are more likely to be women the employment of part-time staff on different conditions to full-time workers was a simple way of discriminating. The directive has been implemented into UK law in the Part-time Workers (Prevention of Less Favourable Treatment) Regulations 2000 (see Chapter 14.6).

Directive 99/70

The Fixed-Term Workers Directive extends the principles of equality and non-discrimination already prevalent in the case of sex and for part-time workers to fixed-term workers. The purpose of the rules is that employers should be prevented from using fixed-term contracts as a means of denying workers access to basic employment protections. The directive has been implemented in UK law in the Fixed-Term Employees (Prevention of Less Favourable Treatment) Regulations 2002 (see Chapter 14.7).

Directive 2000/43

The Race Directive was introduced to ensure equal treatment between employees irrespective of their race or ethnic origin. There were already quite extensive rules on race discrimination in the Race Relations Act 1976 which was drafted in very similar terms to the Sex Discrimination Act 1975. The directive in fact introduced a quite different definition of indirect discrimination which was much more beneficial to employees bringing such a claim. Race is now a protected characteristic under the Equality Act 2010 and claims can be brought in respect of all the types of prohibited conduct identified in the Act and in respect of all stages of employment (see Chapter 12).

Directive 2000/78

The Framework Directive on Equal Treatment in Employment and Occupation is a far reaching and far sighted directive which extends the whole scope of discrimination law. As a result Member States were required to extend basic principles of equal treatment to age, disability, religion or belief and sexual orientation. These were initially implemented into UK law in the Disability Discrimination Act 1995 (Amendment) Regulations 2003, the Employment Equality (Religion or Belief) Regulations 2003, the Employment Equality (Sexual Orientation) Regulations 2003, and the Employment Equality (Age) Regulations 2006. Now all of these are protected characteristics under the Equality Act 2010 and subject to regulation of the prohibited conduct identified in the Act. There are slightly different rules for different protected characteristics (see Chapter 13 and Chapters 14.2, 14.4 and 14.5).

Directive 2008/104

The Agency Workers Directive provides a range of rights for temporary agency workers so that they receive equal treatment to permanent employees where they are assigned. Clearly one way for an employer to avoid a worker receiving rights would be to hire temporary agency workers since these are rarely considered to be employees under the various tests of employment status (see Chapter 4.4). The directive has been implemented in UK law in the Agency Workers Regulations 2010 (see Chapter 14.8).

As can be seen from the above, EU law is significant to many of the chapters that follow and therefore to a very wide range of employment protections.

2.3.2 The development of EU labour law

Originally EU law was more concerned with the economics of the single market, up until fairly recently referred to as the common market. There was very little in the original Treaties that related to employment rights. In the original EC Treaty there was only quite limited reference to employment issues.

Article 118 (later Articles 137–140 following the Amsterdam Treaty but subsequently repealed following the Lisbon Treaty) stipulated that: without prejudice to the other provisions of this Treaty and in conformity with its general objectives, the Commission shall have the task of promoting close cooperation between Member States in the social field, particularly in matters relating to: employment, labour law and working conditions; basic and advanced vocational training; social security; prevention of occupational accidents and diseases; occupational hygiene; the right of association, and collective bargaining between employers and workers. However, there was no real movement on Article 118 until after the Single European Act 1986.

The other major provision in the original Treaty was Article 119 which is now Article 157 of the Treaty on the Functioning of the European Union (TFEU). This was a much narrower principle with a narrower context of equal pay between men and women for equal work. This did have significant implications and is discussed in detail in Chapter 10.3. It also developed through Directive 76/207 (now in the Recast Directive 2006/54) into equal working conditions for men and women.

The next significant development was the Social Action Programme in 1974. The aims of the programme were to achieve full employment, to improve the standard of living and improved working conditions of all workers and to develop social dialogue in the workplace. However, the depressed economic conditions of the 1970s and 1980s meant that little progress was made. It was with a new Social Action Programme in 1984 and the Single European Act 1986 that further developments were made. This introduced Article 118A which provided as follows:

ARTICLE

The Working Time Directive was passed under this Treaty Article although it was argued by the UK government as being social policy which the UK had been allowed to opt out of because of protocols inserted in the Treaty on European Union 1992. It also was the basis for many other developments in health and safety law.

Brian Bercusson in *European Labour Law* (Butterworths, 1996, p. 70) argues that there are in fact three possible interpretations of Article 118A:

SECTION

'(i) as limited to the protection of working activity in the strictest sense;
(ii) as including all conditions of work which have or could have effects on the safety and health of workers, including duration of work, its organisation and its content (so as to cover, for example, night work and various forms of "atypical" work);
(iii) as including the working environment in the widest sense of the term, including workers' welfare and well-being, as well as occupational accidents and illness and protection of health at the workplace.'

It is inevitable that Member States would try to protest for the narrowest interpretation while the ECJ would interpret the provision that would bring the greatest number of EU citizens within the protection.

Another significant development of the time was the Community Charter for the Fundamental Social Rights of Workers 1989. Under the Charter the community (now the EU) was obliged to provide for the development of fundamental social rights of workers under a series of categories:

- free movement of workers;
- employment and remuneration;
- improvement of living and working conditions;
- social protection;
- freedom of association and collective bargaining;
- vocational training;
- equal treatment for men and women;
- information and consultation and participation of workers;
- health protection and safety in the workplace;
- protection of children and adolescents;
- the elderly;
- disabled persons;
- Member States' action.

The Charter could not at the time be integrated into the Treaty because of the opposition of the UK government. The UK did eventually accept the Charter, but only following a change of government in 1997. Nevertheless, a new Social Action Programme was launched and the Charter was in fact instrumental in a number of initiatives in employment and industrial relations policy, which resulted in a number of directives during the 1990s. Included in these are directives on pregnancy and maternity (see Chapter 8.4), on working time (see Chapter 16.4.3), and on the framework agreements on parental leave (see Chapter 8.5), part-time work (see Chapter 14.6) and fixed-term work (see Chapter 14.7). Besides this the Charter also anticipated much of the potential of the fundamental individual employment rights in the Charter of Fundamental Rights of the European Union, adopted in Nice in December 2000. The Charter can in any case be used as a tool for interpretation by the European Court of Justice in cases involving social and employment rights

Into the 1990s the Commission became more focused on problems associated with unemployment and with trying to tackle unemployment. It introduced a White Paper in 1993 entitled 'Growth, Competitiveness and Employment'. More significantly the Amsterdam Treaty 1999 inserted employment in Article 2 EC Treaty (now Article 3 TFEU) as one of the tasks of the 'Community'.

ARTICLE

'Article 2
The [EU] shall have as its task, by establishing a common market and an economic and monetary union and by implementing common policies or activities . . . a high level of employment and of social protection, equality between men and women, sustainable and non-inflationary growth, a high degree of competitiveness and convergence of economic performance, a high level of protection and improvement of the quality of the environment, the raising of the standard of living and quality of life, and economic and social cohesion and solidarity among Member States.'

The more recent significant developments have been the Framework Race and Equal Treatment Directives which have extended the scope of discrimination into many more areas (see Chapter 14.1–14.5).

2.3.3 The effects of EU labour law

Membership of the EU has been amongst the most significant factors in developing employment protections. This has been particularly so in the case of modern statutory protections on maternity which previously existed in UK law but has expanded significantly as a result of EU law. EU law has also introduced rights in parental leave, paternity and adoption leave and pay for these also. It has also introduced the concept of dependant care leave. So there are a wide range of what have become known as the 'family friendly policies' that exist only as a result of EU law.

In the area of discrimination law the EU has had a massive influence on English law. Legislation on equal pay and later sex discrimination only arose in the first place because of application for membership and the need to be compatible with Treaty requirements of the time. Discrimination law of course has expanded massively since its origins in the simple proposition that men and women should receive equal pay for equal work. The ECJ was instrumental on numerous occasions in correcting the errors and shortcomings of UK implementation of EU discrimination law and the Commission also produced a logical definition of sexual harassment at a point where women claiming in England had to try to make a catch all principle in sex discrimination fit their particular circumstances. In the twenty-first century the EU has expanded the scope of discrimination law to cover age, disability, gender reassignment, marriage and civil partnership, pregnancy and maternity, race (where it has introduced a significantly wider definition of indirect discrimination than was the case with English law), religion or belief and sexual orientation. On gender reassignment and sexual orientation the Court of Justice had already identified that English law was inferior in dealing with the problems.

QUOTATION

Brian Bercusson in *European Labour Law* (Butterworths, 1996, p. 29), suggests: 'The impact of [EU] labour law on UK labour law has been greatest in the field of equality between the sexes.'

In its widening of discrimination law the EU has moved on at a pace since this.

In the case of atypical workers such as part-time workers, fixed-term employees and temporary agency workers directives have introduced rights of equal treatment with comparable employees that were otherwise absent from English law. In the case of part-time workers again rulings of the ECJ had already developed some protections.

In health and safety at work the EU has had an enormous influence. It has developed protections for young workers. It has introduced rules on working time which includes mandatory daily rest periods, a full day without work each week, and a minimum of four weeks paid holiday annually. It has also through a series of directives introduced the concept of compulsory risk assessment, regulation of the work environment, use of equipment and of personal protective equipment as well as modernising the use of display screen equipment.

The idea of protection of employment rights on the transfer of a business was created by the EU and dealt with the formerly abusive practice of employers who colluded on the sale and purchase of the business with the new employer being able to change all of the contractual rights and obligations of the workforce or even sack them with neither employer picking up any bill for redundancy payments. The EU has also in any case been instrumental in developing controls on redundancies, particularly collective redundancies and introducing the requirement for consultation.

QUOTATION

Brian Bercusson in *European Labour Law* (Butterworths, 1996, p. 30), suggests: 'Perhaps the clearest example of the UK government's minimalist approach to [EU] labour law combining with its overall market philosophy to produce inadequate implementation of [EU] law has been the case of the Acquired Rights Directive 77/187. The UK Transfer of Undertakings (Protection of Employment) Regulations 1981 excluded non-commercial ventures. This gave a clear passage to the privatisation policies of the government during the 1980's largely premised on the ability of private contractors for formerly public services to compete by reducing existing pay and labour standards.'

Much of this was overcome by decisions of the ECJ. However, the current government, following the report of venture capitalist Adrian Beecroft has announced that it plans to review the regulations to remove the protection from workers whose jobs have been outsourced.

The history of the EU has been a history of a continuous tension between the EU institutions striving to achieve the objectives of the EU and the national self-interest of the Member States.

QUOTATION

Ian Ward in *A Critical Introduction to European Law 3rd edition* (Cambridge University Press, 2009), makes the following comment: 'so wedded is the Union to the basic tenets of liberal political economy that it seems to be quite unable to appreciate the nature of the what is possibly the most pervasive form of discrimination of all; that which is suffered by those who are excluded, either totally or in large part, from an effective capacity to engage in the activities of the [single] market itself'. Ward goes on to also comment: 'no free society can claim to be free so long as it presumes that the presence of a free market suffices for a public philosophy'. He goes on to identify: 'the present neoliberal vision of the free market is ethically perverted, governed by a majority of the uncaring "affluent" which appears to be quite unwilling to accept a collective responsibility for the disempowered minority'. He also identifies: 'Devoid of … a progressive conception of social justice, markets simply become instruments of tyranny and terror.'

The EU has provided and for the last forty years has been the major provider of much needed developments of employment protections in the UK. EU employment law is only as good as the willingness of Member States to use and be bound by it and UK governments have shown a fair amount of reluctance over the years to embrace these developments.

It is common to see commentators on TV news and current affairs programmes suggesting that current economic and employment problems could be eased by a reduction in regulation and to blame the EU for the amount of regulation. Politically there has always been a rump of euroscepticism throughout UK membership. There is also a significant likelihood that there will in the near future be a referendum on membership and a greater likelihood of withdrawal from the EU than at any time before. It is important to remember that withdrawal from the EU would almost certainly be followed almost immediately by repeal of the various employment protections that have built up as a result of membership.

KEY FACTS

UK membership of the EU	Case/statute
• All existing EU law is automatically English law and all future EU law will become so	*S2(1) European Communities Act 1972*
• Any Act of Parliament passed or to be passed, shall be construed and have effect	*S2(4) European Communities Act 1972*

The supranational legal order	Case/statute
EU instruments	
• regulations are generally applicable and directly applicable	*Article 288 TFEU*
• directives are binding as to the result to be achieved (so are implemented by Member States within set time)	*Article 288 TFEU*

Supremacy	
• membership creates a 'new legal order' by which Member States have partially surrendered sovereignty	*Van Gend en Loos v The Netherlands*
• so EU law 'cannot be overridden by domestic legal provisions, however framed'. And prevails over all inconsistent national law	*Costa v ENEL*
• and allows judges to suspend operation of a national legislative provision	*R v Secretary of State for Transport ex parte Factortame Ltd*

Direct effect	
• certain measures should be enforceable by citizens of Member States – if they were clear, precise and unconditional, and conferred rights on individuals	*Van Gend en Loos v The Netherlands*
• direct effect can be vertical (against the state) or horizontal (against another citizen)	*Defrenne v SABENA*
• Directives can be directly effective if date for implementation passed	*Pubblico Ministero v Ratti*
• but only vertically against the state – there can be no horizontal direct effect	*Marshall v Southampton and S W Hants AHA (No 1)*
• or against an emanation of the state	*Foster v British Gas*

Indirect effect	Article 4(3) TEU
• because of Member States' obligations to EU national judge may sympathetically interpret national law to be harmonious with the directive	*Von Colson and Kamann v Land Nordrhein-Westfalen*

State liability	Article 340 TFEU
• follows liability of institutions to compensate citizens who suffer loss because of their acts	
• possibly where right is clearly identifiable, the breach of EU law by the Member State is sufficiently serious, and there is a causal link between the breach and the damage	*Brasserie du Pecheur v Germany; R v Secretary of State for Transport, ex parte Factortame (No 2)*
• failure to implement a directive is always sufficiently serious	*Dillenkofer and others v Germany*
• in all other cases it must be proved	*R v Ministry of Agriculture, Fisheries and Food, ex parte Hedley Lomas*

Implementation of EU law	Case/statute
• Significant implementation in Acts of Parliament	*European Communities Act 1972*
• But also in many directives	*Equality Act 2010*
• Equal pay	*Directive 75/117 (now Recast Directive 2006/54) – Equal Pay Act 1970, Equal Pay (Amendment) Regulations 1983 (now in Equality Act 2010)*
• Collective redundancies	*Directive 75/129 (now 98/59) – Trade Union and Labour Relations (Consolidation) Act 1992*
• Equal treatment	*Directive 76/207 (now Recast Directive 2006/54) – Sex Discrimination Act (now in Equality Act 2010)*
• Acquired rights	*Directive 77/187 (now Directive 2001/23) – Transfer of Undertakings (Protection of Employment) Regulations 2006*

• Equal treatment in social security	*Directive 79/7 (now in Recast Directive 2006/54)*
• Working time	*Directive 93/104 (now Directive 2003/88) – Working Time Regulations 1998*
• Protection of young people at work	*Directive 94/33 – Management of Health and Safety at Work Regulations 1999, Working Time Regulations*
• Parental leave	*Directive 96/34 – (now Parental Leave Directive 2010/18) – Maternity and Parental Leave (Amendment) Regulations 2001, Paternity and Adoption Leave Regulations 2002, Additional Paternity Leave Regulations 2010, Employment Rights Act 1996*
• Part-time workers	*Directive 97/81 – Part-time Workers (Prevention of Less Favourable Treatment) Regulations 2000*
• Health and safety at work	*Directive 89/391 – Management of HASAW Regulations 1999 (amended 2006), Workplace (Health and Safety at Work) Regulations 1992, Provision and Use of Work Equipment Regulations 1998, Personal Protection Equipment at Work Regulations 1992, Manual Handling Operations Regulations 1992, Health and Safety (Display Screen) Equipment Regulations 1992*
• Fixed-term work	*Directive 99/70 – Fixed-Term Employees (Prevention of Less Favourable Treatment) Regulations 2001*
• Race discrimination	*Directive 2000/43 – Equality Act 2010*
• Equal Treatment in Employment and Occupation	*Directive 2000/78*
• Agency workers	*Directive 2008/104 – Agency Workers Regulations 2010*

The development of EU labour law	Case/statute
• Originally there was little employment law in the Treaties – equal pay for men and woman was the most obvious – with developments in equal working conditions	*Article 119 (now Article 157 TFEU)* *Directive 76/207*
• Rules on health and safety was one of the next significant developments	*Article 118A EC Treaty*
• A Charter of Fundamental Social Rights was also created – but originally the UK opted out only joining in 1998 after a change of government and this has led to many directives on discrimination, equality for atypical workers and health and safety	
• A high level of employment and of social protection, equality between men and women, and the raising of the standard of living and quality of life was added as a task of the EU	*Article 2 EC Treaty (inserted by the Amsterdam Treaty)*

The effects of EU labour law	Case/statute
• Membership of the EU has resulted in the development of employment protections in family friendly policies, discrimination law, rights for part-time, fixed-term and temporary agency workers, health and safety law, retaining rights on the transfer of a business and also on redundancy, particularly collective redundancies • The history of the EU has been one of a tension between the EU institutions trying to achieve the objectives of the EU Treaties and national self-interest • One of the consequences of withdrawal from the EU would be the loss of employment protections that have resulted from membership	

SUMMARY

- The UK joined the EU (formerly the EC) by signing the Treaties and by passing the European Communities Act 1972 which incorporates it into English law and provides for all existing and future EU law to be part of English law.
- EU legislation is also significant in the form of Regulations which are automatically law and directives which have to be implemented by a set date.
- EU law is supreme so prevails over inconsistent national law.
- EU law can be enforced through the process of direct effect – but directives cannot be enforced horizontally only against the state so indirect effect is possible or if the citizen suffers a loss resulting from the Member State's breach of EU law state liability is also a possibility.
- EU law has been implemented into EU law in some limited cases as a result of Treaty Articles but there are numerous directives that have introduced a variety of employment rights and protections into English law.
- Originally EU employment law was quite limited, equal pay between men and women being the most significant right.
- This extended out into equal treatment of men and women in other conditions of employment.
- Significant health and safety laws were introduced following the Single European Act.
- A Charter of Fundamental Rights was also created – originally the UK was able to opt out of this but adopted it with a change of government in 1998.
- Many developments in protection of different types of atypical workers in the scope of discrimination law and health and safety law have resulted from the policies that developed from the Charter.
- Achieving a high level of employment and of social protection, equality between men and women, sustainable and the raising of the standard of living and quality of life is now a task of the EU inserted in the Treaty.

Further reading

Emir, Astra, *Selwyn's Law of Employment 17th edition*. Oxford University Press, 2012, Chapter 1.
Sargeant, Malcolm and Lewis, David, *Employment Law 6th edition*. Pearson, 2012, Chapter 1.3.
Storey, Tony and Turner, Chris, *Unlocking EU Law 3rd edition*. Hodder Education, 2011, Chapters 1, 4, 8 and 9.

3

Institutions and procedures

AIMS AND OBJECTIVES

After reading this chapter you should be able to:

- Understand which cases hear claims or appeals on employment law issues
- Understand that the Court of Justice of the European Union only hears references from a Member State court or tribunal on employment law issues or infringement proceedings against a Member State that breaches its EU obligations
- Understand the role of other important institutions
- Understand the various procedural elements of a claim on an employment law issue
- Understand the available remedies
- Critically analyse the area
- Apply the law to factual situations and reach conclusions

3.1 Courts and tribunals hearing employment disputes

Disputes at first instance involving issues of employment law can be heard in employment tribunals, the County Court and the High Court. Where the case is heard depends on the issue in question. In general terms cases involving statutory employment protections will be brought as claims in employment tribunals. This could include numerous types of claim such as equal pay, discrimination, redundancy, unfair dismissal, maternity rights and others. Disputes involving a breach of contract and a claim for damages will usually go to court, although following the Employment Tribunals Extension of Jurisdiction (England and Wales) Order 1994 it is possible for some breach of contract claims to be brought in tribunals where the maximum award would be £25,000.

3.1.1 Employment tribunals

Employment tribunals were originally established under the Industrial Training Act 1964 and until 1998 were known as industrial tribunals. Procedure in employment tribunals is now governed by the Employment Tribunals (Constitution and Rules of Procedure) Regulations 2004 as amended and the Employment Tribunals Act 1996.

They comprise an employment judge and two lay members. The employment judge can be a barrister or solicitor and can sit either full-time or part-time. The lay members only sit part-time and one will represent employers' associations and one will represent employee associations so that there is a balance of views and expertise. It is possible also for the employment judge to sit with only one lay member if both parties to the dispute agree. It is also possible for the employment judge to sit alone in unfair dismissal cases. The employment judge should be impartial and not have any connection with any of the parties that appear before him.

Employment tribunals have wide jurisdiction to hear cases including the following statutory provisions:

- the Employment Agencies Act 1973;
- the Health and Safety at Work etc Act 1974;
- the Industrial Training Act 1982;
- the Trade Union and Labour Relations (Consolidation) Act 1992;
- the Employment Rights Act 1996;
- the National Minimum Wage Act 1998;
- the Employment Relations Act 1999;
- the Equality Act 2010;
- the Suspension from Work (on Maternity Grounds) Order 1994;
- the Working Time Regulations 1998;
- the National Minimum Wage Regulations 1999;
- the Maternity and Parental Leave Regulations 1999;
- the Part-time Workers (Prevention of Less Favourable Treatment) Regulations 2000;
- the Fixed-Term Employees (Prevention of Less Favourable Treatment) Regulations 2002;
- the Paternity and Adoption Leave Regulations 2002;
- the Flexible Working (Eligibility, Complaints and Remedies) Regulations 2002;
- the Transfer of Undertakings (Protection of Employment) Regulations 2006;
- the Agency Workers Regulations 2010.

There is no financial legal assistance available for representation in employment tribunals. A claimant might be able to gain support and representation from their trade union and help may possibly be available from a Citizens Advice Bureau or from a Law Centre. In limited circumstances in discrimination claims the Equality and Human Rights Commission might fund a case or provide representation. However, this does indicate yet another imbalance in the employment relationship.

3.1.2 County Court and High Court

Claims arising from statutory employment protections are heard in employment tribunals. Claims involving breach of contract can be made in the normal courts, either the County Court or the High Court.

In many cases such claims will be brought in the County Court but where the case is heard depends on the amount of damages which are being sought. In practice there is a presumption that where damages will be less than £25,000 then the claim will be heard in the County Court. Similarly there is a presumption that where damages will be more than £50,000 then the claim will be heard in the High Court.

The High Court will also hear actions by employers to gain injunctions to prevent strike action. It is likely also that applications to secure injunctions to prevent a restraint of trade will be heard in the High Court.

On the other hand it must also be remembered that much industrial health and safety law concerns criminal sanctions so in these instances the Crown Court and the Magistrates' Courts could be involved in employment matters.

3.1.3 The Employment Appeal Tribunal

The Employment Appeal Tribunal (EAT) was originally created in 1975. It comprises High Court judges and other members who have specialist knowledge of industrial relations. These are of two types: those that represent employers' organisations and those that represent employee organisations.

The EAT is an appeal court and a superior court of record. It has civil jurisdiction to hear the following appeals:

- appeals on points of law on most areas falling within the jurisdiction of employment tribunals (this does not include appeals relating to improvement notices and prohibition notices because these involve criminal offences and so any appeal would have to be on a point of law to the Divisional Court of the Queen's Bench Division of the High Court);
- appeals from the decisions of the Certification Officer (where an appeal could also be based on fact as well as law);
- appeals from the Central Arbitration Committee.

Appeals are heard by a judge and either two or four lay members so that there are an equal number representing employer organisations and employee organisations. This can be varied with the consent of both parties. Also, where a tribunal hearing has been presided over by a single employment judge rather than a full panel, the appeal in the EAT does not have to be in front of a full panel.

A party can appear in person or be represented by a lawyer or a representative of either a trade union or an employers' association or by any other representative that the party selects.

If the Registrar thinks that an appeal has no reasonable prospect of success or that it amounts to an abuse of process then he can inform the appellant that the appeal will not proceed.

In respect of precedent the EAT is not bound by its own previous decisions. However, it is of course bound by applicable precedents of the Court of Appeal and the Supreme Court (and of course any of the former House of Lords). It will also have to apply principles of laws decided by the Court of Justice of the European Union.

3.1.4 The Court of Appeal (Civil Division)

An appeal against a decision of a County Court, the High Court or the Employment Appeal Tribunal could go to the Court of Appeal (Civil Division). Practicality and cost would mean that in most instances the Court of Appeal is likely to be the final appeal.

3.1.5 The Supreme Court

The Supreme Court was created by the Constitutional Reform Act 2005 and it replaced the House of Lords in October 2009. It is the highest court in the English court hierarchy except where a case concerns an issue which is governed by EU law in which case the Court of Justice of the European Union is the superior court.

The court hears appeals and is the final appeal court in the court hierarchy. It hears appeals on points of law generally where an existing precedent is in question or where there is an issue of statutory interpretation.

3.1.6 The Court of Justice of the European Union

The Court of Justice could be involved in UK employment law in either of two ways.

First the court has jurisdiction under Article 267 TFEU to hear references from courts or tribunals of Member States for preliminary rulings on the proper interpretation of provisions of EU law.

- Under the reference procedure in Article 267(2) any court or tribunal may make a reference to the Court of Justice where it is necessary for the resolution of the dispute.

- By Article 267(3) a court of last resort must make a reference where it is necessary to resolve the case.

The court provides its answer to the question posed by the national court or tribunal and it is then for the national court or tribunal to apply the legal principle as explained by the Court of Justice to the facts of the case. There are numerous examples of cases involving a reference to the Court of Justice in many of the chapters that follow.

Second the Court of Justice could become involved where a Member State, for the purposes here the UK, is in breach of its EU obligations for example by failing to implement at all or to fully implement a directive. In that situation the Commission can institute infringement proceedings under Article 258 TFEU. In practice there would be an attempt to persuade the Member State first to follow its obligations before the issue would actually end up in the court as Article 258 proceedings. A classic early example of this was *Commission v UK* 61/81 where the Equal Pay Act 1970 was found to be deficient since it failed to provide a means of bringing an action for equal pay for work of equal value as required by the then Equal Pay Directive 75/117 (now subsumed in the Recast Directive 2006/54). The outcome of the proceedings was that the UK government passed the Equal Pay (Amendment) Regulations 1983 and inserted a new section 2(4) in the Equal Pay Act 1970.

3.1.7 Other significant institutions in employment law
The Advisory, Conciliation and Arbitration Service (ACAS)

ACAS was created as an independent body in the Employment Protection Act 1975. It is now governed by the Trade Union and Labour Relations (Consolidation) Act 1992.

Its work is directed by a council which comprises a chairman, three members who are appointed after consultation with employers' associations, three members who are appointed after consultation with workers' associations and three neutral appointments that are usually academics. There are also two further members who can be appointed by the Secretary of State.

While ACAS is publicly funded and performs functions on behalf of the Crown, it is nevertheless not subject to any ministerial control. Under section 209 Trade Union and Labour Relations (Consolidation) Act 1992 its role is to promote the improvement of industrial relations. There are four key aspects to its work:

- promoting good practice;
- providing advice and information;

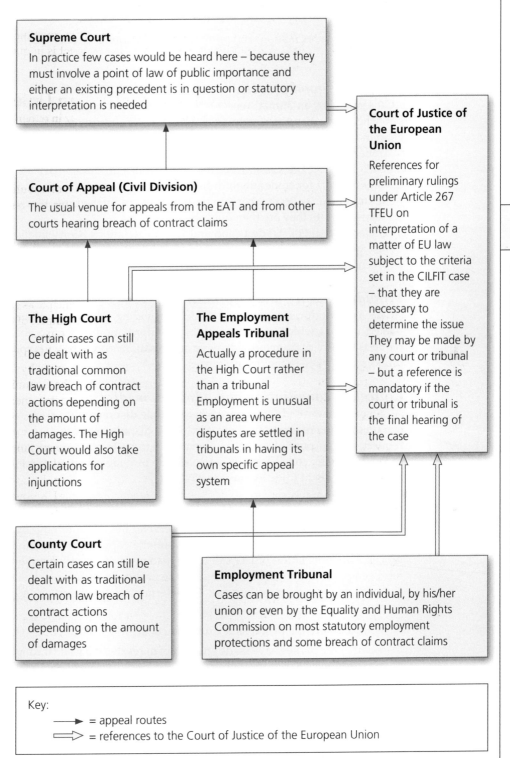

Figure 3.1 Diagram illustrating the courts or tribunals hearing employment cases

- preventing and resolving disputes through collective conciliation and advisory mediation;
- providing conciliation and arbitration in disputes brought before employment tribunals.

Promoting good practice

ACAS produces an annual report which is presented to Parliament but which is also published and therefore freely available. It also produces numerous publications on good industrial practice in a variety of contexts.

Under sections 199–202 Trade Union and Labour Relations (Consolidation) Act 1992 it also produces Codes of Practice including Codes on disciplinary and grievance procedure, time off for trade union duties and activities, and disclosure of information to trade unions for collective bargaining purposes. After the Codes are approved by the Secretary of State they are then published.

Under section 207 Trade Union and Labour Relations (Consolidation) Act 1992 the Codes are admissible in tribunal hearings. While they are not legally binding they can be taken into account by tribunals when they are arriving at decisions.

Providing advice and information

ACAS also produces numerous booklets providing advice on different employment related matters which are vital sources of information. It is also able to respond to requests for advice from individuals or organisations and to provide specific advice as it thinks appropriate in the circumstances.

Collective conciliation and advisory mediation

ACAS can also provide assistance where a trade dispute either exists or is imminent. It can do so at the request of either party to the dispute or indeed can intervene without request. The purpose of ACAS involvement is to try to reach an appropriate settlement of the dispute by conciliation. It is also able to provide conciliation services in disputes over recognition of trade unions.

Conciliation and arbitration in claims before employment tribunals

A conciliation officer from ACAS can intervene in claims to employment tribunals. When a claim has been lodged with a tribunal a copy is then sent to the conciliation officer. The conciliation officer can then try to promote a settlement either because he has been requested to do so by either of the parties or because he believes that he has a reasonable prospect of success. In determining the issue ACAS will take into account:

- whether there is a prima facie cause of action;
- whether the parties have made an attempt to resolve the issue through internal grievance or disciplinary procedures;
- whether intervention by ACAS might undermine any existing agreements or procedures;
- the cost of intervention bearing in mind the number of disputes that ACAS might be called on to intervene in at that time.

There is also a pre-claim conciliation service where employers or employees can contact ACAS and seek help in an unresolved dispute prior to any formal claim being lodged with a tribunal.

In unfair dismissal claims only section 212A Trade Union and Labour Relations (Consolidation) Act 1992 allows for the claim to be heard by a single independent arbitrator if both parties have agreed to this and have signed a COT3 or have reached a compromise agreement. In such circumstances the parties waive their rights to argue jurisdictional issues. As a result the procedure is not suitable for those claims which include jurisdictional or other complex issues. The parties submit a written statement to the arbitrator. The process is then inquisitorial and the decision of the arbitrator is binding in most instances.

The Central Arbitration Committee

The Committee was first created in the Employment Act 1975 but is now governed by section 259 Trade Union and Labour Relations (Consolidation) Act 1992. It comprises a chairman, ten deputy chairmen, twenty-seven representatives of employers' associations and twenty-three representatives of employee associations.

It acts as an independent source of arbitration dealing with statutory recognition or derecognition of trade unions for collective bargaining purposes, complaints from trade unions over failures by employers to disclose matters for collective bargaining purposes.

It can also arbitrate in disputes referred to it by ACAS where both parties have agreed to submit themselves to arbitration.

The Certification Officer

This post was first established in 1975 and is now governed by section 254 Trade Union and Labour Relations (Consolidation) Act 1992. The Certification Officer has a number of roles in relation to trade unions. He maintains a list of independent trade unions issuing them with certificates of independence as well as keeping records of their membership, copies of their rules and records of their finances. He also has powers to investigate complaints relating to election of trade union officials or other ballots and to oversee the setting up of political funds, as well as being able to investigate allegations of fraud.

The Equality and Human Rights Commission

The Commission was created in the Equality Act 2006 and replaced the former Equal Opportunities Commission (EOC), Commission for Racial Equality (CRE) and Disability Rights Commission (DRC). It does, however, have much wider powers than any of the former bodies.

The Commission has a general duty identified in section 3:

SECTION

'3. General duty

The Commission shall exercise its functions under this Part with a view to encouraging and supporting the development of a society in which –

(a) people's ability to achieve their potential is not limited by prejudice or discrimination,

(b) there is respect for and protection of each individual's human rights,

(c) there is respect for the dignity and worth of each individual,

(d) each individual has an equal opportunity to participate in society, and

(e) there is mutual respect between groups based on understanding and valuing of diversity and on shared respect for equality and human rights.'

The Commission also has more specific duties with relation to equality in section 8:

SECTION

'8. Equality and diversity

(1) The Commission shall, by exercising the powers conferred by this Part –
    (a) promote understanding of the importance of equality and diversity,
    (b) encourage good practice in relation to equality and diversity,
    (c) promote equality of opportunity,
    (d) promote awareness and understanding of rights under the equality enactments,
    (e) enforce the equality enactments,
    (f) work towards the elimination of unlawful discrimination, and
    (g) work towards the elimination of unlawful harassment.'

The Commission is responsible for promoting equality and tackling discrimination in all those areas identified as protected characteristics in the Equality Act 2010 (see Chapters 9, 11, 12, 13 and 14), and also for promoting human rights under the Human Rights Act 1998.

The Commission is staffed by sixteen Commissioners and has the power to appoint advisory committees and to issue Codes of Practice. It also prepares a strategic plan for its activities as well as preparing a three-yearly report which outlines problem areas and suggests proposals for improvement. It also has powers to carry out investigations and to issue unlawful act notices.

The Health and Safety Executive

The Health and Safety Executive (HSE) was originally created in the Health and Safety at Work etc Act 1974 together with the Health and Safety Commission. In 2008 the two bodies were merged. The HSE comprises eleven non-executive members, three appointed following consultation with employers' associations, three following consultation with employee associations, one after consultation with local authorities and four following consultation with professional bodies.

The HSE makes arrangements for the general purpose of promoting and ensuring health and safety at work. In particular the HSE's role includes:

- researching health and safety issues;
- introducing Codes of Practice on health and safety at work;
- suggesting new health and safety regulations;
- providing and promoting education and training on health and safety;
- providing advice and information on health and safety issues;
- assisting people to pursue matters related to health and safety at work.

The HSE also has powers of investigation using local authority inspectors and of enforcement of the statutory provisions through improvement notices and prohibition notices. It can also bring prosecutions for breaches of health and safety laws (see Chapter 16.4).

ACTIVITY

Self-assessment questions

1. Which courts or tribunals hear claims on employment related matters?
2. In what circumstances would an employment related claim be heard in a court rather than in a tribunal?
3. What is the usual composition of an employment tribunal?
4. What is the Employment Appeal Tribunal and how is it comprised?
5. In what circumstances would an appeal on an employment related matter go to the Supreme Court (or the former House of Lords)?
6. In what circumstances could the Court of Justice of the European Union be influential in relation to claims on employment related matters?
7. What is ACAS?
8. What are the principal roles of ACAS?
9. In what ways could ACAS be involved in a claim over an employment related matter?
10. What does the Central Arbitration Committee generally do?
11. What is the role of the Certification Officer?
12. What are the general duties and the more specific duties of the Equality and Human Rights Commission?
13. What are the basic powers of the Health and Safety Executive?

3.2 Employment tribunal procedure

3.2.1 Time limits

Time limits govern employment tribunal procedure in exactly the same way that they govern any other form of civil dispute resolution procedure. An employee seeking to enforce an employment right or claiming a breach of any such right must bring his claim within the strict time limits that are imposed by law.

In general the rule is that claims must be presented to the tribunal within three months of the act complained about. There are, however, some exceptions to this basic rule:

- a claim for interim relief should be made within seven days of the dismissal;
- a claim for a redundancy payment should be made within six months of the termination (although under section 164 Employment Rights Act 1996 the tribunal has a discretion to extend this by up to a further six months if it is just and equitable to do so in the circumstances);
- a claim concerning a dismissal because of official industrial action should be brought within six months of the dismissal;
- a claim against a trade union for unlawful exclusion or expulsion should be brought within six months of the unlawful act;
- a claim for equal pay should either be brought during the employment or within six months of the termination of the contract of employment.

Time limits are mandatory and an employment tribunal has no jurisdiction to hear a claim that is brought out of time. In *Rogers v Bodfari (Transport) Ltd* [1973] IRLR 172 a claim for unfair dismissal was brought out of time but the tribunal actually held that the dismissal was unfair. The employer then raised the issue that the claim was brought out of time and that the tribunal therefore had no jurisdiction to hear the claim. The Employment Appeal Tribunal agreed that this was the case and has subsequently made the same point in *Kudjodji v Lidl* [2011] UKEAT/0054/11/CEA.

There are two limited circumstances where the time limit might be extended:

■ where it was not reasonably practicable to bring the claim in time;
■ where it is just and equitable for the limit to be extended.

Not reasonably practicable to bring the claim in time

In this instance the tribunal will have to consider the reasons why it was not reasonably practicable to submit the claim in time and determine whether these are sufficient to justify extending the limit.

CASE EXAMPLE

John Lewis Partnership v Charman [2011] UKEAT/0079/11/ZT

The claimant had been summarily dismissed and was out of time bringing his claim to the tribunal because he had pursued an internal appeal which only took place ten weeks later with a decision being made four weeks after that and the claimant was unaware about the time limits and thought it would be sensible to await the outcome of the internal appeal before bringing his claim. The tribunal heard the claim because it held that it had not been reasonably practicable for the claimant to present his claim until after the internal appeal and he had presented his claim within a reasonable time. The employer appealed on the issue of jurisdiction and the EAT agreed with the tribunal that if the employee was reasonably ignorant of the time limits it would not be reasonably practicable for him to bring his claim in time. If, on the other hand he had been represented by legal advisers or trade union advisers who should be aware of the time limit then the answer would be different.

It is inevitable also for the tribunal to determine whether a claimant acts reasonably in bringing his claim promptly once he knows of the time limit.

CASE EXAMPLE

James W Cook Ltd v Tipper [1990] IRLR 386

Shipyard workers were dismissed by their employer but reasonably believed that they had a good prospect of being re-employed. They only later learned that the shipyard at which they worked was to close down so their claims were brought out of time. The employer then appealed the decision to allow the claims to go ahead out of time. The EAT held that it had not been reasonably practicable for the claimants to complain of unfair dismissal until the closure of the business, which only occurred after the time limit had passed, because the employees had been misled.

JUDGMENT

Neill LJ commented: 'As has been emphasised in the authorities, the expression 'reasonably practicable' must be looked at in a common sense way.'

Just and equitable to extend the time limit

In some claims such as discrimination claims a tribunal might have more leeway to extend the time limit under the just and equitable head than it would on the basis of the not reasonably practicable test.

CASE EXAMPLE

Department of Constitutional Affairs v John Grant Jones [2007] EWCA Civ 894; [2008] IRLR 128

The claimant was chief executive of a Magistrates' Courts Committee and was suspended from work on 28 July 2004 because of allegations of serious financial irregularities. He was then diagnosed as suffering from anxiety and depression. His doctors then recommended that he was unable to attend a disciplinary hearing both because of his severe depression but also he had broken his leg. The hearing was held in his absence and he was dismissed for gross misconduct. The police then raided his home. He brought an action for unfair dismissal and breach of contract and later brought an action for disability discrimination but this was brought out of time. The tribunal was prepared to allow the claim out of time when it was demonstrated that the delay was partly because the claimant was reluctant to admit that his illness in fact amounted to a disability. The Court of Appeal held that the Chairman of the tribunal was entitled to extend the time limit in the circumstances.

JUDGMENT

Pill LJ explained: 'the Chairman was entitled to have in mind the series of misfortunes which the respondent suffered ... from the police raid, to the broken ankle, to the knowledge that disciplinary proceedings were being conducted in an absence of his supported by the appellants' own doctor, factors were operating on his mind which make it more likely to be just and equitable that a modest extension of time should be granted ... I am far from stating any general principle that a person with mental health problems is entitled to delay as a matter of course in bringing a claim. What I am sure about is that upon the careful consideration given by this Chairman, he was entitled to reach the conclusion he did on the particular facts and combination of circumstances present in this case.'

In *Chohan v Derby Law Centre* [2004] IRLR 685 the EAT identified that wrong advice by a legal adviser may also be sufficient to allow a tribunal to extend the time limit under the just and equitable reasoning, although a fault by a legal adviser in failing to lodge an appeal in the EAT on time is not generally grounds to exercise the discretion. In general solicitors and other legal advisers should be aware of all time limits and keep track of whether a claim is submitted in time. In *Camden v Islington Community Services NHS Trust v Kennedy* [1996] IRLR 381 the claim had to be made by 27 December. The solicitor posted the completed claim form on 19 December and should have received acknowledgement by 5 January but failed to check whether the claim was received until 30 January. It had not been received and the tribunal could not receive a later submission.

In the case of unfair dismissal claims time runs from the effective date of termination (ETD) so it is vital to know when this is:

- If the dismissal is with notice then it is when the notice expires.
- If it is without notice then it is the date on which the termination takes effect.
- If it is a fixed or limited-term contract then it is the date on which the termination occurs.

3.2.2 Originating procedure (bringing a claim)

With some limited exceptions all claims should be submitted to the regional employment tribunal office on the appropriate form, the ET1. The claim should include a proscribed range of information:

- the nature of the claim e.g. discrimination, unfair dismissal;
- the claimant's personal details i.e. name and address;
- details of any representation if appropriate;
- the employer's details;
- the details of the claimant's employment i.e. job description, length of service, hours of work, pay, etc.;
- the details of the claim giving as much precise detail as possible;
- the remedy sought (ordinarily this will be a form of compensation but it could involve other remedies such as for instance reinstatement or re-engagement in an unfair dismissal claim).

The form is reasonably easy to complete and there is extensive guidance on the website http://justice.gov.uk/forms/hmcts/employment.

The fact that some minor details are missing from the claim form will not necessarily prove fatal to the claim and prevent it from proceeding. However, it is possible for the tribunal secretary to refuse to accept the claim if some important detail is missing.

The Regional Tribunal Office checks the claim and allots it a case number and sends an acknowledgement of receipt to the claimant. It then sends a copy of the claim form and a response form (ET3) to the employer. Again guidance on completing the response form is available on the website http://justice.gov.uk/forms/hmcts/employment.

The employer is then bound to return the completed response form within twenty-eight days. If the employer is defending the claim then the response form should contain sufficient information to indicate the basis on which the claim is being resisted. If the employer fails to return the response form in time or has not been successful in gaining an extension to the time limit then a default judgment will be made. The employer could apply within fourteen days to have the default judgment set aside. If the completed response form has not been returned or it contains insufficient information then the tribunal secretary may refuse to accept it and may refer the matter to an employment judge who may then invite the parties to a pre-hearing review.

If both claim form and response form are appropriately completed then they are passed on to a conciliation officer. At the request of either party or on his own volition because he feels that it may be successful the conciliation officer will try to reach a settlement between the parties.

3.2.3 Conciliation, settlements and compromise arrangements

ACAS has a statutory duty to help parties to reach a voluntary settlement which would avoid the need for a tribunal hearing. It does this through the process of conciliation. A settlement that is reached through the conciliation officer could then be binding on the parties whereas in general an employee cannot waive his statutory rights so that a settlement between an employer and employee which does not involve the conciliation officer is not binding. Communications with the conciliation officer are not then admissible in the tribunal unless both parties consent.

There are two main ways in which a settlement can be reached without a tribunal hearing. The first of these is a settlement made on form COT3. This is a voluntary settlement reached with the conciliation officer. The settlement only applies to the matters that are identified in the COT3 so that a later claim on another ground is still possible. A claim is also possible where it is based on facts of which the employee was unaware at the time the settlement was made. Otherwise the settlement is binding on both parties.

The other type of settlement is a compromise agreement. This must:

- be in writing;
- relate to particular proceedings;
- only occur after the employee has received independent legal advice either from a qualified lawyer or from a trade union official who is certified as being a competent adviser and in either case the adviser must have legal professional indemnity insurance;
- identify who the adviser is;
- state that the statutory conditions regulating the compromise agreement are satisfied.

Compromise agreements can be made in respect of most matters within the jurisdiction of employment tribunals, an exception being failure to consult with a trade union during a redundancy situation.

Compromise agreements only act as settlement of those disputes that have been raised when the agreement is reached but they are binding on both parties. Because compromise agreements amount to a contractual agreement connected with employment they can be enforced in a tribunal.

3.2.4 Case management

An employment judge has extensive case management powers by virtue of the Employment Tribunals (Constitution and Rules of Procedure) Regulations 2004 as amended. If a party fails to comply with a direction then the employment judge may make an order for costs or indeed may make an order to strike out all or part of either the claim or the response to it if the failure to comply with the direction means that a fair trial of the claim is then impossible.

The employment judge can use his powers to ensure that the case is dealt with as fairly and expeditiously as possible and that both parties are on an equal footing.

Either party can request further and better particulars or an order for discovery of documents. However, there is no automatic procedure for making such orders. The employment judge may make such an order only where the party requesting it would otherwise be unfairly prejudiced. Discovery cannot be used as a 'fishing expedition' or in other words as the means of establishing the existence of a claim. Where disclosure has been ordered the order continues right up to the end of the tribunal hearing.

Privilege from disclosure only applies to communication between clients and their professional legal advisers. If privilege is claimed then the potential injustice of non-disclosure must be balanced against what is in the public interest.

3.2.5 Pre-hearing review

The provision to hold a pre-hearing review was originally made in the Industrial Tribunal (Constitution and Rules of Procedure) Regulations 1993 and is now in the Employment Tribunal (Constitution and Rules of Procedure) Regulations 2004 as amended.

The original purpose of the pre-hearing review was to assess whether either the claim or the response to it were unsustainable rather than this being discovered in the tribunal. At the pre-hearing review the employment judge may do a variety of things:

- He can decide on preliminary matters and issue directions.
- He can decide that, while a claim or the response to it is still arguable, it has little prospect of success, in which case he can order that party to pay a deposit (currently set at £500) in order to continue: if the deposit is then not paid within a set time the claim or response can be struck out.
- He can decide that the claim or the response to it is so weak that it has no reasonable prospect of success, in which case he can stop it proceeding to the tribunal.

■ He can also strike out a claim or the response to it where it is vexatious, or where the manner in which it has been conducted is vexatious, or where there has been intentional and contumelious (meaning insulting) fault by the claimant, or where there has been such delay by the claimant that there is a substantial risk that a fair trial would not be possible.

Restricted reporting orders can also be made at the pre-hearing review. These are possible for example in discrimination cases where information of a personal nature might be revealed.

3.2.6 The procedure at the hearing

Employment tribunal hearings are public so the public and the press are entitled to attend, although restricted reporting orders can be made in certain cases. There are limited circumstances where a tribunal can sit in private:

■ where it would be against the interests of national security for the evidence to be heard in public;

■ where a person could not give evidence in public without breaching a statutory provision;

■ where the evidence had been communicated to the person in confidence;

■ where the evidence if given in public could cause substantial injury to the employer.

Some evidence may also be given in private to comply with Article 8 European Convention on Human Rights, the right to respect for private or family life.

A closed material procedure is also possible where the claimant and his representatives are excluded from part of the proceedings in the interests of national security. It has been identified in *Home Office v Tariq* [2011] UKSC 34 that this does not breach either EU law or the European Convention on Human Rights.

The composition of a tribunal panel is a legally qualified employment judge, a member drawn from a panel approved by the Secretary of State representing employers' associations and a member drawn from a panel approved by the Secretary of State representing a recognised trade union or other employee association. In unfair dismissal claims an employment judge sits alone.

The order of proceedings resembles court proceedings in many ways. However, the rules of evidence are different to those applied in courts and much more matters can be introduced.

CASE EXAMPLE

Docherty v Reddy [1977] ICR 365

The employee had been dismissed for a minor theft and when making the decision to dismiss the employer took into account that the employee had been suspected of stealing small sums on previous occasions. Suspicion would not be accepted as evidence in a normal court and even evidence of past theft would not be introduced since it would be more prejudicial than probative. However, the issue for an employment tribunal is whether the employer has acted reasonably in the circumstances. On this basis the EAT held that the claimant's prior conduct was a factor that could be taken into account in reaching a decision.

Burden of proof also operates slightly different to it would in usual civil claims. In general the burden of proof does lie on the claimant who would therefore normally present his case first which can then be rebutted by the employer. In certain claims in employment tribunals, however, the burden is in effect reversed. In unfair dismissal claims if the dismissal is admitted it is then for the employer to establish the exact reason for the dismissal, that it fell within one of the five potentially fair reasons for dismissal and that it was also fair in fact falling within the reasonable range of responses test (see Chapter 22.5.1). Also under the Equality Act 2010 section 135 the burden of proof is also reversed in discrimination claims (see Chapter 15.1).

The role of the tribunal is to consider the facts, listen to the witnesses, study all of the evidence and then reach a decision on the basis of the relevant legal provisions. The duty of the tribunal is to apply the law as laid down by Parliament. In this respect the tribunal can take into account interpretations of law made by the EAT and the other superior courts. However, ultimately it is the statutory provision which must be followed.

In practice employment tribunals are bound to give a reasoned decision. They will usually give an oral decision in the hearing and then put it in writing at a later date. About 95 per cent of all decisions in employment tribunals are unanimous.

The employment tribunal will also provide the appropriate remedy. Financial remedies vary with the particular type of claim and there are also special rules for claims that are brought on the basis of EU law. Awards also attract interest on a daily basis until they are paid. In the case of unfair dismissal claims reinstatement and re-engagement are also possible remedies (see Chapter 22.7).

3.2.7 Appeals

An appeal from a decision of an employment tribunal is made to the Employment Appeal Tribunal (EAT). The appeal must be made within forty-two days of the date when the written reasons for the decision was sent to the appellant. It is only in very rare and exceptional circumstances that the EAT will relax this rule and allow an extension.

Once the appeal is submitted there is a preliminary hearing/directions. An appeal can only be on a point of law so the appeal will only be allowed to proceed to the EAT if it can be shown that it is reasonably arguable that the tribunal made an error in law. If it can then directions are made to ensure that the appeal is determined efficiently and effectively. If there is no arguable point of law then the appeal is dismissed at this stage.

An appeal cannot be made on a point of law that was not raised in the tribunal unless it would be unjust to let the other party get away with a deception or unfair conduct; or there is a glaring injustice in not permitting an unrepresented party to rely on evidence that could have been given to the tribunal; or if it is of particular public importance for a legal point to be decided on.

For the appeal to succeed one of the following must apply:

- The tribunal misdirected itself in law.
- The tribunal entertained the wrong issue.
- The tribunal misapprehended or misconstrued the evidence.
- The tribunal took into account matters that were irrelevant to the decision.
- The tribunal reached a decision which no reasonable tribunal properly directing itself in law could have reached.

The appellant should state in precise terms which point of law is being questioned. Merely stating in general terms for instance that there is a misdirection or an error in law is insufficient.

Any further appeals are to the Court of Appeal and then on to the Supreme Court. Where an issue of EU law is involved and would resolve the case a reference may be made at any stage to the ECJ if it is necessary.

ACTIVITY

Self-assessment questions

1. What is the usual time limit for bringing claims in an employment tribunal?
2. What are the exceptions?
3. What are the only situations in which the time limit can be extended?
4. What is the difference between the two?
5. What details should a claimant put on his ET1?
6. What is the difference between a settlement and a compromise agreement?
7. What is case management?
8. What happens at a pre-hearing review?
9. How are the rules of evidence different in an employment tribunal to the courts?
10. In what circumstances does the burden of proof shift to the employer?
11. On what grounds can an appeal be made to the EAT?

KEY FACTS

Courts and tribunals hearing employment disputes	Case/statute
Employment tribunals	
• rules on procedure • composition = a qualified employment judge and two lay members representing employer associations and employee associations • hear cases on all statutory protections – and now can hear some breach of contract claims	*Employment Tribunals (Constitution and Rules of Procedure) Regulations 2004* *Employment Tribunals Act 1996*
County Court and High Court	
• hear breach of contract actions – claims below £25,000 in County Court and above £50,000 in High Court • High Court also hears applications for injunctions	
Employment Appeal Tribunal	
• is part of the High Court • hears appeals on points of law on most areas falling within the jurisdiction of employment tribunals, and from the decisions of the Certification Officer, and from the Central Arbitration Committee	
Court of Appeal (Civil Division)	
• hears appeals on points of law from the EAT and the courts	
Supreme Court	
• hears appeals from the Court of Appeal	

Court of Justice of the EU	
• hears references from Member State courts where a preliminary ruling on a point of EU law is necessary to resolve the case	

Other significant institutions in employment law	Case/statute
ACAS	
• role to promote the improvement of industrial relations • promotes good practice by producing Codes of Practice • provides advice and information, collective conciliation and advisory mediation, and conciliation and arbitration in employment tribunal claims • in unfair dismissal claim can be heard by a single independent arbitrator if both parties have agreed to this and have signed a COT3 or have reached a compromise agreement.	*S209 Trade Union and Labour Relations (Consolidation) Act 1992* *S199–202 TULR(C)A 1992* *S212A Trade Union and Labour Relations (Consolidation) Act 1992*
Central Arbitration Committee	
• provides arbitration on statutory recognition or derecognition of trade unions for collective bargaining purposes, complaints from trade unions over failures by employers to disclose matters for collective bargaining purposes	*S259 Trade Union and Labour Relations (Consolidation) Act 1992*
Certification Officer	
• maintains a list of independent trade unions, keeps records of membership, rules and finances, investigates complaints	*S254 Trade Union and Labour Relations (Consolidation) Act 1992*
Equality and Human Rights Commission	
• general duty to encourage diversity and discourage discrimination • specific duty to promote understanding of the importance of equality and diversity, encourage good practice, promote equality of opportunity, promote awareness and understanding of equality legislation, enforce the equality enactments, try to eliminate unlawful discrimination,	*S3 Equality Act 2006* *S8 Equality Act 2006*
Health and Safety Executive	
• enforces health and safety law and investigates health and safety breaches and issues improvement notices and prohibition notices through local inspectors • also researches health and safety issues, introduces Codes of Practice, proposes new regulations, provides education and training, and advice and information	*Health and Safety at Work etc Act 1974*

Employment tribunal procedure	Case/statute
Time limits	
• generally three months – but seven days for interim relief, six months for redundancy claims, dismissal for TU activities, and exclusion or expulsion from a TU, and equal pay either during employment or within six months of leaving • can only extend the time limit if it was not reasonably practicable to bring it in time • or can extend where it is just and equitable to do so	*John Lewis Partnership v Charman* [2011] *Department of Constitutional Affairs v John Grant Jones* [2007]
Bringing a claim	
• claim is on an ET1 which should include: nature of claim, claimant's personal details, details of any representation, employer's details, details of claimant's employment, details of the claim giving as much precise detail as possible and remedy sought • employer responds on ET3 within twenty-eight days or judgment in default • both then sent to Conciliation Officer	
Conciliation, settlements and compromise agreements	
• can have a settlement without tribunal on COT3 • or could reach a compromise agreement	
Case management	
• employment judge has wide powers to ensure case is dealt with as fairly and expeditiously as possible and both parties on equal footing • discovery is discretionary	*Employment Tribunals (Constitution and Rules of Procedure) Regulations 2004*
Pre-hearing review	
• employment judge may decide on preliminary matters and issue directions, • decide that, while a claim or the response to it is still arguable, it has little prospect of success and order a deposit is paid • decide that the claim or the response to it is so weak that it has no reasonable prospect of success, and stop it proceeding to the tribunal • and strike out claims or response which are vexatious, or conduct is vexatious, or where there has been intentional and contumelious fault by the claimant, or delay by claimant means a fair trial is not possible	*Employment Tribunals (Constitution and Rules of Procedure) Regulations 2004*

Procedure at hearing	
• hearings are public although some can be in private • composition is legally qualified chair (employment judge) and two lay members, an employer organisation representative and an employee association representative • rules of evidence are more relaxed • burden of proof shifts with type of claim e.g. in unfair dismissal or discrimination claims • must give effect to the law as laid out by Parliament • oral decision given followed by reasoned decision later	*Docherty v Reddy* [1977]
Appeals	
• to the EAT only on law: tribunal misdirected itself in law, or entertained the wrong issue, or misapprehended or misconstrued the evidence, or took into account matters that were irrelevant to the decision, or reached a decision which no reasonable tribunal properly directing itself in law could have reached • further appeals are to the Court of Appeal and then to the Supreme Court • references can be made to the Court of Justice on issues of EU law where necessary to resolve the case	

SUMMARY

- A number of courts and tribunals hear employment cases.

- Most first instance cases are in employment tribunals which have wide jurisdiction to hear cases on all statutory employment protections – they can also hear some breach of contract cases up to £25,000 worth of damages.

- Otherwise breach of contract cases such as wrongful dismissal go to either the County Court or the High Court depending on the value of the claim – actions for injunctions are also heard in the courts.

- Appeals from tribunals are to the Employment Appeal Tribunal (EAT) – appeals from there and from court go to the Court of Appeal (Civil Division) and appeals from there are to the Supreme Court.

- References for a preliminary ruling on an interpretation of EU law can be made to the Court of Justice where it is necessary.

- Other important institutions include ACAS, the Central Arbitration Committee, the Certification Officer, the Equality and Human Rights Commission and the Health and Safety Executive.

- The usual time limit for bringing a claim in a tribunal is three months – but there are some exceptions.

- The time limit can only be extended where it was not reasonably practicable to bring the claim in time, or where it is just and equitable.
- Claims should be made to the Regional Office on form ET1 which is sent to the employer who returns a response form (ET3).
- Both are then sent to a conciliation officer who will see if it is possible to reach a settlement or a compromise agreement.
- The employment judge has extensive powers of case management and there is a pre-hearing review to weed out weak claims or responses.
- Hearings resemble court hearings but the rules of evidence are different and the burden of proof is reversed in some instances.
- Appeals are to the EAT on a point of law only.

Further reading

Emir, Astra, *Selwyn's Law of Employment 17th edition*. Oxford University Press, 2012, Chapters 1 and 20.

Sargeant, Malcolm and Lewis, David, *Employment Law 6th edition*, Pearson, 2012, Chapter 1.

4

Employment status

AIMS AND OBJECTIVES

After reading this chapter you should be able to:

- Understand the basic character of employment
- Understand the limitations of the statutory definition
- Understand the differences between an employee and an independent contractor
- Understand the purposes of distinguishing between employees and independent contractors (the self-employed)
- Understand the tests for establishing whether someone is an employee or not
- Understand those types of situations where work is atypical and the tests do not easily apply
- Distinguish between employees and independent contractors
- Assess the impact of the distinction on the individual and the person hiring their service
- Critically analyse the concepts of employment, self-employment and atypical workers, the reasons for distinguishing and the impact on the employment relationship and on employment rights
- Apply the tests to factual situations to determine whether an individual is an employee
- Apply the outcome to a variety of rights

4.1 Introduction

There are a multitude of rights and responsibilities that exist in the employment relationship. However, before we can begin to study or understand them we need first to consider to whom they apply because in most instances they apply only to employees and employers, and at all times we must distinguish an employee from an independent contractor, a self-employed person.

On the face of it the distinction may seem simple but it is not always so. While most people work they do so in different circumstances and under different conditions.

With certain types of working situations it is not possible to determine at first sight whether in fact a person is employed under a contract of service or not. It will often be in the interest of an 'employer' to deny that the relationship is one of employment to avoid responsibility for employment protection rights. Definitions such as that contained in the Employment Rights Act (see 4.2.1 below) that the employer is a person employed under a contract of employment are not really of much use in determining whether a person is in fact an employee. It has also been suggested in *WHPT Housing Association Ltd v Secretary of State for Social Services* [1981] ICR 737 that the distinction lies in the fact that the employee provides himself to serve while the self-employed person only offers his services. This is no greater help in determining whether or not a person is employed.

Besides this a number of different types of working relationship are not so easy to define. 'Lump' labour was common in the past, particularly the 1960s and 1970s. The lump, as it was called at that time, referred to practice where workers in many trades in industries like construction such as carpenters, bricklayers and painters for example would move from site to site without formally being taken on as employees of contractors hiring labour but would simply work for cash in hand. This gave the 'employee' the advantage of not paying any tax or National Insurance. It gave the 'employer' the advantage of possibly paying less in wages but certainly also of not paying the employer's National Insurance contributions. In effect it defrauded the revenue. Casual and temporary employment is possibly even more prevalent today and many major companies and organisations rely on the use of agency staff or casual labour.

Over the years the courts have devised a number of methods of testing employee status. They all have shortcomings. Some are less useful in a modern society than others.

4.2 Distinguishing between employment and self-employment

4.2.1 The employment relationship

The effective starting point when deciding whether employment law rights apply in any given situation is to ask the question first: is the person an employee? Following the Industrial Revolution, the only relationship that existed was that between the 'master and servant'. Therefore a person's employment status was easy to define. Today, however, the question of whether an individual is an employee is not always easy to answer.

On the surface it seems as though it should be simple and straightforward. However, even a brief examination of the statutory definition shows that it is not.

SECTION

'230 Employees, workers, etc.
(1) In this Act "employee" means an individual who has entered into or works under (or, where the employment has ceased, worked under) a contract of employment.
(2) In this Act "contract of employment" means a contract of service or apprenticeship, whether express or implied, and (if it is express) whether oral or in writing.'

The statutory definition is therefore fairly ambiguous and does not really help to provide any understanding as to who is actually an employee. Under the definition in s230(2), a person is an employee if he works under a contract of service. However, there is no statutory definition of a *contract of service* and the common law has developed rules to help distinguish it from a *contract for services*. In basic terms an employee working under a contract of service agrees to serve another whereas someone who is an independent contractor or self-employed works under a contract for services and agrees to provide certain services to another.

An employer could be a sole trader, a partnership, a company, an unincorporated association or even a private individual. Employers' needs can also vary enormously when hiring 'labour'. They may want permanent staff or only temporary, part-time or casual staff, and they need highly skilled staff for specific tasks. This all impacts on the nature of the employment relationship.

The picture has become even more confused in recent years as a new statutory status of 'worker' has evolved. A worker is defined under s230(3) ERA 1996:

SECTION

'230

(3) In this Act "worker" (except in the phrases "shop worker" and "betting worker") means an individual who has entered into or works under (or, where the employment has ceased, worked under) –

(a) a contract of employment, or

(b) any other contract, whether express or implied and (if it is express) whether oral or in writing, whereby the individual undertakes to do or perform personally any work or services for another party to the contract whose status is not by virtue of the contract that of a client or customer of any profession or business undertaking carried on by the individual; and any reference to a worker's contract shall be construed accordingly.'

In *Byrne Brothers (Formwork) Limited v Baird* [2002] IRLR 496 the EAT stated that a 'worker' had a lower set of qualifying criteria than an 'employee'. So a person may not qualify as an employee but still be entitled to certain rights by being qualified as a worker. Where a person is, on balance, classed as self-employed but there are some factors which point towards employment, it may be possible for him to qualify as a worker. While workers have less extensive employment protection rights than employees, increasingly new statutory employment protections cover workers as well as employees, for example working times and the National Minimum Wage.

The section, as it goes on, is no more illuminating.

SECTION

'230

(4) In this Act "employer", in relation to an employee or a worker, means the person by whom the employee or worker is (or, where the employment has ceased, was) employed.

(5) In this Act "employment" –

(a) in relation to an employee, means (except for the purposes of section 171) employment under a contract of employment, and

(b) in relation to a worker, means employment under his contract; and "employed" shall be construed accordingly.'

The common law tests of employment status are therefore very important.

4.2.2 The purpose of distinguishing between employment and self-employment

Distinguishing between who is classed as an employee and who is an independent contractor is important for a number of reasons. Examples include:

- Implied duties – employers and employees have obligations that are implied into the contract between them (for example, the mutual duty of trust and confidence, the duty of faithful service, etc.).

- Employment protection – the majority of the core legal protections only apply to employees, most particularly the rights on termination of employment granted under ERA 1996, the right not to be unfairly dismissed and the right to a statutory redundancy payment. 'Workers' enjoy limited protection under employment law – for example, the right not to have unlawful deductions from wages, minimum wage, rest breaks, paid leave and data protection.

- Health and Safety – employers owe employees statutory duties relating to health and safety. Independent contractors may not be covered under these duties. They will be covered, however, under the employer's common law duty of care.

- Vicarious liability – an employer is vicariously liable for acts done by an employee in the course of his employment. This vicarious liability does not usually extend to independent contractors or self-employed individuals (although it may do if the employer has directed the independent contractor to commit the tort *Ellis v Sheffield Gas Consumers Co* [1853] 2 E & B 767).

- Taxation – the tax and social security treatment of a person providing services depends on their status. Employers make deductions for income tax under schedule E (PAYE) from salaries and the self-employed are taxed under schedule D annually on a previous year basis and are able to set off certain expenses against tax.

- Insurance – an employer is required to take out employer's liability insurance to cover the risk of employees injuring themselves at work. Self-employed individuals or independent contractors may not be covered by this insurance and may need to take out their own insurance.

- VAT – an independent subcontractor may have to register their business for Value Added Tax.

Independent contractors may be better off financially but can be disadvantaged if injured. While the self-employed benefit by taking all of the profit from their work they also stand any losses and also have to find their own work. Employees have relative security by contrast and know that they receive a wage each pay period but they lack independence. So there are advantages and disadvantages in both classifications.

The differences are generally determined by the consequences of whatever classification. As a result there is inconsistency in the methods of testing employee status according to who it is that is doing the testing. For instance the tax authorities, when testing employee status, are only interested in determining the nature of the person's liability to pay tax, and not any other purpose. So the fact that a person is paying Schedule D tax is not necessarily definitive of their status as self-employed. In the case of industrial safety inspectors investigating breaches of health of safety law they may have less concern with whether an injured person is an employee and more with the fact that the regulations have been breached and caused injury.

4.3 Tests of employment status

4.3.1 Introduction

Because there is no adequate statutory definition of employment a variety of tests for establishing employment status have been devised by the courts over many years.

The diverse and increasingly complex and technical character of work means that it is difficult for any test to be seen as an absolute test or one that will be definitive in all

	EMPLOYEES	SELF-EMPLOYED
Contractual terms	A contract of employment includes express terms (many of which are required to be included by statute) but also many duties implied by common law	A contract for services is usually only subject to its express terms agreed by the parties
Statutory employment rights	Employees enjoy many protections e.g. redundancy, maternity etc. (see e.g. Employment Rights Act 1996)	Most protections are denied to self-employed
Discrimination	Employees are covered by discrimination law	Self-employed are also covered by discrimination law
Health and safety	A high level of care is owed to employees – both in statute (Health and Safety at Work Act 1974), and in common law	There is a lower duty and virtually no common law duty – because independent contractors have the expertise to guard their own safety and in any case would be bound to take out their own insurance
Breach of a statutory duty	Some statutes, particularly in industrial safety law, may provide a civil action for breach of a duty, as well as commonly imposing criminal sanctions e.g. fencing machinery	Such duties are rarely applicable to independent contractors. If there is a non-delegable duty to ensure equipment is used as well as provided it will be owed both to employees and self-employed
Vicarious liability	Employers are commonly liable for the torts of their employees committed in the course of their employment	Such liability will rarely operate in respect of hired independent contractors – unless the hirer directed the contractor to do the tort
Taxation	Schedule E. PAYE. Deducted at source on each pay period	Schedule D. Annual payment following submission of accounts. Advantage of setting off expenses. But self-employed may be liable to register for VAT
Welfare benefits	Class 1 NI contributions deducted from wages. Employees may claim all available welfare benefits	Class 2 or Class 4 contributions made by the self-employed person. Minimal welfare benefits available
Insolvency/ bankruptcy	Employees are preferential creditors and can recover money owed from the liquidator as well as applying for redundancy payments from the Secretary of State	Self-employed are not. As well as losing the money they may be owed – they may in turn be forced out of business as a result
Benefits to the employer	Greater degree of control over the work. Possibility of greater diversification among the workforce. Possibly greater disciplinary powers. Collective bargaining more available	Reduced expenditure on administration. No levy for industrial training. Trade unions are less likely to recruit among the self-employed. Easier to dismiss the worker

Figure 4.1 Chart illustrating the consequences of distinguishing between employees and self-employed

circumstances. The tests having originated under the old 'master and servant laws' (see Chapter 1.4.1) are in part not really relevant in more modern circumstances and some have been discarded.

Whichever test may seem appropriate in a given situation, the general approach in modern times has been for judges to treat each case on its merits and to consider all of the various factors that may point to either employment or self-employment and to balance those factors accordingly.

The tests are nevertheless important as many of them may still be appropriate in particular circumstances.

There have been four tests:

- the control test;
- the integration or organisation test;
- the economic realty or multiple test;
- the mutuality of obligations test.

4.3.2 The control test

The control test is the oldest test for establishing employment status and it comes from a time when the only employment relationship that existed was that between the 'master' and 'servant'. It considers the degree of control and supervision that is exerted by the employer over their staff. The classic definition of the master servant relationship comes from the judgment in *Limland v Stephens* [1801] 3 Esp. 269:

JUDGMENT

Lord Kenyon stated that there were: 'reciprocal duties between master and servant. From the servant is due obedience and respect; from the master protection and good treatment'.

The control test was based very firmly on this style of relationship. An early definition was given in *Yewens v Noakes* [1880] 6 QB 530 where in a tax law case, the Court of Appeal held that a clerk who earned £150 a year did not fall within the definition of servant.

JUDGMENT

In his judgment Bramwell LJ identified that a servant was: 'a person subject to the command of his master as to the manner in which he shall do his work'.

The test was then further developed and explained in:

CASE EXAMPLE

Performing Rights Society Ltd v Mitchell and Booker (Palais de Danse) [1924] 1 KB 762

The case involved a band of musicians which, under its contract, was bound not to play anything that was subject to copyright when performing. In fact the band did so and the claimant sued the company which had hired the musicians. The court held that the musicians had acted within the scope of their employment and so the company that had hired them was liable for the breach of copyright.

JUDGMENT

McArdie J stated: 'the final test, if there is to be a final test, and certainly the test to be generally applied, lies in the nature of the detailed control over the person alleged to be a servant'.

Often a worker would have been unable to gain a remedy without proving that the test applied. In *Walker v Crystal Palace Football Club Ltd* [1910] 1 KB 87 a footballer was considered to be an employee of the club and therefore able to claim compensation for an injury received in a match accident under the Workmen's Compensation Act 1906.

JUDGMENT

Relying on *Yewens v Noakes* Cozens-Hardy MR stated that Walker: 'is bound according to the express terms of his contract to obey all general directions of the club'.

The implication is that the master not only controlled what was to be done and when it was to be done, but also the manner in which the work was done. In the case of simple forms of employment prevalent when the master and servant laws were developed, such as farm labouring or domestic service, then clearly this level of control could be easily identified and the test worked well.

However, the test is still important as in today's employment market an employee would normally be subject to some form of control or supervision by the employer. Lord Thankerton in *Short v J W Henderson Ltd* [1946] 62 TLR 427 identified many key features that would show that the master had control over the servant. These included the power to select the servant, the right to suspend and dismiss, the payment of wages and the right to control the method of working (this has sometimes been referred to as the indicia test – it has also been criticised as inadequate because the first three only point to a contract not necessarily to employment and the last is merely the control test). There is also the power to terminate and, in particular, to subject the employee to disciplinary procedures and to manage the relationship by issuing orders and directions. Many of the cases, however, have tended to focus on the extent to which the individual is controlled in the manner in which they carry out their tasks.

CASE EXAMPLE

Motorola v Davidson and Melville Craig Group Ltd [2001] IRLR 4

Davidson was recruited by Melville employment agency who supplied temporary workers to Motorola. Davidson was bound by contract with Melville to comply with all reasonable requests made by Motorola. Motorola terminated Davidson's assignment and he claimed unfair dismissal. He was considered to be an employee of Motorola as there was sufficient degree of day-to-day control.

Such a test is virtually impossible to apply accurately in modern circumstances. Nevertheless, there are circumstances in which a test of control is still useful; in the case of borrowed workers.

CASE EXAMPLE

Mersey Docks & Harbour Board v Coggins and Griffiths (Liverpool) Ltd [1947] AC 1

Here the test was usefully applied when a crane driver negligently damaged goods in the course of his work. In this case the Harbour Board hired out both a crane and the crane driver to stevedores to act as their servant. Under the contract between the Board and the stevedores the crane driver was still to be paid by the Board and only they had the right to dismiss him, but for the duration of the contract he was to be regarded as the employee of the stevedores. The Harbour Board was still held to be liable for his negligence, however, since he would not accept control from the stevedores.

JUDGMENT

In the case above Lord Porter gave a very clear explanation of the control test: 'the most satis-factory [test] by which to ascertain who is the employer at any particular time, is to ask who is entitled to tell the employee the way in which he is to do the work upon which he is engaged … it is not enough that the task to be performed should be under his under his control, he must control the method of performing it'.

However, even in the nineteenth century in the case of more sophisticated types of work requiring technical knowledge and expertise that was likely to be beyond that enjoyed by the master then it was apparent that such a simple test was not really workable. As technology advanced in the twentieth century certain work became even more special-ist. The classic example of this is in medicine. Hospitals very often employ managerial and administrative staff with backgrounds for example in retailing or in financial serv-ices or other businesses. It would be difficult to say that these people had the expertise to be able to 'control' surgeons carrying out highly complex surgical procedures or even to understand what was going on if they attended operations. This is shown in *Cassidy v Ministry of Health* [1951] 2 KB 343 where it had to be decided who was in fact liable and the court felt that hospitals and health services should always be responsible for the work done in them.

4.3.3 The integration or organisation test

The degree of integration into the employer's business was identified as a test in the early 1950s by Lord Denning.

> **Is the alleged employee subject to the detailed control of the person for whom he works?**
> • he can be told what work he must do
> • he can also be directed in the way in which he does the work

YES

> **ACCORDING TO THE CONTROL TEST HE MAY BE CLASSED AS AN EMPLOYEE**

Figure 4.2 Diagram illustrating the operation of the control test

CASE EXAMPLE

Stevenson, Jordan & Harrison v MacDonald & Evans [1952] 1 TLR 101

An accountant had sold the copyright of a book which he had written partly using information that he had gained generally during his employment but also partly through a particular assignment that he had been given and without which he would not have had the knowledge. The employer sought to restrain the transfer of copyright. The Court of Appeal held that the employer could only restrain those parts of the manuscript that related to the specific knowledge gained during employment, not to that using general knowledge.

JUDGMENT

Lord Denning explained: 'under a contract of service a man is employed as part of the business and his work is done as an integral part of the business but under a contract of services his work, although done for the business, is not integrated into it but only accessory to it'.

The basis of the test is that someone will be an employee whose work is fully integrated into the business, whereas if a person's work is only accessory to the business then that person is not an employee. In other words he is considered to be 'part and parcel' of the employer's organisation. A self-employed person or an independent contractor is more likely to perform duties which are ancillary to the main business of the employer.

Lord Denning explained that, according to this test, the master of a ship, a chauffeur and a reporter on the staff of a newspaper are all employees, where the pilot bringing a ship into port, a taxi driver and a freelance writer are not. The test can work well in some circumstances particularly in the case of very skilled employees where the control test may not be adequate, doctors being an obvious example.

CASE EXAMPLE

Whittaker v Minister of Pensions and National Insurance [1967] 1 QB 156

A trapeze artist broke her wrist and needed to show that she was an employee in order to claim an industrial injuries benefit. The artist had duties to perform other than merely her own special act. She also travelled with the circus and was subject to a considerable degree of domestic control. The court considered that she was therefore an integral part of the circus.

JUDGMENT

Mocatta J considered: 'had she only been obliged to perform her trapeze act, even if she had also been under various constraints and controls in relation thereto, there would have been grounds for holding her contract to have been one for services'.

However, there are still defects. For instance part-time examiners may be classed as employed for the purposes of deducting tax, but it is unlikely that the exam board would be happy to pay redundancy when their services were no longer needed. Another problem in modern employment is that many businesses outsource parts of their work and this would make application of the test difficult.

Is the alleged employee integrated into the business of the person for whom he works?
- he is a part of the business organisation
- he is not merely accessory to the business organisation

YES

↓

ACCORDING TO THE INTEGRATION TEST HE MAY BE CLASSED AS AN EMPLOYEE

Figure 4.3 Diagram illustrating the operation of the integration test

4.3.4 The economic reality or multiple test

The courts later recognised that a single test of employment is not satisfactory and may produce confusing results. As a result a new test, the economic reality test, was developed. This is sometimes known as the multiple test since all the various factors need to be considered.

CASE EXAMPLE

Ready Mixed Concrete (South East) Ltd v Minister of Pensions and National Insurance [1968] 2 QB 497

Under a revised contract drivers who had formerly been employees were obliged to use vehicles, which they bought on hire purchase agreements from the company. The vehicles were in the company colours and bore the company logo. The vehicles also had to be maintained according to set standards and drivers were only allowed to use them on company business. The drivers' hours were flexible and their pay was subject to an annual minimum rate based on the amount of concrete they hauled. The contract also permitted them to hire drivers in their place. The question for the court was who paid National Insurance contributions, the company or the drivers. The court held that the terms of the contract were inconsistent with a contract of employment and that the driver in question was self-employed, although this might be seen to have operated unfairly on the claimant. The case is important because McKenna J developed the economic reality test in determining their lack of employment status.

JUDGMENT

McKenna J explained the elements of the test: '(i) The servant agrees that in consideration of a wage or other remuneration he will provide his own work and skill in the performance of some services … (ii) he agrees, expressly or impliedly, that in the performance of that service he will be in the other's control in a sufficient degree to make that other master; (iii) the other provisions of the contract are consistent with it being a contract of service.'

So the answer under the test is to consider whatever factors may be indicative of employment or self-employment. In particular, three conditions should be met before an employment relationship is identified:

- The employee agrees to provide work or skill in return for a wage.
- The employee expressly or impliedly accepts that the work will be subject to the control of the employer.

- All other considerations in the contract are consistent with there being a contract of employment rather than any other relationship between the parties.

In respect of this last point the test has been developed over time so that all the relevant factors in the relationship should be considered and weighed according to their significance. It is not a case of simply totalling up factors which indicate employment and factors which indicate self-employment and running with the one with the most factors. The factors that will be considered include:

- The method of payment – an employee usually receives a wage, regular payments for a defined pay period whereas a self-employed person will usually be paid a price for a whole job.

- Tax and National Insurance contributions – an employee usually has tax deducted out of wages under the PAYE scheme under schedule E and also has Class 1 National Insurance contributions also deducted by the employer from wages each pay period, so an employee has no choice but to pay tax and National Insurance and is usually unable to claim expenses against tax. A self-employed person on the other hand usually pays tax annually under schedule D on a previous year basis and is able to set expenses off against tax, and makes National Insurance contributions by buying Class 2 stamps or Class 4 beyond a certain level of income.

- Ownership of tools or plant or equipment – an employee is less likely to own the plant and equipment with which he works particularly when this involves large expensive items, however, the self-employed will very often need to provide their own tools although with large expensive equipment this may mean hiring it.

- Self-description – a person may describe himself as one or the other and this will usually, but not always, be an accurate description. So self-description may be strong but not necessarily definitive evidence of employment status. Courts look more to the substance of the relationship rather than just accepting the description as can be seen in the following two cases. In *Massey v Crown Life Insurance* [1978] IRLR 31 an employee arranged with his employer to carry on the same work but to do it on a self-employed basis and a new agreement was drawn up. He paid tax under schedule D and self-employed National Insurance contributions which obviously benefited him, although there was no issue of trying to defraud the revenue. When he was later dismissed he tried to claim unfair dismissal but failed since he was in fact self-employed. The description in the new agreement accurately matched the relationship. In contrast in *Young & Woods Ltd v West* [1980] IRLR 201 a skilled sheet metal worker reached a similar agreement with his employer for tax purposes but the court held that the self-employed description did not match the reality of the situation. In all other respects the worker was an employee.

- Level of independence – probably one of the most significant indicators that a person is self-employed is the extra degree of independence in being able to take work from whatever source and turn work down.

- Another test could be to determine who has the benefit of any insurance cover that might be available (see *British Telecommunications plc v James Thompson & Sons (Engineers) Ltd* [1999] 1 WLR 9).

- Another test could be to consider what any job advertisement or contract for the position states.

All of these are useful in identifying the status of the worker but none of them are an absolute test or are definitive on their own. As a result the 'multiple test' considers other factors.

CASE EXAMPLE

Market Investigations v Minster of Social Security [1969] 2 QB 173

Interviewers were employed on a casual basis by a market research company which also had permanent staff. The court needed to determine whether they were employees which would mean that the company should pay National Insurance contributions. The interviewers worked as and when required. They were obliged to complete their surveys within an allotted time and were given set questions to ask. However, they were able to select their own times of working. The court weighed all the factors in the case and held that the interviewers were employees rather than independent contractors. Control was one element but did not wholly determine employment status.

JUDGMENT

Cooke LJ commented: 'No exhaustive list has been compiled and perhaps no exhaustive list can be compiled of considerations which are relevant in determining [employment status] . . . control will no doubt always have to be considered, although it can no longer be regarded as the sole determining factor; and that factors, which may be of importance, are . . . whether the man performing the services provides his own equipment, whether he hires his own helpers, what degree of financial risk he takes, what degree of responsibility for investment and management he has, and whether and how far he has an opportunity of profiting from sound management in the performance of his task.'

The Privy Council in *Lee v Chung and Shun Shing Construction & Engineering Co Ltd* [1990] IRLR 236 also followed this approach and held that the fundamental issue was whether the person was performing services as a person in business on his own account. Factors that could be considered include:

- the degree of risk the person takes;
- the degree of responsibility for investment and management that the person has;
- whether the person makes a profit;
- whether the person hires people himself.

The approach was also developed in *Hall (Inspector of Taxes) v Lorimer* [1994] IRLR 171 where the Court of Appeal identified other factors that could be relevant:

- the duration of the engagement;
- the number of people by whom the individual is employed;
- the degree of independence from the person paying the wages.

Not every factor will apply in every case. In *Hall v Lorimer* the court identified that rather than simply going through a checklist a detailed analysis of every situation should be considered in each case.

4.3.5 The mutuality of obligations test

Mutuality of obligations is a reasonably straightforward principle that has developed out of the multiple factor approach. The test identifies that for employment status there must be an obligation on the part of the employer to provide work for the employee and there must be a complimentary obligation on the part of the employee. Without these it is unlikely that a person could be classed as an employee.

Does the economic reality point to an employment relationship?
- the person provides skill or work in return for a wage from the person for whom he works
- the person expressly or impliedly accepts that his work will be subject to the control of the person for whom he works
- there is nothing inconsistent with there being a contract of employment

YES
↓

ACCORDING TO THE ECONOMIC REALITY TEST THE PERSON DOING THE WORK MAY BE CLASSED AS AN EMPLOYEE

Figure 4.4 Diagram illustrating the operation of the economic reality test

The test has developed out of disputes involving agency workers, casual staff and volunteers.

CASE EXAMPLE

O'Kelly v Trust House Forte [1984] QB 90

The company used a large number of casual catering staff to work at its large banquets. It employed only thirty-four permanent staff but between 200 and 300 casual staff. It kept two lists of staff around 100 of which, including O'Kelly, were given preference when work was available, and a list of other staff who were used less regularly. O'Kelly argued that he and other members of staff had been unfairly dismissed for being members of a trade union and for having taken part in its activities. To make such a claim they obviously needed to prove that they were employees. The tribunal considered eighteen separate factors in trying to determine whether they were employees. Two factors that proved decisive were first, that it was not custom or practice in the hotel industry to create employment relationships and, second, that there was no mutuality of obligation between the parties. As casual workers they were subject to individual contracts for services and were therefore not employees and not eligible under unfair dismissal law.

JUDGMENT

Ackner LJ stated: 'the assurance of preference in the allocation of any work which regulars enjoyed was no more than a firm expectation in practice. It was not a contractual promise.'

Sir John Donaldson MR identified: 'giving the claimants' evidence its fullest possible weight, all that could emerge was an umbrella or master contract *for*, not *of*, employment. It would be a contract to offer and accept individual contracts of employment and, as such, outside the scope of the unfair dismissal provisions.'

It follows that if a person is able to refuse work then their level of independence makes it unlikely that they can be considered to be an employee. In *Carmichael v National Power plc* [2000] IRLR 43 the House of Lords (now the Supreme Court) reinstated the view adopted by the tribunal that, as casual workers, the claimants were not in any contractual relationship with CEGB when they were not acting as guides, and they also failed the mutuality of obligations test so that therefore they were not employees.

CASE EXTRACT

In this case extract a significant section of the judgment has been reproduced in the left hand column. Individual points arising from the judgment are briefly explained in the right hand column. Read the extract including the commentary in the right hand column and complete the exercise that follows.

Extract adapted from the judgment in *Carmichael v National Power plc* [2000] IRLR 43	
Facts	*These are the significant facts*
The two claimants both worked on a 'casual' as required basis for the Central Electricity Generating Board as guides at a power station as stated in documents inviting applications for the posts. They had worked for CEGB for more than six years and had latterly done as much as twenty-five hours per week. Initially the tribunal held that as casual workers, they were not in any contractual relationship with CEGB when they were not acting as guides, and therefore they were not employees. The Court of Appeal then stated that the extent and the regularity of the working relationship meant that CEGB had an obligation to offer them a reasonable amount of work and they had a corresponding obligation to accept a reasonable amount of work, in other words, they had a contract of employment. The House of Lords (now the Supreme Court), however, reinstated the position taken by the tribunal and identified that one of the most critical issues was that there was no obligation on the CEGB to provide work, nor was there any requirement for the guides to accept it.	*This was the initial finding of the tribunal that they were not employees* *The Court of Appeal said that they were employees because there was mutuality of obligations* *The House of Lords said that they were not employees because the employer was not obliged to provide them with work*
Judgment	*The evidence used by the tribunal in reaching its decision*
LORD IRVINE OF LAIRG LC: The tribunal made this finding on the basis of (a) the language of the March 1989 documentation, (b) the way in which it had been operated and (c) the evidence of the parties as to how it had been understood. For reasons I will amplify later, this was in my judgment the correct approach. In substance it held that the documents did no more than provide a framework for a series of successive ad hoc contracts of service or for services which the parties might subsequently make; and that when they were not working as guides they were not in any contractual relationship with the CEGB. The parties incurred no obligations to provide or accept work but at best assumed moral obligations of loyalty in a context where both recognised that the best interests of each lay in being accommodating to the other. The decision therefore was: that by accepting an 'offer of employment as a station guide on a casual as required basis', Mrs Leese and Mrs Carmichael were doing no more than intimate that they were ready to be invited to attend for casual work as station guides as and when the CEGB required their services. Just as the CEGB was not promising to offer them any casual work, but merely intimating that it might be offered, so also they were not agreeing to attend whenever required	*A series of ad hoc contracts for services is not a single contract of service* *No contract when not working* *No mutuality – no obligation to provide or accept work*

In my judgment it would only be appropriate to determine the issue in these cases solely by reference to the documents in March 1989, if it appeared from their own terms and/or from what the parties said or did then, or subsequently, that they intended them to constitute an exclusive memorial of their relationship. The industrial tribunal must be taken to have decided that they were not so intended but constituted one, albeit important, relevant source of material from which they were entitled to infer the parties' true intention, along with the other objective inferences which could reasonably be drawn from what the parties said and did in March 1989, and subsequently.

Only what was in writing and how the parties behaved was relevant

The documents contained no provisions governing when, how or with what frequency guide work would be offered; there were no provisions for notice of termination on either side; the sickness, holiday and pension arrangements for regular staff did not apply; nor did the grievance and disciplinary procedures. Significantly, as Kennedy LJ in his dissenting judgment with which I agree emphasised, in 1994, for example, Mrs Carmichael was not available for work on seventeen occasions nor Mrs Leese on eight (p. 1174D). No suggestion of disciplining them arose. The objective inference is that when work was available they were free to undertake it or not as they chose. This flexibility of approach was well suited to their family needs. Just as the need for tours was unpredictable so also were their domestic commitments. Flexibility suited both sides. As Mrs Carmichael said in her application form, 'the part-time casual arrangement would suit my personal circumstances ideally!' The arrangement turned on mutual convenience and goodwill and worked well in practice over the years. The tribunal observed that Mrs Leese and Mrs Carmichael had a sense of moral obligation to the CEGB, but would infer no legal obligation. Mr Lovatt also gave evidence for the CEGB that 'neither ladies are required to work if they do not wish to do so'. In my judgment, therefore, the industrial tribunal was well entitled to infer from the March 1989 documents, the surrounding circumstances and how the parties conducted themselves subsequently that their intention neither in 1989 nor subsequently was to have their relationship regulated by contract whilst Mrs Leese and Mrs Carmichael were not working as guides. The industrial tribunal correctly concluded that their case 'founders on the rock of absence of mutuality'. I repeat that no issue arises as to their status when actually working as guides.

There were no details in the agreements which would normally be associated with an employment contract

No discipline involved

Moral obligation but no legal obligation to attend

No intention to create an employment contract

Fails the mutuality of obligations test

Thus, even if the words, 'employment will be on a casual as required basis' in the March 1989 documentation were, as Mr Langstaff QC contends, capable of imposing an obligation to undertake guide work when required – and in my judgment they are not – that interpretation is negated by the findings of the industrial tribunal. So also, even if the March 1989 documentation was capable of bearing the primary constructions which found favour with Ward LJ and Chadwick LJ – and in my judgment they are not – the terms which each implied, by invoking business efficacy may not be implied because there may be no implication on that ground unless into a relationship itself contractual.

Employment contract cannot be implied either

Once it is accepted that tribunal's finding as to the lack of mutuality of obligation between the respondents and the CEGB cannot be disturbed, it follows that the engagement of the respondents as guides in 1989 cannot have constituted in itself a contract of employment. It laid down the terms upon which it was expected that they would from time to time work for the CEGB and it may well be that when performing that work, they were being employed. But that would not be enough for the respondents. They could succeed only if the 1989 engagement created an employment relationship which subsisted when they were not working. On the findings of the Tribunal, it did not in itself give rise to any legal obligations at all and the respondents' claim must therefore fail.

Could only be employment if contractual obligations continued when not working

ACTIVITY

In the key points list that follows try to insert the two points made in the judgment that are missing from the list below using the commentary in the right hand column in the extract above to help you.

Key points from the case of *Carmichael v National Power plc* [2000] IRLR 43 above:

- A series of ad hoc contracts for services is not a single contract of service and so is not a contract of employment.
- When there are no obligations on either side when the person is not working then it is not a contract of employment.
- The nature of the relationship should be taken from what was in the agreement and how the parties behaved.
- If there are only moral obligations to accept work but no legal obligation then there is no employment contract.
- For there to be an employment contract there must be some evidence of intention to create such a contract.

Nevertheless, it is possible to infer mutuality from how the contract between the parties operates over a period of time.

CASE EXAMPLE

Prater v Cornwall County Council [2006] IRLR 362

A teacher worked from home teaching pupils who could not attend school. Despite the fact that the council was not obliged to send her pupils and she was not obliged to accept the pupils that were sent to her she had numerous such individual contracts over a period of ten years and was found to be an employee.

Another aspect of mutuality of obligations is the requirement of personal service on the part of the worker. One of the factors that defeated the claimant in the *Ready Mixed Concrete* case was the fact that the new agreement identified that drivers could own more than one lorry and could use substitute drivers. So where the worker is not bound absolutely to perform the services personally but can substitute another person to carry out the work then the worker who can do that is much more likely to be self-employed because of the level of independence.

Is there mutuality of obligations between the two parties?
• the one party is bound to provide work
• the other party is bound to do the work

YES

ACCORDING TO THE MUTUALITY OF OBLIGATIONS TEST THE PERSON DOING THE WORK MAY BE CLASSED AS AN EMPLOYEE

Figure 4.5 Diagram illustrating the operation of the mutuality of obligations test

ACTIVITY

Quick quiz

Consider whether each of the following would be classed as employees using the tests above:

1. Sarah, a machinist, who works from home stitching shirts from pieces of cloth pre-cut and delivered by her employer, Tej, who also deducts National Insurance payments from her pay, but leaves her to settle her own tax. Tej owns the sewing machine that Sarah uses.
2. Eric, a plasterer, who travels round building sites and works for cash payments. Neither he nor builders that he works for pay tax or NI for him. He uses his own tools.
3. Coco, a circus clown, who also sells tickets before performances and helps to pack up the big top when the circus goes on to the next town. He also drives one of the lorries that transport the circus. The circus owner says that Coco is self-employed.
4. Alistair is a consultant orthopaedic specialist. He is paid a full-time salary by an NHS Trust but spends three days per week seeing private patients.

Test of employment status	Strengths	Weaknesses
Control test	• Simple to use • Can be applied in situations where an element of subservience is obvious • Can be useful in the case of lent employees	• Difficult to apply where work is very skilled and management is generic • Does not always provide an answer on its own
Integration (organisation) test	• Relatively simple to apply • Can be easier to apply than the control test in the cased of skilled workers	• Outcome may depend on purpose of testing • Does not really work in the case of outsourcing
Economic reality (multiple) test	• Weighs up all factors so has more chance of being accurate • Recognises the significance of independence as part of the test	• Could be quite a complex process • Depends on a lot of factors none of which is an absolute test
Mutuality of obligations test	• Relatively simple to apply • Recognises the significance of independence	• Could be said to be just a part of the other tests

Figure 4.6 Chart illustrating the relative merits of the four tests

ACTIVITY

Self-assessment questions

1. What is the principal purpose of distinguishing between employment and self-employment?
2. How adequate is the statutory definition in section 230 Employment Rights Act 1996?
3. What is the difference between a 'contract of service' and a 'contract for services'?
4. To what extent does the reason for testing a person's employment status play a part in determining that status?
5. How effective can the control test ever be in a modern working environment?
6. Are there any situations where the control test could be used by itself?
7. How effective is the integration test on its own without considering other factors?
8. Why is MacKenna's test known as the multiple test, and why is it also known as the economic reality test?
9. Why should factors be weighed rather than counted in this test?
10. To what extent is the method of payment of tax and National Insurance contribution a deciding factor in determining employment status?
11. Why should self-description not be assumed to be an accurate test of employment status?
12. What is the essential feature of the mutuality of obligations test?

4.4 Non-standard categories of work

In many if not most instances an employment relationship is straightforward. Certain types of work, however, are less clear cut and more likely to defy easy definition. This is why the tests in Chapter 4.3 have been developed. Over time judges and tribunal panels have been required to make decisions on employment status, sometimes based on the factors that have been identified above. Often the answer will depend on the purpose of the case. In this way the court might seek to bring a person within industrial safety law although they appear to be self-employed.

Outworkers

This group, sometimes also referred to as homeworkers, refers to people who work from home. They are usually women with young children and represent a disadvantaged sector of the workforce. They have traditionally tended to work for little pay and with few employment rights or protections. There is obviously little control over the hours that they work. Nevertheless, working in areas such as the garment industry, they normally fall into a general framework of organisation. They were in the past always considered to be independent contractors, which is well illustrated in the case law. However, some cases have suggested otherwise.

CASE EXAMPLE

Nethermere (St Neots) Ltd v Taverna & Gardiner [1984] IRLR 240

Women working from home in the garment industry had no fixed hours but did use machine and equipment that was provided for them. The only rule that they was subject to was that they were bound to complete sufficient work to make it worthwhile for the company driver to collect it. The Court of Appeal held that they were employees because it was felt that they were doing the same work as employees in the factory, they were merely doing it at a different location, at home. It was held that the long-standing relationship meant that there was mutuality of obligations. The company was bound to provide work and they were bound to do it.

JUDGMENT

Dillon LJ explained: 'There was a regular course of dealing between the parties for years under which garments were supplied daily to the outworkers, worked on, collected and paid for. If it is permissible on the evidence to find that by such conduct a contract had been established ... I see no necessity to conclude that the contract must have been a contract for services and not a contract of service.'

In such circumstances courts have identified that an umbrella contract can exist if a practice of dealing has been built up over years with expectations and obligations on each side. So it is because there is a mutuality of obligation that there is a contract of service rather than individual contracts for services.

CASE EXAMPLE

Airfix Footwear Ltd v Cope [1978] IRLR 396

A company supplied parts of shoes, glue and other materials to outworkers, including the claimant, for them to make up at home as well as providing them with training. Although there was no specific requirement as to where the work was done, she worked from home and the patterns and materials were brought to her each afternoon. She worked five days a week and if she did not finish the work she completed it the following day. She had done the work for seven years for five days a week, with occasional breaks when demand was low. The work had previously been done in the factory. The tribunal found that the volume of work varied from time to time according to seasonal demand. The claimant was given weekly 'wages' and an annual statement of the wages she had earned. The company instructed her how to do the work and that the glues were highly inflammable; and that she must ensure that there was adequate ventilation. There was no holiday or sick pay and no provisions on notice of termination of employment. The EAT held that the tribunal was correct in identifying a continuing contract of service because of the continuing relationship that had built up over the years.

JUDGMENT

Slynn J explained: 'it may well be that if the arrangements between a company and a person are such that ... the company may provide or not, as it chooses and the other person may accept or not, as he pleases, it may well be that this is not properly categorised as a contract of employment. If in such a situation the company only delivers work sporadically from time to time, and from time to time the worker chooses to do it, so that there is a pattern of an occasional week done a few times a year, then it might well be that there comes into existence on each of these occasions a separate contract of service, or contract for services, but that the overriding arrangement is not itself a contract of employment, either of service or for services. But these matters must depend upon the facts of each particular case.'

Casual workers

Casual workers have traditionally been viewed as independent contractors rather than as employees. This may be of particular significance since modern employment practices tend towards less secure and less permanent work. It is obviously vital to consider all the relevant factors. In *O'Kelly v Trust House Forte plc* [1983] 3 WLR 605 (see 4.3.5 above) it was important for 'wine butlers', employed casually at the Grosvenor House Hotel, to show that they were employees in order that they could claim for unfair dismissal. They had no other source of income and they were able to show a number of factors consistent with employment. However, the tribunal took the view that, since there was no regular wage, sick pay or pension entitlement, the employer had no obligation to provide work and since they could if they wished work elsewhere then there was no mutuality of obligations and they were not employed.

One argument used in trying to establish that such workers are employees is that instead of there being a series of independent contracts that there is a global contract. However, without being able to show mutuality of obligations this has had little success.

CASE EXAMPLE

Clark v Oxfordshire Health Authority [1998] IRLR 125

The claimant wished to bring a claim for unfair dismissal and needed to show that she was an employee. She worked as part of a 'Nurse Bank' as a Staff Nurse who could be contacted on a daily basis to stand in for absent staff. She was given a document entitled 'Statement of Employment'. Tax and National Insurance were deducted from her pay at source but she was not paid when she did not work and she received no holiday or sick pay. She was subject to the Health Authority's disciplinary and grievance procedures and also to Whitley Council health service conditions which identified that bank nurses were not regular employees. The Court of Appeal found that there was no mutuality of obligations. The Health Authority was not bound to offer her work and she was not obliged to accept offers of work. She was not an employee and not eligible for unfair dismissal proceedings.

JUDGMENT

Sir Christopher Slade explained: 'the mutual obligations required to found a global contract of employment need not necessarily and in every case consist of obligations to provide and perform work. To take one obvious example, an obligation by the one party to accept and do work if offered and an obligation on the other party to pay a retainer during such periods as work was *not* offered would in my opinion, be likely to suffice … however … *some* mutuality of obligation is required to found a global contract of employment. In the present case I can find no such mutuality.'

In *Carmichael v National Power plc* [1998] ICR 1167 (see 4.3.5 above) the then House of Lords also confirmed that lack of mutual obligations in casual work will mean that the arrangement is unlikely to be seen as employment. While the tour guide at a nuclear power station was given work as required and paid for the work done and tax and National Insurance contributions were also deducted, the court decided that the critical factors were that there was no obligation to provide work and no obligation on the woman's part to accept any that was offered.

However, there are still situations in which mutuality of obligations can be inferred from how the contract between the parties operates over a period of time. In *Prater v Cornwall County Council* [2006] IRLR 362 (see 4.3.5 above) the teacher had so many individual contracts over a period of ten years teaching excluded pupils from home that she was found to be an employee.

Agency staff

Many large companies now hire staff through employment agencies. The employer identifies to an agency posts that it needs filling. The agency generally has workers on its books with particular skills and can then send the required number of workers to the employer. On past cases they have not always been seen as employees either of the agency or of the business hiring their services. In *Wickens v Champion Employment* [1984] ICR 365 it was held that the agency workers were not employees since the agency was under no obligation to find them work and there was no continuity and care in the contractual relationship consistent with employment.

There is in fact a relatively confused situation with regard the employment status of agency workers and their employment status varies with the circumstances of the individual case. There are in any case three possibilities:

- They are employees of the agency.
- They are employees of the business hiring them from the agency.
- They are not employees at all.

Clearly how the worker is defined in the contract with the employment agency is important but it is not absolutely definitive and it has been stated that there is no single factor that points to employment or self-employment: all of the relevant factors must be taken into account.

CASE EXAMPLE

McMeechan v Secretary of State for Employment [1997] IRLR 353

A temporary worker was on the books of an employment agency for almost a year and during this time he was given a series of assignments for work by the agency. When the agency became insolvent, he wanted to recover from the Redundancy Fund, under s122 of the Employment Protection (Consolidation) Act 1978, the unpaid earnings that were due to him from his last assignment. The Department of Employment refused his claim arguing that he was an independent contractor not an employee. The tribunal accepted this argument but its decision was reversed by the EAT. The Court of Appeal also found that he was an employee of the agency on the basis that it had the power to dismiss him and make deductions from his pay.

On the other hand courts applying the control test have often found that there is no employment relationship between the agency and the agency worker. In *Montgomery v Johnson Underwood Ltd* [2001] IRLR 269 the Court of Appeal held that an agency worker was not employed by the agency because she was not under its control while she was at work. Using the control test it has also been held that the agency worker is not an employee of the hirer or the agency.

CASE EXAMPLE

Bunce v Postworth trading as Skyblue [2005] EWCA Civ 490; [2005] IRLR 557

The claimant was a welder, who entered into an agreement with the agency which arranged regular welding work for him with Carillion Rail and other companies, amounting to 142 assignments during the year before the termination of his contract. Under his contract with the agency he was bound to accept the supervision of clients to whom he was assigned. At one point Carillion complained about his work and the agency terminated its contract with him. He claimed unfair dismissal. Both the tribunal and the EAT held that he was not an employee. The Court of Appeal agreed that he could not be an employee of the agency because it had no control over the manner in which he did his work and he was not an employee of Carillion as he had no contractual relationship with the company.

It has also been held that an agency worker is not an employee, that he is hired out by the agency because there is no contractual connection between them.

CASE EXAMPLE

Hewlett Packard Ltd v O'Murphy [2002] IRLR 4

The claimant was a computer specialist who set up his own limited company which then contracted with an agency for provision of work. The agency hired him out to the company under an arrangement that lasted several years. His eventual claim for unfair dismissal failed on the basis that there was no contractual connection between him and the company that had hired his services. In fact there were too many intermediaries for him to have a direct employment relationship with the company that hired his services.

On the other hand a contract of employment has been identified between the agency worker and the client hiring from the agency in circumstances where it can be shown that the agency worker has become integrated into the hirer's business.

CASE EXAMPLE

Dacas v Brook Street Bureaux [2004] EWCA Civ 217; [2004] ICR 1437

The claimant had been supplied by the agency to a local council for whom she had worked as a cleaner for over four years when the council asked the agency to remove her. The agency then terminated its agreement with her and she claimed unfair dismissal against the agency. The agency paid her wages and was entitled to discipline her under its agreement with her. The tribunal found that she was not an employee of either body. The EAT held that she was an employee of the agency. In the agency's appeal the Court of Appeal held that there was an implied contract with the council because of mutuality of obligations and length of service but she was not an employee of the agency because there was no mutuality of obligations. The agency had no control over her day-to-day work and she was not in any case obliged to accept any work from it.

JUDGMENT

Mummery LJ explained: 'what the Council was paying for was not the work done by Mrs Dacas and her fellow workers but the services supplied to it by Brook Street in accordance with the Specification and the other contractual documents. The monies paid by the Council to Brook Street were not payments of wages, nor were they calculated by reference to the wages payable by Brook Street to Mrs Dacas and her fellow workers. There was no mutuality.'

Courts have also stated that whether an agency worker is an employee or not should be decided on the facts of the case and the principles of implied contracts rather than whether an irreducible minimum of obligations exists.

CASE EXAMPLE

James v London Borough of Greenwich [2008] IRLR 302

The claimant had worked for the council as a housing support worker for several years being hired through an agency. When the council replaced her with another worker supplied by the agency following a period of sickness absence she claimed unfair dismissal which obviously meant that she needed to show that she was an employee of the council. The tribunal, the EAT and the Court of Appeal all held that she was not an employee and none were prepared to accept that a contract of employment was implied in the circumstances.

JUDGMENT

Mummery LJ identified: 'the question whether an "agency worker" is an employee of an end user must be decided in accordance with common law principles of implied contract and, in some very extreme cases, by exposing sham arrangements. Just as it is wrong to regard all "agency workers" as self-employed temporary workers outside the protection of the 1996 Act, the recent authorities do not entitle all "agency workers" to argue successfully that they should all be treated as employees in disguise ... there is a wide spectrum of factual situations.... In many cases agency workers will fall outside the scope of the protection of the 1996 Act because neither the workers nor the end users were in any kind of express contractual relationship with each other and it is not necessary to imply one in order to explain the work undertaken by the worker for the end user.'

Workers' co-operatives

Workers' co-operatives were quite common in the early 1980s after the government of the time had abandoned a lot of traditional industries that were run or supported by the state. Most of the mining industry disappeared during that time but steelworks, heavy engineering and other traditional industries were also affected. It was not unusual for groups of workers to collect together their redundancy payments and to buy the businesses for which they had worked and run them collectively with representatives of the workforce acting also as the management of these businesses. Again it is uncertain whether such workers would be employees or not. Usually we would expect them to be so. However, there are instances where such workers have been classed as an association of self-employed people.

CASE EXAMPLE

Addison v London Philharmonic Orchestra Ltd [1981] ICR 261

The orchestra operated as a co-operative. The musicians were individually able to accept other work on their own account. It was held that they were subjecting themselves to a disciplined arrangement rather than actually being subject to control as employees. In essence they were independent and so were not employees.

Trainees

Because of the definition in section 230 Employment Rights Act 1996 (see 4.2.1 above) it is possible for an apprentice to be classed as an employee. However, apprenticeships were traditionally subject to their own distinct rules (although there are few of these traditional types of apprenticeship now in existence). In the case of trainees the major purpose in their relationship with the 'employer' is to learn their trade rather than to actually provide work. As a result there have been instances where they have not been classed as employees.

CASE EXAMPLE

Wiltshire Police Authority v Wynn [1980] QB 95

A female police cadet tried to claim unfair dismissal. In order to do so she needed to prove first that she was an employee. While she had been placed on various attachments, was paid a wage, was prevented from taking offers of other work and had set hours, the court accepted that she was only undergoing training with a view to becoming a police officer and was not yet at a point where she was an employee.

Crown servants

People working for the crown were traditionally viewed as not being under a contract of employment. This meant that they had very restricted rights. The trend in modern times has been to move away from this position. They may be classed as employees but may have more selective employment protection rights than other employees. Most of the provisions of the Employment Rights Act 1996 apply to Crown employees except those relating to notice periods and redundancy payments and there are restrictions on disclosure of information. They also fall under the provisions of the Equality Act 2010. They are also covered by most of the provisions in the Trade Union and Labour Relations (Consolidation) Act 1992.

Office holders

An office is basically a position that exists independently of the person currently holding it. The categories of people who can be classed as office holders are declining but it might include ministers of the church and justices of the peace as well as other offices. The picture on these is confused. Certainly they may have privileges not available to normal employees, an example being judges who hold office during good behaviour and can only be removed by a resolution passed by both Houses of Parliament. An office holder might in this sense have a greater job security than an ordinary employee would have.

CASE EXAMPLE

Lincolnshire County Council v Hopper [2002] All ER (D) 401

The case concerns a registrar and whether or not she could be dismissed by the council. She worked for and was paid by the council, which also regulated her hours of work and provided a pension. However, registrars are also governed by the Registration Services Act 1953. Section 6(4) of the Act states: 'Every superintendent registrar and every registrar of births and deaths shall hold office during the pleasure of the Registrar General.' In this way the registrar could not be dismissed by the council and in this respect was in a better position than an employee.

Directors

A director may or may not also be an employee of the company. This will inevitably depend on the terms of the individual contract. In general an executive director is likely also to be an employee of the company. An executive director is one who is involved in the day-to-day running of the business. In the case of non-executive directors it is less likely that they will be regarded as employees. Non-executive directors are ones that usually only act in an advisory capacity.

Health service workers

One issue for people engaged in healthcare which could be critical was whether or not the health service employer was vicariously liable for torts committed by them during their work. The traditional view in *Hillyer v Governor of St Bartholomews Hospital* [1909] 2 KB 820 was that a hospital should not be vicariously liable for the work of doctors. Taking into account the age of the case the position was justified on the grounds that hospitals generally lacked adequate finance before the creation of the National Health Service. However, in *Cassidy v Ministry of Health* [1951] 2 KB 343 it was suggested that hospitals and health services should be responsible for the work done in them. A resident surgeon had performed an operation negligently and the patient sued. The issue for the court was whether the surgeon could be said legitimately to be under the employer's control because, if not, this would limit the patient's ability to receive compensation. It was held that hospitals must inevitably be vicariously responsible for the tortious acts of all doctors who are permanent members of staff despite the difficulties associated with applying the traditional control test, since to do otherwise would generally be to deny wronged patients an effective claim.

JUDGMENT

Lord Somervell saw the difficulty by contrasting with the master of a ship: 'The master may be employed by the owners in what is clearly a contract of service and yet the owners have no power to tell him how to navigate his ship.' Lord Denning stated: 'authorities who run a hospital, be they local authorities, government boards, or any other corporation, are in law under the self-same duty as the humblest doctor. Whenever they accept a patient for treatment, they must use reasonable care and skill to cure him of his ailment.'

In respect of employment rights and protections health service employees now have all of the rights in the legislation.

Police
While police officers are employed they have few employment rights. They are effectively excluded from most employment rights by section 200 of the Employment Rights Act 1996. These include for instance the right to an itemised pay statement, guarantee pay, rights under the Working Time Regulations, rights in protected disclosure situations, time off for public duties and many others. They are also excluded from unfair dismissal claims. However, they do have a full range of rights under the Equality Act 2010.

Probationary employees
Probationary employees by definition are serving a probationary period to establish their suitability for the post. They are aware from the start that their permanent employment is dependent on satisfactory completion of the probation.

One potential problem with probationers is the length of the probationary period. In *Weston v University College Swansea* [1975] IRLR 102 a lecturer was appointed for a probationary period of three years and then not given a permanent appointment. It was held that he was able to pursue an unfair dismissal claim.

KEY FACTS

The statutory definition of employee	Case/statute
• Employee means an individual who has entered into, works under, or worked under a contract of employment.	*S230 Employment Rights Act 1996*

The reasons for distinguishing between employees and the self-employed	Case/statute
• Employed duties do not apply to self-employed • Most statutory employment protections do not apply to self-employed • Health and safety… • Employers not vicariously liable for the wrongs of independent contractors unless they hire them to commit the tort	*Ellis v Sheffield Gas Consumers Co*

- Employed tax by PAYE schedule E, self-employed annually schedule D and may have to pay VAT
- National Insurance contributions Class 1 taken at source for employees, self-employed make their own contributions Class 2 or Class 4 – self-employed eligible for less welfare benefits
- Employees are preferential creditors on an employer's insolvency – self-employed are not

The tests of employment status	Case/statute
Control	
• a person subject to the command of his master as to the manner in which he shall do his work	*Yewens v Noakes*
• still useful in case of lent employees	*Mersey Docks & Harbour Board v Coggins and Griffiths (Liverpool) Ltd*
• and possibly in agency situations	*Motorola v Davidson*
Integration	
• employee is integral part of the business but self-employed is only ancillary to it	*Stevenson, Jordan & Harrison v MacDonald & Evans*
• works well in highly skilled occupations where control test would not	*Whittaker v Minister of Pensions and National Insurance*
Economic reality	
• three part test – employee agrees to provide work or skill in return for a wage; employee expressly or impliedly accepts that the work will be subject to the control of the employer; all other considerations in the contract are consistent with a contract of employment	*Ready Mixed Concrete (South East) Ltd v Minister of Pensions and National Insurance*
• must consider and weigh all factors	*Market Investigations v Minster of Social Security*
Mutuality of obligations	
• the employer is bound to provide work and the employee is bound to do it	*Carmichael v National Power plc*
• can infer mutuality from long term behaviour	*Prater v Cornwall County Council*
Non-standard categories of work	Case/statute
Outworkers	
• traditionally self-employed unless regular course of dealing over long time	*Nethermere (St Neots) Ltd v Taverna & Gardiner*
• depends on degree of independence	*Airfix Footwear v Cope*
Casual workers	
• traditionally seen as self-employed	*O'Kelly v Trust House Forte*
• because no mutuality of obligations	*Carmichael v National Power plc*
Agency workers	
• how the worker is defined in the agency agreement is not definitive	*McMeechan v Secretary of State for Employment*
• under the control test agency workers have been found to be employees of neither the agency nor the hirer of their services	*Bunce v Postworth trading as Skyblue*

• and agency workers have been said not to be employees of the hirer because there is no contractual relationship between them	*Hewlett Packard Ltd v O'Murphy*
• but it is possible they are employees of the hirer where they become integrated into the business	*Dacas v Brook Street Bureaux*
• ultimately status should be decided on the circumstances of each case	*James v London Borough of Greenwich*
Workers' co-operatives	
• uncertain but possibly an association of self-employed people	*Addison v London Philharmonic Orchestra Ltd*
Trainees	
• only learning trade so probably not employees	*Wiltshire Police Authority v Wynn*
Crown servants	
• traditionally not seen as employees but now covered by most employment rights	*Employment Rights Act 1996 (except notice periods, redundancy payments and restrictions on disclosure of information. Equality Act 2010. Trade Union and Labour Relations (Consolidation) Act 1992.*
Office holders	
• office is independent of person doing it so may have privileges not enjoyed by employees	*Lincolnshire County Council v Hopper*
Directors	
• generally employees if executive	
Health service workers	
• suggestion that employer is always vicariously liable	*Cassidy v Ministry of Health*
Police	
• generally denied most employment rights • but are protected from discrimination	*S200 Employment Rights Act 1996 Equality Act 2010*
Probationers	
• generally denied employment rights	

SAMPLE ESSAY QUESTION

ESSAY 'No test on its own is adequate and employment status can only be determined by examining all of the relevant facts and circumstances.' Critically analyse the tests for employment status in the light of the above statement.

Explain that there are different reasons why employment status may need to be established

- To establish employment protections for example under the Employment Rights Act 1996.
- To determine whether an employer is vicariously liable for the misdeeds of a worker.
- To determine liability for health and safety at work.
- To determine whether an employer is liable to make pay tax at source and make employer's NI contributions.

Explain that there are four main tests

- The control test.
- The integration (organisation) test.
- The economic reality (multiple factor) test.
- The mutuality of obligations test.
- Refer possibly also to the indicia test and the entrepreneurial test.

Explain the control test

Person is subject to the command of his master as to the manner in which he does his work *Yewens v Noakes*.

Discuss the strengths and weaknesses of the control test

- Still useful in case of lent employees *Mersey Docks & Harbour Board v Coggins and Griffiths (Liverpool) Ltd*.

- And possibly in agency situations *Motorola v Davidson*.
- But not really appropriate in the case of highly skilled work *Cassidy v Minister of Health*.
- And does not always provide an answer on its own.

Explain the integration test

Employee is integral part of the business but self-employed is only ancillary to it *Stevenson, Jordan & Harrison v MacDonald & Evans*.

Discuss the strengths and weaknesses of the integration test

- Works well in highly skilled occupations where control test would not *Whittaker v Minister of Pensions and National Insurance*.
- But the outcome may depend on purpose of testing.
- And does not really work in the case of outsourcing.
- And still depends on mutuality.
- So probably an incomplete test on its own.

Explain the economic reality test

Employee agrees to provide work or skill in return for a wage; expressly or impliedly accepts control of the employer; everything else is consistent with a contract of employment *Ready Mixed Concrete (South East) Ltd. v Minister of Pensions and National Insurance*.

Discuss the strengths and weaknesses of the economic reality test

- Considers all factors and weighs them so probably more accurate.
- Recognises the significance of independence so test of self-employment as well as employment.
- But could be quite a complex process.
- And depends on a lot of factors none of which is an absolute test.

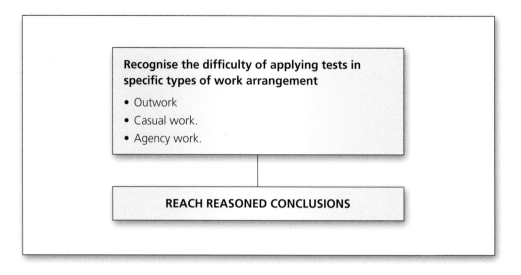

Recognise the difficulty of applying tests in
specific types of work arrangement

• Outwork
• Casual work.
• Agency work.

REACH REASONED CONCLUSIONS

ACTIVITY

Applying the law

Using the guide to answering legal problem questions in Appendix 2, attempt the following
problem question.

Ann Britton is engaged by Quickstitch as a skilled tailor's cutter. She is supplied with patterns, materials, tools and equipment in order for her to do the work. She has never received
any specific agreement as to where her work should be done, however, in practice she works
at home and has done so for the past twelve years since the birth of her first child. Patterns
and materials sufficient for twelve garments are brought to her house at about 4.00 p.m. each
afternoon by the company. Ann works each day for five generally between 9.00 a.m. and
3.00 p.m. when her children are at school. On occasions when she has been unable to finish
the work she completes it after 10.00 p.m. when her children have gone to bed.

When Ann began working for the company she had done some dress making but was not
particularly skilled. The company paid for her to have initial training and she has progressed
since. She is paid a weekly 'wage' and at the end of a year she is given a statement referring
to 'the wages' she had earned. She is told by the company how to do the work, and is also
obliged to follow the company's health and safety rule book.

She does not receive holiday pay or sick pay but on very rare occasions when the company
has had no work for her because of low demand it has still paid her, although this only
amounts to a few days over the twelve years. She has never had any income tax deducted, and
the company has not paid National Insurance contributions on her behalf. There are also no
provisions as to notice of termination of the arrangement between her and the company.
Three years ago Ann was offered a better paid contract working for another firm but only for
ten hours per week. Ann asked Quickstitch if she could reduce her hours to take on the other
work but it refused and said that she could work only for them or she could leave.

Using the various tests of employment status consider Ann's employment status in the light
of the above.

SUMMARY

- Section 230 Employment Rights Act 1996 defines an employee as someone who works under a contract of employment – but this is vague and not really helpful.
- Most workers are straightforwardly employees, but there are certain classes of worker whose status is uncertain – the law traditionally distinguishes between a person who is under a contract of service (an employee) and a person who has a acontract for services (a self-employed person or independent contractor).
- The law has developed a number of tests to determine which a particular classification worker falls under.
- There are a number of reasons why it is important to know whether the worker is an employee not least that most employment protections are only available to employees.
- These include: the control test, based on the level of detailed control the employer has over the manner in which the worker does his work; the integration test which identifies that employees are integral to the business where the self-employed are only ancillary to it; the economic reality test under which an employee is identified as being paid a wage in return for work, having subjected himself to the control of the employer, and there are no factors that are inconsistent with a contract of employment; the mutuality of obligations test which identifies that there is an employment relationship when the employer is bound to offer the worker work and the worker is bound to accept it.
- There are also a range of non-standard categories of work where it is less easy to ascertain whether the worker is an employee, although in many of these case law has often established that employment or self-employment applies to the particular category – these include outworkers, casual workers, agency workers, but also some more specific groups such as workers' co-operatives, trainees, crown servants, office holders, directors, health service workers, the police and probationers.

Further reading

Emir, Astra, *Selwyn's Law of Employment 17th edition*. Oxford University Press, 2012, Chapter 2.
Pitt, Gwyneth, *Cases and Materials on Employment Law 3rd edition*. Pearson, 2008, Chapter 3.
Sargeant, Malcolm and Lewis, David, *Employment Law 6th edition*. Pearson, 2012, Chapter 2.

5

The contract of employment

AIMS AND OBJECTIVES

After reading this chapter you should be able to:

- Understand the basic contractual requirements for a contract of employment to exist
- Understand the scope and significance of the statutory statement under section 1 Employment Rights Act 1996
- Understand the ways in which express terms are incorporated into the contract and their significance
- Understand how collective agreements become part of the contract of employment and their significance
- Understand the significance of works rules to the contract and of the job description
- Understand the rules regarding variation of terms in employment contracts
- Critically analyse the law on the contract of employment
- Apply the law to factual situations and reach conclusions

5.1 Formation of the employment contract

5.1.1 The form of the contract of employment

Although much of employment law is statutory it is also said to be based on the law of contract, and almost all working relationships are governed by contracts. The law of contract generally presumes that the parties have equal bargaining power. However, the employment relationship in reality is very unequal and in general an employee has no choice but than to accept employment on whatever terms the employer dictates, unless the person has a particular skill that is highly in demand. Therefore, the organisation has far more bargaining power. Much of employment law was created through legislation (often from membership of the EU) in an attempt to redress (i.e. to compensate for) this imbalance of power.

The employment contract conforms to the general rule that writing is not needed to create a valid contract, and contracts of employment can be made orally or by conduct. The main exceptions are contracts for apprenticeships and merchant seamen, who must have individual written agreements. It is of course also possible for the contract to be implied from the fact of the parties dealing with each other over a period of time.

CASE EXAMPLE

Dacas v Brook Street Bureau [2004] EWCA Civ 217; [2004] ICR 1437

The claimant was an agency worker who had been supplied by the agency to a local council for whom she had worked as a cleaner for over four years. The council then asked the agency to remove the claimant and the agency terminated its agreement with the claimant as a result. She claimed unfair dismissal against the agency and the council. The tribunal had found that the claimant was not an employee of either body. She appealed to the EAT but only on the agency not the council. The EAT held that she was an employee of the agency. The agency appealed and the Court of Appeal held that there was no contract of service between the agency and the claimant because there was no mutuality of obligations and the written agreement between them was quite precise. The agency also had no control over her day-to-day work and she was not in any case obliged to accept any work from the agency. The court suggested, however, that there could be an implied contract between the claimant and the council because of mutuality of obligations and length of service.

JUDGMENT

Mummery LJ commented: 'in future cases of this kind the Employment Tribunal should, in my judgment, at least consider the possibility of an implied contract of service. The result of the consideration will depend on the evidence in the case about the relationship between the applicant and the end-user and how that fits into the other triangular arrangements. In general, it would be surprising if, in a case like this, the end-user did not have powers of control or direction over such a person in such a working environment. The end-user is the ultimate paymaster. The arrangements were set up and operated on the basis that the end-user was paying the agency ... for the work done by Mrs Dacas under its direction and for its benefit.... The decision of the Employment Tribunal rejecting the claim by Mrs Dacas against the Council must stand, however, as it was not appealed to the Employment Appeal Tribunal or to this court. If it had been appealed, I would have remitted it to the Employment Tribunal to determine whether there was an implied contract between Mrs Dacas and the Council, and, if so, whether it was a contract of service under which she worked for the Council. In dealing with cases of this kind in the future Employment Tribunals should not determine the status of the applicant without also considering the possibility of an implied contact of service and making findings of fact relevant to that issue.'

Like all contracts, an employment contract requires certain key elements of formality. It will require an offer and acceptance, consideration and an intention to be legally bound. For example, the offer can be revoked at any time before it is accepted and can be conditional on medical examination, reference or subject to the enhanced criminal records check for sensitive jobs. An employment contract must also be free from vitiating factors, importantly illegality, for example attempting to defraud HM Revenue and Customs.

5.1.2 The requirement of writing

There is no general requirement that the contract of employment be in writing although of course an employment contract does require written evidence of certain terms in the required statutory statement from section 1 Employment Rights Act 1996. So a contract of employment could be implied by the conduct of the parties. While it could result from an exchange of correspondence between the parties for instance a written advertisement in a publication advertising the vacancy, responded to in letter requesting an application form, the filling in and returning of the application form, a letter inviting an applicant to interview, written notes taken at the interview, a written offer of a job following the interview, a written acceptance and a letter of appointment, it could be informally made following a casual conversation and a verbal indication of a likely starting date.

There are of course a number of exceptions where the contract must be in writing or at least elements of the agreement must be evidenced in writing. These include:

- Contracts of apprenticeship must generally not only be in writing but they must also be signed by both parties to the apprenticeship deed.

- Employees who operate under fixed-term contracts may in certain circumstances elect to exclude certain of their statutory rights for example to a redundancy payment; if they do so this has to be done in writing.

- The Merchant Shipping Acts require that seamen's contracts must be in writing and must be signed by both the employee and the employer.

- There are also a complex set of rules in respect of rights in regard of maternity, and now paternity and adoption leave – generally an employer is entitled to request that employees seeking to exercise such rights state their full intention in writing for instance where a woman having exercised additional maternity leave states in writing her intention to return to work.

5.1.3 Formalities in the contract

As with all aspects of contract law a contract can only be formed where there is an agreement, in this case the employer has offered work and the employee has unconditionally accepted it, both parties must have promised consideration, in this case the promise of work in return for a wage, and finally both the employer and the employee intend that the employment relationship should be legally binding on them.

There is no particular form in which the offer and acceptance must be made. The offer could result from a formal written offer but it could be made orally. It is also of course the case that the means by which the potential employee finds out about the vacancy can vary. It could be that the applicant goes to the employer's workplace asks if work is available and is told that it is. It could also of course arise through an advertisement, in which case, since the employer wishes a wide range of people to know of the vacancy so that he can select the best possible candidate, the principle in *Carlill v The Carbolic Smokeball Co Ltd* [1893] 1 QB 256 must also apply that the offer can be made to the whole world.

Inevitably an offer of employment can also be made subject to a condition precedent, for example a satisfactory reference or medical examination.

CASE EXAMPLE

Wishart v National Association of CAB'x Ltd [1990] IRLR 393

The claimant had been offered a position subject to satisfactory references. One of the references was from his existing employer which included information about several sickness absences. The employer who offered the claimant the job then withdrew the offer. The claimant sought an injunction to restrain that employer from taking on anyone else and enforcing his original job offer. Initially the injunction was granted. However, on appeal this was reversed. The Court of Appeal held that the job offer had been given subject to a condition: the receipt of satisfactory references. The employer's only obligation then was to consider the reference in good faith.

Another interesting point is what happens when an employer makes an offer of employment and then, before the employee in fact commences work, the employee withdraws the offer without any lawful justification. The issue is important of course because the employee may well have handed in notice with a previous employer and be without work but have no chance of a remedy in unfair dismissal not having completed the necessary two years of continuous service with the new employer (see Chapter 22.2), in fact having no service with the new employer.

CASE EXAMPLE

Sarker v South Tees Acute Hospitals NHS Trust [1997] IRLR 328

In this case the claimant was offered employment as an ultrasound manager with an NHS Trust. On 25 August 1995 she was sent a letter of appointment and a formal document setting out the particulars of her employment. Both documents required two months' notice from the claimant to terminate her employment and she accepted the terms. Before she even started work, however, the Trust contacted her and tried to vary the terms of the agreement. Following a telephone call between the parties, the offer of employment was then withdrawn by the Trust and the claimant brought a claim for breach of contract for the notice she was due under the contract. The tribunal had ruled that it could not hear the claim because there had been no termination of employment because she had not actually started work and it therefore rejected her claim on those grounds. Overturning this decision, the EAT said the claim did arise or was outstanding on the termination of employment. There was a contract, one that would start at a later date, and that contract had been broken the EAT ruled. The breach of contract claim would be for the period of notice to which the employee was entitled, although an unfair dismissal would be unavailable.

The case reiterates an earlier decision *Taylor v Furness, Withy & Co Ltd* [1969] 6 KIR 488 which involved a dock worker being prevented from taking up new employment because his union membership had lapsed.

As has already been indicated, acceptance of an offer of employment could in fact come in any form. While it might involve the applicant replying to the employer in writing it could also of course be no more than a handshake at the factory gate.

There must be consideration for the agreement which would be executory, the promise of work in return for the promises of wages.

According to *R v Lord Chancellor's Department ex p Nangle* [1992] 1 All ER 897 the parties must intend to create legal relations. In consequence a person agreeing to do voluntary work may not have a contract of employment.

CASE EXAMPLE

Mellhuish v Redbridge CAB [2005] IRLR 419

The claimant was a voluntary worker for a Citizens Advice Bureau who, while not receiving any wage of any kind was reimbursed for necessary expenses. Besides this the claimant had also received free training. The claimant brought an action for unfair dismissal. The tribunal and the EAT held that he was not an employee as there was no mutuality of obligations since the CAB was not obliged to find him any work (in fact he had only ever attended for a maximum of two days a week and this had dropped to one day a week occasionally), there was no contract of employment and in fact the only contractual obligation that could be identified was the agreement to reimburse him for any expenses that he incurred.

5.1.4 Minority and the contract of employment

The position on minority is the same as the standard position for minors in contracts generally. Obviously a minor (a person under the age of eighteen) may well need to work to support himself and so must be able to legitimately enter contracts of employment. Even as early as the nineteenth century the courts recognised that an employment contract would only be binding on the minor if on balance the terms of the contract were substantially to the benefit of the minor.

CASE EXAMPLE

Clements v London and North Western Railway Company [1894] 2 QB 482

A minor gained a position as a porter with the railway company. He agreed to join the company's insurance scheme as a result of which he would relinquish any rights he might have under the Employer's Liability Act 1880. In the event of an accident the statutory scheme would be of greater benefit to the minor since it covered a wider range of accidents for which compensation could be claimed, although the levels of compensation were lower. When the minor tried to claim that he was not bound by the employer's scheme he failed. Viewing the whole contract on balance it was generally to his benefit.

In contrast if the contract is made up of terms, which are predominantly detrimental to the minor, then the contract is unlikely to be enforceable by the employer.

CASE EXAMPLE

De Francesco v Barnum [1890] 45 Ch D 430

A fourteen year old girl entered into a seven year apprenticeship to be taught stage dancing. Under the apprenticeship deed the girl agreed that she would be at the master's total disposal during the seven years of the apprenticeship, and would not accept professional engagements except with his express approval. The master had no obligation to maintain her or to employ her but if he did so the scales of pay were very low. The girl could also not marry except with his permission. The master was also able to terminate the arrangement without notice. The girl then found work and the master sought to enforce the terms of the apprenticeship deed but failed. The provisions of the apprenticeship deed were held to be unfair, not substantially for the girl's benefit and so were unenforceable against her.

The courts have subsequently taken an even more progressive view of those circumstances which can be classed as a beneficial contract of service.

CASE EXAMPLE

Doyle v White City Stadium Ltd [1935] 1 KB 110

Here the principle was extended to cover a contract between a minor who was a professional boxer and the British Boxing Board of Control. Under the agreement the minor would lose his 'purse' (the payment for the fight) if he were disqualified. The agreement was held to be binding on the minor since it was not only to encourage clean fighting but also proficiency in boxing, and was therefore for the benefit of the minor.

5.1.5 Illegality and the contract of employment

As with contracts generally it is the usual rule that a court or tribunal will not enforce an illegal contract because such contracts are contrary to public policy at common law and may even be prohibited by statute. In either case the contract may prove to be unenforceable by either party.

CASE EXAMPLE

Salvesen v Simons [1994] IRLR 52

An employee, at his own request, was paid partly through an annual salary with all of the usual deductions and partly through a consultancy that he operated with his wife and this was without any deductions. When the business changed hands his new employer was not prepared to continue with the arrangement and partly because of this the employee then claimed constructive dismissal. Even though tax lost was in fact relatively small the agreement was nevertheless designed to defraud the revenue and so it was tainted with illegality, and the EAT, reversing the decision of the tribunal, held that no unfair dismissal claim was therefore possible in the circumstances.

JUDGMENT

Lord Coulsfield explained: 'it would be very difficult ... to reach the conclusion that public policy did not require that the contract ... should be treated as unenforceable. It may be said that the consequence is that the [employee] suffers a severe penalty for a minor illegality which cannot, in all probability, have cost the Revenue any significant sum in lost tax: but ... it is difficult to imagine that the [employee] did not appreciate that the contractual arrangement which was made did involve some effects on the taxation position, and that it is not necessarily inequitable that persons who seek to take advantage out of the tax system, misguidedly or otherwise, should not be entitled to be treated as if they were employed under a normal contract of employment.'

So where an employment contract is tainted by illegality and the employee is aware of that it is likely that the employee will lose statutory rights as a result.

CASE EXAMPLE

Cole v Fred Stacey Ltd [1974] IRLR 73

The employee was paid an additional sum of money on top of his wages that he was aware was not being taxed. When he was later made redundant it was held that he could not enforce his normal right to a redundancy payment. His contract was in part a contract to defraud the revenue and as a result it was tainted with illegality.

A contract that is legally formed but then is illegally performed in some manner is not automatically unenforceable and the fact that some aspects are tainted with illegality will not necessarily make the whole contract unenforceable.

CASE EXAMPLE

Coral Leisure Group Ltd v Barnett [1981] IRLR 204

The employee was a public relations executive. Amongst his duties he allegedly looked after rich gamblers by providing them with the services of prostitutes. When he was later dismissed the issue was whether or not the contract was tainted with illegality and if so whether this meant that he would have no claim in unfair dismissal. The court held that an immoral or illegal act would not necessarily make the whole contract illegal unless the contract was entered into with the specific purpose of carrying out the illegal acts.

It is usually the employee's knowledge of the illegality which leads to a loss of rights under the contract but where it was intended that the employment should be carried out lawfully but some of the work is then tainted with illegality the question for the courts is then whether it is possible to sever the illegal parts from the main contract to avoid the employee losing rights altogether.

CASE EXAMPLE

Blue Chip Trading Ltd v Helbawi [2009] IRLR 128

Under the terms of his immigration permit a foreign student was allowed to work no more than twenty hours per week during term time but had in fact done so on some occasions. When the student brought a claim against his employer that the employer was not paying him the National Minimum Wage the employer tried to plead that the contract was tainted with illegality and he was not therefore bound by it. The court held that he was entitled to the minimum wage for all weeks where he had complied with the immigration requirements but not those where he had not.

In general a contract that has the purpose of defrauding the revenue is tainted with illegality and will result in a loss of rights for the employee.

CASE EXAMPLE

Hyland v JH Barker (North West) Ltd [1985] IRLR 403

The employee was given a tax free lodging allowance for four weeks while he was commuting. This was enough to taint the contract with illegality to the extent that it prevented the employee from gaining sufficient continuous service to qualify to make a claim for unfair dismissal.

However, if what the employee receives without payment of tax cannot be said to be part of the regular wages then this may not be classed as defrauding the revenue and will not therefore taint the contract with illegality. In *Lightfoot v D & J Sporting Ltd* [1996] IRLR 64 an arrangement to pay part of the employee's salary to his wife was held to be tax avoidance rather than tax evasion and was therefore not unlawful. The difference between tax evasion where a person takes steps to not pay tax that he is already bound to pay and which is unlawful, and tax avoidance whereby people in a position to hire an accountant and therefore do not pay the tax that they might be expected to is an interesting distinction which the current government is still trying to explain to the electorate. In the case of most working people the distinction would be lost since their tax is paid at source on a PAYE basis so that they would not be in a position to try either.

It is usually the employee's knowledge of the illegality which leads to the employee losing rights under the contract of employment.

CASE EXAMPLE

Tomlinson v Dick Evans U Drive Ltd [1978] IRLR 77

An employee claimed unfair dismissal and a redundancy payment. During her employment she had received a weekly cash payment of £15, on which no tax was paid. She understood that this was put through the books as an expense in order to defraud the Revenue. The EAT held that her contract of employment was tainted by the illegality in which she had participated and so her claim failed. The EAT said that even where a junior employee 'goes along' with the fraud in circumstances where the employer is primarily to blame, the employee's contract is not enforceable.

However, the fact that the employee knows of the illegality will not in every case prevent the employee from enforcing the contract. This is particularly so where the employee will not benefit from the illegality in any way.

CASE EXAMPLE

Hewcastle Catering Ltd v Ahmed and Elkamah [1991] IRLR 473

This case involved a number of employees who cooperated with Her Majesty's Revenue and Customs in relation to an investigation of fraudulent VAT receipts charged on customers' bills but not paid over to the revenue. The employer was prosecuted as a result of their cooperation and the employees were dismissed. The court held that the employees were not caught by the illegality even though they knew of it. They had not benefited in any way from the fraud.

It is also the case that the illegality must be linked to the actual subject of the claim for the claim to be affected by the illegality. In this way for instance it may still be possible to bring discrimination claim even though aspects of the employment involve an illegality.

CASE EXAMPLE

Hall v Woolston Hall Leisure Centre Ltd [2001] 1 WLR 225 CA

The claimant was dismissed because of her pregnancy and so claimed under the then Sex Discrimination Act 1975. Her contract of employment was in fact tainted with illegality because she knew that after she had been promoted part of her salary had been paid without proper deductions for tax and NI. The Court of Appeal held that her acquiescence over the illegality was not fatal to her claim of discrimination since it was not causally linked to the discrimination claim and so did not prevent her from gaining compensation.

JUDGMENT

Peter Gibson LJ explained: 'the salient facts are that the fraud was not Mrs Hall's. She was in effect simply confronted with it. She may have had little real choice but to submit. Bearing in mind the imbalance which may often exist in the bargaining positions of employer and employee, it would be strange if the [Equal Treatment Directive] did not ... protect employees from discrimination in such circumstances. Otherwise, employers – having, in effect, imposed on their employees unlawful pay conditions as a condition of employment or continued employment – could thereafter discriminate against them on grounds of sex with impunity ... I see no basis on which any involvement on Mrs Hall's part in illegal performance of her contract of employment can or should lead to her forfeiting any claim to damages for financial loss arising from the sex discrimination involved in her dismissal. Her claim is not to enforce the contract.'

ACTIVITY

Self-assessment questions

1. Do the requirements for formation of a contract of employment differ in any way from the usual rules on formation of contracts?
2. Which contracts if any have to be in writing or evidenced in writing?
3. What happens if an employer withdraws the offer of employment after having made it but before the successful applicant actually starts work?
4. Is minority a major issue in employment?
5. What is the basic rule on employment contracts that are tainted with illegality?
6. When will a contract tainted with illegality prevent an employee from exercising rights under the contract?

5.2 The statutory statement

5.2.1 The legal status of the statement

As we have already seen in 5.1.1 there is no general requirement for a contract of employment to be in writing. Nevertheless, to avoid a dispute, it is useful for the employer and new employee to record the terms in writing which limits the scope of any later dispute about the terms of the contract.

In order to ensure that all new employees receive details of the essential terms of their employment, section 1 of the Employment Rights Act 1996 requires that employers must provide employees whose employment is to continue for more than one month with a written statement of particular terms of their contract. This written statement must be given to employees no later than two months after their employment begins. Section 1 indicates a variety of information which must be provided in the statement or which the statement must indicate where they can be found. These are listed in Figure 5.1.

WRITTEN PARTICULARS REQUIRED IN THE S1 STATEMENT
Section 1 Employment Rights Act 1996 – within eight weeks of employment the employer must provide the employee with a written statement of particulars containing the following:

If there are any changes to any of the particular terms within the written statement then under section 4 Employment Rights Act 1996 the employer is bound to give the

Basic information	a) the names of both employer and employee b) the date of commencement of employment c) the date of commencement of continuous employment (this may be different to the exact date when employment commenced for instance because previous employment may be taken into account for continuous employment – as is the case in teaching in schools)
Information to be given at a specified date not more than seven days before the statement is given	a) the scale of remuneration, the method of calculating pay and the pay period b) terms concerning the expected hours of work c) holiday entitlements (including public holidays and holiday pay); provisions for sickness an any sick pay; pension rights and occupational pension schemes d) periods of notice on both sides e) the job title and possibly a brief job description f) the period of employment if not permanent g) the place or places of work (which may include a mobility clause) h) details of collective agreements affecting conditions I) specific details for overseas working for more than one month (this should include details of the period of such work, the currency in which employees will be paid, any special benefits to be given while they work abroad and terms relating to their return to the UK)
Other key factors	1) If no particulars are to be entered under any of these heads then that fact should be stated 2) the statement may refer the employee to other documents which give more detailed explanations; but only where the employee will have adequate access to these during his employment 3) the statement must be given even though the employment is terminated within the two months
Additional information	a) details of disciplinary rules; b) details of grievance procedure.
	N.B. changes to matters specified in the statement should be made known to the employee within one month of the change.

Figure 5.1 Chart illustrating the information that must be contained in the statement of particulars of employment as required by section 1 Employment Rights Act 1996

employee a new written statement containing details of the change at the earliest opportunity but no later than one month after the change.

The written statement required by section 1 is not a contract of employment.

JUDGMENT

As Lord Parker CJ stated in *Turriff Construction Ltd v Bryant* [1967] ITR 292: 'it is of course quite clear that the statement … is not the contract; it is not even conclusive evidence of the contract'.

This was later confirmed in *System Floors (UK) Ltd v Daniel* [1982] ICR 54.

CASE EXAMPLE

System Floors v Daniel [1981] IRLR 475

The claimant had signed a document which it was accepted was mere acknowledgement of receipt of the statutory statement provided by the employer (this practice obviously protects the employer who is able to show that the statutory statement was given to the employee by the correct date). The claimant later brought a claim for unfair dismissal and so needed to establish the precise date that employment began. The date was disputed by the parties and the precise status of the section 1 statement had to be established by the court. The EAT held that the section 1 statement is not definitive of the contractual terms unless the parties stipulate that it is. It is very strong but not conclusive evidence of terms in the contract. However, it does place a heavy burden on the employer to show how and why the terms of the contract differ from those identified in the statement.

JUDGMENT

Browne-Wilkinson P explained: 'the statutory statement ... provides very strong prima facie evidence of what were the terms of the contract between the parties, but does not constitute a written contract between the parties. Nor are the statements of the terms finally conclusive: at most, they place a heavy burden on the employer to show that the actual terms of the contract are different from those which he has set out in the statutory statement.'

A contract creates the rights and duties of the parties. The written statement required under section 1 merely declares what they are after they have been agreed, but these can be inaccurate. The statement therefore meets the employer's statutory obligations, but is not a contractual document. If the document was held to be a written contract it would be presumed to be an accurate record of what was agreed. It would therefore be difficult to persuade a court otherwise.

As a result section 1 can only be seen as evidence of the contractual terms not the contract itself. Although of course it could prove to be quite powerful evidence.

CASE EXAMPLE

Gascol Conversions Ltd v Mercer [1974] IRLR 155

Under a national agreement formed with employers in the industry and a recognised trade union employees were expected to work forty hours per week plus overtime if necessary. In contrast under a local agreement formed with the employer itself the working week was stated as being fifty-four hours per week. The claimant was later made redundant and the issue in dispute was on which of the two agreements his redundancy payment should be calculated. The Court of Appeal held that the national agreement had been incorporated into his contract and took precedence over the local agreement because it had in fact been referred to in the section 1 statement.

It follows that, while the section 1 statement can be evidence of terms in the contract it will not actually be contractually binding on its own unless the parties agree that it is contractually binding. One way that this could be done is by the employee signing to accept that it is contractual.

CASE EXAMPLE

Robertson v British Gas [1983] ICR 351

By his letter of appointment a gas meter reader was promised that he would be included in an incentive bonus scheme which had been negotiated with the trade union. The employer later withdrew this bonus scheme and the fact of this was inserted in a new section 1 statement, although the claimant did not in fact receive this for seven years. The employee claimed for full arrears of the bonus. The Court of Appeal held that the letter of appointment created a binding contractual term in relation to the bonus. Despite the collective agreement between the employer and the union having no legal force as between the signatories it was incorporated into the employee's contractual terms. The withdrawal of the bonus scheme was thus a unilateral change to the contract. The case shows that unless signed as a contract of employment the s1 statement is only evidence of contractual terms. Other evidence includes the letter of appointment. So it is important to look at all evidence to establish what the terms of the contract actually are.

An example of a written statement of particulars is given below.

5.2.2 Enforcement of the statement

If an employer fails to provide a written statement, or provides an inaccurate or incomplete statement or fails to provide an employee with a statement of changes, then under section 11 Employment Rights Act 1996 the employee may complain to an employment tribunal. The employee could continue in employment and do this or, if the contract has been terminated, then it would have to be within three months of the date of termination.

Where this is the employee's only claim then the only remedy will be a declaration from the tribunal which either confirms the written particulars or amends them but the tribunal cannot merely substitute its own of what the terms should be. In *Cuthbertson v AML Distributors* [1975] IRLR 228 for example the tribunal felt that it was not appropriate to state what notice was reasonable for a senior executive.

If the employee has succeeded in another claim, for example for unfair dismissal, then, in addition to the declaration, under section 38 Employment Act 2002 the employee may also receive compensation of between two and four weeks' pay.

ACTIVITY

Self-assessment questions

1. What is the section 1 statement?
2. What type of information is required to be in the statement?
3. What happens when the employer later makes changes to the contract?
4. If the section 1 statement is not actually the contract of employment how useful is it in establishing what is in the contract?
5. When will the section 1 statement be contractual?
6. What is the position when an employer has not provided a section 1 statement?

5.3 The incorporation of the express terms

5.3.1 The range and character of express terms

All contracts contain terms that have been incorporated into them which set out the obligations of the parties and this is no different in contracts of employment. Express terms are

Statement of Terms of Employment

This statement of the terms of your employment is as required by section 1 of the Employment Rights Act 1996.

Commencement of employment

1. Your employer is [employer's name]. Your employment commenced on [date]. No employment with a previous employer counts towards your period of continuous employment with us.

Job title & Place of work

2. You are employed as [job title].
3. Your normal place of work is [location]. You will not be required to work outside the UK for more than one month per year during your employment.

Salary

4. Your basic salary is £[amount] per year which shall be payable monthly in arrears on the [date] of each month directly into your bank or building society account.

Hours of work

5. Your normal hours of work are between [time] and [time], [Mondays] to [Fridays] with a lunch break of one hour. You may be required to work overtime as is necessary for the proper performance of your duties without extra payment.

Holidays

6. You will be entitled to [number] days' holiday during each holiday year in addition to public holidays. The holiday year runs between [date] and [date]. Full regulations are available for your inspection at [location].

Sickness absence

7. If you are absent from work for any reason you must notify [manager] of the reason for your absence as soon as possible but no later than [time] on the end of the first day of absence. Full regulations are available for your inspection at [location].

Pensions

8. You are entitled to become a member or the [name] Pension Scheme, subject to satisfying certain eligibility criteria and subject to the rules of such scheme as amended from time to time. Full regulations are available for your inspection at [location].

Termination and notice period

9. You are required to give one week's prior written notice to terminate your employment. You will be entitled to one week's notice for any period of continuous employment up to two years. Thereafter you will be entitled to one week's additional notice for each completed year of continuous employment up to a maximum of 12 weeks' notice.
10. Nothing in these terms and conditions prevents us from terminating your employment summarily without notice in the event of gross misconduct or if you commit a serious breach of your obligations as an employee.

Disciplinary and grievance procedures

11. Your attention is drawn to the disciplinary and grievance procedures applicable to your employment, a copy of which is available for your inspection at [location]. If you wish to appeal against a disciplinary decision you may apply in writing to [manager] in accordance with our disciplinary procedure. If you wish to raise a grievance you may apply in writing to [manager] in accordance with our grievance procedure.

Collective agreement

12. There is no collective agreement which directly affects your employment.

Signed ....
For and on behalf of [employer]

I acknowledge receipt of a copy of this written statement and agree that the terms set out in it and the documents referred to form the basis of my contract of employment

Signed ....
[employee]

Figure 5.2 Sample statutory statement of particulars

those that have been written into the contract or they may have been agreed by the parties orally. Express terms usually deal with such matters as pay, hours or work and holiday entitlement and they are often in any case affected by statutory rights and restrictions, for example, the right to equal pay, the minimum wage, and the rules on working time all affect what the employer can put into the contract on these matters. As a result express terms can be overridden by implied terms, particularly when these are statutory.

The parties to an employment contract could agree on any terms, although except in very rare cases the terms would be dictated by the employer. They must of course be subject to general principles of law, so as we have seen in 5.1.5 there would be implications if the contract was based on illegality and an employee might find it difficult to enforce such a contract. Similarly the contract may reflect an inadequate balance between the parties but it could not be based on slavery.

The express terms usually contain the same information as that which is included in the written statement of particular terms required by section 1 Employment Rights Act 1996, so they may include details on pay, holiday entitlement, duties required notice and many others. The express terms would usually be of three distinct types:

- specific terms agreed by the parties;
- everything required to be in the section 1 statement;
- terms contained in other documents specifically referred to in the section 1 statement (an example of this latter might be details of paid holiday entitlement in excess of that required by law).

These terms can be discovered in the case of dispute by looking at what the parties said or wrote when they made the agreement. Obviously they are simpler to find if they are in writing. However, even where they are expressed, it is still for courts and tribunals to interpret them and they will do so by looking at the general practices in the particular industry. Where terms are not expressed they may be implied.

5.3.2 The significance of the express terms

Not all terms are expressed in a written agreement or even indicated orally in negotiations, many are implied either by custom, by law or by statute or other statutory provision. The range of possible terms can be illustrated in diagram form as in Figure 5.3.

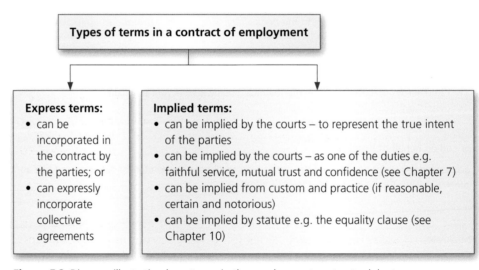

Figure 5.3 Diagram illustrating how terms in the employment contract originate

It is always preferable for express terms to be in writing so that there is no disputing them and they are clear to all parties, including a tribunal in the case of a dispute. In *Stubbs v Trower, Still & Keeling* [1987] IRLR 321 there was a dispute when a firm of solicitors failed to properly express the requirement of passing the necessary professional qualifications before a post could be taken up. So the written statement needs to accurately represent the actual agreement between the parties to avoid disputes.

CASE EXAMPLE

Nelson v BBC (No 2) [1980] IRLR 346

Under his contract an employee was required to work when and where the corporation demanded. When the employer closed down its Caribbean service it tried to make him redundant on the basis that it was implied in the contract that he was only required for that service. The Court of Appeal held that there was no such implied term. The express term in the contract on place of work was absolutely clear and unambiguous. Therefore there could be no redundancy on the grounds suggested.

It is possible for either party to accept breaches of the terms of the contract by the other party. In the case of a breach of terms by the employee the employer could count this as grounds for dismissal. In the case of a breach of the terms by the employer the employee could claim for constructive dismissal. In either case established tests of fairness or unfairness will be used. This can be seen in two contrasting cases.

CASE EXAMPLE

Martin v Solus Schall [1979] IRLR 1

In the claimant's contract there was a requirement that he should work a particular amount of overtime. He had in fact signed the contract which included this term so that when he refused to do overtime and was dismissed in consequence the dismissal was held to be fair because overtime was a contractual obligation.

CASE EXAMPLE

Redbridge London Borough Council v Fishman [1978] IRLR 69

The claimant was a teacher in charge of a resource centre. Her head teacher consistently required that she do a greater and greater amount of teaching and when she eventually refused she was dismissed. Her dismissal was held to be unfair because teaching was ancillary to her main role and the extent of the teaching that she was being asked to do was unreasonable.

In general advertisements may be indicative of express terms in the contract of employment and so be a means of a tribunal determining what the express terms are in the event of a dispute. However, if these are inconsistent with the express terms they will not override them.

CASE EXAMPLE

Deeley v British Rail Engineering Ltd [1980] IRLR 147

Here the job advert was for a 'Sales Engineer (Export)'. In fact the role under the express terms in the written contract was 'Sales Engineer'. The claimant who had been appointed to the post later tried to claim that the job was limited to a role involving only exports. It was held that this was not the reality of the contract.

It is possible, however, that express oral terms can override details provided in the statutory statement and present a more accurate representation of the contract.

CASE EXAMPLE

Hawker Siddeley Power Engineering Ltd v Rump [1979] IRLR 425

An HGV driver signed a contract saying that he would travel all over the country. He was reluctant for domestic reasons to work outside Southern England, but was assured that he would not have to do so. This assurance was never put in writing. However, he later received a written statement of his terms and conditions which included a mobility clause. Again it was promised that he would not have to move outside the Bristol area. He was then dismissed when he refused to make a trip to Scotland. The employer relied on the mobility clause to justify the dismissal. The EAT held that there was a valid oral agreement that the claimant would not be required to work outside Southern England and this had the effect of varying the written contract. The claimant's signature on the statement of particulars was still insufficient because there was evidence that he would not actually have agreed to the mobility requirement.

5.3.3 Interpreting the express terms

Whatever the parties may have agreed which can then be classed as the express terms of the contract it is inevitable that, if there is a dispute then the courts will be called on to decide if an alleged term is in fact consistent with the employment relationship.

CASE EXAMPLE

Cole v Midland Display Ltd [1973] IRLR 62

This was a case heard by the National Industrial Relations Court. The claimant was employed as a manager and his employment was described being 'on a staff basis'. When he was called on to work overtime and asked to do so without any pay he refused. This resulted in his dismissal and he challenged this as unfair on the basis that there could be no contractual requirement for him to work unpaid overtime. At the time people regarded as staff were treated very differently to people who were not. For instance workers who were not staff very often at that time had no holiday entitlement, had no pay during sickness and in this instance it was accepted by the court that the claimant would receive pay even if there was no work for him. On that basis it was held that it was not unreasonable for him to be asked to work some overtime without receiving any additional pay and his dismissal was therefore fair.

However, despite the fact that tribunals and courts will be called on to interpret the precise meaning of terms, however, well or badly expressed, one thing that they cannot do is to reach decisions that would in effect change the job description, and thus the contractual terms.

CASE EXAMPLE

Redbridge LBC v Fishman [1978] IRLR 69

As we have seen in 5.3.2 the claimant was a teacher in charge of a resource centre who was asked to do an excessive amount of teaching and who was dismissed when she eventually refused. The fact was that her principal role was as director of the resource centre and the tribunal could not change that fact.

The tribunal is of course entitled to consider extrinsic material such as job advertisements in order to ascertain the meaning of terms. In *Tayside Regional Council v McIntosh* [1982] IRLR 272 for instance the EAT held that a requirement for 'qualifications' need not be expressly stated in a contract of employment, as it may be inferred from the job advertisement or even from the nature of the job. However, as we have seen in 5.3.2 such material cannot be used to override express terms as in *Deeley v BREL* [1980] IRLR 147 where the actual role was Sales Engineer and the use of the word Export in the job advertisement was not definitive.

The traditional view was that, if the employee agreed a term then he was bound by it, however, harshly it might apply. However, the modern view is that they should also express terms that should be exercised reasonably and they should not be inconsistent with the implied duty of mutual trusts and respect (see Chapter 7.2.5).

CASE EXAMPLE

United Bank Ltd v Akhtar [1989] IRLR 507

An employee's contract included a mobility clause. The employer notified the employee that he was to transfer from the Birmingham branch to the Leeds branch about 120 miles away and he was given only three days' notice of this. Despite the employee requesting a brief delay in his transfer because of his wife's serious illness at the time and in order to sort out arrangements for accommodation and removal the employer refused. The employee left and claimed constructive dismissal. The EAT held that, even though there was a mobility clause in the contract, there was an implied term that it should be affected in a reasonable manner. As a result the employee's claim for unfair dismissal succeeded.

The courts will not accept that an ambiguous provision in the contract can act to the employee's detriment. Similarly courts will not allow an employee to enforce anything that is too vague or ambiguous.

CASE EXAMPLE

Judge v Crown Leisure Ltd [2005] EWCA Civ 571

The employee attended a staff Christmas party during which he was promised to be put on 'roughly' the same pay scale as other managers. When he remained on the same pay scale he claimed breach of contract. The Court of Appeal held that there was no contractual arrangement so there could be no breach. The words used were too vague to be contractually binding and this merely reflects the basic rule of contract law that an offer must be certain as to its terms.

5.3.4 The advantages and disadvantages of express terms

Advantages

- Where the parties have expressed themselves on the terms of the contract, and particularly where the terms have been put in written form then there is likely to be less room for dispute. If the terms are clear then there should not in fact be any room for dispute.

- If this is the case then inevitably there is a consequent saving of time and money because there is no point an employee arguing about something that he had agreed to at the time of making the contract or at least was plainly aware of at the time of contracting.

- Express terms can be broadly stated, and we have seen this in the case of mobility clauses and so may give much greater scope to the employer for flexibility. Obviously employers wish to get the greatest productivity from employees. A well drafted written contract of employment with clearly stated express terms provides the greatest chance of this unless of course express terms conflict with the implied duties (see Chapter 7) or any statutory provisions which may override them.

Disadvantages

Great care should be taken in drafting a written contract of employment otherwise an employer might actually end up creating more problems – there are two obvious ones:

- The express terms may be drafted too narrowly to cover the employer's actual needs – then if the employer tries to extend what he requires from the employee he may be in breach of contract.

- Alternatively, even though the express terms may be drafted well they may still be subject to narrow interpretation by the tribunal – in which case the employer still has not achieved the desired flexibility from the contract.

Conclusion

Since the employer is obliged in any case to provide a written statement of particulars and give this to the employee within eight weeks of the commencement of employment it is possibly better to provide a more detailed written contract at the commencement of employment. The employee is then in no doubt what the terms of his employment are and it avoids later disputes. The employer will clearly benefit by including as broad terms as are possible.

ACTIVITY

Self-assessment questions

1. What types of terms will usually be found as express terms in the contract?
2. Why are express terms significant?
3. In what way do the express terms have to operate fairly?
4. What is the significance of job advertisements in determining what the express terms are?
5. Will terms agreed orally by the parties ever override terms that are identified in the section 1 statement?
6. What is the significance of cases such as *United Bank Ltd v Akhtar* to the interpretation of the express terms?

5.4 Collective agreements

5.4.1 The nature of collective agreements

A collective agreement is defined in section 178 Trade Union and Labour Relations (Consolidation) Act 1992 as 'any agreement or arrangement made by or on behalf of one or more trade unions and one or more employers or employers' associations'. It is an agreement made through collective bargaining between the unions and the employers and such agreements are generally presumed to have no effect in law unless they are incorporated into the contract. There are three ways in which they may be incorporated into the contract and become binding on the employer and employees:

- If they are expressly incorporated into the contract – this would be in a clause identifying that the employee is bound by the agreement and there may also be reference to collective agreements in the section 1 statement.
- There might be implied incorporation through conduct for instance which would in effect be custom and practice.
- Incorporation of collective agreements might result from the trade union negotiating with the employer, in effect being the agent of the employees and acting on their behalf.

Collective agreements may define the relationship between the trade union and the employer which will not usually form part of the contract of employment, but they can also define the terms and conditions of those employees who fall within the agreements reached between trade unions and the employer. Often such agreements are made on a national scale but there can also be local agreements which may be specific to a branch of a trade union and a specific workplace. These are still covered by the same rules.

5.4.2 Express incorporation of collective agreements

The most obvious way for terms from a collective agreement to be incorporated in the contract of employment is for an express provision to be inserted in the contract to that effect.

CASE EXAMPLE

Jewell v Neptune Concrete [1975] IRLR 147

The employee's wage rates were determined by a national agreement and this was indicated in the section 1 statement. This was held not to automatically incorporate other aspects of the national agreement into his contract.

The section 1 statement is of course another obvious method by which the collective agreement can be incorporated into the contract.

CASE EXAMPLE

Camden Exhibition & Display Ltd v Lynott [1966] 1 QB 555

The statement given to employees indicated that their contractual terms were in line with the rules of the national joint council for the industry. Under these rules it was identified that the working of overtime was required by direct arrangement and mutual agreement with the employer. During a dispute over a wage award employees then refused to work overtime but the court held that working overtime was a contractual requirement.

In order for the terms arising from collective agreements which affect the employee's working conditions to be incorporated they clearly must represent the actual contractual intention of the parties.

CASE EXAMPLE

Alexander v Standard Telephones and Cables plc [1990] IRLR 55

A collective agreement between management and a trade union had determined that in the case of compulsory redundancies being carried out the criteria for selection for redundancy would be based on a last in first out (LIFO) basis. The company did then engage in a redundancy situation but wished to retain employees on the basis of their skills and flexibility rather than the accepted criteria. The claimant sought an injunction to prevent this. The EAT accepted that the agreement was incorporated into his contract so that any remedy could only be for breach of the contract, if indeed there was any breach in the circumstances.

One of the benefits of express incorporation of an arrangement with trade unions and therefore collective agreements made with them is that this may mean that the contract need not be amended on each re-negotiation. The employer will simply have stated in the contract that the employee is subject to the collective agreements negotiated with that trade union.

CASE EXAMPLE

N.C.B. v Galley [1958] 1 WLR 16

Here the contract of employment identified that the employee's conditions were subject to national agreements made with the relevant trade unions which were 'for the time being in force'. Under these agreements employees were required to work a certain amount of overtime. The claimant refused but it was held that the collective agreement had been expressly incorporated into the contract of employment and the employee's refusal was therefore a breach of contract.

It is of course true that not every collective agreement is in fact always suitable for incorporation into the contract of employment as they may simply concern the relationship between the employer and the trade union.

CASE EXAMPLE

British Leyland UK Ltd v McQuilken [1978] IRLR 245

At the time it was not uncommon for employers and trade unions to reach agreements which included a clause which at the time became known as TINALEA (this is not a legally enforceable agreement) clauses. In the case the employer was closing down a department and skilled employees were being given the choice of retraining as an alternative to redundancy. Some employees had at first chosen redundancy but then wanted to change their minds. However, they were being told by management that they could not do so. They argued that this refusal was in contravention of a collective agreement which obviously required them proving that the collective agreement had been incorporated into their contracts. The court held that it had not it was merely a policy agreement between union and employer, not one that produced rights for employees.

It would also be true that an employee cannot rely on a term in a collective agreement when the term is in fact procedural rather than conferring any substantive individual rights on employees.

CASE EXAMPLE

Griffiths v Buckinghamshire CC [1994] ICR 265

A redundancy agreement between an employer and a trade union had recommended that twelve months' notice of any redundancy scheme was appropriate. However, the court held that it was merely procedural so it did not create rights that were incorporated into the contract of employment.

Where the terms of national and local agreements conflict then one approach has been that the most recent in time should prevail. This is how the problem was resolved in *Clift v West Riding CC* [1964] The Times 10 April 1964 where the employee was paid less under a local agreement than he might have been under a national agreement but because the local agreement was made after the national agreement it was the local agreement that the employee was held to be bound by.

However, it is a question of fact in each case which agreement will be taken as the one which prevails.

CASE EXAMPLE

Gascol Conversions Ltd v Mercer [1974] IRLR 155

Here we have seen in 5.2.1 that under the national agreement employees were expected to work forty hours per week plus overtime if necessary whereas under the local agreement there was a fifty-four hour week. When the claimant was made redundant the Court of Appeal held that the national agreement had been incorporated into his contract for the purpose of calculating his redundancy payment. This was because it had in fact been referred to in the section 1 statement.

5.4.3 Implied incorporation of collective agreements

Collective agreement can also be incorporated in the contract of employment by implication which will usually involve operation of the 'officious bystander test' (see Chapter 7.1.2). This could occur because in certain industries there is almost an assumption that the terms developed from agreements between the recognised trade unions and management become contractual. Terms resulting from collective agreements are likely to be implied into contracts of employment where there is long term acceptance of the process.

CASE EXAMPLE

Wilton v Peebles [1994] UKEAT 835 93 2607

Here the claimants were arguing that they should have increases in wages in 1992 and 1993 under the Thermal Insulation Contractors Agreement which allowed for rates agreed from time to time between the Thermal Insulation Contractors' Association on the one hand, and the General Municipal Boilermaker and the Transport and General Workers Union, on the other hand. The employer had refused to make these increases in pay and the employees were claiming that this amounted to an unlawful deduction in wages and they also complained that they had not been issued with particulars of employment as required. The EAT held that there was an implied term that their wages should be those in the Thermal Insulation Contractors Agreement because this was a long-standing practice in the trade. It also held that the fact that there were no written particulars did not prevent the agreement, and therefore the wage rises, being incorporated into their contract of employment.

It is also possible that terms agreed in a collective agreement can be incorporated into the contract of employment by custom and practice following the principle in *Sagar v Ridehalgh* [1931] 1 Ch 310 that the practice is reasonable, certain and notorious (see Chapter 7.1.2).

CASE EXAMPLE

Carlton Henry & Others v London General Transport Services Ltd [2002] EWCA Civ 488

The employer had engaged in negotiations for privatisation under a management buy-out and prior to the sale of the business negotiations with the appropriate trade union took place. The employer then reached an agreement referred to as a 'framework agreement' with the Transport and General Workers Union (T&GWU), which was the recognised trade union. Under this framework agreement the terms and conditions of employment were revised and the changes to the existing terms involved reductions in pay. Notices were displayed stating the changes to pay and conditions of service and all members of staff were asked to sign individual statements of changed terms and conditions. After holding meetings with employees the trade union informed management that the majority of employees had agreed to the changed conditions which were then later put into effect. A number of employees at the Stockwell Bus Station had objected to the reductions in pay and now brought claims in the tribunal for unlawful deductions in pay. The Court of Appeal held against these employees and identified that the changed conditions were contractual and the employees were bound by them. The fact that the employees' contracts had traditionally over many years been subject to collective bargaining between the T&GWU and the employer meant that the so-called framework agreement was incorporated into their contracts by custom.

5.4.4 The effect of collective agreements on non-union members

A trade union may well be the agent of its members but of course it has no real relationship with employees who are not members. As a result collective agreements will only be contractually binding on employees who are not members of the trade union or who are members of a different trade union to the one that is recognised by the employer if they have been expressly incorporated into the contracts of those employees. If they have not been expressly incorporated then the terms reached under a collective agreement cannot apply to those employees.

CASE EXAMPLE

Singh v British Steel Corporation [1974] IRLR 131

The claimant had originally been a member of the recognised trade union but then had left the union. At a later point after the claimant had left the union the employer negotiated a new shift system with the union. This involved a shift over seven days. The claimant refused to work to the new shift pattern and the employer dismissed him as a result. The court acknowledged that the agreement with the union could not affect the claimant's contract without negotiation with him and then express incorporation of the agreement into the contract. Interestingly, however, since the rest of the workforce had accepted the new terms as members of the union the dismissal was in fact fair for some other substantial reason (see Chapter 22.4.5).

Singh concerned an employee who was no longer a member of a union. It is also possible to apply the principle to an employee who is a member of a trade union other than the one with which the collective agreement has been reached.

CASE EXAMPLE

Miller v Hamworthy Engineering Ltd [1986] IRLR 461

Two trade unions including the one which the claimant was a member of negotiated a change to working hours. The union to which the claimant did not belong then reached another agreement with the employer which the claimant would not adhere to. It was held that he should be treated as a non-member and could only be bound by the agreement if it was expressly incorporated in his contract after negotiation with him.

It could of course be possible for there to be implied incorporation of the agreement (see *Carlton Henry & Others v London General Transport Services Ltd* [2002] EWCA Civ 488 in 5.4.3 above).

5.4.5 No strike clauses

Such clauses are now covered by section 180 Trade Union & Labour Relations (Consolidation) Act 1992 which identifies the restrictions on their use.

SECTION

'180 Effect of provisions restricting right to take industrial action.
(1) Any terms of a collective agreement which prohibit or restrict the right of workers to engage in a strike or other industrial action, or have the effect of prohibiting or restricting that right, shall not form part of any contract between a worker and the person for whom he works unless the following conditions are met.
(2) The conditions are that the collective agreement –
   (a)   is in writing,
   (b)   contains a provision expressly stating that those terms shall or may be incorporated in such a contract,
   (c)   is reasonably accessible at his place of work to the worker to whom it applies and is available for him to consult during working hours, and
   (d)   is one where each trade union which is a party to the agreement is an independent trade union;
      and that the contract with the worker expressly or impliedly incorporates those terms in the contract.'

So provisions limiting industrial action arising out of a collective agreement are only incorporated if:

▨ the collective agreement is in writing;

▨ the agreement expressly states that the no-strike clause is incorporated into the contract and it is actually incorporated;

▨ the notification of the agreement is reasonably accessible in the workplace in working hours.

Besides this of course a strike is always a breach of contract so this may in fact reduce the impact of section 180.

5.4.6 Changing or ending collective agreements

The agreement if incorporated cannot be unilaterally varied or ended. This can be seen in *Robertson v British Gas* [1983] ICR 351 in 5.2.1 above. Despite the collective agreement between the employer and the union having no legal force as between the signatories it was incorporated into the employee's contractual terms and the withdrawal of the bonus scheme was therefore a unilateral change to the contract which the employee had no entitlement to make.

Unilateral termination may, however, be possible where the contract in fact allows for it.

CASE EXAMPLE

Cadoux v Central Regional Council [1986] IRLR 131

A term in the claimant's contract of employment was that his 'post was subject to the Conditions of Service laid down by the National Joint Council for Local Authorities' Administrative, Professional, Technical and Clerical Services (Scottish Council) and as supplemented by the Authorities' Rules and as amended from time to time'. Originally the claimant was entitled to participate in a non-contributory life assurance scheme in accordance with the Authorities' Rules. However, his employers then unilaterally withdrew the scheme, thereby depriving the claimant of any benefits under the scheme. The Scottish Court of Session concluded from an examination of the Rules that they were created unilaterally and not bilaterally. As a result the employer was also entitled to alter them unilaterally, since they were not agreed rules, but the employer's rules. The claim was dismissed on the basis that the claimant did not have an irrevocable right to participate in the non-contributory scheme.

It is of course possible to change or end the agreement through a lawful agreement and a lawful notice of the agreement to the employees affected.

ACTIVITY

Self-assessment questions

1. What is a collective agreement?
2. In what ways can collective agreements be incorporated into the contract of employment?
3. What is the benefit of methods of express incorporation of collective terms into the contract?
4. How will the situation be resolved when there are conflicting national and local collective agreements?
5. In what circumstances can it be implied that a collective agreement is incorporated into the contract of employment?
6. In what circumstances can an employee who is not a member of the trade union with whom the employer has an agreement be bound by the terms in that agreement?
7. When can no strike clauses be enforced?
8. Are there any circumstances in which the terms of a collective agreement can be unilaterally changed or ended by the employer?

5.5 Works rules

5.5.1 The nature and effect of works rules

All employers have works rules and some present these in handbooks which are sometimes given to employees but in any case are available to employees. The works rules could include a variety of issues to do with the employment which may even include references to disciplinary proceedings, health and safety as well as sickness procedure and holiday entitlement. The problem with handbooks is that they may mix contractual and non-contractual matter. The distinction is clearly important because contractual terms of employment can only be changed by agreement with employees whereas non-contractual rules are seen as management prerogative and can be changed unilaterally.

CASE EXAMPLE

Cadoux v Central Regional Council [1986] IRLR 131

As can be seen in 5.4.6 above the claimant was subject to a collective agreement as supplemented by the Council's own rules. When his employers unilaterally withdrew a non-contributory life assurance scheme depriving the claimant of any benefits under the scheme the Scottish Court of Session held that since the rules were created unilaterally and not bilaterally they could also be altered unilaterally.

If the provisions of the rule book are seen as merely rules rather than contractual terms then the employer is entitled to change the rules and introduce new rules and employees would not be able to challenge this even though the changes may be significant.

CASE EXAMPLE

Bateman v Asda Stores Ltd [2010] IRLR 370

The employer's staff handbook stated that the employer 'reserved the right to review, revise, amend or replace the contents of this handbook, and introduce new policies from time to time reflecting the changing needs of the business'. Significantly the handbook also provided details of pay and other conditions of employment. The employer then proposed to introduce a new pay structure, which in fact was already operated in relation to most of its employees and after extensive consultation with employee representatives this was indeed implemented. Around 9,300 staff moved on to the new pay structure leaving about 8,700 on whom it was imposed. More than 700 staff then challenged the changes as amounting to an unlawful deduction of pay contrary to section 13 Employment Rights Act 1996 and some even claimed unfair dismissal. Both the tribunal and the EAT dismissed the claims and held that because of the precise wording of the handbook there was no breach of contract on the part of the employer.

In this way the fact that changes in the rules acts harshly on particular employees is of no real consequence. There is no automatic repudiation of contract by an employer based purely on making changes to the works rules.

CASE EXAMPLE

Dryden v Greater Glasgow Health Board [1992] IRLR 469

It is important to note for the avoidance of confusion that this case occurred prior to legislation which has subsequently prohibited smoking in public places including in the workplace except in exterior shelters of a particular design. The employer in the case had previously allowed smoking only in designated smoking areas. The employer then, after extensive consultation with staff, introduced a total ban on smoking within the workplace. The claimant, a nursing auxiliary, usually smoked up to thirty cigarettes per day and had previously been used to smoking while at work in those areas that had been set aside for that purpose. She decided that she could no longer remain at work following the total prohibition on smoking in the workplace, and her job meant that she was unable to leave the premises to smoke. She claimed constructive dismissal. The court held that there was no breach of contract since there was neither any implied term nor any customary term that employees should be allowed to smoke. The rule was introduced for a legitimate purpose and it did not prevent the employee from performing her contract.

Often where there are a large number of detailed rules in the rule book dealing with practical issues, then a court may simply infer that these are not contractual but merely a set of instructions to the employee on how the contract should be carried out. However, a court might still see a failure to carry out the rules as having contractual consequences.

CASE EXAMPLE

Secretary of State for Employment v ASLEF (No 2) [1972] 2 QB 455

During an industrial dispute over pay railway workers engaged in a so-called 'work to rule'. This involved not working overtime including rest days. The action was clearly designed to cause inconvenience to the employer that depended on such flexibility to run its services effectively. Under the then Industrial Relations Act 1971 the Secretary of State was empowered to bring action against trade unions in disputes that might cause harm to the national economy. One of the obvious problems for the court was that if the employees were genuinely sticking to the rule book and this was in fact part of their contract then they could only be said to be honouring their contractual obligations. However, the court made reference to another part of the rule book which required that employees should 'make every effort to facilitate the working of trains and prevent unavoidable delay'. As such the employees were required to interpret the rules reasonably and not in such a way that would disrupt services and they were thus in breach of contract. This was despite the fact that Lord Denning identified that the rules were not in fact terms of the contract.

In *Peake v Automotive Products* [1977] QB 780 (later *Automotive Products Ltd v Peake* [1977] IRLR 365 in the Court of Appeal) the EAT identified that works rules were in fact no more than non-contractual administrative arrangements. Nevertheless, provisions in works rules have still been enforced by courts even against blameless employees and leading to what may be seen as relatively harsh results.

CASE EXAMPLE

Jeffries v BP Tanker Co Ltd [1974] IRLR 260

A rule in the company handbook identified that employees with a history of cardiac disease would not be allowed to work as radio officers at sea. The claimant had two heart attacks and was then dismissed. The court held that it was a fair dismissal even though the employee had made a full recovery and despite the fact that the rule was in essence only a company policy rather than an enforceable contractual requirement.

Rules should be clear and unambiguous and should still be reasonable in character so that an autocratic approach to the rulebook may not be accepted by the court. In *Talbot v Hugh Fulton Ltd* [1975] IRLR 52 which involved a works rule that led to an employee being dismissed for having long hair, the court suggested that such rules must have some justification for example based on hygiene or safety.

The courts have found in certain circumstances that works rules can be contractual in nature despite their unilateral character.

CASE EXAMPLE

Briggs v Imperial Chemical Industries Ltd [1968] 5 KIR 492

A process worker at a cyanide plant was asked to move to another plant when management decided that the plant where he worked was to be demolished and replaced. He refused to move and claimed that he should be entitled instead to a redundancy payment. The court analysed his contract of employment. This stated that his rate of pay could be changed according to the job he was to do. As well as this the works rules identified that the employer had a right to transfer him to another job and they also made reference to wage rates being variable according to whether the work was day work, night work or shift work. As such the court concluded that these amounted to terms in his contract.

In general works rules are more likely to be seen as contractual where express mention of the rules is made in the contract itself.

CASE EXAMPLE

Singh v Lyons Maid Ltd [1975] IRLR 328

An employee who was a Sikh grew a beard which was in keeping with his religious beliefs. He did so despite knowing of the existence of a works rule which in fact prohibited the growing of beards. The rule was in place to maintain high standards of hygiene in a food processing industry. His refusal to observe the rule led to his dismissal and he claimed unfair dismissal.

The dismissal was held to be fair. In effect the employee had disobeyed a lawful and reasonable order which was necessary to the maintenance of proper conditions within the process. It was not merely a works rule but was also a contractual requirement.

The ultimate analysis of whether a works rule is in fact incorporated into the contract is for the tribunal or court to determine and this analysis may turn on the character of the clause.

CASE EXAMPLE

Keeley v Fosroc Ltd [2006] EWCA Civ 1277

The company handbook contained a clause under a section entitled 'Employee benefits and rights', which said: 'Those employees with two or more years' continuous service are entitled to receive an enhanced redundancy payment from the Company.... Details will be discussed during both collective and individual consultation.' The dispute involved whether or not this could be enforced which would depend on it being contractual. The Court of Appeal (reversing the trial judge) held that it was incorporated and so gave rise to a contractual entitlement. The court looked at the clause in its context as part of the employee's total remuneration package. Redundancy exercises were common in the company and enhanced redundancy payments were also common. The fact that the handbook gave no details of amount did not matter.

JUDGMENT

The Court of Appeal identified: 'A provision of that sort, even if couched in terms of information or explanation or expressed in discretionary terms, may still be apt for construction as a term of his contract.'

5.5.2 The significance of the job description

It is common for employers to produce a document detailing the employee's duties and this is generally referred to as the 'job description'. Indeed it is also common for potential applicants for posts to receive this along with an application form when they first enquire about the job. The advantage of the potential applicant receiving the job description before applying is that they will be able to decide whether or not they have the necessary skills and aptitude so that they are capable first of being given the job and second of doing it.

There is no required format for a job description but sensible employment policy would suggest that it should achieve two significant purposes:

- first it should be sufficiently specific that an applicant and indeed an employee is able to identify the precise details of the work;

- second it should also be in language that is sufficiently flexible to allow the employer to make reasonable variations to the work.

Particularly with small businesses rigid demarcation lines between particular duties are unrealistic and the workforce would need to be reasonably flexible both in terms of the work done and the circumstances surrounding it. (In the 1950s through to the 1970s it was not uncommon for a stoppage to occur because a particular worker was not allowed to carry out another worker's work. For example a maintenance engineer having repaired a piece of machinery might be prevented from cleaning up the resulting mess because this was the job of a labourer. Inevitably this had a major effect on productivity. Small businesses simply could not afford for this to happen now.)

In this respect the scope of the contract is inevitably different to and broader than the scope of the job description so that the job description is not contractual although it can be strong evidence of contractual terms. On this basis the job description can develop over time and can be unilaterally altered as long as it still falls within the scope of the contract.

However, the mere fact that the employer includes a flexibility clause in the job description does not necessarily mean that the employer is able to change the fundamental nature of the work without consulting the employees. Where an employer tries to make changes to the employees' duties without their agreement these must fall within the scope of the contract to be lawful and binding on the employee.

CASE EXAMPLE

Land Securities Trillium Ltd v Thornley [2005] IRLR 765

This involved an architect who worked for the BBC as a Senior Project Leader in the Construction Management Department. Her duties were identified in her job description. The BBC then decided to outsource work and much of the Construction Management Department including qualified staff like Mrs Thornley was transferred to Land Securities Trillium Ltd. This company had indicated before the transfer that within a few months the nature of the work would change significantly. With the BBC Mrs Thornley had engaged in full architectural duties, in other words overseeing projects from start to finish. With her new employer the duties eventually became quite different and she did not have the same opportunity to see all stages of a project. She left and claimed constructive dismissal on the basis that the change in her duties had the effect of deskilling her as an architect and was therefore a fundamental breach of her contract and that as a result she was entitled to a redundancy payment. Both the tribunal and the EAT agreed.

ACTIVITY

Self-assessment questions
1. What are works rules?
2. In what circumstances will works rules be seen as contractual?
3. Is it generally possible for the employer to unilaterally change works rules without consulting employees?
4. What would be the justification for allowing employers to change works rules unilaterally?
5. In what circumstances could an employee be in breach of contract for following the works rules?
6. What is the significance of the job description?

5.6 Variation of contractual terms

Over the course of most employment relationships, an employee's terms of employment are bound to change in a number of ways. While the recession may have limited annual pay increases (particularly those that bring the wage in line with inflation), they are quite common. Employees are often promoted which will normally mean quite a significant change to their contract of employment. However, these types of changes will normally happen by mutual consent and are unlikely to cause any legal or practical problems for employers.

Occasionally, however, an employer may wish to make other changes to the contract of employment that the employee is less happy to accept. There are two main reasons when an employer will wish to change terms in a contract, the first being economic circumstances resulting in a need to reorganise the employer's business. This may result in specific changes to the terms of an employment contract, such as changes to pay rates, bonus and commission structures, job content and the place where an employee is required to work. The second reason where change is normally apparent is where the employer is going through a programme of harmonisation of terms of employment across the business. The employer may wish to move all employees on to standard terms of employment, where previously they were all on a variety of different contracts. This may have been the result of a previous business merger for example.

At common law an employment contract like any other contract may be amended only in accordance with its terms or with the agreement of all parties. The law will not allow employers to use their greater bargaining position to impose contractual variations on employees against their will.

5.6.1 Bilateral variations

An express agreement is the most effective way of varying a contract of employment. From a legal and practical perspective, obtaining the agreement of the employee to the change is the simplest option for employers.

The employee's express agreement to a variation of the terms of the contract must be given voluntarily and should be free from duress. A verbal agreement to the change could be sufficient but employers should try to obtain a written confirmation of the agreement. The terms of an employment contract are determined at the start of the employment relationship and strong evidence of mutual agreement will be required to establish that they have been varied. This does not mean, however, that the written evidence will always take precedence over what has been said and done by the parties.

CASE EXAMPLE

Simmonds v Dowty Seals Ltd [1978] IRLR 211

The employee was able to show that the employer had orally agreed to a change from day shift to night shift working, even though the change was not reflected in a change to his written particulars of employment. As a result the employee was successful in his claim for constructive dismissal when new management tried to make the employee revert to the day shift arrangement.

Ultimately express terms in the contract might allow the employer to make significant variations in the terms and the employee would be bound by the changes.

CASE EXAMPLE

Bex v Security Transport Ltd [1972] IRLR 68

A clause in the employer's contract allowed the employer to even change the nature of the work done by the employee. The employer did alter the post held by the employer to different work which the employee considered amounted to an effective demotion. The employee resigned and argued that there was a breach of contract. The court held that the terms of the contract meant that the employer was entitled to make the change.

Clearly the easiest way for the employer to vary the terms of the contract is to include a flexibility clause in the contract. However, because these clauses aim to give the employer wide discretion to change any term of the employment relationship, so as to evade the general rule that changes must be mutually agreed, courts and tribunals will only rarely enforce such clauses which remove rights gained under the contract.

CASE EXAMPLE

Baynham and Others v Phillips Electronics (UK) Ltd [1995] TLR 421

The employer was unable to rely on an express contractual term which entitled it 'to vary the contract from time to time' in order to withdraw healthcare cover from a group of pensioners after they had retired. The High Court held that the clause was only intended to cover matters such as a change in job description and could not extend to accrued rights, including in this case post termination healthcare cover.

Changes in terms of employment which are negotiated by an independent trade union may be effective in amending an employee's contracts of employment. This will generally occur where the contract terms include an express provision giving effect to the results of collective bargaining. Any changes to terms which are agreed through that process may be binding on employees. This may even apply to employees who are not members of the relevant trade union.

CASE EXAMPLE

Parry v Holst [1968] 3 ITR 317 DC

An employee in the construction industry was employed under a contract which was subject to a collective agreement under which the employer had the discretion to move an employee to a different job. The work that the employee was doing in South Wales finished and the employer then wished the employee to move to work in Somerset. The employee refused and tried to claim a redundancy payment. He failed since the collective agreement was incorporated into his contract.

In the absence of an express provision giving effect to the results of collective bargaining, a term to that effect may be implied as a result of a custom or practice of collectively negotiating important changes to individual contracts of employment. Clear evidence is required to establish such a custom, but the standard of proof required is the balance of probabilities (see *Carlton Henry & Others v London General Transport Services Ltd* [2002] EWCA Civ 488 in 5.4.3 above).

5.6.2 Unilateral variations

An employer who imposes a contractual change without the employee's express or implied agreement will be in breach of contract and, as a matter of law, the original terms of the contract will remain in place. If the employee, however, continues working under the new terms, without protesting in any way for a number of weeks, the employer can argue that the employee has implicitly accepted the changes through their actions. This is otherwise known as 'acceptance through practice'. This practice is evidence that the court or tribunal will accept.

Where the employee does not accept the unilateral change, they may respond to the breach in a number of ways. First they could continue to work under protest. So the employee should make it clear that they are not accepting the change. An employee will not lose the opportunity to remain in employment and sue on the employment contract just because the employer's actions in imposing the change amount to a repudiatory breach of contract which would entitle the employee to resign and claim constructive dismissal.

CASE EXAMPLE

Rigby v Ferodo Ltd [1988] ICR 29

The employer cut the employees' wages despite indications from the union on behalf of the employees that the reduction was not agreed. The claimant continued working under protest for well over a year and then claimed the shortfall in his wages for the whole of the period of underpayment. The court held that the employer's liability for the underpayment was not limited to the employee's notice period because, even though the breach was repudiatory, the contract had not been terminated.

The employee could also refuse to work under the new terms which would only be possible where the new terms affect the employee's day-to-day working arrangements such as job duties and working hours. If an employee refuses to accept a change in terms but does not resign as a result, the employer is left with a predicament over what to do with the obstructive employee. The employer may be forced to dismiss the employee.

CASE EXAMPLE

Robinson v Tescom Corporation [2008] IRLR 408

The employer unilaterally imposed new terms and conditions on the employee which would dramatically affect the area he served and therefore his daily travel. The employee took advice from ACAS and wrote to the employer stating that he agreed to the changed work arrangements and would work under the changes but only under protest and that he treated the contract as breached by the employer. In fact he did not work under the change of arrangements and the employer then dismissed him. The dismissal for failing and refusing to abide by the new terms was held to be fair.

5.6.3 Implied variations

A variation can also be implied where it can be inferred from the conduct of the parties.

CASE EXAMPLE

Armstrong Whitworth Rolls v Mustard [1971] 1 All ER 598

After a fellow employee left the claimant was asked to change from eight-hour shifts over five days a week, which was from a national agreement, to twelve-hour shifts over five days a week, which he did. When he was later made redundant the court accepted that his payment should reflect a sixty-hour week. Even though this had not been altered in any written agreement it was evident from the conduct of the parties.

Statute may also result in employers having to make changes to contracts of employment. For instance the National Minimum Wage Act 1998 allows the Secretary of State to pass secondary legislation which changes the National Minimum Wage that workers receive. This change does not need the agreement of either the employer or worker. The Working Time Regulations 1998 also have the same effect of requiring changes to be made to contracts of employment. These changes have had a significant effect on pay rates, annual leave entitlement, rest breaks, working hours and night work.

ACTIVITY

Self-assessment questions

1. Why would an employer wish to vary the terms of the employment contract?
2. What is the basic principle on variation of the terms of the contract of employment?
3. By what methods could an employer vary the terms of the contract which would be accepted as being with the agreement of the employees?
4. Can the terms of the contract be changed as the result of collective agreements between management and trade unions?
5. If an employer unilaterally varies the terms of the contract what is the best course of action for the employee to take?
6. When can a variation of the terms of the contract be legitimately implied?

KEY FACTS

The form of the employment contract	Case/statute
• No particular form is required – the contract can arise from conduct or be implied • Certain things must be in writing or evidenced in writing e.g. apprenticeship deeds, contracts of merchant seamen	*Dacas v Brook Street Bureaux*

The formation of the employment contract	Case/statute
Formalities in the contract	
• there must be an offer of work – which could be dependent on a condition precedent such as a satisfactory medical • if the offer is accepted but then withdrawn before the employee commences work an action for breach of contract is possible • consideration is executory • there must be intention to create legal relations so this may exclude purely voluntary work	*Wishart v National Association of CAB'x Ltd* *Sarker v South Tees Acute Hospitals NHS Trust* *Mellhuish v Redbridge CAB*

Minority and the contract of employment	
• employment contracts involving minors are enforceable if they are substantially for the benefit of the minor • but they are not bound by employment contracts that mainly work to their detriment	*Clements v London and North Western Railway Company* *De Francesco v Barnum*

Illegality and the contract of employment	
• in general employment contracts that are tainted with illegality are unenforceable • so the employee may also lose statutory rights • a contract that is legally formed but then is illegally performed in some manner is not automatically unenforceable • in general a contract to defraud the revenue is illegal and unenforceable • usually it is the employee's knowledge of the illegality that causes them to lose rights • but not if they gain no benefits from the illegality • and an employee may not lose rights if there is no causal connection between the illegality and the claim	*Salvesen v Simons* *Cole v Fred Stacey Ltd* *Coral Leisure Group Ltd v Barnett* *Hyland v JH Barker (North West) Ltd* *Tomlinson v Dick Evans U Drive Ltd* *Hewcastle Catering Ltd v Ahmed and Elkamah* *Hall v Woolston Hall Leisure Centre Ltd*

The statutory statement	Case/statute
• S1 Employment Rights Act requires that a variety of information e.g. commencement date, place of work pay rates, be provided in a written statement of particulars • The section 1 statement is not the contract • It can be evidence of contractual terms • It may be contractual if it is signed by the employer as being so	 *System Floors Ltd v Daniel* *Gascol Conversions Ltd v Mercer* *Robertson v British Gas*

The incorporation of express terms	Case/statute
Express terms are: • specific terms agreed by the parties • everything required to be in the section 1 statement • terms contained in other documents specifically referred to in the section 1 statement Express terms should accurately reflect the agreement to avoid disputes • job adverts that are inconsistent with express terms will not override them • but express oral terms can override an inconsistent statutory statement Courts must decide if the express terms are consistent with the employment relationship • they cannot rewrite the terms • but should ensure that they are exercised reasonably • they should not enforce anything that is too ambiguous	 *Nelson v BBC (No 2)* *Deeley v British Rail Engineering Ltd* *Hawker Siddeley Power Engineering Ltd v Rump* *Cole v Midland Display Ltd* *Redbridge LBC v Fishman* *United Bank Ltd v Akhtar* *Judge v Crown Leisure Ltd*

Collective agreements	Case/statute
Express incorporation	
• the easiest method is a written provision in the contract • the section 1 statement could also be used • must represent the intention of the parties • benefit of express incorporation is that contract need not be renegotiated with employees • procedural terms are not incorporated • where national and local agreements conflict which is incorporated is based on the facts in each case	*Jewell v Neptune Concrete* *Camden Exhibition & Display Ltd v Lynott* *Alexander v Standard Telephones and Cables plc* *N.C.B. v Galley* *Griffiths v Buckinghamshire CC* *Gascol Conversions Ltd v Mercer* *Wilton v Peebles*
Implied incorporation	
• implied incorporation of collective agreements is possible where the practice of negotiation between trade union and employer is long-standing • it can also occur because of custom if the practice is reasonable, certain and notorious	*Carlton Henry v London General Transport Services Ltd*
Collective agreements and non-union members	
• non-members are only bound if the agreement is incorporated in their contracts after negotiation with them • the same principle applies to members of trade unions other than the one the collective agreement has been made with • No-strike clauses must be incorporated to have effect	*Singh v British Steel Corporation* *Miller v Hamworthy Engineering Ltd* *S180 Trade Union & Labour Relations (Consolidation) Act 1992*
Varying or ending collective agreements	
• this cannot generally be done unilaterally by the employer • but it is possible if the contract indicates so	*Robertson v British Gas* *Cadoux v Central Regional Council*
Works rules	*Case/statute*
The nature and effect of works rules	
• contractual terms of employment can only be changed by agreement with employees where works rules can be changed unilaterally • where the works rules are not contractual the employee can make even significant changes • even where this appears to be harsh on the employee • an employee is still bound to follow the works rules in a way that will not harm the employer • works rules can still be contractual • particularly where they are also indicated in the contract • and analysis by the court or tribunal	*Cadoux v Central Regional Council* *Bateman v Asda Stores Ltd* *Dryden v Greater Glasgow Health Board* *Secretary of State for Employment v ASLEF (No 2)* *Briggs v Imperial Chemical Industries Ltd* *Singh v Lyons Maid Ltd* *Keeley v Fosroc Ltd*

The significance of the job description	
• this should be sufficiently precise to identify the details of the work – but should also be flexible to allow for reasonable changes to be made • the job description is not generally contractual – but where changes are made to the work these should be within the scope of the contract	*Land Securities Trillium Ltd v Thornley*

Variation of terms	Case/statute
• A bilateral variation is possible even where the parties have agreed to it orally • Or express terms in the contract might allow for variation • Employers often insert flexibility clauses in contracts • They can also result from collective agreements • Unilateral variations are unlawful so an employee can continue to work stating that this is under protest • But refusing to work may result in dismissal • Variations can be implied from the conduct of both parties	*Simmonds v Dowty Seals Ltd* *Bex v Security Transport Ltd* *Baynham and Others v Phillips Electronics (UK) Ltd* *Parry v Holst* *Rigby v Ferodo Ltd* *Robinson v Tescom Corporation* *Armstrong Whitworth Rolls v Mustard*

SAMPLE ESSAY QUESTION

ESSAY Discuss the significance of the section 1 statement, works rules and the job description to the contract of employment.

Explain what the section 1 statement is

• Explain that it is required by section 1 Employment Rights Act 1996.
• All employers must provide employees whose employment is to continue for more than one month with a written statement of particular terms of their contract.

Explain what should be included in the section 1 statement

• Pay scale, means of calculating pay, and pay period.
• Hours of work.

- Holiday entitlements (including public holidays and holiday pay); provisions for sickness and any sick pay; pension rights and occupational pension schemes.
- Periods of notice on both sides.
- Job title and description.
- Period of employment if temporary.
- Place or places of work.
- Any collective agreements.
- Details of overseas working.
- Possibly reference to discipline and grievance procedures.

Discuss the significance of the section 1 statement to the contract of employment

- It is not contractual.
- But it can be powerful evidence of the terms of the contract.
- It may be contractual if the employee signs to say that it is the contract.
- If the employer fails to provide one or it is deficient then under section 11 Employment Rights Act 1996 the employee can complain to a tribunal.
- The tribunal can declare what the terms of the contract are but not substitute its own.
- Under section 38 ERA 1996 the employee can also receive compensation.

Explain what works rules are

- Works rules are sometimes in handbooks which are sometimes given to employees.
- They should be available to employees.
- Can include procedural rules or how to do the job.
- But might also include references to disciplinary proceedings, health and safety, sickness procedure, holiday entitlement.
- They are generally not contractual.

Discuss the significance of works rules to the contract of employment

- The works rules are generally not contractual.
- So the employer will be able to change them unilaterally without consulting employees.
- This will be the case even if this acts harshly on particular employees.
- But works rules have been enforced against employees.
- And employees should be careful of 'working to rule' since this might breach implied duties.
- Works rules can be contractual where there is some indication of that in the contract.

Explain what the job description would usually include

- It would usually indicate what the job is and the duties that the job involves.
- It is not generally contractual.

Discuss the significance of the job description to the contract of employment

- Needs to be sufficiently precise to identify the details of the work.
- Employer will also want it to be flexible enough to allow for reasonable changes to be made.
- Can provide evidence of the terms of the contract.
- If an employer tries to change the job description should have employee's agreement or the changes should be allowed by the contract.

REACH REASONED CONCLUSIONS

SUMMARY

- An employment contract in general does not need to be in any particular form – in some cases they can be implied – but some do have to be in writing e.g. apprenticeships.
- The usual contractual formalities apply – there must have been an offer of work which was unconditionally accepted by the employee, there must be consideration, the post in return for the wage, and there should be an intention on the part of both employer and employee to create a legally binding relationship.
- Minors are able to enter employment contracts that are substantially to their benefit.
- Illegality misrepresentation and mistake can all vitiate the contract of employment.
- Section 1 Employment Rights Act 1996 requires that within eight weeks of commencing employment an employee must be given a written statement of particulars.
- This is not the contract itself but can be evidence of contractual terms.
- The contract will include express terms which are specific terms agreed by the parties, everything required to be in the section 1 statement and other terms contained in other documents specifically referred to in the section 1 statement.
- It is always best if express terms are in writing.
- In disputes over the express terms courts will interpret them to provide consistency with the employment relationship.
- Some terms result from collective agreements between employers and recognised trade unions where these have actually been incorporated in the contract.
- Employers also have works rules which are only contractual if they are actually incorporated in the contract so the employer can otherwise change these unilaterally.
- The job description while not generally contractual can be good evidence of contractual terms.
- An employer cannot vary the terms of the contract unilaterally so changes in the terms of the contract can only generally be made by agreement with the employees.

Further reading

Emir, Astra, *Selwyn's Law of Employment 17th edition*. Oxford University Press, 2012, Chapter 3.

Pitt, Gwyneth, *Cases and Materials on Employment Law 3rd edition*. Pearson, 2008, Chapter 4, pp. 154–167, p. 172.

Sargeant, Malcolm and Lewis, David, *Employment Law 6th edition*. Pearson, 2012, Chapter 3.5.2.2–3.5.2.3.

6

Garden leave and restraint of trade

AIMS AND OBJECTIVES

After reading this chapter you should be able to:

- Understand the process of garden leave
- Understand the nature of post termination restraint of trade clauses
- Understand the basic principle in relation to restraint of trade
- Understand the limited range of interests that can be protected by restraint of trade clauses in employment contracts
- Understand the tests of reasonableness which may validate restraint of trade clauses
- Understand how such clauses are enforced
- Critically analyse the area
- Apply the law to factual situations and reach conclusions

6.1 Garden leave clauses

One very basic right of employers on giving notice of termination of the employment contract is to insist that the employee works through the notice period. Of course if the employee refuses to work then there are limited remedies since a mandatory injunction would not be available. Courts rarely grant mandatory injunctions because of the difficulty of enforcing them. Mandatory means making somebody doing something and making an employee work would be beyond the ability of the court to enforce. The employee would of course lose rights to pay.

On some occasions, however, the employer, while being prepared to pay the employee, actually wants the employee not to work and this is generally referred to as garden leave. The reasons for this are that the employer wants:

- first for the employee to have no further access to the business; and

- second to prevent the employee from working for a competitor during the notice period – the payment of wages during the garden leave period means that the employer is entitled to extract from the employee an agreement not to work for the competitor, in essence it is consideration in return for the promise of the employee.

So garden leave is in a way connected to post termination restraint of trade clauses.

While there is no obligation on an employer to provide work during the notice period (subject to the exceptions identified later in 7.2.2) garden leave can only be imposed where there is a clause to that effect in the contract.

CASE EXAMPLE

William Hill Organisation Ltd v Tucker [1998] IRLR 313

The employee, a senior member of staff, was required to give six months' notice under his contract. In fact he only gave one month's notice and he wished to join a competitor of the employer. The employer placed him on 'garden leave', with pay but with the instruction not to return to work or to join the competitor during the six months' notice period. The employee refused to abide by the garden leave restrictions and argued that the failure to provide him with work was a breach of contract releasing him from his obligations. The employer sought an injunction to restrain him from working for the competitor. The employer was denied the injunction on three grounds:

- First it was stated that an employee who holds a 'specific and unique post' is entitled to work to carry out his skills.
- Second, and more importantly, there was no express power in the contract permitting garden leave.
- Third the same basic principles apply to garden leave as to restraint of trade clauses (see 6.2.1 below) which must be reasonable in their extent and duration and used only to protect a legitimate business interest.

The terms of the contract reinforced the first point since the employee was required to work the hours necessary to carry out his duties in a full and professional manner.

JUDGMENT

Morritt LJ stated: 'When an employer … whilst continuing to pay remuneration, insist[s] that [the employee] stays away from work for the duration of the notice period … it is not disputed that he may do so if there is an express contractual term to that effect.' On the issue of denying work during the notice period he stated: 'If the employer were to be entitled to keep his employee in idleness, the investment in its staff might be as illusory as the limited power of suspension would be unnecessary.'

It is clear then that, whenever an employer tries to use a garden leave clause, he will also have to justify the clause itself and particularly the length of notice on the basis of the employee's access to confidential information, the connection with customers and the effect that the employee's absence has on the rest of the workforce.

CASE EXAMPLE

Evening Standard Co Ltd v Henderson [1987] ICR 588

The contract of employment provided for twelve months' notice on either side. Besides this, the employee also agreed not to work for any rival newspaper during this period. The employee in fact gave only two months' notice and indicated that he intended to join a rival newspaper for the remainder of his contractual notice period. The employer sought an injunction to restrain him from working for the competitor during that period and succeeded. The employer was prepared to pay him during the notice period in order to protect a legitimate business interest. As a result the garden leave restrictions were reasonable.

It also follows that a garden leave clause will only be enforced by the courts where it would be appropriate having regard to the length of the notice period indicated in the clause, the extent to which it may deprive the employee of the right to exercise necessary skills and of course whether the employer is merely protecting a legitimate business interest.

CASE EXAMPLE

Provident Financial Group plc v Hayward [1989] IRLR 84

A financial director employed by estate agents had a clause in his contract of employment which required that during his employment he would not work for anyone else. The contract also required him to give twelve months' notice of termination of his contract. In fact, in agreement with his employer, he actually gave only six months' notice. He worked for two months but then the employer decided that there was no more work for him and so an agreement for paid garden leave was reached. One month later he announced his intention to work for another estate agent. The employer sought an injunction to prevent him from doing so during the remaining four months of the notice period. The court refused to grant the injunction, first because by this time there was only ten weeks of the six months' notice period left, and second because evidence showed that taking up the new post could not cause any damage to the employer.

One benefit to an employer in using garden leave clauses is that, unlike with restraint of trade clauses, tribunals seem willing to modify clauses that are drafted in terms that are too wide. In *Symbian Ltd v Christiensen* [2001] IRLR 77 CA a clause preventing the employee from taking up any employment during the garden leave was too wide but was modified to apply only to a named competitor, making it reasonable. In *GFI Group Inc v Eaglestone* [1994] IRLR 119 a garden leave period was reduced from twenty weeks to thirteen weeks making it more reasonable.

Garden leave clauses are clearly problematic since they are in essence restraints of trade. They can also be very easily abused, particularly where they involve very long periods of notice as in some of the cases above.

ACTIVITY

Self-assessment questions

1. What is garden leave?
2. What are the major reasons why an employer will try to enforce a period of garden leave?
3. What conditions must apply for a court to allow garden leave?

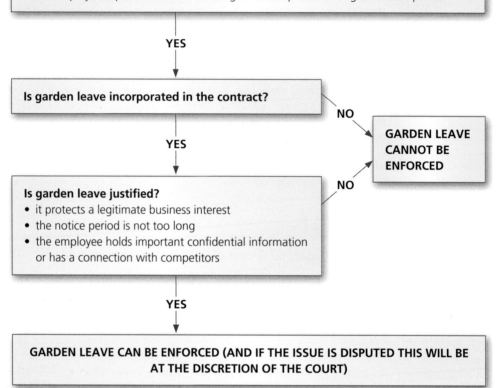

Figure 6.1 Flow chart illustrating the conditions under which garden leave may be granted

KEY FACTS

Garden leave – requirements	Case/statute
• Defined as where the employer wants the employee not to work during the notice period	
• But an employee who holds a 'specific and unique post' may be entitled to work to carry out his skills	*William Hill Organisation v Tucker*
• A common requirement is also for the employee not to work for a competitor during the notice period	*William Hill Organisation v Tucker*
• The requirement of garden leave must be contained in the contract and be justified – length of notice period, employee's access to confidential information, connection with competitors etc.	*Evening Standard Co Ltd v Henderson*
• Enforcement is within the discretion of the court – and must involve protecting a legitimate business interest	*Provident Financial Group plc v Hayward*

6.2 Post termination restraint of trade clauses

6.2.1 The definition and character of restraint of trade clauses

A restraint of trade clause, sometimes referred to in the context of employment as a post termination restrictive covenant, is quite simply a term in a contract under which one party agrees to limit or restrict his ability to carry on his trade, business or profession. In the context of employment contracts such clauses have been characterised as: 'a legal device to attempt to hold the balance between two competing factors, an employee's freedom to take employment as and when he wishes, and an employer's interest in preserving certain aspects of his business from disclosure or exploitation by an employee, or, more usually, an ex-employee'.

In basic contract law restraint of trade clauses also occur in other contexts:

- Vendor restraints – these occur where the purchaser of a business seeks to prevent the seller of the business from unfairly competing after the sale of the business.

- Agreements of mutual recognition between businesses – these are restraints by which parties agree to regulation that restricts their trade but for a mutual benefit.

Judges have always viewed restraint of trade clauses as prima facie void, particularly in employment contracts. There are two principal reasons:

- They are reluctant to endorse an arrangement whereby an employee in effect gives up his right to earn a living, even if only temporarily, as part of a contractual requirement imposed on him by what in any case is the stronger party to the contract, the employer.

- They are just as reluctant to allow the public to be deprived of the employee's skill or expertise (and of course in times of economic depression to allow employees to be prevented from working may add an additional financial burden on the country's resources).

On the other hand judges have also always been eager to protect the idea of freedom of contract and only intervene in a contractual relationship reluctantly (as we have seen in Chapter 1.1.3, 1.4.1 and 1.4.2). The result is that, although restraint of trade clauses are prima facie void, they may be enforced where they can be shown to be reasonable.

JUDGMENT

Lord Macnaghten explained the position in *Nordenfelt v Maxim Nordenfelt* [1894] AC 535 HL: 'The public have an interest in every person's carrying out his trade freely: so has the individual. All interference with individual liberty of action in trading, and all restraints of trade themselves, if there is nothing more, are contrary to public policy and therefore void. That is the general rule. But there are exceptions: restraints of trade and interference with individual liberty of action may be justified by the special circumstances of a particular case. It is a sufficient justification, and indeed it is the only justification, if the restriction is reasonable.'

There are two aspects to what is reasonable:

- The restraint must be reasonable as between the parties, the employer and the employee. This means that the restraint must be no wider than is needed to protect the legitimate interests of the employer. Where the employer is merely using a restraint clause to prevent legitimate competition then the clause is void and will be unenforceable.

JUDGMENT

Lord Parker explained this in *Herbert Morris Ltd v Saxelby* [1916] 1 AC 688 HL: '[for] a restraint to be reasonable in the interests of the parties it must afford no more than adequate protection to the party in whose favour it is imposed.'

- The restraint must also be reasonable in the public interest or at least it must not be harmful to the public interest. Thus a restraint would not be considered reasonable if it deprived the public of a benefit that might otherwise be freely enjoyed or if it unduly restricted choice. There are therefore two key issues in assessing restraint of trade clauses:

- what amounts to the employer's legitimate business interests (because only these can be protected);

- the measures that the courts use to determine whether a restraint is reasonable

6.2.2 Interests that can be protected by the employer

During the course of employment the employer will often seek to protect its legitimate business interests and it will do so through the implied term of faithful service, or fidelity (see Chapter 7.3.4). Restraint of trade on termination involves many of the same interests. What is certainly the case for both is that it is only those legitimate business interests that can be protected by the restraint.

The restraint must be no wider than is necessary to protect the legitimate business interests of the employer.

An employer may only use a restraint clause to protect his legitimate business interests, not to prevent competition. In order to determine what rights may require protection; the employer must look at the nature of its business and the employee's position in that business.

JUDGMENT

In *Herbert Morris Ltd v Saxelby* [1916] 1 AC 688, Lord Parker stated: 'I cannot find any case in which a covenant against competition by a servant or apprentice has as such ever been upheld by the court. Wherever such covenants have been upheld it has been on the grounds, not that the servant or apprentice would, by reason of his employment or training, obtain the skill or knowledge necessary to equip him as a possible competitor in the trade, but that he might obtain such personal knowledge of, and influence over, the customers of his employers, or such an acquaintance with his employer's trade secrets as would enable him, if competition were allowed, to take advantage of his employer's trade connection or utilise information confidentially obtained.'

In *Office Angels Ltd v Rainer-Thomas & O'Connor* the Court of Appeal expanded on this reasoning and highlighted what legitimate proprietary interests may be protected.

CASE EXAMPLE

Office Angels Ltd v Rainer-Thomas & O'Connor [1991] IRLR 214

The ex-employee of an employment agency was subject to two restraints which the employer was seeking to enforce. The one was that for six months after leaving employment the employee would not solicit custom from any person who was a client of the company during his employment. On the facts this was excessively wide. The potential client base during that period was towards 7,000 but the employee had had contact with only about 100 by telephone. The Court of Appeal held that the extent to which an employer can restrain the activities of ex-employees is limited. The general rule is that all contractual restraints on an ex-employee's freedom to work where he pleases, often known as restrictive covenants or post termination covenants, are void as being in restraint of trade and contrary to public policy, unless they can be shown to be reasonable. A restriction may be found to be reasonable and therefore enforceable if it gives adequate, but no more than adequate, protection to the legitimate business interests of the employer. Such interests include some 'advantage or asset' in the employer's business which, in a general sense, can properly be regarded as the employer's property and as justifying protection against employee appropriation.

Legitimate business interests include the employer's customers or client base (trade connections) as well as its confidential information (trade secrets). These interests must be distinguished from general competition, since an employer will never be entitled to protection against competition pure and simple by means of a restrictive covenant.

CASE EXAMPLE

Strange v Mann [1965] 1 All ER 1069

The employee had agreed that on leaving employment he would not engage in 'bookmaking' within twelve miles of his employer's business. In fact he set up his own business within that radius. The restraint clause was, however, held to be unenforceable because betting within the employer's business had been done by telephone and the employer had no real contact with the client base. The purpose of the restraint in this instance then was merely to prevent competition.

Within the two broad headings above, four main legitimate business interests have been considered as protectable by the courts:

- trade secrets
- client connection
- competing
- soliciting other employees away from the employment.

Trade secrets
It is understandable that an employer may wish to protect confidential information that, if revealed to a competitor, might well damage its business interests. This is limited to processes, ingredients or other factors which are specific to the business.

CASE EXAMPLE

Forster & Sons Ltd v Suggett [1918] 35 TLR 87

A clause in the contract of an engineer in the glass industry prevented him from working for any competitor in the United Kingdom for five years and from divulging any part of his employer's manufacturing process on leaving his employment. The court held that the manufacturing process was so specialist, since it was only used by the ex-employer, that it amounted to a trade secret and the glass manufacturer was entitled to the protection of the clause. It was held to be reasonable in the circumstances and was enforceable.

However, a restraint which covers the general knowledge of the particular trade or industry or general organisation will usually not be enforceable. To enforce such restraints would usually only have the effect of preventing the employee from working.

CASE EXAMPLE

Herbert Morris Ltd v Saxelby [1916] 1 AC 688

The employee was prevented in a clause in his contract from involvement with the sale or manufacture of pulley blocks, overhead runways or overhead travelling cranes for a period of seven years after leaving his employment. The restraint clause covered the whole range of the employer's business and also all of the employee's potential expertise. This was held to be too wide because it would have had the effect of preventing the ex-employee from taking any employment opportunities that related to his skills and experience.

Inevitably an employee will gain knowledge of the employer's business as part of his employment. An employer will find it difficult to prevent an employee from using all of the knowledge gained by the employee. The courts have provided guidance on what amounts to trade secrets which can be protected and knowledge which cannot.

CASE EXAMPLE

Commercial Plastics Ltd v Vincent [1965] 1 QB 623, [1964] 3 All ER 546

The employee was restrained by a clause in his contract from working for any competitor in the field of PVC calendar sheeting for one year after leaving his employment. In fact he had only been employed in the making of calendar sheeting for adhesive tape, a small part of the calendar sheeting industry. As such the court held that the restraint was too wide in that it was not protecting a legitimate business interest and it was unenforceable. The Court of Appeal classified the knowledge or information gained by an employee at work into different types:

- skill, aptitude and general technical knowledge with regard to the production of the commodity;
- the business organisation and methods;
- secret specifications, confidential test reports and other confidential documents; and
- confidential information not recorded in documents which gives the possessor a competitive advantage.

The court concluded that the first two of these are essentials to an employee to be able to work and therefore he cannot be restrained from using this information. The third, it considered, would in any case be protected by copyright laws, etc. The court felt that it was only the fourth that could legitimately be protected by the use of a restraint of trade clause, and only then if it was found to be reasonable.

The restraint must be against activities only, which would protect the employer's legitimate interests. Any attempt to widen the clause to activities not relevant to the employee's actual work will be void.

CASE EXAMPLE

(JA) Mont (UK) Ltd v Mills [1993] IRLR 172 (CA)

This restraint clause was against a forty-three year old managing director in the paper tissue industry and was contained in a severance agreement. The clause restrained him from working for any company in the paper industry for twelve months after leaving his employment. The court decided that it was too wide. Rather than protecting the employer's legitimate interests it in effect prevented him from working in the paper industry at all which was the only industry he knew. All that the clause needed to do was to prevent him from revealing confidential information.

What amounts to a trade secret depends on the facts of each case. In general it covers information which is confidential to the employer. Information which is publicly available and general organisational methods cannot be protected. However, in *SBJ Stephenson Ltd v Mandy* [2000] IRLR 233 the identity of customers, prices, market information and other organisational information protected from disclosure by a restraint clause was accepted as protectable.

Client connection

In general, the rule is that an employer is able to protect both his trade secrets and his client contact. The client connection is the so-called 'goodwill' of the business and if an employer has built up a relationship with clients it is possible that he could damage the goodwill by luring clients away. A clause that prevents the employee from soliciting those clients will be upheld provided that it is not too wide.

CASE EXAMPLE

Hanover Insurance Brokers Ltd and Christchurch Insurance Brokers Ltd v Schapiro [1994] IRLR 82

Certain insurance brokerages including Hanover Insurance Brokers (HIB) were sold to another company, Christchurch. Following the sale three directors of HIB left, started their own business and were then accused of soliciting clients from their former employer. A clause in their contract prohibited them from soliciting clients of Hanover Associates (of which HIB was a subsidiary) and all its other subsidiaries. The ex-directors argued that the clause was too wide and should be declared void since they had only worked for HIB. The court accepted this, but held also that since the purpose of the restraint was to prevent soliciting of insurance clients, and only HIB engaged in this activity, then the clause could be upheld against them in respect of the clients of HIB.

On this basis a clause restraining ex-employees from soliciting clients of the employer is more likely to be enforced if it is limited to those employees that the ex-employee had contact with.

CASE EXAMPLE

Home Counties Dairies Limited v Skilton [1970] 1 All ER 1227

A milk roundsman's contract of employment included two restraints. One prevented him from entering any employment connected with the dairy business. This was clearly too wide as it would effectively prevent him from working in a wide range of jobs. The second clause prohibited him from working as a roundsman on his former area or serving any existing customer for a period of one year after leaving his employment. The second clause was enforceable since it only protected a legitimate business interest and it was for only a short period of time.

A restraint clause may be declared void because in any case the effect is to prevent the employee from future employment rather than merely protecting a legitimate interest.

CASE EXAMPLE

M & S Draper v Reynolds [1957] 1 WLR 9

A salesman was restrained by a clause in his contract of employment from soliciting all clients of the firm on leaving the employment for a period of five years. The restraint covered a great many clients that the employee had actually brought with him on entering the employment and was declared void on this basis. The court accepted that the salesman's own client contact could also in effect be the tools of his trade and to allow the restraint would seriously damage his prospects of further work.

It might also be the case that there is no unfair competition if the employee is not known to the client contact that he later solicits. In this case the clause will be void.

CASE EXAMPLE

Austin Knight v Hinds [1994] FLR 2

The court accepted evidence to show that the employee who was the subject of the restraint could have had contact with no more than one-third of the employer's client base despite the fact that the restraint was general and prevented the soliciting of any clients of the business. The restraint clause was declared void. It was not in effect protecting a legitimate interest but was merely preventing legitimate competition on the employee leaving.

The Court of Appeal in *Marley Tile Company Limited v Johnson* [1982] IRLR 75 stated that where the employee cannot reasonably be expected to come into contact with all the employer's customers during his employment, a restrictive covenant which protects the whole of the employer's customer base will be unreasonably wide.

However, where it is clear that the employee may have gained an unfair advantage from his position in employment then the clause may well be reasonable and therefore valid.

CASE EXAMPLE

G W Plowman & Son Ltd v Ash [1964] 2 All ER 10

A sales representative was restrained by a clause in his contract from soliciting work from any farmer or market gardener for a period of two years after terminating his employment. The clause was upheld as reasonable and therefore valid in the case because evidence showed that he had had the opportunity to solicit these clients of the business during his employment with them.

Working for competitors

Generally courts will not grant injunctions that in effect compel an employee to remain in his existing employment as this amounts to compulsory labour and restricts freedom of contract.

A restraint clause which prohibits an employee from carrying on or being employed in a particular business will therefore be difficult to justify. The employer must therefore be able to show that some lesser form of protection would not have been adequate.

CASE EXAMPLE

Littlewoods Organisation Ltd v Harris [1978] 1 All ER 1026

The employee worked in a senior position for a catalogue mail order business. His contract of employment included a restraint clause that prevented him from working for his employer's main competitor, Great Universal Stores, anywhere in the world for twelve months after leaving. He then left the company with the intention of taking up a position with the competitor and his employer sought to enforce the restraint clause. The Court of Appeal was prepared to enforce the clause even though it was drafted very widely because of the confidential information he possessed about the mail order side of the business. The court construed the clause only to the extent that it protected the mail order part of the business.

As with other protectable interests, the clause must be no wider than is necessary to protect the legitimate business interest. If it exceeds this and is too wide then it is merely preventing the ex-employee from working and will be void. We have already seen this in *Commercial Plastics Ltd v Vincent* [1965] 1 QB 623, [1964] 3 All ER 546 under trade secrets. Here the court would not enforce the restraint that applied to the calendar sheeting industry generally when the employee had only been involved in adhesive tape production. To have done so would merely have prevented the ex-employee from working in the field in which his competence and experience lay.

Soliciting other employees away from the business

Other employees in the employer's business are an important part of its continued stability. Inevitably employers may therefore include clauses in contracts seeking to prevent a former employee from soliciting other employees. This may merely be seen as protecting a legitimate business interest in the stability of the workforce. In *Ingham v ABC Contract Services Ltd* (unreported) 12 November 1993, the Court of Appeal held that the employer 'had a legitimate interest in maintaining a stable trained workforce in what is acknowledged to be a highly competitive business'.

This was later confirmed by the Court of Appeal in *Dawnay, Day & Co Ltd v de Braconier d'Alphen* [1997] IRLR 442 where the court upheld a covenant in the defendants' service agreements which prevented them from soliciting or enticing away any director or senior employee for a year after the termination of their employment.

JUDGMENT

The Court said: 'an employer's interest in maintaining a stable, trained workforce is one which he can properly protect within the limits of reasonableness. . . . The employer's need for protection arises because the ex-employee may seek to exploit the knowledge which he has gained of their particular qualifications, rates of remuneration and so on.'

However, restraints that seek to prevent ex-employees from enticing other employees to leave will generally be held to be void.

CASE EXAMPLE

Hanover Insurance Brokers Ltd and Christchurch Insurance Brokers Ltd v Schapiro [1994] IRLR 82

As well as the restraints on client contact we have seen above the contract also contained a clause that the employee would not 'solicit or entice any employees of the company' for twelve months after leaving the employment. This restraint was not enforced by the courts on the basis that a person must have the freedom to work for whoever they choose. The restraint applied to all employees irrespective of their role or status in the company. However, the position may be different if the restraint was applied only in respect of senior employees.

Again the point is that the restraint must do no more than is necessary to protect a legitimate business interest. Any clause that goes beyond that will be considered unreasonable and unenforceable.

CASE EXAMPLE

TSC (Europe) Ltd v Massey [1999] IRLR 22

A clause in an ex-employee's contract restrained him from inducing any employee to leave the company. The clause was not enforceable because first it applied to all employees not just those with particular status or particular skills within the business, and second it included employees who had joined after the employee left.

One further limitation is that employees will not be able to engineer what amounts to a restraint by an agreement between them not to appoint employees currently working for the other.

CASE EXAMPLE

Kores Manufacturing Co v Kolok Manufacturing Co [1959] Ch 108

Two companies agreed that neither of them would hire employees of the other firm for a period of five years after the employee leaving. It was obvious that the agreement would have exactly the same effect as a restraint clause would have. As a result the agreement was held to be void and unenforceable.

6.2.3 The possible scope of post termination restraints

While an employer is only able to protect a legitimate business interest as we have seen in 6.2.2, it is also the case that such interests even then are only protectable if the restraint clauses in which they are contained are held to be reasonable. The courts have developed means of establishing whether clauses are reasonable. There are four main contexts for establishing reasonableness:

- the geographical area covered by the restraint;
- the duration for which the restraint will last;
- the nature of the business or the work;
- the status of the employee.

The geographical area covered by the restraint

The area that the employer wishes to protect is critical in considering the reasonableness of any clause. Often the geographical area will serve no purpose other than to restrict competition and in some cases the area of the clause bears no resemblance to the nature of the employer's business.

CASE EXAMPLE

Office Angels v Rainer-Thomas and O'Connor [1991] IRLR 214

Here the restraint attempted to stop the defendants, who worked in the Bow Lane London Office, from working within 3,000 metres of their office and from opening an office within 1.2 square miles of their former office. This included most of the City of London. The Court of Appeal would not enforce the covenant on this basis because it was considered too wide. Besides this the extent of the area covered was not necessary. Much of the work that the employee had performed was conducted by telephone and therefore the site of the office that they worked in was completely irrelevant.

In contrast, quite a broad radius for a restraint to operate, even as much as ten miles has been held by the Court of Appeal to be reasonable, taking into account all of the circumstances in which the restraint operates.

CASE EXAMPLE

Hollis & Co v Stocks [2000] IRLR 712

The employee worked as an assistant solicitor for a firm based in Nottinghamshire. A restraint clause in his contract prohibited him from working within a ten-mile radius of the office from which he worked for twelve months after leaving his employment and from advising clients in nearby police stations and magistrate courts. The clause was held to be a reasonable restriction for an assistant solicitor, because there were several large urban centres where the employee could have worked which were close to but outside the area covered by the restraint.

Again whether the geographical extent covered by the restraint is considered to be reasonable will depend on the circumstances of the case and the extent to which the employer is protecting a legitimate business interest or on the contrary is merely preventing the ex-employee from working, possibly in competition.

CASE EXAMPLE

Spencer v Marchington [1988] IRLR 392

Marchington owned two employment agencies, one in Banbury and one in Leamington Spa, of which Mrs Spencer had been the manager. Her contract of employment contained a clause which restricted her, for two years after employment ended, from being 'engaged or concerned or interested in the business of any employment agency within a radius of twenty-five miles of the office address, Banbury, Oxfordshire, and within ten miles of 47th Parade, Leamington Spa'. The High Court considered that the area covered by the clause was too wide as all Mrs Spencer's existing customers lived within twenty miles. Besides this, prospective customers outside the twenty-five-mile radius who would normally look to Oxford or Northampton to find an employment agency, would be deprived of the possibility of going to an agency there with which Mrs Spencer was concerned.

Often duration and area will be considered together. The geographical area must still not be wider than necessary to protect the legitimate interest of the employer, otherwise the restraint clause will not be enforced.

CASE EXAMPLE

Fitch v Dewes [1921] 2 AC 158

A solicitor's clerk had a restraint clause in his contract that prevented him from operating in the same capacity within a seven-mile radius of Tamworth town hall for life. The restraint was nevertheless upheld as reasonable by the court. At the time Tamworth was quite a small rural community and there would only be a restricted amount of work for an individual solicitor's practice within the town. In any case the clerk was well acquainted with the employer's client contact and therefore could have been in a position to damage its business. Besides this, Tamworth was within easy travelling distance of Birmingham where there would have been many opportunities in the same field.

By contrast where the local population is much larger the geographical extent of the restraint clause may have to be much narrower to be reasonable or the clause may well be considered void and unenforceable.

CASE EXAMPLE

Fellowes v Fisher [1976] QB 122

This case involved a similar restraint that had been incorporated into the contract of a conveyancing clerk and which prevented him from taking up similar employment in the Walthamstow area of London. This was held to be unreasonable by Lord Denning since the clerk was relatively unknown and the area was quite densely populated by contrast. There were also personal circumstances which necessitated the employee taking up employment in the area.

In general though where the clause applies to a locality rather than a broad area it is more likely to be enforced.

CASE EXAMPLE

Greer v Sketchley Ltd [1979] IRLR 445

At the time of the case the company only operated in the London area and the Midlands. However, the restraint clause prevented the employee from working in a similar business anywhere in the United Kingdom. As such the clause was too wide to be protecting a legitimate business interest and was unenforceable.

It is clearly also possible that, while a court might find aspects of the restraint clause such as geographical extent and duration to be reasonable, that other aspects of the clause mean that it is unreasonable and cannot be enforced.

CASE EXAMPLE

Allan Jones LLP v Johal [2006] IRLR 599

This again involved a person employed as an assistant solicitor. The restraint clause in her contract prevented her from practising as a solicitor for twelve months after leaving employment within a six-mile radius of the office where she had worked. Another clause prevented her from dealing with clients of her employers for one year. When she left and went into partnership with another solicitor one-and-a-half miles away from her ex-employer and solicited former clients for business the court held that the first clause was mainly to prevent her from competing and was invalid. However, the clause preventing her from soliciting clients was enforceable.

The duration of the restraint

The duration of the restraint must be no longer than is actually necessary to protect the legitimate interest of the employer. A longer period than is necessary means that the clause will be considered void and unenforceable. Inevitably there is an element of subjectivity in determining what is a reasonable length of time and by contrast what is unreasonable.

CASE EXAMPLE

Fitch v Dewes [1921] 2 AC 158

The restraint on the conveyancing clerk that we have seen above was actually for an unlimited duration. Nevertheless the restraint was still upheld as reasonable because of the rural nature of the community and the inevitable significance of the clerk's contact with the solicitor's client base.

Although the scope of the clause content may be reasonable it may be that the duration of the clause may not. Although there is an element of interplay between the two, if the employer wants a restraint to cover a wide geographical area it may need to limit the duration and vice versa. A comparison here can be drawn between *Herbert Morris Ltd v Saxelby* [1916] 1 AC 688 where a seven-year restraint was considered void and *Nordenfelt v Maxim Nordenfelt Guns and Ammunition Co Ltd* [1894] AC 535. In this case, Thorsten Nordenfelt, a manufacturer specialising in armaments, had sold his business to Hiram Stevens Maxim. They had agreed that Nordenfelt 'would not make guns or ammunition anywhere in the world, and would not compete with Maxim in any way for a period of twenty five years'. The House of Lords held that the duration of the clause was reasonable having regard to Nordenfelt's worldwide business and the value that had been paid to him. The latter case is a vendor rather than an employee restraint but the principle applies.

Generally then shorter periods are preferred by the courts. In fact in modern times it would be rare for a restraint to be for more than six months. Clearly this is because shorter periods have less chance of interfering with an employee's livelihood and merely preventing him from working.

CASE EXAMPLE

Home Counties Dairies Ltd v Skilton [1970] 1 WLR 526

The milk roundsman, as we have seen above under client connection, had an employment contract containing two restraints. The first prevented him from entering any employment connected with the dairy business which was inevitably void and unenforceable. The second provided only that he should not work as a roundsman or serve any existing customer for a period of one year after leaving the employment. This latter clause was successful since it only protected legitimate interests and it was for only what the court considered to be a reasonable period of time in the circumstances.

Whether or not the work is specialised

In cases where the work or indeed the business of the employer is highly specialised the restraint is more likely to be seen as reasonable. Where the employee's work is commonplace then the restraint is unlikely to be seen as reasonable.

CASE EXAMPLE

Forster v Suggett [1918] 35 TLR 87

A glass manufacturer included in the contracts of employees a clause that prevented them from working for any competitor on leaving their employment with him. The court held that the skill was so specialist at the time of the case that it amounted to a trade secret and the glass manufacturers were entitled to the protection of the clause. It was reasonable in the circumstances and the restraint was enforceable.

The position held by the employee in the employer's business
The higher the position held by the employee and the more important he is to the business then the more likely it is that inclusion of the restraint will be held to be reasonable in the circumstances.

CASE EXAMPLE

Herbert Morris Ltd v Saxelby [1916] 1 AC 688 HL

The restraint clause in the employee's contract prevented him on terminating his employment from involvement with the sale or manufacture of pulley blocks, overhead runways or overhead travelling cranes for a period of seven years after leaving. In short this covered both the whole range of the employer's business and indeed the employee's potential expertise. As such it was held to be too wide to succeed despite the key position held by the employee and despite the experience that he had gained from the employment. It would have had the effect of depriving him of any employment opportunities.

6.2.4 Interpreting post termination restraints
The clear message for an employer or his legal advisers is not to draft restraint clauses too widely or to attempt to cover every possibility. A restraint that is drafted excessively broadly in the context of the interest that is being protected will be declared void and unenforceable.

CASE EXAMPLE

Home Counties Dairies Ltd v Skilton [1970] 1 WLR 526

Here one clause in the milk roundsman's employment contract restricted him from any employment at all connected with the dairy business. This clause was clearly far too wide to be reasonable. The potential areas of employment within the dairy industry were vast and the clause would have prevented the employee from taking up a wide range of employment well beyond the work that he had actually done for the employer and with no chance of damaging his employer's interests. Such a clause could not be enforced.

Reasonableness and public policy
As well as having a legitimate proprietary interest, the protection sought must not be more than is reasonable having regard to the interests of the parties and the public interest.

In *Herbert Morris Ltd v Saxelby* [1916] 1 AC 688 Saxelby was an engineer and had a restraint of trade clause in his contract that restricted him from engaging anywhere in the UK in any business which carried on similar work to that of his former employer for seven years. The then House of Lords held that the clause was unreasonable and therefore void because:

- the content of the clause was too wide and would prevent him from doing any kind of work;
- the duration of the clause was too long in time;
- the area covered by the clause was too wide geographically.

Thus to decide whether a clause is reasonable the judge must consider the content, the duration and the area covered by the clause.

The restrictive covenant clause, in addition to being reasonable, must also be in the interests of the public. This has been something that has not generally been considered in employment restrictive covenants. However, in *Esso Petroleum Co Ltd v Harper's Garage (Stourport) Ltd* [1968] AC 269 the then House of Lords stated that some of the cases regarding employment restrictive covenant clauses should have been decided on the basis of public policy.

In *Bull v Pitney-Bowes Ltd* [1967] 1 WLR 273 the employee's contract of employment contained the rules of the pension scheme. It gave the employer the right to cancel rights and benefits if the employee competed with the employer after termination of employment. The court considered this to be unenforceable and therefore void as it was against public policy to allow an employee to be threatened by the employer in this way.

Content

The content of the clause is also important. The protection sought must be no more than is reasonable to protect the employer's legitimate proprietary interest. If the employer tries to draft the restraint too wide it will become void and therefore unenforceable.

CASE EXAMPLE

Attwood v Lamont [1920] 2 KB 146

The employer was carrying on a business as a draper, tailor and general outfitter at Kidderminster. A restraint of trade clause written into the employee's contract of employment, stated that he would not, at any time thereafter 'either on his own account or on that of any wife of his or in partnership with or as assistant, servant or agent to any other person, persons or company carry on or be in any way directly or indirectly concerned in any of the following grades or businesses, that is to say, the trade or business of a tailor, dressmaker, general draper, milliner, hatter, haberdasher, gentlemen's, ladies' or children's outfitter at any place within a radius of ten miles of Kidderminster'. The defendant, however, subsequently set up business as a tailor at Worcester, outside the ten miles limit, but obtained and executed tailoring orders in Kidderminster. When the employer brought an action, the defendant argued that the agreement was illegal and could not be enforced. It was held that the content of the clause was too wide.

A further example can be seen in *Fellowes v Fisher* [1976] QB 122. Here the conveyancing clerk was restrained from working in the legal (or associated) profession, anywhere within the postal district for five years, and from working with clients he had met whilst working there. This was considered void. Although the clause covered a small geographical area and had a short duration, the content of the clause was too wide. It prevented the employee not just from working as a conveyancing clerk but also the entire legal and associated professions.

Achieving restraint through other means

It is not uncommon for employers to seek other means of restraining their employees. It will also then generally be classed as unreasonable where the employer does not actually insert a restraint clause into the contract of employment but attempts to achieve the same restraint but through other means.

One possibility is garden leave which has been discussed in 6.1.

One way that has been tried is to use other different parts of the contract with the purpose of achieving the same end.

CASE EXAMPLE

Bull v Pitney Bowes [1966] 1 WLR 273

There was no restraint clause in the contract of employment. However, there was a clause whereby an employee would forfeit pension rights in the event of taking up work with a competitor of the employer. The court held that to all intents and purposes the provision was a part of the contract having the same purpose as a restraint. It was held to be void for public policy.

Other employers have attempted to achieve the same purpose as a restraint by agreements among themselves not to employ ex-employees. Because such agreements amount to a disguised restraint they will still be declared void as unreasonable restraints.

CASE EXAMPLE

Kores Manufacturing Co v Kolok Manufacturing Co [1959] Ch 108

Two electronics companies reached an agreement that neither of them would hire employees of the other firm for a period of five years after their leaving. The court held that his had exactly the same effect as a restraint clause and the agreement was held to be void and unenforceable.

A further possibility is that the rules of associations are used to achieve the same purpose as a restraint. Again this is seen as quite similar to an agreement between employers and such agreements may be unenforceable against the ex-employee.

CASE EXAMPLE

Eastham v Newcastle United FC Ltd [1964] Ch 413

Here George Eastham, a well-known footballer of the time, challenged the rules of the Football Association on the legitimacy of the transfer system as it then existed. The FA rules meant that a club could retain a player's registration even after his contract had ended and so effectively the rules could be used to prevent him from playing again. Besides this at the time players could be placed on the transfer list against their will. The court determined that these rules did amount to an unlawful restraint of trade and were unenforceable. (Of course subsequently the whole area of the transfer market has become subject to control under Art 45 TFEU following the Bosman ruling.)

6.2.5 Enforcement and remedies

Severance

The courts will not re-write a covenant to make it enforceable if it is too broad. Neither will a court construe a wide (and void) restriction as having implied (and valid) limitations; to do so would mean that employers would have no incentive to pay attention to the accurate drafting of restrictive covenants. This was clearly explained in *J A Mont (UK) Ltd v Mills* [1993] IRLR 172. This is, however, a potentially harsh and damaging situation for the employer. If the employer fails to protect his legitimate proprietary interest he may suffer a significant detriment.

The court will therefore seek to interpret a covenant in a way that gives effect to the intention of the parties. For example, a court will treat separate promises as severable, so if a clause contains what, in the court's view, are two separate promises, only one of which is unenforceable, it will uphold the enforceable promise and strike out the other. This was stated in *Mason v Provident Clothing and Supply Co Ltd* [1913] AC 724. This is what is commonly known as the 'blue-pencil' test, a blue line is drawn through the severable unenforceable part of the restrictive covenant.

In *Sadler v Imperial Life Assurance Company of Canada Ltd* [1988] IRLR 388 three conditions that were necessary for the 'blue-pencil' test to be used were laid down:

- the unenforceable part of the clause can be removed without needing to add or change the remaining part;
- the remaining terms and conditions continue to make sense; and
- the removal of the words does not change what the clause set out to do.

The blue-pencilling test has been affirmed by the Court of Appeal in *Beckett Investment Management Group Limited v Hall* [2007] EWCA Civ 613 which held that the threefold test identified in *Sadler* should be adopted in approaching questions of severability.

If there are some aspects of the clause that are too wide but some that are not and which do protect legitimate business interests then it may be possible for the offending parts to be removed and the remaining parts to stand and be enforced.

CASE EXAMPLE

Lucas v Mitchell [1974] Ch 129

A sales representative agreed that on leaving his employment he first would not deal in any similar goods and second would not solicit orders from his employer's customers both for a set period. The first was clearly too broad because it merely prevented competition. The second, however, could protect a legitimate business interest and be enforced so blue-pencilling was used to sever the first and save the second.

In any case the test actually only reflects judicial traditional judicial attitudes.

CASE EXAMPLE

Attwood v Lamont [1920] 2 KB 146

Where the restraint included a lengthy list covering the whole of the employer's business there was no way that the list could be reduced without altering the meaning. As a result it was void and unenforceable.

Remedies

An employer seeking to enforce restrictive covenants may take steps to obtain an interim injunction. If the clause is enforceable then this is the common method of obtaining a remedy.

The test for whether an injunction will be granted is that in *American Cyanamid v Ethicon* [1975] 1 All ER 504 often referred to as the balance of convenience test:

- Is there a serious issue to be tried?
- Would damages be an appropriate remedy?
- What is the likelihood of the claimant succeeding at trial?

CASE EXAMPLE

Lansing Linds Ltd v Kerr [1991] IRLR 80

The Court of Appeal refused an injunction concerning a restraint against working for a competitor for twelve months since by the time of trial the period had mostly expired.

It also has to be remembered that an injunction is a discretionary remedy subject to the maxims of equity. As a result it will only be granted where it is both appropriate and necessary.

CASE EXAMPLE

GFI Group Inc v Eaglestone [1994] IRLR 119

The employee in this case was bound to give twenty weeks' notice of leaving. He left his employment in breach of this agreement and set up with a competitor with two colleagues who were only required to give four weeks' notice. The court would not enforce the clause on notice because it would achieve nothing. The damage had already been done with those employees who could leave after four weeks and equity will do nothing in vain.

Besides this it must be remembered that an injunction to enforce a contract of employment will generally not be given.

CASE EXAMPLE

Lumley v Wagner [1852] 42 ER 687

An opera singer, Joanna Wagner, had entered into a contract that contained an express stipulation that during the three months for which she was contracted she would not take up work with any other theatre. When she did enter another contract that would run simultaneously with her contract with Wagner she was successfully restrained from doing so by grant of the injunction. Bearing in mind the brief duration of the contract it in no way interfered with her general ability to earn a living and was reasonable and enforceable in all the circumstances. However, granting of such mandatory injunctions is rare.

Alternatively, or if it is not successful in obtaining an injunction, the employer may also seek damages from the employee for breach of the covenants. In deciding whether to award damages the court will consider:

- whether the covenant was enforceable;
- if so, whether the employee had breached the covenant;

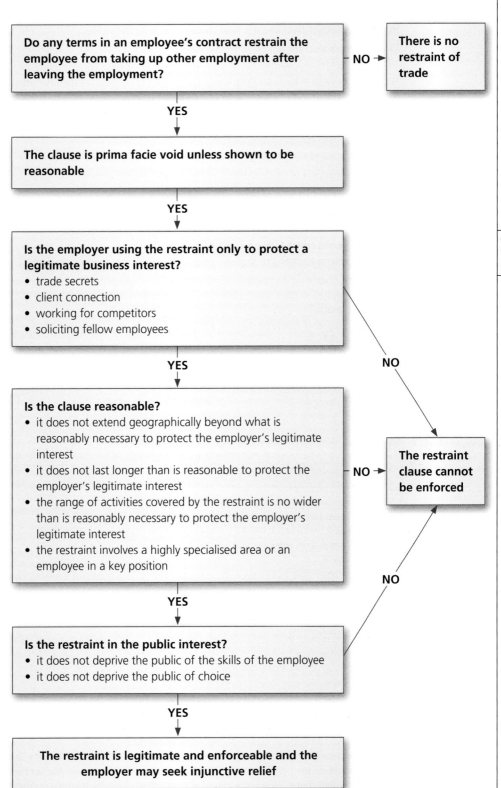

Figure 6.2 Flow chart illustrating how a court determines the legitimacy of a restraint of trade clause in a contract of employment where the employee fails to abide by the restraint

■ if so, whether that breach had caused the employer loss;

■ if so, how that loss should be assessed.

A further way in which an employer can protect his own legitimate proprietary interests is to incorporate into the employee's contract of employment a garden leave clause (discussed in 6.1).

ACTIVITY

Self-assessment questions

1. What is a restraint of trade clause?
2. Why are restraint clauses generally considered to be prima facie void?
3. When will a restraint clause be enforced?
4. What are the interests that an employer is able to protect through a restraint of trade clause?
5. What factors does a court take into account in assessing whether or not a restraint clause is reasonable?
6. Why was the restraint clause not enforced in *Office Angels Ltd v Rainer-Thomas & O'Connor*?
7. How does 'blue-pencilling' work?
8. What are the remedies available to an employer who succeeds in enforcing a restraint of trade clause against an ex-employee?

KEY FACTS

The definition of restraint of trade clauses	Case/statute
• Defined as a contractual device limiting ex-employees to protect an employer's business interests • Prevent a person from earning a living so are prima facie void • Unless reasonable as between the parties and in the public interest	 *Nordenfelt v Maxim Nordenfelt*

The protectable interests	Case/statute
• Can only protect legitimate business interests • Some 'advantage or asset' in the employer's business which, in a general sense, can properly be regarded as the employer's property and as justifying protection against employee appropriation. Includes: • Trade secrets – which if revealed to a competitor, might well damage its business interests – but does not include general knowledge of the trade – a test can be found in • Client connection – where the clause is not drafted too widely – so more likely to succeed if only applies to clients ex-employee had actual contact with	*Herbert Morris Ltd v Saxelby* *Office Angels Ltd v Rainer-Thomas & O'Connor* *Forster & Sons Ltd v Suggett* *Herbert Morris Ltd v Saxelby* *Commercial Plastics Ltd v Vincent* *Hanover Insurance Brokers Ltd and Christchurch Insurance Brokers Ltd v Schapiro* *Home Counties Dairies Limited v Skilton*

• Working for competitors – which will be hard to justify if it merely prevents the ex-employee from working in the trade	*Littlewoods Organisation Ltd v Harris*
• Soliciting other employees away from the business – generally be held to be void – may be different if the restraint was applied only in respect of senior employees	*Hanover Insurance Brokers Ltd and Christchurch Insurance Brokers Ltd v Schapiro*

Factors indicating reasonableness	Case/statute
• Geographical area covered by the restraint – will depend on the circumstances of the case and the extent to which the employer is protecting a legitimate business interest or merely preventing the ex-employee from working – but must not be out of proportion with the ex-employee's actual employment	Contrast *Fitch v Dewes* with *Fellowes v Fisher* *Office Angels Ltd v Rainer-Thomas & O'Connor*
• Duration of the restraint – generally shorter periods are preferred by the courts, e.g. six months – but even unlimited duration is possible if necessary to protect the employer's business	*Home Counties Dairies Limited v Skilton* *Fitch v Dewes*
• Whether the work is specialised – the more specialised the more reasonable the restraint	*Forster & Sons Ltd v Suggett*
• The status of the employee – the higher the position the more likely the restraint is reasonable	*Herbert Morris Ltd v Saxelby*

Construing restraint of trade clauses	Case/statute
• A restraint that is drafted too broadly in the context of the interest that is being protected is void	*Home Counties Dairies Limited v Skilton*
• Some disputes over restraint clauses will be decided by public policy – what is in the public interest	*Esso Petroleum Co Ltd v Harper's Garage (Stourport) Ltd*
• The protection sought must be no more than is reasonable to protect the employer's legitimate proprietary interest	*Attwood v Lamont*
• Other parts of the contract cannot be used to achieve a restraint of trade	*Bull v Pitney Bowes*
• Nor different types of agreement between different employers	*Kores Manufacturing Co v Kolok Manufacturing Co*
• Nor rules of associations of employers	*Eastham v Newcastle United FC Ltd*

Remedies	Case/statute
• Courts will not re-write a covenant to make it enforceable if it is too broad – but may sever (blue-pencil) if possible	Compare *Attwood v Lamont* with *Lucas v Mitchell*
• Blue-pencilling is only possible if the unenforceable part of the clause can be removed without needing to add or change the remaining part, the remaining terms and conditions continue to make sense, and the removal of the words does not change what the clause set out to do	*Beckett Investment Management Group Limited v Hall*
• An injunction will only be granted where it is both appropriate and necessary	*GFI Group Inc v Eaglestone*
• And an injunction to enforce a contract of employment will generally not be given	*Lumley v Wagner*

SAMPLE ESSAY QUESTION

ESSAY Discuss the extent to which the rules on restraint of trade are a real attempt to balance an employee's freedom to take employment as and when she or he wishes, and an employer's right to protect his legitimate business interests.

Explain the basic rule on restraint of trade

- Offends public policy.
- So *prima facie* void.
- Unless reasonable – as between both parties – and in the public interest.
- And can only protect a legitimate business interest.

Explain what is considered a legitimate business interest

- Trade secrets.
- Client connection.
- Non-competition.
- Not soliciting existing employees.

Discuss whether this balances the employee's freedom and the employer's rights

- Trade secrets limited to unique information which can only be gained in the employment – so cannot protect general knowledge in the trade – seems to be fair to both sides.
- The employee must have had actual contact with clients, not just clients of the business generally – so again seems fair.
- Generally an employer is prevented from stopping an ex-employee from working for a competitor unless it involves a key employee – so probably favours the employee.
- Generally there is nothing to stop other employees leaving – so difficult to prevent them from being lured away unless they are key employees – again may be damaging to the employer.

Explain how reasonableness is measured

- Geographical extent.
- Duration.
- Nature of business.
- Status of employee.

Discuss whether the tests create a balance

- Geographical extent could be whole of UK but normally restricted to area covered by business or even the specific business interest – so probably fair to both sides.
- Courts usually restrict duration to six months sometimes longer – could still be adverse to employee but generally protects employer – but again depends on other factors.
- More likely to validate a clause where business is very specialised – so necessary to protect employer – but can in effect prevent employee from working.
- Restraint clauses more likely to succeed where employee is high level or holds unique role so significant to the business – so necessary to protect employer but could be unfair to employee.

Explain construction and remedies

- Possible effect of public policy.
- Possibility of blue pencilling.
- Usual remedy is injunction.

Discuss effect of construction and remedies

- Public policy will usually be used to invalidate the clause – so will work in employee's favour.
- Blue pencilling (severance) is narrowly used – so clauses drafted too wide will be void – if cannot sever and retain sense of restraint then will be void – so generally protects employee.
- Mandatory injunctions are not granted nor ones that tie the employee to the employer – so protects employee.

REACH REASONED CONCLUSIONS

- Garden leave is a period during which an employee is serving a notice period, is paid but is usually not working the notice period and is prevented from working for a competitor.
- It is to protect the employer's property and to avoid unfair competition.
- But it can only be enforced if there is a contractual basis for it.
- Contracts in restraint of trade, sometimes called post termination covenants, are terms inserted in the contract to protect the employer.
- Because they may have the effect of preventing the employee from earning a living they are prima facie void but they may enforced if they are accepted as reasonable as between the parties, and in the public interest.
- An employer can only protect a legitimate business interest – these include trade secrets, client contact, not competing and not soliciting other employees away from the business.
- What is reasonable depends on the geographical extent of the restraint, the duration of the restraint, the nature of the business and the status of the employee.
- It may be possible to sever void parts of a restraint clause if the clause still makes sense – this is known as 'blue-pencilling'.
- The usual remedy sought is an injunction.
- But an injunction cannot be granted where it merely forces an employee to stay with the employer.

Further reading

Emir, Astra, *Selwyn's Law of Employment 17th edition*. Oxford University Press, 2011, Chapter 19.

Sargeant, Malcolm and Lewis, David, *Employment Law 6th edition*. Pearson, 2012, Chapter 3.5.2.2–3.5.2.3.

7

Implied terms

AIMS AND OBJECTIVES

After reading this chapter you should be able to:

- Understand the nature of implied terms and how terms are implied into contracts by statute or by common law
- Understand why the common law implies terms into employment contracts
- Understand the duties owed by employers to employees
- Understand the duties owed by employees to employers
- Be able to critically analyse the concept of implied duties
- Be able to apply individual categories of implied terms to factual situations

7.1 The process of implying terms

7.1.1 The nature of implied terms

As we have already seen, while employment law is an area that is heavily influenced by statute as well as by EU law it is also in essence a specific area of contract law. All contractual relationships are based on terms either agreed by the parties before entering the contract or implied by process of law by the courts or by statute.

All implied terms are of two types:

Common law implied terms	Statutory implied terms
Those inserted into contracts by the courts (and in the case of contracts of employment possibly also by tribunals) with the benefit of hindsight • in general they represent what the court believes is the presumed but unexpressed intent of the parties when contracting • but they may be inconsistent with the express terms and so may be overridden depending what the parties have agreed because they are what would reasonably be included in an employment contract	Those imposed by statute (which increasingly in modern times may be to comply with a provision of EU law) • they generally involve employment protection • they take precedence over any inconsistent express term in the contract • as such they may not represent what at least one party (and this will generally be the employer) would have agreed to at the time of contracting

Statutory implied terms in the employment contract

Implied terms appear throughout contract law and, because of the nature of the employment relationship, have a significant role to play in employment law. Employment law, and in particular employment protections, have traditionally been subject to regulation by statute and subject also to continuous change. Inevitably this reflects the different attitude of conservative and socialist governments to employment. Many of the subsequent chapters of this book in effect deal with the insertion of terms into employment contracts through statutory intervention and by which both parties to the contract are bound. A classic example of a statutory implied term is the insertion of the so-called 'equality clause' into all contracts of employment by s1(1) of the Equal Pay Act 1970, which has now been overtaken by the Equality Act 2010 to reflect developments in EU law.

Common law implied terms in the employment contract

A simple scan of a chapter on terms in any contract law text will also identify that terms can be implied by the courts, either as a question of fact or by process of law. Implied terms of this type have developed in a very specific way in employment law and we generally refer to them as the 'implied duties' of both employers and employees.

The basic proposition is that, in those circumstances where the parties (which in the case of employment contracts almost inevitably means the employer) have failed to insert an express term into the contract to meet a particular contingency or a particular aspect of the specific employment relationship, the court or tribunal will, if necessary, imply terms into the contract to cover that contingency or the particular feature of the employment relationship which is in dispute.

This point can easily be illustrated in two contrasting cases:

CASE EXAMPLE

Stevenson v Teesside Bridge and Engineering Ltd [1971] 1 All ER 296

A steel erector refused to transfer to a new site some distance from his home and away from a site that was very close to his home. There was no written mobility clause in the employee's contract of employment. However, it is in the nature of the work that steel erectors move from site to site to whatever new building they are erecting the framework for. It would be impossible for an employer to guarantee that the work would always be located near to an employee's home. Besides this there were provisions in the written terms for travel expenses and subsistence allowances so it was implicit from the express terms that the employee was expected to travel. The court identified that the contract contained an implied mobility clause and that the employee's refusal was found to be unjustified and unlawful.

Clearly the court is basing its judgment on the facts of the case and the circumstances of the particular type of employment. In this way the courts will not automatically imply mobility clauses into all employment clauses, only those where the actual working practices reflect a real need for mobility. A contrasting outcome can therefore be illustrated in another case.

CASE EXAMPLE

O'Brien v Associated Fire Alarms Ltd [1969] 1 WLR 1916

An electrician who had always worked exclusively in and around Liverpool for his employer was asked to transfer to another of the employer's offices in Barrow-in-Furness. There had been a reduction of work in the Liverpool branch which nevertheless was part of the employer's north-western region which also included the Barrow branch. The employer was therefore arguing, as Barrow was within the same region, there was an implied mobility clause in the contract to the effect that employees were bound to work anywhere within the north-western region. The Court of Appeal rejected this argument holding that while there could be implied into the contract a clause requiring employees to work anywhere within daily travelling distance, since Barrow was 120 miles away, it could not reasonably apply in the particular circumstances.

7.1.2 The process of implying terms into contracts

It is inevitable that courts and tribunals will only be asked to imply terms into a contract, including a contract of employment, when a dispute has already arisen between the parties and the parties are in disagreement as to what the actual terms of the contract are.

The court is then being asked to look at the contractual agreement with hindsight in order to determine what the presumed mutual intention of both parties was at the time the contract was formed. This is necessarily an artificial process because the parties clearly already have different viewpoints so that one at least is going to be disappointed with the result.

The original justification for implying a term into a contract by fact was expressed as the need to give business efficacy to the contract. In other words the contract would be rendered commercially meaningless if the term was not included in the contract even though no express mention had been made of it at the time when the contract was formed.

CASE EXAMPLE

The Moorcock [1889] 14 PD 64

In a contract for mooring a vessel in a wharf the court held that there was an implied undertaking that the ship would not be damaged, without which the whole purpose of the contract would be defeated.

JUDGMENT

Bowen LJ explained: 'the implied term must be founded on presumed intention and upon reason'.

JUDGMENT

In *Luxor (Eastbourne) Ltd v Cooper* [1941] AC 108 Lord Wright explained that the implied term is: 'some term not expressed but necessary to give to the transaction such business efficacy as the parties intended'.

The other classical test for determining how and when a term will be implied into a contract is that developed by McKinnon LJ in *Shirlaw v Southern Foundries Ltd* [1939] 2 KB 206 CA, the so-called 'officious bystander test'.

JUDGMENT

'Prima facie that which in any contract is left to be implied and need not be expressed is something so obvious that it goes without saying; so that if, while the parties were making their bargain, an officious bystander were to suggest some express provision for it in their agreement, they would testily suppress him with a common "Oh, of course!"'

The language is somewhat strange but the point is simple and straightforward, terms can be implied into a contract where they are so obvious to the effective completion of the contract that they 'go without saying'.

In determining what would obviously be included as a term in the employment contract despite a failure to incorporate it expressly courts and tribunals have been prepared, for instance, to look at trade custom. In this way courts have accepted that certain terms can be implied where they are 'certain, notorious, and reasonable'.

CASE EXAMPLE

Sagar v Ridehalgh [1931] 1 Ch 310

A weaver complained when his employer deducted one shilling (now 5p but obviously worth a great deal more at the time) from his wages for work that the employer had decided was not up to standard. It was accepted by the court that this was a customary practice in the Lancashire cotton mills and that a term could therefore be implied in the contract by custom. The required features were all in place because the practice was 'reasonable, certain and notorious'.

JUDGMENT

Lawrence LJ stated: 'I am of the opinion that the [practice] is not unreasonable. The deductions are not arbitrary deductions at the will and pleasure of the employers; they are limited to cases where there has been bad work, and they are limited to an amount which does not exceed the actual or estimated damage or loss occasioned to the employer by the act or omission of the workman.' He added: 'a trade [practice] allowing an employer to make deductions for bad work at his discretion not exceeding a certain defined limit does not ... render [it] uncertain ... and it is reasonable that employers should not exact the full amount of the loss.... A Lancashire weaver knows, and has for very many years past known, precisely what his position was as regards deductions for bad work.'

However, the employee must be aware of the precise custom and have accepted it as part of the employment contract and this must be demonstrated for the court's satisfaction for it to be enforceable against him. It is not sufficient merely that the employee is working at the same time as being aware of the custom.

CASE EXAMPLE

Samways v Swan Hunter Shipbuilders [1975] IRLR 190

In this contrasting case the employee was a labourer who was then promoted to the position of charge hand with a consequent increase in pay. Because of a shortage in work he was then asked to revert to his previous job with a consequent reduction in his pay. The man argued that he had been made redundant but the employer tried to show that ups and downs in orders in the industry was common and that other employees had been promoted and demoted in the way that the claimant had here, so that such reductions in pay and status were customary. The tribunal rejected this argument.

The process of implication of terms has in any case moved on in the field of employment contracts and the argument very often now, rather than involving either what produces 'business efficacy' or what is the presumed intention of the parties, focuses instead on what is reasonable in all the circumstances of the case.

QUOTATION

As Smith and Wood identify the tribunal may have to: 'insert a term based on all the evidence of the relationship between the parties and what had happened in practice since the employment began'.

I T Smith and G H Thomas *Smith & Wood's Industrial Law*, Butterworths, 2009

CASE EXAMPLE

Mears v Safecar Security Ltd [1982] IRLR 183

The employee in this case complained about the fact that he received no pay during a period of sickness absence. One problem was that there was in fact no reference to sick pay in the written terms. The court considered that, before a term is implied into a contract, the correct process was to consider all of the relevant circumstances. It also considered that this includes looking at the way that the parties had behaved during the contract. The court did feel that in general in circumstances where there was insufficient information then the dispute should be settled in favour of the employee. In the case itself, however, there was evidence that there had been no intention to include such a term in the contract and as a result any such term should have been included in the written terms to have effect. Now the same problem would not apply since the Social Security Contributions and Benefits Act 1992. Because of this all employees are now eligible for Statutory Sick Pay.

Again both the history of what has gone on during the contract and what is reasonable in the circumstances are both relevant in deciding the outcome.

CASE EXAMPLE

Courtaulds Northern Spinning Ltd v Sibson [1988] IRLR 305 CA

The contract of employment did not include an express mobility clause. However, when the employee tried to claim a constructive dismissal after he refused to transfer to another site, the court was prepared to imply a mobility clause in the contract in rejecting his argument. There were two key factors influencing the court's decision: first the new site was within daily travel for the employee, and second he had already worked on that site on previous occasions.

JUDGMENT

Slade LJ explained: 'the court does not have to be satisfied that the parties, if asked, would in fact have agreed the term before entering into the contract. The court merely has to be satisfied that the implied term is one which the parties would probably have agreed if they were being reasonable.'

As a result in many cases the courts are able to imply terms quite easily based on what is reasonable in the circumstances.

CASE EXAMPLE

Prestwick Circuits Ltd v McAndrew [1991] IRLR 191

Here the employee was subjected to a move to a factory that was fifteen miles away. This could appear reasonable enough in itself since this obviously would fall under a definition of reasonable daily travel. However, the Court of Session was prepared to accept that giving only one week's notice of the impending move was a breach of an implied term that reasonable notice was required thus justifying a claim of constructive dismissal.

The precise effect of implied terms on the express terms has also been subject to a change of attitude by the courts. In *Rank Xerox Ltd v Churchill* [1988] IRLR 280 the attitude of the EAT was that where the contract of employment included an unambiguous mobility clause then this could not be modified purely by inclusion of an implied term that such a clause should be exercised reasonably. However, a significant turning point in the attitude of the courts has been not just to accept the inclusion of such implied terms but also to see them as overriding the express terms.

CASE EXAMPLE

United Bank Ltd v Akhtar [1989] IRLR 507

The employee's contract of employment included an express mobility clause to the effect that he could be moved to any of the bank's branches anywhere in the UK. The bank chose to transfer Akhtar from a branch in Leeds to a branch in Birmingham, giving him only six days' notice of the intended move. The bank then also refused to accept Akhtar's request for a short postponement of the move, which he had asked for because of his wife's current illness. The EAT held that, not only had the bank acted unreasonably in failing to give appropriate notice of the move, thereby inserting an implied term of reasonable notice in the contract, but in view of its conduct, had breached the implied term of trust and respect (see 7.2.5 below). In doing so the EAT acknowledged that in certain circumstances implied terms could produce overriding obligations which would stand even if inconsistent with the express terms of the contract.

JUDGMENT

The court stated: 'in the field of employment law it is proper to imply an overriding obligation which is independent of ... the terms of the contract'.

A much broader view has then been taken in the context of employment law to the implication of terms. This broader view has also in effect modified the original test of business efficacy. In this way the test, in an employment context has now has been widened to the extent that certain terms will be implied simply because the relationship of employment exists and, as Lord Bridge described it in *Scally v Southern Health & Social Services Board* [1991] IRLR 522 HL, the term is one:

JUDGMENT

'which the law will imply as a necessary incident of a definable category of contractual relationship'.

CASE EXAMPLE

Scally v Southern Health & Social Services Board [1991] IRLR 522; [1991] 3 WLR 778

Statutory provisions allowed doctors employed in Northern Ireland to make, as the doctors had in England, contributions to a superannuation scheme. A collective agreement further gave the doctors the right to improve their pensions by buying additional years, but this had to be done within a prescribed time limit. The doctors had not done so because they had not been informed of this right before the time limit expired. The House of Lords accepted that the employees were not in a position to exercise their rights without being given the necessary information, so that the employer had breached an implied term requiring the employer to take reasonable steps to inform employees of such rights gained under collective agreements.

This builds on the comment already made by Lord Reid in *Sterling Engineering Co Ltd v Patchett* [1955] AC 534:

JUDGMENT

'the phrase "implied term" can be used to denote a term inherent in the nature of the contract which the law will imply in every case unless the parties agree to vary or exclude it'.

This category of implied terms has been developed in a very structured way in employment contracts and we now refer to these implied terms as 'duties'. These duties are of two different types:

- implied duties owed by the employer to the employee
- implied duties owed by the employee to the employer.

It must be remembered, however, that the categories of implied terms, while currently falling into neat established groupings, are not absolutely fixed but are in fact expanding.

While the employer, for instance, owes employees trust and respect (see 7.2.5 below), this basic duty has been developed and expanded so that now it is also possible to say that the employer should not treat his employee arbitrarily or vindictively.

CASE EXAMPLE

Robinson v Crompton Parkinson Ltd [1978] ICR 401; [1978] IRLR 61 EAT

Falsely accusing the employee of theft was a breach of the implied term because, without justification, it was vindictive.

CASE EXAMPLE

Gardiner Ltd v Beresford [1978] IRLR 63 EAT

Denying the employee a pay increase that had been granted to other employees was arbitrary and a breach of the implied duty.

CASE EXAMPLE

Warner v Barbers Stores [1978] IRLR 109 EAT

Refusing an employee's request for time off to deal with a domestic emergency was a breach of the implied term because it was an obviously unreasonable stance by the employer.

Indeed some terms are now implied irrespective of intention of parties because they are considered to be so important in the context of the employment relationship. A classic example of this is the development of a law on protection of the mental health and psychiatric well-being of the employee (see Chapter 16.3). As such they may automatically override express terms in the contract, even though the test is less absolute for other implied terms.

CASE EXAMPLE

Johnstone v Bloomsbury Health Authority [1992] QB 333; [1991] ICR 269; [1991] IRLR 118

A junior doctor was required under express terms in his contract to be on call for at least forty-eight hours per week on top of his existing forty hours per week on normal duty. He argued that this was a breach of an implied term to take reasonable care for his safety. The Court of Appeal upheld his claim and accepted that such an implied term in fact existed. While Leggett LJ, dissenting, took the orthodox view that the junior doctor was bound by the express terms in his contract so that no such implied term could override it, the majority upheld the claim, though giving different reasons. Browne-Wilkinson VC identified that the argument could succeed because there is no absolute obligation to work overtime, although this certainly contradicts the reality of this and other contracts. Stuart-Smith LJ simply accepted that there was an implied term that employers should take care of their employees in the way argued by the employee.

ACTIVITY

Self-assessment questions

1. Why are the 'officious bystander' and business efficacy test insufficient on their own when implying terms into employment contracts?
2. In what way is the concept of reasonableness significant in implying terms into employment contracts?
3. What is the basic difference between implied terms and the implied duties in employment contracts?
4. When will custom affect a contract of employment?
5. In what ways has *Johnstone v Bloomsbury HA* developed the principles of implied terms in employment contracts?

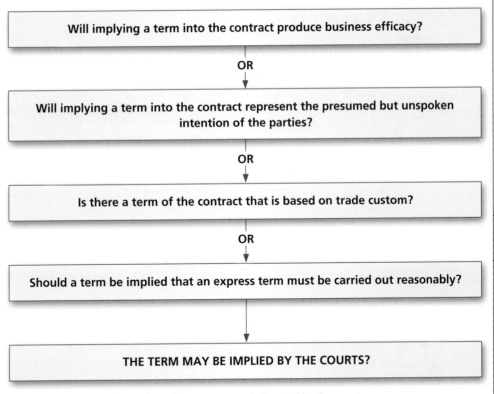

Figure 7.1 Diagram illustrating when terms may be implied by the courts

7.2 The implied duties of employers

As identified above, a variety of implied terms have been accepted by the courts over a period of time which can be categorised into groups, known as the implied duties of the employer.

7.2.1 The payment of wages

The duty to pay wages is still a fundamental common law principle, although the area is now heavily regulated by statute. Every employee should receive an itemised pay statement (see Chapter 6.1). However, in the absence of express details in the contract or related documentation such as collective agreements, the court will declare a reasonable amount on a *quantum meruit* (literally for the amount earned).

CASE EXAMPLE

Way v Latilla [1937] 3 All ER 759

The defendant had promised the claimant that he would 'look after his interests' if the claimant secured gold mining concessions for the defendant. This was done and the concessions produced a million pound profit for the defendant who nevertheless failed to honour the vague promise. The House of Lords held that the claimant could recover £5,000 commission on a *quantum meruit*.

Moreover, an employee who is ready and willing to work may be entitled to wages even though there is no work currently available.

CASE EXAMPLE

Beveridge v KLM (UK) Ltd [2000] IRLR 765

The employee had been absent from work with a long term illness but had informed her employer that she was fit to return to work. However, the employer then refused to allow her to return until its own doctor had certified her as being fit to return, which delayed her return for six weeks during which time she was not paid. The EAT held that she was entitled to be paid as she was willing to work, unless there was an express clause to the contrary in the contract of employment, which there was not here.

The same principle can be seen operating in a slightly different way in the case of *Devonald v Rosser* [1901] 2 KB 653 (see 7.2.2 below) where it was held that pieceworkers should be given enough work to make their normal earnings.

7.2.2 The provision of work

The basic traditional view was that there is no absolute 'right to work'. As a consequence there is similarly no obligation on the employer to provide work for the employee.

CASE EXAMPLE

Collier v Sunday Referee Publishing Co [1940] 2 KB 647

A newspaper sub-editor was kept on after the business was sold out to another business but, even though he was still paid, he was given no work to do. He argued that the employer had breached an implied term of the contract by failing to provide work. The court recognised that there was no overall obligation to provide work. Nevertheless, it also accepted that there are specific circumstances in which an employer would be obliged to provide work.

JUDGMENT

Asquith J, commenting on the notion of a 'right to work' stated: 'It is true that a contract of employment does not necessarily, or perhaps normally, oblige the master to provide the servant with work. Provided I pay my cook her wages she cannot complain if I choose to take any or all of my meals out.'

As an example of the principle this was possibly meaningless to the average employee of the time. Nevertheless, the court did recognise that the basic principle inevitably had exceptions where the failure to provide work could amount to a breach of duty by the employer:

■ Where there was an existing obligation to provide work.

■ Where the employee gained his income solely from, for example, commission or piecework, meaning that it would be impossible to earn a wage unless work was provided. The point has been established in the case of commission *Turner v Goldsmith* [1891] QB 544 and in the case of piecework *Devonald v Rosser & Sons* [1906] 2 KB 728, where the claimant, a pieceworker, in other words paid by the 'piece' of work rather than a set wage, was given one month's notice but no work to do after his employer ceased trading and he successfully sued for damages.

■ Where public performance was an essential feature of the contract and a failure to provide work might lead to a loss of reputation.

This is particularly true of employment in a theatrical, musical or entertainment context because the opportunity to work may have a value independent of pay.

CASE EXAMPLE

Herbert Clayton & Jack Waller Ltd v Oliver [1930] AC 209 HL

An actor was given a leading role in a musical which was then taken off him and substituted for a minor role in the production. Even though the actor kept the same wage the employer was held to have breached the contract because of the potential impact on the actor's reputation and future chances of work. The court held that there was an implied duty on the part of the employer to provide him with appropriate work. He was also awarded damages for the loss of opportunity that would result from his lowered reputation.

The categories have subsequently been added to by the courts to reflect the realities of modern employment situations.

- Where expert employees with specific skills are involved.

This has developed out of the 'garden leave' cases (see Chapter 6.1). Employers often impose lengthy notice periods on highly specialist employees on full pay but with no work, possibly to prevent the employee going to a rival company and carry with them recent expertise or expert knowledge. In *Provident Financial Group plc and Whitegates Estate Agency Ltd v Hayward* [1989] IRLR 84 the Court of Appeal identified that the employer could only impose such conditions if there was a clause to that effect in the contract. It also recognised that the publicity exception could extend beyond actors and musicians to other areas of skilled and specialist work. This has subsequently been accepted.

CASE EXAMPLE

William Hill Organisation Ltd v Tucker [1998] IRLR 313

The employee held a unique position within the organisation and had specialist skills. When he resigned his post to take up a post with a rival organisation he was put on six months' 'garden leave' with no work. The employer then sought an injunction to prevent him working for the competitor during the notice period. There was no actual express term in the employment contract allowing for 'garden leave' and the Court of Appeal held that an employee who holds a 'specific and unique post' is entitled to work in order to carry out his skills. This was evidenced in the contract which required the employee to work the hours necessary to carry out his duties in a full and professional manner. As a result in the circumstances there was an obligation on the employer to provide work which it had breached thus meaning that the employee could immediately repudiate his contract and take up the other employment.

JUDGMENT

Morritt LJ explained it in simple terms: 'if the employer were to be entitled to keep his employee in idleness, the investment in its staff might be as illusory as the limited power of suspension would be unnecessary'.

The point has been expanded since in *SG & R Valuation Service v Boudrais* [2008] IRLR 770. Here the court qualified the position in that those with a right to work in such circumstances hold it subject to a breach of contract indicating that they are not willing and ready to work.

Another and even more interesting approach was taken by the Court of Appeal in *Langston v AUEW* [1974] ICR 180.

CASE EXAMPLE

Langston v AUEW [1974] ICR 180

The claimant had refused to join a trade union which he had every right to do by law at the time. Other employees who were members of the union then threatened to strike in protest at Langston's refusal. In order to avoid the strike, the employer then suspended Langston on full pay for an indefinite period. As a result Langston sued the union for inducing a breach of contract and arguing that he was being denied the right to work. The Court of Appeal acknowledged that, in certain circumstances, an employee may in fact have a right to work. Part of its reasoning was that it would enable the employee to achieve job satisfaction. It also commented that it would make no difference that the employee is being paid full wages at the same time as being denied work.

JUDGMENT

Explaining this reasoning Lord Denning commented: '[a] man should be given the opportunity of doing his work when it is available and he is ready and willing to do it. A skilled man takes a pride in his work. He does not do it merely to earn money. He does it so as to make his contribution to the well-being of all. He does it so as to keep himself busy, and not idle. To use his skill, and to improve it. To have the satisfaction which comes of a task well done.'

7.2.3 The care of the employee

A basic duty has developed to take care of the health, safety and welfare of the employee and this has expanded significantly in recent years. Health and safety law is a massive area in its own right and is covered in detail in Chapter 13.

There has been intervention both by domestic statutes and as a result of EU law. There has also developed, however, a basic common law duty owed under the contract. This may be significant since the measure of damages is obviously different between contract and tort.

However, the House of Lords (now the Supreme Court) has held in *Tai Hing Cotton Mill Ltd v Chong Hing Bank Ltd* [1986] that the courts should not simply find the existence of a duty in tort where the same duty exists in contract. The basic obligation is that the employer must provide a safe system of work, safe premises, safe work colleagues and safe plant and equipment.

CASE EXAMPLE

Wilsons & Clyde Coal Co Ltd v English [1938] AC 57

Owing to negligent maintenance of a pit a miner was injured and sought compensation for his injuries. The pit owner tried to avoid liability, arguing that it had delegated its responsibilities and therefore also its liability under various industrial safety laws to its Colliery Manager. It had done so by contractually making the manager entirely responsible for safety. The court held that the owner was liable on the basis that its personal liability could not be delegated to a third party, who was in any case an employee. It was a non-delegable duty of care. The court also indicted the scope of the duty: to provide competent working colleagues, safe plant and equipment, a safe place of work and a safe system of work (see later Chapter 13).

The duty has developed over time so that it includes the psychiatric well-being and general welfare of the employee.

CASE EXAMPLE

Walker v Northumberland County Council [1995] 1 All ER 737

A senior social worker suffered a nervous breakdown as a result of work related stress. His return to work agreement included a phased return to a full workload. However, his workload actually increased and he suffered another breakdown causing him to leave work permanently after he was dismissed on sickness grounds. The court held that because after the first break-down the employer was aware of his susceptibility to stress and did nothing to relieve it he was placed under even more stressful conditions, and the employer was liable.

JUDGMENT

As Colman J explained: 'there is no logical reason why risk of psychiatric damage should be excluded from...'

However, the duty is towards the employee so there is no duty to care for his property.

CASE EXAMPLE

Deyong v Shenburn [1946] KB 227; [1946] 1 All ER 226, CA

Here the employee's clothing was stolen from a theatre in which he worked. It was held that there was no liability on the employer to compensate for the loss.

A logical development of this is that there is no duty to care for the employee's general economic well-being.

CASE EXAMPLE

Crossley v Faithful and Gould Holdings Ltd [2004] EWCA Civ 293

A senior employee asked to take early retirement due to ill health. His employer did not inform him that his entitlement under a permanent health insurance scheme would be adversely affected as a result. The employee claimed that the employer had breached an implied term to warn him about the effects of his retirement. The court held that there was no such term. As a senior employee he should have been aware of the implications and had enjoyed access to specialist advice. To imply a term that an employer was responsible for financial advice would be unreasonable. (Although in *Scally v Southern Health and Social Services Board* [1992] 1 AC 294 the House of Lords (now the Supreme Court) had identified that an employer does owe a duty to take reasonable steps to bring benefits of schemes to the attention of employees who could not be reasonably expected to be aware of these schemes themselves.)

There is also no duty to provide personal accident insurance for an employer working abroad, or to provide any specific advice *Reid v Rush & Tompkins Group* [1989] IRLR 265 CA.

(N.B. Much more detailed consideration of this area of the duty is given in Chapter 16 on common law health and safety law.)

7.2.4 The duty to indemnify

The employer is under a duty to indemnify the employee for all expenses that are necessarily incurred in the course of employment. In many ways this is a very straightforward duty. It obviously applies to all expenses that naturally arise out of the employment. This quite commonly includes, for example, travel expenses where it is required to travel during work hours, board and lodging or hotel bills, and even purchases necessarily made in the course of employment. Quite often the payment of such expenses is agreed beforehand and may be identified as an express term of the contract.

The situation may be more complex where the expense involves the payment of fines or defending legal proceedings against the employee.

CASE EXAMPLE

Gregory v Ford [1951] 1 All ER 121

Here the claimant had been injured through the negligent driving of the employee. Contrary to the legal requirement of compulsory third party insurance (now under the Road Traffic Act 1988) the employer carried no such insurance, hence the private claim. The court held that the employer was liable for the damages. It considered that a reasonable employer would not expect an employee to act in an illegal manner on his behalf and as a result there was an implied term that the employer would indemnify the employee in such situations.

The same basic principle can be adopted in other situations where the employee is facing legal proceedings in respect of something that occurred during the course of the employment and was therefore done on behalf of the employer.

CASE EXAMPLE

Re Famatina Development Corporation Ltd [1914] 2 Ch 271

The employee worked as a consultant engineer for the company. He was asked to prepare a report about a managing director. This report later became the basis of a libel action against him. Since the report had been requested by the employer and was therefore part of the employee's duties the company was bound to indemnify him for the cost of defending the legal action against him.

7.2.5 The duty of mutual trust and respect

The duty of mutual trust and respect is probably the widest and most significant of the employer's duties. The actual width will vary from employment to employment. However, it essentially means that the employer must be conscious of good personnel practice, take appropriate steps towards training and improving standards, and fair and appropriate disciplinary procedures.

The duty has its origins in the nineteenth century, at which point it was very limited in scope. Inevitably, with the introduction of unfair dismissal and constructive dismissal, the concept has grown as the traditional idea of hire and fire at will has disappeared.

In short the basis of the duty is that the employee should be treated fairly and with respect by the employer. It is therefore, a breach of the duty where the employer does anything that would undermine the relationship and prevent the contract from continuing in the manner which was envisaged when it was formed.

CASE EXAMPLE

United Bank Ltd v Akhtar [1989] IRLR 507

The employee's contract included a mobility clause, in effect that he could be transferred to any of the bank's branches at short notice. The employer gave the employee three days' notice that he was to transfer from the Birmingham branch to the Leeds branch about 120 miles away. Despite his request for a brief delay in the transfer because of his wife's serious illness at the time and in order also to sort out relocation arrangements, the employer refused. He claimed constructive dismissal. The court held that, despite the mobility clause in the contract, there was a fundamental breach of an implied term that the transfer should be carried out in a reasonable manner, and not in a way that would undermine the trust and confidence in the relationship. The claim of unfair dismissal succeeded.

The duty can apply in many situations. An obvious example from *Arden v Bradley* [1994] IRLR 490 is that the employer should not unilaterally change the pay or status of an employee.

Obviously the personal relationships within an employment environment are significant in maintaining a good working environment as well as maintaining trust and respect. Criticising an employee in front of colleagues is clearly damaging to the relationship.

CASE EXAMPLE

Isle of Wight Tourist Board v Coombes [1976] IRLR 413

A director was overheard saying to an employee that his personal secretary was 'an intolerable bitch on a Monday morning'. The secretary became very upset and resigned her post. It was held that the director's action amounted to a breach of the duty of mutual trust and respect.

A rational extension of the principle is swearing at staff or using abusive language, or indeed of provoking the employee into anger or frustration where he might use abusive language as a result.

CASE EXAMPLE

Wilson v Racher [1974] ICR 428; IRLR 114 CA

A head gardener was wrongly accused of failing to do his job properly. This led to an argument in which the gardener used abusive language and he was then summarily dismissed by the employer. Even though the gardener's behaviour could amount to gross misconduct, it was held that it was caused by the employer's provocative behaviour and there was, therefore, a wrongful dismissal in the circumstances.

Another logical extension of the principle is that the employer should not be deliberately provocative towards an employee. In *Donovan v Invicta Airways Ltd* [1970] 1 Lloyd's Rep 486 CA the employee resigned claiming a number of instances where he had been treated unfairly. Although the court held these to be an irritation rather than sufficiently substantial to amount to a breach, it did hold that an employer should show sufficient courtesy and consideration to his employee to allow the contract to continue.

It could also be a breach of the implied duty if the employer treats employees differently by providing one or more with a benefit that is barred to others. In *BG plc v O'Brien* [2002] IRLR 444 an employee was denied the opportunity given to other employees of signing a changed contract which contained better redundancy payments. This was a breach of the implied duty because, as it was suggested, this could damage the trust and confidence between employer and employee, and may even be calculated to do so.

Harassment, and more precisely a failure to deal with it, could also amount to a breach of the duty. Where this leads to a claim of constructive dismissal by the employee who feels unable to continue work in the circumstances it could also amount to an unfair dismissal.

CASE EXAMPLE

Bracebridge Engineering Ltd v Darby [1990] IRLR 3

A single sexual assault was held to be sexual discrimination. The employer was vicariously liable because the harassers were currently in disciplinary supervision and the acts fell within the course of their employment.

The later case of *Reed & Bull Information Systems Ltd v Stedman* [1999] IRLR 299 EAT identified that, if an employer has reason to suspect harassment, it has a duty to investigate and take action, not wait for a formal complaint.

The duty inevitably also has a context in respect of the employee's reputation. As a result where the actions of the employer may impact on the employee's future prospects this may also be a breach of the duty.

CASE EXAMPLE

Malik v Bank of Credit and Commerce International [1997] IRLR 462

The bank was accused of fraudulent, dishonest and corrupt dealing and went into liquidation as a result. The claimant, who had been an employee of the bank, then found it almost impossible to find new employment. He argued that this was because having worked for the bank had destroyed his own personal reputation by association. He appealed to the House of Lords (now the Supreme Court) against an earlier decision not to award him compensation. The House held that the corrupt and fraudulent practices of the bank did in fact amount to a breach of the implied duty of mutual trust and confidence.

JUDGMENT

Lord Nicholls explained: 'the bank was under an implied obligation to its employees not to conduct a dishonest or corrupt business. This implied obligation is no more than one particular aspect of the ... general obligation not to engage in conduct likely to undermine the trust and confidence required if the employment relationship is to continue in the manner the employment contract implicitly envisages.'

7.2.6 The duty of confidentiality

The duty of confidentiality owed by an employer mirrors that owed by the employee. The employer is under a duty not to pass on information to third parties which is relevant only to the employment and not public knowledge.

CASE EXAMPLE

Dalgleish v Lothian & Borders Police Board [1991] IRLR 422

It is obvious that an employer will be in possession of the names and addresses of all its employees. The employer here was asked to provide this information to a local council that wished to use the information to find out the names of people who had not paid what was then called the 'poll tax' (similar to the current council tax – but which was a controversial subject at the time). The claimants successfully sought an injunction restraining the release of this information since it was given to the employer only for the purposes of the employment relationship.

The EC Data Protection Directive 95/46 and the Data Protection Act 1998 also offer similar protections.

7.2.7 The duty to deal with grievances promptly

While grievance procedure is a separate issue dealt with in Chapter 15.1 of this book, it has also been accepted that there is an implied duty to deal with grievances promptly. Where an employee raises a formal grievance within his employment the subject of the grievance is clearly something that is causing distress. For this reason it is important for maintaining a good working relationship that the issue is sorted out as quickly as possible to avoid further distress. In fact Codes of Practice confirm this point.

CASE EXAMPLE

W A Goold (Pearmak) Ltd v McConnell [1995] IRLR 516

Under their contract of employment two sales representatives were paid partly through a salary and partly on a commission basis. The company then appointed a new managing director at a point when the company was facing certain financial difficulties. The new managing director introduced a new payment system which caused a significant reduction in the two men's pay. They approached their own line manager who identified that he could not do anything about it. They also approached the new managing director who was not prepared to listen to any complaints from them. After they had raised the issue on numerous occasions they left and claimed that they had been constructively dismissed. They then brought a claim for unfair dismissal in a tribunal. It was later held in the Employment Appeals Tribunal that the failure by the company to provide any form of grievance procedure through which the men could raise the issue properly was in fact a fundamental breach of the contract (the required starting point for a claim of constructive dismissal. As a result they were successful in their claim for unfair dismissal.

JUDGMENT

Morison J illustrated the duty in the following terms: 'good industrial relations requires employers to provide their employees with a method of dealing with grievances in a proper and [timely] manner'. He goes on to add why a prompt procedure is necessary: 'the right to obtain redress against a grievance is fundamental for very obvious reasons. The working environment may well lead to employees experiencing difficulties, whether because of the physical conditions under which they work, or because of a breakdown in human relationships, which can readily occur when people of different backgrounds and sensitivities are required to work together, often under pressure.'

7.2.8 The giving of references

Another of the duties owed by employers to their employees has largely developed in fairly recent times. This is the duty to take care and not be negligent in the drafting of references that they provide.

CASE EXAMPLE

Spring v Guardian Assurance plc [1995] 3 WLR 354

An employee of an insurance company was dismissed and then prevented from gaining a position with another company because of a negligently prepared and highly unfavourable reference provided by his existing employer. He claimed damages for a negligently prepared reference. The House of Lords (now the Supreme Court) held that employers owe a duty of care to their employees and that this includes a duty not to make negligent references. As a result the employer was liable. Interestingly the House was divided on whether the duty arose under the principle on negligent misstatements from *Hedley Byrne v Heller & Partners Ltd* [1964] AC 465.

The case was a significant development for employees since previously their only remedy would have been through defamation law where they would have been prevented from seeing the reference unless they could prove malice. In negligence, however, they would be entitled to thorough discovery of documents.

The approach to dealing with negligently prepared references has since been developed by the Court of Appeal. In *Bartholomew v London Borough of Hackney* [1999] the court increased the duty to ensuring that information provided is accurate and that the reference does not create any unfair impression. It has also been developed still further.

CASE EXAMPLE

Cox v Sun Alliance Life Ltd [2001] IRLR 448

A branch manager of an insurance company was suspended for reasons not related to dishonesty. An allegation of dishonesty was made during negotiations for a termination agreement. However, the investigation was abandoned and company agreed that in any references it would make no mention of the allegation. It did, however, do so in one reference which cost the claimant a job. The claimant sued successfully for negligence. Lord Justice Mummery explained the required procedure for avoiding liability. Before divulging information that is unfavourable to an ex-employee in a reference, an employer must (i) believe in the truth of the information, (ii) have reasonable grounds for that belief and (iii) make a reasonably thorough investigation before providing the reference.

ACTIVITY

Self-assessment questions

1. What is significant about the case of *Beveridge v KLM (UK) Ltd* to the duty to pay wages?
2. Can it be said in general that there is a right to work?
3. In what circumstances will an employer owe a duty to provide work?
4. What are the various aspects of the employer's duty to care for the employee?
5. Precisely what must an employer indemnify for an employee?

6. In what way will the duty of mutual trust and respect affect the way that an employer carries out his business?
7. What is the character of information about the employee that the employer must keep confidential?
8. What problems might occur if an employer fails to deal with employees' grievances promptly?
9. In what way was *Spring v Guardian Assurance* such a landmark case for employees?

ACTIVITY

Quick quiz

In the following situations identify which implied duty of an employer is involved and consider whether it may have been breached.

1. The headmaster of the Duddleberry Academy has given all of the teachers' addresses and home phone numbers to an academic book publisher. Kirsty is complaining because she has been inundated with mail and phone calls from the publisher.
2. Brian, the managing director of a company, repeatedly tells Viv, an administrator for the company, that she is useless and not worth the money that she is paid every time he walks through the office where she works, and in front of her colleagues. Viv becomes very depressed and is on medication. Whenever she takes time off sick Brian calls her a sickly little wimp in front of her colleagues. Viv then suffers a nervous breakdown.
3. Gordon is instructed by his manager, Hayden, to take an important contract to be signed by a client in London and to use the train. Hayden refuses to pay for the train fare.

7.3 The implied duties of employees

7.3.1 The duty to obey lawful and reasonable instructions

The duty to obey lawful and reasonable instructions originates with the master and servant rules developed in the nineteenth century, which also at that time included a master's right to chastise (see Chapter 1.4.1). Now it is much more to do with the necessity of cooperation in order to satisfy the needs of the contract.

Obviously provided the order is both lawful and reasonable then it should be obeyed and a refusal could amount to a breach of the contract justifying dismissal. In this respect the contract itself is significant.

CASE EXAMPLE

United Kingdom Atomic Energy Authority v Claydon [1974] ICR 128

Here an express mobility clause was contained in the written terms of the contract. Under this the employee was required to work anywhere in the United Kingdom. He was asked to transfer to another site and when he refused he was dismissed as a result. It was held that the instruction was both lawful and reasonable because it was included in the express terms of the contract.

Express mobility clauses have, however, been the subject of some controversy and of different treatment by the courts. In *Bass Leisure Ltd v Thomas* [1994] IRLR 104 the EAT held that the principle on mobility clauses from *Claydon* should not automatically be followed. In *High Table Ltd v Horst* [1998] ICR 409 it was suggested that the proper test was a factual one so that the existence of a mobility clause in a contract did not mean that an employee could automatically be transferred if his current place of work was his expected place of work. Besides this, in *United Bank Ltd v Akhtar* [1989] IRLR 507 (see 7.2.5 above) suggested that mobility clauses, in any case, should be exercised reasonably.

Clearly a dismissal for a breach of the duty can be justified because in essence it destroys the basis of the contract and makes it unworkable.

CASE EXAMPLE

Laws v London Chronicle [1959] 1 WLR 698

The claimant was employed as an assistant to an advertising manager of a newspaper. After only working for the newspaper for three weeks she accompanied her line manager to an editorial meeting and followed him when he walked out of the meeting, despite being ordered to stay by the managing director. She was dismissed without notice for disobedience and claimed wrongful dismissal. The court did not accept that her actions were either wilful or sufficiently serious to amount to breach of the implied duty to obey lawful and reasonable orders, and upheld her claim for wrongful dismissal.

JUDGMENT

Lord Evershed MR explained: 'it is no doubt … generally true that wilful disobedience of an order will justify summary dismissal, since wilful disobedience of a lawful and reasonable order shows a disregard – a complete disregard – of a condition essential to the contract of service, namely the condition that the servant must obey the proper orders of the master and that, unless he does so, the relationship is … struck at fundamentally.'

By definition, of course, this means that there is no obligation on an employee to obey an order that is unlawful. In fact the employee could be said to be under a duty to disobey such instructions.

CASE EXAMPLE

Morrish v Henly's Ltd [1973] ICR 482

The employee was a store's driver and was bound to fill his vehicle with fuel as required. On one day he filled up with five gallons and recorded it. When he filled up the next day he saw that this had been changed to seven gallons so he changed it back. This was then repeated it until he discovered a record showing that two gallons had been put into his vehicle that had not in fact. In an argument with his manager who was making the changes he would not accept the instruction to leave the changes to the record and so he resigned and claimed unfair dismissal. The court held that the employee was only bound to obey reasonable and lawful orders. Since what the employee was asked to do was unlawful, disciplinary action arising from that was also unlawful and the dismissal was unfair.

JUDGMENT

Sir Hugh Griffiths commented: 'The employers contended that ... it was a common practice to alter the records ... to cover deficiencies [and] his refusal to do so was an unreasonable refusal to obey an order, which justified dismissal. We cannot accept this submission. It involves the proposition that it is an implied term ... that he should accept an order to connive at the falsification of one of his employer's records. The proposition [is] untenable ... the employee was fully entitled to refuse.'

It is equally clear that there is equally no obligation on an employee to obey an order which is unreasonable.

CASE EXAMPLE

Ottoman Bank v Chakarian [1930] AC 277

The employee was ordered to go to Constantinople (now Istanbul) by his employer, where he was in fact in threat of being killed. Since the order might obviously expose him to danger or to the risk of loss of liberty or life, the order was unreasonable and he was not obliged to obey it.

However, the risk must also be a real one. In *Walmsley v Udec Refrigerators Ltd* [1972] IRLR 80 an employee was dismissed after refusing to travel to a place in Ireland. His argument that it was hotbed of IRA activists and he was therefore in danger could not be substantiated so his refusal was a breach of his contract.

What is reasonable may also have to be measured against good industrial relations. In *Payne v Spook* [1984] IRLR 219 EAT a foreman was asked to compile a merit table of the performance of employees and send out warnings to those on the bottom of the table. Since he did not see all of the employees each week he refused and was threatened with dismissal. Since the system was unfair a dismissal for refusing to apply it was unfair also. However, in *Robinson v Flitwick Frames Ltd* [1975] IRLR 261 a dismissal for a refusal to work overtime, which was not a contractual obligation, was fair because all the other workers complied and this would have in effect meant different employees operating on different terms.

One other important point is that it is the refusal itself which amounts to a breach rather than necessarily the manner in which the refusal is made.

CASE EXAMPLE

Pepper v Webb [1969] 1 WLR 514

A domestic gardener, with a history of insolence and inefficiency, was asked what arrangements he had made concerning a greenhouse during his absence. The gardener replied 'I couldn't care less about your bloody greenhouse or your sodding garden' and then walked off resulting in his dismissal. His dismissal was justified since his behaviour made continued employment impossible.

JUDGMENT

Harman LJ stated: 'Now what will justify an instant dismissal? – something done by the employee which impliedly or expressly is a repudiation of the fundamental terms of the contract.'

7.3.2 The duty to exercise reasonable care and skill

An employee, on appointment, undertakes to perform the work competently and taking all reasonable care and skill. A failure to show such competence and skill can therefore amount to a breach of the implied duty. This was identified at an early point in *Harmer v Cornelius* [1858] 5 CBNS 236 (although the case actually involves a representation by the worker that he had the necessary skill to carry out the work).

So an employer might be able to recover for incompetence or lack of skill by the employee that has caused a loss to the employer.

CASE EXAMPLE

Janeta Bank v Ahmed [1981] ICR 791

A branch manager of a bank had offered mortgages and loans over a period of time to clients who were in fact bad credit risks, causing a loss to his employer of £34,640. The employer argued that his conduct had been negligent, dismissed him and successfully claimed for the amount. It was held that he had failed to exercise the proper care and skill that his job demanded.

Another aspect of the duty obviously involves taking appropriate care of the employer's property.

CASE EXAMPLE

Superlux v Plaidstead [1958] The Times 12 December 1958

The employee was entrusted with his employer's van and the property inside it as part of his contract. When his negligence led to the property being stolen from the van this justified his dismissal.

7.3.3 The duty to adapt

In an ever changing economy and with technology constantly developing it is inevitable that working practices change over time. The duty to adapt is not an absolute duty on the employee without qualification as this would be to demand of an employee what he never contracted for in the first place. However, where an employer does need to change working practices, unless the changes are so fundamental as to change the very nature of the job, then employees should be willing to adapt to necessary changes.

CASE EXAMPLE

Cresswell v Board of Inland Revenue [1984] 2 All ER 713

For many years an employee had carried out his clerical duties using paper filing systems. With the rise in technology it was only logical for greater efficiency that the employer chose to move to a computerised system of storing information and in wider communication. The employee refused to accept training towards using the computerised systems and was obstructive about the change. In doing so the employee argued that there was an implied term in his contract that he should not be required to carry out his work in a manner other than that which he had been used to. As a result he claimed that the employer was in breach of the contract by expecting him to change. The court rejected the suggestion that such a term existed. On the contrary it held that there was an implied duty on an employee to adapt to all necessary changing circumstances in the work environment. This necessarily included adapting to new skills and methods as required. However, it was obviously also for the employer to provide training which the employer had done.

JUDGMENT

Walton J explained: 'it will in all cases, be a question of pure fact whether the training involved the acquisition of such esoteric skills that it would not be reasonable to expect the employee to acquire them. In an age when the computer has forced its way into the school room and where electronic games are played by schoolchildren in their own home as a matter of everyday occurrence, it can hardly be considered that to ask an employee to acquire basic skills as to retrieving information from a computer or feeding such information into a computer is something in the slightest esoteric, or even nowadays, unusual.'

On the basis of this it was accepted by the court in *Connor v Halfords Ltd* [1972] IRLR 109 that a dismissal for a refusal to attend training necessary to adapt to new methods is a fair dismissal. Such a refusal is a straightforward breach of contract by the employee.

7.3.4 The duty of faithful service

The duty of faithful service, sometimes known as the duty of fidelity again goes back to the development of master and servant rules in the nineteenth century (see Chapter 1.4.3).

The original aspects of the duty included:

- the duty to be honest;
- the duty not to compete with the employer;
- the duty of confidentiality;
- the duty to disclose misconduct.

There has also been suggested a general duty not to harm the employer's business in any way.

The duty to be honest

The duty could include simple acts of dishonesty. For instance in *Denco Ltd v Joinson* [1992] IRLR 63 the employee was dismissed when it was found that he had used a password without authorisation to gain access to confidential records in a computer. The dismissal was fair.

It could also include acts which while the employee might argue are not dishonest in fact could be seen as a breach of good faith. For instance in *Sinclair v Neighbour* [1967] 2 QB 279 an employee borrowed money from a till. Even though he intended to pay it back and had left an IOU, it was held to be a breach.

Another aspect of the duty is that the employee should not make a secret profit or bribe out of his employment.

CASE EXAMPLE

Boston Deep Sea Fishing and Ice Co v Ansell [1888] 39 Ch D 339

Here a managing director of a company placed orders from another company from whom he was receiving a commission. He challenged the decision to dismiss him. The court held that the actions were a breach of the implied duty of faithful service or fidelity justifying dismissal. One aspect of the duty is not to make a secret profit, commission, gift or bribe from the employment because otherwise there is a conflict of interest. The employee, as a director, was also under a fiduciary duty.

The duty not to compete with the employer

In general the courts accept that an employee can do whatever he likes in his spare time. On this basis they dislike prohibiting spare time activities unless they harm the employer.

CASE EXAMPLE

Hivac Ltd v Park Royal Scientific Instruments Ltd [1946] Ch 169

Two highly skilled employees of a company involved in a technologically advanced business worked for a direct competitor on weekends. The company then sought an injunction to prevent this competition. The court granted the injunction in the circumstances, even though there had been no breach of confidentiality. The court identified that an injunction would not be available where employees worked part-time in a different type of business which was not a competitor. To do so would be to interfere with the employee's right to earn a living.

While an employee may be able to indicate a future intention to compete with his employer, for instance in a business capacity, it would be a breach of the duty of fidelity if the employee was to compete during employment. In *Adamson v B & L Cleaning Services Ltd* [1995] IRLR 193 EAT a foreman tendered for the renewal of a cleaning contract which his employer currently held. His dismissal for refusing not to tender was fair, as he had breached his duty.

The duty of confidentiality

The general duty is not to misuse confidential information. There may be a difference in the application of the rule between existing employees and ex-employees. In the case of existing employees the rule is strict and may cover the employee's own skill and knowledge. In *Bents Brewery Co Ltd v Hogan* [1945] 2 All ER 570 Lynsey J stated:

JUDGMENT

'It is quite clear that an employee is under an obligation to his employer not to disclose information obtained by him in the course of his employment.'

To decide if information is confidential leading to a breach, if it is disclosed it must:

- have the necessary quality of confidence;
- be imparted to the employee in circumstances which create an obligation of confidence;
- involve an unauthorised use of the information to the disadvantage of the employer.

In *Foster v Scaffolding Ltd* [1973] IDS Brief 13 a dismissal was upheld as fair when an employee had passed information to a rival company to the disadvantage of his employer.

Where the employee has left the employment then restrictions on disclosure are probably limited to trade secrets and client contact. These may then be the subject of a valid restraint of trade clause if reasonable (see Chapter 6).

CASE EXAMPLE

Faccenda Chicken v Fowler [1986] ICR 297

The ex-employee was a sales manager for a company selling fresh chickens. He developed a new sales strategy involving a door to door service. He then left to set up his own business in competition with his former employer which sought an injunction to restrain him from doing so.

The employer failed to gain the injunction because it had not included an express restraint clause in the contract to protect its business interest.

It will, however, be a straightforward breach of the duty where the ex-employee in effect 'poaches' clients away from his ex-employer. In *Sanders v Parry* [1967] 2 All ER 803 an assistant solicitor set up in independent practice by taking one of his ex-employer's main clients with him. This was a clear breach of the duty.

In the case of employee inventions the traditional position was that the employer is entitled to the inventions of the employee if made during the course of employment and are referable to the employment. In *British Syphon Co Ltd v Homewood* [1956] 1 WLR 1190 the company discovered a new type of soda siphon and the chief technician applied to patent it but failed.

The position is now covered by s39 Patents Act 1977 under which employee inventions only belong to the employer if (a) they were specifically assigned, whether made in the course of employment or not, or (b) they were made during the course of employment and the employee was under an obligation to further the employer's interests. Under the Copyright Designs and Patents Act 1988 an employer may be the first owner of copyright of literary, dramatic, musical and artistic work.

Of course there are also situations which act as exceptions to the basic rule where an employee might be obliged to breach confidentiality. One such instance would be where the employee is under a legal duty to provide necessary information to a health and safety inspector under the Health and Safety at Work, etc. Act 1974. Another example is the duty of a doctor, not only to his patient's confidentiality, but to the public good. In *W v Egdell* [1990] Ch 359 Scott J recognised that there was not only a duty of confidentiality to a patient but also a duty to the public in situations where failure to disclose information might expose the patient or someone else to the risk of death or serious harm.

There is also an exemption to the principle under the Public Interest Disclosure Act 1998 in the case of a so-called 'protected disclosure' (sometimes called 'whistle-blowing'). This is one where the employee has disclosed confidential information and has been dismissed and has disclosed information that is confidential to his employment because he reasonably believes:

- that a criminal offence has been, is being or is likely to be committed; or
- that a person has failed, is failing or is likely to fail to comply with legal obligations; or
- that a miscarriage of justice has occurred, is occurring or is likely to occur; or
- that the health and safety of an individual has been, is being or is likely to be damaged; or
- that the environment has been, is being or is likely to be damaged; or
- that information relating to any of the above has been, is being or is likely to be deliberately concealed.

The employee only needs a reasonable belief in any of the above and the disclosure must be made to:

- the employer or another responsible person; or

- a legal adviser; or
- a Minister of the Crown (if the employee was appointed by such); or
- a prescribed person e.g. a local authority.

(N.B. the issue of 'whistle-blowing' will be considered again in Chapter 22 under unfair dismissal.)

The duty to disclose misconduct

While there is no general absolute duty on an employee to disclose misconduct, it could in specific circumstances be seen as a breach of the duty of faithful service. This area of the law has certainly developed as an element of the fiduciary duty of directors who, while executives, are still employees. It was certainly an issue that was raised in the cases below.

CASE EXAMPLE

Bell v Lever Bros [1932] AC 161

The company appointed Bell to be chairman of a subsidiary company that was failing in order to improve its performance. He succeeded in doing so well within the time set under his contract. As a result the subsidiary was then merged with another company within the group. The employer then reached a settlement of £30,000 for the termination of Bell's contract as it did not require two chairmen. After reaching this settlement it then discovered, from Bell himself, that he was in breach of an express clause in his contract which prohibited him from dealing in stocks privately and sued for return of the money it had paid Bell. The House of Lords (now the Supreme Court) held that Bell was not under any duty to reveal his own misconduct, although he may have been if he had been directly questioned about it. The employer had argued that it had only paid the money as a result of a common mistake, but it was held that there was no such mistake which would make the contract void because the mistake was not operative, it not being the reason why Lever had agreed the settlement. In fact the settlement was to reward Bell for the early termination of a completed contract which would have been part of its duty to pay for the work Bell had done.

The case has been distinguished in similar circumstances but where there was a genuine mistake of fact which was the basis on which the contract was formed. On this basis the mistake would be operative.

CASE EXAMPLE

Sybron Corporation v Rochem Ltd [1983] ICR 801

Under a contractual agreement the company paid money into the pension fund of its European Manager and when he took early retirement he received pension and insurance benefits. It was only after his retirement that the company discovered that he had conspired with other colleagues to set up a business in direct competition with the company so it then sought restitution of money it had paid him. The company argued that, if it had known of the misconduct while the manager was still working for it, it could have dismissed him for gross misconduct which also amounted to a breach of the implied duty of fidelity. It was held that the money could be recovered since it was given under a mistake of fact and the breach of duty would have given rise to a right to dismiss the manager summarily.

JUDGMENT

Stephenson LJ stated: 'there is no general duty to report a fellow-servant's misconduct or breach of contract; whether there is such a duty depends on the contract and on the terms of employment of the particular servant'. He also then agrees with Walton J (the judge at first instance) who said: 'I do not think that there is any general duty resting upon an employee to inform his master of the breaches of duty of other employees; the law would do industrial relations no great service if it held that such a duty did in fact exist in all cases. The duty must ... depend upon all the circumstances of the case, and the relationship of the parties to their employer and <u>inter se</u>.'

The duty not to harm the employer's business in any way

One final aspect of the duty of faithful service that has been considered by the courts concerns the extent to which an employee has to cooperate with the employer. The question is of obvious sensitivity when set against trade union rights and trade union action. Courts in dealing with the issue have been keen to show that an employee should not be doing anything that is harmful to the employer's business.

CASE EXAMPLE

Secretary of State for Employment v Associated Society of Locomotive Engineers and Firemen (No 2) [1972] 2 QB 455

Railway workers in an industrial dispute then engaged in a so-called 'work to rule'. The action meant that they were refusing to work any overtime including rest days. The action was clearly designed to put pressure on the employer by causing disruption to services. The employer depended on the employees being flexible. At the time the Industrial Relations Act 1971 was in force and under its provisions the Secretary of State was empowered to bring action against trade unions in disputes that might cause harm to the national economy and did so. One problem for the court was that if the employees were only sticking to the works rules and these were contractual, then they could only be said to be honouring their contractual obligations. However, the court actually referred to another part of the rule book which stated that employees should 'make every effort to facilitate the working of trains and prevent unavoidable delay'. The court held that the employees were bound to interpret the rules reasonably and not in such a way that would disrupt services and they were thus in breach of the implied duty of faithful service.

JUDGMENT

Lord Denning explained it in the following terms: 'I quite agree that a man is not bound positively to do more for his employer than his contract requires. He can withdraw his goodwill if he pleases. But what he must not do is wilfully to obstruct the employer as he goes about his business. That is plainly the case where man is employed singly by a single employer.... It is equally the case where he is employed, as one of many, to work in an undertaking which needs the service of all. If he, with the others, takes steps wilfully to disrupt the undertaking, to produce chaos so that it will not run as it should, then each who is a party to those steps is guilty of a breach of his contract.'

The potential consequences of applying this aspect of the duty go beyond the issue of fair or unfair dismissals, and the principle has been extended in more recent times.

CASE EXAMPLE

Ticehurst v British Telecommunications plc [1992] IRLR 219 CA

The claimant, a union official, had taken part in a number of one day strikes, and instructed members to withdraw goodwill, in effect to do nothing outside their strict contractual obligations. The employer then demanded that employees sign an undertaking that they would work normally and anyone who refused would be sent home and their pay deducted. The claimant would not sign, was sent home and sued for the lost pay. Her claim failed since her withdrawal of goodwill amounted to a breach of the implied term of faithful service, as it was disruptive of the employer's business.

In fact another extension of the principle is that a wrongful act by an employee that harms the employer may still be a breach of the duty even if it does not benefit the employee in any way (as the railwaymen's action above could have done if it had succeeded). For instance, in *Dalton v Burton's Gold Medal Biscuits Ltd* [1974] IRLR 45 a dismissal of an employee who clocked in a fellow employee falsely was upheld as fair.

ACTIVITY

Self-assessment questions

1. What is the significance of the written terms of a contract of employment in determining whether an order is reasonable?
2. What is the effect on a dismissal which is for refusing to obey an unlawful order?
3. Why are employees under a duty to exercise reasonable care and skill in their work?
4. What impact do changing working practices have on an employee's duties to the employer?
5. What are the various aspects of an employee's duty of faithful service?
6. What is the justification for limiting the freedom of an employee to do what he wants in his spare time?
7. Why is there a difference between the duty of confidentiality during employment and after employment?
8. In what circumstances will an employee be bound to disclose the misdeeds of fellow employees?
9. What problems could result from there being an apparent duty not to disrupt or harm the employer's business?

ACTIVITY

Quick quiz

In the following situations identify which implied duty of an employee is involved and consider whether it may have been breached.

1. Under pressure to get an order of components made to meet a tight deadline, Greg has assembled 500 incorrectly so that they all have to be done again. Despite not having been shown the correct process Greg is dismissed.
2. Terry, a law lecturer at the Woolberry University, works part-time on weekends delivering pizzas. He has been given a written warning by his employer, even though there is nothing in his written terms about part-time working.
3. Jaz, a works driver is instructed to give a lift to a manager, Ken, who has to go to an important meeting in town. When they arrive at the venue for the business meeting it is raining heavily so Ken tells Jaz to park outside the building and wait till he comes back. As there are only double yellow lines outside the building Jaz tells Ken that he cannot do this. When they return to work later Ken gives Jaz his notice of termination of his contract.

Figure 7.2 Do the implied duties help to create a balance in the employment relationship?

KEY FACTS

The process of implying terms	Case
• Traditionally measured by the 'officious bystander test' • Or by custom if 'certain, notorious, and reasonable' • Original justification was need for business efficacy • Now is 'necessary incident of definite category of contractual relationship' • And may be based on what is reasonable • Effect on express terms is disputable • Now terms can be implied despite intent of parties	*Shirlaw v Southern Foundries* *Sagar v Ridehalgh* *The Moorcock* *Scally v Southern Health & Social Services Board* *Mears v Safecar Security* compare *United Bank v Akhtar* with *Rank Xerox Ltd v Churchill* *Johnstone v Bloomsbury Health Authority*

The implied duties of employers	Case
To pay wages	*Way v Latilla*
To provide work for e.g. actors, pieceworkers	*Herbert Clayton & Jack Waller Ltd v Oliver*
To take reasonable care of employee:	
• provide safe system, plant, premises, colleagues	*Wilson & Clyde Coal Co. v English*
• not cause psychiatric harm	*Walker v Northumberland*
• but no duty to property	*Deyong v Shenburn*
To indemnify for all reasonable expenses	*Gregory v Ford*
To give mutual trust and respect:	
• treat employee reasonably	*United Bank v Akhtar*
• not be abusive or provocative	*Wilson v Racher*
• not to harm employee's reputation	*Malik v BCCI*
• protect from sexual harassment	*Bracebridge Engineering v Darby*
To protect confidentiality	*Dalgleish v Lothian & Borders Police Board*
To deal properly with grievances	*W A Goold (Pearmark) Ltd v McConnell*
To make any references accurate	*Spring v Guardian Assurance*

The implied duties of employees	Case
To obey lawful and reasonable instructions	*United Kingdom Atomic Energy Authority v Claydon*
• but not unlawful ones	*Morrish v Henlys*
• nor unreasonable ones	*Ottoman Bank v Chakarian*
To exercise care and skill	*Superlux v Plaidstead*
To adapt to necessary changes	*Cresswell v Board of Inland Revenue*
To give faithful service:	
• to be honest – and not make a secret profit	*Boston Deep Sea Fishing and Ice Co v Ansell*
• or to compete with employer	*Hivac v Park Royal Scientific Instruments*
• or to misuse confidential information	*Faccenda Chicken v Fowler*
• to disclose misdeeds of colleagues	*Sybron Corporation v Rochem*
• not harm employer's business	*Secretary of State for Employment v ASLEF*

ESSAY Discuss the extent to which the implied duties of both the employer and the employee help to balance the relationship.

Explain the background to the implied terms

- Terms have been implied to give effect to the presumed intention of the parties – the officious bystander test.
- And terms have been implied to give effect to business efficacy and because of trade custom and to ensure that the express terms are carried out reasonably.
- Some terms are now implied irrespective of intention of parties because they are considered to be so important in the context of the employment relationship.

Identify the implied duties owed by employers to their employees

- To pay wages.
- To provide work in some limited circumstances.
- To take care of the employee.
- To indemnify the employee for necessary expenses.
- To show mutual trust and respect.
- To respect the employee's confidentiality.
- To deal with grievances promptly.
- Not to give negligently prepared or inaccurate references.

Identify and explain the implied duties owed by employees to their employers

- To obey lawful and reasonable instruction.
- To exercise reasonable care and skill.
- To adapt where necessary and reasonable.
- To give faithful service.

Discuss the relative weight of the implied duties

- There are more duties owed by the employer than by the employee.
- But the remedy for breach of an implied duty by the employer is likely only to be a sum of compensation – and this may mean in any case that the employee no longer has a job.
- On the other hand the remedy for a breach of an implied duty by the employee is likely to mean some form of disciplinary proceedings against him and it may even result in his dismissal.

Discuss the relative significance of the different duties

Employer's implied duties

- Paying a wage is not a burden since the employer is gaining the benefit from the employee's work.
- The employer is only bound to provide work in limited circumstances where it involves reputation, commission or piece work – so there is no fundamental right to work.
- Taking care of the employee is tied up with health and safety and it is questionable whether statute is now more important.
- It is only fair that an employer should indemnify the employee for expenses incurred in the course of employment and to respect confidentiality, hear grievances promptly and not prepare references negligently but an employer is not bound to give a reference and this could be a problem for the employee.
- The duty of mutual respect may mean that an employer has to treat an employee reasonably but may also often mean that the employee has to claim constructive dismissal for a remedy and then is without a job.

Employee's implied duties

- Obeying instructions is obviously necessary and balance is created by it only applying to lawful and reasonable ones.
- Exercising reasonable care and skill, adapting where necessary and giving faithful service are also necessary but a breach may result in dismissal.

REACH REASONED CONCLUSIONS

SUMMARY

- Like with any contract terms can be implied by fact or law.
- Traditionally this would have been according to the 'officious bystander' and to give business efficacy.
- Now in employment it is more based on the specific relationship and the specific circumstances – and term will be measured against what is reasonable.
- Implied terms in employment contracts have developed as duties owed by both employer and employee.
- The employer's duties are: to pay wages;to provide work for e.g. actors, piece-workers, etc.; to take reasonable care of employees; to indemnify for all reasonable expenses; to give mutual trust and respect; to protect the confidentiality of the employee; to deal with grievances properly; to be accurate where references are provided.
- The employee's duties are: to obey lawful and reasonable instructions; to exercise care and skill; to adapt to necessary change; to give faithful service which includes honesty, not competing, preserving confidentiality; in some cases disclosing the misdeeds of colleagues; in general not doing anything to harm the employer's business.

Further reading

Emir, Astra, *Selwyn's Law of Employment 17th edition*. Oxford University Press, 2012, Chapter 3, pp. 97–101.

Pitt, Gwyneth, *Cases and Materials on Employment Law 3rd edition*. Pearson, 2008, Chapter 4, pp. 172–212.

Sargeant, Malcolm and Lewis, David, *Employment Law 6th edition*. Pearson, 2012, Chapter 3.3–3.5.

8

Statutory employment protections

AIMS AND OBJECTIVES

After reading this chapter you should be able to:

▥ Understand the rules relating to wages, deductions from wages and the National Minimum Wage

▥ Understand what is meant by a guarantee payment and the circumstances where they are made

▥ Understand the rules relating to sickness, medical suspension and paid sick leave

▥ Understand the rules relating to maternity, leave during maternity, maternity payments, and dismissal and discrimination because of pregnancy or maternity

▥ Critically analyse the area

▥ Apply the law to factual situations and reach conclusions

8.1 Wages

8.1.1 The meaning of wages

The basic obligation on an employer to pay wages is clearly a contractual one. This is the consideration element of the bargain (see Chapter 5.1.3). The employee will agree to provide work in return for a wage. This does not necessarily have to be a set wage since it is possible to be employed on a commission only basis or on a piecework basis, in which case remuneration could be variable.

Statutory protection of pay originally came in the Truck Acts 1831 and 1896 which made it an offence for an employer to contract to pay wages other than in current 'coin of the realm' and workmen could recover for sums paid in a different form (see Chapter 1.3.1). The Acts were repealed in the Wages Act 1986 which also introduced rules on deductions from wages (see 8.1.2 below). Now the rules on wages are in the Employment Rights Act 1996.

Wages are defined quite broadly in section 27(1) Employment Rights Act 1996 as amended.

SECTION

'27 Meaning of "wages", etc.

(1) In this Part "wages", in relation to a worker, means any sums payable to the worker in connection with his employment, including –

   (a) any fee, bonus, commission, holiday pay or other emolument referable to his employment, whether payable under his contract or otherwise,

   (b) statutory sick pay...

   (c) statutory maternity pay...

      (ca) ordinary statutory paternity pay or additional statutory paternity pay...

      (cb) statutory adoption pay...

   (d) a guarantee payment...

   (e) any payment for time off ... for carrying out trade union duties, etc....

   (f) remuneration on suspension on medical grounds ... and remuneration on suspension on maternity grounds...

      (fa) remuneration on ending the supply of an agency worker on maternity grounds...

   (g) any sum payable in pursuance of an order for reinstatement or re-engagement...

   (h) any sum payable in pursuance of an order for the continuation of a contract of employment...

   (j) remuneration under a protective award...

      but excluding any payments within subsection (2).'

The definition is potentially very wide, although perhaps not as wide as the EU definition of pay in Article 157(2) (see Chapter 10.3.2). It can obviously include things such as overtime payments, shift payments and also accrued holiday payments.

CASE EXAMPLE

Greg May (Carpet Fitters and Contractors) Ltd v Dring [1990] IRLR 19

The employee was entitled to accrued holiday pay on termination of his contract, but his contract of employment also identified that this would not apply if he was dismissed for gross misconduct. The employer did then dismiss him for gross misconduct and refused to pay any accrued holiday pay. The claimant was seeking payment of the money. The EAT held that the arrangement in respect of the holiday pay was contractual and was therefore was subject to his dismissal actually being for gross misconduct. Since the tribunal had found that it was not gross misconduct he was entitled to the holiday pay which was part of his wages.

It can also include discretionary bonuses that are on the face of it non-contractual payments.

CASE EXAMPLE

Kent Management Services Ltd v Butterfield [1992] IRLR 394

On termination of his contract an employee received a letter informing him that he would receive four weeks' salary in lieu of notice along with the monies due to him for outstanding annual holiday entitlement but also stating that 'As the commission and bonus schemes are discretionary and non-contractual, we shall not be exercising our discretion in your favour in respect of any outstanding commissions.' In his claim the employee was arguing that the *ex gratia* discretionary bonus payments should be counted as wages and that he was therefore entitled to them. The EAT accepted that the payments could be classed as wages because both parties contemplated that such payments would be made where appropriate under the scheme. The court also suggested *in obiter* that if such payments were only to be paid on satisfactory performance or for some other stipulation that this should be clearly expressed in the contract.

It does not include payment in lieu of notice since this in law is damages paid in respect of the breach of the contract and is a payment in respect of the termination not the employment. In *Delaney v Staples t/a De Montfort Recruitment* [1990] IRLR 86 the House of Lords (now the Supreme Court) identified that payment in lieu of wages, where it relates to the period after employment, are not wages, which are for services rendered, but damages in anticipation of a breach of the contract by termination.

There are also certain payments which the Act indicates do not count as wages. These are found in section 27(2).

SECTION

'27

(2) Those payments are –
  (a) any payment by way of an advance under an agreement for a loan or by way of an advance of wages (but without prejudice to the application of section 13 to any deduction made from the worker's wages in respect of any such advance),
  (b) any payment in respect of expenses incurred by the worker in carrying out his employment,
  (c) any payment by way of a pension, allowance or gratuity in connection with the worker's retirement or as compensation for loss of office,
  (d) any payment referable to the worker's redundancy, and
  (e) any payment to the worker otherwise than in his capacity as a worker.'

Section 27(5) also explains that in most instances benefits in kind are not classed as wages.

SECTION

'27

(5) For the purposes of this Part any monetary value attaching to any payment or benefit in kind furnished to a worker by his employer shall not be treated as wages of the worker except in the case of any voucher, stamp or similar document which is –
  (a) of a fixed value expressed in monetary terms, and
  (b) capable of being exchanged (whether on its own or together with other vouchers, stamps or documents, and whether immediately or only after a time) for money, goods or services (or for any combination of two or more of those things).'

So this is really limited to things like luncheon vouchers but most benefits in kind would not be classed as wages.

8.1.2 Deductions from pay

The rules regarding deductions from pay extended to include all workers and are now contained in sections 13–27 of the Employment Rights Act 1996.

Section 13(3) defines what a deduction is.

SECTION

'13 Right not to suffer unauthorised deductions.

(3) Where the total amount of wages paid on any occasion by an employer to a worker employed by him is less than the total amount of the wages properly payable by him to the worker on that occasion (after deductions), the amount of the deficiency shall be treated for the purposes of this Part as a deduction made by the employer from the worker's wages on that occasion.'

So a deduction in effect covers any situation where the employer is paying the employee less than the employee is rightly due under the contract of employment.

CASE EXAMPLE

Bruce v Wiggins Teape (Stationery) Ltd [1994] IRLR 536

In order to meet business needs the employer agreed to pay enhanced overtime rates to workers on a 'rolling night shift' which were double that which was paid to ordinary night shift workers. It made these payments for four years then decided to pay the rolling night shift workers the same overtime rates as the other night shift workers. The workers and their trade union objected to this unilateral change in pay and the workers then worked under protest and brought a claim in the tribunal (at that time under the Wages Act 1986) for unlawful deductions from their wages. The EAT, reversing the decision of the tribunal held that the enhanced overtime rates did count as wages and that the decision to unilaterally reduce the rate was an unlawful deduction.

JUDGMENT

Mummery J identified: 'The crucial question is ... what was the amount of wages "properly payable" to the workers? On the facts ... this point is clear. Wiggins Teape agreed to pay the enhanced rate of overtime to ... the workers, on the rolling night shift.... There was no provision in the contract of employment or in the particulars of employment which entitled Wiggins Teape to reduce the wages of their workers unilaterally.'

Wages are defined in section 27 Employment Rights Act 1996. The definition is broad and includes 'any sums payable to worker by his employer in connection with his employment': as a result there are a number of ways in which a deduction could occur and it could obviously include a total failure to pay some or all remuneration that could be described as wages, so the deduction must relate to something that falls within the definition of wages.

CASE EXAMPLE

Delaney v Staples t/a De Montfort Recruitment [1990] IRLR 86

The claimant was summarily dismissed and was given a cheque as payment. This included £55 which was for commission and also holiday pay and £82 which was a payment in lieu of notice. The employer then stopped the cheque before it could be cashed and justified this on the basis that the employee had taken confidential information with her. The claimant brought a claim for unlawful deduction from her wages. One of the significant issues at the time was whether the claim could be made in a tribunal or whether it had to be made in court. On this basis it had to be decided whether a payment in lieu of wages counted as wages. The House of Lords (now the Supreme Court) identified that on a literal interpretation the £55 was wages and there was therefore an unlawful deduction from wages. However, it also held that a payment in lieu of wages, where it relates to the period after employment, is not wages, which are for services rendered, but in fact amount to damages in anticipation of a breach of the contract by termination. Lord Browne-Wilkinson listed four circumstances where a lieu payment would be appropriate:

(i) the employer gives the appropriate notice but does not require work from the employee (garden leave);

(ii) under the contract the employer is entitled to terminate the contract with notice or summarily on payment of a sum of money in lieu of notice;

(iii) an agreement between employer and employee to terminate the contract for an agreed payment;

(iv) the employer dismisses the employee summarily with a lieu payment.

Since the Employment Tribunals Extension of Jurisdiction Order 1994 such actions can be heard in tribunals so the specific problem in the case has been removed.

A deduction can also be identified in circumstances where the employer has used other methods to hide a deduction. In *McCree v London Borough of Tower Hamlets* [1992] IRLR 56 the employer in fact attempted to achieve an actual deduction in pay by absorbing it into a pay increase which obviously should have been greater. The EAT acknowledged that it was still an unlawful deduction from wages.

It has also been accepted by the courts that a reduction in work which in consequence leads on to reduction in pay is a deduction from wages which without proper authority is an unlawful deduction under section 13.

CASE EXAMPLE

International Packaging Corporation (UK) Ltd v Balfour [2003] IRLR 11

The employer introduced short-time working because of falling orders. This inevitably resulted in the earnings of the employees being reduced from what they otherwise would have been if working to full capacity. The EAT held that because there was no power in the contract and the change had not been agreed to by the employees that it was an unlawful deduction under section 13.

JUDGMENT

Lord Johnston explained: 'Reduction in working hours is plainly a variation of a contract of employment and, unless expressly catered for within that contract, or allowed by implication again within the terms of the contract, any actual deduction of wages, even if related to the hours worked, is not authorised by the statute and can only be achieved by agreement.'

Section 13(1) also identifies the only deductions from pay that can be made lawfully by the employer.

'13 Right not to suffer unauthorised deductions.

(1) An employer shall not make a deduction from wages of a worker employed by him unless –

    (a) the deduction is required or authorised to be made by virtue of a statutory provision or a relevant provision of the worker's contract, or

    (b) the worker has previously signified in writing his agreement or consent to the making of the deduction.'

So lawful deductions are really of three types:

- those authorised by statute – this would obviously include deductions for tax and National Insurance contributions but it could also include attachment of earnings orders;

- those authorised by the contract of employment – this need not be in writing but the employee must have been given notification of the deduction;

CASE EXAMPLE

Kerr v Sweater Shop (Scotland) Ltd [1996] IRLR 424

The EAT held that a notice in a factory which had been posted by the employer and which stated that accrued holiday pay would not be given to employees who were dismissed for gross misconduct was not sufficient written notification to the workers of a contractual term to authorise a deduction from their wages.

- those authorised by employee in writing before the deduction is made – in which case the written agreement must state that the deduction is to be made from wages or it will be an unlawful deduction.

CASE EXAMPLE

Potter v Hunt Contracts Ltd [1992] IRLR 108

This involved an agreement under which the employer agreed to pay the cost of an HGV driving course but the employee was liable to repay a proportion of the training course fee to his employer if his employment was terminated within two years. The employee in fact left after one month and so the employer did not pay him any wages. The EAT held that this was an unlawful deduction from wages since the agreement did not specifically authorise repayment by way of a deduction from wages.

Another significant point is that as well as being authorised by whatever means, the deduction must also be justified in fact.

CASE EXAMPLE

Fairfield Ltd v Skinner [1993] IRLR 4

A van driver was subject to requirements that deductions would be made from his wages for any private phone calls that he made, for any private mileage that he did in the employer's van and for any excess insurance payments arising from damage to the van. After the employee was dismissed the employer deducted £305 from his final wage with half of this being for damage done to the van and the other half being a notional fee for private phone calls. The employee claimed that this was an unlawful deduction (at that time under the Wages Act 1986). The tribunal identified that the employee had personally paid for damage to the van and that there was no evidence to show how the deductions for private phone calls had been calculated so that the deductions were indeed unlawful. The EAT held that although an employer may have a right to make deductions that a deduction can only be made if it can be justified in fact. Since the employer's allegations were unsubstantiated there was no justification for the deduction.

Section 14 Employment Rights Act 1996 identifies a number of deductions which are in fact exempt from the provisions in section 13 and so if an employee is seeking a remedy in respect of any of these it would have to be done in a breach of contract action in the courts rather than in the tribunal.

- A deduction to reimburse the employer in respect of an overpayment of wages or of expenses incurred in the course of the employment (section 14(1)).
- A deduction made in consequence of any disciplinary proceedings if those proceedings were held by virtue of a statutory provision (section 14(2)).
- A deduction in pursuance of a requirement imposed on the employer by a statutory provision to deduct and pay over to a public authority amounts determined by that authority as being due to it from the worker if the deduction is made in accordance with the relevant determination of that authority (section 14(3)).
- A deduction which is then paid over to a third party at the employee's request (for example trade union subscriptions) (section 14(4)).
- A deduction where the worker has taken part in a strike or other industrial action and the deduction is made by the employer on account of the worker having taken part in that strike or other action.
- A deduction agreed by the worker which is to satisfy an order of a court or tribunal requiring the payment of an amount by the worker to the employer.

Under section 17 Employment Rights Act 1996 there are also special rules that exist in retailing in respect of shop workers for the employee to recover for cash shortages or stock shortages. The provision can also include other workers such as bank tellers and petrol station employees.

For this to be lawful it must first be included in the contract so that the employee must have agreed to it beforehand. Second the deduction must not amount to more than 10 per cent of gross wages payable.

ACTIVITY

Self-assessment questions

1. How are wages defined in the Employment Rights Act?
2. Why does the definition of wages not include a payment made in lieu of notice?
3. When will a benefit in kind be classed as wages?
4. How is a deduction from pay defined in the Employment Rights Act?
5. What sorts of things can be classed as deductions?
6. What are the only types of deductions that can be considered lawful?
7. What deductions are exempt from the provisions?
8. How would an employee seek a remedy in respect of those deductions?

ACTIVITY

Quick quiz

Consider whether there has been an unlawful deduction from wages in each of the following situations and suggest whether any action would occur in a tribunal or in court.

1. Conrad is a retail manager and has been summarily dismissed for stealing money from his employer's tills over a period of months. The employer did not make any payment in lieu of notice and after investigation has assessed the loss at more than Conrad's normal monthly pick up pay so has refused to pay Conrad anything.
2. Denzil has complained that his employer has unlawfully deducted £20 per month for each of the last three months. Denzil is the subject of an attachment of earnings order which is for maintenance for his ex-wife.
3. Euan has not received production bonuses for the last twelve months which he is entitled to under the terms of his written contract of employment.
4. Frank, a university librarian at the Middlebits University, recently completed a six month course to qualify as a law librarian. His employer paid the cost of the course expecting that Frank would remain in post and have additional skills but Frank handed in his notice and took up work in another university. Middlebits University has deducted the cost of the course from Frank's final salary payment.

8.1.3 The National Minimum Wage

The idea of legislation to protect the low paid is not a new concept. The Conditions of Employment and National Arbitration Order 1940 was aimed at enforcing collective agreements on pay in specific trades. The scope of the order was extended by the Employment Protection Act 1975 which in Schedule 11 provided an action in respect of workers who received less favourable wages than comparable workers in the same trade. Over decades Wages Councils also existed and regulated conditions in many low paid jobs. However, these were abolished in the Trade Union Reform and Employment Rights Act 1993.

The National Minimum Wage Act 1998 which gained force on 1 April 1999 introduced minimum rates of pay for all those workers who qualify. Under section 1 these:

▨ are engaged under a contract of employment; or

▨ are engaged under any other contract where they are required to do the work personally, other than as a client or customer of any business, profession or undertaking (so this includes agency workers, home workers unless they are genuinely self-employed and foreign workers working in Britain).

There are a number of groups that are not covered by the legislation. These are identified in section 3 which includes:

▨ share fishermen;

▨ genuine voluntary workers;

▨ members of the armed forces;

▨ those on government funded training schemes and work experience;

▨ live-in au-pairs, nannies and companions where there is no deduction for board and they are treated as the employer's family;

▨ resident workers in religious communities;

▨ undergraduates on sandwich courses or on teaching practice.

The major exclusion of course is the genuinely self-employed.

How the hourly rate is calculated in order to establish whether the worker is receiving minimum wage is identified in Regulation 14 of the National Minimum Wage Regulations. This is done by taking the total remuneration paid the worker in the period and dividing it by the number of hours of time work, salaried hours work, output work and unmeasured work.

- Time work is where the worker is paid by the hour for a number or set of varying hours.
- Salaried hours work is where the worker is paid for a number of set hours per year and is entitled to an annual sum which is paid by dividing it into pay periods.
- Output work is where the worker is paid by reference to performance of specific tasks or the specific value of sales made. So this could include pieceworkers as well as commission paid workers.
- Unmeasured work is where none of the above applies and the worker is required to work as and when work is available and will be paid accordingly.

The Act was a cornerstone of New Labour's first term in office. One of its principal aims was to ensure that young workers in particular should get a fair wage and are not exploited by employers. This is particularly significant at present with youth unemployment standing in excess of 20 per cent and with such high percentages of young people staying on in further education and then a significant number in higher education. If the current government's policies on education, removing the Education Maintenance Grant and trebling the tuition fees in higher education, depress the numbers of young people in education then youth employment will rise even higher and without the legislation young people competing for work might be forced to accept even lower rates of pay. When it was introduced, the National Minimum Wage immediately raised the pay of 1.9 million low-paid British workers despite the fact that at that time the highest rate was only £3.60 an hour. The minimum rates have subsequently risen each year.

The minimum rates in operation from 1 October 2013 are shown in Figure 8.1.

An employee who thinks that he is not being paid the National Minimum Wage can complain to a tribunal for an unlawful deduction from wages under section 13 Employment Rights Act 1996 or for breach of contract. Under section 9 Minimum Wage Act 1998 the employer must keep records, and must be able to prove that he is paying the minimum wage if an employee complains to the tribunal that it has not. The burden of proof is reversed.

An employee is also entitled not to be subjected to a detriment for asserting rights under the National Minimum Wage Act 1998. In this way a dismissal for asserting the

Age (years)	Min. hourly wage	Weekly wage*	Yearly salary*
21+	£6.31	£252.40	£13,124.80
18-20	£5.03	£201.20	£10,462.40
16-17	£3.72	£148.80	£7,737.60
Apprentice	£2.68	£107.20	£5,574.40
*Based on forty hours a week, fifty-two weeks a year			

Figure 8.1 Chart of the rates of pay under the National Minimum Wage

right to minimum pay is automatically unfair (see Chapter 22.3). There is also enforcement procedure which can be carried out by Her Majesty's Revenue and Customs (HMRC) in the form of enforcement notices and also criminal penalties are available to enforcement officers in the form of fines.

It is important to make the point that even in the case of the top rate it would be difficult to construe this as a living wage. Presently, £13,124 is under half of the average salary for full-time workers in the UK, which is currently around £26,000 a year. Since average pay of chief executive officers of listed companies stands at around 145 times average wage this means that the low paid, with the limited protection that they enjoy, are on a rate which is 1/290th of the wage of the most privileged in society.

When the National Minimum Wage was first mooted many employers, economists and right-wing politicians argued that it would have a depressive effect on employment as it would discourage employers from taking on new staff, particularly young people trying to break into the job market. The reality of the years from its introduction up to the banking crisis was different since there were high levels of employment at that time.

In the face of the current recession such commentators are returning to the argument and asking for the repeal of the National Minimum Wage Act because it is destructive to employers and depresses employment. It is suggested that alternative arguments are that first since the minimum wage is so low in relative terms that in fact if an employer is not in a position to hire employees except at a lower rate that he does not in fact have a viable business model. Second since many employees paid minimum wage rates will receive some form of benefits, if only housing benefits, that those employers who pay at such low rates are merely exploiting the tax payer in order to make a profit.

ACTIVITY

Self-assessment questions

1. Why was the National Minimum Wage Act introduced?
2. What classes of worker are entitled to the minimum wage?
3. What classes of worker are excluded from the National Minimum Wage provisions?
4. What are time work, salaried hours work, output work and unmeasured work?
5. How would an employee bring an action to enforce the minimum wage?

8.2 Guarantee payments

Guarantee payments relate to lay-offs and short-time working. These are defined in section 147 Employment Rights Act 1996. A lay-off is defined as a week when an employee receives no pay due to him under his contract of employment. Short time is defined as a week when an employee receives less than half the pay that he is entitled to under his contract of employment. Both situations may eventually lead to redundancy rights (see Chapter 20.6).

There are a variety of reasons why either lay-offs or short time might occur which could include lack of orders, recession, natural breaks in production and seasonal variations in trade. They were also traditionally quite common in specific industries such as the construction industry and shipbuilding.

The uncertainty of the original common law position and the need for employees to be able to maintain an income led to the development of guarantee payments under statute. These were originally developed in the Employment Protection Act 1975 but they are now found in the Employment Rights Act 1996 in sections 28–35. The basic right is in section 28.

SECTION

> '28 Right to guarantee payment.
>
> (1) Where throughout a day during any part of which an employee would normally be required to work in accordance with his contract of employment the employee is not provided with work by his employer by reason of –
>
>   (a) a diminution in the requirements of the employer's business for work of the kind which the employee is employed to do, or
>
>   (b) any other occurrence affecting the normal working of the employer's business in relation to work of the kind which the employee is employed to do, the employee is entitled to be paid by his employer an amount in respect of that day.'

So the right to a guarantee payment exists where the employee has been continuously employed for at least one month and either:

- there is no work of the type that he normally does; or

- there is something else which affects the employer's business in relation to that work.

If the lack of work is for another reason then no guarantee payment is available. This could clearly be the case for instance where the reason that the employee is not working is because of a trade dispute.

CASE EXAMPLE

Garvey v J & J Maybank (Oldham) Ltd [1979] IRLR 408

The claimant was a lorry driver. Along with other colleagues he had refused to cross a picket line during a dispute, in which he was not involved, which was between a trade union and his employer, despite the employer's instructions that the lorry drivers should work normally and therefore cross the picket line. As a result of the picket the employer in fact received insufficient supplies to continue work and so laid-off workers, including the claimant. The claimant then argued that he was entitled to a guarantee payment by law. The court held that guarantee payments during lay-offs are not available if the workless day occurs because of a trade dispute involving any employee of the employer or associated employers. Since the lay-off occurred because of the refusal by the drivers to cross the picket line it was due to such a trade dispute and as a result there was no entitlement to a guarantee payment.

Guarantee payments are designed to encourage employers to act responsibly so that any contractual payments are set off against the statutory scheme and employers can gain exemption.

Employees will qualify for a payment if certain conditions are met. These are identified in sections 29 and 35 Employment Rights Act 1996:

- They must have at least one month's continuous service prior to the day for which a guarantee payment is claimed.

- They will be unable to claim for a workless day – this could be the result of a strike or other industrial action.

- They will be unable to claim a guarantee payment where suitable alternative employment has been offered and refused.

■ They will also be unable to claim when they ignore reasonable attendance requirements made by the employer.

■ There is also a provision for exclusions where collective agreements have been made.

The amount of the guarantee payment is calculated by multiplying the normal working hours by the guaranteed hourly rate. However, this is subject to statutory maximum which in 2013 was set at £24.20. The maximum period for which a guarantee payment can be claimed is five days for any three month period. On this basis the maximum claim in a year would be twenty days. When this is multiplied by the maximum payment the resulting £484 would appear to in fact have little impact on most people.

In the event that an employer fails to pay all or part of a payment due the employee should complain to the tribunal within in three months of the failure to pay. The tribunal can require the employer to make the payment but no other sanctions are available.

ACTIVITY

Self-assessment questions

1. What is a guarantee payment?
2. In what circumstances should a guarantee payment be made?
3. What qualifications are there before an employee can receive a guarantee payment?
4. When will a guarantee payment not be available?

8.3 Sickness

8.3.1 Sick leave

Inevitably there will be occasions where an employee is absent from work because of illness or sickness. Apart from Statutory Sick Pay arrangements concerning sickness absence are usually contractual. An employee is entitled to know the arrangements made for absence through sickness including any rights to contractual pay during the sickness absence. This is identified in section 1 Employment Rights Act 1996. The information does not have to be included in the statutory statement but it must identify where the information will be found and this must be reasonably accessible to the employee (see Chapter 5.2).

There are certain legal requirements which may apply during a sickness absence. Under the Health and Safety at Work etc Act 1974 and subsidiary legislation as well as the basic common law duty of care the employer will owe a duty to protect the employee on her or his return to work and the duty could apply during the sickness absence (see Chapter 16). If the sickness absence relates to a disability then under section 15 Equality Act 2010 the employer has a duty not to treat the employee unfavourably because of the disability and under section 20 Equality Act 2010 the employer may have to make reasonable adjustments on the employee's return to work. The other provisions on indirect discrimination, harassment, victimisation also apply (see Chapter 13.3). If the employer dismisses the employee because of ill health then this may be frustration of the contract (see Chapter 20.1) but it may also be a potentially fair dismissal. If it fails the reasonable range of responses test then this may amount to unfair dismissal (see Chapter 22.4.1 and 22.5.1). An employer is also bound to comply with the Data Protection Act 1998. If a sickness absence record contains specific medical information relating to the employee then this is deemed sensitive data and the employer will have to satisfy the statutory conditions for processing such data.

8.3.2 Medical suspension

Under section 64(2) Employment Rights Act 1996 a suspension on medical grounds occurs where the employee is suspended as a result of a statutory requirement or a recommendation made in a Code of Practice issued or approved under section 16 of the Health and Safety at Work etc Act 1974. These include:

- the Ionizing Radiations Regulations 1999;
- the Control of Lead at work Regulations 2002;
- the Control of Substances Hazardous to Health Regulations 2002.

Where a health risk occurs in relation to one of these then the employer must suspend the employee.

Under section 64(1) where an employee is suspended from work on medical grounds he is entitled to be paid by his employer for a period not exceeding twenty-six weeks. To qualify for a payment the employee must have been continuously employed by the employer for at least one month before the medical suspension began. Also the payment will only be made if the employee is fit for work: if he is not then he would be subject to other rules on payment during sickness absence.

If the employer fails to make a payment then the employee can bring a claim in a tribunal within three months of the failure to pay. If the claim is successful then the tribunal will order the employer to make the payment.

If an employee is dismissed for a reason which in effect is because of medical suspension then there is only a one month qualifying period of continuous employment for an unfair dismissal claim.

8.3.3 Pay during sick leave

There is no automatic right that an employee will be paid his wages by his employer during periods of sickness absence. As a result at common law the position is entirely contractual and any entitlement will be found in the contract of employment. If there is no express term in the contract then there is no presumption that payment of wages during sickness absence should be implied into the contract. In *Mears v Safecar Security Ltd* [1982] IRLR 183 in fact the Court of Appeal did suggest that the tribunal could assess all of the circumstances and decide whether there is an entitlement or not. The employee had been absent through sickness for six months during which time he did not send in any medical certificates or ask for payment. The Court of Appeal held that there was no entitlement to pay. It was well known that the employer never made such payments and the claimant had only asked for pay seven months after leaving the employment. This rather creative approach has subsequently been disapproved in *Eagland v British Telecommunications plc* [1992] IRLR 323.

JUDGMENT

Parker LJ commented that in *Mears* the court: 'agreed that the tribunal is under a statutory duty to invent terms if there are no materials upon which they can say a term could be found to be agreed expressly or by implication or by the general conduct of the parties . . . in my judgment they have no power to impose on an employer any such terms if it be the fact . . . that either it had been agreed that there should be no pension, sick pay, holiday pay or disciplinary rules, or the matter had not been agreed at all.'

It may be that the contract of employment does provide for full or part payment of wages during sickness absence and this is clearly beneficial to the employee. The general common law position, however, has possibly become of less significance since the introduction, originally in the Social Security and Housing Benefits Act 1982, of Statutory Sick Pay (SSP). This now falls under the Social Security Contributions and Benefits Act 1992 and the Statutory Sick Pay (General) Regulations.

The employer is bound to pay SSP to the employee for the first twenty-eight weeks of a sickness absence. Originally the employer could recover all of the payments made to the employee by deducting it from its National Insurance payments and there was relief also for small businesses. Now a threshold is used and the employer can recover SSP paid in a tax month where it exceeds 13 per cent of its National Insurance liability for that month.

Eligibility

To qualify for SSP an employee has to meet certain requirements:

- There must be a day of incapacity for work – that is the employee must be suffering from some illness, disease or injury which renders him incapable of doing his work.
- This must be in a period of incapacity for work – which must be at least four days.
- The day must fall within a period of entitlement – which starts with the first day of incapacity for work and ends either when the incapacity ends or when the twenty-eight weeks is over if the employee is still incapacitated or if the contract of employment is terminated or in the case of a pregnant woman who becomes disqualified under the provisions.
- The day of incapacity must be a qualifying day – this is one where the employee would normally be expected to work under his contract.

Exclusions

Not all employees are entitled to a payment. The following are excluded:

- Those who are incapacitated for less than four days.
- Those who earn less than a set lower earnings level averaged over an eight-week period – from April 2012 the lower earnings limit was set at £107 per week.
- Those pregnant women whose first day of sickness brings them within the restricted period where they fall under the regulations on maternity.
- Those employees who are engaged in an industrial dispute.
- Those employees who are currently in legal custody.
- Those employees whose first day of sickness falls within eight weeks of a claim for a number of state benefits.

Self-certification and certification by a doctor

Employees have been obliged to self-certify for the first seven days of their sickness absences since 1982. After that employees who are still sick will need to gain certification from a doctor.

Until April 2011 doctors routinely signed sick notes which explained the medical reason for the employee being unable to return to work. This has now been replaced with the 'fit for work note'. GPs will identify in the note what tasks at work the employee would be capable of. The move is aimed at reducing sickness absence as well as reducing the number of employees claiming incapacity benefit. Employers will have to be careful under the system with long term sickness absentees. If these can be identified as disabled and the employer has failed to make reasonable adjustments then the employer could be liable for claims of unfair dismissal (see Chapter 13.4).

ACTIVITY

Self-assessment questions

1. Why does sickness absence have implications for health and safety law and also for discrimination law?
2. Why does long term sickness have implications for termination of the contract of employment whether through dismissal or by other means?
3. In what circumstances will an employee be subject to medical suspension?
4. What are the basic rights of an employee who has been suspended on medical grounds?
5. If there are references to payment during sickness absence in the contract of employment what will the employee be entitled to?
6. What is Statutory Sick Pay?
7. In what circumstances is an employee on sickness absence entitled to a payment of Statutory Sick Pay and who will pay it?
8. In what circumstances are certain employees excluded from the scheme?
9. What is a 'fit to work note'?

8.4 Maternity

Traditionally in English law women enjoyed a range of rights relating to maternity. In the late twentieth century the law actually became quite confused following the Pregnant Workers Directive 92/85. In fact prior to the Directive there was legislation in most European nations providing rights and benefits for pregnant women and those that had recently given birth, although there was wide variation between country and country.

Measures protecting pregnant women were first introduced in the UK in 1948 when National Insurance rules provided a maternity allowance for women who gave up work to have a baby and this was gradually increased so that women were entitled to a sum representing 90 per cent of their earnings for up to thirteen weeks. The later Employment Protection Act 1975 also introduced the right for women with two years' continuous service to delay their return to work for twenty-nine weeks after the birth of their child.

Directives are harmonising legal instruments and Directive 92/85 aimed to produce a consistent approach amongst Member States and to adopt a minimum standard. The former provisions under English law differed from those in the Directive in the qualifying period for maternity leave, in the length of available leave and on payments during maternity.

Since in many ways provisions in English law exceeded the minimums set in the Directive the original approach of the government at the time was simply to graft the EU provisions on to the existing UK law so that the area was quite confused. Changes since have made the position clearer.

Developments of rights for pregnant workers have really had three main strands. First they have provided administrative machinery that is simpler than it formerly was and complies with the requirements of EU law. Second they have advanced the health and safety of pregnant workers and aimed to eliminate or minimise risk to pregnant workers. Third they have dealt with the unfair situation of women suffering discrimination even to the point of dismissal because of their pregnancy.

8.4.1 Time off for ante-natal care

Section 55 Employment Rights Act 1996 gives a woman the right not to be unfairly denied time off work to keep appointments if advised by doctor, midwife or health visitor.

SECTION

'55 Right to time off for ante-natal care.
(1) An employee who –
  (a) is pregnant, and
  (b) has, on the advice of a registered medical practitioner, registered midwife or registered nurse made an appointment to attend at any place for the purpose of receiving ante-natal care, is entitled to be permitted by her employer to take time off during the employee's working hours in order to enable her to keep the appointment.'

One reasonable qualification of the right identified in section 55(2) is that if requested the woman should provide her employer with evidence of the appointment, although this does not apply to the first appointment.

SECTION

'55
(2) An employee is not entitled to take time off under this section to keep an appointment unless, if her employer requests her to do so, she produces for his inspection –
  (a) a certificate from a registered medical practitioner, registered midwife or [F1 registered nurse] stating that the employee is pregnant, and
  (b) an appointment card or some other document showing that the appointment has been made.'

The right arises from the moment that the woman commences employment and is available regardless of whether the woman is full-time or part-time, or the size of the employer's business. The right is not available in the case of:

- women who are not working under a contract of employment;
- share-fisherwomen;
- police women.

Under section 56 Employment Rights Act 1996 the right also includes the right to receive normal payment at the usual rate of pay.

The right is not to be unreasonably refused time off for ante-natal care so it could possibly be argued that it is in fact more reasonable for the woman to make appointments out of works time for example where the woman works only limited hours. If the woman is refused reasonable time off or her employer fails to pay her in accordance with section 56 Employment Rights Act 1996 then under section 57(5) the woman can make a complaint to a tribunal and must do so within three months of the appointment in question. The tribunal can then make a declaration of her right to time off for ante-natal care and award her any pay that she should have received.

8.4.2 Suspension on maternity grounds

This area is now under the Management of Health and Safety at Work (Amendment) Regulations 2006 under which employers are obliged to carry out risk assessments on pregnant women. This is to ensure the health and safety of pregnant women or those that have recently given birth and will involve, if necessary, suspending them from work.

Earlier regulations were essentially criminal in essence but the provisions now also create civil rights and so create a potential cause of action for the employee.

CASE EXAMPLE

Day v T Pickles Farms Ltd [1999] IRLR 217

The claimant was a counter assistant at a sandwich shop and cooked chicken and other foods. She had recently had a miscarriage when she became pregnant again. She had severe morning sickness and told her manager at the shop that she was pregnant. The smell of the food made her feel nauseous and was so bad that she consulted her doctor who certified her unfit for work and she gave a doctor's certificate to her employer. She then left work and did not return. She claimed constructive dismissal arguing that her employer should have carried out a risk assessment. The EAT returned the case to the tribunal for certain facts to be established. However, it did accept that a failure to carry out a risk assessment on a pregnant woman could amount to unlawful discrimination and also a repudiatory breach of contract by the employer.

Section 66 Employment Rights Act 1996 follows Directive 92/85 and in fact requires employers to suspend women in two precise circumstances:

- where the work is of a kind that there is a risk to the health of an expectant or recent mother or her unborn child and it is impossible to alter her work to remove the risk (the risk may involve any agent which is likely to cause foetal lesions or disrupt the pregnancy so this could include exposure to shocks and movement, extreme heat or cold, exposure to certain biological or chemical agents or ionisation or radiation or to lead, it also could involve working underground or under water, but it can also include extreme fatigue);

- where the work involves night shifts and doctor or midwife certifies that it is unsafe and that she should not for any period identified be working

Another aspect of the risk assessment is to establish what measures must be taken to avoid the risk to health which obviously may involve suspension on maternity grounds. There are also two further significant rights.

First under section 67 Employment Rights Act 1996 the employer must offer suitable alternative work if there is any available. A failure by an employer to offer suitable alternative work where it is available could lead to the woman bringing a claim in a tribunal which could then award her compensation. The alternative work offered should also obviously be on terms that are not substantially less favourable than those of her existing employment. In *British Airways (European Operations at Gatwick) Ltd v Moore and Botterill* [2000] IRLR 296 female air crew transferred to ground duties when they were pregnant and were not entitled to flying allowance during this time. The EAT held that they had been given suitable alternative work and that their terms were not substantially less favourable. In fact they had selected the posts that they wished to transfer to and accepted the pay in those jobs.

On the other hand an unreasonable refusal to accept an offer of suitable alternative work may result in the woman losing any right to pay during suspension.

Second under section 68 Employment Rights Act 1996 where the woman is subject to medical suspension on maternity grounds the employer must pay the woman her normal rate of pay while she is suspended.

It is also worth noting that these rights do not require any minimum qualifying period of continuous employment in contrast to a suspension on medical grounds where there is a one month qualifying period.

8.4.3 Maternity leave

There are now three possible periods of maternity leave:

- compulsory maternity leave;
- ordinary maternity leave;
- additional maternity leave.

Compulsory maternity leave

Under section 72 Employment Rights Act 1996 a woman is prevented from returning to work within two weeks of giving birth. An employer allowing a woman to return earlier can be subject to a fine. Besides allowing a woman to return to work in a factory within four weeks of giving birth may offend health and safety law under the Health and Safety at Work etc Act 1974.

Ordinary maternity leave

Prior to amendments to the law women were entitled to maternity leave and also to what was then described as maternity absence which was the right to delay return to work up to twenty-nine weeks after childbirth if the woman had the qualifying period of two years' continuous employment. Following implementation of Directive 92/85 this became ordinary maternity leave and additional maternity leave but certain benefits only applied during ordinary maternity leave. Now under the Maternity and Parental Leave Regulations 1999 (as amended by the Maternity and Parental Leave and the Paternity and Adoption Leave (Amendment) Regulations 2008) the differences have effectively been removed.

Under section 71 Employment Rights Act 1996 a woman employee is now entitled to twenty-six weeks of ordinary maternity leave irrespective of her length of service or whether she is a permanent or temporary employee.

There are a number of conditions that the woman must satisfy:

- She must notify her employer no later than the end of the fifteenth week before the expected week of confinement of her pregnancy, the expected week of childbirth and the date on which she expects her ordinary maternity leave to commence.
- She must provide a doctor's certificate or a notice from a midwife which states the expected week of childbirth if the employer requests this under section 75 Employment Rights Act 1996.
- If it is not reasonably practicable to give this notice then she should inform her employer as soon as is reasonably practicable to do so (this obviously covers the situation where the woman has to go into hospital because of complications with the pregnancy or where the birth has been premature).
- Also if she wishes to vary the start date of her ordinary maternity leave she should give twenty-eight days' notice of this or if it is not reasonably practicable to do so she must do so as soon as it is.

There are two exceptions from the normal notification requirements:

- when the maternity leave starts on the day following the first day after the beginning of the fourth week before the expected week of confinement because she is absent wholly or partly because of pregnancy; or

- when the maternity begins with the day following the birth of the child (which will obviously be because it is earlier than the expected date of confinement).

On receiving the information from the woman the employer must within twenty-eight days inform her of the date on which her additional maternity leave will end.

Ordinary maternity leave can commence in a number of ways:

- on the date that the woman has already notified her employer that she expects the ordinary maternity leave to start; or

- on the day following the first day after the beginning of the fourth week before the expected week of confinement when the woman is absent from work wholly or partly due to her pregnancy; or

- on the day following the day of the birth.

In essence the start of the ordinary maternity period is whichever is the earliest of these alternatives.

The woman is entitled to all of her normal contractual rights during the ordinary maternity leave with the exception of her normal wage which is replaced by SMP (see 8.4.4 below). So this could include amongst other things any mortgages or loans that she would normally entitled to, any pension contributions that she is entitled to or any private medical entitlement.

Additional maternity leave

The traditional rules that allowed a woman to delay her return to work were modified in 1993 to fall in line with Directive 92/85 and this period is now called additional maternity leave. A woman is entitled to additional maternity leave if she is entitled to ordinary maternity leave.

The period of additional maternity leave commences the day after ordinary maternity leave finishes and is for twenty-six weeks. The only real difference from ordinary maternity leave now is that the woman will not be entitled to accrued pension rights during the last thirteen weeks. She is entitled to a more limited range of her normal contractual rights, for instance normal notice and it will count towards continuous employment for statutory employment rights.

Return to work

A woman who wishes to return to work after her ordinary maternity leave is entitled to return to the job she left on the same terms.

CASE EXAMPLE

Blundell v St Andrew's Catholic Primary School [2007] IRLR 652

The claimant had taught the reception class in a primary school before she went on maternity leave. On her return, because of a policy of rotation of teachers every two years, she was asked to teach year 2 and argued that she had not been properly returned to the job she was doing before she took her leave as required. The EAT held that she had in fact been returned to her job that of primary school teacher. The exact teaching class was irrelevant to the protection offered.

8.4.4 Payment during maternity

Under the Statutory Maternity Pay (General) Regulations 1986 (as amended) there is a statutory scheme for payment during maternity. This is called Statutory Maternity Pay (SMP). It is paid by the employer who pays it for a maximum of thirty-nine weeks to women employees who satisfy the qualifying conditions. Employers recoup payments from their National Insurance liability at the rate of 92 per cent or 105 per cent for small firms.

There are a number of qualifying conditions for a woman to receive SMP:

- The woman must have been an employed earner – this means she must be paying Class 1 National Insurance contributions and be paying tax under Schedule E.

- She must have been employed for twenty-six weeks immediately prior to a qualifying week – this is the fifteenth week before the expected date of confinement.

- She must qualify under the earnings rule – this means that her average earnings (which can include things like overtime normally worked) must be at or above the lower earnings limit above which employees make National Insurance contributions: in 2013 this is set at £109 per week.

- She must provide her employer with a medical certificate which identifies the expected week of confinement and give her employer a minimum of twenty-eight days' notice of the expected date that payment of SMP will commence.

SMP involves two different rates of pay:

- For the first six weeks a woman should receive 90 per cent of her average weekly earnings (AWE) before tax.

- For the remaining thirty-three weeks the payment is either 90 per cent of AWE or the statutory maximum (in 2013 set at £136.78), whichever is the lower.

A woman is not entitled to SMP when she is actually working. It is possible of course that a woman may have contractual entitlements also during pregnancy. The woman is bound by these while they do not conflict with SMP payment.

CASE EXAMPLE

North Western Health Board v McKenna C-191/03 [2005] IRLR 895

The claimant was absent from work for most of her pregnancy and for some time after because of pregnancy related illness. Her employer operated a scheme where employees were paid full pay for the first 183 days of sickness then half pay for the rest of any eighteen month period. It also covered pregnancy related illness prior to maternity leave. As a result the claimant spent some absence on half pay and argued that this was discrimination. The ECJ held that [EU] law did not require full pay during periods of pregnancy related illness so long as pay rates during such periods did not defeat the objective of protecting pregnant workers.

Women who are not eligible for SMP may nevertheless be eligible for what is known as a Maternity Allowance under the Social Security Contributions and Benefits Act 1992. This is paid by the Department of Work and Pensions. To qualify the woman must show that:

- she is pregnant and has reached the start of the eleventh week before the expected week of confinement;

- she was employed or self-employed for at least twenty-six weeks in the sixty-six weeks prior to the expected week of confinement – although this need not be continuous;

- her average weekly earnings are not less than the maternity allowance threshold (this is currently set at £30 per week).

Payment is for thirty-nine weeks and mirrors the second period of SMP, so is 90 per cent of average weekly earnings or the current maximum of £136.78, whichever is the lower.

8.4.5 Discrimination and dismissal because of pregnancy

One of the areas that originally caused some controversy was discriminatory treatment of a pregnant woman. The traditional view in English courts was the so-called like with like approach. The argument was that since a man cannot become pregnant then a woman could not be treated less favourably than a man if the alleged discrimination was because of her pregnancy.

The ECJ took a completely different approach, the so-called automatic approach, which recognised that because only women can become pregnant then any differential treatment that results from their pregnancy must be discrimination based on their sex. In this way the ECJ has identified that discriminatory treatment of a woman during the process of applying for work is unlawful if it is because of the pregnancy.

CASE EXAMPLE

Dekker v Stichting Vormingscentrum voor Jong Wolvassenen (VJV Centrum) Plus [1990] (C-177/88) ECR 1-3941

A woman applying for a job happened to tell the interview panel that she was pregnant and her application was then rejected. The ECJ held that, even though all applicants were in fact women, the fact that she had been rejected purely because of her pregnancy was a breach of the then Equal Treatment Directive 76/207 (now part of the Recast Directive 2006/54).

JUDGMENT

The Court identified: 'A refusal of employment on account of the financial consequences of absence due to pregnancy must be regarded as based, essentially on the fact of pregnancy [and] cannot be justified on grounds relating to the financial loss which an employer who appointed a pregnant woman would suffer for the duration of her maternity leave.'

All discrimination in employment against women because of pregnancy or maternity is contrary to EU law and the ECJ has also identified that a dismissal on the grounds of pregnancy or maternity is also unlawful and a breach of the former Equal Treatment Directive 76/207 (which is now subsumed within the Recast Directive 2006/54).

CASE EXAMPLE

Webb v EMO Air Cargo (UK) Ltd (No 2) [1995] UKHL 13; [1995] 4 All ER 577

The claimant was employed to replace a pregnant employee on maternity leave. She then found out that she was also pregnant and her baby was due at about the same time as the woman whose maternity leave she was covering. When the employer found out she was dismissed. She claimed that her dismissal was discrimination on the ground of sex. The tribunal, the EAT, the Court of Appeal and the then House of Lords (now the Supreme Court) all held that on a proper construction of the relevant provision of the then Sex Discrimination Act 1975 the dismissal was not discriminatory. However, the House of Lords was bound to make a reference for a preliminary ruling from the ECJ on whether it amounted to a breach of the Equal Treatment Directive 76/207. The ECJ held that there could be no comparison made with a man who was ill, the traditional approach of the English courts which would have defeated her claim for the lack of a comparator, and that a dismissal purely on grounds of pregnancy would be a breach of Directive 76/207.

JUDGMENT

The ECJ concluded: 'Directive 76/207 ... precludes dismissal of an employee who is recruited for an unlimited term with a view, initially, to replacing another employee during the latter's maternity leave and who cannot do so because, shortly after her recruitment, she is herself found to be pregnant.'

JUDGMENT

Lord Keith commented: 'The ... European Court ... set out a more precise test of unlawful discrimination, and the problem is how to fit the terms of that test into the ruling. It seems to me that the only way of doing so is to hold that, in a case where a woman is engaged for an indefinite period, the fact that the reason why she will be temporarily unavailable for work at a time when to her knowledge her services will be particularly required is pregnancy is a circumstance relevant to her case, being a circumstance which could not be present in the case of the hypothetical man. It does not necessarily follow that pregnancy would be a relevant circumstance in the situation where the woman is denied employment for a fixed period in the future during the whole of which her pregnancy would make her unavailable for work, nor in the situation where after engagement for such a period the discovery of her pregnancy leads to cancellation of the engagement.'

Subsequently the ECJ in *Jiménez Melgar v Ayuntamiento de Los Barrios* C-438/99 [2001] ECR 1–6915 and *Teledenmark v Handels-og Kontorfuntionaerernes Forbund i Danmark* C-109/00 [2001] ECR 1-6993 has held that no distinction should be drawn between pregnant workers on indefinite contracts and those on temporary contracts

The ECJ has also held that where a works rule applies equally to men and women but adversely affects women because of their pregnancy then this is discriminatory and a breach of the Equal Treatment Directive 76/207 (now subsumed in the Recast Directive 2006/54).

CASE EXAMPLE

Brown v Rentokil Ltd [1998] CMLR 1049; [1998] IRLR 445

The claimant had a series of pregnancy related illnesses and was absent because of them for more than twenty-six weeks. One of the employer's works rules was that any employee who was absent because of sickness for more than twenty-six weeks would be dismissed and in consequence of this the employer dismissed the claimant. The Court of Justice held that it was discriminatory to dismiss a woman for any absence because of pregnancy or pregnancy related illness.

JUDGMENT

The ECJ explained: 'Where it is relied on to dismiss a pregnant worker because of absences due to incapacity for work resulting from her pregnancy, such a contractual term, applying both to men and to women, is applied in the same way to different situations since,... the situation of a pregnant worker who is unfit for work as a result of disorders associated with her pregnancy cannot be considered to be the same as that of a male worker who is ill and absent through incapacity for work for the same length of time. Consequently, application of that contractual term in circumstances such as the present constitutes direct discrimination on grounds of sex.'

However, there are situations in which there is no discrimination. In *British Telecommunications plc v Roberts and Longstaffe* [1996] IRLR 601 two women wanted to return to work after their maternity leaves on a job sharing arrangement. Because this would involve them working on Saturday mornings they complained that this was discrimination. The court held that since job sharing did not come under the protections offered to women during pregnancy and maternity leave therefore there was no issue of discrimination.

Pregnancy and maternity is now a protected characteristic under the Equality Act 2010. The provisions relating to discrimination against a woman at work because of her pregnancy or maternity are in section 18 Equality Act 2010.

SECTION

'18 Pregnancy and maternity discrimination: work cases.
(1) This section has effect for the purposes of the application of Part 5 (work) to the protected characteristic of pregnancy and maternity.
(2) A person (A) discriminates against a woman if, in the protected period in relation to a pregnancy of hers, A treats her unfavourably –
(a) because of the pregnancy, or
(b) because of illness suffered by her as a result of it.
(3) A person (A) discriminates against a woman if A treats her unfavourably because she is on compulsory maternity leave.
(4) A person (A) discriminates against a woman if A treats her unfavourably because she is exercising or seeking to exercise, or has exercised or sought to exercise, the right to ordinary or additional maternity leave.'

The word used is unfavourable rather than less favourable as is the case with most of the other protected characteristics so there is no comparator. Any unfavourable treatment of a woman because of her pregnancy during the protected period is discrimination. The protected period is identified in section 18(6) Equality Act 2010.

'18

(6) The protected period, in relation to a woman's pregnancy, begins when the pregnancy begins, and ends –

   (a) if she has the right to ordinary and additional maternity leave, at the end of the additional maternity leave period or (if earlier) when she returns to work after the pregnancy;

   (b) if she does not have that right, at the end of the period of 2 weeks beginning with the end of the pregnancy.'

The unfavourable treatment can obviously be in the recruitment and selection process, as in *Dekker v Stichting Vormingscentrum voor Jong Wolvassenen (VJV Centrum) Plus* [1990] (C-177/88) ECR 1-3941 above, or during employment, as in *British Telecommunications plc v Roberts and Longstaffe* [1996] IRLR 601 or on dismissal.

CASE EXAMPLE

O'Neill v Governors of St Thomas More School [1997] ICR 33

The claimant, who was unmarried, was employed as a teacher of religious education at a Roman Catholic voluntary aided school in Bedford and was expected 'to make the ideologies and teachings of the Roman Catholic faith clear to the pupils in order to maintain the ethos of the school as a Roman Catholic school'. She became pregnant during a relationship with a Roman Catholic priest known in the locality and at the school, to which he made regular visits to give advice and guidance to pupils and teachers. The governors initially felt that she should not return to the school and that she should be dismissed. After her child was born the claimant gave written notice to the governors of her intention to return to full-time employment in the post of a religious education teacher at the school. She was not allowed to return to the school which also stopped paying her salary. She claimed a repudiatory breach of her contract of employment and payment of arrears of salary. The EAT held that she had indeed been discriminated against on grounds of her pregnancy.

JUDGMENT

Mummery J explained: 'The critical question is whether, on an objective consideration of all the surrounding circumstances, the dismissal or other treatment complained of by the applicant is on the ground of pregnancy. It need not be only on that ground. It need not even be mainly on that ground. Thus, the fact that the employer's ground for dismissal is that the pregnant woman will become unavailable for work because of her pregnancy does not make it any the less a dismissal on the ground of pregnancy. She is not available because she is pregnant. Similarly, in the present case, the other factors in the circumstances surrounding the pregnancy relied upon as the "dominant motive" are all causally related to the fact that the applicant was pregnant – the paternity of the child, the publicity of that fact and the consequent untenability of the applicant's position as a religious education teacher are all pregnancy based or pregnancy related grounds. Her pregnancy precipitated and permeated the decision to dismiss her. It is not possible, in our view, to say ... that the ground for the applicant's dismissal was anything other than her pregnancy.'

Section 18 provides quite extensive protection as a result of which there is no provision for indirect discrimination or harassment, nor is an occupational requirement possible. Claims of direct discrimination and victimisation are possible.

ACTIVITY

Self-assessment questions

1. What is the basic right to time off for ante-natal care?
2. In what circumstances will an employer have to suspend an employee on maternity grounds?
3. What are the woman's rights during this suspension?
4. What is the difference between ordinary maternity leave and additional maternity leave?
5. What is compulsory maternity leave?
6. What is a woman's entitlement to payment during maternity leave?
7. In what ways has membership of the EU been significant in terms of discrimination against women who are pregnant?
8. How is maternity and pregnancy dealt with under the Equality Act 2010?
9. At which stages in employment is discrimination against a pregnant woman prohibited?

8.5 Other entitlement to leave or time off

8.5.1 Parental leave

A development again led by the EU, parental leave is now available to both parents, either a mother or father, if they qualify. It is governed by sections 76–80 Employment Rights Act 1996 and the Maternity and Parental Leave Regulations 1999 and the Maternity and Parental Leave (Amendment) Regulations 2001. Unlike maternity leave (or paternity leave, below) it is not paid leave but the right is additional to those rights.

A parent is eligible to take parental leave if:

- they have been continuously employed for one year; and
- they have responsibility for a child (the definition of parental responsibility is taken from that in section 3 Children Act 1989 (as amended)).

SECTION

'3 Meaning of "parental responsibility".
(1) In this Act "parental responsibility" means all the rights, duties, powers, responsibilities and authority which by law a parent of a child has in relation to the child and his property.'

However there is also a definition in the regulations themselves.

The entitlement is to leave of up to thirteen weeks (eighteen weeks if the child is disabled) to care for the child. The right exists in respect of each child and can be taken any time from the birth of the child up the child reaching five years old.

During parental leave the employee's terms and conditions of employment are the same as those during additional maternity leave (see 8.4.3 above).

If an employer unreasonably refuses parental leave or causes it to be postponed the employee has a right to make a complaint in a tribunal which may award compensation.

An employee is also entitled not to suffer a detriment because of parental leave so a dismissal for taking parental leave would be automatically unfair (see Chapter 22.3).

8.5.2 Paternity leave

Paternity leave is governed by the Paternity and Adoption Leave Regulations 2002 (as amended). A father is entitled to take two weeks' paid leave in order to help the mother and it has to be taken within eight weeks of the birth of the child, although it can be taken as a single two week period or two periods of one week. It cannot be taken as odd days.

To qualify the man must have been employed for twenty-six weeks by the end of the fifteenth week before the expected date of confinement.

Paternity leave is paid. This is in the form of statutory paternity pay (SPP) which is at the same rate as Statutory Maternity Pay, either 90 per cent of average earnings or the statutory maximum which in 2013 is £136.78.

An employee is entitled to all the contractual terms that he would have been entitled to if he had not been on paternity leave. An employee is also entitled not to suffer a detriment because of paternity leave so that a dismissal for taking paternity leave is an automatically unfair dismissal (see Chapter 22.3).

CASE EXAMPLE

Atkins v Coyle Personnel plc [2008] IRLR 420

The claimant was on paternity leave during which he also worked and was available to answer phone calls. He was woken up from one phone call from his manager having only had three hours' sleep. This led to a series of angry e-mails and an angry phone call after which he was dismissed. He claimed that was unfair dismissal. The tribunal identified that, for unfair dismissal purposes, the dismissal must be connected to the paternity leave. This was during the paternity leave but actually resulted from the angry exchanges and therefore was not connected to the paternity leave and was not therefore an automatically unfair dismissal.

From 3 April 2011 it is also possible to have additional paternity leave of twenty-six weeks. This is governed by the Additional Paternity Leave Regulations 2010 and means that the father can in effect take what would have been the mother's additional maternity leave. Obviously it means that it is only available to the father if the mother returns to work.

The father will be eligible if he has at least twenty-six weeks' continuous employment and with earnings equal to or above the lower earnings limit (currently set at £109 per week) during the eight weeks prior to the fifteenth week before the baby is due. The mother must provide written confirmation that he is the father and he must inform his employer at least eight weeks before the start of the leave period.

Paternity leave can also be taken by a partner in a civil partnership, so in this sense paternity leave can be taken by a woman.

8.5.3 Adoption leave

Adoption leave is governed by the Paternity and Adoption Leave Regulations 2002. In essence it involves very similar rights to paternity leave. There is an entitlement to twenty-six weeks' ordinary adoption leave and twenty-six weeks' additional adoption leave.

In order to qualify the employee must have been in employment with the employer for twenty-six weeks prior to being informed that a suitable match has been made.

During ordinary adoption leave statutory adoption pay (SAP) is paid at the same rates as for statutory paternity pay.

During ordinary adoption leave the employee is entitled to the same contractual rights as if she or he was not on leave.

8.5.4 Time off for dependant care

Dependant care leave is governed by section 57A Employment Rights Act 1996. Section 57A(1) identifies the only circumstances in which the employee can take dependant care leave.

SECTION

'57A Time off for dependants.
(1) An employee is entitled to be permitted by his employer to take a reasonable amount of time off during the employee's working hours in order to take action which is necessary –
   (a) to provide assistance on an occasion when a dependant falls ill, gives birth or is injured or assaulted,
   (b) to make arrangements for the provision of care for a dependant who is ill or injured,
   (c) in consequence of the death of a dependant,
   (d) because of the unexpected disruption or termination of arrangements for the care of a dependant, or
   (e) to deal with an incident which involves a child of the employee and which occurs unexpectedly in a period during which an educational establishment which the child attends is responsible for him.'

Under section 57A(2) dependant care leave can only be taken if the employee tells her employer the reason for her absence as soon as reasonably practicable, and except where it is impossible until after the employee has returned to work, she tells her employer for how long she expects to be absent.

The definition of dependant is in section 57A(3) and is either the employee's spouse or civil partner, or child, or parent, or a person who lives in the same household as the employee, other than an employee, tenant, lodger or boarder. Under section 57A(4) dependant can also include any person who reasonably relies on the employee to make arrangements for the provision of care.

Illness or injury includes physical as well as mental illness or injury.

There is no qualification for dependant care leave in terms of continuous employment. There is also no requirement on an employer to pay an employee who takes dependant care leave although some contracts of employment might include reference to payment during such absence.

The right in essence is aimed at emergency situations so the length of dependant care leave is not unlimited and will be dictated by the immediate circumstances.

CASE EXAMPLE

Qua v John Ford Morrison [2003] IRLR 184

A legal secretary had a number of absences from work during a short period. She claimed that this was justified under dependant care leave provisions as the absences were almost entirely to do with her son's medical problems. The EAT gave guidance on the application of dependant care leave. It held that such leave covered the immediate critical points where a child became ill and arrangements needed to be made, but did not include continuous on-going care. In other words there is no right to unlimited time off for dependant care needs and a dismissal in such circumstances would not be classed as automatically unfair.

In a similar way in *Forster v Cartwright Black* [2004] IRLR 781 the EAT identified that leave on the death of a dependant was in order to make the funeral and other necessary arrangements and for attending the funeral but it did not extend to taking time off to overcome grief.

8.5.5 Time off for public duties

Under section 50 Employment Rights Act 1996 it is also possible for an employee to take time off work to undertake a wide range of public duties. The bodies for which time off is available are identified in section 50(1) and 50(2).

SECTION

'50 Right to time off for public duties
(1) An employer shall permit an employee of his who is a justice of the peace to take time off during the employee's working hours for the purpose of performing any of the duties of his office.
(2) An employer shall permit an employee of his who is a member of –
  (a) a local authority,
  (b) a statutory tribunal,
  (c) a police authority established under section 3 of the Police Act 1996 or the Metropolitan Police Authority,
  (d) an independent monitoring board for a prison or a prison visiting committee,
  (e) a relevant health body,
  (f) a relevant education body.'

Time off for the public bodies identified in section 50(2) must be for activities identified in section 50(3):

■ attendance at a meeting of the body or any of its committees or sub-committees; and

■ the doing of any other thing approved by the body, or anything of a class so approved, for the purpose of the discharge of the functions of the body or of any of its committees or sub-committees.

The employee is only allowed a reasonable time to discharge his public duties and there is no obligation on the employer to pay for this time.

ACTIVITY

Essay writing

Using the guide on planning and writing essays in Appendix 1 answer the following essay question:
Discuss whether the growth of rules on family friendly areas including maternity, paternity, adoption and dependant care makes conditions of employment more fair and balanced or whether they are an unfair and unnecessary burden on employers.

KEY FACTS

Wages	Case/statute
The meaning of wages	
• includes any fee, bonus, commission, holiday pay or other emolument referable to his employment, whether payable under his contract or otherwise, statutory sick pay, maternity pay, paternity pay, adoption pay, guarantee payments, payment for time off, for carrying out trade union duties, pay on suspension on medical and maternity grounds, pay in pursuance of an order for reinstatement or re-engagement, or for continuation of a contract of employment, or pay under a protective award	*S27(1) Employment Rights Act 1996*
• and can include overtime payments, shift payments and accrued holiday payments	*Greg May (Carpet Fitters and Contractors) Ltd v Dring*
• and some discretionary bonuses	*Kent Management Services Ltd v Butterfield*
• it does not include a loan or by way of an advance of wages, expenses incurred by the worker in carrying out his employment, a pension, allowance or gratuity in connection with the worker's retirement or as compensation for loss of office, redundancy pay, any payment to the worker otherwise than in his capacity as a worker, or most benefits in kind except things like luncheon vouchers	*S27(2) Employment Rights Act 1996* *S27(5) Employment Rights Act 1996*
Deductions from pay	
• deduction is defined as where the total amount of wages paid on any occasion by an employer to a worker employed by him is less than the total amount of the wages properly payable by him to the worker on that occasion	*S13(3) Employment Rights Act 1996*
• but must relate to something that can be defined as wages	*Delaney v Staples*
• and a reduction in work leading to a lowering in wages can be an unlawful deduction if not authorised	*International Packaging Corporation (UK) Ltd v Balfour*
• there are only three types of lawful deductions – those authorised by statute, those in the contract and those agreed by the employee	*S13(1) Employment Rights Act 1996*
• but the deduction must also be justified in fact	*Fairfield Ltd v Skinner*
• some deductions are exempt and should be enforced in court – for overpayments of wages, in respect of disciplinary proceedings, to pay back a public body, where the employee agrees in order to pay a third party, because of a strike or to satisfy an order of the court	*S14 Employment Rights Act 1996*

The National Minimum Wage	
• all workers who are engaged under a contract of employment; are engaged under any other contract where they are required to do the work personally, other than as a client or customer of any business, profession or undertaking are entitled to the National Minimum Wage	*S1 National Minimum Wage Act 1998*
• certain workers are excluded including share fishermen, genuine voluntary workers, members of the armed forces, those on government funded training schemes and work experience, live-in au-pairs, nannies and companions where there is no deduction for board and they are treated as the employer's family, resident workers in religious communities, undergraduates on sandwich courses or on teaching practice	*S3 National Minimum Wage Act 1998*
• employees can claim an unlawful deduction from wages where they do not receive minimum wage	*S13 Employment Rights Act 1996*
• employers are obliged to keep records	*S9 National Minimum Wage Act 1998*

Guarantee payments	Case/statute
An employee may receive a guarantee payment:	
• when on a normal working day there is no work of the type that he normally does; or there is something else which affects the employer's business in relation to that work	*S27 Employment Rights Act 1996*

Qualifications for a payment	
• they must have at least one month's continuous service prior to the day for which a guarantee payment is claimed	*SS29 and 35 Employment Rights Act 1996*
• they will be unable to claim for a workless day – this could be the result of a strike or other industrial action	
• they will be unable to claim a guarantee payment where suitable alternative employment has been offered and refused	
• they will also be unable to claim when they ignore reasonable attendance requirements made by the employer	
• an employee is entitled to a maximum of five days in a three month period – and there is a maximum payment	

Sickness	Case/statute
Sick leave	
• provisions for sickness have to be included in the statutory statement of particulars	*S1 Employment Rights Act 1996*

Medical suspension	
• possible under HASAW 1974 or other statutory provisions	*S64(2) Employment Rights Act 1996* *The Ionizing Radiations Regulations 1999* *The Control of Lead at work Regulations 2002* *The Control of Substances Hazardous to Health Regulations 2002*
• the suspended employee is entitled to pay up to twenty-six weeks	*S64(1) Employment Rights Act 1996*

Pay during sick leave	
• can be contractual • or Statutory Sick Pay • to qualify for SSP employee must have a day of incapacity for work, in a period of incapacity for work, falling within a period of entitlement, and which is a qualifying day • excluded are: incapacitated for less than four days, earn less than lower earnings level, pregnant women in the restricted period, employees on strike, employees in custody, claim falls within eight weeks of a claim for a number of state benefits	*Social Security Contributions and Benefits Act 1992* and the *Statutory Sick Pay (General) Regulations.*

Maternity	Case/statute

Time off for ante-natal care	
• a woman is entitled to keep appointments for ante-natal care • and to receive normal pay • if she is unreasonably refused she can bring a complaint in a tribunal within three months of the refusal	*S55 Employment Rights Act 1996* *S56 Employment Rights Act 1996* *S57(5) Employment Rights Act 1996*

Suspension on maternity grounds	
• a pregnant woman should be suspended on full pay when her work involves exposure to a range of dangerous processes or substances or she is required to work nights and a medical practitioner is advising that this is dangerous – and in either case there is no suitable alternative work • the alternative work must be on the same terms • the right can give rise to a civil remedy	*S66 Employment Rights Act 1996* *British Airways (European Operations at Gatwick) Ltd v Moore and Botterill* *Day v T Pickles Farms Ltd*

Maternity leave	
• there are now two periods – ordinary maternity leave of twenty-six weeks – and additional maternity leave of a further twenty-six weeks • the woman must notify the employer no later than the start of the fifteenth week before the EWC – unless she is absent through pregnancy in the last four weeks or gives birth – in which case she should notify the employer when reasonably practicable • there is also now compulsory maternity leave for the two weeks after the birth	

Payment during maternity leave	
• SMP is available to employees paying class 1 NI, employed for twenty-six weeks immediately prior to fifteenth week before EWC, over the earnings limit, and must provide employer with medical certificate identifying EWC • rate is 90 per cent of wages up to a statutory maximum for thirty-nine weeks • those not entitled may be eligible for Maternity Allowance	

Discrimination and dismissal during maternity	
• unlawful not to employ because of pregnancy • or to dismiss because of pregnancy • and maternity and pregnancy is now a protected characteristic • and prohibited conduct can arise at any point in employment	*Recast Directive 2006/54* *Dekker v Stichting Vormingscentrum voor Jong Wolvassenen (VJV Centrum) Plus* *Webb v EMO Air Cargo (UK) Ltd (No 2)* *S18 Equality Act 2010*

Other entitlement to leave or time off	Case/statute
Parental leave	
• parental leave of up to thirteen weeks between the birth of the child and the child's fifth birthday • it is available to those with parental responsibility • an employee can challenge an unreasonable refusal in the tribunal • a dismissal for taking parental leave is automatically unfair	*Maternity and Parental Leave (Amendment) Regulations 2001* *S3 Children Act 1989*
Paternity leave	
• the father is entitled to two weeks' paid leave during the first eight weeks after the birth • must have been employed for twenty-six weeks prior to the fifteenth week before the EWC • Statutory Paternity Pay is at same rates as SMP • entitled to all normal contractual benefits and dismissal for taking paternity leave is automatically unfair • can also take twenty-six weeks' additional paternity leave in place of the mother's additional maternity leave • must have twenty-six weeks' continuous employment prior to the relevant date and be above the lower earnings limit	*Paternity and Adoption Leave Regulations 2002* *Additional Paternity Leave Regulations 2010*
Adoption leave	
• entitled to twenty-six weeks' ordinary adoption leave and twenty-six weeks' additional adoption leave • must have been employed for twenty-six weeks prior to a suitable match being made • Statutory Adoption Pay at same rates as maternity during ordinary adoption leave	*Paternity and Adoption Leave Regulations 2002*

Time off for dependant care	
• an employee is entitled to time off where it is necessary to help when a dependant falls ill, gives birth or is injured or assaulted, or to make arrangements for care of an ill or injured dependant, or death of a dependant, or unexpected disruption or termination of arrangements for the care of a dependant, or something unexpected to do with a child's education	*S57A(1) Employment Rights Act 1996*
• dependant includes spouse or civil partner, child, parent, a person who lives in the same household as the employee, other than an employee, tenant, lodger or boarder	*S57A(3) Employment Rights Act 1996*
• can also include any person who reasonably relies on the employee to make arrangements for the provision of care	*S57A(4) Employment Rights Act 1996*
• the right is not to an unlimited amount of time	*Qua v John Ford Morrison*

Time off for public duties	
• there is a statutory right to take time off for public duties, as a magistrate, or for a local authority, statutory tribunal, police authority, independent monitoring board for a prison or a prison visiting committee, relevant health body, relevant education body	*S50(1) Employment Rights Act 1996*
• must be for attendance of meetings or other things for discharging the functions of the body	*S50(1) Employment Rights Act 1996*
• the right is only to time off that is reasonable in the circumstances and there is no obligation on the employer to pay during this leave	

SAMPLE ESSAY QUESTION

ESSAY Discuss the extent to which the rules on deductions from pay are fair to both employer and employee.

Explain the definition of pay

• Any fee, bonus, commission, holiday pay or other emolument referable to his employment, whether payable under his contract or otherwise, statutory sick pay, maternity pay, paternity pay, adoption pay, guarantee payments, payment for time off for carrying out trade union duties, pay

on suspension on medical and maternity grounds, pay in pursuance of an order for reinstatement or re-engagement, or for continuation of a contract of employment, or pay under a protective award.
- And some overtime payments, shift payments, accrued holiday payments and some discretionary bonuses wages.

Explain how deduction from pay is defined

- Statutory definition is where the total amount of wages paid on any occasion by an employer to a worker employed by him is less than the total amount of the wages properly payable by him to the worker on that occasion.
- Courts have stated that it must relate to something that can be defined as wages.
- Identify that this could also mean that a reduction in work leading to a lowering in wages can be an unlawful deduction if not authorised.

Discuss whether the definitions of pay and deduction are fair to employer and employee

- Pay is defined broadly so gives wide scope to the employee – but an employer might argue that it is too broad.
- Definition of deduction is very clear and should be clear to both parties.
- The fact that the courts have stated that the deduction must be in respect of something identifiable as wages offers some protection to the employer.
- The fact that it can also be classed as a reduction in work which lowers pay is also a significant protection for the employee.

Explain the types of deductions that fall within the legislation

- There are only 3 types of lawful deductions.

- Those authorised by statute (so could include tax and national insurance paid at source).
- Those in the contract (so these are known about before employment).
- Those agreed by the employee.
- So anything else is unlawful and an action can be brought in the tribunal.

Discuss whether this is fair to employer and employee

- The range of lawful deductions are either necessary or agreed.
- But have to remember imbalance in relationship in respect of those in contract and those agreed with the employee as there may have been no real choice.
- But the fact that the deduction has to be justified in fact makes it fairer for the employee.

Discuss the exemptions that are exempt from section 13 and covered by section 14

- For overpayments of wages, in respect of disciplinary proceedings, to pay back a public body, where the employee agrees in order to pay a third party (e.g. trade union subscriptions), because of a strike, or to satisfy an order of the court.
- So the categories all seem fair to both parties.
- The only difference is that the action would have to be in court not the tribunal.

REACH REASONED CONCLUSIONS

SUMMARY

- Wages are defined as any sums payable to the worker in connection with his employment and statute adds other specific payments such as maternity pay and sick pay.
- Wages can also include things like discretionary bonuses but will not include loans made to employees, expenses, pension contributions, redundancy payments and most benefits in kind except luncheon vouchers.

- Deductions from pay are unlawful unless they are authorised by statute (for example tax and National Insurance contributions), authorised by the contract of employment or agreed beforehand by the employee.

- A reduction in work could also lead to an unlawful deduction from wages.

- Actions for certain deductions would need to be brought in a court rather than a tribunal including overpayment of wages, one made in consequence of any disciplinary, one made in pursuance of a statutory requirement to pay a public authority, one paid over to a third party (for example trade union subscriptions), one in respect of strike action, one to satisfy an order of a court or tribunal.

- The National Minimum Wage applies to a number of employees except for share fishermen, genuine voluntary workers, members of the armed forces, those on government funded training schemes and work experience, live-in au-pairs, nannies and companions where there is no deduction for board and they are treated as the employer's family, resident workers in religious communities, undergraduates on sandwich courses or on teaching practice.

- Guarantee payments are possible where employees are laid off or working short time.

- Where employees are absent through sickness arrangements for dealing with this are generally contractual.

- How sickness is dealt with could have implications under the Health and Safety at Work Act and associated regulations as well as common law and also where disability is a possibility it might also have implications under the Equality Act 2010 – however, long term sickness could also lead to the contract being frustrated or be seen as a potentially fair head of dismissal.

- It is also possible for employees working in particular industries with certain dangerous substances to be suspended with pay in certain circumstances.

- Payments may be made during sick leave under the contract but there is also a system of payments under the Statutory Sick Pay scheme for those who are eligible.

- There are now extensive rules on pregnancy and maternity.

- Women have the right to time off to keep antenatal appointments, and should be suspended on full pay where their jobs might prove too dangerous to the woman or foetus and there is no suitable alternative work.

- There are now three possible periods of maternity leave, ordinary maternity leave for twenty-six weeks, additional maternity leave for a further twenty-six weeks, but the first two weeks after the birth is compulsory maternity leave.

- Under EU law and now under the Equality Act 2010 maternity and pregnancy is a protected characteristic and discrimination at any point in employment for reason of the pregnancy is prohibited.

- Parental leave which is additional to any maternity or paternity leave is possible for either parent for up to thirteen weeks from the child's birth up to the child's fifth birthday.

- A father also can have two weeks' paid paternity leave within the first eight weeks after the birth and can also have twenty-six weeks' additional paternity leave in place of the mother's additional maternity leave.

- Adoption leave is very similar to paternity leave and with similar rights.

- There is also a right to dependant care leave which is generally unpaid leave and in reality covers emergency situations involving dependants who the employee cares for.

- It is also possible to have time off for a range of public duties.

Further reading

Emir, Astra, *Selwyn's Law of Employment 17th edition*. Oxford University Press, 2012, Chapters 6, 7 and 8.

Pitt, Gwyneth, *Cases and Materials on Employment Law 3rd edition*. Pearson, 2008, Chapter 6.

Sargeant, Malcolm and Lewis, David, *Employment Law 6th edition*. Pearson, 2012, Chapters 7 and 8.

9

Protection from discrimination

Introduction (the Equality Act 2010)

AIM AND OBJECTIVES

After reading this chapter you should be able to:

- Understand the background to the law on discrimination in employment and its limitations prior to the Equality Act 2010
- Understand the protected characteristics under the Equality Act 2010
- Understand the different types of prohibited practices under the Equality Act 2010
- Understand the nature of occupational requirements
- Understand the contexts in which discrimination might occur in employment
- Critically analyse the area
- Apply the law to factual situations and reach conclusions

9.1 The origins of UK discrimination law

Before the first Race Relations Act in 1965 discrimination in effect was perfectly lawful in the UK. This is not to say that individuals or institutions had not previously been conscious of or attempted to introduce measures to remove some of the worst excesses of inequality. However, in the case of women, it was as late as 1873 that the first woman, Elizabeth Garrett Anderson, gained membership of the British Medical Association and she was the sole female member for another nineteen years. It was not until the Representation of the People Act 1918 that women over the age of thirty who met a property qualification to vote won the right to vote in Parliamentary elections. Although 8.5 million women met the age and property criteria, this still only represented 40 per cent of women. It was not until the Equal Franchise Act of 1928 that women over twenty-one were able to vote and that women eventually achieved the same democratic rights as men. It was not until the Sex Disqualification (Removal) Act of 1919 that women were allowed to join the civil service and the profession of solicitor.

Parliament moved slowly in the twentieth century in introducing equality and the judiciary often demonstrated innate conservatism and hostility to the concept. In *Roberts v Hopwood* [1925] AC 578 Poplar Council decided to pay all of its council workers a minimum wage of £4 a week, whether they were men or women and regardless of the job they did. When this was challenged Lord Atkinson in the then House of Lords commented:

JUDGMENT

'the council would, in my view, fail in their duty if … [they] allowed themselves to be guided in preference by some eccentric principles of socialist philanthropy, or by a feminist ambition to secure the equality of the sexes in the matter of wages in the world of labour'.

Laws protecting against sex discrimination really begin with the Equal Pay Act 1970 which was only passed to advance the UK's application for membership of the EU (at that time the EEC later EC). This was later supplemented by the Sex Discrimination Act 1975. However, even after more than forty years of sex equality law statistics show that women's conditions of work are still poorer than men's.

The Race Relations Act 1965 was later supplemented and extended by the Race Relations Act 1968. The first Act, while relatively ineffectual, was much needed. The second was a significant development as it also covered discrimination in employment. Unfortunately judges were still able to identify colour bars as legal despite the Acts as in *Dockers' Labour Club and Institute Ltd v Race Relations Board* [1976] AC 285 (see Chapter 12.1). This was a time when there had been a large influx of Caribbean immigrants and colour prejudice was common and accepted and there were race riots in London, Bristol and the Midlands. The Act made discrimination on grounds of colour, race, or ethnic or national origins unlawful.

In the case of religion, discrimination against Roman Catholics was perfectly legal until the Papists Act 1778 and it was not until the Roman Catholic Relief Act 1829 that there was any meaningful equality. When in 1830 there was debate on extending the same protections to Jews a large vocal group of Tory MPs lobbied against this and some meaningful acceptance of different religious viewpoints was not achieved until the Religious Opinions Act 1846 and this was quite limited.

Other than certain protections of child workers from abuse in the nineteenth century (see Chapter 1.3) there has been little or no protection from age discrimination which of course can have a major impact in the workplace.

In the case of gay employees and transsexual employees case law shows that these had almost no rights at all (see Chapter 14.2 and 14.3).

The most significant developments in protection from discrimination have resulted from EU law emanating from the social policy. It is worth noting that until the change of government in 1997 the UK effectively could opt out of social policy developments. Key in these developments were the Framework Directive 2000/78 and the Race Directive 2000/43. In the case of pay and conditions of work in the case of sex discrimination the original Equal Pay Directive 75/117 and the Equal Treatment Directive 76/207 have now also been replaced with the Recast Directive 2006/54.

The UK initially implemented many of the reforms from the Framework Directive in numerous regulations. Subsequently the law has been consolidated in the Equality Act 2000. The Equality Act 2006 has repealed much of the previous statutory discrimination law including the Equal Pay Act 1970, the Sex Discrimination Act 1975, the Race Relations

Act 1976, the Sex Discrimination Act 1986, the Disability Discrimination Act 1995 as well as various Regulations on religion and belief, sexual orientation, gender discrimination and age.

9.2 The Equality Act 2010 and the protected characteristics

The Equality Act gives effect to the Framework Directive 2000/78 and the Race Directive 2000/43 in a single comprehensive piece of legislation. In keeping with EU social policy it aims to harmonise the law on prevention of discrimination and to promote equality. The Act identifies the range of protected characteristics in section 4 Equality Act 2010.

SECTION

'4 The protected characteristics.
The following characteristics are protected characteristics –

age;
disability;
gender reassignment;
marriage and civil partnership;
pregnancy and maternity;
race;
religion or belief;
sex;
sexual orientation.'

The characteristics are ones that had already been identified in former statutory provisions. However, some of the definitions have been modified by the Act. Section 4 lists the protected characteristics in alphabetical order and that is reflected in the section numbering.

Age is defined in section 5 Equality Act 2010.

SECTION

'5 Age.
(1) In relation to the protected characteristic of age –
   (a) a reference to a person who has a particular protected characteristic is a reference to a person of a particular age group;
   (b) a reference to persons who share a protected characteristic is a reference to persons of the same age group.
(2) A reference to an age group is a reference to a group of persons defined by reference to age, whether by reference to a particular age or to a range of ages.'

The definition clearly covers specific ages or specific age groups so it is not limited to the old or the young. Clearly one area of significance concerns the removal of the previous default age for retirement. Age discrimination is covered in Chapter 14.5.

Disability is defined in section 6.

SECTION

'6 Disability.
(1) A person (P) has a disability if –
   (a) P has a physical or mental impairment, and
   (b) the impairment has a substantial and long-term adverse effect on P's ability to carry out normal day-to-day activities.
(2) A reference to a disabled person is a reference to a person who has a disability.
(3) In relation to the protected characteristic of disability –
   (a) a reference to a person who has a particular protected characteristic is a reference to a person who has a particular disability;
   (b) a reference to persons who share a protected characteristic is a reference to persons who have the same disability.
(4) This Act (except Part 12 and section 190) applies in relation to a person who has had a disability as it applies in relation to a person who has the disability; accordingly (except in that Part and that section) –
   (a) a reference (however expressed) to a person who has a disability includes a reference to a person who has had the disability, and
   (b) a reference (however expressed) to a person who does not have a disability includes a reference to a person who has not had the disability.'

Clearly the first significant issue with disability is being able to show that the claimant falls within the definition of disability in section 6(1) which means showing:

- that he suffers from a physical or mental impairment;
- which has a substantial and long term effect;
- on his ability to carry out normal day-to-day activities.

Section 6(5) goes on to identify that a Minister of the Crown may issue guidance about matters to be taken into account in deciding any question for the purposes of subsection (1). There are also some specific additional areas of discrimination in relation to disability where for instance an employer fails to make reasonable adjustments to accommodate the disability. Disability discrimination is covered in Chapter 13. The area has some difficulties and is supplemented by a Schedule to the Act and guidance from the Equality and HR Commission
   Gender reassignment is defined in section 7 Equality Act 2010.

SECTION

'7 Gender reassignment
(1) A person has the protected characteristic of gender reassignment if the person is proposing to undergo, is undergoing or has undergone a process (or part of a process) for the purpose of reassigning the person's sex by changing physiological or other attributes of sex.
(2) A reference to a transsexual person is a reference to a person who has the protected characteristic of gender reassignment.
(3) In relation to the protected characteristic of gender reassignment –
   (a) a reference to a person who has a particular protected characteristic is a reference to a transsexual person;
   (b) a reference to persons who share a protected characteristic is a reference to transsexual persons.'

The section in this way covers transsexuals who include anybody who is proposing to undergo, or is currently undergoing or has already undergone a process (or part of a process) for the purpose of reassigning their sex by changing their physiological or other attributes. Disability on the ground of gender reassignment is covered in Chapter 14.3.

Marriage and civil partnership is defined in section 8 Equality Act 2010.

SECTION

'8 Marriage and civil partnership
(1) A person has the protected characteristic of marriage and civil partnership if the person is married or is a civil partner.
(2) In relation to the protected characteristic of marriage and civil partnership –
   (a) a reference to a person who has a particular protected characteristic is a reference to a person who is married or is a civil partner;
   (b) a reference to persons who share a protected characteristic is a reference to persons who are married or are civil partners.'

These are fairly straightforward definitions which obviously reflect the fact that the claimant has either gone through a legitimate marriage ceremony or a legitimate civil partnership ceremony. Discrimination on the ground of marriage or civil partnership is covered in Chapter 11.5.

Race is defined in section 9 Equality Act 2010.

SECTION

'9 Race.
(1) Race includes –
   (a) colour;
   (b) nationality;
   (c) ethnic or national origins.
(2) In relation to the protected characteristic of race –
   (a) a reference to a person who has a particular protected characteristic is a reference to a person of a particular racial group;
   (b) a reference to persons who share a protected characteristic is a reference to persons of the same racial group.
(3) A racial group is a group of persons defined by reference to race; and a reference to a person's racial group is a reference to a racial group into which the person falls.'

This is somewhat different to the definitions of race in the previous Acts.

The section also goes on to identify in section 9(4) that the fact that a racial group comprises two or more distinct racial groups does not prevent it from constituting a particular racial group. Section 9(5) also identifies that a Minister of the Crown may by order amend the section so that caste can also be seen as an aspect of race. Race discrimination is covered in Chapter 12.

Religion or belief is defined in section 10 Equality Act 2010.

'10 Religion or belief.

(1) Religion means any religion and a reference to religion includes a reference to a lack of religion.

(2) Belief means any religious or philosophical belief and a reference to belief includes a reference to a lack of belief.

(3) In relation to the protected characteristic of religion or belief –

(a) a reference to a person who has a particular protected characteristic is a reference to a person of a particular religion or belief;

(b) a reference to persons who share a protected characteristic is a reference to persons who are of the same religion or belief.'

As can be seen from section 10 the definition covers quite a broad range. It would cover all formal religions. It would also cover specific philosophical beliefs. More importantly it covers lack of religion and lack of a philosophical belief so that an atheist would have just as much protection from the Act as a Christian, a Muslim or a Jew or indeed a Buddhist. Discrimination on the ground of religion or belief is covered in Chapter 14.4.

Sex is defined in section 11 Equality Act 2010.

SECTION

'11 Sex.

In relation to the protected characteristic of sex –

(a) a reference to a person who has a particular protected characteristic is a reference to a man or to a woman;

(b) a reference to persons who share a protected characteristic is a reference to persons of the same sex.'

It is obviously one of the simplest definitions and a well-established area of discrimination law. Sex discrimination is covered in Chapter 11.

Sexual orientation is defined in section 12 Equality Act 2010.

SECTION

'12 Sexual orientation.

(1) Sexual orientation means a person's sexual orientation towards –

(a) persons of the same sex,

(b) persons of the opposite sex, or

(c) persons of either sex.

(2) In relation to the protected characteristic of sexual orientation –

(a) a reference to a person who has a particular protected characteristic is a reference to a person who is of a particular sexual orientation;

(b) a reference to persons who share a protected characteristic is a reference to persons who are of the same sexual orientation.'

This is one of the newer areas of discrimination law but all sexual orientations enjoy the same protection under the Act by virtue of the section, whether the person is gay, heterosexual or bisexual. Discrimination on grounds of sexual orientation is covered in Chapter 14.2.

Pregnancy and maternity is defined in section 18 of the Equality Act 2010.

SECTION

'18 Pregnancy and maternity discrimination: work cases.

(1) This section has effect for the purposes of the application of Part 5 (work) to the protected characteristic of pregnancy and maternity.

(2) A person (A) discriminates against a woman if, in the protected period in relation to a pregnancy of hers, A treats her unfavourably –

  (a) because of the pregnancy, or

  (b) because of illness suffered by her as a result of it.

(3) A person (A) discriminates against a woman if A treats her unfavourably because she is on compulsory maternity leave.

(4) A person (A) discriminates against a woman if A treats her unfavourably because she is exercising or seeking to exercise, or has exercised or sought to exercise, the right to ordinary or additional maternity leave.

(5) For the purposes of subsection (2), if the treatment of a woman is in implementation of a decision taken in the protected period, the treatment is to be regarded as occurring in that period (even if the implementation is not until after the end of that period).

(6) The protected period, in relation to a woman's pregnancy, begins when the pregnancy begins, and ends –

  (a) if she has the right to ordinary and additional maternity leave, at the end of the additional maternity leave period or (if earlier) when she returns to work after the pregnancy;

  (b) if she does not have that right, at the end of the period of 2 weeks beginning with the end of the pregnancy.

(7) Section 13, so far as relating to sex discrimination, does not apply to treatment of a woman in so far as –

  (a) it is in the protected period in relation to her and is for a reason mentioned in paragraph (a) or (b) of subsection (2), or

  (b) it is for a reason mentioned in subsection (3) or (4).'

As can be seen from the section pregnancy and maternity have more specific protections than the other protected characteristics. Pregnancy and maternity is in any case subject to extensive provision and is covered in Chapter 8.4.

9.3 The Equality Act 2010 and the areas of prohibited conduct

9.3.1 Direct discrimination

Direct discrimination is defined in section 13 Equality Act 2010.

SECTION

'13 Direct discrimination.

(1) A person (A) discriminates against another (B) if, because of a protected characteristic, A treats B less favourably than A treats or would treat others.'

This is reasonably straightforward, if the employer treats the employee less favourably because of his or her protected characteristic then he would treat others then this is direct discrimination. Obviously in this respect a claimant must have an identified comparator to claim direct discrimination. The wording of the section means that it also includes associative discrimination that the person has been discriminated against because of association with a person with the protected characteristic. It also will not matter that the employee does not have the protected characteristic if the employer believes that he does. The motive for the discrimination is not relevant.

The section also goes on to make some qualifications in relation to particular protected characteristics.

SECTION

'13
(2) If the protected characteristic is age, A does not discriminate against B if A can show A's treatment of B to be a proportionate means of achieving a legitimate aim.
(3) If the protected characteristic is disability, and B is not a disabled person, A does not discriminate against B only because A treats or would treat disabled persons more favourably than A treats B.
(4) If the protected characteristic is marriage and civil partnership, this section applies to a contravention of Part 5 (work) only if the treatment is because it is B who is married or a civil partner.
(5) If the protected characteristic is race, less favourable treatment includes segregating B from others.
(6) If the protected characteristic is sex –
   (a) less favourable treatment of a woman includes less favourable treatment of her because she is breast-feeding;
   (b) in a case where B is a man, no account is to be taken of special treatment afforded to a woman in connection with pregnancy or childbirth.
(7) Subsection (6)(a) does not apply for the purposes of Part 5 (work).'

9.3.2 Indirect discrimination

Indirect discrimination is defined in section 19 Equality Act 2010.

SECTION

'19 Indirect discrimination.
(1) A person (A) discriminates against another (B) if A applies to B a provision, criterion or practice which is discriminatory in relation to a relevant protected characteristic of B's.
(2) For the purposes of subsection (1), a provision, criterion or practice is discriminatory in relation to a relevant protected characteristic of B's if –
   (a) A applies, or would apply, it to persons with whom B does not share the characteristic,
   (b) it puts, or would put, persons with whom B shares the characteristic at a particular disadvantage when compared with persons with whom B does not share it,
   (c) it puts, or would put, B at that disadvantage, and
   (d) A cannot show it to be a proportionate means of achieving a legitimate aim.'

So this means that an employer discriminates against an employee when he:

- subjects the claimant to a provision, criterion or practice which is discriminatory in relation to his or her protected characteristic (classic examples of such provisions, criteria or practices might include for example company policies and dress codes);

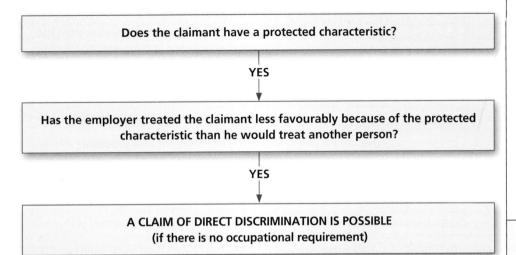

Figure 9.1 Diagram illustrating the elements of a claim for direct discrimination

- which applies to other employees not sharing the characteristic but puts the claimant at a disadvantage compared with persons who do not share his protected characteristic;
- and it cannot be shown to be a proportionate means of achieving a legitimate aim.

It is possible for the employer to justify the discrimination by showing that it is a result of a genuine business need and is a proportionate means of achieving a legitimate aim. In deciding whether the requirement does indirectly discriminate it must strike an objective balance between the discriminatory effect and the reasonable needs of the business. For example, if the Fire Service had a rule of 'No headgear whilst on service' this would indirectly discriminate against Sikh men. However, it may well be justified if fire fighters were required to wear helmets for safety reasons.

Section 19(3) identifies that the protected characteristics that are protected from indirect discrimination are age, disability, gender reassignment, marriage and civil partnership, race, religion or belief, sex and sexual orientation.

9.3.3 Harassment

Harassment was not covered by UK equality law until quite late. When the first complaints of sexual harassment arose the only mechanism under the Sex Discrimination Act 1975 was under section 6(2)(b) being subjected to 'any other detriment'. As a result a woman could only bring a successful action if she could show that she had suffered a detriment which was not always possible. In *Stewart v Cleveland Guest Engineering Ltd* [1994] IRLR 440 the EAT held that female nude pinups from magazines and calendars posted on the walls of a factory were gender neutral, and men as well as women might be offended by them so that there was no detriment and the claimant had not suffered less favourable treatment. At one point it was also suggested that a claim would fail if both women and men were subjected to the same treatment. In *Balgobin and Francis v London Borough of Tower Hamlets* [1987] IRLR 401, EAT a woman's claim failed because she could not prove the harassment and it held that without proof a man suffering homosexual advances would have been treated the same so there could be no less favourable treatment. Subsequently the EAT in *Driskel v Peninsula Business Services Ltd* [2000] IRLR 151 identified that if the conduct complained of is of a sexual nature then the fact that men and women are subjected to the same treatment is irrelevant.

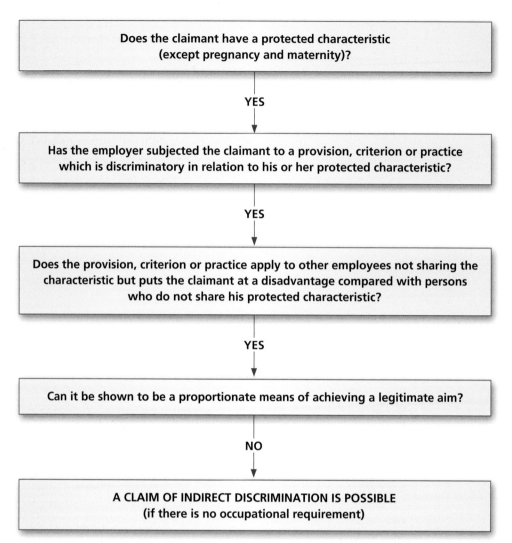

Figure 9.2 Diagram illustrating the elements of a claim for indirect discrimination

The EU Commission in any case had developed a comprehensive definition of harassment and this was later inserted in the Framework Directive 2000/78. Article 2(3) of the directive provided the following definition of harassment:

ARTICLE

'**3. Harassment** shall be deemed to be a form of discrimination within the meaning of paragraph 1, when unwanted conduct related to any of the grounds referred to in Article 1 takes place with the purpose or effect of violating the dignity of a person and of creating an intimidating, hostile, degrading, humiliating or offensive environment. In this context, the concept of harassment may be defined in accordance with the national laws and practice of the Member States.'

This was later supplemented by a further definition in Directive 2002/73 which temporarily replaced the Equal Treatment Directive 76/207 until the Recast Directive 2006/54 gained force. This added the following:

ARTICLE

'2. For the purposes of this Directive, the following definitions shall apply:

harassment: where an unwanted conduct related to the sex of a person occurs with the purpose or effect of violating the dignity of a person, and of creating an intimidating, hostile, degrading, humiliating or offensive environment,

sexual harassment: where any form of unwanted verbal, non-verbal or physical conduct of a sexual nature occurs, with the purpose or effect of violating the dignity of a person, in particular when creating an intimidating, hostile, degrading, humiliating or offensive environment.'

Now harassment is one form of prohibited conduct under the Equality Act 2010. Harassment is defined in section 26 which gives statutory effect to the EU definition.

SECTION

'26

(1) A person (A) harasses another (B) if
   (a) A engages in unwanted conduct related to a relevant protected characteristic, and
   (b) the conduct has the purpose or effect of
       (i) violating B's dignity, or
       (ii) creating an intimidating, hostile, degrading, humiliating or offensive environment for B.'

There is a second form of harassment which is identified in section 26(2).

SECTION

'26

(2) A also harasses B if –
   (a) A engages in unwanted conduct of a sexual nature, and
   (b) the conduct has the purpose or effect referred to in subsection (1)(b).'

There is also a third type of harassment identified in section 26(3).

SECTION

'26

(3) A also harasses B if –
   (a) A or another person engages in unwanted conduct of a sexual nature or that is related to gender reassignment or sex,
   (b) the conduct has the purpose or effect referred to in subsection (1)(b), and
   (c) because of B's rejection of or submission to the conduct, A treats B less favourably than A would treat B if B had not rejected or submitted to the conduct.'

So the common features of all three are:

▨ that the conduct is unwanted; and

▨ that it has the purpose or effect of violating the claimant's dignity or subjecting them to an intimidating, hostile, degrading, humiliating or offensive environment.

It was identified in *Insitu Cleaning Co Ltd v Heads* [1995] IRLR 4 that conduct is unwanted if it is unwelcome or uninvited (see Chapter 11.2.3). It is also possible that a claim can be brought for a single incident of harassment if it is sufficiently serious as was the case in *Bracebridge Engineering Ltd v Darby* [1990] IRLR 3 which involved a single but unsavoury sexual assault.

Section 26(4) also goes on to identify a more specific explanation of what must be taken into account by a court or tribunal in deciding whether the conduct has the purpose or effect in section 26(1)(b):

SECTION

'26

(4) In deciding whether conduct has the effect referred to in subsection (1)(b), each of the following must be taken into account
   (a) the perception of B;
   (b) the other circumstances of the case;
   (c) whether it is reasonable for the conduct to have that effect.'

This subsection helps to remove the problem of the so-called 'hyper sensitive claimant'.

Section 26(5) also identifies that harassment applies to the protected characteristics of age, disability, gender reassignment, race, religion or belief, sex, and sexual orientation.

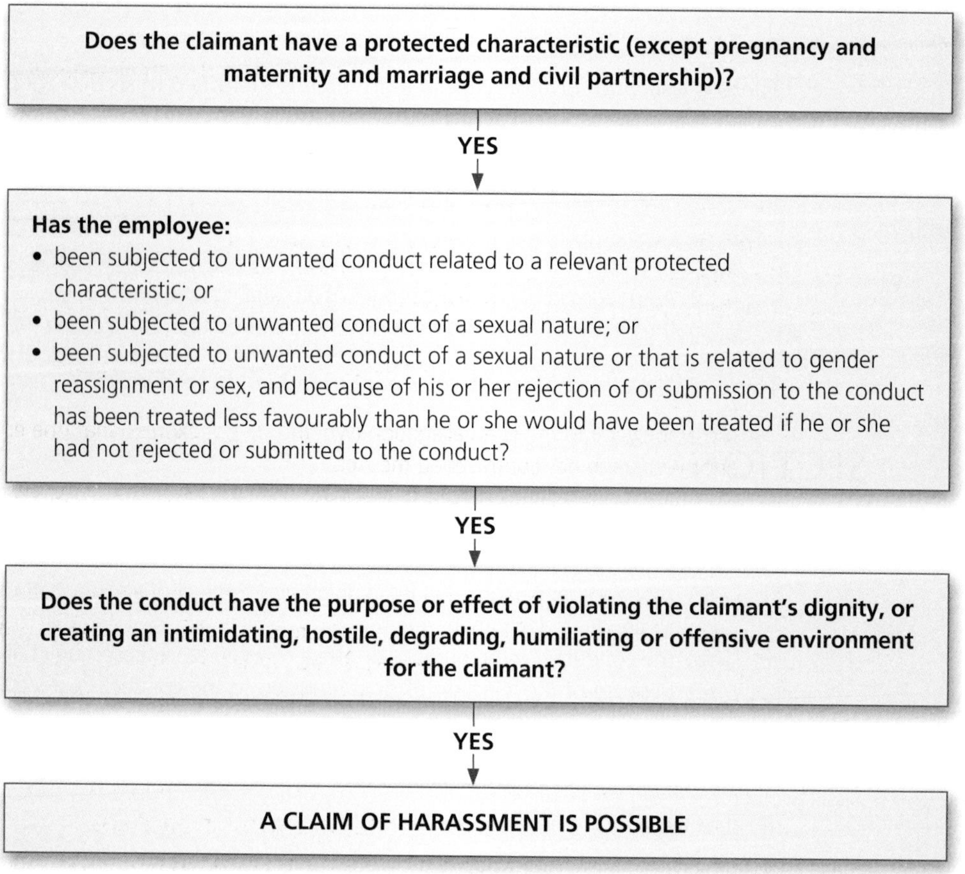

Does the claimant have a protected characteristic (except pregnancy and maternity and marriage and civil partnership)?

YES

Has the employee:
- been subjected to unwanted conduct related to a relevant protected characteristic; or
- been subjected to unwanted conduct of a sexual nature; or
- been subjected to unwanted conduct of a sexual nature or that is related to gender reassignment or sex, and because of his or her rejection of or submission to the conduct has been treated less favourably than he or she would have been treated if he or she had not rejected or submitted to the conduct?

YES

Does the conduct have the purpose or effect of violating the claimant's dignity, or creating an intimidating, hostile, degrading, humiliating or offensive environment for the claimant?

YES

A CLAIM OF HARASSMENT IS POSSIBLE

Figure 9.3 Diagram illustrating the elements of a claim for harassment

It is worth noting that harassment covers a very broad range of conduct from a single inappropriate and offensive comment in *Insitu Cleaning Co Ltd v Heads* [1995] IRLR 4 (see Chapter 11.2.3) to the brutal and sadistic physical abuse in *Jones v Tower Boot Co Ltd* [1997] IRLR 168 (see Chapter 12.2.3).

9.3.4 Victimisation

Victimisation is defined in section 27 of the Equality Act 2010.

SECTION

'27 Victimisation

(1) A person [the employer] victimises another person [the employee] if [the employer] subjects [the employee] to a detriment because –
   (a) [the employee] does a protected act, or
   (b) [the employer] believes that [the employee] has done, or may do, a protected act.
(2) Each of the following is a protected act –
   (a) bringing proceedings under this Act;
   (b) giving evidence or information in connection with proceedings under this Act;
   (c) doing any other thing for the purposes of or in connection with this Act;
   (d) making an allegation (whether or not express) that [the employer] or another person has contravened this Act.'

Does the claimant have a protected characteristic?

YES

Has the employee done a protected act under the Act?
- the employee has brought proceedings under the Act; or
- the employee has given evidence or information in connection with proceedings under the Act; or
- the employee has done any other thing for the purposes of or in connection with the Act; or
- the employee has made an allegation (whether or not express) that [the employer] or another person has contravened the Act.

YES

Has the employer subjected the employee to a detriment because the employee did a protected act under the Act?

YES

A CLAIM OF VICTIMISATION IS POSSIBLE

Figure 9.4 Diagram illustrating the elements of a claim for victimisation

Victimisation is a relatively straightforward concept. In essence it occurs whenever the employee is disadvantaged or subjected to a detriment because of exercising a right under the Act in connection with his protected characteristic. In *St Helens Metropolitan Borough Council v Derbyshire* [2007] UKHL 16 the employer sent letters to all staff two months before the claimant's equal pay claim was to be heard expressing concern at the effect the claim would have on the staff. Women who had settled their claims could obviously show disapproval to the claimants so the letters amounted to victimisation (see Chapter 11.2.4).

9.4 Occupational requirement

Occupational requirement replaces the old defence of genuine occupational qualification (GOQ) that was found in section 7 of the Sex Discrimination Act and section 4 of the Race Relations Act 1976. These listed a variety of specific situations which would amount to a defence to discrimination, for example both Acts included a GOQ of authenticity of physiology.

Now occupational requirement is a general provision of the Equality Act 2010 in schedule 9.

SECTION

'1(1)   A person [an employer] does not contravene a provision … by applying in relation to work a requirement to have a particular protected characteristic, if [an employer] shows that, having regard to the nature or context of the work –
(a) it is an occupational requirement,
(b) the application of the requirement is a proportionate means of achieving a legitimate aim, and
(c) the person to whom [an employer] applies the requirement does not meet it (or [an employer] has reasonable grounds for not being satisfied that the person meets it).'

So an employer can rely on an occupational requirement if it is a proportionate means of achieving a legitimate aim and the claimant does not meet the requirement. There are individual occupational requirements for the different protected characteristics. Occupational requirements can provide a defence to all aspects of employment under section 39(1) and (2), on recruitment and selection, during employment and on dismissal. They can provide a justification for direct discrimination under section 13 and indirect discrimination under section 19 but not to harassment under section 26 or victimisation under section 27.

9.5 Discrimination in employment

Section 39 places discrimination in the context of employment and explains the points at which unlawful discrimination in employment might occur:

SECTION

'39 Employees and applicants
(1) An employer (A) must not discriminate against a person (B) –
(a) in the arrangements A makes for deciding to whom to offer employment;
(b) as to the terms on which A offers B employment;
(c) by not offering B employment.

(2) An employer (A) must not discriminate against an employee of A's (B) –
  (a) as to B's terms of employment;
  (b) in the way A affords B access, or by not affording B access, to opportunities for promotion, transfer or training or for receiving any other benefit, facility or service;
  (c) by dismissing B;
  (d) by subjecting B to any other detriment.'

So there are three points at which discrimination in employment might be an issue:

- in recruitment and selection
- during employment
- on dismissal.

ACTIVITY

Self-assessment questions

1. For what reasons was the Equality Act 2010 passed?
2. What are the protected characteristics under the Act?
3. How are the different types of discrimination described in the Act and what are they?
4. What has to be proved for a claim of indirect discrimination?
5. How has the area of harassment improved from the Sex Discrimination Act 1975 and Race Relations Act 1976?
6. What is an occupational requirement?

KEY FACTS

Origins	Case/statute
Developed from EU social policy	*Framework Directive 2000/78* *Race Directive 2000/43*
Protected characteristics	**Case/statute**
Age	
• a person of a particular age group which is defined by reference to a particular age or to a range of ages	*S5 Equality Act 2010*
Disability	
• a person has a disability if he or she has a physical or mental impairment, which has a substantial and long term adverse effect on his or her ability to carry out normal day-to-day activities	*S6 Equality Act 2010*
Gender reassignment	
• a person who is proposing to undergo, is undergoing or has undergone a process (or part of a process) for the purpose of reassigning their sex by changing physiological or other attributes (a transsexual person)	*S7 Equality Act 2010*
Marriage and civil partnership	
• a person who is married or is a civil partner	*S8 Equality Act 2010*

Race	
• a person of a particular colour, nationality, ethnic or national origin	*S9 Equality Act 2010*
Religion or belief	
• a person who has a particular religion or no religion or who has a particular philosophical belief or no belief	*S10 Equality Act 2010*
Sex	
• a man or a woman	*S11 Equality Act 2010*
Sexual orientation	
• a person's sexual orientation towards persons of the same sex, or persons of the opposite sex, or persons of either sex	*S12 Equality Act 2010*
Pregnancy and maternity	
• the protected period begins when the pregnancy begins, and ends at the end of additional maternity leave period or (if earlier) when she returns to work after the pregnancy; or if the woman has no right to ordinary and additional maternity leave two weeks after the end of the pregnancy	*S18 Equality Act 2010*
The different types of prohibited conduct (discrimination)	**Case/statute**
Direct discrimination	
• the person is treated less favourably than a person who does not share their protected characteristic	*S13 Equality Act 2010*
Indirect discrimination	
• the claimant is subjected to a provision, criterion or practice which is discriminatory in relation to his or her protected characteristic which puts him or her at a disadvantage compared with persons who do not share his protected characteristic and it cannot be shown to be a proportionate means of achieving a legitimate aim	*S19 Equality Act 2010*
Harassment	
• the claimant is subjected to unwanted conduct related to his or her protected characteristic, with the purpose or effect of violating his dignity, or subjecting him or her to an intimidating, hostile, degrading, humiliating or offensive environment	*S26 Equality Act 2010*
Victimisation	
• the claimant was subjected to a detriment because he or she brought proceedings under the Act, or gave evidence or information in connection with proceedings or did anything else for the purposes of or in connection with the Act, or made an allegation (whether or not express) that his or her employer or another person has contravened the Act	*S27 Equality Act 2010*

Occupational requirement	Case/statute
An employer can lawfully discriminate where it can be shown: • that this is because of an occupational requirement • which is a proportionate means of achieving a legitimate aim, and • the person to whom the employer applies the requirement does not meet it (or [an employer] has reasonable grounds for not being satisfied that the person meets it)	*Schedule 9, para 1(1) Equality Act 2010*
Discrimination in employment	**Case/statute**
There are three points where unlawful discrimination might occur in employment in relation to a specific protected characteristic:	
Recruitment and selection	
• in the way in which it is decided who to employ • by offering employment on different terms • by refusing to offer employment	*S39(1) Equality Act 2010*
During employment	
• in applying different terms and conditions • in the way the employer affords access to opportunities for promotion training or transfer or any other facility, benefit or service or by not affording access to any of these	*S39(2) Equality Act 2010*
On dismissal	*S39(1) Equality Act 2010*

SUMMARY

- The Equality Act 2010 has evolved from EU social policy and in particular the Framework Directive 2000/78 and the Race Directive 2000/43.
- It groups together all of the former areas of discrimination law and adds to them those areas indicated in the Directives.
- These are now referred to as 'protected characteristics' and include age, disability, gender reassignment, marriage and civil partnership, race, religion or belief, sex, sexual orientation, pregnancy and maternity.
- There are extensive definitions given to each.
- The Act also identifies four forms of prohibited behaviour: direct discrimination, indirect discrimination, harassment and victimisation.
- Direct discrimination is defined as where a person is treated less favourably than a person who does not share their protected characteristic.
- Indirect discrimination is defined as where the claimant is subjected to a provision, criterion or practice which is discriminatory in relation to his or her protected characteristic which puts him or her at a disadvantage compared with persons who do not share his protected characteristic and it cannot be shown to be a proportionate means of achieving a legitimate aim.
- Harassment is defined as where the claimant is subjected to unwanted conduct related to his or her protected characteristic, with the purpose or effect of violating his dignity, or subjecting him or her to an intimidating, hostile, degrading humiliating or offensive environment.

- Victimisation is defined as where the claimant was subjected to a detriment because he or she brought proceedings under the Act; or gave evidence or information in connection with proceedings or did anything else for the purposes of or in connection with the Act; or made an allegation (whether or not express) that his or her employer or another person has contravened the Act.

- It is also possible for there to be occupational requirements where discrimination is possible but justified – this occurred in the previous law and includes things like authenticity where a film producer wants a woman to play a woman's role, and insisting on a particular sex for example to preserve decency.

- Discrimination covers all aspects of employment: recruitment and selection, during employment and dismissal.

Further reading

Emir, Astra, *Selwyn's Law of Employment 17th edition*. Oxford University Press, 2012, Chapter 4.
Sargeant, Malcolm and Lewis, David, *Employment Law 5th edition*. Pearson, 2010, Chapter 5.

10

Protection from discrimination (1) equal pay

AIMS AND OBJECTIVES

After reading this chapter you should be able to:

- Understand how the concept of equal pay for men and women doing the same or equal work originated
- Understand how the equality clause in the Equality Act 2010 works
- Understand who will be a comparator
- Understand the concepts of like work, work rated equivalent and work of equal value
- Understand the circumstances in which pay differentials between men and women can be justified and the concept of material factor defence
- Understand how equal pay claims are brought and the available remedies
- Understand the significance of Article 157 TFEU
- Understand the definition of pay in the Article
- Understand the concept of objective justification for indirect discrimination
- Critically analyse the area
- Apply the law to factual situations and reach conclusions

10.1 The origins of equal pay

Equal pay law in the United Kingdom began with the Equal Pay Act 1970, although this did not gain force until 1975. Together with the Sex Discrimination Act 1975, as well as later additional enactments and amendments, the Act was aimed first at complying with the requirements of what was then Article 119 EC Treaty (now Art 157 TFEU) and second at remedying what was unjustifiable discrimination against women.

The concept of equal pay developed not from English law but as part of what is now EU law. The concept of equal pay between men and women for equal work was inserted into the original Treaty because of the potential problems that would arise from the single market with no internal barriers to trade. Member states such as France, which has had the principle of equality from the time of the revolution, may well have suffered from an inability to compete with cheap imports from countries where there was large disparity between the pay of men and women at the time the Treaties were drafted. Equality developed as a general principle of EU law, so that in cases equality is an underlying principle which the judges would consider. Since the Treaty on European Unity (TEU) it is also established in the Treaties.

A number of potential problems did originally exist from having both EU and domestic law on equal pay.

- First EU law is supreme over all inconsistent national law, and by the processes of direct effect, indirect effect and state liability EU law is enforceable in national courts.

- Both principles originated in the 1962 case *Van Gend en Loos v Nederlandse Administratie der Belastingen* 26/62 so were established long before UK membership. As a result it is often necessary to consider both sets of law.

- EU law in general is based on much broader principles than UK law. The driving force in case law in the Court of Justice is achieving the objectives of the Treaties, which are in any case broadly stated, and therefore there is much more room for interpretation. The Court of Justice inevitably looks for the broadest interpretation which will achieve the Treaty objectives for the greatest number of citizens. National law is likely to be interpreted more narrowly.

- The EU method of interpretation is teleological or purposive so the ultimate question for the court is whether the objectives of the Treaties are being satisfied. This has been one of the reasons for a gradual change in emphasis from literal to purposive interpretation in English courts.

- While there is no system of precedent in EU law, rulings on law in the ECJ inevitably become precedent for English courts.

- Traditionally in EU law there was not the strict demarcation between pay and conditions of work that existed within the framework of the Equal Pay Act 1970 and the Sex Discrimination Act 1975. In fact now both are covered by Directive 2006/54.

- The definition of pay in the Treaty was traditionally much broader and has been generously interpreted by the ECJ (see 10.3.2 below).

- Certainly some of the case law shows a reluctance to embrace EU principles absolutely. It is also often questioned whether, despite the legislation true equality has been achieved. Women's pay is on average around 80 per cent of men's, it represents a smaller share of household income, women are often referred to as a secondary workforce and their jobs are often the first under threat in times of economic hardship, and reference is still made to the so-called 'glass ceiling' in access to higher paid employment.

10.2 The Equality Act 2010

10.2.1 The equality clause

Section 66 Equality Act 2010 now contains an equality clause.

SECTION

'66 Sex equality clause.

(1) If the terms of A's work do not (by whatever means) include a sex equality clause, they are to be treated as including one.

(2) A sex equality clause is a provision that has the following effect –

(a) if a term of A's is less favourable to A than a corresponding term of B's is to B, A's term is modified so as not to be less favourable;

(b) if A does not have a term which corresponds to a term of B's that benefits B, A's terms are modified so as to include such a term.'

So it is implied that a woman will receive equal treatment to a man doing equal work and, if a term in a woman's contract is less favourable than a term in the man's contract then the contract will be modified so as make both contracts as favourable as each other. This mirrors the equality clause that was originally in section 1 Equal Pay Act 1970.

Under section 65 Equality Act 2010 the work of fellow employees is equal if it is:

- like work

- work rated as equivalent

- work of equal value.

SECTION

'65 Equal work.

(1) For the purposes of this Chapter, A's work is equal to that of B if it is –

(a) like B's work,

(b) rated as equivalent to B's work, or

(c) of equal value to B's work.'

These are examined respectively in 10.2.3, 10.2.4 and 10.2.5 below.

The right approach for the court or tribunal is obviously to view the compared contracts term by term and to modify any term that is unfavourable. One problem that has surfaced is the 'whole contract' approach, the attitude posed by employers that the contract should not be viewed term by term but as a whole and if, even though she gets less pay than her male comparator, because a woman is getting different benefits that a man does not get that on the whole they are equally treated. This was an argument put forward in *Hayward v Cammell Laird Shipbuilders Ltd (No 2)* [1988] ICR 464. The argument was accepted by the tribunal which rejected the claim for equal pay. However, the House of Lords (now the Supreme Court) accepted that this would be to interfere with her rights under Article 157 TFEU (at the time Article 119 EC Treaty) (see 10.2.5 below).

One of the inevitable consequences of the approach is that it could result in a so-called 'piggy-back claim' where a man relies on a man making a claim for equal pay with a woman who has succeeded in a claim using a higher paid male comparator. This has recently been confirmed in *Hartlepool Borough Council v Llewellyn* [2009] IRLR 796.

JUDGMENT

The EAT commented: 'in truth the issue is straightforward, and in our view not difficult to decide in the light of our conclusion on the claim under the 1970 Act. In circumstances where, as we have held, the Councils would have been obliged, had the claims proceeded to a decision, to pay the same sums (both by way of arrears and for the future) to male and female claimants, it would be remarkable if they were entitled to discriminate between them in any offer to compromise the selfsame claims.'

Other contractual entitlements besides simply pay are also covered by the equality clause so should be considered in determining whether to grant equal pay. This can for example cover things such as concessionary travel facilities for the families of retired railway workers as in *Garland v BREL* 12/81; [1983] AC 751. The principle has also been applied in the case of unequal treatment in the case of contributions to pension schemes.

CASE EXAMPLE

Worringham & Humphries v Lloyds Bank Ltd 69/80 [1981] ECR 767

The employer made supplementary payments to male employees under the age of twenty-five as contributions to an occupational pension scheme. The same payments were not given to female employees of the same age and they challenged this disparity as a breach of Article 157 TFEU (at the time Article 119 EC Treaty). The ECJ held that sums included in calculating an employee's gross salary which are used to directly determine the calculation of other benefits such as redundancy payment, family credit etc., all count as pay for the purposes of the Article. Since women below the age of twenty-five were denied the subsidy this was a clear breach of the Article.

10.2.2 The comparator

A primary requirement of bringing a claim for equal pay is that the comparator must be with a person of the opposite sex who is working in the same or associated employment. The principle is now contained in section 79 Equality Act 2010.

SECTION

'79 Comparators.
(1) This section applies for the purposes of this Chapter.
(2) If A is employed, B is a comparator if subsection (3) or (4) applies.
(3) This subsection applies if –
   (a) B is employed by A's employer or by an associate of A's employer, and
   (b) A and B work at the same establishment.
(4) This subsection applies if –
   (a) B is employed by A's employer or an associate of A's employer,
   (b) B works at an establishment other than the one at which A works, and
   (c) common terms apply at the establishments (either generally or as between A and B).'

The Comparator should be employed at the same establishment or employed by an associated employer or at establishments which have common terms and conditions. The comparator must be typical with no personal considerations such as red circling or geographical considerations such as London weighting. The issue of common conditions was discussed in the case below.

CASE EXAMPLE

Leverton v Clwyd C.C. [1989] IRLR 28

A female nursery nurse claimed equal pay with eleven comparators, ranging from a male clerk to a caretaker working at a different establishment for the same Council. The female worked for thirty-two hours per week and had seventy days' annual holiday. A male comparator worked thirty-seven hours per week and had only twenty days' annual holiday. On the basis of these differences the Court of Appeal stated that the male was not therefore a valid comparator. However, the then House of Lords held that because both employees were covered by the same collective agreements then they were under the common terms required under the Act.

The original interpretation of associated employer from the Equal Pay Act 1970 was also much more restrictive in the case of public sector workers than would be the case under EU law.

CASE EXAMPLE

Scullard v Knowles [1996] IRLR 344

A female manager of a training unit run by a regional education council sought to compare herself with higher paid male managers of training units run by different regional education councils. Originally the tribunal had denied her claim on the basis that the woman did not work for an associated employer to the men. The EAT reversed this decision using EU principles. All of the Councils were funded by what was at that time the Department of Employment and all employees were subject to the same collective agreement.

The more recent test in establishing whether the claimant and comparator can be said to be in the same or associated employment when they work at different establishments is whether their pay generates from the same source. This was the issue on the interpretation of Article 157 TFEU (at the time Article 119 EC Treaty) in *Lawrence v Regent Office Care Ltd, Commercial Catering Group and Mitie Secure Services Ltd* (Case C–320/00) [2002] ECR I–7325 (see 10.3.1 below). In *Armstrong v Newcastle-upon-Tyne NHS Hospital Trust* [2006] IRLR 124 female health service employees working for one NHS Trust were unable to use male workers in a different NHS Trust hospital as their comparators because the Trusts were independent of each other and there was not a single source for setting pay rates. In contrast in *South Ayershire Council v Morton* [2002] ICR 956 a teacher working for one local authority was able to use a male teacher working for a different local authority as a comparator because their pay was set by the same national agreement.

A claim is not possible against a hypothetical comparator as a result of which the original view of the UK courts was that the male comparator must be in contemporaneous employment with the female claiming equal pay. This was inevitably out of step with the broader interpretation of the ECJ.

CASE EXAMPLE

Macarthys Ltd v Smith [1980] ICR 672

A stockroom manageress discovered that a former male employee whose role she now occupied had received significantly higher wages for the same job that she now did and so pursued a claim for equal pay using her predecessor as her male comparator. The Court of Appeal held that there was no claim as there was no contemporaneous male in the same employment but made a reference to the ECJ. The ECJ held that comparison could be made with any male doing the same work for the same or an associated employer and there was no need for contemporaneous employment. However, it did confirm that a hypothetical male comparator could not be used. The Advocate-General in his reasoned opinion also suggested that 'equal work' could include jobs with a high degree of similarity while not exactly the same.

JUDGMENT

The Court stated: 'the principle of equal pay enshrined in [Article 157 TFEU] applies to the case where it is established that, having regard to the nature of her services, a woman has received less pay than a man who was employed prior to the woman's period of employment and who did equal work for the employer'.

The EAT in *Diocese of Hallam Trustees v Connaughten* [1996] 3 CMLR 93 applied the same principle to a female employee using the male who took over her job at much higher pay as a comparator. The disparity of pay in the case was extreme with the female being paid £11,138 per annum and her male successor receiving £20,000 per annum. Such comparisons are in any case now also indicated in section 64(2) Equality Act 2010 which identifies that a claim is not restricted to a comparator in contemporaneous employment.

A woman is also not prevented from selecting a comparator in a claim for work of equal value simply because there is a token male who the employer has engaged in the same role as the woman on the same pay. In *Pickstone v Freemans plc* [1988] ICR 697 the court held that the fact that there was a man on the same rate of pay as the woman was irrelevant if there was a genuine male comparator. The House of Lords acknowledged that the alternative would be to encourage unscrupulous behaviour by employers who would then have a mechanism to always avoid equal pay (see 10.2.5 below).

10.2.3 Like work

Work is defined as like work if it is the same or broadly similar in nature and any differences are of no significance. This is identified in section 65(2) Equality Act 2010.

SECTION

'65(2) A's work is like B's work if –
(a) A's work and B's work are the same or broadly similar, and
(b) such differences as there are between their work are not of practical importance in relation to the terms of their work.'

So the work should be broadly similar and not necessarily identical and there can be differences as long as they are not significant.

CASE EXAMPLE

Capper Pass Ltd v Lawton [1977] ICR 83

A directors' cook had responsibility for producing meals for between ten and twenty people each day. Since her pay was lower, she claimed equal pay [under the then section 1(4) Equal Pay Act 1970] with male chefs who worked in the works canteen and who produced around 350 meals per day over six separate sittings, two each for breakfast, lunch and tea. The male chefs worked forty-five hours to the woman's forty. She was unsupervised while the men were supervised by a head chef. The EAT acknowledged that there were some minor differences but held that work did not have to be identical as long as it was broadly similar which it was in the case. It accepted her claim to equal pay.

JUDGMENT

Phillips J explained: 'in most cases the inquiry will fall into two stages. First, is the work ... "of a broadly similar" nature ... secondly ... it is then necessary to go on to consider the detail and to enquire whether the differences between the work being compared are of "practical importance in relation to the terms and conditions of employment".... There seems to be a tendency ... to weigh up the differences by references to such questions as whether one type of work is or is not suitable for women.... The only differences which will prevent work which is of a broadly similar nature from being "like work" are differences ... reflected in the terms and conditions of employment.'

A court or a tribunal obviously needs to take a broad view of the work done and ignore insignificant differences. Where differences are significant then they might be reflected in different pay rates. There are three usual examples.

Different hours of work
A difference in working hours might justify different pay even though in other respects the work is broadly similar.

CASE EXAMPLE

Dugdale v Kraft Foods Ltd [1977] ICR 48

Four women who worked as quality control inspectors claimed equal pay [under s1(4) EPA 1970] using six male quality control inspectors as their comparators. The men received a significantly higher basic rate of pay. While the women only worked mornings and afternoons, the men also worked compulsory evening shifts, and also on Sunday mornings, although this was voluntary, but for which they also received a 25 per cent shift allowance. At the time women were prevented by law from working night shifts unless there was a specific statutory exemption (such as there was for nurses) but there was no such exemption for the work in question. The tribunal had decided that the men and women were engaged in similar work but that the working at night was such a significant difference in working conditions that the men and women could not be said to be doing like work. The EAT took the view that while the time at which the work was done was not a bar to equal pay there was also no reason why the men should not be compensated for the more onerous hours through a shift allowance.

JUDGMENT

Phillips J stated: 'There seems to be no reason why the women should not have equality of treatment in respect of the basic wage, or in respect of the day shift payment (if any). In a case in which the men are not paid a shift payment or premium for night working or Sunday working, but are paid an enhanced basic wage to reflect their readiness to work at nights or on Sundays, there seems to us to be no reason why, in giving effect to the equality clause in accordance with s1(2)(a) [Equal Pay Act 1970] the terms in the women's contract as to remunneration should not be so modified as to take account of the fact that the men do, and they do not, work at night or on Sunday.'

Different duties
A difference in the duties performed might obviously justify different pay since the two employees would not in that case be engaged in like work.

CASE EXAMPLE

Noble v David Gold & Son (Holdings) Ltd [1980] IRLR 253

Noble and her male comparators were all employed in a warehouse. While the men's duties involved loading and unloading supplies, the women were generally engaged in lighter duties such as sorting, packing and labelling goods. The Court of Appeal considered that the difference in the duties was significant and meant that the women could not be said to be doing work that was broadly similar to the work of the men.

However, the court or tribunal must consider what actually happens in practice before deciding that there are different duties which might justify a difference in pay as can be seen in the following two cases.

CASE EXAMPLE

Electrolux Ltd v Hutchinson [1977] ICR 252

Male and female workers were on different rates of pay despite doing broadly similar work. The employer tried to justify the pay differential on the basis that the men had additional contractual obligations to work compulsory overtime when required, and to work evening and weekend shifts when required. The EAT accepted that the reality of the situation was that the men were rarely if ever called on to perform the additional duties and that this could be dealt with by additional payments when they did. An award of equal pay was made.

CASE EXAMPLE

Shields v E Coomes Holdings Ltd [1978] IRLR 263

A female counter clerk in a betting shop was paid only 62p per hour while her male comparator was paid a rate of £1.06 per hour. The employer tried to justify this on the basis that the man had additional duties of dealing with unruly customers and also had to transport cash between shops. The Court of Appeal accepted that there was no history of unruly customers in the betting shop and that taking money to other shops had no practical significance at the time. There was no justification for the unequal pay rates.

Different responsibilities

Where a male employee has different, meaning greater, responsibilities than a female employee then a difference in pay might be justified.

CASE EXAMPLE

Eaton Ltd v Nuttall [1977] IRLR 71

Male and female employees performed broadly similar work as production schedulers responsible for ordering materials for the production process. However, while the woman only dealt with goods that were £2.50 and less in value, the man dealt with goods that were between £5 and £1,000. The man was on a higher rate of pay and the woman claimed equal pay. The EAT accepted the employer's argument that the man had greater responsibility and if he were to make a mistake it would create a greater loss for the company. It was therefore appropriate to take into account the greater responsibility.

Clearly to justify a difference in pay any alleged responsibility must be regular one not just an occasional one.

CASE EXAMPLE

Redland Roof Tiles v Harper [1977] ICR 349

The male and female employees performed like work. However, the male employee deputised for the transport manager for five weeks each year as a result of which he received a higher rate of pay. The additional responsibility could have been dealt with by additional pay during the weeks in which he had the additional responsibility. It could not justify a continuous difference in pay.

10.2.4 Work rated equivalent

An action for work rated equivalent was originally under section 1(5) Equal Pay Act 1970. This was where an employer had voluntarily engaged in a job evaluation study which had identified that the jobs of male and female comparators would be of equal value and the pay should therefore be equal and would be if it were not based on a sex-specific system of values. The action is now under Section 65(4) Equality Act 2010.

SECTION

'65(4) A's work is rated as equivalent to B's work if a job evaluation study –
(a) gives an equal value to A's job and B's job in terms of the demands made on a worker, or
(b) would give an equal value to A's job and B's job in those terms were the evaluation not made on a sex-specific system.'

Job evaluation studies rate jobs according to the demands made upon the individual employee in various set factors including skill, effort, responsibility, decision making. Job evaluation studies are gender neutral where a sex specific system sets different values for men and women.

Where a genuine scheme has occurred then its findings should be implemented.

CASE EXAMPLE

Arnold v Beecham Group Ltd [1982] IRLR 307

A job classification study was carried out in 1978 in which a female catering supervisor was rated a grade lower than a male vending supervisor. Because of government pay restraint policy an agreement was not reached on how salaries should be attached to the different grades. A later weighted points system carried out in 1980 found that the female catering supervisor and the male vending supervisor should be classified on the same grade and therefore should receive equal pay. The management then failed to implement the findings of the study following objections from some male staff. Instead it based its wage settlement on the 1978 study and the female catering supervisor brought an equal pay claim. She initially failed in the tribunal on the basis that the conclusions of the 1980 study had not been completely acceptable to the management, the unions and the employees so comparisons made under it were not feasible. The EAT reversed this on the basis that at a meeting in May management and employees had agreed to the validity of the study.

Different types of study have been developed as was pointed out by the EAT in *Eaton Ltd v Nuttall* [1977] IRLR 71 such as job ranking, paired comparisons, job classification, points assessment and factor comparison.

JUDGMENT

In *Eaton v Nuttall* it was said that a genuine study should be: 'thorough in its analysis and capable of impartial application'.

Any genuine study then must be objectively applied and analytical with the separate factors in each job compared, so 'whole job' comparisons are not really adequate for this purpose.

CASE EXAMPLE

Bromley v H & J Quick Ltd [1988] IRLR 249

The employer carried out a job evaluation study using the paired comparison system. This is a very cheap and simple method where each job is measured as a whole according to whether its overall importance is judged to be equal or unequal and points are then awarded and a rank order of different jobs is produced. Female claimants argued that the study was invalid and that their work was in fact of equal value to the men's. The Court of Appeal agreed that the study was not objective and was therefore invalid.

JUDGMENT

Dillon LJ explained: 'it is clear from the decision of the European Court of Justice *Rummler v Dato-Druck GmbH* [1987] that the consideration of any job, and of the qualities required to perform that job, under a job evaluation study must be objective ... it is necessary, in my judgment, that both the work of the woman ... and the work of the man who is her chosen comparator should have been valued in such terms of demand made on the worker under various headings ... the method used ... must necessarily be analytical ... the process of dividing a physical or abstract whole into its constituent parts to determine their relationship or value ... the jobs of each worker must have been valued in terms of the demand made on the worker under various headings'.

10.2.5 Work of equal value

The definition of a claim for equal pay for work of equal value is now contained in section 65(6) Equality Act 2010.

SECTION

'65 (6) A's work is of equal value to B's work if it is –
(a) neither like B's work nor rated as equivalent to B's work, but
(b) nevertheless equal to B's work in terms of the demands made on A by reference to factors such as effort, skill and decision-making.'

A claim for equal pay for work of equal value was actually inserted into the Equal Pay Act as section 2A(1)(a) by Regulation 2 of the Equal Pay (Amendment) Regulations 1983. This extra head of claim was added because it was lacking in the original Equal Pay Act and the UK then failed to fully implement the requirements of Article 119 EC treaty (now Article 157 TFEU) as expanded in the then Equal Pay Directive 75/117 (now part of the Recast Directive 2006/54). This subsequently led to infringement proceedings in the European Court of Justice in *Commission v UK 61/81*. In the case the argument made by the UK that the concept of 'equal value' was too abstract to stand application was rejected by the court.

An action for equal pay for work of equal value, as section 65(6) Equality Act 2010 identifies, may be brought when there is no male comparator doing like work or there is no work rated as equivalent in a genuine job evaluation study.

The process is now governed by section 131 Equality Act 2010 and regulations contained in Schedule 6 of the Employment Tribunals (Constitution and Rules of Procedure) (Amendment) Regulations 2004 which also set maximum timescales of twenty-five weeks if no independent expert is used and thirty-seven weeks if independent experts are used. The previous procedure was long-winded and full of potential delays with the average time taken to complete claims being two-and-a-half years, a real disincentive to claiming.

Claims can obviously be quite complex and take time to resolve because a number of comparators may be used.

CASE EXAMPLE

Hayward v Cammell Laird Shipbuilders Ltd (No 2) [1988] ICR 464

Julie Hayward was a cook working for Cammell Laird Shipbuilders was paid a lower rate of pay than many skilled male workers in the factory. However, she did enjoy certain benefits that they did not which included better sickness pay, paid meal breaks and better holidays. An independent job evaluation survey had concluded that her work was of equal value to her male comparators. As a result she claimed equal pay with three named male comparators, a painter, a thermal engineer and a joiner. Her claim for equal pay for work of equal value was in fact the first ever to be heard in the UK. The tribunal rejected her claim explaining that, taken as a whole, her conditions were not less favourable than her male comparators. As such it held that pay was not the only consideration but that other terms and conditions in the contract must be taken into account in determining the outcome. The House of Lords (now the Supreme Court), however, rejected this approach and held that each and every term of the contract should be compared and be equal, not that the terms should not be overall less favourable. On this basis if there is a difference in pay it should be adjusted which would otherwise be to deny the woman of her rights under EU law in Article 157 (at the time Article 119 EC Treaty).

JUDGMENT

Lord Goff commented: 'this may, in some cases, lead to what has been called mutual enhancement or leap-frogging, as terms of the woman's contract and the man's contract are both ... upgraded to bring them into line with each other ... if the construction ... does not accord with the true intention of Parliament, then the appropriate course ... is to amend the legislation to bring it into line with its true intention. In the meantime, however, the decision ... may have the salutary effect of drawing to the attention of employers and trade unions the absolute need for ensuring that the pay structures for the different groups of employees do not contain any element of sex discrimination.'

It is possible for a woman to pursue a claim for equal pay for work of equal value despite there being other men on the same wage provided that there is a male comparator on a higher wage.

CASE EXAMPLE

Pickstone v Freemans plc [1989] AC 66

The claimant worked as an operative in the defendant catalogue company. She claimed that her work was of equal value to a male 'checker warehouse operative' who was on a significantly higher rate of pay. One obstacle that she faced was that there were male operatives on the same rate of pay as her and the employer argued that as a result there was no discrimination. The House of Lords (now the Supreme Court) upheld her claim on the basis that the fact that there was a man on the same rate of pay as the woman was irrelevant if there was a genuine need for equal pay with another male comparator. The House acknowledged that the alternative would be that unscrupulous employers would always be able to avoid equality by placing a token male on the same low pay as a woman.

JUDGMENT

Lord Keith said that reaching a different interpretation would: 'leave a large gap in the equal work provision, enabling an employer to evade it by employing one token man on the same work as a group of potential women claimants who were deliberately paid less than a group of men employed on work of equal value with that of the women. This would mean that the United Kingdom had failed yet again fully to implement its obligations under Article 119 of the Treaty [now Article 157 TFEU] and the equal pay directive, and had not given full effect to the decision of the European Court of Justice in Commission of the European Communities v United Kingdom Of Great Britain and Northern Ireland (1982).'

ACTIVITY

Quick quiz

Explain the type of equal pay claim which is appropriate in each of the following:

1. Alison, a female, works for the *Middlington Weekly Journal* as the fashion feature editor. Alison's annual salary is £35,000 and Alison believes that she should be on the same annual salary as the politics editor, the international news editor and the sports editor. All of these are male employees and receive annual salaries of £45,000.
2. Brenda works in a call centre for an energy company. Brenda works part-time, sixteen hours per week and is paid an hourly rate of £8.50 as are all part-time staff in the same role. Full-time staff are paid a monthly salary which is equivalent to a rate of £10 per hour and also receive an annual bonus. While the full-time staff are mostly men all of the part-time staff are women.
3. Caitlin works as a waitress for a hotel which holds regular functions such as weddings and conferences. The hotel chain recently carried out a job evaluation study which identified that Caitlin should be on the same pay grade as male employees who are paid considerably more than Caitlin.

10.2.6 Justifications for unequal pay

Traditionally an employer had a defence to an equal pay claim where he could show that the difference in pay was due to a genuine material factor where the difference in pay was not based on the person's sex. This defence is now contained in section 69 Equality Act 2010.

SECTION

'69 Defence of material factor.

(1) The sex equality clause in A's terms has no effect in relation to a difference between A's terms and B's terms if the responsible person shows that the difference is because of a material factor reliance on which –

   (a) does not involve treating A less favourably because of A's sex than the responsible person treats B, and

   (b) if the factor is within subsection (2), is a proportionate means of achieving a legitimate aim.'

There have been a variety of contexts in which employers have argued that a genuine material factor justifies differences in pay.

Geographical location

Geographical location may be a justification for differences in pay. This operates where national employers have employees at different locations around the country and living costs can vary. A classic example was the challenge to what is known as London weighting in *NAAFI v Varley* [1976] The Times 25 October. Men and women might be doing the same work but in different parts of the country where living costs are much higher and therefore employers have to offer better rates of pay to attract staff.

Different responsibilities

We have seen in 10.2.3 above that different duties and responsibilities may mean that the work is not in fact taken as being broadly similar.

CASE EXAMPLE

Capper Pass v Allan [1980] IRLR 236

A female employee was not given productivity bonus. She claimed equal pay with a male comparator who did but failed. The man had to work shifts on unsocial hours which she did not. He took care of money and he was also responsible for stock control. Even though their jobs were similar, the man had additional responsibilities justifying the additional pay.

Different productivity

This has particularly risen in relation to different treatment of part-time employees by contrast to their full-time counterparts and has been considered also by the ECJ.

CASE EXAMPLE

Jenkins v Kingsgate Clothing Productions Ltd [1981] IRLR 388; ECR 911

An employer in the clothing industry paid different and lower hourly rates of pay to part-time employees than to full-time employees. The employer argued that this was necessary on the basis that machines were unused for part of the week as a result of hiring part-time staff and that therefore the effective productivity was greater in the case of full-timers. The difference in pay was to encourage more full-time employees and increase net production. A reference under Article 177 (now Article 267 TFEU) was made by the EAT to the ECJ. The latter accepted that the reason could justify different pay rates if it was not merely discriminatory.

Economic necessity (market forces)

The need to attract staff with particular skills or where skills are scarce can also be a factor that has been accepted as justifying paying higher rates than might be the case with the existing workforce.

CASE EXAMPLE

Rainey v Greater Glasgow Health Board (Eastern District) [1987] AC 224

The case concerned prosthetics technicians working for the Health Board (prosthetics are essentially artificial body parts such as limbs). The Board needed to employ more prosthetists but when there was a shortage of skilled staff in the area it in fact had to then appoint applicants from private practice who were on much higher rates of pay than the standard NHS rates that existing staff received. One existing female employee claimed equal pay with one of the new male recruits. The House of Lords accepted that the difference in pay was due to a genuine material factor that was unrelated to sex.

JUDGMENT

Lawton LJ commented: 'where there is no question of intentional sex discrimination whether direct or indirect (and there is none here) a difference which is connected with economic factors affecting the efficient carrying on of the employer's business or other activity may well be relevant'.

However, there are limits to how far an argument of market forces will be accepted when the reality is that the pay differential is in fact discriminatory.

CASE EXAMPLE

Ratcliffe v North Yorkshire County Council [1995] IRLR 439

The Council had developed a direct services organisation after the introduction of compulsory tendering for provision of school meals. The work of its dinner ladies had been rated as equivalent with other male council employees including those involved in refuse collection. When the direct service organisation then could not make a competitive bid in a compulsory tender without reducing the women's pay it made pay cuts. It argued that the cuts were for economic reasons and were therefore covered by a genuine material factor defence. This was accepted by the Court of Appeal. However, the then House of Lords held that the difference of pay was in fact a difference based on the sex of the claimants and was therefore not covered by the defence. The defence was effectively tainted by sex discrimination because the catering industry had a history of low pay and traditionally had been predominantly staffed by women.

JUDGMENT

Lord Slynn identified the pay cut as: 'the very kind of discrimination in relation to pay that the Act sought to remove'.

Inconvenience

It may also be possible to argue that the difference in pay is justified because the nature of the man's role involves unsocial elements and inconvenience not present in the woman's.

CASE EXAMPLE

Calder v Rowntree Mackintosh Confectionary [1993] IRLR 212

Here male and female employees were on the same basic wage but the male staff got a shift allowance which the women did not. The women's argument for equal pay was partly based on the fact that they worked some unsocial hours as the men did. The Court of Appeal, however, accepted that there was a defence since the men worked a rotating shift system while the women did not. Part of the shift allowance was paid for unsocial working hours but much of it related to the rotating shift pattern.

The decision is possibly at odds with the principle that a woman employed in a female dominated occupation can still bring a claim using a comparator from a male dominated occupation.

CASE EXAMPLE

Enderby v Frenchay Health Authority [1994] ICR 112

Speech therapists employed by a health authority made a claim for equal pay for work of equal value using male pharmacists and male clinical psychologists as comparators. Both of these occupations were predominantly male while speech therapy was predominantly female. The difference in pay resulted from separate pay negotiating machinery. The employers justified the difference on a market forces argument, that they needed the higher pay to attract and keep highly skilled employees. On a reference to the ECJ the court identified that a woman in a female dominated occupation is entitled to compare herself with a male from a male dominated occupation where there was evidence to show statistical differences in pay. It would then be for the employer to show that there was an objective justification for the difference (see 10.3.3 below).

Red circling

This involves salaries that are protected for some reason. This will usually occur where an employee has had to accept redeployment into a lower paid job or because the employee is unable to continue in the same role, for instance because of health issues. The employer wishes to retain the employee and keeps him on the same pay even though he is working in a role on a lesser pay grade.

It may be possible to justify this and use it as a defence if the decision to 'red circle' the previous wage was not made on a discriminatory basis.

CASE EXAMPLE

Methven v Cow Industrial Polymers Ltd [1980] IRLR 289

A male employee was temporarily doing the same clerical work as the female claimant but retained the salary from his previous high profile role which was much greater than the woman's. The man was in fact being temporarily rested following a period of illness on a gradual return to duties so there could be a defence.

However, 'red circling' is not a guarantee of a defence of genuine material factor and an employer should not think that there is an automatic right to carry on such a practice since it is also potentially offensive to the remainder of the workforce. A temporary situation is more likely to succeed than a permanent situation. In any case the significant question is why the pay has been 'red circled' and whether or not this is discriminatory. If it is then the defence is not available.

CASE EXAMPLE

Snoxell v Vauxhall Motors Ltd [1977] ICR 700

The employer had traditionally had different pay grades for men and women. It then introduced a new structure with equal pay. However, it had not properly regraded one formerly male-grade position and when this was realised the post was moved on to the appropriate scale but the pay of the men doing the work was then 'red circled'. The employer argued that this was a genuine material factor, to preserve the pay of the men. The EAT disagreed. The reason for the 'red circling' was the original discrimination.

Incremental pay grading

Many forms of employment use incremental pay scales. Employees get an incremental increase in salary for each year of service until they reach the top of the pay scale. This may justify differences in pay since it is recognition of the extra experience that the employee has and therefore could be linked to productivity or capability.

However, the practice could also be discriminatory to women in the sense that since because of maternity and the child care responsibilities it is possible at any given time that there are a greater number of male employees with advanced service. The ECJ has considered this in detail and determined that while the practice may be justified it must be objectively justified.

CASE EXAMPLE

Cadman v Health and Safety Executive [2006] ICR 1623

A female head of a unit employed by the Health and Safety Executive (HSE) had an annual salary of £35,000 while four male employees in the same pay band, earned between £39,000 and £44,000 because of their position on the incremental pay scale which the HSE argued justified the difference. On a reference to the ECJ the court held that different lengths of service could justify different pay rates for otherwise similar jobs, although this was not conclusive. It would not be so 'where the worker provides evidence capable of giving rise to serious doubts as to whether ... the criterion of length of service is, in the circumstances, appropriate'. The case clearly shows that, while incremental pay scales may be justified where length of experience indicates greater capability that too many increments may be both unjustified and potentially discriminatory.

ACTIVITY

Quick quiz

Consider whether the employer will have a defence of genuine material factor available in each of the following situations:

1. Christine, a female, and David, a male, are lecturers in a privately run college and are subject to an incremental pay scale. Christine is at point 4 on the incremental pay scale while David is at the top of the scale at point 20. As a result, even though they teach the same subject and have the same qualifications, David's pay is £17,600 per annum more than Christine's.

2. Elaine, a female, and Frank, a male, are both shop assistants in an off-licensed liquor store. While they work the same number of hours, Frank works on evenings and weekends while Elaine does not. Elaine receives £8 per hour while Frank receives £12 per hour.

3. Six years ago George, a male sales manager, was given clerical duties in the customer accounts department following a long term sickness absence with stress and depression. Clerical workers in the department who are all female receive pay of £16,000 per annum. George has kept his former salary of £72,000.

10.2.7 Making equal pay claims

A claim for equal pay must be brought to the tribunal during the course of employment or within six months of leaving. Application is made on the same forms as for other claims. There is no right to extend this limit. However, the period may be extended if it is shown that the employer deliberately concealed information and that without this the employee could not have reasonably been expected to bring the claim in time.

The procedure for making a claim for equal pay for work of equal value is now governed by section 131 Equality Act 2010 and regulations contained in Schedule 6 of the Employment Tribunals (Constitution and Rules of Procedure) (Amendment) Regulations 2004 which set maximum timescales of twenty-five weeks if no independent expert is used and thirty-seven weeks if independent experts are used.

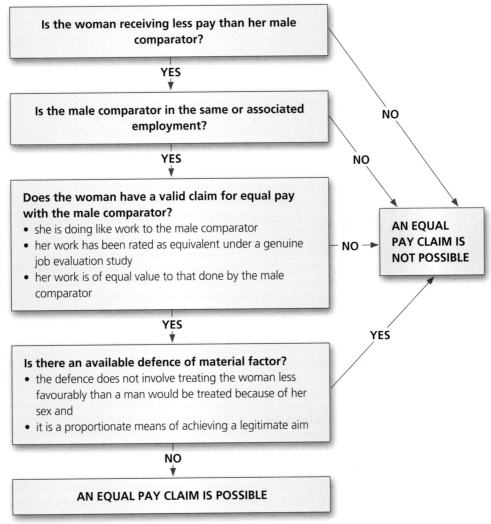

Figure 10.1 Diagram illustrating the elements of an equal pay claim under the Equality Act 2010

The procedure has two stages. Stage 1 will apply to all claims and the tribunal determines whether the claim should proceed and also whether to hear it itself or whether to appoint independent experts from ACAS. In Stage 2 any disputed facts are resolved and experts, if used will prepare a report. After this there is a full hearing at which the issue whether to award equal pay is decided.

10.2.8 Remedies

There are essentially two aspects to any award for equal pay:

- first if the claim has succeeded then the tribunal will issue a declaration to that effect and stating that the employee is entitled to equal pay and ordering the employer to increase the pay;
- second the tribunal will make an order for arrears of pay. This could include any other benefits or bonuses or other perks.

Thus the contractual obligations of the employer and rights of the employee are in effect changed.

The arrears can be backdated for a period of up to six years from the date when the claim was brought. This follows the change made by the Equal Pay Act (Amendment) Regulations 2003 to the old maximum of two years. This change arose because of the finding in the ECJ in *Preston and Others v Wolverhampton Healthcare NHS Trust* (C-78/98) [2000] ECR I-3201 that the then restriction was in breach of EU law.

ACTIVITY

Self-assessment questions

1. What mechanism does the Equality Act 2010 use in seeking to achieve equal pay?
2. How does this mechanism operate?
3. What is the 'same or associated employment'?
4. What problems might a woman have traditionally encountered in selecting a male comparator?
5. How did the courts overcome these problems?
6. What is the effect of putting a token male into a particular job in order to defeat equal pay?
7. What are the three major heads of claim in equal pay?
8. In what circumstances will an employer be able to avoid a claim for equal pay?
9. What different types of material factor have been accepted by the courts?
10. What remedies are possible in an equal pay claim?
11. What defect was present in the Equal Pay Act 1970 in comparison to EU (at that time EC) law?

10.3 Article 157 TFEU

10.3.1 The basic protection

Originally Article 119 of the EC Treaty identified that men and women should receive equal pay for equal work. Following renumbering under the Amsterdam Treaty this became Article 141 EC Treaty. Following the replacement of the EC Treaty with the Treaty on the Functioning of the European Union (TFEU) the principle is now contained in Article 157 TFEU.

ARTICLE

'Art 157

(1) Each Member State shall ensure that the principle of equal pay for male and female workers for equal work or work of equal value is applied.'

The principle is a simply stated one and was originally under Article 119 EC Treaty mainly a part of the economic agenda of securing a single market (at that time referred to as the common market). It was established at a relatively early stage that the Article was directly effective (see Chapter 2.2.3) and therefore is enforceable by a citizen of the EU in a national court of a Member State.

CASE EXAMPLE

Defrenne v SABENA (43/75) [1976] 2 CMLR 98

A woman employed as an air stewardess by the Belgian national airline was paid at a significantly lower rate than was the case for male cabin crew doing the same work. At the time she was prevented from claiming equal pay under Belgian law as there was no legislation on equal pay. She then attempted to bring her action in the Belgian court under Article 157 TFEU (at that time Article 119 EC Treaty). The Belgian authorities, mirroring the argument made several years earlier in *Van Gend en Loos v Nederlandse Administratie der Belastingen* 26/62, argued that the Article only affected the state and gave no rights to individuals. The Court of Justice held that, since the Article complied with all of the *Van Gend en Loos* criteria for direct effect, in the absence of any appropriate national law she was able to bring her action under the Article as the basis for claiming equal pay. The court also identified that the Article was both vertically and horizontally directly effective and so could be used both against private individuals and the state.

JUDGMENT

The Court stated that the prohibition on discrimination in pay: 'applies not only to the actions of public authorities but also extends to all agreements which are intended to regulate paid labour collectively, as well as to contracts between individuals'.

One sad aside to the case followed representations made to the court by both the UK and Ireland who feared the effect the ruling could have. Following these representations the Article was held to be only prospectively, rather than retrospectively, directly effective as should have been the case. As a result many women in those Member States lost out on potential and justifiable claims which they otherwise might have made.

One important limitation on the scope of Article 157 was also identified by the ECJ in the case, that Article 157 can only be used in respect of 'equal work which is carried out in the same establishment or service'. In consequence a woman cannot claim equal pay with a man employed by a different employer even if they are doing exactly the same work. This was later confirmed and explained by the court.

CASE EXAMPLE

Lawrence v Regent Office Care Ltd, Commercial Catering Group and Mitie Secure Services Ltd (Case C–320/00) [2002] ECR I–7325

A group of female employees had worked for the Council until 1993, preparing school meals and cleaning schools. In 1993 the Council then tendered out the work to private companies which were then the new employers of the females. The females then brought a claim for equal pay for work of equal value using as their comparators male employees who had been retained by the Council and who were on higher rates of pay than themselves. The ECJ held that Article 157 TFEU (at that time Article 141 EC Treaty) could not apply as the women were no longer the employees of the same or an associated employer.

JUDGMENT

The Court stated: 'Where the differences identified in the pay conditions of workers performing equal work or work of equal value cannot be attributed to a single source, there is no body which is responsible for the inequality and which could restore equal treatment. Such a situation does not come within the scope of [Article 157]. The work and the pay of those workers cannot therefore be compared on the basis of that provision.'

The same principle was also later applied in a situation involving a comparison between permanent employees and agency workers.

CASE EXAMPLE

Allonby v Accrington & Rossendale College [2004] IRLR 224

A college dismissed all of its part-time lecturers, two-thirds of whom were women. The college then rehired them through an agency. The women were paid less and lost pension rights and other benefits. One of the women brought an action under Article 157 TFEU (at that time Article 141 EC Treaty) using as comparators a group of full-time lecturers, most of whom were male, who were employed by the college itself. Despite the fact that the permanent employees and agency staff worked in the same college doing the same work, following the dismissals they had different employers and in consequence an action using the Article could not succeed.

10.3.2 The definition of pay

The EC Treaty also defined pay quite broadly. The definition is now in Article 157(2) TFEU.

ARTICLE

'Art 157
(2) For the purpose of this Article, "pay" means the ordinary basic or minimum wage or salary and any other consideration, whether in cash or in kind, which the worker receives, directly or indirectly, in respect of his employment from his employer. Equal pay without discrimination based on sex means:
  (a) that pay for the same work at piece rates shall be calculated on the basis of the same unit of measurement;
  (b) that pay for work at time rates shall be the same for the same job.'

The definition of pay in the Article is not limited to 'wages' or 'salary'. It can include any form of remuneration which does not have to be in the form of money. The definition has also been very broadly construed by the ECJ in case law. Examples of what has been accepted as pay for the purposes of Article 157 have included the following:

- perks e.g. concessionary rail fares for retired railway workers, *Garland v BREL* 12/81 – the ECJ held that it was irrelevant that the benefits were not laid down in the employment contract;

- supplementary payments into an occupational pension scheme, *Worringham & Humphries v Lloyds Bank Ltd* 69/80;

- sick pay, *Rinner-Kuhn v FWW Spezial Gebaudereinigung GmbH & Co. KG* 171/88;

- paid leave for training, *Arbeiterwohlifahrt der Stadt Berlin v Botel* – the ECJ stated that remuneration could amount to 'pay' 'irrespective of whether the worker receives it under a contract of employment, by virtue of legislative provisions or on a voluntary basis';

- contractual non-contributory occupational pension schemes, supplementing state schemes, denied to part-timers, *Bilka-Kaufhaus v Weber von Hartz* 170/84;

- unequal retirement ages, *Marshall v Southampton & South West Hampshire AHA (Teaching) (No 1)* 152/84;

- redundancy payments, *R v Secretary of State for Employment ex parte Equal Opportunities Commission* [1995] 1 AC 1 (HL);

- 'contracted out' pension schemes which depend for operation on different retirement ages, *Barber v Guardian Royal Exchange Assurance Group* 262/88 – the case is also important in identifying that Art 157 is infringed if pension rights are deferred in a person made compulsorily redundant to retirement age (if different to person of opposite sex) – so applies *Marshall* logic to contracted out schemes – but had prospective direct effect like *Defrenne*;

- in Royal Copenhagen case (C–400/93) [1995] ECR I–1275, the ECJ was asked whether pay on a 'piece-work' basis – where the level of pay is wholly or partially dependent on the individual employee's output – was covered by Article 157 and the court held that it was;

- severance payments, *Kowalska* [1990] ECR I–2591 – these payments are designed to help employees who became unemployed involuntarily, for example, following retirement or disability, to adjust to their new situation;

- compensation for unfair dismissal, *Seymour-Smith & Perez* [1999] ECR I–623 – the ECJ described it as 'a form of deferred pay to which the worker is entitled by reason of his employment but which is paid to him on termination of the employment relationship with a view to enabling him to adjust to the new circumstances arising from such termination';

- bonuses, *Krüger* (Case C–281/97) [1999] ECR I–5127, involved annual Christmas bonus;

- a monthly salary supplement, awarded by an employer on an ad hoc basis to reflect the quality of individual's work, *Brunnhofer* (Case C–381/99) [2001] ECR I–4961;

- maternity pay, *Gillespie v Northern Health and Social Services Board* (Case C–342/93) [1996] ECR I–475;

- occupational pensions – this area has possibly provided some of the more contentious application of the definition in Article 157(2).

CASE EXAMPLE

Bilka Kaufhaus GmbH v Weber von Hartz (Case 170/84) [1986] ECR 1607; [1987] ICR 110

Harz, a female employee, had been employed by Bilka Kaufhaus, a large department store, for ten years full-time after which she reduced to part-time. A total of 27.7 per cent of women were on part-time contracts while only 10 per cent of male employees worked part-time. Harz complained that the occupational pension scheme was only available to employees who had worked full-time for fifteen of the last twenty years as a result of which she was excluded from the scheme. The store argued that, while this was discriminatory, it nevertheless represented a genuine need of the business since part-timers were less likely to work late afternoons and Saturdays. The ECJ held that the rule could amount to indirect discrimination. Although the court accepted that the provision was gender neutral it nevertheless thought that it could adversely affect women because of the greater percentage of part-time employees who were female. In the context of Article 157(2) (at the time Article 119 EC Treaty) it also identified that the right to enter an occupational pension scheme could be classed as pay.

The occupational pension scheme in the *Bilka Kaufhaus* case was one that supplemented the state pension scheme. In a later judgment the ECJ identified that the definition under Article 157(2) also covered so-called 'contracted out' schemes, ones designed in effect to replace the state scheme.

CASE EXAMPLE

Barber v Guardian Royal Exchange (Case 262/88) [1990] ECR-1 8889; [1990] ICR 616

Barber had been made redundant at age fifty-two. His employer paid him the statutory redundancy payment but would not pay him an early retirement pension available under the firm's contracted out scheme since under its rules this was only available to men over the age of fifty-five when made redundant. However, those covered by the scheme could take an early pension at age fifty. Barber argued that this was in breach of Article 157 (at that time Article 119 EC Treaty). The ECJ held that money paid out under such schemes was pay for the purposes of the Article and so there was an unjustified breach. The ECJ also held that the nature of the scheme was irrelevant. Occupational pension schemes would come within the scope of the Article whether they were employer schemes which supplemented the State's retirement scheme (as in *Bilka-Kaufhaus*) or the so-called 'contracted out' schemes as was the case here.

JUDGMENT

The Court stated: 'Although it is true that many advantages granted by an employer also reflect considerations of social policy, the fact that a benefit is in the nature of pay cannot be called into question where the worker is entitled to receive the benefit in question from the employer by reason of the existence of the employment relationship.'

The ruling proved quite controversial and, because of the potential effects on contracted out schemes the court decided to apply the ruling prospectively and not retrospectively. The case also led to several preliminary rulings, mainly from the UK and the Netherlands.

10.3.3 Indirect discrimination and objective justification

Pay was originally covered by the Equal Pay Directive 75/117. This is now in the Recast Directive 2006/54.

The Court of Justice has identified in *Macarthys Ltd v Smith* (Case 129/79) [1980] ECR 1275,that 'equal work' does not necessarily have to mean identical work but work with a high degree of similarity.

In the case of work of equal value this is a question of fact for the national court to determine whether work is of equal value. Although determining exactly how different jobs should be assessed has been problematic. Article 4 of Directive 2006/54 (the recast Directive) gives some guidance. It states that 'where a job classification system is used for determining pay, it must be based on the same criteria for both men and women and so drawn up as to exclude any discrimination on grounds of sex'.

CASE EXAMPLE

Rummler v Dato-Druck GmbH [1987] ICR 774

A female packer who was graded under her employer's job evaluation scheme below the level that she thought her work merited challenged the criteria used. These included muscular effort, physical hardship and fatigue. The ECJ held that the criteria used in job evaluation schemes must not differ according to whether the job is carried out by a man or by a woman. It also stated that it must not be organised in such a manner that it has the practical effect of discriminating against one sex. The criteria must be objectively justified and to be so they must be appropriate to the tasks to be undertaken and also correspond to a genuine need of the business. However, it also stressed that it would be possible to have criteria which included factors which favoured one sex over another provided that these criteria were part of an overall package which included factors that did not. In the scheme in question other criteria which were non-discriminatory included knowledge, training and responsibility. Logically, however, physical strength would appear to be a criterion that naturally discriminates against women and in favour of men.

JUDGMENT

The ECJ held that such a system: 'must be based on criteria which do not differ according to whether the work is carried out by a man or by a woman and must not be organised, as a whole, in such a manner that it has the practical effect of discriminating against workers of one sex'.

The ECJ has also developed the test for how to measure what is objective justification for differences in pay. In *Bilka Kaufhaus GmbH v Weber von Hartz* [1987] ICR 110 the ECJ held that national courts should decide whether there is a real need to apply different rules for part-timers, but that there must be objective justification. It identified the criteria for establishing objective justification:

- the measure must correspond to a genuine need of the business;
- it must be suitable for obtaining the objective;
- it must be necessary for that purpose.

It is also important to note that the court will not accept that the mere fact that a system for job classification for determining salary scales is apparently neutral guarantees that it is not discriminatory.

Handels-og Kontorfunktionaernes Forbund i Danmark v DanskArbejdsgiver-forening (acting for Danfoss) [1991] ICR 74

A Danish trade union challenged pay rate criteria set by the Danish Employers Association and how they had been applied by an employer, Danfoss. The criteria included flexibility and seniority. However, despite the minimum pay for each grade being the same for both men and women, the average pay for women within each grade was lower than for that of men. The ECJ held that, even though neutral criteria for setting appears on the surface to be neutral and therefore non-discriminatory, if the criteria can be shown to result in systematic discrimination this naturally implies that the employer applied the criteria in a discriminatory manner.

One significant failing in equal pay legislation is that, while it may lead to an aggrieved party gaining equal pay this does not necessarily mean that she gains the pay that she deserves in the light of the evidence.

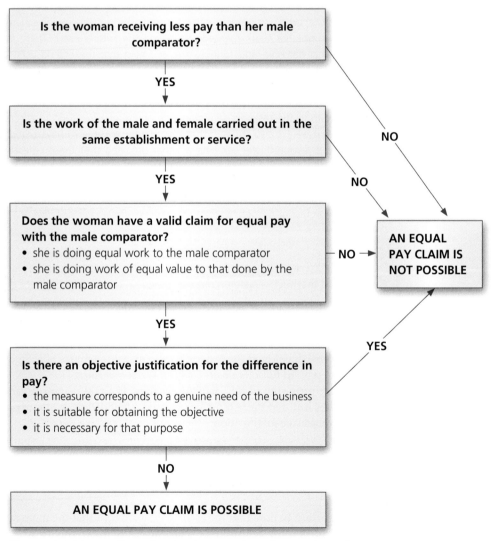

Figure 10.2 Diagram illustrating the elements of equal pay under EU law

CASE EXAMPLE

Murphy v Bord Telecom Eireann [1988] ECR 673; [1988] IRLR 267

A female factory worker and twenty-eight female colleagues discovered that they were paid significantly less than a male store labourer in the same factory. It was discovered during her claim for work of equal value that in fact the women's work was of greater value to the employer. As a result of this difference in value it was suggested that a claim for equal pay for work of equal value could not succeed. In a reference to the ECJ, the Court stated that although Article 157 (at the time Article 119 EC Treaty) concerned equal pay for equal work, and for work of equal value, but not to work of unequal value, it was bound to apply the principle here.

JUDGMENT

The Court said that to: 'adopt a contrary interpretation would be tantamount to rendering the principle of equal pay ineffective and nugatory … an employer would easily be able to circumvent the principle [of equal pay] by assigning additional or more onerous duties to workers of a particular sex, who could then be paid a lower wage'.

The anomaly here is that the women received equal pay with the men when they should in fact and in fairness have been receiving higher pay.

ACTIVITY

Self-assessment questions

1. What are the two types of equal pay identified in Article 157?
2. What unfairness resulted from the decision of the court in *Defrenne v SABENA*?
3. How has the ECJ defined who may be a comparator for the purpose of Article 157?
4. How is pay defined in Article 157(2)?
5. What sorts of benefits have been classed as pay by the ECJ?
6. In what ways is the EU definition of pay wider than a UK definition?
7. Why was *Barber v Guardian Royal Exchange* considered to be controversial?
8. What are the criteria for measuring objective justification for differences in pay?
9. How different are a 'genuine material factor' and an 'objective justification'?
10. What is one of the major defects of equal pay law that is shown up in *Murphy*?

KEY FACTS

The Equality Act 2010 – the equality clause	Case/statute
Under the equality clause (1) an equality clause is implied into every contract of employment (2) if a term of A's is less favourable to A than a corresponding term of B's is to B, A's term is modified so as not to be less favourable (b) if A does not have a term which corresponds to a term of B's that benefits B, A's terms are modified so as to include such a term	*S66 Equality Act 2010*

The Equality Act 2010 – the comparator	Case/statute
Can only be person of the opposite sex in the same or associated employment	*Leverton v Clwyd CC*
• but can be the woman's predecessor	*Macarthys Ltd v Smith*

The Equality Act 2010 – the three types of claim	Case/statute
Like work	*S65(2) Equality Act 2010*
• work must be broadly similar	*Capper Pass Ltd v Lawton*
• and no significant differences	*Electrolux Ltd v Hutchinson*
Work rated equivalent under a job evaluation study	*S65(4) Equality Act 2010*
• follows objective job evaluation study	*Bromley v H & J Quick*
• result of study must be implemented	*Arnold v Beecham Group Ltd*
Work of equal value	*S65(6) Equality Act 2010*
• originally inserted in Equal Pay Act by Equal Pay (Amendment) Regulations 1983 after infringement proceedings against UK for failure to implement then Directive 75/117	*Commission v UK 61/81*
• decided by tribunal or independent experts from ACAS	*Hayward v Cammell Laird Shipbuilders*

Equality Act 2010 – material factor defence	Case/statute
Difference may be justified by a 'genuine material factor'	*S69 Equality Act 2010*
• location	*NAAFI v Varley*
• different responsibilities	*Capper Pass v Allan*
• inconvenience	*Calder v Rowntree Mackintosh*
• different productivity	*Jenkins v Kingsgate Clothing*
• economic necessity	*Rainey v Greater Glasgow HB*
• red circling	*Methven v Cow Industries*
But not	
• reducing wage to create competitive rates	*Ratcliffe v North Yorkshire CC*
• woman accepts less	

Bringing claims and remedies	Case/statute
Claims must be brought during employment or within six months of leaving	
The period can only be extended if it is shown that the employer deliberately concealed information and that without this the employee could not have reasonably been expected to bring the claim in time	
There are 2 stages for equal value claims	*131 Equality Act 2010*
• stage 1 decides whether claim should be heard – stage 2 disputed facts are resolved and experts may produce a report	*Schedule 6 of the Employment Tribunals (Constitution and Rules of Procedure) (Amendment) Regulations 2004*
• then a full hearing	
• remedies include a declaration and order for arrears of pay	
• can have back pay of up to six years	Equal Pay Act (Amendment) Regulations 2003 *Preston and Others v Wolverhampton Healthcare NHS Trust*

EU law – Article 157	Case/statute
Basic principle is that men and women should receive equal pay for equal work • is directly effective both vertically and horizontally	*Article 157(1)* *Defrenne v SABENA*

EU law – the meaning of pay	Case/statute
Defined as 'the ordinary basic or minimum wage or salary or any other consideration, whether in cash or in kind, which the worker receives directly or indirectly, in respect of his employment from his employer' So has included • perks e.g. concessionary rail fares for retired railway workers • supplementary payments into an occupational pension scheme • sick pay • paid leave for training • contractual non-contributory occupational pension schemes, supplementing state schemes, denied to part-timers • unequal retirement ages • redundancy payments (HL) • 'contracted out' pension schemes which depend for operation on different retirement ages	*Article 157(2)* *Garland v BREL 12/81* *Worringham & Humphries v Lloyds Bank Ltd 69/80* *Rinner-Kuhn v FWW Spezial Gebaudereinigung GmbH & Co. KG 171/88* *Arbeiterwohlifahrt der Stadt Berlin v Botel* *Bilka-Kaufhaus v Weber von Hartz 170/84* *Marshall v Southampton & South West Hampshire AHA (Teaching) (No 1) 152/84* *R v Secretary of State for Employment ex parte Equal Opportunities Commission [1994]* *Barber v Guardian Royal Assurance Group 262/88*

EU law – objectively justifying inequality	Case/statute
It is possible to justifying discrimination in pay provided there is an 'objective justification' which it will be if it • corresponds to a genuine need of the enterprise • is suitable for obtaining the objective pursued by the enterprise • and it is necessary for that purpose	*Bilka-Kaufhaus v Weber von Hartz 170/84*

ESSAY Discuss the extent to which UK equal pay law has in the past been inconsistent with the EU law principles from which it derives and is obliged to follow.

Explain the basis of a claim originally under the Equal Pay Act 1970 and now under the Equality Act 2010

- Based on an equality clause – every term in a woman's contract should be no less favourable than each term in a man's.
- There must be a male comparator in the same or associated employment.
- There are three types of claim: like work; work rated equivalent under a job evaluation study; work of equal value.

Discuss the differences with equal pay under Article 157

- Men and women should receive equal pay for equal work – simpler proposition.
- There must be equal work done by men and women which is carried out in the same establishment or service – seems to be more straightforward than UK law and the issue has been the subject of references.
- A claim can be for equal work or work of equal value – the UK original got this wrong so that an action for work of equal value had to be included later by amendment following infringement proceedings.

Discuss the broader definition of pay under Article 157

- '… the ordinary basic or minimum wage or salary or any other consideration, whether in cash or in kind, which the worker receives directly or indirectly, in respect of his employment from his employer…'

- Consider what has been acknowledged as pay e.g. occupational pensions.
- Comment that this has caused references and controversy.

Discuss the types of claim

- ECJ has taken a broader view on the comparator – and allowed for a claim using a predecessor.
- UK law disallows a like work claim if there are different hours, different duties, different responsibilities – EU law.
- In UK law there was originally no equal value claim at all – and was introduced because of infringement proceedings.
- UK in effect has an additional type of claim.

Discuss the different defences under UK law and EU law

- UK has a defence of genuine material factor.
- Equal value claims the defence used to be genuine material difference.
- EU has a defence of objective justification.
- UK courts have accepted many factors including market forces.
- EU is likely to take a more restrictive view – but leaves it to the national court to decide.

Discuss the number of changes to UK principles resulting from references to ECJ

- Definition of pay.
- No need for contemporaneous comparator.
- Insertion of equal value claim.
- Definition of same or associated employment.
- Incremental pay scales.
- Equal value claims where the women's work is of greater value than the men's.

REACH REASONED CONCLUSIONS

- The first Equal Pay Act was passed in 1970 in anticipation of application for membership of what was then the EEC, now the EU.
- The origin of equal pay is in Article 157 TFEU (originally Article 119 EC Treaty).
- The Equality Act 2010 includes an equality clause meaning that any term in a woman's contract should be as favourable as any term of a male comparator in the same or associated employment.
- Actions can be brought for three types of claim: like work, work rated as equivalent by a genuine job evaluation study, or work of equal value.
- There is a defence of material factor which may justify differences in pay e.g. because of market forces or 'red circling'.
- Claims must be brought in the employment or within six months of leaving employment and remedies are a declaration of equal pay and an award of arrears of pay.
- Pay is broadly defined under EU law.
- Under EU law pay of men and women should be equal where they are doing equal work or work of equal value.
- Differences of pay may be valid under EU law if there is an objective justification for the difference.

Further reading

Emir, Astra, *Selwyn's Law of Employment 17th edition*. Oxford University Press, 2012, Chapter 5.

Pitt, Gwyneth, *Cases and Materials on Employment Law 3rd edition*. Pearson, 2008, Chapter 7.

Sargeant, Malcolm and Lewis, David, *Employment Law 6th edition*. Pearson, 2012, Chapter 5.3.

Storey, Tony and Turner, Chris, *Unlocking EU Law 3rd edition*. Hodder Education, 2011, Chapter 18.

11

Protection from discrimination (2) sex discrimination

AIMS AND OBJECTIVES

After reading this chapter you should be able to:

▦ Understand the background to the law on sex discrimination in employment and its limitations prior to the Equality Act 2010

▦ Understand the definition of sex under the Equality Act 2010

▦ Understand the different types of prohibited practices under the Equality Act 2010 as they relate to employees

▦ Understand the contexts in which discrimination on grounds of sex can occur in employment

▦ Understand the nature of occupational requirements in relation to sex

▦ Critically analyse the area

▦ Apply the law to factual situations and reach conclusions

11.1 The origins and aims of sex discrimination law

Prior to the Equal Pay Act 1970 there was no protection against discrimination on sex. UK sex discrimination law arose because of application for membership of the EU (at the time the EC). In EU law protection from sex discrimination came in the Equal Treatment Directive 76/207. Now this is contained in the Recast Directive 2006/54.

Occupational sexism could be any discriminatory practices, statements, actions or behaviour based on a person's sex that occurs in the context of employment. One form of occupational sexism is wage discrimination (see Chapter 10). Eurostat found a persisting gender pay gap of 17.5 per cent on average in the 27 EU Member States in 2008. Similarly, the Organization for Economic Cooperation and Development (OECD) found that female full-time employees earned 17 per cent less than their male counterparts across OECD countries in 2009.

In 2008, the OECD found that while female employment rates have expanded considerably and the gender employment and wage gaps have narrowed virtually everywhere, on average, women still have 20 per cent less of a chance to have a job and are paid 17 per cent less than men. The report also stated: '[In] many countries, labour market discrimination – i.e. the unequal treatment of equally productive individuals only because they belong to a specific group – is still a crucial factor inflating disparities in employment and the quality of job opportunities ... Evidence presented in this edition of the Employment Outlook suggests that about 8% of the variation in gender employment gaps and 30% of the variation in gender wage gaps across OECD countries can be explained by discriminatory practices in the labour market.'

11.2 The different types of sex discrimination

Sex is now a protected characteristic under section 4 of the Equality Act 2010. Section 11 defines who is included within this protected characteristic.

SECTION

'11 Sex.
In relation to the protected characteristic of sex –
(a) a reference to a person who has a particular protected characteristic is a reference to a man or to a woman;
(b) a reference to persons who share a protected characteristic is a reference to persons of the same sex.'

While it may commonly be expected that women are more likely to be discriminated against, as section 11(a) identifies the Act applies equally to both sexes and this was the case in the Sex Discrimination Act 1975. If a man is subjected to a detriment because of his sex then he will have a possible claim.

CASE EXAMPLE

Ministry of Defence v Jeremiah [1979] IRLR 436

The claimant worked in an ordnance factory for the Ministry of Defence. While there were both male and female employees, the men were required to take turns working in a part of the factory called the 'colour-bursting shell shop'. The work in this department was dusty and dirty and workers needed to wear protective clothing and take a shower at the end of the shift. So it was very uncomfortable working conditions. Female workers did not have to work in the 'colour-bursting shell shop'. The claimant brought an action under what was then section 6(2)(b) Sex Discrimination Act 1975, that he had been subjected to a detriment. The employer's argument was that there was no discrimination because the men were compensated by being paid extra when they worked in the shop and by being allowed three-quarters of an hour overtime pay when they finished work in the shop. The Court of Appeal upheld the decisions of both the tribunal and the EAT that the claimant had been discriminated against. The additional pay compensated him for the unpleasant nature of the work but it did not alter the fact that he was being treated less favourably than the female employees by being forced to work in the shop when they were not.

The test for whether something is discriminatory is an objective one so that the motive for the discrimination is irrelevant, the test being whether the claimant would have been treated the same if it was not for their sex.

CASE EXAMPLE

James v Eastleigh Borough Council [1990] 2 AC 751

The claimant and his wife who were both aged sixty-one went one day to a public swimming pool run by the local council. At the time there were different retirement ages in the UK for men and women. Men retired at age sixty-five but women retired earlier at age sixty. The claimant's wife was admitted into swimming baths free because she was over sixty. However, the claimant had to pay 75p for admission to the baths because he had not yet reached sixty-five. He then brought proceedings against the council for sex discrimination under the Sex Discrimination Act 1975. The council gave concessions for both pensioners and children under the age of three but the House of Lords held that this did not alter the fact that its policy was discriminatory, the motive, however good, was irrelevant.

11.2.1 Direct discrimination

Applying the full definition in Chapter 9.3.1 under section 13 Equality Act 2010 a person would be directly discriminated against because of their sex if:

- he or she is treated less favourably than a person of the opposite sex would be.

Direct discrimination can arise in a variety of ways. It can inevitably concern denying a woman an opportunity that would be available to a man simply because of her sex. Providing that the claimant is treated less favourably than an employee of the opposite sex then there could be direct discrimination.

CASE EXAMPLE

Grieg v Community Industry [1979] IRLR 158

The claimant and another young woman were given jobs in a painting and decorating team on a scheme aimed at tackling high unemployment amongst young people. The claimant turned up for work but the other young woman dropped out. As a result the management of the scheme decided that, in her own interest, the claimant should be dropped from the scheme rather than be the only woman on a team that was otherwise all male. The EAT held that the motive for being prevented from continuing on the scheme was irrelevant. The correct test was had she been treated less favourably because she was a woman and she had.

The claimant has to show that there is less favourable treatment. As a result there logically has to be a comparator of the opposite sex. The courts have considered the situation where there is no appropriate comparator.

CASE EXAMPLE

Shamoon v Chief Constable of the Royal Ulster Constabulary [2003] IRLR 285

The claimant, a female chief inspector, had been relieved of her counselling and appraisal duties after being the subject of complaints, and she claimed discrimination on the basis that she had been treated less favourably than two male chief inspectors who had kept their counselling responsibilities. The problem for the court was whether it was actually comparing like with like which it felt it was not. The court felt that the appropriate comparator in the case was a hypothetical comparator, a male chief inspector in the same position of the claimant having had complaints against him and to consider whether he would have been treated differently.

JUDGMENT

The court concluded: 'although she suffered a detriment by being stopped from doing appraisals, the appellant failed to prove that [her employer had] discriminated against her by treating her less favourably than he treated or would have treated a man in the same circumstances'.

It has even been questioned in the past whether, even though there has been direct discrimination, the matter is too trivial or not deserving of a remedy.

CASE EXAMPLE

Automotive Products Ltd v Peake [1977] IRLR 365

The claimant worked at a factory where all employees finished at the same time but female employees were allowed to leave the factory five minutes earlier than the men to prevent them being jostled or hurt in the rush from the factory. The arrangement had been agreed between management and unions. The claimant, a male employee, complained that this was direct discrimination under the then Sex Discrimination Act 1975. He lost in the tribunal, won his claim in his appeal to the EAT, but on the employer's appeal to the Court of Appeal Peake was again unsuccessful.

JUDGMENT

In his judgment Phillips J initially commented: 'Our first impression, unaided by a detailed consideration of the provision of the Sex Discrimination Act 1975, was that Mr. Peake's application was most unreasonable, and it seemed to us to be absurd to say that it was sex discrimination to make a sensible arrangement which enabled the women to leave the factory in comfort and convenience before the men.' He did go on to say: 'despite our impression when we entered upon this case, it seems to us that Mr. Peake has made out his claim. Guiding ourselves by the ideas implicit in the Sex Discrimination Act 1975, we can see that there is here, in the practice which has been adopted in this factory for so many years, a sort of sex discrimination; for it is a case in which men and women in comparable situations are being treated differently on the ground of sex.'

11.2.2 Indirect discrimination

Applying the full definition in Chapter 9.3.2 under section 19 Equality Act 2010 a person would be indirectly discriminated against because of their sex if:

■ he or she is subjected to a provision, criterion or practice which is discriminatory in relation to his or her sex;

■ which applies to other employees not sharing the characteristic but puts the claimant at a disadvantage compared with persons of the opposite sex;

■ and it cannot be shown to be a proportionate means of achieving a legitimate aim.

Obviously the first part of the test for indirect discrimination is whether there is a provision, practice or criterion which is common to both men and women. The fact that will make it discriminatory is that a person of one sex has a lesser chance of complying because of their sex.

CASE EXAMPLE

Price v Civil Service Commission [1978] ICR 27

The claimant was a thirty-five year old mother. She had joined the Civil Service as a Clerical Officer when she was seventeen, and served for two years. At the age of twenty she then married, and had two children doing various part-time work as her children grew up. She then saw an advertisement inviting applications for appointment in the Civil Service as Executive Officer in which no mention was made of any age limits for entry. At the time in fact the Civil Service had a scheme of direct entry at Executive Officer level for applicants with certain qualifications. An advertisement stated that only people between the ages of seventeen and twenty-eight were eligible to apply in such a way. The claimant argued that this was discrimination as she was prevented from applying. The EAT held that this was indirect discrimination. Although the requirement applied irrespective of gender, because they were more likely to be involved in child care arrangements fewer women would be able to comply with the conditions. The question was the extent to which women would be unable to comply with the requirement.

JUDGMENT

Phillips J identified: 'it is safe to say that the condition is one which it is in practice harder for women to comply with than it is for men … there are undoubtedly women of whom it may be properly said … that they "cannot" comply with the condition, because they are women; that is to say because of their involvement with their children…. The difficulty we have is in saying whether the proportion of women who can comply with the condition is *considerably smaller* than the proportion of men who can comply with it.'

It is plain that, because it is mostly women who are associated with child care arrangements that provisions, practices or criteria in their daily working arrangements that might interfere with their ability to manage those child care arrangements may well be seen as indirect discrimination. Inevitably there would have to be a disadvantage suffered.

CASE EXAMPLE

London Underground v Edwards [1999] ICR 494

The claimant was a single mother who was employed as a tube train driver and had worked for the company for ten years. She had always worked a shift system that allowed her to look after her child out of school hours. The employer then introduced a new variable shift system which made it impossible for the claimant to continue with the same child care arrangements. The employer would not be flexible so she resigned and claimed indirect discrimination. The court accepted that it was. There were only twenty-one females out of a workforce of 2,000. Bearing in mind the claimant's length of service and that her child was growing older and would eventually need less care the employer should have tried to reach a compromise with her.

Of course the other part of the definition of indirect discrimination concerns whether the practice or criterion is a proportionate means of achieving a legitimate aim. It is then possible to show that the discrimination was justified.

CASE EXAMPLE

Hardys & Hansons plc v Lax [2005] IRLR 726

The claimant was employed as a retail recruitment manager for a brewery. She went on maternity leave and asked if she could return to work on a part-time basis and the employer refused justifying this on the basis that there was an operational need for full-time employees. She claimed indirect discrimination. The tribunal had found with her as it felt that there was no real difficulty in the circumstances in allowing her to work part-time. The employer appealed arguing that the tribunal should have applied the 'reasonable range of responses' test (see Chapter 22). The Court of Appeal rejected the employer's view that the tribunal was bound only by the reasonable range of responses test. It concluded that the tribunal was entitled also to make its judgment based on the strength of the justification presented by the employer, the burden being on the employer to show that the decision (here not to allow the claimant to work part-time) was objectively justified despite having a discriminatory effect.

JUDGMENT

Pill LJ explained: 'The principle of proportionality requires the tribunal to take into account the reasonable needs of the business. But it has to make its own judgment, upon a fair and detailed analysis of the working practices and business considerations involved, as to whether the proposal is reasonable necessary.'

The significant fact is that there is less favourable treatment. If a policy applies regardless of the employee's sex then it is unlikely to be indirect discrimination.

CASE EXAMPLE

British Telecom plc v Roberts [1996] IRLR 601

Two women returning from maternity asked to return on a job share arrangement but were turned down by their employer. Both women wanted to return to work, but because they had young babies to look after: they decided that they would like to share jobs so they would have more time for their children. Prior to their maternity leave they had been full-time which had been sufficient to man the Customer Service Department. Due to increased customer demand the employer found it necessary to extend the original hours of the department to include Saturdays, and also to extend the hours during the week. The court held that there was no indirect discrimination. Their request for job share had been rejected because the requirement that the work be done full-time was necessary in the circumstances and a man would have also been expected to work full-time.

11.2.3 Harassment

Sex is one of the protected characteristics identified in section 26(5) Equality Act 2010 and therefore an action for sexual harassment is possible.

Applying the full definition in Chapter 9.3.3 under section 26 Equality Act 2010 a person would suffer sexual harassment if:

- he or she was subjected to unwanted conduct related to his or her sex; and

- the conduct had the purpose or effect of violating his dignity, or subjecting him or her to an intimidating, hostile, degrading humiliating or offensive environment.

This is a significant development from the original law on sexual harassment. Traditionally there had been no distinct provision made for sexual harassment in the Sex Discrimination Act 1975. The only possibility was under section 6(2)(b) that the person had been subjected to 'any other detriment'. As a result women could only bring a successful action if they could show that they had suffered a detriment. In contrast the EU (at the time EC) did produce a Code of Practice containing a definition 'unwanted conduct of a sexual nature, or other conduct based on sex affecting the dignity of women and men at work'.

In the early claims the problem for a woman alleging sexual harassment was that she had to show that she had been treated less favourably than a man in the same circumstances would be and that she had suffered a detriment

CASE EXAMPLE

Strathclyde Regional Council v Porcelli [1986] IRLR 134

The claimant worked as a laboratory technician in a school run by the Regional Council. She alleged a deliberate campaign of lewd comments and behaviour, including touching, by two colleagues which had forced her into seeking a transfer to another school and that the Regional Council was liable under what was then section 4(1) Sex Discrimination Act 1975. The tribunal held that a man who was disliked by his colleagues would have been treated equally badly if not in the same way so that there was no less favourable treatment of the claimant. The EAT rejected this and found for the claimant and in the employer's appeal to the Court of Session the court held that even if only some of the behaviour was of a sexual nature then there was less favourable treatment on grounds of sex.

Any form of unwanted conduct which is unwelcome and offensive may be seen as harassment and give rise to a claim of sexual discrimination. The perception of the claimant is also significant. The case above the detriment involved the creation of an unwanted and hostile environment, but harassment can also occur as a result of the humiliation of the claimant.

CASE EXAMPLE

Insitu Cleaning Co Ltd v Heads [1995] IRLR 4

Heads, a female area supervisor for a contract cleaning firm attended a management meeting. A manager, who was also the son of two of the company's directors, said to her, 'Hiya, big tits' which she found embarrassing and distressing, particularly because she was nearly twice the man's age. Apparently neither of the other two people present heard the remark, and the employer took the view that if Mrs Heads wished to pursue a complaint, she should invoke the grievance procedure and they would conduct an investigation. She thought that this was unsatisfactory and resigned. She also claimed that the man had made grossly offensive remarks to her of a sexual nature on three previous occasions. The EAT held that a comment about a woman's breasts is sexual in nature and rejected the argument that it was comparable with a remark about a man's bald head, and that a single act of verbal sexual harassment was sufficient to amount to a detriment.

A significant problem for women trying to bring claims for sexual harassment at this time was the argument that was often accepted by tribunals that certain behaviour was gender neutral. The extension of the argument is that a man could be as offended by it as a woman as a result of which there would be no detriment and no less favourable treatment of the woman.

CASE EXAMPLE

Stewart v Cleveland Guest Engineering Ltd [1994] IRLR 440

Here men in a factory posted female nude pinups from magazines and calendars on the walls. The female claimant took offence and objected at the practice to management. They initially ordered that they be removed but then reversed their decision when they were approached by other workers who claimed that they did not object. The claimant then argued that she had been sexually harassed by the behaviour. The EAT upheld the view of the tribunal that there was no harassment because the materials could be considered as gender neutral, and men as well as women might be offended by it so that there was no detriment and no less favourable treatment.

JUDGMENT

The tribunal had identified: 'the display itself was neutral. A man might well find this sort of display as offensive as the applicant did'. The EAT concluded that: 'no one is better placed to make a decision on the facts of a particular case than the.... Tribunal. It heard evidence from the witnesses, saw the material which Miss Stewart found to be offensive and considered the detailed arguments on the law and the facts. There is, of course, room for disagreement among different groups of people, such as Tribunals, as to what is or is not less favourable treatment and as to the extent to which women in the workplace are *vulnerable to such treatment*.'

The argument completely misses the point. The nude pictures were of women and therefore it is arguable whether there was any gender neutrality and only women would feel vulnerable as a result of the situation. Because a detriment was required it is also the case that a claim could be defeated by reference to the woman's attitudes to sexual matters and her own sexual history.

CASE EXAMPLE

Snowball v Gardner Merchant Ltd [1987] IRLR 397

A female catering manager alleged that she had been sexually harassed by her male district manager. She was cross-examined on her sexual attitudes with the aim of showing that she had not suffered a detriment. The chair of the tribunal then allowed the employer to introduce witnesses who identified that she spoke freely with her work colleagues about sexual matters. The Employment Appeal Tribunal held that the tribunal had not exceeded its power by admitting the evidence since it was relevant not only to credibility but also to detriment and hurt to feelings.

CASE EXAMPLE

Wileman v Minilec Engineering Ltd [1988] IRLR 144

A female employee complained of harassment by a company director which included sexual remarks such as a suggestion that she should go topless, as well as being rubbed up against by him. The employer argued that she had not suffered any detriment since she had posed in flimsy clothing for a newspaper and would be unaffected by the man's behaviour. The court held that, while the woman might accept sexual remarks from one person that this may not apply in the case of others. She had been discriminated against. The EAT did identify that the wearing of provocative clothes could be taken into account by a tribunal in determining whether there was a detriment suffered.

11.2.4 Victimisation

Applying the full definition in Chapter 9.3.4 under section 27 Equality Act 2010 a person would have been victimised against because of their sex if:

- he or she has been subjected to a detriment;

- because he or she has brought proceedings under the Act; or

- he or she has given evidence or information in connection with proceedings under the Act; or

- he or she has done anything else for the purposes of or in connection with the Act; or

- he or she has made an allegation (whether or not express) that his or her employer or another person has contravened the Act.

For a claim of victimisation the claimant only has to show that she has suffered a detriment because she has done one of the protected acts under section 27.

CASE EXAMPLE

St Helens Metropolitan Borough Council v Derbyshire [2007] UKHL 16

Derbyshire was one of thirty-nine women, who had successfully brought a claim of equal pay against their employer, the council. They then claimed, in separate proceedings, that during their claim for equal pay they had been subjected to victimisation by the Council because they had persisted in pursuing that claim. Two months before their equal pay claim was to be heard the Council had sent letters to all staff in which it stated that it was concerned at the effect that the claim would have on the staff. The letters went to other women who had settled their claims which could obviously then create an adverse reaction to Derbyshire who claimed successfully on victimisation.

JUDGMENT

Lord Bingham commented: 'The right to seek effective legal redress conferred on a person who is or claims to be the victim of proscribed discriminatory conduct would itself be of limited value and perhaps no value if the alleged discriminator were free, otherwise than by defeating the claim on its merits, to frustrate or interfere with the conduct of the proceedings in a way that undermined the integrity of the judicial process to which the claim had given rise.'

However, it will not be victimisation where the employer acts reasonably in trying to reach a compromise in a dispute with an employee in trying to get them to reach a settlement.

CASE EXAMPLE

Cornelius v University College of Swansea [1987] IRLR 141

A female employee of the university made a complaint of sexual discrimination and while she was awaiting the proceedings in a tribunal asked to be either transferred or given access to the College's internal grievance procedure, but was informed by the university registrar that neither could occur until the outcome of the proceedings was known. She then claimed victimisation arguing that but for her tribunal proceedings her request would have been treated differently. The House of Lords disagreed.

JUDGMENT

Bingham LJ explained the reasoning of the court: 'There is no reason whatever to suppose that the decisions of the registrar and his senior assistant on the applicant's requests for a transfer and a hearing under the grievance procedure were influenced in any way by the facts that the appellant had brought proceedings or that those proceedings were under the Act. The existence of proceedings plainly did influence their decisions. No doubt, like most experienced administrators, they recognised the risk of acting in a way which might embarrass the handling or be inconsistent with the outcome of current proceedings. They accordingly wished to defer action until the proceedings were over. But that had, so far as the evidence shows, nothing whatever to do with the appellant's conduct in bringing proceedings under the Act.'

ACTIVITY

Quick quiz

Consider which type of discrimination may have occurred in each of the following situations:

1. Emma, an eighteen year old female clerical assistant, works in her employer's general office. Emma is distressed because the Accounts Manager and the Marketing Manager who are both more than twice Emma's age both regularly make lewd and suggestive remarks to her and often rub up against her when she is at the photocopier. Emma has complained to the General Manager but nothing has been done about it.
2. Fiona, a single mother, is employed in a warehouse for a distribution company which has recently seen a significant increase in business. Fiona is distressed because the company has now introduced a variable shift pattern for all employees which is going to make child care arrangements impossible.
3. Georgina a female qualified electrician has applied for a promotion to site supervisor but has been told her application will not be considered because the workforce, which is predominantly male, would 'not take kindly to being told what to do by a woman'.
4. Helen approached a lawyer with a view to issuing discrimination proceedings against her employer. The employer has now given Helen one month's notice of termination of her contract.

11.3 The situations in which discrimination is prohibited in employment

Section 39 Equality Act 2010 deals with discrimination in employment. The section makes the following provisions.

SECTION

'39 Employees and applicants
(1) An employer (A) must not discriminate against a person (B) –
  (a) in the arrangements A makes for deciding to whom to offer employment;
  (b) as to the terms on which A offers B employment;
  (c) by not offering B employment.

(2) An employer (A) must not discriminate against an employee of A's (B) –

  (a) as to B's terms of employment;
  (b) in the way A affords B access, or by not affording B access, to opportunities for promotion, transfer or training or for receiving any other benefit, facility or service;
  (c) by dismissing B;
  (d) by subjecting B to any other detriment.'

There are clearly three points in relation to employment where discrimination could be a significant issue:

- in the recruitment and selection of staff;
- during employment;
- on termination of employment.

11.3.1 Recruitment and selection of staff

Applying the full definition from section 39(1) Equality Act 2010 an employer is not allowed to discriminate:

- in the way in which it decides who it will offer employment;
- in the terms on which the employment is offered;
- by not offering a person employment.

Jobs should clearly be available generally to both sexes unless there is an occupational requirement. If the selection procedure is not impartial then this is likely to be discriminatory.

CASE EXAMPLE

Brennan v J H Dewhurst Ltd [1984] ICR 52

The claimant, who had two years' experience as a butcher's assistant, applied for a job in the defendant's shop in Torquay. The initial interview was with the shop manager but any subsequent appointment would be made by the District Manager. The claimant argued that she had been subjected to discriminatory questioning at the interview and that the shop manager had made it plain that he had no desire to employ a woman assistant. She had been told that the vacancy had been filled when in fact it had been frozen and was later filled by transfer within the company. The EAT held that, since the shop manager in effect had the role at the interview stage of filtering applicants before the final process under the District Manager, that the manner in which he conducted the interview meant that no female applicant would go forward and there was indeed sexual discrimination.

In this respect questions at interviews can be critical since they must only relate to the actual work and be gender neutral unless sex is a genuine determining factor.

CASE EXAMPLE

Saunders v Richmond-upon-Thames London Borough Council [1978] ICR 75

A female professional golfer attended an interview for a position as a professional golfer. She was asked numerous questions and comments were passed that on the surface appeared to discriminate such as 'Are there any women golf professionals in clubs?' 'So you'd be blazing a trail would you?' 'Do you think men respond as well to a woman golf professional as to a man?'

'If all this is true, you are obviously a lady of great experience but don't you think this type of job is rather unglamorous?' 'Don't you think this is a job with rather long hours?' 'I can see that you could probably cope with the playing and teaching side of the job but I am rather concerned as to whether you could cope with the management side.' 'If some of the men were causing trouble over the starting times on the tee, do you think you would be able to control this?' When she was informed that she had not made it to the final shortlist she claimed that this was due to discrimination in the questioning that she had been subjected to. The EAT identified that there may be practical reasons for asking such questions and gave the example of a man being interviewed for a position as a head teacher in a girls' school being asked questions about his ability to relate to girls. As a result the asking of such questions was not discriminatory. The EAT did, however, consider that some of the questions asked at the interview reflected an out-of-date and proscribed attitude of mind.

On the other hand in *Gates v Wirral Borough Council* (unreported) a woman was asked at her job interview, about her relationship with her husband and whether she intended to have a family in the near future. Since the same questions were not put to any male candidate the tribunal found that the questions were discriminatory.

Clearly it would also be discrimination to refuse a person solely because of their sex. In *Batisha v Say* [1977] IRLR 6 a woman was turned down for a job as a cave guide because, as it was explained, 'it is a man's job'. This was a clear act of discrimination. Of course if the refusal to employ is actually for another reason then there is unlikely to be discrimination. In *Steere v Morris Bros* a woman was refused work as an HGV driver and claimed discrimination. The defendant was able to show that the refusal was because the woman lived too far away from their premises.

The ECJ in *Dekker v Stichting Vormingscentrum voor Jong Wolwsassenen (VJV Centrum) Plus* [1990] (C-177/88) ECR 1-3941 also identified that a refusal to appoint a woman because she was pregnant was in breach of the then Equal Treatment Directive 76/207 and so amounted to sex discrimination. Pregnancy and maternity is now a protected characteristic under section 18 Equality Act 2010 (see Chapter 9.2). There are extensive rules covering pregnancy and maternity. These are covered in Chapter 8.4.

11.3.2 During employment

Applying the full definition from section 39(2) Equality Act 2010 during employment an employer is not allowed to discriminate:

- by giving the claimant less favourable terms than that of an employee of the opposite sex;
- in the way that it provides opportunities for promotion, transfer, training or any other benefit, service or facility;
- by subjecting the claimant to any other detriment.

Any form of differential treatment during employment based on sex could amount to discrimination. This is an area where EU law has been significant in developing rights, originally under the Equal Treatment Directive 76/207.

CASE EXAMPLE

Marshall v Southampton and South West Hampshire AHA (No 1) 152/84 [1986] QB 401

A woman who was forced to retire by her employer because of her age and the fact that at the time there were different retirement ages for men and women in the UK. She argued that this different treatment amounted to discrimination contrary to the then Equal Treatment Directive 76/207. The problem was whether the Directive could be enforced through direct effect. The ECJ confirmed that the UK had failed to fully implement the Directive and identified that the woman could only rely on the improperly implemented Directive against her employer because it was the health service, an organ of the state. The Court recognised that Directives are only capable of vertical direct effect.

Originally the fact that directives could only be vertically directly effective against the state or an emanation of the state meant that there was an anomaly in the law in that the possibility of enforcing rights given in a directive would not be available where the employer was a private body.

CASE EXAMPLE

Duke v GEC Reliance Ltd [1988] AC 618

The case has similar facts to *Marshall* above where another woman did not wish to retire at the state retirement age. Unfortunately, in contrast to *Marshall* the woman was employed by a private body, not by the state. As a result the House of Lords (now the Supreme Court) held that it was not bound to apply Directive 76/207 because of the principle in *Marshall* that directives can never be horizontally directly effective, against another citizen or private body. Despite the UK being at fault for failing to fully implement the directive the availability of a remedy then was entirely dependent on the identity of the employer. It also rejected a request to make a reference to the ECJ to consider whether the principle of indirect effect from *Von Colson and Kamann v Land Nordrhein-Westfalen* 14/83 [1984] ECR 1891 could be used. It held that it was bound by the criterion in *CILFIT 283/81* that a reference is not necessary where there is an existing interpretation because the principle of *acte clair* applies and there was an existing interpretation in *Marshall* on horizontal direct effect.

The problem was later overcome by the ECJ in developing the principle of state liability. Equal treatment now falls under the Recast Directive 2006/54. While the cases above are illustrating EU law principles of direct effect as well as concerning discrimination during employment they are also significant in illustrating that the English court was prepared to allow an injustice to occur where the ECJ was not.

Any denial of similar opportunities for promotion or training or transfer that are enjoyed by employees of the opposite sex are likely to amount to discrimination.

CASE EXAMPLE

Wallace v South Eastern Education and Library Board [1980] IRLR 193

A part-time female visual aids technician applied for a new full-time post and was interviewed believing that the interview was a formality and that she would get the post. A man was then appointed to the post. The woman then discovered that the man's qualifications and experience were inferior to hers but could find no actual evidence that the appointment had been based on sex. The Northern Ireland Court of Appeal held that in cases involving access to employment or promotion the appointment of a less qualified man over a more qualified woman raises a prima facie case of discrimination. It also identified that in that instance it would be for the employer to show evidence showing that there was no discrimination.

Similarly, imposing conditions on one sex that are not imposed on the opposite sex may be discriminatory if they cannot be justified.

CASE EXAMPLE

Moyhing v Barts & London NHS Trust [2006] IRLR 860

A male student nurse claimed discrimination when he was required to be chaperoned when carrying out an ECG on female patients which would mean him touching the patient's chest but female nurses were not chaperoned when giving treatment requiring similar intimate contact. He argued that there was a culture which treated male nurses effectively as second class citizens because there was a widespread assumption that female nurses were automatically suitable to provide care, including intimate care, to anyone, whereas the assumption was that it was inappropriate for male nurses to provide intimate care to female patients. The Trust argued that the policy was to avoid claims of assaults by male nurses. The EAT held that the motive for the policy was irrelevant and it was still discrimination.

JUDGMENT

Elias J explained: 'We have much sympathy for the dilemma in which this decision places the respondent and other hospital trusts who have adopted similar policies for good and objective reasons. Assuming that the risk of … false allegations by male patients really is virtually non existent … it seems a waste of potentially scarce resources in the health service to require a chaperone system to be extended to females … unless and until a specific legislative exception is made for this situation or the concept of justification is extended so that exceptionally it could apply to direct discrimination, we see no legal basis for treating male and female student nurses differently.'

Another area that may give rise to claims of discrimination is differential dress codes for men and women. If there is no detriment or there is a justification then they may be unsuccessful. In *Schmidt v Austicks Bookshops Ltd* [1977] IRLR 360 the employer's dress code included a prohibition on female staff wearing trousers. This was held not to be discrimination since there was no detriment.

JUDGMENT

In the EAT Phillips J explained: 'if one considers the situation of the men and the situation of the women there was no comparable restriction which could be applied to the men, equivalent to that applied to the women preventing them from wearing trousers, which could make it possible to lead to the conclusion that the women were being treated less favourably than the men'.

In *Burrett v West Birmingham Health Authority* [1994] IRLR 7 a nurse claimed that having to wear a hat which was stiff and was of no practical significance when a male nurse did not have to wear such a hat was discrimination. When she complained she was then transferred to a different department where she had less chance of overtime. The EAT held, however, that it was not less favourable treatment, the mere fact that men and women had different dress codes was not in itself discriminatory.

Traditionally sexual harassment claims were based on less favourable treatment and suffering a detriment. It has been accepted that even a single act of harassment could be both and thus be the basis of a claim.

CASE EXAMPLE

Bracebridge Engineering Ltd v Darby [1990] IRLR 3

The claimant was subjected to a single indecent assault. The court had to decide whether this amounted to discrimination and whether the employer could be held responsible. The court held that a single act can amount to harassment, and did in the circumstances because of its serious nature. The perpetrators were involved in disciplinary proceedings at the time and were also under supervision, As a result their acts were seen as being in the course of their employment and the employer's failure to treat the allegation of sexual harassment seriously was a breach of the implied term to maintain the trust and confidence of the employee, which entitled her to treat the contract as having been repudiated. The employer was liable.

11.3.3 On termination of employment

A discriminatory dismissal is identified also in section 39(2). Clearly any dismissal based on a person's sex would be unacceptable. The claimant must show that the dismissal was for reasons of his or her sex for a successful claim. In *Grieg v Community Industry* [1979] IRLR 158 (see 11.2.1 above) the young women was dismissed on the first day of work but it was specifically because of her sex and so was a discriminatory dismissal.

In sexual harassment cases a woman may feel that she has no choice but to resign because the behaviour is unacceptable. This would be a constructive dismissal (see Chapter 19) and could amount to a discriminatory dismissal. This was the case in *Insitu Cleaning Co Ltd v Heads* [1995] IRLR 4 (see 11.2.3 above).

As has already been identified in 11.3.2 dress codes can also be discriminatory if they have the result that they treat a person of one sex less favourably than a person of the other sex would be.

CASE EXAMPLE

Smith v Safeway plc [1996] IRLR 456

The employer had different rules on hair length for men and women. The rule for men was that they should have hair that was not below the collar and that they should not have any unconventional hair style. The claimant wore his long hair in a ponytail and was dismissed when he would not have his hair cut. He claimed direct discrimination. He succeeded in the EAT which held that the rule was discriminatory because it extended beyond work. However, the Court of Appeal held that it was not discrimination.

JUDGMENT

Philipps LJ stated: 'there is an important distinction between discrimination between the sexes and discrimination against one or other of the sexes. It is the latter that is forbidden by the Sex Discrimination Act 1975. A code which applies conventional standards is one which, so far as the criteria of appearance is concerned applies an even handed approach between men and women, and not one which is discriminatory.' He also stated: 'Rules concerning appearance will not be discriminatory because their content is different for men and women if they enforce a common principle of smartness or conventionality, and taken as a whole and not garment by garment or item by item, neither gender is treated less favourably in enforcing that principle.'

The judgment would appear to be based on a value judgment of what constitutes smartness and convention rather than on an objective standard applied regardless of gender. Again perceptions or prejudices of employers might be an issue leading to discrimination.

Another common prejudice is that men are breadwinners of families. This could be factually accurate but it is dangerous to base a discriminatory practice on it.

CASE EXAMPLE

Gubala v Crompton Parkinson [1977] IRLR 10

A young woman with a family was selected for redundancy rather than a man. Despite the woman having longer service than the man the employer made the decision based on the age of the man, who was fifty-eight, and the fact that a man would be the breadwinner of the family. This argument was rejected and the dismissal was therefore discriminatory.

11.4 Lawful justifications for sex discrimination

Applying the full definition in Chapter 9.3.5 under schedule 9 Equality Act 2010 an employer will be able to justify the alleged discrimination when:

- there is an occupational requirement;
- the application of the requirement is a proportionate means of achieving a legitimate aim;
- the person to whom the employer applies the requirement does not meet it or the employer has reasonable grounds for not being satisfied that the person meets it.

There were a variety of 'genuine occupational qualifications' under section 7 of the Sex Discrimination Act 1975. Some of these will survive as occupational requirements under schedule 9 of the Equality Act 2010 if they are a proportionate means of achieving a legitimate aim.

One is where the job requires authenticity of physiology. This will obviously be the case with films and plays where the producer requires a female actor to play a female role and a male actor to play a male role.

Another is where the nature of the job requires it to be done by one sex in order to preserve decency or privacy. This could be because it could prove objectionable for there to be contact with a member of the opposite sex. Two cases illustrate the same point but involving different sexes.

CASE EXAMPLE

Etam plc v Rowan [1989] IRLR 150

The EAT would not accept that there was an occupational requirement when a man was rejected in an application for sales assistant in a shop selling women's clothing. The employer argued that it needed a woman because a man would not have been able to help customers in the changing rooms. The EAT stated that this aspect of the work could have been carried out by a female employee and it would not have stopped the man from doing other aspects of the job.

CASE EXAMPLE

Wylie v Dee & Co (Menswear) Ltd [1978] IRLR 103

A woman was turned down in an application for a job as a shop assistant in a menswear shop. The employer argued that this was an occupational requirement because the job could involve taking men's inside leg measurements. Again the argument was rejected since a male assistant could have covered this aspect of the work.

On the contrary where the job requires that the employees are in close contact in a state of undress then it will be accepted that this is a necessary occupational requirement for preserving decency and privacy

CASE EXAMPLE

Sisley v Britannia Security Systems [1983] IRLR 404

The employer installed and maintained security systems. It set up a new security control centre and advertised for operatives. Two operators worked three different shifts including a twelve hour shift. The operators had to change into uniforms at work and needed to strip to underwear during rest periods to prevent their uniforms from becoming crumpled. The claimant had applied for a job and then found out that the company was operating a female only team of operators and later advertised for female operators. The claimant alleged sex discrimination. In order for the defence to apply there had to be a need for some form of residence where employees would be called on to sleep over and would be likely to be in close proximity with one another in a state of relative undress and so a single sex requirement would be appropriate in order to preserve decency. The women here had rest periods sometimes amounting to five hours. The EAT identified also that the state of undress had to be reasonably incidental to the job. In this case it was reasonable to have a rest period during a long rest and the EAT accepted that it was also reasonable for the women to undress during that rest and therefore there was an occupational requirement justifying a women only team.

Another possible occupational requirement concerns private residencies. If the job involves living in a private home and needs to be done by a person of a particular sex because objection might reasonably be taken to allowing someone of the opposite sex the degree of personal contact or knowledge of the employer's private affairs which the job necessarily entails. This could obviously cover professional carers.

Another is where the job involves performance of duties in another country the laws or customs of which would make it difficult for one particular sex to do the work. This is usually going to be a woman.

CASE EXAMPLE

O'Connor v Kontiki Travel (Unreported)

A woman was turned down in her application for a position of coach driver. The justification given by the employer was that the job involved driving through Muslim countries where there may have been objection to a woman doing the work. This was not accepted as an occupational requirement when it was identified that the only Muslim country that she would have had to drive through was Turkey. Since Turkey was a secular state and had no objection to women drivers there was no justification for the discrimination.

Another interesting possibility has been discussed within the context of EU law.

CASE EXAMPLE

Johnston v Chief Constable of the Royal Ulster Constabulary [1987] ICR 83

A female officer in the Royal Ulster Constabulary argued that not issuing firearms to female officers was a breach of the right of equal treatment under what was then Directive 76/207 (but would now fall under the Recast Directive 2006/54). She argued that in effect the policy acted as a bar to promotion for female officers. The RUC claimed that its policy was justified on public safety and national security grounds and was also authorised by a statutory instrument. It also argued that allowing women to carry arms increased their risk of becoming targets for assassination and that the derogation in Article 2(2) of Directive 76/207 would apply. Now contained in Article 14(2) of the Recast Directive 2006/54 the derogation identifies that different treatment based on sex is not discriminatory if 'because of the nature of the particular occupational activities concerned or of the context in which they are carried out, such a characteristic constitutes a genuine and determining occupational requirement'. The ECJ held that there was no general public safety exemption in the Directive and that the only derogation available was that in Article 2 on occupational activities which by nature required that the sex of the worker is a determining factor. It held that the derogation should be applied strictly but accepted that the principle of proportionality should also be applied. The policy could fall within the derogation because of the politically sensitive situation that existed at the time in Northern Ireland. The ECJ did, however, recognise that the effect of the strict rules in the policy was to deprive female officers of the right to a judicial hearing or indeed any remedy. As such it was a breach of their human rights.

ACTIVITY

Quick quiz

Consider whether it may be a defence to a claim of discrimination in each of the following situations:

1. Daniel, a male nurse, has applied for the position of private nurse to a wealthy disabled woman. The job involved intimate care and Daniel was told he could not be appointed because he was a man.
2. Gemma is a female engineer with lengthy experience of site management. Her employer has a contract to install machinery in a factory in Iran and Gemma wishes to be the site manager. Her employer has told her that this will probably be impossible.
3. Stephen is producing a play about the life and death of Marilyn Monroe, a famous actress of the 1950s and 1960s. He is only auditioning female actresses for the part.

ACTIVITY

Self-assessment questions

1. In what ways is EU law on discrimination superior to UK law?
2. What is the basis of direct sex discrimination?
3. What has to be proved for a claim of indirect discrimination?
4. What needs to be shown in a claim for direct discrimination?
5. What problems confronted women trying to claim sexual harassment under the Sex Discrimination Act 1975?
6. In what ways has the Equality Act 2010 improved the position?
7. Why was the claim of victimisation unsuccessful in *Cornelius v University College of Swansea*?
8. How does the Sex Discrimination Act protect men?
9. In which aspects of employment does the Act apply?
10. How is an employer's right to recruit whom he chooses restricted by the Act?
11. When can an employer ask discriminatory questions?
12. To what extent can an employer dictate the dress of employees?
13. Are there any connections between the different types of occupational requirement?

Has the claimant been the victim of direct discrimination?
- the claimant has been treated less favourably than a person of the opposite sex

OR

Has the claimant been the victim of indirect discrimination?
- the claimant has been subjected to a provision, criterion or practice which is discriminatory in relation to his or her sex
- which applies to all sexes but puts him or her at a disadvantage compared with persons of different sex
- and it cannot be shown to be a proportionate means of achieving a legitimate aim

—OR→

Has the claimant been the victim of harassment?
- the claimant was subjected to unwanted conduct related to his or her sex, and
- the conduct had the purpose or effect of violating his or her dignity, or subjecting him or her to an intimidating, hostile, degrading humiliating or offensive environment

Has the claimant been the victim of victimisation?
- the claimant has been subjected to a detriment
- because he or she has brought proceedings under the Act; or
- he or she has given evidence or information in connection with proceedings under the Act; or
- he or she has done anything else for the purposes of or in connection with the Act; or
- he or she has made an allegation (whether or not express) that his employer or another person has contravened the Act

YES

Is there a legal justification for the discrimination?
- there is an occupational requirement
- the application of the requirement is a proportionate means of achieving a legitimate aim
- the person to whom the employer applies the requirement does not meet it or the employer has reasonable grounds for not being satisfied that the person meets it
- In the case of indirect discrimination the provision, criterion or practice would also need to be a proportionate means of achieving a legitimate aim or it would not be lawful

YES

YES

A CLAIM FOR DISCRIMINATION ON GROUNDS OF SEX IS POSSIBLE

Figure 11.1 Flow chart illustrating the requirements for a claim of discrimination on grounds of sex

11.5 Discrimination on marital status

Discrimination on marital status was originally unlawful under section 3(1) Sex Discrimination Act 1975. Now marital status and civil partnership are a protected characteristic under section 4 of the Equality Act 2010. Section 8 defines who is included within this protected characteristic.

SECTION

'8 Marriage and civil partnership.
(1) A person has the protected characteristic of marriage and civil partnership if the person is married or is a civil partner.
(2) In relation to the protected characteristic of marriage and civil partnership –
    (a) a reference to a person who has a particular protected characteristic is a reference to a person who is married or is a civil partner;
    (b) a reference to persons who share a protected characteristic is a reference to persons who are married or are civil partners.'

Direct discrimination

Applying the full definition in Chapter 9.3.1 under section 13 Equality Act 2010 a person would be directly discriminated against because of his or her marital status or civil partnership if:

■ he or she is treated less favourably than a single person would be.

Obviously, in the context of employment this less favourable treatment could either be in the recruitment and selection of staff, during the employment or on dismissal. So it could involve failing to employ somebody because of their marital status, subjecting them to different terms of employment because of their marital status or dismissing them because of their marital status.

An example of discrimination during employment might result from a failure to promote the employee because of his or her marital status.

CASE EXAMPLE

Chief Constable of the Bedfordshire Constabulary v Graham [2002] IRLR 239

A female police inspector had applied for a promotion. The only reason that she did not get the promotion was that she was married to a chief superintendent in the same division where the promoted post was and it was thought that there could be difficulties in having a married couple working together at such a high level. The EAT accepted that she had been treated less favourably than a single person applying for the promotion would have been and so there was direct discrimination.

The employer in the above case was making prejudiced assumptions about whether a married couple can work together. The example of a discriminatory dismissal below is also interesting because it features a similar prejudice.

CASE EXAMPLE

Coleman v Sky Oceanic Ltd [1981] IRLR 398

A man and a woman who worked for different, competitive travel companies then married. The employers were both worried about the confidentiality of their separate businesses despite the fact that the woman had expressly promised not to divulge any of the company's business. Management from the two companies met and decided that the woman would be dismissed because of the assumption that the man would be the breadwinner in the relationship and she was dismissed the day after her wedding. She claimed both sex and marital discrimination under the Sex Discrimination Act 1975. The EAT reversed the finding of the tribunal and held that there was no marital discrimination because the same issue of worry over confidentiality might have occurred in the case of single people in a relationship. She appealed to the Court of Appeal on sex discrimination and the court agreed that a dismissal based on the assumption that men are more likely to be the breadwinners is sex discrimination.

Indirect discrimination

Indirect discrimination is also possible. Applying the full definition in Chapter 9.3.2 under section 19 Equality Act 2010 a person would be indirectly discriminated against because of their marital status or civil partnership if:

- he or she is subjected to a provision, criterion or practice which is discriminatory in relation to his or her marital status or civil partnership;
- because it puts him or her at a disadvantage compared with single people;
- it cannot be shown to be a proportionate means of achieving a legitimate aim.

In *Chief Constable of the Bedfordshire Constabulary v Graham* [2002] IRLR 239 above the EAT also decided that there could have been indirect discrimination because evidence showed that there was a higher proportion of female officers in relationships than male officers.

Indirect discrimination might also result from a practice or criterion which is based on the prejudice of the employer.

CASE EXAMPLE

Hurley v Mustoe [1981] IRLR 208

The claimant had four children and had worked for four years at nights as a waitress while her husband looked after the children. She applied for a waitressing job in a bistro and had only worked there for one night when she was dismissed after the owner of the bistro discovered that the claimant had children. It was a policy that he did not employ women with children because he thought them to be unreliable. The EAT held that it was direct sex discrimination but was also indirect discrimination on grounds of marital status. The employer had argued that his policy was necessary as he had only a small business. The EAT felt that he was applying double standards because he only questioned whether married women with children were reliable rather than married people with children.

Harassment

Harassment will only apply in relation to marital status under section 26(2) Equality Act 2010 where a person suffers harassment because of his or her marital status or civil partnership if:

- he or she was subjected to unwanted conduct of a sexual nature related to his or her marital status or civil partnership; and
- the conduct had the purpose or effect of violating his or her dignity, or subjecting him or her to an intimidating, hostile, degrading, humiliating or offensive environment.

Victimisation

Finally victimisation also applies in the case of marital status. Applying the full definition in Chapter 9.3.4 under section 27 Equality Act 2010 a person would have been victimised against because of his or her marital status or civil partnership if:

- he or she has been subjected to a detriment;
- because he or she has brought proceedings under the Act; or
- he or she has given evidence or information in connection with proceedings under the Act; or
- he or she has done anything else for the purposes of or in connection with the Act; or
- he or she has made an allegation (whether or not express) that his employer or another person has contravened the Act.

| **Has the claimant been the victim of direct discrimination?**
• the claimant has been treated less favourably than a single person
OR
Has the claimant been the victim of indirect discrimination?
• the claimant has been subjected to a provision, criterion or practice which is discriminatory in relation to his or her marital status
• which applies to married and single people but puts him or her at a disadvantage compared with single persons
• and it cannot be shown to be a proportionate means of achieving a legitimate aim | **Has the claimant been the victim of harassment?**
• the claimant was subjected to unwanted conduct related to his or her marital status, and
• the conduct had the purpose or effect of violating his dignity, or subjecting him or her to an intimidating, hostile, degrading, humiliating or offensive environment
Has the claimant been the victim of victimisation?
• the claimant has been subjected to a detriment
• because he or she has brought proceedings under the Act; or
• he or she has given evidence or information in connection with proceedings under the Act; or
• he or she has done anything else for the purposes of or in connection with the Act; or
• he or she has made an allegation (whether or not express) that his employer or another person has contravened the Act |

OR

YES ↓   YES ↓

A CLAIM FOR DISCRIMINATION ON THE GROUNDS OF MARITAL STATUS IS POSSIBLE

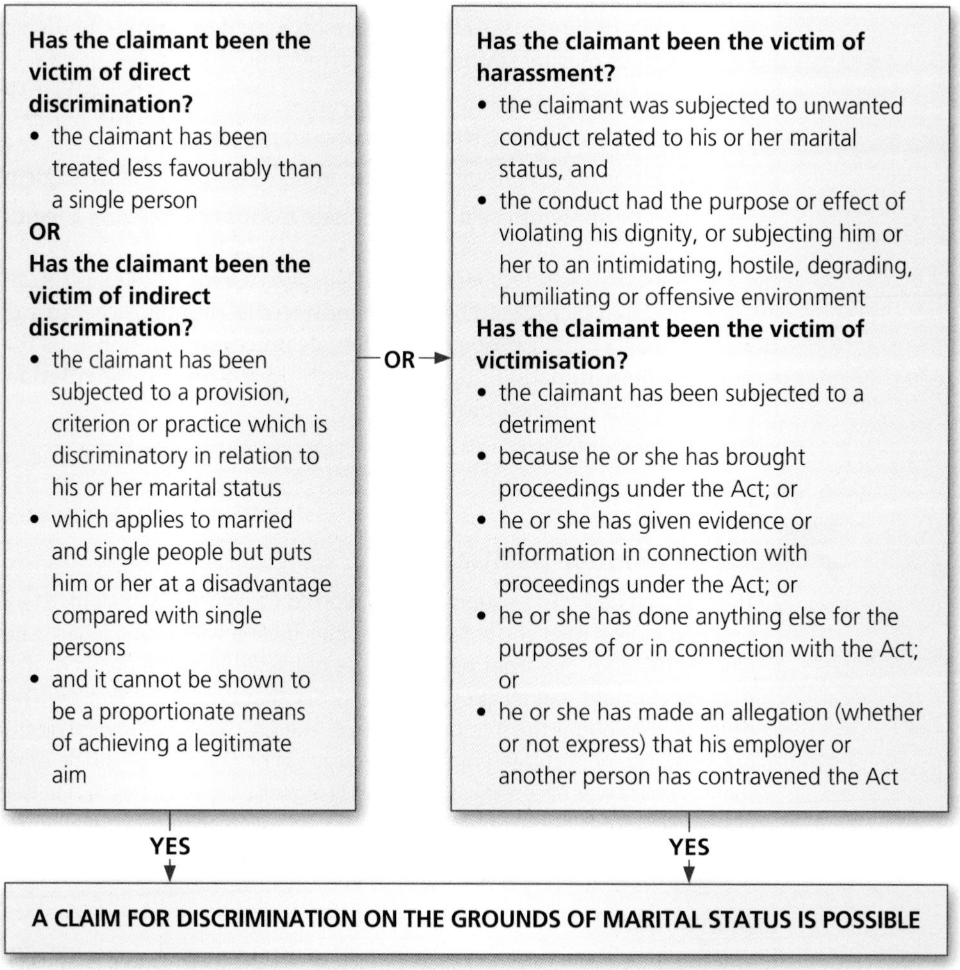

Figure 11.2 Flow chart illustrating the requirements for a claim of discrimination on the grounds of marital status or civil partnership

Single employees

While marital status is a protected characteristic, being single or unmarried is not, so it has always been possible to discriminate against a single person. In *Sun Alliance & London Insurance Co v Dudman* [1978] IRLR the court identified that, where a firm makes preferential mortgage facilities available to married men then it must do so also for married women, otherwise there would be discrimination. On the other hand it was perfectly permissible to exclude single employees from the scheme.

Similarly in *Bavin v NHS Pensions Trust Agency* [1999] ICR 1192 which involved survivor pension rights for unmarried partners the surviving unmarried partner of the female deceased was a transsexual who had undergone gender reassignment from female to male. The partners were unmarried because under the law at that time neither same sex couples nor transsexuals could marry. The EAT held that in law the transsexual was a female and had been discriminated against only on the basis of her single status which was perfectly legal. The reason for the single status was considered irrelevant to the issue by the court.

KEY FACTS

Origins	Case/statute
Developed in 1960s	*Sex Discrimination Act 1975* *Sex Discrimination Act 1986*

The different types of sex discrimination	Case/statute
Direct discrimination	
• the person is treated less favourably than a person of the opposite sex would be • the motive for the discrimination is irrelevant, the test being whether the claimant would have been treated the same if it was not for their sex	*S11 Equality Act 2010* *James v Eastleigh Borough Council* [1990]
Indirect discrimination	
• the claimant is subjected to a provision, criterion or practice which is discriminatory in relation to his or her sex, which puts him or her at a disadvantage compared with persons of the opposite sex; and it cannot be shown to be a proportionate means of achieving a legitimate aim • a person of one sex has a lesser chance of complying because of their sex	*S19 Equality Act 2010* *Price v Civil Service Commission* [1978]
Harassment	
• the claimant is subjected to unwanted conduct related to his or her sex, with the purpose or effect of violating his or her dignity, or subjecting him or her to an intimidating, hostile, degrading, humiliating or offensive environment • which can occur because of the humiliation of the claimant • and occurs because there is an intimidating, hostile or offensive environment	*S26 Equality Act 2010* *Insitu Cleaning Co Ltd v Heads* *Strathclyde Regional Council v Porcelli*

Victimisation	
• the claimant was subjected to a detriment because he or she brought proceedings under the Act; or gave evidence or information in connection with proceedings or did anything else for the purposes of or in connection with the Act; or made an allegation (whether or not express) that his or her employer or another person has contravened the Act	*S27 Equality Act 2010* *St Helens Metropolitan Borough Council v Derbyshire*
• the detriment could be as extreme as a dismissal	*Gubala v Crompton Parkinson*

Sex discrimination in employment	Case/statute
Recruitment and selection	
• could occur in the way who is offered employment is decided; or in the terms on which the employment is offered; or by not offering a person employment	*S39(1) Equality Act 2010*
• so could involve making the job only available to a certain sex	*St Helens Metropolitan Borough Council v Derbyshire*
During employment	
• could occur by giving the claimant poorer terms than that of an employee of the opposite sex; or in the way that opportunities for promotion, transfer, training or any other benefit, service or facility are provided; or by subjecting the claimant to any other detriment	*S39(2) Equality Act 2010*
• which may be imposing different conditions on different sexes without justification	*Moyhing v Barts & London NHS Trust*
Dismissal	
• by dismissing an employee for a discriminatory reason	*S39(2) Equality Act 2010*
• which will generally be for applying different criteria	*Smith v Safeway plc*

Justifications for sex discrimination	Case/statute
Discrimination can be lawful if there is an occupational requirement; the application of the requirement is a proportionate means of achieving a legitimate aim; and the person to whom the employer applies the requirement does not meet it or the employer has reasonable grounds for not being satisfied that the person meets it	*Schedule 9 Equality Act 2010*
Which may be where the job is done by one sex in order to preserve decency or privacy	*Sisley v Britannia Security Systems*

Discrimination on marital status or civil partnership	Case/statute
Direct discrimination	
• the person is treated less favourably than an unmarried person would be	*S11 Equality Act 2010*
• which could be a failure to promote	*Chief Constable of the Bedfordshire Constabulary v Graham*

Indirect discrimination	
• the claimant is subjected to a provision, criterion or practice which is discriminatory in relation to his or her marital status, which puts him or her at a disadvantage; and it cannot be shown to be a proportionate means of achieving a legitimate aim	*S19 Equality Act 2010*
• which may result from prejudiced assumptions	*Hurley v Mustoe*
Harassment	
• the claimant is subjected to unwanted conduct related to his or her marital status, with the purpose or effect of violating his or her dignity, or subjecting him or her to an intimidating, hostile, degrading, humiliating or offensive environment	*S26 Equality Act 2010*
Victimisation	
• the claimant was subjected to a detriment because he or she brought proceedings under the Act; or gave evidence or information in connection with proceedings or did anything else for the purposes of or in connection with the Act; or made an allegation (whether or not express) that his or her employer or another person has contravened the Act	*S27 Equality Act 2010*
Single people are not protected from discrimination	*Sun Alliance & London Insurance Co v Dudman*

SAMPLE ESSAY QUESTION

ESSAY Discuss the ways in which the Equality Act 2010 has improved the law on sex discrimination and the extent to which EU law has been instrumental in developing the law.

Explain the background to sex discrimination law

- UK introduced legislation firstly in the Equal Pay Act 1970 in advance of application for EU (then EC) membership.
- Sex discrimination first in Sex Discrimination Act 1975.
- EU Equal Treatment Directive 76/207 required equal treatment in conditions of employment including equal access to promotion, training and transfer.

Explain the basis of a claim under the Sex Discrimination Act

- Direct – where the woman was treated less favourably than a man would be.
- Indirect – where measure applied to both sexes but more difficult for the woman to comply with.
- Victimisation – suffering a detriment because of asserting a right under the Act.

Discuss the limitations under the 1975 Act

- Need for comparator of opposite sex for direct.
- Limited scope of indirect.
- Nothing on part-time although more women worked part-time.
- No provision for harassment – had to use s6(2)(b) being caused to suffer any other detriment.
- So could be defeated by claim of treatment being gender neutral and had to show actual detriment.
- Wide range of Genuine Occupational Requirements under the Act.
- Did not fully implement EU law – *Marshall*.

Explain the changes introduced in the Equality Act 2010

- Introduces protected characteristics – of which sex is one.
- Identifies and defines four types of prohibited conduct.
- Direct similar – less favourable treatment.
- But indirect is where there is a practice, provision or requirement which puts the person at a disadvantage because of their sex and it cannot be shown to be a proportionate means of achieving a legitimate aim.
- Introduces statutory definition of harassment – claimant is subjected to unwanted conduct related to his or her sex, with the purpose or effect of violating his or her dignity, or subjecting him or her to an intimidating, hostile, degrading humiliating or offensive environment.

- Victimisation is similar – claimant was subjected to a detriment because he or she brought proceedings under the Act; or gave evidence or information in connection with proceedings or did anything else for the purposes of or in connection with the Act; or made an allegation (whether or not express) that his or her employer or another person has contravened the Act.

Discuss whether there are any improvements
- Puts all protected characteristics in the same or similar framework.
- Indirect definition is broader than SDA definition and requires objective justification.
- Harassment claim based on statutory definition and does not involve the same hurdles.

Discuss the impact of EU law
- Required objective discrimination for different treatment.
- Introduced definition of harassment in Code of Practice.
- Court of Justice rulings on shortcomings in SDA.
- Following Amsterdam Treaty expanded scope of law.
- Revised Directive 76/207 in Recast Directive 2006/54.
- Together with Framework Directive 2000/78 resulted in Equality Act 2010.

REACH REASONED CONCLUSIONS

SUMMARY

- Laws concerning discrimination on grounds of sex were originally in the Sex Discrimination Act 1975.
- There was a further Act in 1986.
- Now sex is a protected characteristic under the Equality Act 2010.
- There are four ways in which discrimination could occur:
  - direct discrimination involves treating the person less favourably because of his or her sex than a person of the opposite sex would be treated;
  - indirect discrimination involves applying a provision, criterion or practice which is discriminatory because it puts the person at a disadvantage because of his or her sex in contrast to a person of the opposite sex and it is not a proportionate means of achieving a legitimate aim;
  - harassment involves unwanted conduct related to a person's sex, with the purpose or effect of violating his or her dignity, or subjecting him or her to an intimidating, hostile, degrading, humiliating or offensive environment;
  - victimisation is subjecting a person to a detriment because he or she has asserted any right under the Act for example taking action or seeking advice.
- Sexual discrimination could occur in employment in the recruitment process, during employment or in the conditions of employment or on dismissal.
- There are some lawful justifications for discrimination known as occupational requirements, one of these is the provision of personal and welfare services.
- Discrimination can also occur in relation to marital status or civil partnership in all four types of discrimination.
- But it is legal to discriminate against a person who is single.

Further reading

Emir, Astra, *Selwyn's Law of Employment 17th edition*. Oxford University Press, 2012, Chapter 4.
Pitt, Gwyneth, *Cases and Materials on Employment Law 3rd edition*. Pearson, 2008, Chapter 3.
Sargeant, Malcolm and Lewis, David, *Employment Law 6th edition*. Pearson, 2012, Chapter 5.

12

Protection from discrimination (3) racial discrimination

AIMS AND OBJECTIVES

After reading this chapter you should be able to:

- Understand the background to the law on discrimination on racial grounds in employment and its limitations prior to the Equality Act 2010
- Understand the definition of race under the Equality Act 2010
- Understand the different types of prohibited practices under the Equality Act 2010 as they relate to employees
- Understand the contexts in which discrimination on racial grounds can occur in employment
- Understand the nature of occupational requirements in relation to race
- Critically analyse the area
- Apply the law to factual situations and reach conclusions

12.1 The origins and aims of race discrimination law

Prior to 1965 discrimination on the grounds of a person's skin colour, race or nationality was not illegal. As early as 1930, a Dr A M Shah had complained to the Home Office that the Streatham Locarno dance hall had refused him admission on the grounds that he was Indian. The Home Office replied that, although it was sympathetic, there was nothing it could do.

During the 1950s the government encouraged immigration from what would now be called the Commonwealth to fill job vacancies in particular occupations. Many migrant workers from the Caribbean travelled to and settled in the UK. By the 1960s what came to be known as 'the colour bar' was an increasingly obvious injustice in British society. In fact in the 1960s colour prejudice and racism were commonplace and a daily part of life in certain areas of the country. Migrant workers were subjected to denial of services, colour bars, because of their colour, and intolerable housing conditions with what came to be known as 'Rachmanism' after Peter Rachman a notorious landlord of low grade housing. There were also race riots in some towns. At a later point migrant workers and their families also suffered the insult of Enoch Powell's so-called 'Rivers of Blood' speech, which was delivered to a Conservative Association meeting in Birmingham on 20 April 1968, Enoch Powell having been a minister in the government that encouraged migration to the UK in the 1950s.

It was obvious that something needed to be done and in 1965, the first Race Relations Act was passed outlawing certain aspects of racial discrimination and creating a Race Relations Board (RRB) to investigate complaints. The Act made it unlawful to refuse to serve a person, to have an unreasonable delay in serving someone or to overcharge someone, on the grounds of colour, race, or ethnic or national origins. The Act was limited in scope, its provisions were weak and it did little to curb discrimination. A further Act the Race Relations Act 1968 was then passed which extended the scope of the previous Act by including employment and housing. It also extended the powers of the Race Relations Board and set up the Community Relations Commission (CRC) to help enforce the new laws. Interestingly the 1968 Act was passed in the same year as the Commonwealth Immigration Act 1968, which actually tightened controls on new migrants. James Callaghan, the Home Secretary of the time who was responsible for introducing both Acts, considered that in conjunction they were a way of creating 'a society in which, although the government might control who came in, once they were in, they should be treated equally'.

The ineffectiveness of the Acts in reducing discrimination can be seen in case law of the time, not concerning employment but still relevant to the point. In *Ealing London Borough Council v Race Relations Board* [1972] AC 342 a Polish man who had fought in the Royal Air Force during the Second World War and had settled in the UK was refused a place on the council waiting list for council housing on the basis that he was not a British national. The House of Lords held that 'national origins' in the Act was not the same as nationality and the Council's actions were lawful. In *Charter v Race Relations Board* [1973] AC 868 a Sikh was refused membership of a Conservative Club because of his colour and his claim that this was discriminatory failed because as the then House of Lords stated the club's members were not 'a section of the public' as was required under the Race Relations Act 1968.

In another case *Dockers' Labour Club and Institute Ltd v Race Relations Board Respondents* [1976] AC 285 a similar 'colour bar' was upheld.

JUDGMENT

> Lord Diplock made the following observations: 'The arrival in this country within recent years of many immigrants from disparate and distant lands has brought a new dimension to the problem of the legal right to discriminate against the stranger. If everyone were rational and humane – or, for that matter, Christian – no legal sanction would be needed to prevent one man being treated by his fellow men less favourably than another simply upon the ground of his colour, race or ethnic or national origins. But in the field of domestic or social intercourse differentiation of treatment of individuals is unavoidable.'

The Race Relations Act 1976 replaced the earlier Acts. It was drafted in almost identical terms to the Sex Discrimination Act 1975 and made discrimination unlawful in employment, training, education, and the provision of goods and services. It also widened the meaning of discrimination to include victimisation, and it also replaced the Race Relations Board with the Commission for Racial Equality (CRE), a much stronger body with wider powers. Subsequent amendments have been made to the Act. Even so these three Acts did not do away with racism or discrimination. For instance the Lawrence inquiry of 1998 into the handling by the police of the investigation into the murder of Stephen Lawrence headed by Sir William Macpherson identified that there was institutional racism within the Metropolitan Police force.

12.2 The different types of racial discrimination

Race is now identified as a protected characteristic under section 4 of the Equality Act 2010. Section 9 defines who is included within this protected characteristic.

SECTION

'9
(1) Race includes (a) colour; (b) nationality; (c) ethnic or national origins.
(2) In relation to the protected characteristic of race –
 (a) a reference to a person who has a particular protected characteristic is a reference to a person of a particular racial group;
 (b) a reference to persons who share a protected characteristic is a reference to persons of the same racial group.
(3) A racial group is a group of persons defined by reference to race; and a reference to a person's racial group is a reference to a racial group into which the person falls.
(4) The fact that a racial group comprises two or more distinct racial groups does not prevent it from constituting a particular racial group.
(5) A Minister of the Crown may by order –
 (a) amend this section so as to provide for caste to be an aspect of race;
 (b) amend this Act so as to provide for an exception to a provision of this Act to apply, or not to apply, to caste or to apply, or not to apply, to caste in specified circumstances.'

So for the purposes of protection under the Equality Act 2010 race includes:

- colour
- nationality
- ethnic origin
- national origin.

Moreover according to section 9(4) a person from a mixed race background is also covered by the provisions

Under the previous Acts what constituted a racial group for the purposes of the legislation had proved controversial. Nationality and national origins were held to be different concepts, as can be seen in *Ealing London Borough Council v Race Relations Board* [1972] AC 342 in 12.1 above.

It has also been accepted by the courts that the term ethnic origin is quite a broad term much wider than race or national origin. In *Mandla v Dowell Lee* [1983] 2 AC 548, a case that actually concerned whether a school uniform requirement discriminated against a Sikh, the issue was whether Sikhs were a distinct ethnic origin. While the Court of Appeal held that they were not an ethnic group but a religious group, the then House of Lords held that they were indeed a distinct ethnic group, despite the unifying religion, because of their long history and distinct culture as a group.

JUDGMENT

Lord Fraser commented on what constituted an ethnic group: 'For a group to constitute an ethnic group ... it must ... regard itself, and be regarded by others, as a distinct community by virtue of certain characteristics.... The conditions which appear to me to be essential are ... (1) a long shared history ... (2) a cultural tradition of its own ... (3) either a common geographical origin, or descent from a small number of common ancestors ... (4) a common language ... (5) a common literature peculiar to the group ... (6) a common religion different from neighbouring groups ... (7) being a minority, or being an oppressed or a dominant group within a larger community.'

Again while there is a unifying religious aspect Jews also have been held to be a distinct ethnic group in *Seide v Gillette Industries* [1980] IRLR 427. In contrast Muslims were assumed not to be a distinct ethnic group in *Walker v Hussain* [1996] IRLR 11. Similarly Rastafarians have also been considered not to be a distinct ethnic group.

CASE EXAMPLE

Dawkins v Crown Suppliers (PSA) [1993] ICR 517

Dawkins had brought an action for discrimination because, while he had been offered a job as a van driver by Crown Suppliers, this was provisional on him getting his hair cut. Dawkins was a Rastafarian and in consequence had long dreadlocks. He claimed that he had been denied the job because of racial grounds and therefore had been discriminated against. The Court of Appeal dismissed his appeal, confirming the decision of the Employment Appeal Tribunal which had reversed the decision of the Tribunal. It held that Rastafarians were not a distinct ethnic group but a twentieth century religious sect.

One thing that links all of these groups is that they would now come under the Act since religion and belief is a protected characteristic.

Ethnic origin is not dependent on and is a different thing to nationality. In this way the Scottish Court of Session was able to hold that Scots are a distinct ethnic group in *BBC Scotland v Souster* [2001] IRLR 150.

JUDGMENT

Lord Cameron of Lochbroom observed: 'Looking to the terms of the Act of 1976 itself, there seems neither reason nor logic in the proposition for which the appellants contend, that the phrase "national origins" means no more than the nationality in the legal sense acquired by an individual at birth. Nor is it supported by any of the cases.'

Nor is ethnic origin absolutely dependent on language. In this way there was held to be no distinction between Welsh speaking Welsh and non-Welsh speaking Welsh and Welsh was a distinct ethnic origin in *Gwynedd County Council v Jones* [1986] ICR 833. In *Commission for Racial Equality v Dutton* [1989] IRLR 8 the Court of Appeal also confirmed gypsies as a distinct ethnic group.

12.2.1 Direct discrimination

Applying the full definition in Chapter 9.3.1 under section 13 Equality Act 2010 a person would be directly discriminated against because of their race if:

- he is treated less favourably than a person of a different colour, nationality, ethnic or national origins would be; and

- less favourable treatment can include segregating him from others.

Direct racial discrimination occurs in any situation where a person is treated less favourably because of his colour, nationality, ethnic or national origins.

CASE EXAMPLE

Owen & Briggs v James [1982] IRLR 502

A black applicant for a job was rejected even though she was better qualified, having a better shorthand speed, than the successful applicant, who was a white girl. It later emerged that the interviewer had said to the successful applicant 'why take on coloured girls when English girls are available'. The Court of Appeal was satisfied that the unsuccessful applicant had been treated less favourably because she was not white, and therefore had been directly discriminated against because of her colour.

As is clear from the definition, another type of direct discrimination is segregating the claimant because of his colour, nationality, ethnic or national origins.

CASE EXAMPLE

Pel Ltd v Modgill [1980] IRLR 142

Here the court was prepared to accept that it was not discrimination to develop an exclusively Asian night shift where it was at the wish of the workers. What would be direct discrimination by segregation would be to insist on a particular race of employees to work on a particular shift to prevent them from being in contact with the rest of the workforce.

It was always the case in the previous law that it could be direct discrimination even though the claimant was not the subject of the racial abuse. It appears that under the wording of section 13 this could still be the case.

CASE EXAMPLE

Showboat Entertainment Centre Ltd v Owens [1984] 1 WLR 384

A white employee was dismissed after refusing to operate a colour bar and not let young black men into an amusement arcade as directed by his employer. The reason for the less favourable treatment, the dismissal, was race. It was irrelevant that it was not to do with the race of the claimant. Similar decisions were reached in *Zarczynska v Levy* [1979] ICR 184 and *Weathersfield Ltd t/a Van & Truck Rentals v Sargent* [1999] IRLR 94.

There can also still be direct discrimination despite the fact that the discrimination occurred for a good motive rather than because of any overt racism. Motive is in fact irrelevant.

CASE EXAMPLE

R v Commission for Racial Equality ex parte Westminster City Council [1985] IRLR 426

Here a black man was given a temporary appointment as a refuse collector. However, it became apparent to the council that other employees objected to working with the man because of his race. The Council fearing that the other workers were about to take industrial action in opposition to the man's appointment withdrew the offer of employment. The motive for the Council's discrimination was irrelevant. The claimant had still been treated less favourably because of his race. It was held that the then Commission for Racial Equality could issue a non-discrimination notice to the employer. Without such enforcement the legislation would have been unworkable.

12.2.2 Indirect discrimination

Applying the full definition in Chapter 9.3.2 under section 19 Equality Act 2010 a person would be indirectly discriminated against because of their race if:

- he is subjected to a provision, criterion or practice which is discriminatory in relation to his colour, nationality, ethnic or national origins;
- which applies to all races but puts him at a disadvantage compared with persons of different colour, nationality, ethnic or national origins;
- it cannot be shown to be a proportionate means of achieving a legitimate aim.

This is somewhat different to the original definition of indirect discrimination under the Race Relations Act 1976. This stated that it would be indirect discrimination if a requirement or condition was applied, such that the proportion of people from one racial group who could comply was smaller than persons of another racial group, and it could not be justified, and was to the person's detriment. EU Directive 2000/43, the Race Directive, included a completely different definition of indirect discrimination which is implemented in the Equality Act 2010. The definition in the Equality Act section 19 is simpler and broader so earlier cases might now be decided differently.

Obviously there must be a provision or criterion or practice which the claimant is bound to comply with and which puts him at a disadvantage because of his colour, nationality, ethnic or national origins, and it must not be a proportionate means of achieving a legitimate aim to succeed in a claim.

CASE EXAMPLE

Meer v London Borough of Tower Hamlets [1988] IRLR 399

In a vacancy for head of a legal department the claimant was put on a 'long list' based on ten criteria for the post. He was then not given the job and complained that he had been discriminated against because the proportion of his racial group that could meet one of the criterion was less than would be the case for other racial groups. This criterion was past experience with the Council. The EAT held that in order to found a claim of indirect discrimination upon the basis of a selection criterion with a disproportionate impact, the criterion must be obligatory and operate as an absolute bar. In the case it was only one of ten criteria so there was no absolute requirement to comply with it.

Obviously there can also be no indirect discrimination if the provision or criterion or practice can be justified. In this case the discrimination would not in fact be because of colour, nationality, ethnic or national origins.

CASE EXAMPLE

Panesar v Nestlé & Co [1980] IRLR 64

A rule in a factory producing chocolate prohibited both beards and long hair. A Sikh employee complained that the rule discriminated against him since he was unable to comply with the rule because his religion required him to have both. The court acknowledged that the rule did discriminate indirectly since it was a condition applying to the whole workforce but having a disproportionate and detrimental effect on Sikhs. Nevertheless his claim still failed because the court accepted that there were valid health and safety and hygiene reasons for the rule and so it was justified.

12.2.3 Harassment

Race is one of the protected characteristics identified in section 26(5) Equality Act 2010 and therefore an action for harassment is possible.

Applying the full definition in Chapter 9.3.3 under section 26 Equality Act 2010 a person would suffer racial harassment if:

- he was subjected to unwanted conduct related to his colour, nationality, ethnic or national origins; and
- the conduct had the purpose or effect of violating his dignity, or subjecting him to an intimidating, hostile, degrading, humiliating or offensive environment.

Clearly the conduct prohibited in section 26 could cover a wide range of behaviour from verbal taunts to physical abuse. The case that follows is a classic example illustrating not only unwanted conduct but an astonishing illustration of a 'purpose or effect of violating his dignity, or subjecting him to an intimidating, hostile, degrading, humiliating or offensive environment'.

CASE EXAMPLE

Jones v Tower Boot Co Ltd [1997] IRLR 168

The claimant was a sixteen year old boy of mixed race who started work in a shoe factory as a last operative. From the very first day of his employment he was subjected to both verbal and physical racial abuse. Severe verbal abuse included being called 'chimp' and 'monkey'. Physical abuse included being whipped on his legs, having metal bolts thrown at his head and even being burnt with a hot screwdriver. He also at one point had a notice stuck on his back which read 'Chipmunks are go'. After four weeks of this treatment he could take no more and left claiming racial harassment (at that time under section 4(2) Race Relations Act 1976 – that his fellow employees had subjected him to a detriment because of his race – and under section 32(1), by failing to stop them, his employer was legally responsible). The employer argued that the actions of the boy's colleagues were not in the course of their employment since they were not authorised. Alternatively it argued that it had done everything in its power possible to stop the acts. That the abuse occurred was not in dispute. When the appeal reached the Court of Appeal the prime focus was whether the abuse had taken place in the course of employment. If it had not then the employer would not be responsible. The court held that common law principles of vicarious liability should not be used in such a way as to defeat the purposes of the legislation on racial equality and that the words 'in the course of employment' should be used in a way that laymen understood them. The employer was found liable.

JUDGMENT

Waite LJ concluded: 'It would be particularly wrong to allow racial harassment on the scale that was suffered by the complainant in this case at the hands of his workmates – treatment that was wounding both emotionally and physically – to slip through the net of employer responsibility by applying to it a common law principle evolved in another area of law to deal with vicarious liability for wrongdoing of a wholly different kind. To do so would seriously undermine the statutory scheme of the Discrimination Acts and flout the purposes which they were passed to achieve.'

Section 26(4) also identifies that, in order to decide whether the harassing conduct has the effect referred to in section 26(1)(b), that it has violated the claimant's dignity, or subjected him to an intimidating, hostile, degrading, humiliating or offensive environment, the court must also take into account:

- the claimant's perceptions; and
- the other circumstances of the case; and
- whether it was reasonable for the conduct to have the effect it had on the claimant.

12.2.4 Victimisation

Applying the full definition in Chapter 9.3.4 under section 27 Equality Act 2010 a person would have been victimised against because of their race if:

- he has been subjected to a detriment;
- because he has brought proceedings under the Act; or
- he has given evidence or information in connection with proceedings under the Act; or
- he has done anything else for the purposes of or in connection with the Act; or
- he has made an allegation (whether or not express) that his employer or another person has contravened the Act.

A claim for victimisation might be brought where the claimant has suffered a detriment in essence for asserting her or his statutory rights under the Act and this might be any of the above.

CASE EXAMPLE

Brown v TNT Express Worldwide (UK) Ltd [2001] ICR 182

An employee asked for time off work to see an adviser from the Commission for Racial Equality with regard to a discrimination claim that he was considering bringing. He was refused despite the fact that requests for time off for personal reasons were usually granted by his employer. He took the time off anyway and he was dismissed as a result. He had made a complaint of racial discrimination which was still outstanding at the time of his dismissal which was held to amount to victimisation.

The detriment does not have to be as extreme as dismissal. It could be disciplinary action of some kind but it could also come in a variety of other ways. However, the alleged victimisation would necessarily be because the claimant has done one of the four things in the section and not for any other reason.

CASE EXAMPLE

Chief Constable of West Yorkshire v Khan [2001] IRLR 830

A detective sergeant of Indian origin applied on several occasions over eleven years for a promotion to Detective Inspector without success. He eventually decided that this was because of his race and issued proceedings for discrimination against his Chief Constable. Before this had been heard he applied for a promotion with another police force. When his Chief Constable failed to provide him with a reference he claimed victimisation. His claim failed because the Chief Constable had only failed to provide a reference because he did not want to prejudice his position in the impending claim of discrimination.

JUDGMENT

Lord Nicholls commented: 'Employers acting honestly and reasonably, ought to be able to take steps to preserve their position in pending discrimination proceedings without laying themselves open to a charge of victimisation. This accords with the spirit and purpose of the Act.... An employer who conducts himself in this way is not doing so because of the fact that the complainant has brought discrimination proceedings. He is doing so because, currently and temporarily, he needs to take steps to preserve his position in the outstanding proceedings.'

ACTIVITY

Quick quiz

Consider which type of discrimination may have occurred in each of the following situations:

1. Klaus, a German migrant worker, is frequently subjected to Nazi salutes by fellow employees in the factory where he works. They also call him Kraut and often throw nuts and bolts at his head.
2. Sukhvinder, a Sikh, is distressed because his application for promotion to office manager has been rejected because a rule of the company prevents managerial staff from having either beards or long hair and he has both.
3. George, who is of Afro-Caribbean descent, wishes to apply for a teaching post in a public school. He has been told that his application will not be considered because the pupils are exclusively white.
4. Lasith, a Sri Lankan, has been subjected to racial taunts by fellow employees. He has told his manager about this on several occasions but his employer has failed to do anything to stop it. As a result he has approached a lawyer with a view to issuing discrimination proceedings. When his employer found out Lasith was given one month's notice of termination of his contract.

12.3 The situations in which racial discrimination is prohibited in employment

Section 39 Equality Act 2010 deals with discrimination in employment. The section makes the following provisions.

'39 Employees and applicants
(1) An employer (A) must not discriminate against a person (B) –
    (a) in the arrangements A makes for deciding to whom to offer employment;
    (b) as to the terms on which A offers B employment;
    (c) by not offering B employment.
(2) An employer (A) must not discriminate against an employee of A's (B) –
    (a) as to B's terms of employment;
    (b) in the way A affords B access, or by not affording B access, to opportunities for promotion, transfer or training or for receiving any other benefit, facility or service;
    (c) by dismissing B;
    (d) by subjecting B to any other detriment.'

There are clearly three points in relation to employment where discrimination could be a significant issue:

- in the recruitment and selection of staff;
- during employment;
- on termination of employment.

12.3.1 Recruitment and selection of staff

Applying the full definition from section 39(1) Equality Act 2010 an employer is not allowed to discriminate:

- in the way in which it decides who it will offer employment;
- in the terms on which the employment is offered;
- by not offering a person employment.

One thing that might indicate that the employer is discriminating in the way in which it decides who will be selected is the job advertisement.

CASE EXAMPLE

Cardiff Women's Aid v Hartup [1994] IRLR 390

A woman complained of discrimination on racial grounds, at that time under section 4(1)(a) Race Relations Act 1976 because of a job advertisement by a charity for a black or Asian information centre worker. She was not applying for the job but according to the Home Office's *Guide to the Race Relations Act* at the time it was not necessary. However, she failed because she had not actually been the victim of discrimination. The EAT distinguished between an 'act of discrimination' and an 'intention to discriminate'.

Similarly a person might bring an action where he has been refused employment or deliberately omitted from an offer of employment because of his colour, nationality, ethnic or national origin.

CASE EXAMPLE

Johnson v Timber Tailors (Midlands) Ltd [1978] IRLR 146

A black Jamaican applied for a job as a wood machinist. A manager of the employer told him that he would be contacted a few days after the interview to be informed how he had got on. After a week no one had contacted him so he rung the employer and was told that the job vacancy had in fact been filled. He then saw a further advertisement for the position for the post and again applied but was told again that the vacancy had been filled. When he then saw a further advertisement for the post and on contacting the employer was told again that the vacancy was filled, he brought an action for discrimination and succeeded.

12.3.2 During employment

Applying the full definition from section 39(2) Equality Act 2010 during employment an employer is not allowed to discriminate:

- by giving the claimant poorer terms than that of an employee of a different colour, nationality, ethnic or national origin;
- in the way that it provides opportunities for promotion, transfer, training or any other benefit, service or facility;
- by subjecting the claimant to any other detriment.

Clearly one area where discrimination on racial grounds could be most significant and most offensive is where a talented person is denied access to promotion purely because of her or his colour, nationality, ethnic or national origin.

CASE EXAMPLE

West Midlands Passenger Transport Executive v Singh [1988] ICR 614

The claimant, who was a Sikh, had worked as an inspector for the employer for more than eleven years. He applied for a promotion to one of thirteen senior inspector posts that were offered and his application was rejected. He brought a claim for discrimination. He then sought disclosure of the qualifications and experience and significantly the ethnicity of all of the fifty-five applicants for the posts. The employer agreed to disclose this but refused to provide the same information for all positions advertised in the same grade bands between 1983 when an equal opportunities policy had been implemented and the time of the claimant's application in 1985. In the appeal the court held that it is possible to have discovery of statistical evidence relating to the engagement and promotion of different ethnicity and race since this is how discrimination might be revealed. The information could be relevant in that first it might reveal that treatment of different races was an effective cause for them not receiving promotion; and second it might enable the employee to counter an argument put by an employer that it was operating an effective equal opportunities policy.

JUDGMENT

Balcombe LJ observed: 'The suitability of candidates can rarely be measured objectively; often subjective judgments will be made. If there is evidence of a high percentage rate of failure to achieve promotion at particular levels by members of a particular racial group, this may indicate that the real reason for refusal is a conscious or unconscious racial attitude which involves stereotyped assumptions about members of that group.'

Traditionally under the 1976 Act 'any other detriment' would have been the mechanism used to bring a claim for harassment such as that in *Jones v Tower Boot Co Ltd* [1997] IRLR 168 but that is now regulated by section 26 Equality Act 2010 (see 12.2.3 above).

12.3.3 On termination of employment

A discriminatory dismissal is identified also in section 39(2). Clearly any dismissal based on a person's race would be unacceptable. What a claimant would need to show of course is that the dismissal was for reasons of his colour, nationality, ethnic or national origins.

CASE EXAMPLE

Sidhu v Aerospace Composite Technology Ltd [2001] EWCA 183

Sidhu, a Sikh, had worked for the company since 1979 and had a good record. He was racially abused by three fellow employees and in fact assaulted by one of them on a works outing after his son had been taunted by other children because of his long hair. Sidhu had then picked up a plastic chair and waved it at his attacker. He did not hit him with it and witnesses agreed that it was an act of self-defence. The management heard about the incident and brought disciplinary proceedings against both men. They were dismissed, without any consideration of the mitigation in Sidh's case, because the company's disciplinary policy identified any form of violence in work as gross misconduct. Sidhu claimed that his dismissal was discriminatory. The tribunal upheld the dismissal but the EAT held that it was direct discrimination since the other employee's actions had been specifically racial in character and so there was no need to show whether a white employee would have been treated more favourably. The Court of Appeal reversed this decision on this very point. The employer's policy was clear and any employee would have been disciplined and dismissed in the same way.

JUDGMENT

Peter Gibson LJ explained the point: 'I of course accept that if discrimination is established, the fact that the discriminator did not act with a discriminatory motive or purpose does not negate that discrimination.... But the question here is whether discrimination has been established and on that question the policy applied by [Aerospace Composite Technology] is plainly of relevance. What the majority of the Tribunal were doing in the passages seized on by the EAT was to say that [Aerospace Composite Technology] was applying the policy. That does not show that the majority, impermissibly, were having regard to motive or intention in finding that an act of discrimination was not discrimination. Rather it showed that there was no less favourable treatment of Mr. Sidhu on racial grounds than other persons and so there was no discrimination.'

12.4 Lawful justifications for racial discrimination

Applying the full definition in Chapter 9.3.5 under schedule 9 Equality Act 2010 an employer will be able to justify the alleged discrimination when:

- there is an occupational requirement;
- the application of the requirement is a proportionate means of achieving a legitimate aim;
- the person to whom the employer applies the requirement does not meet it or the employer has reasonable grounds for not being satisfied that the person meets it.

The Race Relations Act 1976 in fact listed a small number of what at that time were referred to as 'genuine occupational qualifications'. It is possible that some of these will survive as occupational requirements.

Authenticity in entertainment

It would be logical to prevent a film director from being able to cast for a specific role from the specific race that the role demanded. This would be particularly true in the case of productions depicting real characters.

To preserve the ambience of places selling food and drink

Clearly this was aimed at restaurants being able legally to advertise and appoint people from particular racial groups to give authenticity to the style of restaurant.

The provision of personal or welfare services to particular racial groups

It is understandable that particular racial groups might feel more comfortable where the person providing the service was from the same racial background. This was certainly accepted under the old law.

CASE EXAMPLE

Tottenham Green Under Fives' Centre v Marshall (No 2) [1991] IRLR 162

A day centre for Afro-Caribbean children had a policy which sought to maintain an ethnic balance between its staff and the children in its care. As a result it produced an advertisement for a position which was stated to be open to Afro-Caribbean workers only. When this was challenged the court was prepared to accept that the centre could rely on a genuine occupational requirement under what was then s5 of the Race Relations Act 1976, of provision of welfare services to a particular racial group. A total of 84 per cent of the children in the centre were of Afro-Caribbean descent. The services needed to be performed personally and the appointed person being able to talk and read in the appropriate dialect was clearly beneficial to the children.

JUDGMENT

Wood J said: 'in construing section 5 it is important not to give too wide a construction, which would enable it to provide an excuse or cloak for undesirable discrimination; on the other hand where genuine attempts are being made to integrate ethnic groups into society, too narrow a construction might stifle such initiatives'.

However, the occupational requirement exists because of the personal nature of the work and the contact between the employee and the person requiring welfare services. It is unlikely that the defence can be used where there is no such context.

CASE EXAMPLE

London Borough of Lambeth v Commission for Racial Equality [1990] IRLR 231

A local council advertised for positions of group manager and assistant head of housing benefits making them available to Asian or Afro-Caribbean applicants only. The council tried to justify this on the basis over half of its tenants were from those racial groups and therefore employees needed to be sensitive to their needs. The Court of Appeal rejected this argument. The posts were managerial in character and the successful applicants would have little in the way of personal contact with the tenants. Therefore they could not claim that there was any provision of personal services.

The public service exemption under Article 45(4) TFEU

One other interesting possibility not in the Equality Act but which to an extent might justify discrimination on grounds of nationality or ethnic or national origins comes from EU law and is the public service exemption under Article 45(4) TFEU.

This allows Member States to restrict access to workers in public service employment on the ground of their nationality. The reasoning behind this provision is to allow Member States to protect sensitive information which might involve things like national security. However, it is not an unlimited restriction. In *Commission v Belgium (Re Public Employees)* 149/79 the ECJ interpreted this provision fairly narrowly, refusing to apply it to all public service and identifying that it only applied in respect of the exercise of civil authority or the security of the state, in essence in situations where the employee is called on to swear some form of oath of allegiance to the state. As a result in *Commission v France (Re French Nurses)* 307/84 the ECJ also identified that a Member State could not reserve posts for nationals in hospitals. In *Bleis v Ministere de l'Education* C-4/91 the same principle was applied in the case of teaching posts.

ACTIVITY

Quick quiz

Consider whether there may be a defence to a claim of discrimination in each of the following situations:

1. The post of personal secretary to the Chief of the General Staff of the armed services is restricted to British nationals only.
2. Fay runs sheltered accommodation for young Asian girls who have run away from home to avoid arranged marriages. Fay will not employ Asian women in the home because of the cultural pressure that they might put on the residents.
3. Danny is producing a film about the life of Nelson Mandela and is only auditioning black South African actors for the part.

ACTIVITY

Self-assessment questions

1. What defects were there in the Race Relations Act 1965?
2. What improvements were made in the Race Relations Act 1968?
3. How is race defined in the Equality Act?
4. According to Lord Fraser in *Mandla v Dowell Lee* what are the characteristics of an ethnic group?
5. What are the four different types of prohibited conduct identified in the Equality Act?
6. In what circumstances could discrimination based on race be justified?

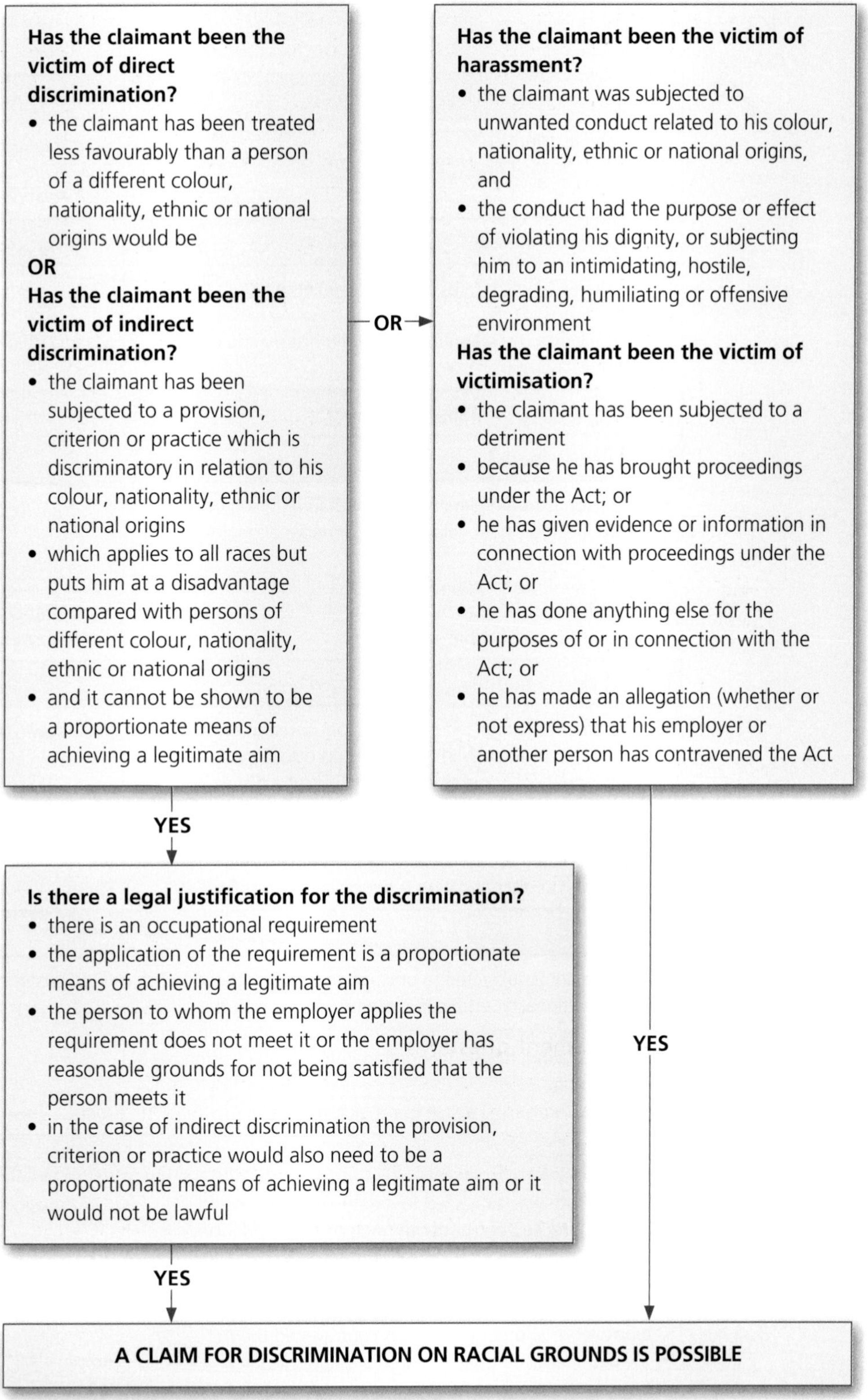

Has the claimant been the victim of direct discrimination?
- the claimant has been treated less favourably than a person of a different colour, nationality, ethnic or national origins would be

OR

Has the claimant been the victim of indirect discrimination?
- the claimant has been subjected to a provision, criterion or practice which is discriminatory in relation to his colour, nationality, ethnic or national origins
- which applies to all races but puts him at a disadvantage compared with persons of different colour, nationality, ethnic or national origins
- and it cannot be shown to be a proportionate means of achieving a legitimate aim

— OR →

Has the claimant been the victim of harassment?
- the claimant was subjected to unwanted conduct related to his colour, nationality, ethnic or national origins, and
- the conduct had the purpose or effect of violating his dignity, or subjecting him to an intimidating, hostile, degrading, humiliating or offensive environment

Has the claimant been the victim of victimisation?
- the claimant has been subjected to a detriment
- because he has brought proceedings under the Act; or
- he has given evidence or information in connection with proceedings under the Act; or
- he has done anything else for the purposes of or in connection with the Act; or
- he has made an allegation (whether or not express) that his employer or another person has contravened the Act

YES

Is there a legal justification for the discrimination?
- there is an occupational requirement
- the application of the requirement is a proportionate means of achieving a legitimate aim
- the person to whom the employer applies the requirement does not meet it or the employer has reasonable grounds for not being satisfied that the person meets it
- in the case of indirect discrimination the provision, criterion or practice would also need to be a proportionate means of achieving a legitimate aim or it would not be lawful

YES

YES

A CLAIM FOR DISCRIMINATION ON RACIAL GROUNDS IS POSSIBLE

Figure 12.1 Flow chart illustrating the requirements for a claim of discrimination on racial grounds

KEY FACTS

Origins	Case/statute
Developed in 1960s	*Race Relations Act 1965* *Race Relations Act 1968* *Race Relations Act 1976*

The definition of race	Case/statute
Race includes (a) colour, (b) nationality, (c) ethnic or national origins	*S9(1) Equality Act 2010*
• an ethnic group is identified by its long history and distinct culture as a group	*Mandla v Dowell Lee*

The different types of discrimination	Case/statute

Direct discrimination	
• the person is treated less favourably than a person of a different colour, nationality, ethnic or national origins would be	*S13 Equality Act 2010*
• which may include segregation	*Pel Ltd v Mogdill*
• and it does not have to be the claimant who is the subject of the racial discrimination	*Showboat Entertainment Centre Ltd v Owens*

Indirect discrimination	
• the claimant is subjected to a provision, criterion or practice which is discriminatory in relation to his colour, nationality, ethnic or national origins which puts him at a disadvantage compared with persons of different colour, nationality, ethnic or national origins and it cannot be shown to be a proportionate means of achieving a legitimate aim	*S19 Equality Act 2010*
• so there is no discrimination if the practice is justified	*Panesar v Nestlé & Co*

Harassment	
• the claimant is subjected to unwanted conduct related to his colour, nationality, ethnic or national origins, with the purpose or effect of violating his dignity, or subjecting him to an intimidating, hostile, degrading, humiliating or offensive environment	*S26 Equality Act 2010*
• can vary from verbal abuse to physical assaults	*Jones v Tower Boot Co Ltd*

Victimisation	
• the claimant was subjected to a detriment because he brought proceedings under the Act; or gave evidence or information in connection with proceedings or did anything else for the purposes of or in connection with the Act; or made an allegation (whether or not express) that his employer or another person has contravened the Act	*S27 Equality Act 2010*
• the detriment could be as extreme as a dismissal	*Brown v TNT Express Worldwide (UK) Ltd*
• but it must be because of one of the four things in the section and not another reason	*Chief Constable of West Yorkshire v Khan*

Race discrimination in employment	Case/statute
Recruitment and selection	
• could occur in the way who is offered employment is decided; or in the terms on which the employment is offered; or by not offering a person employment	*S39(1) Equality Act 2010*
• so could involve making the job only available to a certain racial group	*Cardiff Women's Aid v Hartup*
During employment	
• could occur by giving the claimant poorer terms than that of an employee of a different colour, nationality, ethnic or national origin; or in the way that opportunities for promotion, transfer, training or any other benefit, service or facility are provided; or by subjecting the claimant to any other detriment	*S39(2) Equality Act 2010*
• denying promotion because of race is an obvious example	*West Midlands Passenger Transport Executive v Singh*
Dismissal	
• by dismissing an employee for a discriminatory reason	*S39(2) Equality Act 2010*
• would not apply where the dismissal would apply regardless of race	*Sidhu v Aerospace Composite Technology Ltd*
Justifications for racial discrimination	**Case/statute**
Discrimination can be lawful if there is an occupational requirement, the application of the requirement is a proportionate means of achieving a legitimate aim, and the person to whom the employer applies the requirement does not meet it or the employer has reasonable grounds for not being satisfied that the person meets it	*Schedule 9 Equality Act 2010*
• one possible occupational requirement is the provision of personal or welfare services	*Tottenham Green Under Fives' Centre v Marshall (No 2)*
• but it must involve personal contact	*London Borough of Lambeth v Commission for Racial Equality*

SAMPLE ESSAY QUESTION

ESSAY Discuss the shortcomings of the early race discrimination law and how these have been overcome by the Equality Act 2010.

Explain the background to the early law
• Developed in the 1960s in the context of some overt racism.

- Race Relations Act 1965 and Race Relations Act 1968 were quite limited – extended to employment in 1968 Act.
- Judges took narrow view of what constituted ethnic background – and also defended colour bars in clubs.
- Race Relations Act 1976 was introduced on similar terms to Sex Discrimination Act.
- Race Relations Act 1976.

Explain the basis of a claim under the Race Relations Act 1976

- Direct – where the person was treated less favourably because of race.
- Indirect – where measure applied universally but more difficult for a person of a particular race to comply with.
- Victimisation – suffering a detriment because of asserting a right under the Act.

Discuss the 1976 Act

- Comparator needed for direct – but otherwise just has to be on grounds of race i.e. someone else's race.
- Limited scope of indirect.
- No provision for harassment – had to show detriment and less favourable treatment.
- Fairly wide range of GOQ's – not as wide as SDA.
- No protection for Muslims, Rastafarians, etc.

Explain the changes introduced in the Equality Act 2010

- Introduces protected characteristics – of which race is one.
- Identifies and defines four types of prohibited conduct.
- Direct similar – less favourable treatment.
- But indirect is where there is a practice, provision or requirement which puts the person at a

disadvantage because of their race and it cannot be shown to be a proportionate means of achieving a legitimate aim.

- Introduces statutory definition of harassment – claimant is subjected to unwanted conduct related to his or her race, with the purpose or effect of violating his or her dignity, or subjecting him or her to an intimidating, hostile, degrading humiliating or offensive environment.
- Victimisation is similar – claimant was subjected to a detriment because he or she brought proceedings under the Act; or gave evidence or information in connection with proceedings or did anything else for the purposes of or in connection with the Act; or made an allegation (whether or not express) that his or her employer or another person has contravened the Act.

Discuss whether these are improvements

- First Act very limited and did not cover employment and colour bars justified by courts.
- Second Act covered employment but definition of ethnic origin subject to narrow interpretations by courts.
- Puts all protected characteristics in the same or similar framework.
- Indirect definition is broader than RRA definition and requires objective justification so much better chance of bringing claim.
- Harassment claim based on statutory definition and does not involve the same hurdles as under RRA.
- Much more in line with EU law following Framework Directive.

REACH REASONED CONCLUSIONS

SUMMARY

- Laws concerning discrimination on racial grounds were as early as 1965 but the Act was limited in scope.
- There were subsequently Acts in 1968 and 1976.
- Now race is a protected characteristic under the Equality Act 2010.
- There are four ways in which discrimination could occur:
  - direct discrimination involves treating the person less favourably because of his colour, nationality, ethnic or national origin than a person of a different colour, nationality, ethnic or national origin would be treated;
  - indirect discrimination involves applying a provision, criterion or practice which is discriminatory because it puts the person at a disadvantage because of his colour, nationality, ethnic or national origin in contrast to a person of a different colour, nationality, ethnic or national origin and it is not a proportionate means of achieving a legitimate aim;
  - harassment involves unwanted conduct related to a person's colour, nationality, ethnic or national origins, with the purpose or effect of violating his dignity, or subjecting him to an intimidating, hostile, degrading, humiliating or offensive environment;
  - victimisation is subjecting a person to a detriment because he has asserted any right under the Act for example taking action or seeking advice.
- Racial discrimination could occur in employment in the recruitment process, during employment or in the conditions of employment or on dismissal.
- There are some lawful justifications for discrimination known as occupational requirements, one of these is the provision of personal and welfare services.

Further reading

Emir, Astra, *Selwyn's Law of Employment 17th edition*. Oxford University Press, 2012, Chapter 4.
Pitt, Gwyneth, *Cases and Materials on Employment Law 3rd edition*. Pearson, 2008, Chapter 2.
Sargeant, Malcolm and Lewis, David, *Employment Law 5th edition*. Pearson, 2010, Chapter 5.

13

Protection from discrimination (4) disability discrimination

AIMS AND OBJECTIVES

After reading this chapter you should be able to:

- Understand the background to disability discrimination in employment and its limitations prior to the Equality Act 2010
- Understand the definition of disability under the Equality Act 2010
- Understand the different types of prohibited practices under the Equality Act 2010 as they relate to disabled employees
- Understand the nature and scope of the duty to make reasonable adjustments for disabled employees
- Understand the processes for making claims for disability discrimination and the available remedies
- Critically analyse the area
- Apply the law to factual situations and reach conclusions

13.1 The origins of disability discrimination law

Disability discrimination is not in fact a new area of law. Rights for disabled employees were originally introduced as early as the Disabled Persons (Employment) Act 1944. However, the scope of this legislation was limited as were the rights gained under it. As a result it may actually have been of only quite marginal effectiveness to disabled employees.

The 1944 Act:

- operated only in respect of employers who employed more than twenty employees – so many small businesses were in fact exempt from the provisions of the Act;
- involved voluntary registration as a disabled person – this might not seem too onerous today when for instance we take great interest in the Paralympics but at the time there would have been a lot more stigma attached to disability than there is now;

- imposed quotas on employers – 3 per cent of the workforce should be disabled – in reality there was only very limited monitoring, enforcement or indeed observance of the provision;
- reserved certain occupations for the disabled.

The Act was ineffective, did little to actually advance employment opportunities for the disabled and was eventually repealed in the Disability Discrimination Act 1995. This Act was only introduced after a great deal of political ill will and following fourteen failed private member bills. In fact prior to the introduction of the Act there had been public criticism of the relevant minister by his own daughter who was also a campaigner for the disabled. The Act was a development from the previous law.

- It provided a definition of disability in section 1 'a physical or mental impairment which has a substantial long term effect on ability to carry out normal day-to-day activities' – although there was a restrictive list of affecting normal activities: 'mobility, manual dexterity, co-ordination, continence, ability to lift or carry, speech, hearing, eyesight, memory, ability to learn or understand, perception of dangers'.
- It provided some indications of what would amount to discrimination – although it made no provision for indirect discrimination.
- It introduced in section 6 the duty to make reasonable adjustments to accommodate disabled workers.

However, like the previous Act, it had a number of limitations:

- It only applied to employers with more than twenty employees – so provided no real opportunities for work with small sized enterprises which with the disintegration of large scale employment in the 1980s had expanded in proportion.
- It covered only employees not the self-employed.
- While the Act did create the National Disability Council this had none of the enforcement powers of the then Equal Opportunities Commission (EOC) and Commission for Racial Equality (CRE).
- The Act in any case was designed to come into force with the introduction of various regulations and this only happened slowly.
- It did nothing to support employees with progressive illnesses in the initial stages of their illness.
- In 2000 RADAR (a disability rights group) published a major report, 'Mind the Gap', which was very critical of the lack of support given in trying to move disabled people into work – it calculated that 2.8 million disabled people were on benefits at the time and further suggested that one million of those wanted to work and that 400,000 could enter work immediately if the major barriers were removed.

The Act has subsequently been replaced in the provisions relating to disability in the Equality Act 2010. This Act, which covers a wide range of areas of potential discrimination, resulted from the wide scale development of EU discrimination law in Framework Directive 2000/78.

The Act introduces the idea of protected characteristics, disability being one, and prohibited conduct. It also incorporates specific requirements for the different protected characteristics. In the case of disability this has involved some changes from the previous law to the definition of disability; to the meaning of discrimination and also to the duty to make adjustments. While the case law under the previous law provides some useful illustration of the concepts, it is also possible that some will be overruled in new case law on the Act.

The Minister is empowered to introduce regulations on conditions proscribed as an impairment, the circumstances in which an effect is considered to be long term, what is considered to be a long term adverse effect, on progressive disability, when a person is considered to no longer have a disability, and can also give guidance on these matters.

There are now three key aspects concerning disability under the Act:

- the definition of disability;
- the types of prohibited behaviour;
- the duty to make reasonable adjustments.

13.2 The Equality Act 2010 and the definition of disability

Introduction

The first requirement before a claim can be made for disability discrimination is that the employee is actually suffering from a disability. Disability is defined in section 6 as well as in schedule 1 of the Equality Act 2010.

SECTION

'6 Disability

(1) A person (P) has a disability if –
    (a) P has a physical or mental impairment, and
    (b) the impairment has a substantial and long-term adverse effect on P's ability to carry out normal day-to-day activities.'

It should be noted that the definition of disability for the purposes of the Equality Act are not necessarily the same as in other contexts, for instance for the purposes of claiming disability living allowance (DLA).

As a result of this definition there are three key aspects that need to be considered in any claim for disability discrimination:

- the claimant has – a physical or mental impairment;
- this impairment has – a substantial and long term adverse effect;
- the effect is – on his ability to carry out normal day-to-day activities.

13.2.1 Physical or mental impairment

First and foremost to qualify as a disability under the Act there has to be a genuine impairment. The impairment can be either physical or mental. Traditionally under the 1995 Act where the claimant was arguing a mental impairment he was required to show that this resulted from a clinically recognised psychiatric illness.

CASE EXAMPLE

McNicol v Balfour Beatty Rail Maintenance Ltd [2002] EWCA Civ 1074; [2002] IRLR 711

The claimant was employed as a trackman on the railways and claimed that a vehicle which he was driving went over a pothole, causing him to be jolted upwards towards the roof. As a result of this he was off work since that time. He claimed to have a continuing injury to his back and lower neck which rendered him disabled and that his employer failed to make any reasonable adjustments to his employment arrangements to ensure that he was not substantially disadvantaged. The tribunal rejected his claim since there was no evidence of any physical organic injury and nor did he introduce any evidence that his back pain was the result of a clinically well-recognised mental illness.

JUDGMENT

Mummery LJ observed: 'The approach of the tribunal should be that the term "impairment" in this context bears its ordinary and natural meaning. It is clear from Schedule 1 to the 1995 Act that impairment may result from an illness or it may consist of an illness, provided that, in the case of mental impairment, it must be a "clinically well-recognised illness".'

Similarly in *Goodwin v The Patent Office* [1999] IRLR 4 the tribunal had concluded that the claimant who suffered from paranoid schizophrenia and who was dismissed for bizarre behaviour did not suffer from a disability. The EAT disagreed and identified that in determining disability the World Health Organization (WHO) international classification of disease should be consulted. Cause was an issue since at that time the disability had to be caused by a clinically recognised illness. Now the presence of actual physical symptoms can be taken as evidence of an impairment without reference to any physical cause.

The cause of the impairment is not relevant as long as there are symptoms.

CASE EXAMPLE

College of Ripon and York St John v Hobbs [2002] IRLR 185

The claimant, a lecturer in cultural studies, brought a claim for disability discrimination against her employer. She had been on sick leave for thirteen months from March 1997 but had then returned to work. She had later had time off work with 'stress reaction' and complained of experiencing slow progressive muscle weakness and wasting. In her claim she did not specify whether this was a physical or mental impairment which she suffered. The issue for the appeal was whether she was disabled so the EAT had to consider the meaning of impairment. In concluding that she was indeed disabled the EAT said that if there are symptoms the cause of the symptoms is irrelevant.

JUDGMENT

Lindsay J explained: '[nothing] in the Act or the Guidance expressly require that the primary task of the ascertainment of the presence or absence of physical impairment has to, or is likely to, involve any distinctions, scrupulously to be observed, between an underlying fault, shortcoming or defect of or in the body on the one hand and evidence of the manifestations or effects thereof on the other. The Act contemplates (certainly in relation to mental impairment) that an impairment can be something that *results from* an illness as opposed to itself being the illness.... It can thus be cause or effect.'

Impairment does not include addictions for example to drink, drugs or tobacco or other like substances. However, it could be that the impairment results from or is aggravated by such addictions.

CASE EXAMPLE

Power v Panasonic UK Ltd [2003] IRLR 151

An area sales manager had the area that she was responsible for considerably enlarged. She then suffered from stress resulting in a lengthy sickness absence and she was then dismissed. It was accepted that during the sickness absence she was both depressed and drinking heavily. The tribunal was concerned with which came first the drinking or the depression in determining the cause of the impairment. The EAT said that it was not necessary to consider cause, merely whether there was an impairment within the meaning of the Act.

Some other conditions such as kleptomania, pyromania, sexual deviancy, exhibitionism are not impairments. Seasonal conditions such as hay fever are not impairments but other conditions which they aggravate could be. Progressive illnesses such as multiple sclerosis and HIV which were not covered by the previous law now can be impairments so this is a significant improvement. HIV is now deemed to be a disability from the point of diagnosis according to the Schedules to the Act.

Even if the adverse effect from the impairment ceases it can still be classed as an impairment for the purposes of the Act if it is likely to recur.

13.2.2 A substantial or long term effect

A substantial long term effect means that the impairment has lasted for twelve months or is likely to last for more than twelve months or is likely to last for the rest of the disabled worker's life.

CASE EXAMPLE

SCA Packaging v Boyle [2009] UKHL 37; [2009] IRLR 746

The claimant had a chronic problem with hoarseness due to nodules on her vocal cords. She had operations to remove them as well as speech therapy and had to undergo a strict regime of resting her voice. These were unsuccessful and a second operation was required followed by a similar regime to avoid them returning. She brought a claim for disability discrimination when her employer threatened to remove a partition which separated her workplace from a larger, noisier area. She was then made redundant and also claimed victimisation. The then House of Lords stated *in obiter* that in the absence of evidence to the contrary if an employee is following a regime on medical advice that without the treatment the impairment is likely to recur. Also if it had a substantial adverse effect on the employee's day-to-day activities before the treatment if it recurs then it is likely to have a substantial long term effect.

There may also be a substantial adverse effect if:

- measures are being taken to treat it or correct the impairment; and
- but for those measures the impairment would be likely to have such an effect.

In assessing whether there is a substantial adverse effect the tribunal will only take into account what the person cannot do or can only do with difficulty, not what he can do.

CASE EXAMPLE

Leonard v Southern Derbyshire Chamber of Commerce [2001] IRLR 19

The claimant, who was a claims adviser, suffered from clinical depression and had been on anti-depressants since 1995. She also suffered memory loss and then panic attacks after she was raped in 1997. She coped with the panic attacks by focusing on her work but had to work extra hard to achieve efficiency but still made errors. Her condition worsened and she went on long term sick leave and her brother then died. Her condition was stabilised with increases in her medication but she was eventually dismissed. The tribunal in questioning her considered that she was not suffering from substantial long term effects. The claimant felt that she was improving slowly and could cope with some tasks but she could not do by the time of the hearing what she was doing before she left work. The tribunal did not accept that she was disabled. The EAT held that just because the symptoms were kept under control through medication this did not mean that she was not suffering a substantial adverse effect on her day-to-day activities.

JUDGMENT

Nelson J explained: 'the Tribunal approached this matter incorrectly by focusing on ... what the Appellant was able to do instead of concentrating upon what she could not do or could only do with difficulty. As a consequence they came to an unreasonable conclusion on the facts in finding that the Appellant was not a disabled person within the meaning of the Act. We are clear that the Appellant's clinical depression amounted to a mental impairment which had a substantial adverse effect on her ability to carry out normal day to day activities ... as a result of her clinical depression with its consequent fatigue she is unable to sustain an activity over a reasonable period and because of the adverse effects of her reduced memory and powers of concentration she has difficulty in dealing with domestic tasks such as reading a recipe in a normal time span.'

However, in *Woodrup v London Borough of Southwark* [2003] IRLR 111 it was said that there was still a need to show there would be an adverse effect without the treatment. Here a claimant who suffered from a psychiatric disorder failed to show that withdrawal of psychotherapy would lead to a substantial adverse effect.

The substantial long term effect applies at the time of work not at the time of trial.

CASE EXAMPLE

Kapadia v Lambeth LBC [2000] IRLR 699

The employee claimed that he was disabled through reactive depression and that this affected his day-to-day activities. He was subjected to a medical examination by his employer's doctor but he then refused to authorise disclosure of the report to his employer. At the tribunal he was not affected because his symptoms were being controlled by medication. The employer argued that the employee had failed to prove that he was disabled and the tribunal agreed. The EAT disagreed, however, as it was sufficient that he could show an impairment, not that it had to be present during trial. It did comment that he should have disclosed the report. Clearly, the employee here would be disabled but for his medication so there was a substantial adverse effect because measures were being taken to treat the impairment and but for that medication the impairment would have had a substantial adverse effect.

13.2.3 Normal day-to-day activities

Under the previous law there was a requirement that the impairment affects normal activities only if it affects: mobility, manual dexterity, coordination, continence, ability to lift or carry, speech, hearing, eyesight, memory, ability to concentrate, learn or understand, perception of dangers. This was a long but not exhaustive list and has not been included in the definitions in the Equality Act 2010. As a result the effect now is not judged only on whether the disabled employee can do his job. Inevitably this is relevant if the duties that the disabled employee engages can be seen as day-to-day activities.

In situations where the impairment fluctuates but is worsened by conditions at work it was identified in *Cruickshank v VAW Motorcast Ltd* [2002] IRLR 24 that whether the impairment has a substantial and long term effect should be assessed against day-to-day activities both at work and at home.

Normal day-to-day activities does not generally apply to specialist skills required in certain employment but can relate to activities found across a range of employment.

CASE EXAMPLE

Chief Constable of Dumfries & Galloway v Adams [2009] IRLR 612

A police officer had a history of ME (the so-called chronic fatigue syndrome), a debilitating condition causing chronic fatigue. He complained when he suffered mobility problems while working on night shift in a treble two shift system involving two day shifts followed by two late shifts followed by two night shifts. In the last few hours of night shift he had difficulty walking and often needed to be driven home after his shift. He then had a period on days in another station and his condition improved. He then went to another station again on a shift system involving nights and his symptoms returned. The employer adjusted the claimant's shifts so he could miss the last few hours but his mobility problems persisted and were usually followed by sickness absence the following day. Eventually he was dismissed and claimed that this was discriminatory because of his disability. The EAT considered that night shift could be construed as a normal day-to-day activity because a number of employees are subject to such requirements. The police officer was held to be disabled for the purposes of the then Disability Discrimination Act 1995 and had been discriminated against because of his disability.

13.3 The Equality Act and the different types of discrimination

13.3.1 Discrimination arising from disability

By contrast to other protected characteristics where the employee is treated less favourably than a person not sharing their protected characteristic, in disability discrimination the reference is to unfavourable treatment so there is no need for a comparator. The definition of unfavourable treatment is in section 15 Equality Act 2010.

SECTION

'15
(1) A person (A) discriminates against a disabled person (B) if –
  (a) A treats B unfavourably because of something arising in consequence of B's disability, and
  (b) A cannot show that the treatment is a proportionate means of achieving a legitimate aim.
(2) Subsection (1) does not apply if A shows that A did not know, and could not reasonably have been expected to know, that B had the disability.'

This is a significant development since under the previous law a lack of an appropriate comparator could defeat a claim. In *London Borough of Lewisham v Malcolm* [2008] UKHL 43 the claimant who suffered from schizophrenia was being evicted because he had moved out of his council flat and sublet it. It was held that the appropriate comparator was an able-bodied person who had done the same. Since the council would still have evicted them in the circumstances there was no discrimination. Section 15 effectively reverses the decision.

There are two strands to section 15:

- the employer treats the disabled employee unfavourably because of something arising in consequence of the disability; and
- this treatment cannot be shown to be a proportionate means of achieving a legitimate aim.

CASE EXAMPLE

Farmiloe v Lane Group plc [2004] PIQR P22

A warehouse worker who suffered from psoriasis was unable to wear safety boots as a result, although there was a possibility of enforcement action by health and safety officials if he failed to wear them. The employer approached a number of different footwear manufacturers but none was able to produce suitable footwear for him. As there was no other suitable alternative work for him the employer had no choice but dismiss him. The EAT held that, although the dismissal was in effect because of his disability and was therefore discriminatory, the health and safety requirements overrode disability discrimination provisions. In any case the employer had gone to great lengths in an attempt to make reasonable adjustments (see 13.5 below) and so the dismissal was fair.

The change from treated less favourably (than an able-bodied comparator) to treated unfavourably obviously makes it easier to bring a claim, although there were instances in the previous law where courts interpreted the provision more liberally.

CASE EXAMPLE

British Sugar v Kirker [1998] IRLR 624

The claimant had a severe visual impairment from birth. He complained that he had suffered discrimination when he was, as he argued, unfairly selected for redundancy when the redundancy exercise was based on a number of physical attributes. For example he gained zero out of ten for promotion potential and zero out of ten for competence. Yet he had never been criticised for his performance and he was not even in a supervisory role. It was held that there need not be a like for like comparator and thus K was treated less favourably. The EAT was satisfied that he had been under marked because of his disability.

13.3.2 Direct discrimination

The definition of direct discrimination is straightforward and is found in section 13 Equality Act 2010.

SECTION

'13 Direct discrimination.
(1) A person (A) discriminates against another (B) if, because of a protected characteristic, A treats B less favourably than A treats or would treat others.'

So it would be direct discrimination where the employer treats the disabled employee less favourably because of his disability. This could be as simple as refusing to give the disabled person a job in the first place or for instance denying the disabled employee access to promotion purely because of the disability.

Section 13(3) also carries on to state that if the protected characteristic is disability, and B is not a disabled person, A does not discriminate against B only because A treats or would treat disabled persons more favourably than A treats B.

13.3.3 Indirect discrimination

This is an entirely new concept which was not present in the previous law under the Disability Discrimination Act 1995. As a result there is not really much in the way of case law. The law is clearly going to be beneficial to disabled employees and this area of the Act is likely to be the subject of many claims and judicial interpretation in the coming years.

Applying the full definition in Chapter 9.3.2 under section 19 Equality Act 2010 a person would be indirectly discriminated against because of their disability if:

- he is subjected to a provision, criterion or practice which is discriminatory in relation to his disability;

- which applies to able-bodied and disabled employees but puts him at a disadvantage compared with able-bodied employees;

- it cannot be shown to be a proportionate means of achieving a legitimate aim.

In *Farmiloe v Lane Group plc* [2004] PIQR P22 the claimant was subjected to a health and safety requirement, to wear safety boots. Because of the nature of the work the practice would have applied to disabled and able-bodied employees alike. However, because of the psoriasis from which the claimant suffered it put him at a disadvantage. However, because the safety requirement was a legal obligation the requirement was a proportionate means of achieving a legitimate aim.

13.3.4 Harassment

Applying the full definition in Chapter 9.3.3 under section 26 Equality Act 2010 a person would suffer harassment because of disability if:

- he was subjected to unwanted conduct related to his disability; and

- the conduct had the purpose or effect of violating his dignity, or subjecting him to an intimidating, hostile, degrading, humiliating or offensive environment.

13.3.5 Victimisation

Applying the full definition in Chapter 9.3.4 under section 27 Equality Act 2010 a person would have been victimised against because of his disability if:

- he has been subjected to a detriment;

- because he has brought proceedings under the Act; or

- he has given evidence or information in connection with proceedings under the Act; or

- he has done anything else for the purposes of or in connection with the Act; or he has made an allegation (whether or not express) that his employer or another person has contravened the Act.

13.3.6 Discrimination in employment

Applying the full definition from section 39(1) Equality Act 2010 an employer is not allowed to discriminate.

In selection and recruitment the discrimination could be:

- in the way in which it decides who it will offer employment;
- in the terms on which the employment is offered;
- by not offering a person employment.

CASE EXAMPLE

Kenny v Hampshire Constabulary [1999] IRLR 76

K suffered from cerebral palsy and needed assistance to go to the toilet. He was originally offered employment but this was then withdrawn when it was found that the necessary type of assistance was not available and would have to be provided by the employer. The offer was withdrawn and it was held that employers have no obligation to provide for personal needs (see also 13.5 below on the duty to make reasonable adjustments).

CASE EXAMPLE

London Borough of Hammersmith v Farnsworth [2000] IRLR 691

An applicant was offered employment subject to a satisfactory medical examination. He had a history of mental illness which was discovered by the occupational health physician. The occupational health physician advised the employer not to appoint the applicant and the employer acted on this advice. When this was challenged the employer tried to rely on a lack of knowledge of the full facts. The EAT held that they had imputed knowledge of the occupational health report.

During employment discrimination could occur:

- by giving the claimant poorer terms than that of an able-bodied employee;
- in the way that it provides opportunities for promotion, transfer, training or any other benefit, service or facility;
- by subjecting the claimant to any other detriment.

Discrimination could occur on dismissal:

- when the employee is dismissed because of the disability.

Farmiloe v Lane Group plc [2004] PIQR P22 is an example of a dismissal which arose because of the employee's disability, although of course it was justified because of the health and safety requirement.

Of course for section 39 to apply the claimant would have to be an employee (although the provisions under the Act apply not just to employees).

CASE EXAMPLE

Sheehan v Post Office Counters Ltd [1999] ICR 734 EAT

S entered into a contract with the Post Office to run a sub-post office. For his claim he needed to show that he was under the then s68(1) of the DDA of 'being under any contractual obligation to perform any work personally'. While he had some administrative duties most of the work was undertaken by other personnel and this role was not the dominant purpose of the contract which was in effect a franchise. On this basis he was not an employee of the Post Office and the Act could not apply.

Occupational requirements (schedule 9) are not discriminatory if they are a proportionate means of achieving a legitimate aim and the disabled person does not meet the requirement

13.4 The duty to make reasonable adjustments

Inevitably there are many features that may make it difficult for a disabled employee to cope with the work environment. On this basis the Equality Act includes a duty to make reasonable adjustments, as did the Disability Discrimination Act 1995 before it. The duty to make reasonable adjustments is now found in section 20 Equality Act 2010.

SECTION

'20 Duty to make adjustments

(2) The duty comprises the following three requirements.

(3) The first requirement is a requirement, where a provision, criterion or practice of A's puts a disabled person at a substantial disadvantage in relation to a relevant matter in comparison with persons who are not disabled, to take such steps as it is reasonable to have to take to avoid the disadvantage.

(4) The second requirement is a requirement, where a physical feature puts a disabled person at a substantial disadvantage in relation to a relevant matter in comparison with persons who are not disabled, to take such steps as it is reasonable to have to take to avoid the disadvantage.

(5) The third requirement is a requirement, where a disabled person would, but for the provision of an auxiliary aid, be put at a substantial disadvantage in relation to a relevant matter in comparison with persons who are not disabled, to take such steps as it is reasonable to have to take to provide the auxiliary aid.'

So there are three key aspects to the duty:

▨ Where some provision, criterion or practice puts a disabled employee at a substantial disadvantage compared to an able-bodied one the employer must take all reasonable steps to avoid the disadvantage (so for example in the case of a rule that in the event of fire employees could not use lifts to evacuate the building, this would be a good rule because employees could end up being trapped in lifts in a fire with no means of exit, but it could also discriminate against employees in wheelchairs as well as visually impaired employees unless alternative measures were taken for their evacuation from the building).

- Reasonable steps must be taken to avoid a disadvantage caused by a physical feature (so an obvious example here would be to ensure that all light switches are set low enough on walls for wheelchair users to reach them).
- Reasonable steps must be taken to provide auxiliary aids or services to avoid disadvantage (so an obvious example of this would be the provision of disabled toilets).

It is discrimination if the employer fails to comply with any of these requirements and the duty is owed also to job applicants.

It will clearly be a breach of the duty where the adjustments are simple to make and involve no cost or burden to the employer.

CASE EXAMPLE

Nottinghamshire County Council v Meikle [2004] EWCA Civ 859

A school teacher who suffered from deteriorating vision eventually lost the sight in one eye and had only limited vision in the other. She was given a timetable of classes that she needed to teach each day and found it difficult to read and asked for one in larger print but this was never done. She was also made to teach in a classroom some distance from her normal classroom and asked if this could be changed to make it easier to get to her class but again this did not happen. She also asked for extra preparation time for her classes again with no response. She had to take time off due to eye strain and eventually claimed constructive dismissal. It was held that the school had failed to make reasonable adjustments. There was nothing excessive or costly in the adjustments that had been asked for. She had therefore been unfairly dismissed.

Reasonable adjustments in any case can involve something as simple as moving the employer to a different department or part of the building or even swapping roles with another employee.

CASE EXAMPLE

Chief Constable of South Yorkshire Police v Jelic [2010] IRLR 744

A police officer developed chronic anxiety syndrome and had a period on sick leave with occupational stress. He returned to work on reduced duties but had further periods of sick leave with stress related illnesses. Doctors then advised that he should return to a non-confrontational role and that a normal operational role would cause him to suffer further illness and he was put in a post that involved very little face to face contact with the public. He then had no further sickness absence for three years. Following a restructure his role would in future involve operational duties which doctors argued was not appropriate and personnel was informed that the claimant fell under the provisions of the then Disability Discrimination Act but he was later retired on medical grounds. He claimed disability discrimination and that the employer had failed to make reasonable adjustments. The EAT identified that the employer was under an obligation to make reasonable adjustments and could have merely transferred him to a different role.

Further guidance on the second aspect of the duty, taking reasonable steps to avoid a disadvantage caused by a physical feature, is provided in sections 20(9) and 20(10).

SECTION

'(9) In relation to the second requirement, a reference in this section … to avoiding a substantial disadvantage includes a reference to –
  (a) removing the physical feature in question,
  (b) altering it, or
  (c) providing a reasonable means of avoiding it.
(10) A reference in this section … to a physical feature is a reference to –
  (a) a feature arising from the design or construction of a building,
  (b) a feature of an approach to, exit from or access to a building,
  (c) a fixture or fitting, or furniture, furnishings, materials, equipment or other chattels, in or on premises, or
  (d) any other physical element or quality.'

This may require adapting premises, modifying equipment or providing specialist facilities, but the duty is only to make 'reasonable' adjustments. So it could involve providing a disabled toilet but not necessarily assistance in going to the toilet.

CASE EXAMPLE

Kenny v Hampshire Constabulary [1999] IRLR 76

The claimant suffered from cerebral palsy and needed assistance to go to the toilet. He was originally offered employment but this was then withdrawn when it was found that the necessary type of assistance was not available and would have to be provided by the employer. The offer was withdrawn and a claim of discrimination was brought. The court held that, while employees may be under an obligation to make reasonable adjustments, this does not extend as far as having to provide for personal needs. The case was heard under the Disability Discrimination Act 1995 which was much more restrictive in the case of disability than the Equality Act 2010. However, the principle in the case probably survives the new Act. Employers are only obliged to make reasonable adjustments, providing in effect an additional employee as a kind of carer for Kenny would have been financially prohibitive.

In assessing what is reasonable the operational needs of the employer as well as the needs of other employees may be taken into account as well as the nature of the activities involved, the size of the employer's business and the financial implications of making the adjustment.

CASE EXAMPLE

O'Hanlon v Commissioner for HMRC [2007] IRLR 404

Over a four year period the claimant, who was employed by HMRC, had a total of 365 days' absence through sickness. Of these 320 related to her disability, depression, and the others were for unrelated illnesses. Because she complained of difficulty in getting to the office where she worked she was transferred to a different office. She then had further sickness absences. While she was paid during these sickness absences the length of them meant that she reduced to a lower rate of pay during some sickness absence. She claimed disability discrimination. The Court of Appeal held that it was not a reasonable adjustment to continue to pay full pay beyond the period indicated in the contract of employment.

Is the claimant disabled?
- the claimant has – a physical or mental impairment
- this impairment has – a substantial and long term adverse effect
- the effect is – on his ability to carry out normal day-to-day activities

YES | **YES**

Has the claimant been the victim of discrimination arising from disability?
- the employer treats the disabled employee unfavourably because of something arising in consequence of the disability; and
- this treatment cannot be shown to be a proportionate means of achieving a legitimate aim

OR

Has the claimant been the victim of direct discrimination?
- the employee has been treated less favourably than a person without a disability

Has the claimant been the victim of indirect discrimination?
- the claimant has been subjected to a provision, criterion or practice which is discriminatory in relation to his disability
- which applies to all employees but puts him at a disadvantage compared with persons
- and it cannot be shown to be a proportionate means of achieving a legitimate aim

─OR→

Has the claimant been the victim of harassment?
- the claimant was subjected to unwanted conduct related to his disability, and
- the conduct had the purpose or effect of violating his dignity, or subjecting him to an intimidating, hostile, degrading humiliating or offensive environment

OR

Has the claimant been the victim of victimisation?
- the claimant has been subjected to a detriment
- because he has brought proceedings under the Act; or
- he has given evidence or information in connection with proceedings under the Act; or
- he has done anything else for the purposes of or in connection with the Act; or
- he has made an allegation (whether or not express) that his employer or another person has contravened the Act

YES | **YES**

Is there a legal justification for the discrimination?
- there is an occupational requirement
- the application of the requirement is a proportionate means of achieving a legitimate aim
- the person to whom the employer applies the requirement does not meet it

Has the employer failed to make a reasonable adjustment?
- employer has not taken steps to remove a substantial disadvantage
- employer has not avoided a disadvantage caused by a physical feature
- employer has not provided auxiliary aids or services to avoid disadvantage

YES | **YES**

A CLAIM FOR DISCRIMINATION ON GROUNDS OF DISABILITY IS POSSIBLE

Figure 13.1 Flow chart illustrating the requirements for a claim of disability discrimination

JUDGMENT

Hooper LJ observed: 'The whole point of a comprehensive pay scale and scheme is that it applies to everyone, so that individual departures are likely to create justified resentment and require the exercise of discretion in both the legal and non-legal sense of the word. It is relevant that the aspect of the scheme with which we are concerned is not a term of a kind which every contract of employment has to contain. An employee who is absent for 6 months or more because of chronic illness, whether or not it amounts in law to a disability, might well find that at common law the contract has been frustrated by illness and that a consequent dismissal is held to be fair. A scheme which preserves the contractual relationship in such circumstances and assures first full pay and then half pay for extended periods of time therefore goes well beyond anything required by law. This is not of course to say that it is permissible, much less justified, to construct or administer such a scheme so that it operates arbitrarily to the disadvantage of the disabled. But any unplanned discriminatory impact may well be justified on the ground that such exceptions as can fairly be made in favour of disabled employees are already programmed into the scheme.'

An employer will also not be bound to make adjustments where the only adjustments that could be made are not practicable. In that instance the adjustments would not be reasonable adjustments to expect an employer to make.

CASE EXAMPLE

Secretary of State for Works and Pensions (Job Centre Plus) v Wilson [2010] UKEAT 0289 09 1902

The claimant who suffered from panic attacks and anxiety was redeployed to another office when the job centre in which she worked was closed. The old office was very near to her home and had involved no travel. She asked her employer to allow her to work from home and stated that this was the only basis on which she was prepared to work. She was dismissed after taking sick leave. The EAT, reversing the tribunal decision, upheld the dismissal. It was not practicable to allow the claimant to work from home and refusing to work at the new office made reasonable adjustments impossible.

JUDGMENT

The EAT concluded: 'the only conclusion which the Tribunal could have come to was that first, the adjustments offered by the Appellant were reasonable adjustments in the circumstances of this case and second, that it would not have been a reasonable adjustment for the Claimant to work at home. There was simply no evidence that that was a feasible option.'

ACTIVITY

Self-assessment questions

1. What defects were there in the Disabled Persons (Employment) Act 1944?
2. What defects were there in the Disability Discrimination Act 1995?
3. What are the key improvements in the Equality Act 2010?
4. How is disability defined in the Equality Act?
5. What is a substantial long term effect?

6. What are the four different types of prohibited conduct identified in the Equality Act?
7. What is the difference between discrimination arising from disability under section 15 and direct discrimination under section 13 Equality Act 2010?
8. In what circumstances could discrimination based on disability be justified?
9. How is making reasonable adjustments defined in the Act?
10. Is the employer always bound to make adjustments?

KEY FACTS

Origins	Case/statute
First provisions applied to employers with more than twenty employees, and required registration as disabled, and 3 per cent of employees to be disabled – but did little to advance employment opportunities for the disabled	*Disabled Persons (Employment) Act 1944*
Included definition of disability and introduced the duty to make reasonable adjustments and the National Disability Council – but this lacked powers, there was no indirect discrimination, small employers still exempt and did nothing for employees with progressive illness	*Disability Discrimination Act 1995*
EU social policy extended discrimination protections to disability	*Framework Directive 2000/78*
Enacted as a protected characteristic with rules on prohibited conduct	*Equality Act 2010*

The definition of disability	Case/statute
The claimant has – a physical or mental impairment • cause is irrelevant if there are actual symptoms	*S6 Equality Act 2010* *College of Ripon and York St John v Hobbs*
• does not include addictions but can include conditions that are caused or aggravated by them	*Power v Panasonic UK Ltd*
This impairment has – a substantial and long term adverse effect • one that has lasted for twelve months or is likely to last for more than twelve months or is likely to last for the rest of the disabled worker's life	*SCA Packaging v Boyle*
• the tribunal will only take into account what the person cannot do or can only do with difficulty, not what he can do	*Leonard v Southern Derbyshire Chamber of Commerce*
• substantial long term effect applies at the time of work not at the time of trial	*Kapadia v Lambeth LBC*
The effect is – on his ability to carry out normal day-to-day activities • does not generally apply to specialist skills required in certain employment but can relate to activities found across a range of employment	*Chief Constable of Dumfries & Galloway v Adams*

The Equality Act and the different types of discrimination	Case/statute
Discrimination arising from disability • the person is treated unfavourably because of his disability; and	*S15 Equality Act 2010*
• it cannot be shown to be a proportionate means of achieving a legitimate aim	*Farmiloe v Lane Group plc*

Direct discrimination	
• the person is treated less favourably because of his disability	*S13 Equality Act 2010* *S19 Equality Act 2010*
Indirect discrimination	
• the claimant is subjected to a provision, criterion or practice which is discriminatory in relation to his or her disability, which applies to able-bodied employees also but puts him or her at a disadvantage by comparison; and cannot be shown to be a proportionate means of achieving a legitimate aim	
Harassment	
• the claimant is subjected to unwanted conduct related to his or her disability, with the purpose or effect of violating his or her dignity, or subjecting him or her to an intimidating, hostile, degrading, humiliating or offensive environment	*S26 Equality Act 2010*
Victimisation	
• the claimant was subjected to a detriment because he or she brought proceedings under the Act; or gave evidence or information in connection with proceedings or did anything else for the purposes of or in connection with the Act; or made an allegation (whether or not express) that his or her employer or another person has contravened the Act	*S27 Equality Act 2010*
Discrimination in employment	
Recruitment and selection	
• could occur in the way who is offered employment is decided; or in the terms on which the employment is offered; or by not offering a person employment	*S39(1) Equality Act 2010* *London Borough of Hammersmith v Farnsworth*
During employment	
• could occur by giving the claimant poorer terms than that of an employee of the opposite sex; or in the way that opportunities for promotion, transfer, training or any other benefit, service or facility are provided; or by subjecting the claimant to any other detriment	*S39(2) Equality Act 2010*
Dismissal	
• by dismissing an employee for a discriminatory reason Occupational requirement is possible if it is a proportionate means of achieving a legitimate aim	*S39(2) Equality Act 2010*
The duty to make reasonable adjustments	**Case/statute**
The duty has three aspects: • where some provision, criterion or practice puts a disabled employee at a substantial disadvantage compared to an able-bodied one the employer must take all reasonable steps to avoid the disadvantage	*S20 Equality Act 2010*

- reasonable steps must be taken to avoid a disadvantage caused by a physical feature
- reasonable steps must be taken to provide auxiliary aids or services to avoid disadvantage

Failure to make simple cheap adjustments is a breach of the duty	*Nottinghamshire County Council v Meikle*
And an adjustment could be moving to another office or switching roles with another employee	*Chief Constable of South Yorkshire Police v Jelic*
But the duty only extends to reasonable adjustments	*Kenny v Hampshire Constabulary*
And operational needs, the needs of other employees and financial implications may be considered	*O'Hanlon v Commissioner for HMRC*
And there is no obligation to make adjustments that are not practicable	*Secretary of State for Works and Pensions (Job Centre Plus) v Wilson*

SAMPLE ESSAY QUESTION

ESSAY Discuss the ways in which the Equality Act 2010 has improved the previous law on disability discrimination.

Explain the scope of the Disabled Persons (Employment) Act 1944

- Only covered employers with more than twenty employees.
- Involved voluntary registration.
- Imposed quotas on employers – 3% of the workforce should be disabled.
- Reserved certain occupations for the disabled.

Discuss the limitations of the 1944 Act

- Small businesses were exempt so limited effect.
- Stigma attached to disability might discourage registration.
- There was only very limited monitoring, enforcement or observance of the quota provision.
- Did little to advance employment prospects of the disabled.

Explain the provisions of the Disability Discrimination Act 1995

- It provided a definition of disability: a physical or mental impairment which has a substantial long term effect on ability to carry out normal day-to-day activities.
- It provided some indications of what would amount to discrimination.
- It introduced the duty to make reasonable adjustments to accommodate disabled workers.

Discuss the limitations of the 1995 Act

- It was only introduced after fourteen failed private members bills and political ill will.
- It only applied to employers with more than twenty employees – so provided no real opportunities for work with small sized enterprises.
- It covered only employees not the self-employed.
- It created the National Disability Council but this had no enforcement powers.
- It was designed to come into force with the introduction of various regulations and this only happened slowly.
- It did nothing to support employees with progressive illnesses in the initial stages of their illness.
- There was a restrictive list of normal activities: 'mobility, manual dexterity, co-ordination, continence, ability to lift or carry, speech, hearing, eyesight, memory, ability to learn or understand, perception of dangers'.
- It made no provision for indirect discrimination.

Explain the provisions in the Equality Act 2010

- Disability is a protected characteristic.
- All prohibited conduct applies – discrimination arising because of disability, indirect discrimination, harassment and victimisation.
- There is also the duty to make reasonable adjustments.
- Applies to all aspects of employment – recruitment and selections, during employment and dismissal.

Discuss any improvements made by the 2010 Act

- Better definition of disability – covers people with progressive illnesses and no need to prove cause and no need to prove recognised clinical psychiatric illness for mental impairment.
- Removes requirement that the impairment affects normal activities only if it affects: mobility; manual dexterity, co-ordination; continence; ability to lift or carry, speech; hearing; eyesight; memory; ability to concentrate, learn or understand; perception of dangers.
- Effect now is not judged only on whether the disabled employee can do his job but also on ability to do other day-to-day activities.
- Discrimination arising from disability refers to unfavourable treatment rather than less favourable treatment in direct discrimination so need for a comparator.
- Introduces indirect discrimination for the first time.
- Expands on duty to make reasonable adjustments.

REACH REASONED CONCLUSIONS

SUMMARY

- There was little early law that actually protected people with a disability.

- The Disability Discrimination Act 1995 gave some limited rights but the law is more comprehensive following the passing of the Equality Act 2010 which gives statutory force to the EU Framework Directive 2000/78.

- The Act provides a full definition of disability – the claimant has a physical or mental impairment which has a substantial and long term adverse effect on his ability to carry out normal day-to-day activities.

- The Act identifies the different types of discrimination.

- Discrimination arising from disability occurs when the person is treated unfavourably because of his disability; and it cannot be shown to be a proportionate means of achieving a legitimate aim.

- Direct discrimination occurs when the person is treated less favourably because of his disability.

- Indirect discrimination occurs when the claimant is subjected to a provision, criterion or practice which is discriminatory in relation to his or her disability, which applies to able-bodied employees also but puts him or her at a disadvantage by comparison; and cannot be shown to be a proportionate means of achieving a legitimate aim.

- Harassment occurs when the claimant is subjected to unwanted conduct related to his or her disability, with the purpose or effect of violating his or her dignity, or subjecting him or her to an intimidating, hostile, degrading, humiliating or offensive environment.

- Victimisation occurs when the claimant is subjected to a detriment because he or she brought proceedings under the Act; or gave evidence or information in connection with proceedings or did anything else for the purposes of or in connection with the Act; or made an allegation (whether or not express) that his or her employer or another person has contravened the Act.

- Discrimination can occur in employment in recruitment and selection, during employment and on dismissal.

- It is possible for an employer to claim that there are occupational requirements if these are a proportionate means of achieving a legitimate aim.

- There is also a duty to make reasonable adjustments for a disabled employee: where some provision, criterion or practice puts a disabled employee at a substantial disadvantage compared to an able-bodied one the employer must take all reasonable steps to avoid the disadvantage; and reasonable steps have been taken to avoid a disadvantage caused by a physical feature; and reasonable steps have been taken to provide auxiliary aids or services to avoid disadvantage.

Further reading

Emir, Astra, *Selwyn's Law of Employment 17th edition*. Oxford University Press, 2012, Chapter 4.
Pitt, Gwyneth, *Cases and Materials on Employment Law 3rd edition*. Pearson, 2008, Chapter 3.
Sargeant, Malcolm and Lewis, David, *Employment Law 6th edition*. Pearson, 2012, Chapter 6.

14

Protection from discrimination (5) recent developments in discrimination law

AIMS AND OBJECTIVES

After reading this chapter you should be able to:

- Understand the background to discrimination in employment and its limitations prior to the Equality Act 2010
- Understand the protected characteristics of sexual orientation, gender reassignment, religion and belief, and age
- Understand the different types of discrimination identified as prohibited conduct in the 2010 Act and how they apply
- Understand how an occupational requirement might apply in each case
- Understand the protections available to part-time employees, employees on fixed-term contracts and agency workers
- Critically analyse the area
- Apply the law to factual situations and reach conclusions

14.1 The background to the wider development of discrimination law

Law on sex and race discrimination and to a lesser extent disability discrimination were well established in English law before the Framework Directive 2000/78 and the Race Directive 2000/43. The Framework Directive 2000/78 as a part of the social policies of the EU has significantly widened the scope of discrimination law by applying it to a wider range of characteristics, including now sexual orientation, gender reassignment, religion and belief, and age. All of these are now protected characteristics under the Equality Act 2010 and protected against different types of prohibited conduct identified in the Act. These four areas are considered in sections 14.2–14.5 below.

Sections 14.6–14.8 concern types of work rather than characteristics of the individual worker, part-time workers, fixed-term employees and agency workers. These are all areas where there was traditionally little if any legal protection and therefore ideal ways of employing workers while avoiding the obligations that employers would owe towards their workforce in a straightforward employment relationship. Again the significant feature characterising the development of employment protections in these areas is that it has been driven by EU directives. The significance of membership of the EU to protection against discrimination then cannot be exaggerated.

14.2 Sexual orientation

Traditionally there was no law protecting a person from discrimination on the basis of their sexual orientation. It was not covered in the Sex Discrimination Act 1975 or in the Equal Treatment Directive 76/207.

Sexual orientation was introduced in EU law in the Framework Directive 2000/78 and therefore required implementation into the law of Member States. In the UK this came in the Employment Equality (Sexual Orientation) Regulations 2003. Prior to the introduction of the Regulations there were attempts to bring claims using the Sex Discrimination Act 1975 and the then Equal Treatment Directive 76/207.

CASE EXAMPLE

Smith v Gardner Merchant Ltd [1996] IRLR 342

The claimant, a male homosexual, was employed as a barman and had a good work record. He was transferred following a reorganisation and was suspended following a complaint from a female member of staff that he had been abusive towards her and had flirted with male customers The claimant alleged that they had a bad relationship because of her attitude towards his homosexuality and because the female used drugs at work making her incapable of doing her duties. The claimant was then dismissed because of his threatening and aggressive behaviour which the company saw as gross misconduct. He brought an action for sex discrimination under the then Sex Discrimination Act 1975 on the basis that his female colleague's allegations would not have been made against a gay woman, that the disciplinary process was discriminatory because his employers believed the woman but not him and he also claimed sexual harassment. The EAT ([1996] IRLR 342) held that, because any discriminatory treatment was based on his sexual orientation and this was not covered by the Sex Discrimination Act 1975 he could not claim that he had been discriminated against on grounds of sex. The later appeal in the Court of Appeal was heard after the case of Grant v South West Trains [1998] IRLR 206 and was influenced by the statements made by the ECJ in that case (see below).

The attitude of the courts was that the Sex Discrimination Act 1975 did not cover sexual orientation and neither did the then Equal Treatment Directive 76/207.

CASE EXAMPLE

R v Ministry of Defence, ex parte Smith [1996] IRLR 100

The policy of the Ministry of Defence at that time was that homosexuality was incompatible with military life. As a result it was also a policy that when employees were found to be gay they would be dismissed. One soldier who had been dismissed because of his homosexuality complained that the policy was a breach of the Equal Treatment Directive 76/207. The Court of Appeal disagreed.

JUDGMENT

Sir Thomas Bingham MR commented: 'I find nothing whatever in the Treaty of Rome or in the Equal Treatment Directive which suggests that the draftsmen of those instruments were addressing their minds in any way whatever to problems of discrimination on grounds of sexual orientation. Had it been intended to regulate discrimination on that ground it could easily have been done, but to my mind it plainly was not.'

It was also the case that the ECJ at that time failed to identify that discrimination on the basis of sexual orientation fell within the scope of EU (then EC) law.

CASE EXAMPLE

Grant v South West Trains [1998] IRLR 206

The claimant argued that the policy of her employer to provide travel concessions to spouses and to 'one common law opposite sex spouse of staff ... subject to a statutory declaration being made that a meaningful relationship has existed for a period of two years or more' was discriminatory since the travel concession was denied to her lesbian partner when it was available to an unmarried partner in a heterosexual relationship. The ECJ identified that same sex relationships did not have to be treated the same as heterosexual relationships.

JUDGMENT

In answering the question put in the reference the court concluded: 'The refusal by an employer to allow travel concessions to the person of the same sex with whom a worker has a stable relationship, where such concessions are allowed to a worker's spouse or to the person of the opposite sex with whom a worker has a stable relationship outside marriage, does not constitute discrimination prohibited by [Article 157 TFEU] or Council Directive 75/117 [now in the Recast Directive 2006/54] on the approximation of the laws of the Member States relating to the application of the principle of equal pay for men and women.'

This then influences the view taken by the Court of Appeal in *Smith v Gardner Merchant Ltd* [1999] ICR 134 of who the comparator is when a claim under sex discrimination involves a gay person.

JUDGMENT

Ward LJ explained: 'One can test the matter this way: if an employer is willing to accept female employees without a university degree, but will not accept male employees for the same job without it, the proper comparator, when unsuccessful male applicant for employment makes his complaint under Section 1 [Sex Discrimination Act 1975], must be a female employee without a university degree. The lack of qualification is the personal characteristic of the applicant which must be regarded as the "relevant circumstance" for the purpose of making the comparison required.... It can be no different if the relevant personal characteristic of the complainant happens to be homosexuality. Accordingly I find that for this part of the case the comparator is a homosexual woman.'

Sir Christopher Slade then explained: 'the only proper way for the Tribunal to compare like with like will be to compare the treatment which [the female employee] directed to the [homosexual male] appellant with the treatment she would have directed to a female homosexual.

If the facts were to show that she had a rooted aversion to homosexuals of either sex and that she would have subjected a female homosexual to the like harassment, the appellant's claim under this head would inevitably fail because no discrimination under section 1(1)(a) [Sex Discrimination Act 1975] would have been established. In my judgment the appellant's only hope of success under this head will lie in satisfying the Tribunal that the harassment occurred because he was a man with a particular relevant personal characteristic rather than a woman with the same relevant characteristic. The relevant characteristic in the present case happens to be homosexuality.'

EU law in the shape of the Framework Directive 2000/78 first introduced sexual orientation as an area that could be protected from discrimination. The UK implemented the directive in the Employment Equality (Sexual Orientation) Regulations 2003 which covered the four types of discrimination, direct discrimination, indirect discrimination, harassment and victimisation. The actual sexual orientation of a claimant is not necessarily relevant to a claim.

CASE EXAMPLE

English v Thomas Sanderson Blinds [2008] EWCA Civ 1421; [2009] IRLR 206

The claimant was subjected by four colleagues at work to harassment regarding his perceived sexual orientation. A colleague had discovered that he had been to a boarding school and lived in Brighton, and so he was called 'faggot', and other lurid comments about him were made in a magazine produced internally within the company. This drove him to leaving the job. In fact he was a heterosexual married man with three teenage children and his fellow employees knew that he was not gay. The tribunal and the EAT both felt that the Regulations did not apply. The Court of Appeal held that he was nevertheless being treated as though he was gay and therefore his perceived sexual orientation was relevant.

JUDGMENT

Lawrence Collins LJ observed: 'there is nothing … to require the court in this type of case to enquire whether the maker of offensive homophobic statements actually thought that the victim was homosexual'.

Sexual orientation is now a protected characteristic under section 4 of the Equality Act 2010. Section 12 defines who is included within this protected characteristic.

SECTION

'12 Sexual orientation
(1) Sexual orientation means a person's sexual orientation towards –
   (a) persons of the same sex,
   (b) persons of the opposite sex, or
   (c) persons of either sex.
(2) In relation to the protected characteristic of sexual orientation –
   (a) a reference to a person who has a particular protected characteristic is a reference to a person who is of a particular sexual orientation;
   (b) a reference to persons who share a protected characteristic is a reference to persons who are of the same sexual orientation.'

Prohibited conduct

All four types of prohibited conduct apply to the protected characteristic of sexual orientation.

In the case of *direct discrimination*, under section 13 Equality Act 2010 a person would be directly discriminated against because of their sexual orientation if he or she is treated less favourably than a person of a different sexual orientation would be. It could also be because of their perceived sexual orientation or because they associate with gay people.

CASE EXAMPLE

Reaney v Hereford Diocesan Board of Finance [2007] ET 1602844

The claimant was a homosexual who applied for a job with the church as a youth worker. At the interview the bishop questioned him about his sexuality. He assured the bishop that he was not currently in a relationship and if he was given the job he would not become engaged in a sexual relationship. Although the claimant was the most suitable candidate the bishop still turned him down. The bishop was not so much concerned about the homosexuality but did not think the claimant would remain celibate and this would conflict with the religious principle that sex outside marriage is wrong. The tribunal held that the refusal to offer him the job was direct discrimination on grounds of sexual orientation and rejected the argument that an occupational requirement applied.

In the case of *indirect discrimination* under section 19 Equality Act 2010 a person would be indirectly discriminated against because of sexual orientation if:

- he is subjected to a provision, criterion or practice which is discriminatory in relation to sexual orientation;
- which applies to any sexual orientation but it puts him or her at a disadvantage;
- and it cannot be shown to be a proportionate means of achieving a legitimate aim.

A claim for *harassment* is also possible which under section 26 Equality Act 2010 would occur if a person:

- was subjected to unwanted conduct related to his or her sexual orientation, and
- the conduct had the purpose or effect of violating his or her dignity, or subjecting him or her to an intimidating, hostile, degrading, humiliating or offensive environment.

CASE EXAMPLE

Grant v HM Land Registry [2011] EWCA Civ 769

The claimant, a male homosexual worked for the Land Registry in Lytham where he had revealed his homosexuality to colleagues. He was promoted to a post in Coventry where he did not initially reveal his homosexuality but wanted to wait until he felt comfortable in doing so. His line manager then told fellow employees that he was gay, made homophobic remarks and gestures to him and was uncooperative regarding the use of fleet cars where she readily made them available to heterosexual colleagues. The tribunal found that there was both direct discrimination and harassment on grounds of sexual orientation but the EAT differed. The Court of Appeal dismissed the claimant's appeal on the basis that the claimant had already revealed that he was gay to his colleagues at Lytham.

A claim of *victimisation* is also possible under section 27 Equality Act 2010 if the person:

* has been subjected to a detriment;
* because he has brought proceedings under the Act; or
* he has given evidence or information in connection with proceedings under the Act; or
* he has done anything else for the purposes of or in connection with the Act; or
* he has made an allegation (whether or not express) that his employer or another person has contravened the Act.

Discrimination in employment

Sexual orientation is also covered by section 39 Equality Act 2010 so a complaint can be made concerning discrimination in the context of employment. Clearly discrimination might occur in employment:

* in selection and recruitment – the way in which the employer decides who it will offer employment, in the terms on which the employment is offered or by not offering a person employment because of their sexual orientation; or
* during employment – by giving the claimant poorer terms than that of an employee of a different sexual orientation, or in access to opportunities for promotion, transfer, training or any other benefit, service or facility, or by subjecting the claimant to any other detriment because of his or her sexual orientation;
* on dismissal if this is because of the person's sexual orientation.

It is also possible that there could be an occupational requirement. One would be where the nature of the employment is such that requiring a person of a particular sexual orientation is a proportionate means of achieving a legitimate aim. A second is where there is a requirement of a particular sexual orientation to comply with specific religious doctrines. This was what was being argued in *Reaney v Hereford Diocesan Board of Finance* [2007] ET 1602844 above. The requirement to abstain from sexual behaviour was to comply with the doctrines of the Church of England and it was also to avoid conflict with the strongly held religious convictions of a significant number of the religion's followers. However, the tribunal held that the bishop had not been reasonable when he did not believe that the claimant could meet the requirement which was why the occupational requirement defence was not available.

ACTIVITY

Self-assessment questions

1. What obvious legal rights were originally denied to gay couples?
2. What problems were there in trying to use the Sex Discrimination Act 1975 to bring a claim?
3. To what extent did EU law differ?
4. How did the ECJ explain the position in relation to the Equal Treatment Directive 76/207?
5. How did the Framework Directive 2000/78 change the position?
6. What is significant about the case of *English v Thomas Sanderson Blinds*?
7. How does the Equality Act 2010 define sexual orientation?
8. Which types of prohibited conduct apply to sexual orientation?
9. On what basis can discrimination on the basis of sexual orientation be justified?

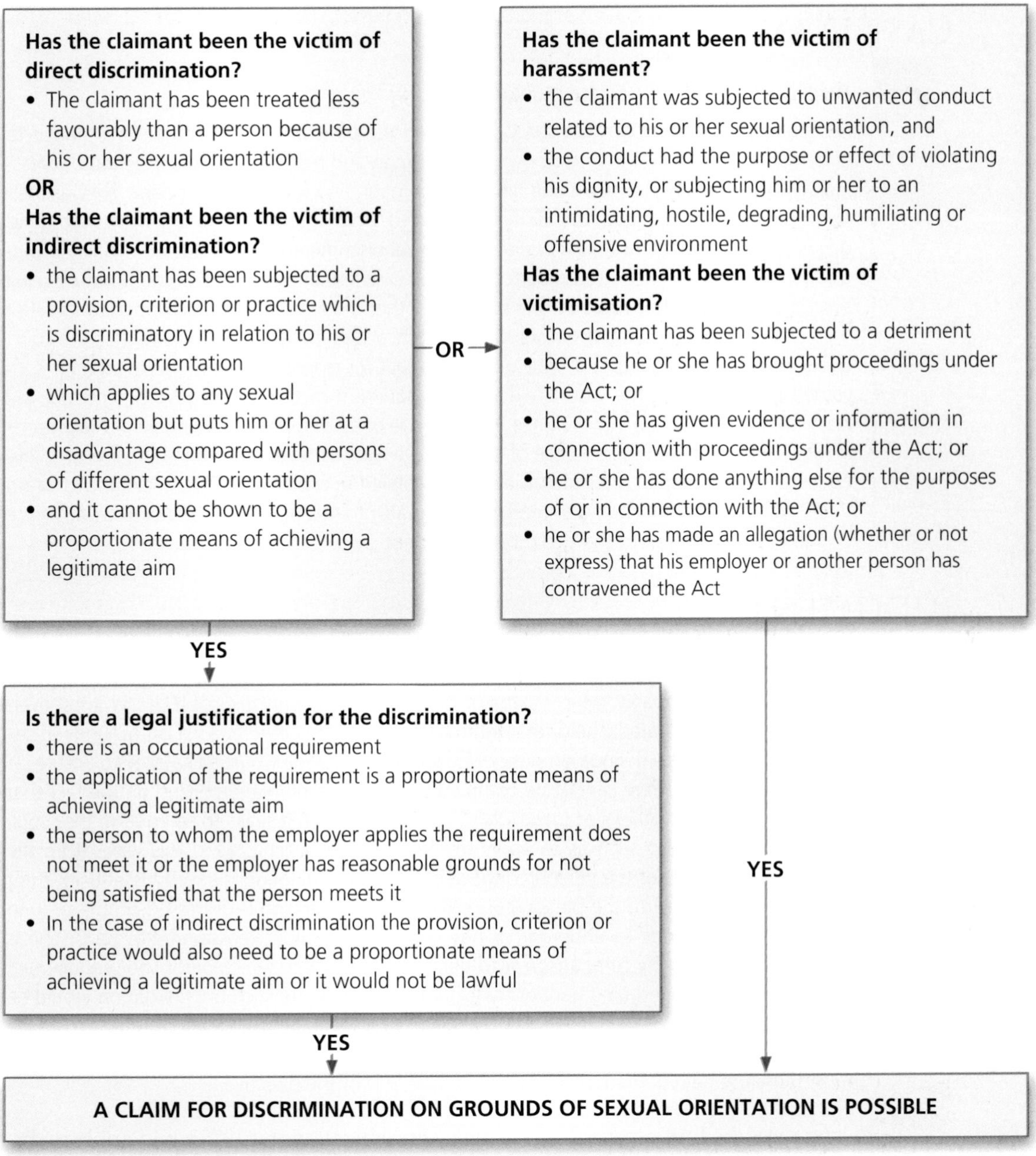

Has the claimant been the victim of direct discrimination?
- The claimant has been treated less favourably than a person because of his or her sexual orientation

OR

Has the claimant been the victim of indirect discrimination?
- the claimant has been subjected to a provision, criterion or practice which is discriminatory in relation to his or her sexual orientation
- which applies to any sexual orientation but puts him or her at a disadvantage compared with persons of different sexual orientation
- and it cannot be shown to be a proportionate means of achieving a legitimate aim

→ OR →

Has the claimant been the victim of harassment?
- the claimant was subjected to unwanted conduct related to his or her sexual orientation, and
- the conduct had the purpose or effect of violating his dignity, or subjecting him or her to an intimidating, hostile, degrading, humiliating or offensive environment

Has the claimant been the victim of victimisation?
- the claimant has been subjected to a detriment
- because he or she has brought proceedings under the Act; or
- he or she has given evidence or information in connection with proceedings under the Act; or
- he or she has done anything else for the purposes of or in connection with the Act; or
- he or she has made an allegation (whether or not express) that his employer or another person has contravened the Act

YES ↓

Is there a legal justification for the discrimination?
- there is an occupational requirement
- the application of the requirement is a proportionate means of achieving a legitimate aim
- the person to whom the employer applies the requirement does not meet it or the employer has reasonable grounds for not being satisfied that the person meets it
- In the case of indirect discrimination the provision, criterion or practice would also need to be a proportionate means of achieving a legitimate aim or it would not be lawful

YES

YES ↓

A CLAIM FOR DISCRIMINATION ON GROUNDS OF SEXUAL ORIENTATION IS POSSIBLE

Figure 14.1 Flow chart illustrating the requirements for a claim of discrimination on grounds of sexual orientation

14.3 Gender reassignment

Traditionally there was no protection against discrimination for transsexuals, people undergoing medical processes to change their original biological sex. In fact the original law was that the person retained the same sex in law regardless of whether they had gone through gender reassignment. This seemed quite unjust in the case of the most ambiguous instances of hermaphroditism. Another consequence of the law of course was that those who had undergone gender reassignment would be unable to marry.

There were cases where courts or tribunals had to consider the issue.

P v S and Cornwall CC [1996] IRLR 347

A male employee at a Cornwall college informed the Director of Studies that he intended to undergo 'gender reassignment' to become a woman and that this involved a period of dressing and behaving like a woman and ultimately an operation for a full sex change. He was then dismissed and argued that the dismissal resulted from informing management about his gender reassignment and that was unlawful sexual discrimination. Management claimed that the dismissal was in fact a redundancy. The Sex Discrimination Act 1975 could not be used since it only applied to people of one sex or the other. As a result P argued under EU law that there was a breach of Directive 76/207. A reference was made to the question for the court being whether dismissal of a transsexual was in fact for reasons of gender as in effect it concerned both genders. The Court rejected the argument of the British government that the dismissal was not discriminatory since it could have equally applied to a female or male transsexual. It identified that the purpose of the Directive was to prevent discrimination and promote equality, a fundamental principle of law to be applied universally. The transsexual was being discriminated against by being treated less favourably than a person of the sex to whom he or she had belonged prior to the gender reassignment.

JUDGMENT

In its judgment the ECJ explained: 'the directive is simply the expression, in the relevant field, of the principle of equality, which is one of the fundamental principles of [EU] law. Moreover, as the Court has repeatedly held, the right not to be discriminated against on grounds of sex is one of the fundamental human rights whose observance the Court has a duty to ensure … the scope of the directive cannot be confined simply to discrimination based on the fact that a person is of one or other sex. In view of … the rights which it seeks to safeguard, the scope of the directive is also such as to apply to discrimination arising, as in this case, from the gender reassignment of the person concerned. Such discrimination is based, essentially if not exclusively, on the sex of the person concerned. Where a person is dismissed on the ground that he or she intends to undergo, or has undergone, gender reassignment, he or she is treated unfavourably by comparison with persons of the sex to which he or she was deemed to belong before undergoing gender reassignment. To tolerate such discrimination would be tantamount, as regards such a person, to a failure to respect the dignity and freedom to which he or she is entitled, and which the Court has a duty to safeguard. Dismissal of such a person must therefore be regarded as contrary to Article 5(1) of the directive.'

In later cases the EAT accepted that the Sex Discrimination Act 1975 could apply to discrimination on the basis of a person's gender reassignment.

CASE EXAMPLE

Chessington World of Adventure v Reed [1997] IRLR 556

A male employee, a rides technician, announced his intention to change gender and was then subjected to prolonged and serious harassment by some male colleagues. This included stealing her tools and coffee mugs, refusal to work with her or assist her with heavy lifting, verbal abuse, defacement of her clothing and other property with lipstick, tampering with her car and motorbike, leaving tampons and sanitary towels on her work bench, leaving a replica coffin inscribed with her name and the letters 'RIP' on her workbench, and telling her that colleagues had saved £100 to be paid to the person who either injured her or got her dismissed. No disciplinary action was taken against the men harassing the claimant and she was given no support. After she attempted suicide the employer dismissed her and she claimed discrimination under the 1975 Act.

JUDGMENT

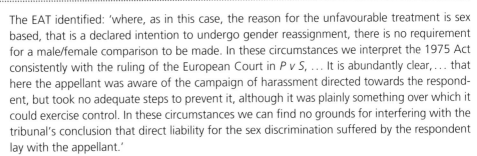

The EAT identified: 'where, as in this case, the reason for the unfavourable treatment is sex based, that is a declared intention to undergo gender reassignment, there is no requirement for a male/female comparison to be made. In these circumstances we interpret the 1975 Act consistently with the ruling of the European Court in *P v S*, ... It is abundantly clear, ... that here the appellant was aware of the campaign of harassment directed towards the respondent, but took no adequate steps to prevent it, although it was plainly something over which it could exercise control. In these circumstances we can find no grounds for interfering with the tribunal's conclusion that direct liability for the sex discrimination suffered by the respondent lay with the appellant.'

Parliament inserted protection in the case of gender reassignment in the Sex Discrimination (Gender Reassignment) Regulations 1999. The EU Framework Directive 2000/78 introduced a number of areas requiring the protection of anti-discrimination legislation including gender reassignment. The UK subsequently passed the Gender Reassignment Act 2004. As a result of the Act transsexuals are able to marry in their acquired gender and can also have an updated birth certificate. In *Chief Constable of Yorkshire v A* [2005] AC 51 it was held that under the 2004 Act once a person has undergone gender reassignment and gained formal recognition under the Act they are entitled to be treated as a person of the acquired gender.

Gender reassignment is now a protected characteristic under section 4 of the Equality Act 2010. Section 7 defines who is included within this protected characteristic.

SECTION

'7 Gender reassignment.
(1) A person has the protected characteristic of gender reassignment if the person is proposing to undergo, is undergoing or has undergone a process (or part of a process) for the purpose of reassigning the person's sex by changing physiological or other attributes of sex.
(2) A reference to a transsexual person is a reference to a person who has the protected characteristic of gender reassignment.
(3) In relation to the protected characteristic of gender reassignment –
    (a) a reference to a person who has a particular protected characteristic is a reference to a transsexual person;
    (b) a reference to persons who share a protected characteristic is a reference to transsexual persons.'

Prohibited conduct

All four types of prohibited behaviour apply – direct discrimination, indirect discrimination, harassment and victimisation – as does section 39 on discrimination in employment.

In the case of *direct discrimination*, under section 13 Equality Act 2010 a person would be directly discriminated against if he or she is treated less favourably because of undergoing gender reassignment within the meaning given in section 7. *P v S and Cornwall CC* [1996] IRLR 347 above is an obvious case of direct discrimination involving a discriminatory dismissal.

In the case of *indirect discrimination* under section 19 Equality Act 2010 a person would be indirectly discriminated against because of undergoing gender reassignment if:

- he is subjected to a provision, criterion or practice which is discriminatory in relation to gender reassignment;

- which applies regardless of gender reassignment but it puts him or her at a disadvantage;

- and it cannot be shown to be a proportionate means of achieving a legitimate aim.

A claim for *harassment* is also possible which under section 26 Equality Act 2010 would occur if a person:

- was subjected to unwanted conduct related to his or her gender reassignment; and

- the conduct had the purpose or effect of violating his or her dignity, or subjecting him or her to an intimidating, hostile, degrading, humiliating or offensive environment.

Chessington World of Adventure v Reed [1997] IRLR 556 is a case of harassment and also involves a discriminatory dismissal.

A claim of *victimisation* is also possible under section 27 Equality Act 2010 if the person:

- has been subjected to a detriment;

- because he has brought proceedings under the Act; or

- he has given evidence or information in connection with proceedings under the Act; or

- he has done anything else for the purposes of or in connection with the Act; or

- he has made an allegation (whether or not express) that his employer or another person has contravened the Act.

Discrimination in employment

Gender reassignment is also covered by section 39 Equality Act 2010 so a complaint can be made concerning discrimination in the context of employment. Clearly discrimination might occur in employment:

- in selection and recruitment – the way in which the employer decides who it will offer employment, in the terms on which the employment is offered or by not offering a person employment because of their gender reassignment; or

- during employment – by giving the claimant poorer terms than that of an employee of the opposite sex to the person's acquired sex or in access to opportunities for promotion, transfer, training or any other benefit, service or facility, or by subjecting the claimant to any other detriment because of his or her gender reassignment;

- on dismissal if this is because of the person's gender reassignment.

An occupational requirement under schedule 9 is also possible. The requirement would obviously have to be as proportionate means of achieving a legitimate aim.

ACTIVITY

Self-assessment questions

1. What were the original difficulties in bringing a successful claim for discrimination because of a person's gender reassignment?
2. How did the ECJ deal with the issue?
3. How does the Act define gender reassignment?
4. During which aspects of the process of gender reassignment is the person protected from discrimination?
5. On what basis could discrimination on gender reassignment be justified?

Has the claimant been the victim of direct discrimination?
- the claimant has been treated less favourably because of their gender reassignment

OR

Has the claimant been the victim of indirect discrimination?
- the claimant has been subjected to a provision, criterion or practice which is discriminatory in relation to his or her gender reassignment
- which applies regardless of gender reassignment but it puts him or her at a disadvantage compared with persons of who have not had a gender reassignment
- and it cannot be shown to be a proportionate means of achieving a legitimate aim

—OR→

Has the claimant been the victim of harassment?
- the claimant was subjected to unwanted conduct related to his or her gender reassignment, and
- the conduct had the purpose or effect of violating his or her dignity, or subjecting him or her to an intimidating, hostile, degrading humiliating or offensive environment

Has the claimant been the victim of victimisation?
- the claimant has been subjected to a detriment
- because he or she has brought proceedings under the Act; or
- he or she has given evidence or information in connection with proceedings under the Act; or
- he or she has done anything else for the purposes of or in connection with the Act; or
- he or she has made an allegation (whether or not express) that his employer or another person has contravened the Act

YES ↓

Is there a legal justification for the discrimination?
- there is an occupational requirement
- the application of the requirement is a proportionate means of achieving a legitimate aim
- the person to whom the employer applies the requirement does not meet it or the employer has reasonable grounds for not being satisfied that the person meets it
- in the case of indirect discrimination the provision, criterion or practice would also need to be a proportionate means of achieving a legitimate aim or it would not be lawful

YES

YES ↓

A CLAIM FOR DISCRIMINATION ON GROUNDS OF GENDER REASSIGNMENT IS POSSIBLE

Figure 14.2 Flow chart illustrating the requirements for a claim of discrimination on grounds of gender reassignment

14.4 Religion and belief

Traditionally there was no law protecting a person from discrimination on the basis of their belief. We have seen this in Chapter 12.2 where in *Mandla v Dowell Lee* [1983] 2 AC 548 the Court of Appeal held that Sikhs were not an ethnic group but a religious group and therefore not covered by discrimination law, although the then House of Lords reversed this. Similarly in *Seide v Gillette Industries* [1980] IRLR 427 Jews were protected because they were seen as a distinct ethnic group as well as a religious one. In contrast Muslims were assumed not to be a distinct ethnic group in *Walker v Hussain* [1996] IRLR 11 and were therefore not covered by discrimination law. Similarly Rastafarians have also been considered not to be a distinct ethnic group. Also in *Dawkins v Crown Suppliers (PSA)* [1993] ICR 517 Rastafarians were held to be a religious cult preventing the claimant from relying on discrimination law.

Religion and belief was introduced in EU law in the Framework Directive 2000/78 and therefore required implementation into the law of Member States. In the UK this came in the Employment Equality (Religion or Belief) Regulations 2003.

Religion and belief is now a protected characteristic under section 4 of the Equality Act 2010. Section 10 defines who is included within this protected characteristic.

SECTION

'10 Religion or belief.

(1) Religion means any religion and a reference to religion includes a reference to a lack of religion.

(2) Belief means any religious or philosophical belief and a reference to belief includes a reference to a lack of belief.

(3) In relation to the protected characteristic of religion or belief –

(a) a reference to a person who has a particular protected characteristic is a reference to a person of a particular religion or belief;

(b) a reference to persons who share a protected characteristic is a reference to persons who are of the same religion or belief.'

The meaning of religion or belief

Clearly the definition is broad enough to cover all religions and indeed section 10(2) shows that it can cover atheism also. All of the established religions should fall within the definition even fringe ones. In *Harris v NLK Automotive Ltd and Matrix Consultancy UK Ltd* [2007] UKEAT 0134 07 0310 held that Rastafarianism could be classed as a philosophical belief for the purposes of the 2003 Regulations. Similarly in *Power v Greater Manchester Police* [2009] UKEAT 0087 10 0810 spiritualism was also held to be a philosophical belief.

Nevertheless, the meaning of 'philosophical belief' might create greater difficulty for interpretation.

CASE EXAMPLE

Grainger Ltd v Nicholson [2010] IRLR 10

The claimant was selected for redundancy. He argued that this was an unfair selection and in fact amounted to unfair dismissal. He claimed that his dismissal was due to his expressed belief that climate change was man made and that this was discriminatory and contrary to the then Employment Equality (Religion or Belief) Regulations 2003. The issue for the EAT was whether or not such beliefs could fall under the regulations. The court held that, provided such beliefs were genuinely held, they could be classed as a 'philosophical belief' for the purposes of the regulations. The EAT also explained the criteria for determining what a belief is:

(a) it must be genuinely held;
(b) it must not merely be an opinion based on fact;
(c) it must be a belief involving a weighty aspect of human life and behaviour;
(d) it must be cogent and have some importance;
(e) it must be worthy in a democratic society, not incompatible with human dignity and not conflict with basic human rights.

JUDGMENT

Burton J commented: 'In my judgment, if a person can establish that he holds a philosophical belief which is based on science, as opposed, for example, to religion, then there is no reason to disqualify it from protection by the Regulations. The Employment Judge drew attention to the existence of empiricist philosophers, no doubt such as Hume and Locke. The best example, as it seems to me, which was canvassed during the course of the hearing, is by reference to the clash of two such philosophies, exemplified in the play *Inherit the Wind*, i.e. one not simply between those who supported Creationism and those who did not, but between those who positively supported, and wished to teach, only Creationism and those who positively supported, and wished to teach, only Darwinism. Darwinism must plainly be capable of being a philosophical belief, albeit that it may be based entirely on scientific conclusions (not all of which may be uncontroversial).

Prohibited conduct

All four types of prohibited conduct apply to the protected characteristic of religion and belief.

In the case of *direct discrimination*, under section 13 Equality Act 2010 a person would be directly discriminated against because of their religion or belief if he is treated less favourably than a person of a different religion or belief would be.

CASE EXAMPLE

Azmi v Kirklees Metropolitan Borough Council [2007] IRLR 484

A Muslim teaching assistant in a primary school complained that a rule preventing her from wearing a full face veil while she was teaching her class amounted to direct discrimination on the grounds of religion. The EAT held that this was not direct discrimination since any woman teacher would have been subjected to the same dress code regardless of her religion. She had not been treated less favourably than a woman of another religion wishing to wear a face veil.

In the case of *indirect discrimination* under section 19 Equality Act 2010 a person would be indirectly discriminated against because of his religion or belief if:

- he is subjected to a provision, criterion or practice which is discriminatory in relation to his religion or beliefs;
- which applies regardless of religion or belief but it puts him at a disadvantage compared with persons of a different religion or belief (which could include no religion or belief);
- and it cannot be shown to be a proportionate means of achieving a legitimate aim.

In *Azmi v Kirklees Metropolitan Borough Council* [2007] IRLR 484 indirect discrimination was also alleged. However, this argument also failed since the requirement that the teacher show her face to her pupils was a necessary and proportionate means of achieving a legitimate aim in that children of such a young age should have a full facial view of their teachers otherwise it would restrict signals that the children might otherwise get from her.

The issue obviously concerns religious symbolism or outward manifestations or belief. For there to be discrimination in this sense the religious symbol would have to be a mandatory requirement of the religion.

CASE EXAMPLE

Eweida v British Airways [2010] IRLR 322; *Eweida v UK* ECHR 48420/10

The claimant, a female employee of the company, claimed that a rule preventing her from wearing a cross outside her uniform to identify her Christian beliefs amounted to indirect discrimination on religious grounds. She was a devout Christian who felt that the cross was a central image of her belief in Christianity and wished to display it. She compared herself with a Sikh who might be permitted to wear a turban. The Court of Appeal held that there was no indirect discrimination and that the two situations were not comparable. For the Sikh it could be seen as a doctrinal religious requirement but there is no requirement in the Christian religion for wearing a cross. The European Court of Human Rights, however, ruled that the interference with her right to manifest her religion under Art 9 of the Convention was disproportionate despite the legitimate aim of her employer.

A claim for *harassment* is also possible which under section 26 Equality Act 2010 would occur if a person:

- was subjected to unwanted conduct related to his religion or belief; and
- the conduct had the purpose or effect of violating his dignity, or subjecting him to an intimidating, hostile, degrading, humiliating or offensive environment.

A claim of *victimisation* is also possible under section 27 Equality Act 2010 if the person:

- has been subjected to a detriment;
- because he has brought proceedings under the Act; or
- he has given evidence or information in connection with proceedings under the Act; or
- he has done anything else for the purposes of or in connection with the Act; or
- he has made an allegation (whether or not express) that his employer or another person has contravened the Act.

Discrimination in employment

Religion and belief is also covered by section 39 Equality Act 2010 so a complaint can be made concerning discrimination in the context of employment. Clearly discrimination might occur in employment:

- in selection and recruitment – the way in which the employer decides who it will offer employment, in the terms on which the employment is offered or by not offering a person employment because of their religion or belief; or
- during employment – by giving the claimant poorer terms than that of an employee of a different religion or belief, or in access to opportunities for promotion, transfer, training or any other benefit, service or facility, or by subjecting the claimant to any other detriment because of his religion or belief;
- on dismissal if this is because of the person's religion or belief.

In selection and recruitment clearly this could be an issue where the employer provides a service that is in some way faith led. If the refusal to employ cannot be justified then it may be discriminatory.

CASE EXAMPLE

Glasgow City Council v McNab [2007] IRLR 476

An atheist teacher who worked in a Roman Catholic school applied for the position of Acting Principal Teacher in Pastoral Care. He was not even considered for an interview because he was not a Catholic. He claimed discrimination on grounds of religion and belief. The local authority responsible for maintaining the school argued that it believed that the church would have thought that being a member of the Catholic faith was a prerequisite for the position. The EAT held that, while the school was a faith school it was not a necessary requirement that the teacher should be of Catholic faith. It was not a reserved post and the local authority could not claim that it had a particular ethos since it would have been responsible for a variety of schools with different ethos.

JUDGMENT

The EAT explained in its judgment: 'an education authority does not, in any event, have a religious ethos. The fact that it operates a statutory system under which it enables denominations to advance their ethos through schools maintained by it, does not mean that they espouse the same ethos at all. An education authority could, under the statute, be maintaining schools for varying denominations at one and the same time. Each denomination could hold a different ethos and it could contradict that of another denomination for which a school is maintained ... the respondents ... have no business seeking to follow or further any particular religious ethos at all.'

In the case of discrimination during employment this was the context of both *Azmi v Kirklees Metropolitan Borough Council* [2007] IRLR 484 and *Eweida v British Airways* [2010] IRLR 322. Both would have argued that they were subjected to a detriment because of their religion or belief, but both failed for the reasons given above.

Any detriment because of the claimant's religion or belief would clearly also be discriminatory. However, the detriment must have resulted from the religion or belief of the claimant and not for any other reason.

CASE EXAMPLE

Ladele v London Borough of Lambeth [2009] EWCA Civ 1357

A registrar of births, deaths and marriages had strong Christian views and was opposed to same sex partnerships. When the Civil Partnership Act 2004 came into force she made it plain that she did not wish to carry out civil partnership ceremonies. Her employer tried to reach a compromise but the registrar changed rosters with colleagues to avoid doing civil partnerships and two gay colleagues objected. She was then disciplined with the threat of dismissal after refusing to marry same-sex couples. She was a committed Christian and argued that she had refused to follow the Council's equality for all policy because it offended her religious beliefs. She claimed that she had been discriminated against under the 2003 Regulations. The court identified that the disciplinary proceedings were not because of her religion but because of a straightforward breach of her contractual obligations. The court also noted that the Sexual Orientation Regulations 2007 took precedence over her right to practise her religious beliefs since this involved her doing so in a discriminatory fashion, ECHR agreed.

A dismissal purely based on the claimant's religion or belief would clearly also be discriminatory. However, the dismissal must have resulted from the religion or belief of the claimant and not for any other reason.

CASE EXAMPLE

McClintock v Department of Constitutional Affairs [2008] IRLR 29

The claimant was a Justice of the Peace who sat on a panel which placed children for adoption and who was a committed Christian. He objected to the possibility that he might have to place a child with a same sex couple arguing that he considered that there was insufficient evidence that this was in the child's best interests and he also felt that the legislation was using children for political correctness. He asked to be relieved from hearing cases which might raise these issues but was refused so he resigned and claimed both direct and indirect discrimination and harassment, contrary to the Employment Equality (Religion or Belief) Regulations 2003. He was unsuccessful.

JUDGMENT

Elias J concluded: 'The Tribunal acknowledged, as do we, that Mr McClintock demonstrated candour and integrity in his handling of what for him was a sensitive issue. However, he expressed his objections on grounds which the Tribunal was entitled to find did not engage the terms of the Religion and Belief Regulations. Even had they done so, the Tribunal found that the Department was fully justified in insisting that magistrates must apply the law of the land as their oath requires, and cannot opt out of cases on the grounds that they may have to apply or give effect to laws to which they have a moral or other principled objection.'

Occupational requirement

Religion and belief is covered by the occupational requirement in schedule 9 Equality Act 2010 so an employer may be able to justify alleged discrimination on the ground of religion or belief if:

■ there is an occupational requirement; and

■ the application of the requirement is a proportionate means of achieving a legitimate aim; and

■ the person to whom the employer applies the requirement does not meet it or the employer has reasonable grounds for not being satisfied that the person meets it.

In *Glasgow City Council v McNab* [2007] IRLR 476 above the local authority was claiming that the requirement for employees to be Catholic which had prevented them from interviewing the claimant for the post of Principal Teacher in Pastoral Care was a genuine occupational requirement. The EAT held that, while the school was a faith school it was not a necessary requirement that the teacher should be of Catholic faith. There was no occupational requirement in the circumstances and the school's actions were unlawful discrimination. Of course had he been applying for the post of say RE teacher, then the decision may well have been different.

JUDGMENT

In its judgment the EAT concluded: 'just because the 1991 agreement specified that a teacher had to be a Roman Catholic for certain posts, that did not mean that that requirement had to be regarded as a genuine occupational requirement for the purposes of regulation 7(2) of the 2003 regulations'.

ACTIVITY

Self-assessment questions

1. How does the Act define religion and belief?
2. What difficulties has this caused in the previous case law?
3. What was the reasoning behind the decision in *Azmi v Kirklees Metropolitan Borough Council*?
4. On what basis could there be no indirect discrimination in *Eweida v British Airways*?
5. Why is *Ladele v London Borough of Lambeth* a significant decision?
6. In what circumstances could discrimination based on religion and belief be justified?

Has the claimant been the victim of direct discrimination?
- the claimant has been treated less favourably because of their religion or belief

OR

Has the claimant been the victim of indirect discrimination?
- the claimant has been subjected to a provision, criterion or practice which is discriminatory in relation to his religion or belief
- which applies regardless of religion or belief but it puts him or her at a disadvantage compared with persons of a different religion or belief
- and it cannot be shown to be a proportionate means of achieving a legitimate aim

—**OR**→

Has the claimant been the victim of harassment?
- the claimant was subjected to unwanted conduct related to his or her religion or belief and
- the conduct had the purpose or effect of violating his or her dignity, or subjecting him or her to an intimidating, hostile, degrading, humiliating or offensive environment

Has the claimant been the victim of victimisation?
- the claimant has been subjected to a detriment
- because he or she has brought proceedings under the Act; or
- he or she has given evidence or information in connection with proceedings under the Act; or
- he or she has done anything else for the purposes of or in connection with the Act; or
- he or she has made an allegation (whether or not express) that his employer or another person has contravened the Act

YES

Is there a legal justification for the discrimination?
- there is an occupational requirement
- the application of the requirement is a proportionate means of achieving a legitimate aim
- the person to whom the employer applies the requirement does not meet it or the employer has reasonable grounds for not being satisfied that the person meets it

YES

YES

A CLAIM FOR DISCRIMINATION ON GROUNDS OF RELIGION OR BELIEF IS POSSIBLE

Figure 14.3 Flow chart illustrating the requirements for a claim of discrimination on grounds of religion or belief

14.5 Age

Traditionally there was very little in the way of protection from discrimination on grounds of age. It is true that the earliest industrial safety law, the Health and Morals of Apprentices Act 1802, was passed to protect child workers and such reforms continued throughout the nineteenth century (see Chapter 1.2.3 and 1.3). Protection from exploitation of children through statute has continued. However, age discrimination can occur in many ways.

QUOTATION

As Brian Willey puts it in *Employment Law in Context 3rd edition* (Pearson, 2009, p. 127): 'experience, know how, educational qualifications, decision making capabilities, emotional maturity and almost any other neutral criterion that might be applicable in the employment context could put persons of a particular age at a disadvantage.'

Inevitably, while discrimination could occur at all ages probably the most discriminated against are the young and the aged. Age discrimination clearly has the potential to be a significant issue in employment. Government statistics show that youth unemployment is currently running at above 20 per cent and the educational reforms and increase in fees is likely to lead to a decrease in the numbers of students in both further and higher education in the next few years which may well show up a bigger problem in youth unemployment. There is also a growing aged population. The Office of National Statistics suggests that by 2020 the proportion of the workforce that is over fifty will have risen to one-third. That there is no longer any default retirement age is likely to mean that people stay in work longer and young people may have even greater difficulty in finding work.

Age was introduced in EU law in the Framework Directive 2000/78 and therefore required implementation into the law of Member States. In the UK this came in the Employment Equality (Age) Regulations 2006. The Regulations followed the Framework Directive and introduced the usual areas of direct discrimination, indirect discrimination, harassment and victimisation. They also removed the upper age limits for unfair dismissal claims and redundancy, provided exemptions from some aged based rules in occupational pensions, and the upper age limits for statutory sick pay.

Age is now a protected characteristic under section 4 of the Equality Act 2010. Section 5 defines who is included within this protected characteristic.

SECTION

'5 Age.
(1) In relation to the protected characteristic of age –
　　(a) a reference to a person who has a particular protected characteristic is a reference to a person of a particular age group;
　　(b) a reference to persons who share a protected characteristic is a reference to persons of the same age group.
(2) A reference to an age group is a reference to a group of persons defined by reference to age, whether by reference to a particular age or to a range of ages.'

Prohibited conduct

All four types of prohibited conduct apply to the protected characteristic of age.

In the case of *direct discrimination*, under section 13 Equality Act 2010 a person would be directly discriminated against because of his age if he is treated less favourably than a person of a different age would be.

CASE EXAMPLE

London Borough of Tower Hamlets v Wooster [2009] IRLR 980

The claimant had been made redundant at aged forty-nine. He was able to show evidence that the decision to make him redundant rather than to redeploy him was so that his employer could avoid him becoming eligible for an early retirement scheme. It was held that this was direct discrimination as the only reason for the claimant's dismissal was in effect his age. The EAT was also concerned that the employer had not considered the other possible alternatives.

JUDGMENT

Underhill J concluded: 'none of the Council's challenges to the Tribunal's reasoning are made good. There was adequate material on which it could have drawn the inference that the Council's conduct in not redeploying the Claimant, or extending his employment, and instead dismissing him when it did, was motivated by a desire to terminate his employment before he reached 50; and its reasons for drawing that inference, though not very well expressed, are again adequate.'

Direct discrimination is clearly problematic in situations like that above where an employee in that age group may find it difficult to find another job because of his age. It is of course a significant problem at the other end of the age spectrum where a young person is dependent on gaining or continuing in employment in order to progress.

CASE EXAMPLE

Wilkinson v Springwell Engineering Ltd [2009] IDS B/851

A teenage female employee was dismissed by her employer because, as it was explained to her at the time she was dismissed, she was too young for the job. At the tribunal the employer tried to argue that the dismissal was actually for lack of capability. The tribunal rejected this argument and accepted her claim for age discrimination. The tribunal also considered that the employer's view about her capability for the work was in fact based on a stereotypical assumption about the link between youth and lack of capability. Having said that because people's capability deteriorates it will always be possible to justify age discrimination according to the particular requirements of the work.

In the case of *indirect discrimination* under section 19 Equality Act 2010 a person would be indirectly discriminated against because of his age if:

▨ he is subjected to a provision, criterion or practice which is discriminatory in relation to his age;

▨ which applies to any age group but it puts him at a disadvantage compared with persons of a different age;

▨ and it cannot be shown to be a proportionate means of achieving a legitimate aim.

As is the case with other protected characteristics indirect discrimination is really concerned with disguised age which put a person at a disadvantage because of their age. The question for the court is whether or not this can be justified.

CASE EXAMPLE

Homer v Chief Constable of West Yorkshire Police [2012] UKSC 15

The claimant had retired from the police force at age fifty-one and then continued to work with the Police National Database as a legal adviser. When he took up this post, a law degree or equivalent was not an essential qualification, and in his case his experience as a police officer was deemed sufficient. However, the criteria were later changed so that a law degree became an essential qualification for first appointment. This did not immediately affect him but a new grade structure was later introduced with three grades. The claimant was unable to be put on the highest grade without a law degree. Since the claimant was age sixty-two at that time (and at that time he was bound to retire at age sixty-five) he argued that it was impossible to complete a law degree in time to reach the highest grade before he retired and that the requirement for a law degree was therefore indirect discrimination on the grounds of his age. The tribunal held that he had been indirectly discriminated against on grounds of age and that this was not objectively justified. The Employment Appeal Tribunal (EAT) disagreed. The Supreme Court held that there was indeed indirect discrimination based on age.

JUDGMENT

Lady Hale commented: 'It is not long ago that it was taken for granted that age was a relevant criterion in deciding how long people should be allowed to go on working. Now that has to be justified. The same is true of apparently neutral criteria which have an adverse impact upon people of a particular age. But both the Age Regulations and the Equality Act recognise that difficult balances have to be struck between the competing interests of different age groups.' The court also considered that the tribunal had not properly considered justification for the discrimination and returned it to the tribunal on that basis.

A claim for _harassment_ is also possible which under section 26 Equality Act 2010 would occur if a person:

- was subjected to unwanted conduct related to his age; and
- the conduct had the purpose or effect of violating his dignity, or subjecting him to an intimidating, hostile, degrading, humiliating or offensive environment.

A claim of _victimisation_ is also possible under section 27 Equality Act 2010 if the person:

- has been subjected to a detriment;
- because he has brought proceedings under the Act; or
- he has given evidence or information in connection with proceedings under the Act; or
- he has done anything else for the purposes of or in connection with the Act; or
- he has made an allegation (whether or not express) that his employer or another person has contravened the Act.

Discrimination in employment

Age is also covered by section 39 Equality Act 2010 so a complaint can be made concerning discrimination in the context of employment. Clearly discrimination might occur in employment:

- in selection and recruitment – the way in which the employer decides who it will offer employment, in the terms on which the employment is offered, or by not offering a person employment because of their age; or

- during employment – by giving the claimant poorer terms than that of an employee of a different age, or in access to opportunities for promotion, transfer, training or any other benefit, service or facility, or by subjecting the claimant to any other detriment because of his age;
- on dismissal if this is because of the person's age.

Homer v Chief Constable of West Yorkshire Police [2012] UKSC 16 above is an obvious example of age discrimination during employment. *London Borough of Tower Hamlets v Wooster* [2009] IRLR 980 above is an obvious example of a discriminatory dismissal on the basis of age.

The occupational requirements under schedule 9 also apply if they are a proportionate means of achieving a legitimate aim. This is an area that has been the subject of some discussion by the ECJ.

CASE EXAMPLE

Wolf v Stadt Frankfurt am Main [2010] IRLR 244

The claimant argued that the policy that applicants for the fire service must be under the age of thirty was discriminatory. The court held that the requirement was a genuine occupational requirement. It was accepted that fire-fighting and rescue duties were traditionally carried out by younger officers so that unlimited recruitment would limit the number of officers who could engage in such duties.

JUDGMENT

In the reference from the German court the ECJ identified: 'the fire-fighting and rescue duties which are part of the intermediate career in the fire service can only be performed by younger officials.... To ensure the efficient functioning of the intermediate career in the fire service, it may be considered necessary for the majority of officials in that career to be able to perform physically demanding tasks, and hence for them to be younger than 45 or 50.... The age at which an official is recruited determines the time during which he will be able to perform physically demanding tasks. An official recruited before the age of 30, who will have to follow a training programme lasting two years, can be assigned to those duties for a minimum of 15 to 20 years. By contrast, if he is recruited at the age of 40, that period will be a maximum of 5 to 10 years only. Recruitment at an older age would have the consequence that too large a number of officials could not be assigned to the most physically demanding duties.... Consequently, it is apparent that national legislation such as that at issue in the main proceedings which sets the maximum age for recruitment to intermediate career posts in the fire service at 30 years may be regarded, first, as appropriate to the objective of ensuring the operational capacity and proper functioning of the professional fire service and, second, as not going beyond what is necessary to achieve that objective.'

Retirement age

From 1 October 2011 the default retirement age of sixty-five was repealed as a result of the Employment Equality (Repeal of Retirement Age Provisions) Regulations 2011. An employer then has the choice either to abolish fixed retirement ages altogether in his organisation or to keep a fixed retirement age. If he does keep a fixed retirement age then this will need to be objectively justified. Objective justification means that the employer must show that the retirement age is a proportionate means of achieving a legitimate aim. There will need to be a sound business reason for the retirement age chosen and the employer will have to produce evidence to show this. Now employees have the choice about whether to retire or not.

ACTIVITY

Self-assessment questions

1. In what ways could age discrimination have a major impact in the employment market?
2. In what ways was the default age for retirement inconsistent with the idea of protection from age discrimination?
3. How did the Framework Directive 2000/78 change the position on age discrimination?
4. What is significant about the case of *Homer v Chief Constable of West Yorkshire Police*?
5. How does the Equality Act 2010 define age?
6. Which types of prohibited conduct apply to age?
7. On what basis can discrimination on the basis of age be justified?

ACTIVITY

Quick quiz

Consider which protected characteristic and which type of discrimination might apply in each of the following situations and whether the individual claims are likely to be successful:

1. Ian, aged sixteen has applied for a position as a sales assistant in a department store. Ian has been told that his application has been rejected because he lacks the necessary experience.
2. James works as a teacher in a large comprehensive. At the start of a new autumn term James has returned with long hair, make-up and wearing a dress and has asked his colleagues to call him Gemma. He has also developed a bust and a more feminine waist and hips and lost his facial hair because of medication that he is taking prior to an eventual operation. The school headmistress has told James that nobody will be calling him Gemma and threatened that he will be suspended if he returns the following day wearing a dress and with make-up on.
3. Danny works as a mechanic in a garage. Danny has been dismissed by his employer after a colleague reported that he had seen Danny in a club dancing with another man in a suggestive and intimate manner.
4. Melissa is employed is a professional ladies hockey player. Melissa is a Christian and is complaining about a rule that prevents her from wearing her cross during training sessions or matches. The club that employs her justifies the rule on the basis that wearing any form of jewellery is potentially dangerous to other players.

14.6 Part-time workers

It is not that long ago in the past that part-time workers had very little in the way of rights. At one time a person working less than eight hours per week had no employment protections and a person working less than sixteen hours per week had very little employment protection.

Protection from discrimination against part-time employees is essential when it is remembered that the majority of part-timers are women and therefore it is a double discrimination. Since the 1980s part-time work has increased dramatically to more than a quarter of the workforce. The significance of this is that more than 40 per cent of part-time employees are women. The significance of the lack of proper protection against part-time employees and the effect on women was recognised in *R v Secretary of State, ex parte Equal Opportunities Commission* [1994] IRLR 176 where the then House of Lords (now the Supreme Court) held that the provisions of the then Employment Protection (Consolidation) Act 1978 (replaced by the Employment Rights Act 1996) under which employees working for under sixteen hours per week were subject to different conditions in qualification for redundancy pay from those applying to employees working more than sixteen hours per week were incompatible with Article 119 EC Treaty (now Article 157 TFEU).

The issue of the treatment of part-time employees had already been considered by the ECJ in a referral from the English courts in a case concerning an equal pay claim.

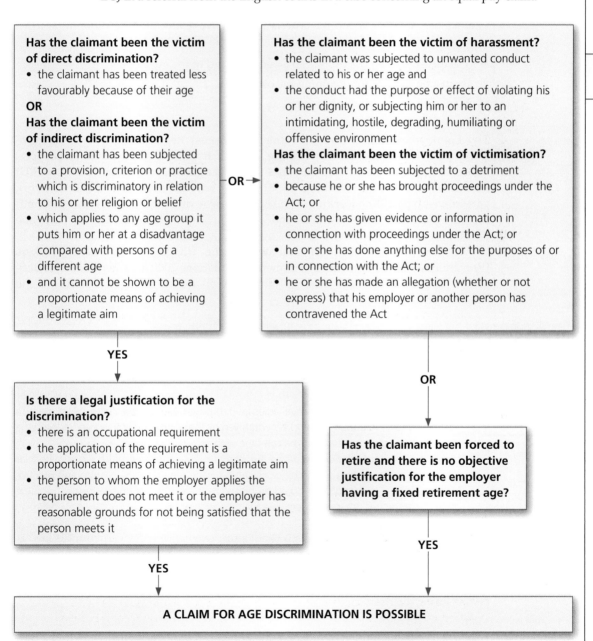

Figure 14.4 Flow chart illustrating the requirements for a claim of age discrimination

CASE EXAMPLE

Jenkins v Kingsgate Clothing Productions Ltd [1981] IRLR 388; ECR 911

A part-time employee in the clothing industry was paid at a different rate to full time employees. In a reference under Article 177 (now Article 267 TFEU) made by the EAT to the ECJ the court identified that differential treatment of part-time employees could amount to discrimination where a greater proportion of women worked part-time. In the event it also accepted that the justification given by the employer could apply if it was objectively justified and not merely discriminatory (see Chapter 11).

The ECJ had also developed the criteria for objective justification for differential treatment in *Bilka Kaufhaus GmbH v Weber von Hartz* [1987] ICR 110 that:

▦ The measure must correspond to a genuine need of the business.

▦ It must be suitable for obtaining the objective.

▦ It must be necessary for that purpose.

The Employment Protection (Part-time Employees) Regulations 1995 were introduced and these removed some of the unequal treatment of part-time employees. However, the significant step towards equal treatment came in the EC (now EU) Directive on Part-time Working 97/81 which resulted from the EC Framework agreement on part-time working. The Directive provided for the removal of discrimination against part-time workers and aimed to improve the quality of part-time work.

The directive has been implemented in the UK in the Part-time Workers (Prevention of Less Favourable Treatment) Regulations 2000 (as amended). The definitions of part-time worker and full-time worker are found in section 2(2) of the Regulations.

REGULATION

'2. Meaning of full-time worker, part-time worker and comparable full-time worker

(1) A worker is a full-time worker for the purpose of these Regulations if he is paid wholly or in part by reference to the time he works and, having regard to the custom and practice of the employer in relation to workers employed by the worker's employer under the same type of contract, is identifiable as a full-time worker.

(2) A worker is a part-time worker for the purpose of these Regulations if he is paid wholly or in part by reference to the time he works and, having regard to the custom and practice of the employer in relation to workers employed by the worker's employer under the same type of contract, is not identifiable as a full-time worker.'

So the definition is quite broad which is not surprising since it derives from EU law. A part-time employee is in essence any worker whose pay is determined by the hours that he works and these are less than a full-time employee. As a result the definition only excludes the genuinely self-employed who would be in a business relationship with the person hiring their services.

As a result of the definition in section 2 the part-time employee will have to find a full-time comparator. The identity of the comparator is explained in section 4.

REGULATION

> '(4) A full-time worker is a comparable full-time worker in relation to a part-time worker if, at the time when the treatment that is alleged to be less favourable to the part-time worker takes place
>
> (a) both workers are
>   (i) employed by the same employer under the same type of contract, and
>   (ii) engaged in the same or broadly similar work having regard, where relevant, to whether they have a similar level of qualification, skills and experience; and
> (b) the full-time worker works or is based at the same establishment as the part-time worker or, where there is no full-time worker working or based at that establishment who satisfies the requirements of sub-paragraph (a), works or is based at a different establishment and satisfies those requirements.'

The test is obviously quite demanding and requires an actual comparator and not a hypothetical one.

CASE EXAMPLE

Carl v University of Sheffield [2009] IRLR 616

The claimant was a part-time worker employed as a teacher of shorthand by the University. She complained that she had been treated less favourably than a named comparator who worked under a full-time University Teacher's contract. The complaint was that the comparator was paid for preparation time while she was not. The issue was whether she was paid less pro rata than the full-time teacher. She alternatively claimed that she was paid less than a hypothetical comparator, a 'generic teacher' on a University Teacher's contract. The EAT held that in the circumstances the named comparator was not an actual comparator and that she could not rely on a hypothetical comparator.

The right not to be subjected to less favourable treatment is found in section 5 of the Regulations.

REGULATION

> '5. Less favourable treatment of part-time workers
> (1) A part-time worker has the right not to be treated by his employer less favourably than the employer treats a comparable full-time worker –
>   (a) as regards the terms of his contract; or
>   (b) by being subjected to any other detriment by any act, or deliberate failure to act, of his employer.
> (2) The right conferred by paragraph (1) applies only if –
>   (a) the treatment is on the ground that the worker is a part-time worker, and
>   (b) the treatment is not justified on objective grounds.'

To bring a claim the part-time worker must show that he works for the same employer as a full-time worker doing broadly similar work and that he has less favourable conditions of work by comparison or is suffering a detriment because of being a part-time worker.

CASE EXAMPLE

Matthews v Kent & Medway Town Fire Authority [2006] IRLR 367

Part-time retained fire-fighters complained that they had been unlawfully discriminated against because their conditions of work were not on the same terms as full-time fire-fighters. Retained fire-fighters often work in rural areas where it would not be economical to maintain a permanent full-time fire service. They attend for limited sessions and are on stand-by to attend any call-outs including fires. The Court of Appeal held that their claim failed because they were not doing broadly similar work to full-time fire-fighters. The then House of Lords disagreed. It identified that the fact that full-time staff do extra duties should not necessarily prevent a part-time worker from claiming. The issue was the importance of their work to the organisation and the extent to which they were doing the same duties and the extent to which the differences were significant.

JUDGMENT

Lord Hope commented: 'I am not confident, however, that the tribunal gave sufficient weight to the extent to which the work on which both groups of fire fighters were engaged was "the same" work...'. Their conclusion that the job of the whole time fire fighter was a fuller wider job than that of the retained fire fighter was not, as they appear to have thought, the end of the exercise. They still had to address the question posed by the statute which was whether, notwith-standing the fact that the job of the whole time fire fighter was a fuller and wider job, the work on which both groups were engaged could nevertheless be described as broadly similar.

Under Regulation 5 a part-time worker is entitled to the same terms and conditions as a full-time worker who is doing broadly the same work. This means that a pro rata principle must be applied and the part-time worker should be paid at the same rate as the full-time worker in proportion to the hours worked. An exception to this principle is overtime. If the employer does not pay overtime to the part-time worker until he has worked the same hours as a full-time worker then this will not amount to less favourable treatment.

CASE EXAMPLE

McMenemy v Capita Business Services Ltd [2007] IRLR 400

The claimant was a part-time worker at a call centre. While the call centre operated seven days a week, the claimant worked only on Wednesdays, Thursdays and Fridays. The contract of employment allowed employees a day off in lieu when they worked on bank holidays. Since most statutory holiday occurs on Mondays the claimant inevitably did not receive as many lieu days as his full-time colleagues and he complained that this was discrimination because of his part-time status. The Court of Session held that the difference of treatment was not because the claimant was a part-time worker but because he did not work on Mondays.

JUDGMENT

Lord Nimmo Smith explained: 'the reason why the appellant received less favourable treatment than did a comparable full-time worker was through the accident of his having agreed with the respondents that he would not work for them on Mondays or Tuesdays.... It is clear ... that ... if a full-time member of the appellant's team worked a fixed shift from Tuesday to Saturday, he would not receive the benefit of statutory holidays which fell on Mondays. Likewise, if the appel-lant, or any other part-time member of his team, worked on Mondays, they would receive the benefit of statutory Monday holidays in exactly the same way as full-time employees would do.'

In *Sharma v Manchester City Council* [2008] IRLR 236 the EAT also identified that the fact that the claimant works part-time need not be the only reason for the different treatment for there to be a claim.

Regulation 7 also makes it an unfair dismissal if the claimant's dismissal is connected with his rights under the Regulations (see Chapter 22.3).

REGULATION

'7. Unfair dismissal and the right not to be subjected to detriment

(1) An employee who is dismissed shall be regarded as unfairly dismissed ... if the reason (or, if more than one, the principal reason) for the dismissal is a reason specified in paragraph (3).

(2) A worker has the right not to be subjected to any detriment by any act, or any deliberate failure to act, by his employer done on a ground specified in paragraph (3).

(3) The reasons or, as the case may be, grounds are –

  (a) that the worker has –

    (i) brought proceedings against the employer under these Regulations;

    (ii) requested from his employer a written statement of reasons under regulation 6;

    (iii) given evidence or information in connection with such proceedings brought by any worker;

    (iv) otherwise done anything under these Regulations in relation to the employer or any other person;

    (v) alleged that the employer had infringed these Regulations; or

    (vi) refused (or proposed to refuse) to forgo a right conferred on him by these Regulations, or

  (b) that the employer believes or suspects that the worker has done or intends to do any of the things mentioned in sub-paragraph (a).'

Where an employee claims under the Regulations there may initially be a hearing with ACAS. In a successful claim a tribunal can award compensation and make recommendations for the employer to remove the discrimination.

14.7 Fixed-term workers

Fixed-term contracts also account for a significant proportion of the workforce. Inevitably people will be prepared to accept a fixed-term contract rather than have no employment at all. It is unlikely in most cases that a person would subject himself to the limited security of a fixed-term contract if an alternative permanent arrangement was available. EU Directive 99/70 concerning the framework agreement on fixed-term work was eventually passed after a lengthy period of trying to persuade Member States, the first proposal having been in 1990.

The purpose of the directive was to:

- improve the quality of fixed-term work by ensuring non-discrimination;
- establish a framework to prevent abuses arising from the use of fixed-term contracts.

A fixed-term employee is one where the termination of the contract of employment is predetermined by objective conditions such as reaching a specific date, completing a specific task or the occurrence of a specific event. So for instance a football manager might be hired by a football club for three years, or an oilfield surveyor might be hired by an oil company only up until such time as the company has struck oil in a particular oilfield.

The directive was initially partly implemented in the Employment Relations Act 1999 which effectively brought fixed-term contracts within the scope of unfair dismissal. Subsequently the directive was implemented in the Fixed Term Employees (Prevention of Less Favourable Treatment) Regulations 2002.

The definition of fixed-term worker is very similar to that of part-time worker and is in Regulation 2.

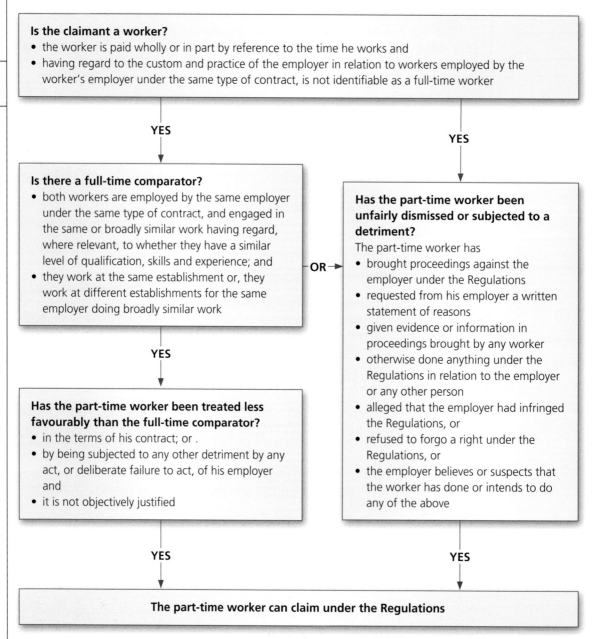

Figure 14.5 Flow chart illustrating the elements of possible claims under the Part-time Workers (Prevention of Less Favourable Treatment) Regulations 2000

REGULATION

'2 Comparable employees

(1) For the purposes of these Regulations, an employee is a comparable permanent employee in relation to a fixed-term employee if, at the time when the treatment that is alleged to be less favourable to the fixed-term employee takes place,

   (a) both employees are –
      (i) employed by the same employer, and
      (ii) engaged in the same or broadly similar work having regard, where relevant, to whether they have a similar level of qualification and skills; and
   (b) the permanent employee works or is based at the same establishment as the fixed-term employee or, where there is no comparable permanent employee working or based at that establishment who satisfies the requirements of sub-paragraph (a), works or is based at a different establishment and satisfies those requirements.'

So again a comparator will be a person with a contract of employment of indeterminate length who works for the same employer at the same establishment or another of the employer's establishments. The distinction from the regulations on part-time workers is that the regulations covering fixed-term contracts apply only to employees. This is likely to exclude large numbers of workers from the protection from discrimination.

The definition of less favourable treatment is in Regulation 3.

REGULATION

'3 Less favourable treatment of fixed-term employees

(1) A fixed-term employee has the right not to be treated by his employer less favourably than the employer treats a comparable permanent employee –

   (a) as regards the terms of his contract; or
   (b) by being subjected to any other detriment by any act, or deliberate failure to act, of his employer.

(2) Subject to paragraphs (3) and (4), the right conferred by paragraph (1) includes in particular the right of the fixed-term employee in question not to be treated less favourably than the employer treats a comparable permanent employee in relation to –

   (a) any period of service qualification relating to any particular condition of service,
   (b) the opportunity to receive training, or
   (c) the opportunity to secure any permanent position in the establishment.

(3) The right conferred by paragraph (1) applies only if –

   (a) the treatment is on the ground that the employee is a fixed-term employee, and
   (b) the treatment is not justified on objective grounds.'

This means comparable treatment in pay, pensions, statutory sick pay, guarantee payments and medical suspension payments. As is identified in Regulation 3(3)(b) differential treatment of fixed-term employees is only possible if it is objectively justified. This defence is identified in Regulation 4.

'4 Objective justification

(1) Where a fixed-term employee is treated by his employer less favourably than the employer treats a comparable permanent employee as regards any term of his contract, the treatment in question shall be regarded for the purposes of regulation 3(3)(b) as justified on objective grounds if the terms of the fixed-term employee's contract of employment, taken as a whole, are at least as favourable as the terms of the comparable permanent employee's contract of employment.'

In the same way as with part-time workers a dismissal that is connected to the rights a fixed-term employee gains under the Regulations will be an automatically unfair dismissal. Regulation 6 on unfair dismissal is phrased in the same terms as Regulation 7 of the Part-time Workers (Prevention of Less Favourable Treatment) Regulations 2000. Again a tribunal can award compensation and make a recommendation for the employer to end the discrimination.

Where there are a series of fixed-term contracts Regulation 8 identifies that if the fixed terms are continually renewed for four years then the contract automatically becomes a permanent contract unless there is an objective justification for the contract not being permanent. However, an employer only has to have a break between successive fixed terms to break continuity of employment and this could make the Regulation ineffective.

14.8 Agency workers

The traditional problem with agency workers is that it depends on the circumstances of each case whether they will be classed as employees (see Chapter 4.4). Therefore traditionally they have generally lacked any employment protections even though, by government figures in 2009 there were estimated to be more than 1.3 million. There are now protections against discrimination in the Agency Workers Regulations 2010. The Regulations only apply to workers who are supplied by a temporary work agency. Workers who are supplied to an employer by an employment agency are not protected by the Regulations since by definition they are seeking to find permanent employment for the people who enlist with them. Regulation 3 identifies in detail which workers come under the Regulations.

REGULATION

'3 The meaning of agency worker

(1) In these Regulations "agency worker" means an individual who –
   (a) is supplied by a temporary work agency to work temporarily for and under the supervision and direction of a hirer; and
   (b) has a contract with the temporary work agency which is –
      (i) a contract of employment with the agency, or
      (ii) any other contract to perform work and services personally for the agency.
(2) But an individual is not an agency worker if –
   (a) the contract the individual has with the temporary work agency has the effect that the status of the agency is that of a client or customer of a profession or business undertaking carried on by the individual; or
   (b) there is a contract, by virtue of which the individual is available to work for the hirer, having the effect that the status of the hirer is that of a client or customer of a profession or business undertaking carried on by the individual.'

There is another significant limitation on which workers can gain the protection from discrimination in the Regulations, a qualifying period of continuous service. This limitation is identified in Regulation 7.

REGULATION

'7 Qualifying period
(1) Regulation 5 does not apply unless an agency worker has completed the qualifying period.
(2) To complete the qualifying period the agency worker must work in the same role with the same hirer for 12 continuous calendar weeks, during one or more assignments.'

Regulation 5 provides that the temporary agency worker is entitled to the same conditions as he would have had if he had been hired directly by the hirer rather than through an agency. On which basis the comparator is a person employed by the hirer doing the same or broadly similar work as the temporary agency worker.

REGULATION

'5 Rights of agency workers in relation to the basic working and employment conditions
(1) Subject to regulation 7, an agency worker (A) shall be entitled to the same basic working and employment conditions as A would be entitled to for doing the same job had A been recruited by the hirer –
    (a) other than by using the services of a temporary work agency; and
    (b) at the time the qualifying period commenced.
(2) For the purposes of paragraph (1), the basic working and employment conditions are –
    (a) where A would have been recruited as an employee, the relevant terms and conditions that are ordinarily included in the contracts of employees of the hirer;
    (b) where A would have been recruited as a worker, the relevant terms and conditions that are ordinarily included in the contracts of workers of the hirer, whether by collective agreement or otherwise, including any variations in those relevant terms and conditions made at any time after the qualifying period commenced.'

The terms and conditions of employment falling under the basic right in Regulation 5 are identified in Regulation 6 and include pay, the duration of working time, night work, rest periods, rest breaks and annual leave.

Under Regulation 6(2) pay means 'any sums payable to a worker of the hirer in connection with the worker's employment, including any fee, bonus, commission, holiday pay or other emolument referable to the employment, whether payable under contract or otherwise, but excluding' a number of possible payments including occupational sick pay, pension, any payment in respect of maternity, paternity or adoption leave, redundancy and guarantee payments.

In the same way as with part-time workers and fixed-term employees a dismissal that is connected to the rights of an agency worker gains under the Regulations will be an automatically unfair dismissal. Regulation 17 on unfair dismissal is phrased in the same terms as Regulation 7 of the Part-time Workers (Prevention of Less Favourable Treatment) Regulations 2000 and Regulation 6 in the Fixed Term Employees (Prevention of Less Favourable Treatment) Regulations 2002. Again a tribunal can award compensation and make a recommendation for the employer to end the discrimination.

ACTIVITY

Self-assessment questions

1. In what way is membership of the EU important to employment protections for part-time workers, fixed-term employees and temporary agency workers?
2. How is a part-time worker defined in the Part-time Workers (Prevention of Less Favourable Treatment) Regulations 2000?
3. Who is the comparator of the part-time worker under the regulations?
4. What is the significance of *Carl v University of Sheffield* in this respect?
5. Who are comparable employees under the Fixed Term Employees (Prevention of Less Favourable Treatment) Regulations 2002?
6. How is less favourable treatment defined under the Regulations?
7. What is an objective justification under the Regulations?
8. Which type of agency workers are not covered by the Agency Workers Regulations 2010 and why?
9. What major limitation in the Regulations will prevent temporary agency workers from gaining rights under them?
10. What terms and conditions are covered by the Regulations?

KEY FACTS

Discrimination on the grounds of sexual orientation	Case/statute
Direct discrimination	
• the person is treated less favourably because of his or her sexual orientation	*S13 Equality Act 2010* *Reaney v Hereford Diocesan Board of Finance*
Indirect discrimination	
• the claimant is subjected to a provision, criterion or practice which is discriminatory in relation to his or her sexual orientation, which puts him or her at a disadvantage compared with persons of different sexual orientation; and it cannot be shown to be a proportionate means of achieving a legitimate aim	*S19 Equality Act 2010*
Harassment	
• the claimant is subjected to unwanted conduct related to his or her sexual orientation, with the purpose or effect of violating his or her dignity, or subjecting him or her to an intimidating, hostile, degrading, humiliating or offensive environment • perceived orientation is possible	*S26 Equality Act 2010* *English v Thomas Sanderson Blinds* *S27 Equality Act 2010*
Victimisation	
• the claimant was subjected to a detriment because he or she brought proceedings under the Act; or gave evidence or information in connection with proceedings or did anything else for the purposes of or in connection with the Act; or made an allegation (whether or not express) that his or her employer or another person has contravened the Act	

Discrimination in employment	
• recruitment and selection – in the way who is offered employment is decided; or in the terms on which the employment is offered; or by not offering a person employment	S39(1) Equality Act 2010
• during employment – by giving the claimant poorer terms than that of an employee of the opposite sex; or in the way that opportunities for promotion, transfer, training or any other benefit, service or facility are provided; or by subjecting the claimant to any other detriment	S39(2) Equality Act 2010
• dismissal – by dismissing an employee for a discriminatory reason	S39(2) Equality Act 2010
• occupational requirement is possible where there is a requirement of a particular sexual orientation to comply with specific religious doctrines	Schedule 9 *Reaney v Hereford Diocesan Board of Finance*

Discrimination on the grounds of gender reassignment	Case/statute
Direct discrimination	
• the person is treated less favourably because of his or her gender reassignment	S13 Equality Act 2010 *P v S and Cornwall CC*
Indirect discrimination	
• the claimant is subjected to a provision, criterion or practice which is discriminatory in relation to his or her sex, which puts him or her at a disadvantage compared with persons of the opposite sex; and it cannot be shown to be a proportionate means of achieving a legitimate aim	S19 Equality Act 2010
Harassment	
• the claimant is subjected to unwanted conduct related to his or her sex, with the purpose or effect of violating his or her dignity, or subjecting him or her to an intimidating, hostile, degrading, humiliating or offensive environment	S26 Equality Act 2010 *Chessington World of Adventure v Reed*
Victimisation	
• the claimant was subjected to a detriment because he or she brought proceedings under the Act; or gave evidence or information in connection with proceedings or did anything else for the purposes of or in connection with the Act; or made an allegation (whether or not express) that his or her employer or another person has contravened the Act	S27 Equality Act 2010
Discrimination in employment	
• recruitment and selection – in the way who is offered employment is decided; or in the terms on which the employment is offered; or by not offering a person employment	S39(1) Equality Act 2010

• during employment – by giving the claimant poorer terms than that of an employee of the opposite sex; or in the way that opportunities for promotion, transfer, training or any other benefit, service or facility are provided; or by subjecting the claimant to any other detriment	*S39(2) Equality Act 2010*
• dismissal – by dismissing an employee for a discriminatory reason	*S39(2) Equality Act 2010* *Schedule 9*
• occupational requirement is possible if it is a proportionate means of achieving a legitimate aim	

Discrimination on the grounds of religion or belief	Case/statute
Direct discrimination	
• the person is treated less favourably than a person of the opposite sex would be	*S13 Equality Act 2010* *Azmi v Kirklees Metropolitan Borough Council*
Indirect discrimination	
• the claimant is subjected to a provision, criterion or practice which is discriminatory in relation to his or her sex, which puts him or her at a disadvantage compared with persons of the opposite sex; and it cannot be shown to be a proportionate means of achieving a legitimate aim	*S19 Equality Act 2010* *Eweida v British Airways*
Harassment	
• the claimant is subjected to unwanted conduct related to his or her sex, with the purpose or effect of violating his or her dignity, or subjecting him or her to an intimidating, hostile, degrading, humiliating or offensive environment	*S26 Equality Act 2010*
Victimisation	
• the claimant was subjected to a detriment because he or she brought proceedings under the Act; or gave evidence or information in connection with proceedings or did anything else for the purposes of or in connection with the Act; or made an allegation (whether or not express) that his or her employer or another person has contravened the Act	*S27 Equality Act 2010*
Discrimination in employment	
• recruitment and selection – in the way who is offered employment is decided; or in the terms on which the employment is offered; or by not offering a person employment	*S39(1) Equality Act 2010* *Glasgow City Council v McNab*
• during employment – by giving the claimant poorer terms than that of an employee of the opposite sex; or in the way that opportunities for promotion, transfer, training or any other benefit, service or facility are provided; or by subjecting the claimant to any other detriment	*S39(2) Equality Act 2010* *Ladele v London Borough of Lambeth*

• dismissal – by dismissing an employee for a discriminatory reason	*S39(2) Equality Act 2010* *McClintock v Department of Constitutional Affairs*
• occupational requirement is possible if it is a proportionate means of achieving a legitimate aim	*Schedule 9 Equality Act 2010* *Glasgow City Council v McNab*

Age discrimination	Case/statute
Direct discrimination	
• the person is treated less favourably than a person of the opposite sex would be	*S13 Equality Act 2010* *London Borough of Tower Hamlets v Wooster*
Indirect discrimination	
• the claimant is subjected to a provision, criterion or practice which is discriminatory in relation to his or her sex, which puts him or her at a disadvantage compared with persons of the opposite sex; and it cannot be shown to be a proportionate means of achieving a legitimate aim	*S19 Equality Act 2010* *Homer v Chief Constable of West Yorkshire Police*
Harassment	
• the claimant is subjected to unwanted conduct related to his or her sex, with the purpose or effect of violating his or her dignity, or subjecting him or her to an intimidating, hostile, degrading, humiliating or offensive environment	*S26 Equality Act 2010*
Victimisation	
• the claimant was subjected to a detriment because he or she brought proceedings under the Act; or gave evidence or information in connection with proceedings or did anything else for the purposes of or in connection with the Act; or made an allegation (whether or not express) that his or her employer or another person has contravened the Act	*S27 Equality Act 2010*
Discrimination in employment	
• recruitment and selection – in the way who is offered employment is decided; or in the terms on which the employment is offered; or by not offering a person employment	*S39(1) Equality Act 2010*
• during employment – by giving the claimant poorer terms than that of an employee of a different age group; or in the way that opportunities for promotion, transfer, training or any other benefit, service or facility are provided; or by subjecting the claimant to any other detriment	*S39(2) Equality Act 2010* *Homer v Chief Constable of West Yorkshire Police*
• dismissal – by dismissing an employee for a discriminatory reason	*S39(2) Equality Act 2010* *London Borough of Tower Hamlets v Wooster*
• occupational requirement is possible if it is a proportionate means of achieving a legitimate aim • there is now no default age for retirement	*Schedule 9 Equality Act 2010* *Wolf v Stadt Frankfurt am Main*

Part-time workers	Case/statute
Part-time worker is one paid wholly or in part by reference to the time he works and in relation to workers employed by the worker's employer under the same type of contract, is not identifiable as a full-time worker Needs a real not hypothetical full-time comparator working for the same employer doing broadly similar work Entitled to the same terms and conditions as a full-time worker who is doing broadly the same work Also entitled not to be dismissed or subjected to a detriment and dismissal connected to rights under the regulations is automatically unfair	*Regulation 2(2) Part-time Workers (Prevention of Less Favourable Treatment) Regulations 2000* *Matthews v Kent & Medway Town Fire Authority* *Regulation 5* *McMenemy v Capita Business Services Ltd* *Regulation 7*

Fixed-term employees	Case/statute
Fixed-term employee is one where termination of his contract is predetermined by objective conditions such as reaching a specific date, completing a specific task or the occurrence of a specific event Comparator is a permanent employee who works or is based at the same establishment as the fixed-term employee and who is doing broadly similar work The fixed-term employee should not be subjected to less favourable treatment in the terms of his contract or be subjected to any other detriment by any act, or deliberate failure to act, of his employer Objective justification for different treatment is possible Dismissal in connection with rights under the regulations are automatically unfair dismissal	*Regulation 2 Fixed Term Employees (Prevention of Less Favourable Treatment) Regulations 2002.* *Regulation 3* *Regulation 4* *Regulation 6*

Agency workers	Case/statute
An agency worker is one who is supplied by a temporary work agency to work temporarily for and under the supervision and direction of a hirer; and has a contract with the temporary work agency which is a contract of employment with the agency, or to perform work and services personally for the agency To claim equal treatment there is a qualifying period of twelve weeks continuous work on the same assignment The temporary agency is entitled to the same terms and conditions as an employee of the hirer Dismissal in connection with rights under the regulations are automatically unfair dismissal	*Regulation 3 Agency Workers Regulations 2010* *Regulation 7* *Regulation 5* *Regulation 17*

SAMPLE ESSAY QUESTION

ESSAY Discuss the problems traditionally associated with trying to bring claims for discrimination by gay people or by people who are undergoing or have undergone gender reassignment and how these have been overcome.

Explain the original law in relation to sexual orientation

- There was no protection in law.
- The only possible claim was under the Sex Discrimination Act 1975 or under the EU Equal Treatment Directive 76/207.

Discuss the problems associated with bringing such claims

- English courts held that the discrimination was not on grounds of sex but on grounds of sexual orientation and so was not covered under the Act – *Smith v Gardner Merchant Ltd*.
- ECJ also identified that sexual orientation was not covered by the Equal Treatment Directive 76/207 *Grant v South West Trains*.
- This meant that discriminatory employment policies against gays were legitimate *R v Ministry of Defence, ex parte Smith*.
- Another consequence was that same sex marriage was impossible.

Explain the original law in relation to gender reassignment

- There was no protection in law.
- The only possible claim was under the Sex Discrimination Act 1975 or under the EU Equal Treatment Directive 76/207.

Discuss the problems associated with trying to gain equality as a transsexual

- People born with confused gender could never change the gender given on the birth certificate.
- This could be particularly significant to hermaphrodites where doctors who determined the actual gender incorrectly.
- It also meant that transsexuals who had undergone gender reassignment were unable to marry a partner of the sex that they had transferred from.

Discuss the problems associated with bringing discrimination claims

- English courts initially held that the Sex Discrimination Act could not apply *P v S and Cornwall CC*.
- This could then justify discriminatory employment practices.

Explain how the problems have been overcome

- ECJ in *P v S and Cornwall CC* took the opposite view.
- EU introduced Framework Directive 2000/78.
- UK introduced various regulations and more recently the Equality Act 2010.

Discuss how these legal developments have removed the problem

- Framework Directive 2000/78 included sexual orientation and gender reassignment within the scope of discrimination law.
- The Directive introduced definitions for direct discrimination, indirect discrimination (which was wider than old UK definition), harassment and victimisation.
- The Equality Act 2010 includes both sexual orientation and gender reassignment as protected characteristics and the four types of prohibited conduct.

REACH REASONED CONCLUSIONS

SUMMARY

- Following the EU Framework Directive a range of other areas where there is a potential for discrimination and where protection is needed have been identified.
- These include age, gender reassignment, religion and belief, and sexual orientation.
- These are now protected characteristics under the Equality Act 2010.
- They are subject to the full range of prohibited conduct under the Act which includes direct discrimination, indirect discrimination, harassment and victimisation.
- Besides this employees are protected in every aspect of employment including recruitment and selection, during employment and on dismissal.
- The EU has also developed protections for part-time workers, fixed-term employees and agency workers.
- The protections generally mean that such workers enjoy the same conditions of work as full-time employees, employees with work of indefinite duration and actual employees of the employer.

Further reading

Emir, Astra, *Selwyn's Law of Employment 17th edition*. Oxford University Press, 2012, Chapter 4.
Pitt, Gwyneth, *Cases and Materials on Employment Law 3rd edition*. Pearson, 2008, Chapter 3.

15

Protection from discrimination (6) pursuing discrimination claims

AIMS AND OBJECTIVES

After reading this chapter you should be able to:

- Understand the processes for submitting a claim
- Understand the time limits, where the burden of proof lies and how information may be obtained
- Understand the available remedies
- Critically analyse the area
- Apply the law to factual situations and reach conclusions

It is worth noting that it was identified in *Lewisham & Guys Mental Health NHS Trust v Andrews (Deceased)* [1999] IRLR 407 that a discrimination claim can survive the death of the claimant and be pursued by the personal representatives of the deceased under the Law Reform (Miscellaneous Provisions) Act 1934.

15.1 Procedure for claiming

Jurisdiction

An employment tribunal has jurisdiction to hear discrimination claims arising from employment under section 39 Equality Act 2010 as well as harassment under section 40, relationships that have ended under section 108, instructing and causing discrimination under section 111, aiding a contravention under section 112, and equality of terms under sections 64–79.

Time limits to making a claim

By virtue of section 123 Equality Act 2010 anyone having one of the protected characteristics identified in sections 4–12 and 18 of the Act can bring a complaint to an employment tribunal which must be within three months of the prohibited conduct about which they are complaining.

In this respect a distinction must be made between an act of continuing discrimination and an act with continuing discriminatory consequences. In a claim based on continuing discrimination the claim must be made within three months of the discriminatory act ceasing.

CASE EXAMPLE

Calder v James Findlay Corporation Ltd [1989] IRLR 55

The employer provided a subsidised mortgage facility but this had never been made available to women. The claimant actually lodged her discrimination claim five months after she was refused the mortgage facility by her employer but the claim was made within three months of her leaving her employment. The court held that the act was one of continuing discrimination and therefore it continued until she left the employment. Her claim was made in time.

In the case of an act of continuing discriminatory consequences the claim must be made to the tribunal within three months of the discriminatory act itself. This can work against the employee where the act is a single act rather than a discriminatory policy for instance.

CASE EXAMPLE

Sougrin v Haringey Health Authority [1992] IRLR 416

A black nurse unsuccessfully appealed against her employer's decision to place her on a particular pay grade although an appeal by a white colleague was successful and she was therefore paid at a higher rate than the claimant. She then made a claim to a tribunal for race discrimination six months later. The Court of Appeal held that the decision on what grade to pay her was a single act with continuing discriminatory consequences rather than a continuing act of discrimination. On this basis her claim was out of time.

On the other hand there are circumstances in which the distinction could work to the benefit of the claimant.

CASE EXAMPLE

Clarke v Hampshire Electro-Plating Co Ltd [1991] IRLR 490

The claimant, a black employee, responded to an advertisement for a promotion to a supervisory role with his employer but was told that he would not be considered for the job. More than three months later a white man was appointed to the post and the claimant brought a claim for discrimination. The tribunal found that his claim had been made out of time. However, the EAT held that the discrimination did not occur until the white person had been appointed and so his claim was in time. It was a single act with continuing discriminatory consequences.

Burden of proof

Section 136 Equality Act 2010 now identifies where the burden of proof lies in a discrimination claim in respect of any of the protected characteristics.

'136 Burden of proof.
(1) This section applies to any proceedings relating to a contravention of this Act.
(2) If there are facts from which the court could decide, in the absence of any other explanation, that a person (A) contravened the provision concerned, the court must hold that the contravention occurred.
(3) But subsection (2) does not apply if A shows that A did not contravene the provision.'

On this basis where the employee brings a claim of discrimination and in the absence of any other explanation the facts indicate that discrimination may have occurred the court will presume that the discrimination has occurred and so the burden of proof shifts to the employer to show that the act complained of was not discriminatory.

A claimant can also ask for details of statistics showing the numbers of people from a particular protected characteristic who have been appointed or promoted or dismissed or one of the other areas where discrimination may have occurred as this may be indicative of discrimination.

Questionnaire procedures and the obtaining of information

Section 138 Equality Act 2010 outlines the procedure for a claimant to obtain necessary information in respect of the claim. A questionnaire is sent to the employer either before the claim is made in the tribunal or within twenty-one days of making the claim.

The questionnaire is designed to help the person making the claim to find the reasons why the discrimination occurred. There are prescribed questionnaires for the different types of discrimination and the answers to the questions are admissible as evidence in the tribunal which can draw inferences from a failure to respond or from evasive answers.

Enforcement powers of the Equality and Human Rights Commission

The Commission has powers under the Equality Act 2006 (as amended) to bring proceedings on behalf of a person who has been discriminated against by direct discrimination under section 13 Equality Act 2010, disability discrimination under section 15 Equality Act 2010, gender reassignment discrimination under section 16 Equality Act 2010, pregnancy and maternity discrimination under section 18 Equality Act 2010, and indirect discrimination under section 19 Equality Act 2010. The proceedings must be commenced within six months of the conduct that is the subject of the complaint.

The Commission has powers to investigate and to issue notices to prevent repetition of the discrimination. It can apply to a court for an injunction to restrain a person from discriminating. It can provide a claimant with assistance in legal proceedings including financial assistance. It can also carry out formal investigations and issue non-discrimination notices.

15.2 Remedies

If a tribunal has found that there has been a breach of one of the provisions identified in section 120, that is the work provisions in section 39, harassment under section 40, relationships that have ended under section 108, instructing and causing discrimination under section 111, and aiding a contravention under section 112, then the tribunal is able to grant one of the remedies outlined in section 124.

'124 Remedies: general.

(2) The tribunal may –

    (a) make a declaration as to the rights of the complainant and the respondent in relation to the matters to which the proceedings relate;

    (b) order the respondent to pay compensation to the complainant;

    (c) make an appropriate recommendation.

(3) An appropriate recommendation is a recommendation that within a specified period the respondent takes specified steps for the purpose of obviating or reducing the adverse effect of any matter to which the proceedings relate –

    (a) on the complainant;

    (b) on any other person.'

So in essence the section identifies three possible orders that the tribunal can make following a successful claim of unlawful discrimination:

- A declaration of the infringement of the employee's rights.
- An award of compensation against the employer.
- A recommendation to end the discrimination within a specified time (and if the recommendation is not complied with then this can result in an award of extra compensation).

A declaration of the infringement of the employee's rights

A declaration is relatively straightforward. It will identify whether an infringement of any of the rights under the Act have been infringed. It will also declare the rights of the employee and the employer in relation to the substance of the claim.

An award of compensation

An award of compensation in discrimination claims is on the tort scale as a result of which damages for injury to feelings is possible where some injury has been sustained and this is attributable to the discrimination.

CASE EXAMPLE

Taylor v XLN Telecom Ltd [2010] IRLR 499

The respondents are a business which provides broadband and other telecom services. The claimant joined them in October 2006. He was promoted to team leader in the broadband division with effect from 1 October 2007 on a three month probationary basis. There was some dissatisfaction expressed with his performance, and the probationary period was extended. On 10 March 2008 the claimant lodged a formal grievance. Although initially his grievance did not allege any kind of racial discrimination, in the course of a grievance appeal meeting on 11 April he complained of racially offensive conduct on the part of one of his managers. The grievance was rejected. Following a probation review meeting on 19 May, the claimant was suspended; and by letter dated 27 May he was dismissed with immediate effect, ostensibly for poor performance. What, however, the tribunal held (so far as the victimisation claim is concerned) was that while the dismissal was indeed partly on perceived performance grounds the respondents were also influenced to a significant extent by the fact that the claimant had brought the grievance that he did and that it included an allegation of racial discrimination

The claimant, a black employee, had issued a grievance and during the grievance procedure made a complaint of racial discrimination by one of his managers. He was then dismissed and the employer claimed that the dismissal was for poor performance. The claimant then suffered a psychiatric illness which he believed was a result of the dismissal. In his claim for unfair dismissal it emerged that while the dismissal was partly because of performance his employer was also influenced to a significant extent by the fact that he had brought the grievance and alleged racial discrimination which obviously amounts to victimisation. The tribunal had not made an award for injury to feelings or personal (psychiatric) injury because he was unaware at the time that it was attributable to the discrimination. The EAT held that this was irrelevant as the psychiatric injury was still attributable to the discrimination and that he should receive compensation for injury to feelings.

Courts have subsequently set guidelines as to how compensation for injury to feelings should be set.

CASE EXAMPLE

Vento v Chief Constable of West Yorkshire (No 2) [2003] IRLR 102

The claimant was a police officer who became divorced and had to combine caring for her three young children with her work responsibilities. She initially had good relationships with her colleagues but then became subjected to aggressive criticism of her character and her personal life. As a result she suffered clinical depression and was off sick for three months. On her return she was subjected to further discrimination and became suicidal. She was eventually dismissed. The tribunal accepted that she had suffered treatment that was less favourable than a hypothetical male would have received and inferred that this was on grounds of her sex. The tribunal's award of £257,844 included £65,000 for injury to feelings. The EAT held that this amount was so excessive as to amount to an error of law. The Court of Appeal set the award for injury to feelings at £18,000. It also identified that awards for injury to feelings should usually fall within three bands.

JUDGMENT

'i) The top band should normally be between £15,000 and £25,000. Sums in this range should be awarded in the most serious cases, such as where there has been a lengthy campaign of discriminatory harassment on the ground of sex or race. This case falls within that band. Only in the most exceptional case should an award of compensation for injury to feelings exceed £25,000.

ii) The middle band of between £5,000 and £15,000 should be used for serious cases, which do not merit an award in the highest band.

iii) Awards of between £500 and £5,000 are appropriate for less serious cases, such as where the act of discrimination is an isolated or one off occurrence. In general, awards of less than £500 are to be avoided altogether, as they risk being regarded as so low as not to be a proper recognition of injury to feelings.'

The case of *Da'Bell v NSPCC* [2010] IRLR 19 identified that the upper limits of the bands should be raised in line with inflation to £30,000, £18,000 and £6,000 respectively.

Traditionally awards were subject to the unfair dismissal maximum level. However, in *Marshall v Southampton & South West Area Health Authority (No 2)* [1993] IRLR 445 it was decided that there should be no upper limit. Now there is no upper limit and the award can include aggravated damages where the discriminatory treatment was malicious, insulting or oppressive. The award for injury to feelings is separate. There have subsequently been some very high levels of compensation awarded. In *Ministry of Defence v Cannock* [1994] IRLR 509 females serving in the armed services were forced to leave when they became pregnant. In their successful claim compensation of £300,000 was awarded.

If there has been indirect discrimination but the tribunal is satisfied that the practice, provision or criterion was not applied with the intention of discriminating then it must not make an award of compensation until it has considered whether to make a declaration or a recommendation.

A recommendation

The tribunal may issue a recommendation which is appropriate to the circumstances of the claim. The recommendation is likely to be that the employer takes specified steps to remove the discrimination within a specified period. It could also indicate improvements that the employer should make which could benefit other employees. If the employer fails to make the adjustments by the time set and has no reasonable excuse for not complying with the recommendation then the tribunal can make an order for additional compensation to be paid. There is no power to make a recommendation in the case of equal pay claims.

KEY FACTS

Procedure for claiming	Case/statute
Jurisdiction	
• an employment tribunal has jurisdiction to hear discrimination claims arising from employment and harassment	S39 Equality Act 2010 S40 Equality Act 2010
• in respect of relationships that have ended, instructing and causing discrimination	S108 Equality Act 2010 S111 Equality Act 2010
• aiding a contravention	S112 Equality Act 2010
• equality of terms	SS64–79 Equality Act 2010
Time limits	
• anyone having one of the protected characteristics can bring a claim within three months	S123 Equality Act 2010
• in a claim based on continuing discrimination the claim must be made within three months of the discriminatory act ceasing	Calder v James Findlay Corporation Ltd
• in the case of an act of continuing discriminatory consequences the claim must be made to the tribunal within three months of the discriminatory act itself	Sougrin v Harringey Health Authority
Burden of proof	
• where in the absence of any other explanation the facts indicate that discrimination may have occurred the court presumes that discrimination has occurred and the burden of proof shifts to the employer to show that it was not discriminatory	S136 Equality Act 2010

Obtaining information	
• a questionnaire is sent to the employer either before the claim is made in the tribunal or within twenty-one days of making the claim	*S138 Equality Act 2010*
Remedies	**Case/statute**
Three possible orders:	
• a declaration identifying any infringement of the employee's rights • an award of compensation • A recommendation e.g. to end the discrimination within a specified time	*S120 Equality Act 2010*
Compensation:	
• can include injury to feelings • there are guidelines for three levels of award for injured feelings • and these should be updated for inflation • the upper level for total compensation is now unlimited	*Taylor v XLN Telecom Ltd* *Vento v Chief Constable of West Yorkshire (No 2)* *Da'Bell v NSPCC* *Marshall v Southampton & South West Area Health Authority (No 2)*

SUMMARY

- An employment tribunal has jurisdiction to hear discrimination claims arising from employment and harassment, in respect of relationships that have ended, for instructing and causing discrimination, for aiding a contravention or for equality of terms.
- Claims need to be brought within three months of the act complained of.
- There is a reversal in the burden of proof in such claims.
- The tribunal can make a declaration identifying any infringement of the employee's rights, award compensation or make a recommendation.

Further reading

Emir, Astra, *Selwyn's Law of Employment 17th edition*. Oxford University Press, 2012, Chapter 4.
Pitt, Gwyneth, *Cases and Materials on Employment Law 3rd edition*. Pearson, 2008, Chapter 2.
Sargeant, Malcolm and Lewis, David, *Employment Law 6th edition*. Pearson, 2012, Chapter 5.4.

16

Health and safety law

AIMS AND OBJECTIVES

After reading this chapter you should be able to:

▨ Understand the non-delegable nature of the employer's common law duty to his employees

▨ Understand the different aspects of the common law duty

▨ Understand the character and scope of the common law duty

▨ Understand the available defences to the common law duty

▨ Understand how the duty has developed in the case of stress at work, and harassment and bullying

▨ Understand the basic statutory duties

▨ Understand the development of the duty through EU law

▨ Be able to critically analyse the area

▨ Be able to apply the law to factual situations and reach conclusions

16.1 Introduction: the significance of health and safety at work

According to the *Health and Safety Statistics 2011/12* published by the Health and Safety Executive, for the period 2011/12:

▨ *1.1 million* working people were suffering from a work-related illness;

▨ *173* workers were killed at work;

▨ *110,000* injuries were reported under RIDDOR (Reporting of Injuries, Diseases and Dangerous Occurrences Regulations 1995);

▨ *212,000* reportable injuries occurred (ones involving more than three days' absence from work);

▨ *27 million* working days were lost due to work-related illness and workplace injury;

▨ workplace injuries and ill health (excluding cancer) cost society an estimated *£13.4 billion* (in 2010/2011).

Besides these, closer examination of the statistics also reveals the following:

- There were *1 million* self-reported injuries at work in the period.
- There were more than *12,000* work related deaths in the period (the largest cause being cancer and the second largest chronic obstructive pulmonary disorder).
- There were over *8,000* deaths (over 5,000 from the construction industry) from work related cancer and *13,000* new cases estimated per year.
- There were *261* occupational asthma cases seen by consultants in 2010, according to GPs there are about *7,000* new cases of work related respiratory disorders each year, and about *4,000* COPD deaths each year caused by past exposure to gases, dust and fumes at work.
- There were *141,000* new cases of work related musculoskeletal disorders with *297,000* pre-existing cases and *7.5 million* working days lost.
- According to GPs there are about *40,000* new cases of work related skin diseases each year with nearly *1,500* dermatitis cases seen in 2010.
- There are about *20,000* new cases of work related noise induced hearing loss each year.
- There are about *1,500* new claims each year for Industrial Injuries Disablement Benefit arising from hand–arm vibration disorders.
- There were *221,000* new cases of work related stress and *10.4 million* working days lost through work related stress.

By any standards the figures are staggering and indicate how significant the area of health and safety at work is and how important it is to ensure health and safety at work, not just because of the human cost to employees and their families but the cost to society as a whole.

This is not to say that these figures are at all comparable with the situation during and immediately following the Industrial Revolution and the desperate need for legislative intervention in the nineteenth century (see Chapter 1.3). However, while it has to be accepted that different types of work involve different dangers, it would nevertheless seem that any death at work or resulting from work ought to be considered unacceptable.

Regulation of health and safety at work involves both statutory provisions, some resulting from membership of the EU, but also common law.

16.2 Common law health and safety at work protections

16.2.1 The origins of liability and the non-delegable duty of care

Employers' liability is a well developed principle that is to be found in both the common law and statute. It developed initially in the nineteenth century through very limited statutory controls following the Industrial Revolution. The very first industrial safety law was Sir Robert Peel's Health and Morals of Apprentices Act 1802 (see Chapter 1.3.1).

Most often those controls applied only to children and sometimes to women and were aimed more at regulating employment practices than at providing legal rights for employees. The first Acts to provide protection for adult male workers were the Factory

Act 1833 (which created a Factory Inspectorate) and the Factory Act 1844 (which introduced the idea of fencing of dangerous machinery) (see Chapter 1.3.2).

So it took a long time for civil liability to develop in the area, not until the Workmen's Compensation Act 1897, and workers rarely had the means of suing or gaining compensation for the injuries that they sustained through negligent practices (see Chapter 1.3.3).

The nature of the development has also meant that the area is quite complex and involves consideration of both common law and statutory provision.

Employment was traditionally seen, as it still is, as a contractual relationship, and so based on freedom of contract, and so originally no remedies were available in tort. Employees were free to negotiate their own contractual terms, at least in theory, and so if no reference to industrial safety was made in the contract then no civil action was available.

The original problems in bringing a claim
In the nineteenth century there were three further major barriers to workers' claims in respect of injuries sustained at work:

- the defence of *volenti non fit injuria* (voluntary acceptance of risk) – the worker in accepting the work was said also to have consented to the risks and dangers inherent in the specific type of work;
- the defence of contributory negligence – this was a complete defence at that time so that if the employer could show that the employee was engaging in unsafe working practices then there could be no claim and this would be the case even though the worker had been directed to pursue those practices by the employer;
- the so-called 'fellow servant rule' and the common law doctrine of common employment – where an employee was injured as the result of an unsafe practices of a fellow employee the employer could disclaim responsibility for that employee's actions and there could be no claim against the employer, and there would be little point in claiming against the 'fellow servant' who would inevitably be a 'man of straw'.

The effects of all of these have already been discussed in Chapter 1.4.5. Certainly industrial workers in the eighteenth and nineteenth centuries worked in very dangerous conditions and were given very little protection from the common law courts.

Development of limitations in the defences
The common law was generally hostile to workers and applied these three defences rigorously. Gradually, however, their severity was limited:

- In *Smith v Baker* [1891] AC 325 the court accepted that *volenti* would only be available if the claimant freely accepted and understood the specific risk.
- The Law Reform (Contributory Negligence) Act 1945 altered the character of the defence of contributory negligence making it a partial defence only affecting the amount of damages to be received rather than removing liability altogether as had formerly been the case.
- Finally in *Groves v Lord Wimbourne* [1898] 2 QB 402 the 'fellow servant' rule was held not to be available as a defence to a breach of a statutory duty; and in the Law Reform (Personal Injuries) Act 1948 the defence was finally abolished altogether.

Developments in industrial safety law
There were also further major positive developments in the law:

- In *Wilsons & Clyde Coal v English* [1938] AC 57 the court identified that the employer owed a personal and non-delegable duty of care towards his employees.

- Employers became liable for defective plant and equipment in the Employers Liability (Defective Equipment) Act 1969.
- The principle of the employer insuring workers against injury that was introduced in the Workmen's Compensation Act 1897 in respect of a limited range of named occupations was at a later stage extended to include all employees by the Employers' Liability (Compulsory Insurance) Act 1969.

The main ways of imposing liability on an employer

Subsequent to all of these developments there are in principle three means by which an employee might impose liability on an employer:

- for a breach of the employer's personal non-delegable duty of care;
- for a breach of a statutory duty e.g. under the Health and Safety at Work Act 1974 or other regulatory provisions where they include civil liability (see Chapter 16.3);
- for the tortious acts of another employee through the principle of vicarious liability.

All three have been subject to significant development. Proving the complexity of the area, in a claim for an injury at work the pleadings will very often involve more than one, and there is the added further complication of being interspersed with a huge number of statutory duties and regulatory provisions, as well as regulations generated by the EU Framework Directive on Health and Safety 89/391 which may also provide civil liability actions.

All of these might prove beneficial to a claimant since commonly with statutory duties liability is strict or the burden of proof is reversed. Often also a common law duty is contained in any case within a statutory provision. For these reasons a claim is often a mixture of both, pleaded as alternatives. With statutory duties there is of course the added complication of demonstrating that the statute does indeed provide a civil remedy.

The basic duty and the employer's non-delegable duty of care

The basic common law duty in essence derives from the judgment of Lord Wright in *Wilsons & Clyde Coal Co Ltd v English* [1938] AC 57. The basic duty is to take reasonable care for the safety of all employees while acting in the course of their employment.

CASE EXAMPLE

Wilsons & Clyde Coal Co Ltd v English [1938] AC 57

A miner was injured due to negligent maintenance of the pit premises. The colliery owner tried to avoid liability by arguing that that it had delegated its responsibilities and liability under various industrial safety laws in place at that time to its Colliery Manager. It had achieved this it argued by contractually making him entirely responsible for safety. The court held that the employer's personal liability could not be delegated to a third party, who was in any case an employee, and found the colliery liable on that basis. It also outlined the possible scope of the duty: to provide competent working colleagues, safe plant and equipment, a safe place of work and a safe system of work

JUDGMENT

Lord Wright identified the duty as personal and non-delegable. He explained: 'the obligation is fulfilled by the exercise of due care and skill. But it is not fulfilled by entrusting its fulfilment to employees, even though selected with due care and skill. The obligation is threefold, the provision of a competent staff of men, adequate material, and a proper system and effective supervision.'

In fact we can separate out these three key aspects and add a fourth:

- the duty to provide competent staff as working colleagues;
- the duty to provide safe plant and equipment;
- the duty to provide a safe system of work;
- the duty to provide a safe place of work.

As the law has developed there has also now been established a general common law duty to protect the health and safety of the worker. This duty extends not only to physical health and well-being but in more recent times has also developed into an obligation to ensure the psychiatric health and well-being of the worker.

One significant fact that must be remembered is that these categories are quite simply stated and do not necessarily fully reflect the complexities of the modern workplace. In this sense the separate duties can quite easily overlap. In any case the likelihood is that a claim that an employer has breached his duties towards an employee will more than likely contain elements of more than one aspect of the duty. Besides this, as has already been indicated, there is likely to be overlap also with many of the statutory duties and, if there are civil remedies attached the claim, will possibly include a range of evidence of the employer's breaches, both common law and statutory.

16.2.2 The duty to provide safe working colleagues

Most employees work within a team of some sort. Many employees work in conditions that include obvious dangers. The clear obligation on the employer is to ensure that all employees are competent to carry out the duties they are required to undertake in the course of their employment, and in that respect to protect their fellow employees.

CASE EXAMPLE

General Cleaning Contractors Ltd v Christmas [1953] AC 180

A window cleaner was injured while cleaning sash windows. The injury was in effect self-inflicted but resulted from having been improperly instructed on the safest and most appropriate method of undertaking the work. The employer was held liable. Since the employer is bound to provide adequate training not only should the claimant have been properly instructed in the work but the employee providing the advice as to the manner of completing the work should have been properly instructed also.

Clearly the competence of a fellow employee will depend also on the extent of training given. The obligation on the employer is also then to train employees so as to avoid the risk of harm.

CASE EXAMPLE

Hawkins v Ross Castings [1970] 1 All ER 180

The claimant was injured when molten metal was spilled on his legs. The accident was partly caused by the inexperience of a young worker who had not been properly trained in carrying molten metal. The employer was liable.

The employer is also bound to ensure the good behaviour of all employees while at work. As a result the employer should not tolerate any unsafe practices including practical jokes that might cause harm to other employees. The employer should deal with such unsafe practices effectively so that an employee who indulges in them should be disciplined and in extreme cases even dismissed.

CASE EXAMPLE

Hudson v Ridge Manufacturing Co [1957] 2 QB 348

An employee was injured following a practical joke by a fellow employee who had wrestled him to the ground breaking his wrist. The employee was already well known for such behaviour. The employer was held to have breached his duty and was thus liable because he had failed previously to discipline the practical joker and prevent him from repeating the behaviour.

JUDGMENT

Streatfield J explained: '[where] a fellow workman is not merely incompetent but, by his habitual conduct, is likely to prove a source of danger to his fellow employees, a duty lies . . . on the employer to remove that source of danger'.

Of course, as with any duty, the duty is based on reasonable foreseeability, so that an employer will not be liable if he is unaware or could not reasonably foresee that the employee causing damage or injury is likely to behave in the manner causing the harm.

CASE EXAMPLE

O'Reilly v National Rail & Tramway Appliances [1966] 1 All ER 499

A gang of labourers was breaking up a disused railway line when they discovered what they believed to be an unexploded shell from the Second World War. It was approximately nine inches long and one inch in diameter. The claimant was injured when he followed the suggestion of his work colleagues that he should hit the object with a sledgehammer. One of them had said 'Hit it: what are you scared of?' The employer could not have foreseen that the employees would behave so recklessly. As a result he escaped liability for the severe injuries sustained by the claimant.

In modern times actions using this basic common law duty are rare because of the principle of vicarious liability. However, it may still be useful when the employee's act causing injury or damage falls outside the scope of employment.

16.2.3 The duty to provide safe plant and equipment

If the tools with which the employee works are not safe then he is clearly at risk of harm. The basic duty on plant and equipment then is that the employer must take reasonable care not only to provide safe plant and equipment but also of course to maintain it properly so that it remains safe.

CASE EXAMPLE

Smith v Baker [1891] AC 325

We have already seen the case in the context of the nineteenth century development of employers' liability (see Chapter 1.4.5). It involved a quarry worker who was hurt when stones fell on him from hoppers that crossed over the quarry bottom on a conveyor system. The employer tried to rely on the defence of *volenti*, that by accepting the work the employee had also accepted the risks of harm that went with it. However, the risk was not a normal consequence of the work. The machinery was not properly maintained and the employee did what he could to avoid harm. The employer was liable.

JUDGMENT

Lord Halsbury LC explained the situation: 'The question of law that seems to be in debate is whether ... on occasion when the very form of his employment prevented him from looking out for himself, he consented to undergo this particular risk ... I do not think the plaintiff did consent at all. His attention was on a drill, and while he was unable to take precautions himself, a stone was negligently slung over his head without due precautions against its being permitted to fall.'

As with safe working colleagues, training is a critical aspect of discharging the duty. The employer's obligation then is not only to provide and maintain safe plant and equipment but also to train employees how to use equipment properly in order that it remains safe.

CASE EXAMPLE

Mountenay (Hazzard) & Others v Bernard Matthews [1993] (unreported)

An employee developed a clinical wrist complaint as the result of continuously handling dead poultry on a production line. There had been no attempt to rotate work to prevent workers constantly using the same wrist actions (see also 16.2.4 – safe system of work) or to educate workers to the natural risks associated with the work. As a result the employer was found liable.

It may not be the fault of the employer that equipment is potentially hazardous. This could result from some defect in its manufacture. Nevertheless, where an employer is aware of defective equipment then it is part of his duty to remove it from use to do everything reasonable to avoid harm. A failure to do so may result in liability for injuries resulting from use of the defective equipment.

CASE EXAMPLE

Taylor v Rover Co Ltd [1966] 1 WLR 1491

The employer had purchased a batch of chisels that were brittle because of manufacturing defects. The employer failed to remove them from use and an employee was injured in the eye when one shattered. The employer was liable for leaving the equipment in use.

An employer can, however, always avoid liability if he is able to show that he has actually provided adequate equipment and that the injury has been caused because the employee has misused the equipment or failed to make proper use of it.

CASE EXAMPLE

Parkinson v Lyle Shipping Co Ltd [1964] 2 Lloyd's Rep 79

Here an employee was badly burned while trying to light a boiler. There was no defect in the boiler. It was quite safe and the employee had been properly instructed in how to light it. So there was no liability.

As with all aspects of the common law duty this aspect has been superseded by statute. Now the provisions of the Employer's Liability (Defective Equipment) Act 1969 are a more likely source of liability. While the Act has a precise definition of equipment in section 1(3) 'any plant and machinery, vehicle, aircraft and clothing', it has still been subject to conflicting interpretation.

CASE EXAMPLE

Coltman v Bibby Tankers [1988] AC 276

In this case the Court of Appeal held that an injury sustained because of a defect in the hull of a ship was not actionable, not falling within the definition. The House of Lords later reversed this and accepted that the definition within the Act could include the circumstances of the case.

As with all statutory provisions the definitions within sections of Acts may be challenged and the court will be called on to interpret. This may lead to some surprising results.

CASE EXAMPLE

Knowles v Liverpool City Council [1993] ICR 21

In this case the court found no problem in bringing a kerbstone within the definition for the purposes of imposing liability under the Act. The employee had been injured because of the negligence of the council in failing to ensure that kerbstones were not raised and it was liable as a result of the broad interpretation accepted by the court.

16.2.4 The duty to provide a safe system of work

The duty to provide a safe system of work is all embracing and concerns all aspects of the work including use of equipment and of protective clothing as well as training and supervision. So it is very much about how the work is organised. There are clearly two key aspects to the duty:

- the creation of a safe system from the outset;
- a proper and continuous implementation of the system.

Creating a safe system

The general duty is to provide an effective system of work which is sufficient to meet any foreseeable dangers.

CASE EXAMPLE

General Cleaning Contractors Ltd v Christmas [1953] AC 180 (see also 16.2.2)

As we have already seen in 16.2.2, holding on to a window sill and without wedges while cleaning sash windows proved to be an unsafe system which led to injury. It was the system that had been explained to the employee by his immediate superior and which he was instructed to follow. The employer was liable because the system was unsafe.

Implementing the system

The duty is not merely to create a safe system of work it is also ensuring that the system is carried out. A safe system is only safe if it is actually followed. Thus, for instance, there is no point in an employer possessing safety equipment if employees are not provided with it.

CASE EXAMPLE

Bux v Slough Metals [1974] 1 All ER 262

The employer had complied with one aspect of the duty by providing safety goggles. However, the employee would not use them because he claimed that they misted up. The employee was then injured by a splash of molten metal. The employer was liable because of failing to ensure that the goggles were worn, the second part of the duty, ensuring that the system is implemented.

Many types of employment are dangerous and the nature of the work or by the people with whom the employee has to work creates a foreseeable risk of harm. The employer's duty is to create a system that will help to avoid the risk of harm. A failure on the part of the employer to operate such a system may then lead to liability when an injury occurs.

CASE EXAMPLE

Cook v Bradford Community NHS Trust [2002] EWCA Civ 1616

The claimant was employed in a psychiatric ward which housed some unstable and dangerous patients. The claimant was assaulted by one violent patient which in itself was a foreseeable risk. Because the systems were inadequate to address the risk involved the employer was liable for the injury.

In recent times it has been possible to bring action for the result of any physical danger in the workplace where the system of work is inadequate and as a result the employer has failed to protect the employee from foreseeable harm.

CASE EXAMPLE

Ingram v Worcestershire County Council [2000] The Times 11 January 2000

A council worker supervised a gypsy camp site as warden and was attacked by residents of the site after the council changed its policies on the treatment of the residents. He had dogs set on him and was also shot at and was unable to work from 1997 onwards. The council was held liable and the employee received considerable damages of £203,000.

It is also insufficient for an employer to argue that he has created a safe system if the employees are unaware of it and therefore do not follow it. One aspect of this is that an employer might be liable for a failure to warn of the dangers associated with the work.

CASE EXAMPLE

Pape v Cumbria CC [1992] 3 All ER 211

The employee's work involved him coming into contact with certain skin irritants. The employer was liable because he failed to warn the employee that not wearing gloves might lead to dermatitis as a result of continuous contact with the irritants.

Many cases involve the provision and use of safety equipment. An employer will inevitably be liable for failing to provide such equipment where it is required. In *Finch v Telegraph Construction and Maintenance Co Ltd* [1949] 1 All ER 452 the employer did provide goggles but had not told the employee where they could be located and was then liable for the employee's injury. It will also lead to liability if the employer fails to ensure that the safety equipment is used. In *Qualcast (Wolverhampton) Ltd v Haynes* [1959] AC 743 safety clothing was available but nothing done to ensure that it was worn but there was no liability because the injury was not sufficiently serious and besides this the risk was one that was obvious. It was the employee's fault for failing to use the safety clothing. By contrast in *Nolan v Dental Manufacturing Co Ltd* [1958] when a chip flew off a grinding wheel an injury caused by not wearing safety goggles was of sufficient seriousness that there was liability.

Advances in modern technology and their effect on systems of work may also impact on working conditions. For instances the use of VDUs is commonplace. There is also a range of provisions under regulations on their use. The common law duty is that systems for using VDUs must not damage the health and safety of the employee.

CASE EXAMPLE

Alexander and Others v Midland Bank plc [2000] ICR 464

Employees worked under high pressure continuously inputting and processing information into computer databases. The employees complained that the employer had consistently increased the work rate demanded and that as a result of unsafe practice they had suffered muscular injuries. They succeeded in their claim.

It is not only contact with dangerous machinery or substances that carries with it a risk of harm. Contact with the public can also be stressful as well as present potential physical hazards to employees (see *Cook v Bradford Community NHS Trust* [2002] EWCA Civ 1616 and *Ingram v Worcestershire County Council* [2000] The Times 11 January 2000 above which both also illustrate this point). An employer might be expected to operate a system of work so that the employee's safety is not unnecessarily threatened by public contact.

CASE EXAMPLE

Rahman v Arearose Ltd [2000] 3 WLR 1184

A restaurant worker was violently assaulted and seriously injured by customers. The employer was liable because it was identified that other members of staff had also been assaulted, the employer was aware of this and had not introduced any effective system to prevent it.

It is also the case that an employer cannot rely on unsafe practice using the argument that it is a common practice. Common practice may be an indication that a duty has not been breached but not if it is an inherently unsafe practice.

CASE EXAMPLE

Re Herald of Free Enterprise [1989] Independent 18 December 1989

A cross-channel ferry capsized after it left port with its bow doors open and several passengers died. In fact the owners of the vessel reached a settlement with the families of the deceased. However, it was identified that it was irrelevant that it was common for bow doors to be left open on roll-on roll-off ferries when entering or leaving port. Vessels could and did capsize as the result of such a practice.

A more recent development of the employer's duty of care to employees (see below 16.3.1) is the duty to ensure that the system of work does not cause undue stress to the employee.

CASE EXAMPLE

Walker v Northumberland CC [1995] 1 All ER 737

A senior social worker had been on long term sick leave with stress caused by unsafe working practices. A second nervous breakdown after returning to work with no change to working practices resulted in liability for the employers. This was because after the first they were aware of his susceptibility to stress and did nothing to reduce his workload or the pressure associated with it.

JUDGMENT

Colman J explained the development: 'It is clear law that an employer has a duty to provide his employee with a safe system of work and to take reasonable steps to protect him from risks which are reasonably foreseeable ... there is no logical reason why risk of psychiatric damage should be excluded from the scope of an employer's duty.'

However, it is also the case that employees owe a duty of care to themselves. In this respect an employee is expected to know of and guard against the risks associated with the job that they are doing.

CASE EXAMPLE

Roles v Nathan [1963] 1 WLR 1117

The Court of Appeal refused to impose liability on occupiers when chimney sweeps died after inhaling carbon monoxide fumes while cleaning flues in an industrial chimney. The sweeps should have accepted the advice of the occupiers to complete the work with the boilers off rather than leaving them lit.

Like the other aspects of the duty owed by employers to their employees, it is also true that the duty to provide a safe system of work has probably now been superseded by statutory provisions, for example by the duty to undertake risk assessment under the 'six pack' and other regulatory requirements on an employer (see 16.4.2).

16.2.5 The duty to provide a safe place of work

While this was not an aspect of the duty stated in Lord Wright's judgment in *Wilsons & Clyde Coal Co Ltd v English*, it is nevertheless an obvious extension of those duties that premises should also be reasonably safe to work in. The general duty is to take all steps that are reasonably practicable in the circumstances to ensure that premises are safe.

CASE EXAMPLE

Latimer v AEC [1957] AC 643

An employee was injured when slipping on a greasy patch on the factory floor following flood damage. The employer was not liable having done everything practicable to ensure that the floor was safe for use. The employer had opened the factory late, had all standing water that could be removed swept out, had cleaned the floor surface and had scattered sawdust around to ensure grip.

It is obvious that in many instances industrial, and in some cases other premises, are potentially hazardous. An employer cannot guarantee safety and must only do what is reasonable to minimise the risk of harm. Where the employee exercises a particular skill or enjoys specific expertise liability may be avoided where the worker has failed to take account of his own safety. All employees exercising a skill should be aware of the risks associated with exercising the skill and guard against those risks themselves.

CASE EXAMPLE

Roles v Nathan [1963] 1 WLR 1117

Chimney sweeps were killed by fumes when they were cleaning flues in an industrial chimney stack while boilers under the chimney were still alight. Their own expert knowledge should have alerted them to the dangers and claims for their deaths failed.

JUDGMENT

As Lord Denning stated: 'These chimney sweeps ought to have known that there might be dangerous fumes ... and ought to have taken steps to guard against them. They ought to have known that they should not attempt to seal up the sweep hole whilst the fire was still alight. They ought to have had the fire withdrawn ... they ought not to have stayed in the alcove too long when there might be dangerous fumes about. All this was known to these two sweeps; they were repeatedly warned about it, and it was for them to guard against it.'

Many employees carry out their work away from their own work premises. A natural extension of the duty in such cases is that the duty extends to other premises on which they carry out their work.

CASE EXAMPLE

Wilson v Tyneside Window Cleaning Co [1958] 2 QB 110

Window cleaners were injured while working on a client's premises. While the employer clearly owed them a duty of care, it was shown that the employer had done everything within his capability to ensure that the men were safe. As a result there was no liability.

Apart from the employer's basic duty of care to his employees, an employer will often also own or rent and therefore be in control of the premises within which employees operate. As a result there can also be liability under the Occupiers' Liability Act 1957. As with other aspects of the common law duty the duty to provide safe premises has been superseded by statutory provisions, particularly those in the so-called 'six pack' of regulations.

ACTIVITY

Quick quiz

Consider which aspect of the employers' duty may have been breached in the following circumstances:

1. On a dark December morning at the start of his shift at 6.00 a.m. on his way into the factory where he works Anton stumbles into a pothole near to the main door. He suffers a broken leg. The entrance to the factory has not been resurfaced for many years and it is very dark because the bulb in the light outside the entrance has gone and has not been replaced.

2. Baljinder suffers a severe back injury when his chair is pulled from under him by a fellow employee, Charlie, just as Baljinder is about to sit down. Fellow employees have repeatedly complained to management that Charlie's practical jokes are likely to injure someone. The employer has never disciplined Charlie or even spoken to him about his behaviour.

3. Denise has had to retire from work at age forty on ill health grounds because of a permanent bronchial complaint. This has been caused as a result of her work drilling panels of a toxic material. Denise has never been provided with a safety mask, there is no mechanism on the machine to prevent dust and she has never had any warnings about the dangers of inhaling the dust or received any health and safety training.

4. Elsie works in a café. Elsie was badly burned when a coffee making machine spurted hot liquid all over her.

16.2.6 The character of the duty

The duty, as already stated, is first and foremost entirely personal to the employer. It cannot be delegated to subordinate employees, however high ranking in the organisation. This means that liability cannot be avoided by claiming that it is the fault of another. It equally means that each and every employee is owed a duty of care.

CASE EXAMPLE

Wilsons & Clyde Coal Co Ltd v English [1938] AC 57

As we have seen in 16.2.1 above, the owner of a colliery claimed to have delegated responsibility for health and safety to its Colliery Manager by contractually making him entirely responsible for health and safety. When a miner was injured due to negligent maintenance of the pit the colliery owner was held liable. The court dismissed its arguments and refused to accept that its personal liability could be delegated to a third party, who was in any case an employee.

Clearly also a higher standard of care is owed to inexperienced employees and an obligation to train sufficiently to do the job safely. A similar point applies in the case of employees who are more vulnerable. In *James v Hepworth and Grandage Ltd* [1968] 1 QB 94 the employee did put up warning signs but owed a greater duty of care to an employee who was unable to read. However, there was no liability since the employee had regularly observed fellow employees wearing the safety clothing. Similarly in *Paris v Stepney Borough Council* [1950]

1 KB 320 an employee who was already blind in one eye was caused complete blindness through an injury when safety goggles had not been provided. Although it was not commonplace for goggles to be used in the work, the employer should have realised that there was a greater risk of substantial harm in the circumstances.

The employer's duty of care only extends to do what is reasonable in the circumstances. Particularly on industrial premises it would be an unreasonable burden to demand that an employee should guarantee the safety of employees and there is no obligation on the employer to go to extraordinary or excessively costly ends in order to avoid harm.

CASE EXAMPLE

Latimer v AEC Ltd [1953] AC 643

The employer's factory was flooded after a torrential rainstorm and the roof caving in during the storm. The water mixed with oil and grease on the floor making the surface very slippery and dangerous. The employer suspended work until the water was swept out and sawdust was spread over the floors for a more secure footing. The employee slipped on an uncovered patch of floor and was injured. The House of Lords held that, in the circumstances, the employer had done everything that could reasonably be done to avoid harm. Balancing out the possible risks of harm, the House felt that it was unreasonable to expect the factory to be closed for a longer period and it held that there was no liability.

One possible argument that an employer might make in defence is that the injury was the result of a customary practice in the trade. It has been identified that, where injuries do occur during the carrying out of such a custom or practice, the employer can only escape liability if the practice itself is a reasonable one. Where practices are inherently dangerous the employer will be liable.

CASE EXAMPLE

Cavanagh v Ulster Weaving Co [1960] AC 145

As part of his employment the employee was required to climb on to pitched roofs. In the particular circumstances he was also being asked to do so while carrying a heavy bag of cement. When the employee fell off the roof and was injured, the employer argued that this was customary practice in the trade. The court held that, despite the custom, the practice was clearly unsafe and as a result the employer was liable.

Accepting the fact that industrial premises inevitably present dangers, it is obvious that an employee might still be injured even though not actually engaged in work at the time. For this reason the law has sensibly concluded that the duty extends beyond the work itself to cover all ancillary activities which are reasonably associated with the work.

CASE EXAMPLE

Davidson v Handley Page Ltd [1945] 1 All ER 235

The employee was not actually working at the time but was on his way to his tea break. He slipped on a greasy duckboard and was injured in the fall. The court accepted that breaks were a necessary part of the working day and even though the break might be out of the course of employment there must be a safe access to wherever the break is taken. As a result the employer was held liable for the injury.

The employer is of course only obliged to guard against foreseeable risks and may take into account the practicability of any possible precautions in trying to avoid harm. There will, however, be liability if precautions taken to avoid a foreseeable risk are inadequate and increase the risk of harm.

CASE EXAMPLE

Charlton v Forrest Printing Ink Co Ltd [1978] IRLR 331

The employee was obliged to take money to the bank by walking there and carrying the money. The employee was then injured in a robbery while he was taking money to the bank. The court held that the employer was liable because much safer precautions could have been taken by which he could have avoided or at least made less likely the risk to the employee.

While the duty is to do what is reasonable to avoid reasonably foreseeable harm, the extent to which an employer is liable may depend on what the judge considers should be foreseen. Two apparently conflicting cases illustrate this. In the first of these the court held that there was no liability since, applying the *Wagon Mound* test, the precise circumstances could not be foreseen.

CASE EXAMPLE

Doughty v Turner Manufacturing Co Ltd [1964] 1 QB 518

Two employees were injured in an explosion when an asbestos lid which had been negligently placed on a chemical tank slipped into the chemicals. The court held that there was no liability because at the time it was not known that the specific chemical reaction causing the injuries would occur.

By contrast in the second case the court took a more liberal view of foreseeability and accepted that neither the precise circumstances nor the precise damage need be foreseen as long as damage of the general kind in the general circumstances of the case could be foreseen.

CASE EXAMPLE

Bradford v Robinson Rentals [1967] 1 All ER 267

Here the employee, a driver for the company, was required to drive from Exeter to Bedford in a blizzard in a van that had no heater and also had a broken window which would not close. The employer tried to claim that the resulting injury, frostbite, was unforeseeable. The court rejected the defence since some form of cold related illness was entirely foreseeable in the circumstances.

As in other areas of tortious liability the 'thin skull' rule also applies so that the employer's duty extends to considering the possible extent of the injury to the particular employee. Interestingly in such circumstances it is the former *Re Polemis* measure of remoteness of damage, that recovery of damages is possible for injury that is a natural and direct consequence of the breach, rather than the *Wagon Mound*, recovery only for foreseeable harm that is used.

CASE EXAMPLE

Paris v Stepney BC [1951] AC 367

The employee, a mechanic, was already blind in one eye. When failure to wear safety goggles resulted in the loss of his sight in his other eye, making him completely blind, the employer was held liable for the full extent of causing total blindness.

The principle can also be seen in *Smith v Leech Brain & Co. Ltd* [1962] 2 QB 405 where an employee suffered a burnt lip as a result of being splashed by molten metal following his employers' negligence. The burn activated a cancer from which the claimant later died. Since some form of harm was foreseeable, the court held that even though the death from cancer was not immediately foreseeable some harm was and the defendant was liable.

The duty is quite wide ranging but, while the duty protects the employee it does not extend as far as protecting his property.

CASE EXAMPLE

Deyong v Shenburn [1946] KB 227

The employee's clothing was stolen from a theatre in which he worked. There was held to be no liability on the employer. The employer owed a duty of care not to injure the employee but was not responsible for the employee's property.

16.2.7 Defences

An action for breach of the common law duty of care is essentially an action for negligence. As with all negligence claims there are a number of possible defences that can be argued by an employer. One very obvious way to defend a claim is by showing that there is in fact no negligence. We have already seen in *Latimer v AEC* (see 16.2.5 above) that, where the employer has done everything reasonably practicable to avoid the risk of harm the duty is not breached and there is no negligence. Similarly, if the harm suffered was solely caused by the employee's fault then there is no breach of duty on the employer and no liability. In *Brophy v Bradfield & Co Ltd* [1955] 1 WLR 1148 an employee died when he was overcome by fumes in a boiler house. The employee was a driver, he had no reason to be in the boiler house and there was no reason why the employer would expect him to be there. The employer could not do anything to guard against the death and was not liable.

There are of course two defences which are always closely connected with negligence claims. They are inevitably defences that appear also very appropriate in the case of employer's liability:

- *volenti non fit injuria* (voluntary assumption of risk);
- contributory negligence.

Volenti non fit injuria *(voluntary assumption of risk)*

Many if not most types of work carry with them their own specific risks and dangers. Certainly since the onset of the Industrial Revolution and the introduction of mechanised processes work became a more dangerous activity (see Chapter 1.2) and it was these increased dangers that ultimately led to the law intervening in and regulating industry (see Chapter 1.3).

The original argument raised by employers was that in accepting the work the employee also accepted the risks that went with it. However, even in the nineteenth century courts showed that they were reluctant to accept the absolute application of the defence of *volenti* in the context of employment (see Chapter 1.4.5).

CASE EXAMPLE

Smith v Baker [1891] AC 325

The employee drilled rock in a quarry bottom. He was injured when rocks that were carried in a crane over his head fell out and dropped on him. The mechanism had been badly maintained by the employer. The court rejected the plea of *volenti* because the worker was given no proper warning of when the crane was in use and so was unaware of the danger. He was aware of the risk of stones falling but there was no voluntary assumption of risk in the circumstances.

JUDGMENT

Lord Halsbury LC explained why the defence could not apply in the circumstances of the case: 'I think that a person who relies on the maxim must shew a consent to the particular thing done ... in order to defeat a plaintiff's right by the maxim relied on ... the jury ought to be able to affirm that he consented to the particular thing being done which would involve the risk, and consented to take the risk upon himself.'

Just because an employee works in a field that exposes him to some risk of harm does not mean that he automatically accepts the risk of harm. The three elements of the defence must still be satisfied:

- The employee is aware of the precise risk of harm.
- The employee is able to exercise free will.
- The employee as a result voluntarily accepts the risk of harm in the circumstances in which he works.

The defence does then have some application where all three are satisfied and the employee fully understands the risks involved and his agreement to take the risk is free from any pressure by the employer.

CASE EXAMPLE

ICI Ltd v Shatwell [1965] AC 656

The employee and his brother both worked in a quarry owned by the defendant. The brothers ignored both the employer's express orders and statutory regulations when they tested detonators without taking the appropriate precautions. One brother was injured in an explosion. He claimed that the employer was vicariously liable because he had been advised by his brother, a fellow employee, not to follow the orders regarding the use of detonators. The court rejected this argument. By ignoring his employer's orders and following instead his brother's unauthorised comments he had assumed the risk of injury by exercising his own free choice and the defence of *volenti* could apply.

Similarly where the employer by his negligence creates emergencies it is not then appropriate to try to apply the principles of *volenti* to the actions of those people responding to the emergency.

CASE EXAMPLE

Baker v T E Hopkins [1959] 3 All ER 225

An employer's workmen were subjected to danger by being exposed to petrol fumes in a confined space when the fumes overcame the men. A doctor attempting to rescue the men died as a result of his own exposure to the fumes. The employer tried to claim *volenti* on the part of the doctor. The court would not accept the application of the defence to the case. The doctor had not agreed to the specific risks involved. He was merely trying to do his best for the unconscious men. He had not consented to the risk of death.

JUDGMENT

The Court of Appeal explained the principle by referring to part of the judgment of Cardozo J in the American case *Wagner v International Railway Co* where he said: 'Danger invites rescue. The law does not ignore these reactions … in tracing conduct to its consequences. It recognises them as normal. It places their effects within the range of the natural and the probable. The wrong that imperils life … is a wrong also to the rescuer.'

In general as a matter of policy the defence of *volenti* is unavailable where there is a breach of a statutory duty. However, in some limited circumstances it is possible to use the defence successfully. This could also be explained as the employee in effect being the sole cause of his injury.

CASE EXAMPLE

Ginty v Belmont Building Supplies Ltd [1959] 1 All ER 414

Under his contract the employee had to climb up and down and work on roofs. He slipped and fell from a roof on which he was working and claimed against his employer for his injuries. The issue in question was the provision and use of certain safety equipment, which in this case was duckboards on which employees could walk safely. The court accepted that these had been provided by the employer and it was the failure by the employee to use the safety equipment that actually led to his injury. In the circumstances the defence of *volenti* applied. It is a complete defence and as a result the employer was not liable.

Contributory negligence

Unlike *volenti*, which is a complete defence and thus absolves liability, contributory negligence is only a partial defence reducing the amount of damages but not absolving liability. We have of course seen that this was not always the case and thus with adverse consequences for employees (see Chapter 1.4.5).

The current basis for the defence is section 1 Law Reform (Contributory Negligence) Act 1945.

SECTION

'where any person suffers damage as the result partly of his own fault and partly of the fault of any other person or persons, a claim in respect of that damage shall not be defeated by reason of the fault of the person suffering the damage, but the damage recoverable in respect thereof shall be reduced to such extent as the court thinks just and equitable having regard to the claimant's share in the responsibility for the damage'.

There are two aspects to proving that the defence applies:

- The employee failed to take care of his own safety.
- This failure is partly the cause of the injury he suffers.

So the defence may be available where although an employer has breached a duty to his employee, the employee has also failed to take care of his own safety and as a result is partly responsible for his injury.

Where the court accepts that the employee has contributed to his own harm and that contributory negligence should apply then damages will be reduced by an amount considered just and equitable by the court according to the extent to which the employee did contribute to his own injury.

CASE EXAMPLE

Jones v Livox Quarries Ltd [1952] 2 QB 608

The employee worked in a quarry and, disobeying his employer's express instructions, he rode on the rear towbar of a 'traxcavator', a vehicle used in quarries. The driver of the vehicle was unaware of the fact and, when another vehicle collided with it the claimant was injured. In his claim the court reduced his damages by 5 per cent for his contributory negligence. While the employer was negligent the employee had contributed to his own injury by riding on the towbar of a traxcavator despite the express prohibition of his employer.

JUDGMENT

Lord Denning explained the application of the defence in the case: 'Although contributory negligence does not depend on a duty of care it does depend on foreseeability. Just as actionable negligence requires the foreseeability of harm to others, so contributory negligence requires the foreseeability of harm to oneself.'

The defence may be available even in extreme situations. Thus where the death of an employee has resulted from negligence by the employer but it is accepted that the employee also contributed to his own harm by failing to take care of his own safety damages may be reduced even though the employer is still liable.

CASE EXAMPLE

Davies v Swan Motor (Swansea) Co Ltd [1949] 2 KB 291

The employee had ridden on the step of a dust-cart while it travelled on public roads. He was well aware that this was a dangerous practice. A bus owned by the defendant overtook the dust-cart and negligently collided with the dustcart. The man was killed in the collision. In the action brought by the dead man's wife both drivers were held to be negligent. The court also accepted that there was contributory negligence because of the dangerous manner in which the man had ridden on the dust-cart.

It has also been accepted, however, that employees may be treated more leniently by the courts when it comes to a finding of contributory negligence. In *Caswell v Powell Duffryn Collieries* [1940] AC 152 the court explained this approach. It is likely that the pressures of work mean that employees may take less than full care of themselves and their sense of danger dulled by familiarity, repetition, noise, confusion and fatigue. In such circumstances the court felt that employees should be protected from their own carelessness, particularly in the case of statutory regulations which are designed specifically to offer such protection and it would be to defeat the object of the provision to do otherwise.

One controversial issue concerns whether it is possible to impose liability on the employer at the same time as declaring 100 per cent contributory negligence on the part of the employee therefore leading to no award of damages.

CASE EXAMPLE

Jayes v IMI (Kynoch) Ltd [1985] ICR 155

Here the employer was liable because a statutory duty in respect of guarding machinery was strict in terms of liability for ensuring that guards were maintained at all times when machines were working. The court held that there was 100 per cent contributory negligence when the employee lost fingers because the employee himself had taken the guard off the machine in order to clear a blockage while the machine was still running.

The decision has been criticised by both judges and academic commentators.

QUOTATION

As John Cooke states: 'The defence … indicates that there must be fault on the part of both parties … a finding of 100% contributory negligence has the same effect as a finding of volenti and would undermine the principle' (John Cooke *Law of Tort 10th edition*, Pearson, 2011).

In *Pitts v Hunt* [1930] 3 All ER 344, the Court of Appeal, reversing the High Court, had already stated that a finding of 100 per cent contributory negligence would be impermissible, and explained its decision on the basis that, under the Act, the claimant must suffer damage partly as a result of his own fault and partly as a result of the defendant's fault, and 100 per cent contributory would indicate fault only on the part of the claimant.

The argument has subsequently continued. In *Reeves v Commissioner of Police for the Metropolis* [1999] UKHL 35; [2000] 1 AC 360 the trial judge held the deceased to be 100 per cent contributorily negligent. A majority of the Court of Appeal agreed but in the then House of Lords damages were reduced by 50 per cent, accepting that the claimant was only partially at fault. In *Anderson v Newham College of Further Education* [2003] ICR 212 the Court of Appeal suggested that *Jayes* was decided *per incuriam* and should not be followed. It is also possible of course to argue that all these commentators are missing the very special circumstances of *Jayes*, which, in the case of statutory duties might be repeated.

16.3 Developments in the duty of care

Over the years judges have developed the employer's duty of care to his employees. They have done so by widening the boundaries of the duty to include other aspects and also by extending the range of injuries covered by the duty.

16.3.1 Stress at work and psychiatric injury

Certainly from the 1980s following mass unemployment and more competitive attitudes to work, stress at work has become a feature which is commonly referred to. Pressure in the workplace and excessive workloads led in the 1990s to the courts accepting work related psychiatric injury as actionable and to the introduction of a general duty to protect not only the health and safety of the employee but also his general well-being and mental health.

CASE EXAMPLE

Johnstone v Bloomsbury Health Authority [1991] 2 All ER 293

A junior doctor claimed against the health authority for whom he worked in just such circumstances. He argued that that being expected as a matter of course to work as much as forty-eight hours' overtime each week and having to be on call had damaged his mental health. The court held that there was a breach of a non-excludable implied term in his contract to take reasonable steps to care for his health, safety and welfare. The employer could not use the express terms of the contract to exclude the duty and was liable.

This led to a whole new field of law on stress related illnesses and psychiatric damage caused at work. The courts accepted that there is a general duty to protect both the psychiatric health and well-being of the employee where harm is foreseeable.

CASE EXAMPLE

Petch v Commissioners of Customs and Excise [1993] ICR 789

An employee claimed damages for a mental breakdown that he alleged was caused by the stressful nature of his working conditions. Dillon LJ in the Court of Appeal held that the employer was not negligent because the event was unforeseeable and also because the employer had done everything possible to try to persuade the employee not to return to work. Nevertheless the court did accept that an employer could be liable if he knows that the employee is susceptible to stress and allows the employee to continue working in stressful circumstances.

Work related stress has been defined as a harmful reaction that employees have to undue pressures and demands placed on them in their employment. The extent of the problem of work related mental illness is illustrated in the *Health and Safety Executive (HSE) statistics*.

The most recent estimates from its Labour Force Survey (LFS) showed that:

- The total number of cases of stress in 2011/2012 was 428,000 out of a total of 1,073,000 for all work related illnesses.

- The number of new cases of work related stress rose from 221,000 to 233,000 in 2010/2011 with 196,000 pre-existing cases (but the change is not statistically significant).

- A total of 10.8 million working days were lost in the period through work related stress.

- The industries that reported the highest rates of work related stress in the three years prior to the survey were health, social work, education and public administration.

- The occupations that reported the highest rates of work related stress in the three years prior to the survey were health and social service managers, teachers and social welfare associate professionals.

The development of this aspect of the duty of care means that an employee is entitled to treat a psychiatric injury caused by negligent work practice in the same way that a physical injury would be dealt with. The courts have developed principles for establishing when the duty is breached.

CASE EXAMPLE

Walker v Northumberland CC [1995] 1 All ER 737

The case was given leave for an appeal to the Court of Appeal but was in fact settled beforehand for £175,000. The significance of the case was that the employee had already suffered a nervous breakdown owing to work related stress. On returning to work he had been promised that his workload would be reduced but he was in fact faced with a huge backlog of work from his absence. As a result he suffered a second breakdown and this caused him to leave work permanently after he was dismissed on sickness grounds. The employer was clearly liable since it placed a person who was already known to suffer from stress under even more stressful conditions, and without having done anything about the under staffing and excess of work that had caused the first breakdown. The *Walker* criteria are straightforward and can be easily applied. An employer will be liable when:

- it is aware of the employee's susceptibility to stress; and
- it has worsened that condition by unsafe practices or unnecessary pressures of work.

JUDGMENT

As Colman J explained: 'It is clear law that an employer has a duty to provide his employee with a safe system of work and to take reasonable steps to protect him from risks which are reasonably foreseeable … there is no logical reason why risk of psychiatric damage should be excluded from the … duty.'

Another context in which stress claims are also likely to occur is redeployment and changing job roles and the effect of these on involved employees. They are obviously stressful circumstances for any employee. If an employer during such processes fails to take care of the employee's general health and welfare then liability is possible provided that the *Walker* test is satisfied.

CASE EXAMPLE

Lancaster v Birmingham City Council [1998] 99(6) QR 4

The claimant was employed in a clerical capacity by a city council. She was redeployed but given no training or guidance in her new position as a housing officer. She then suffered three separate absences through stress and the employer failed to do anything about the problem so that she eventually had to retire on health grounds. The defendant council admitted liability 'in the door of the court' and compensated the claimant.

The *Walker* test also applies in a relatively straightforward way to changes in working practices. Again the employer will be liable if it is aware of the employee's susceptibility to stress related illness and falls below the standard of care that is appropriate to the duty by imposing stressful or unsafe working practices thereby worsening the employee's condition.

CASE EXAMPLE

Young v Post Office [2002] EWCA Civ 661

After changes in work practices which involved a change to computer systems but without adequate training the employee became stressed, was put on anti-depressants. He then suffered a nervous breakdown and was absent from work for months. The employer then agreed that the employee should return with a gradual reintroduction to work. In fact he had to attend a week's residential training course, and cover for a manager in his absence and suffered more stress forcing him to leave permanently. The employer was liable because it did not follow its own agreed treatment of the employee.

In some cases courts applied a stricter standard indicating that a duty only arises when an ordinary bystander would foresee that the stress suffered is likely to be of such a degree as to cause a recognised psychiatric disorder.

CASE EXAMPLE

Rorrison v West Lothian College & Lothian Regional Council [2000] (Scottish Court of Session) IDS Brief 655 February 2000

The claimant was a nurse responsible for welfare duties and first aid in a college. A new personnel officer disciplined her, allegedly for no particular reason, took her first aid role off her and changed the usual method of dealing with sick students without ever informing her. The claimant's GP then diagnosed anxiety depression and gave her sick notes for six weeks. When she returned to work the personnel officer gave her mainly clerical duties, allegedly harassed her and frequently changed her duties afterwards. At one point she was given thirty minutes to accept a change of contractual terms or be fired. She then suffered distress, panic attacks and depression and was given beta blockers by her doctor. The court stated that her action against her employers could only succeed if she was able to show an identifiable psychiatric illness rather than mere stress and was not prepared to accept anxiety depression as being the same as clinical depression. It was also suggested that the illness resulting from the work conditions should be foreseeable to a reasonable bystander rather than to a doctor to succeed. The case is only persuasive but it demonstrates a harsh application of the principles in *Walker*.

In any case *Walker* criteria must be satisfied before a successful claim can be made. This means that it is for the claimant to show that it is the actions of the employer, knowing of the employee's existing illness that has caused the later illness.

CASE EXAMPLE

Sparks v HSBC plc [2002] EWCA Civ 1942

The claimant had worked for the bank for many years when he began to suffer depression. The bank offered him retirement but instead he chose to work part time. Mistakes were found in his work but he was not disciplined and eventually he was also promoted. He suffered further depression and his work deteriorated and he was seen by the occupational therapist who recommended support although this was not given. He later retired on health grounds and claimed loss of earnings. The Court of Appeal would not accept his claim that the employer had caused or worsened the illness.

Because the area is a difficult one for judges to determine the Court of Appeal later produced guidelines for determining liability. These guidelines seem much stricter than the basic *Walker* test and appear to make it very difficult for claimants to bring successful claims for stress related psychiatric injuries.

CASE EXAMPLE

Sutherland v Hatton and Others [2002] EWCA Civ 76

This was a number of joined appeals on stress related illnesses at work. Two claims involved teachers. One concerned a local authority administrator and one a factory worker. All claimed that they had been forced to stop working because of stress related psychiatric illnesses caused by their employers. The Court of Appeal issued some important guidelines.

▓ The basic principles of negligence must apply including the usual principles of employers' liability.

▓ The critical question for the court to answer is whether the type of harm suffered was foreseeable.

▓ Foreseeability depends on what the reasonable employer knew or ought reasonably to have known.

▓ An employer is entitled to assume that an employee is able to cope with the pressures normally associated with the job unless the employer has specific knowledge that an employee has a particular problem and may not cope.

▓ The same test should apply whatever the employment.

▓ The employer will be obliged to take steps to prevent possible harm when the possibility of harm would be obvious to a reasonable employer.

▓ The employer will be liable if (s)he then fails to take steps that are reasonable in the circumstances to avoid the harm.

▓ The nature of the employment, the employer's available resources, the counselling and treatment services provided are all relevant in determining whether the employer has taken effective steps to avoid the harm, and in any case the employer is only expected to take steps that will do some good.

▓ The employee must show that it is the breach of duty by the employer that has caused the harm not merely that the harm is stress related.

▓ Where there is more than one cause of the harm the employer will only be liable for that portion of damages that relates to the harm actually caused by his breach of duty.

▓ Damages will in any case take account of any pre-existing disorder.

QUOTATION

Andrew Collender QC (in Stress in the Workplace, *New Law Journal*, 22 February 2003, pp. 248, 250) identifies one of the problems recognised by the court in *Hatton*: 'whilst it is possible to identify some jobs that are intrinsically physically dangerous, it is rather more difficult to identify which jobs are intrinsically so stressful that physical or psychological harm is to be expected more often than in other jobs'.

He also comments on the judgment in *Hatton*: 'With that guidance, courts are likely to be all the more willing to apportion and limit damages, to take account of the factors noted and if they do, the decision … will mark a significant development in the law.'

The Court of Appeal has more recently re-emphasised the point that a successful claimant must show that it was reasonably foreseeable that (s)he would suffer a psychiatric illness as a result of the employer's breach of duty, not just that (s)he would suffer from stress.

CASE EXAMPLE

Bonser v RJW Mining (UK) Ltd [2003] EWCA Civ 1296

The claimant was employed as a Technical Support and Training Manager. She often was forced to work beyond her contractual hours and the court accepted that her supervisor was overbearing and insensitive to her stress. This was despite the fact that her reference on taking up the post had said that she might not cope in a highly stressful environment. In 1996 she was reduced to a public display of tears when it looked as if the unreasonable demands by her supervisor were likely to lead to her having to cancel a holiday. Eventually in 1997 she suffered a stress related psychiatric illness and was forced to give up work. The trial judge held that, while in 1997 when the illness became obvious it was too late at that time for the employer to take steps to help the claimant, steps could have been taken after the crying episode in the previous year. They had not been and the employer was therefore liable. The Court of Appeal, however, applied the *Hatton* criteria and held that there was insufficient evidence in either the reference or the tears of 1996 to put the employer on notice of the foreseeability of a psychiatric illness resulting and found that the employer could not be liable in the circumstances.

The House of Lords (now the Supreme Court) subsequently had the opportunity to review the principles laid down in *Hatton*.

CASE EXAMPLE

Barber v Somerset County Council [2004] UKHL 13; 1 WLR 1089

This appeal involved one of the original claimants in the joined appeals in *Hatton*, having lost his appeal in the Court of Appeal. The claimant was a maths teacher who was given additional coordinating and managerial responsibilities in order to maintain his current income following a restructuring of the school in which he worked. As a result his working hours increased to between sixty-one and seventy hours a week and after some months of trying to cope he complained of being overloaded to his deputy head teacher. Nothing was done and a few months later, after consulting his GP for stress and enquiring into the possibility of early retirement, he suffered a bout of stress and depression and was absent from work for three weeks. Again nothing was done by the school to address his problems and he continued to see his doctor for stress. He finally broke down, shook a pupil and left the school permanently. Psychiatrists agreed that he was suffering moderate to severe depression. The claimant had won at first instance on the basis that the school ought to have appreciated that the risk to the claimant's health was significantly greater than to another teacher with a high workload and yet had done nothing. This was reversed by the Court of Appeal in the joined *Hatton* appeals. The House of Lords held that the Court of Appeal had failed to pay sufficient attention to the claimant's three week sickness absence and the medical reasons for it and held that the local authority was in breach of its duty of care by being aware of the difficulties that the increased workload was having on the claimant and the medical consequences but failing to do anything to remedy it.

Following *Barber* the Court of Appeal applied the *Hatton* criteria to individual cases in joined appeals, *Hartman v South Essex Mental Health & Community Care NHS Trust, Best v Staffordshire University, Wheeldon v HSBC Bank Ltd, Green v Grimsby & Scunthorpe Newspapers Ltd, Moore v Welwyn Components Ltd, Melville v The Home Office* [2005] EWCA Civ 06.

In a later case *Daw v Intel Corporation (UK) Ltd* [2007] EWCA Civ 76 the Court of Appeal held that 'indications of impending harm to health were plain enough for the [employer] to realise that immediate action was required'. The claimant had sent many notes to her employer drawing their attention to stress caused by overwork and confused lines of communication. The court also held that the mere fact of offering counselling was not sufficient to avoid liability.

The employer owes a personal, non-delegable duty of care to the employee:
- to provide safe working colleagues
- to provide safe plant and equipment
- to provide a safe system of work
- to provide safe premises
- to protect the psychiatric health and general welfare of the employee

The employer breaches its duty of care to the employee:
- by failing to ensure that working colleagues are safe; or
- by having unsafe plant and equipment; or
- by having an unsafe system of work; or
- by having unsafe premises; or
- by causing the employee foreseeable psychiatric injury or by failing to take care of the general welfare of the employee

The employer causes harm to the employee:
- usually in the form of injury
- which could be in the form of psychiatric injury
- but the employee has no duty of care towards the employee's property

There is no available defence:
- *volenti non fit injuria* (voluntary assumption of risk) – complete defence employer is not liable
- contributory negligence – partial defence defendant is liable but claimant is partially to blame and damages are reduced to the extent that the court thinks is equitable in the circumstances

Employer is liable

Figure 16.1 Diagram illustrating the employer's common law liability for failures to take care of the health, safety and welfare of the employee

16.3.2 Bullying and the Protection from Harassment Act 1997

Quite obviously bullying and harassment in the workplace can also lead to psychiatric harm. As a result where the employer fails to deal with the bullying this can amount to a breach of its duty and lead on to liability.

CASE EXAMPLE

Ratcliffe v Dyfed County Council [1998] The Times 17 July 1998

Here a claim for a stress related injury was accepted when a head teacher was found to have bullied a junior member of staff. The court applied the general duty to protect the health, safety and welfare of the employee.

An important development in this respect came when the courts showing willingness to impose vicarious liability where there is a breach of a statutory duty imposed on the individual employee rather than also on the employer. In this way a successful claim of vicarious liability can be made under s3 Protection from Harassment Act 1997.

CASE EXAMPLE

Majrowski v Guy's and St Thomas' NHS Trust [2006] UKHL 34; [2006] All ER (D) 146

The claimant who was employed by the NHS trust claimed that he had been bullied and harassed by his departmental manager because of his homosexuality. He complained internally and following investigation his complaints were accepted and the Trust accepted that there had indeed been harassment. The claimant brought an action against the Trust under s3 Protection from Harassment Act 1997. At first instance the claim was struck out but the claimant won his appeal in the House of Lords.

There has been much recent case law with quite different results. The best publicised of these cases is *Green*.

CASE EXAMPLE

Green v DB Group Services (UK) Ltd [2006] EWHC 1989

The claimant worked as an assistant company secretary for Deutsche Bank. She was subjected to constant abuse by a group of female staff, was constantly undermined by a male colleague and despite reporting this to her manager and seeking help the company did nothing to support or help her. She suffered a period of sickness with depression as a result and on returning to work suffered a relapse and was unable to return to work. The judge awarded her £800,000 for personal injury and loss of future earnings for the mental illness resulting from the bullying. The award was based on both negligence and breach of the 1997 Act.

However, in *Merilie v Newcastle PCT* [2006] EWHC 1433 a dentist failed in a claim for harassment against her former employers because she suffered a lifelong personality disorder making her evidence unreliable since it was based only on her own perceptions.

ACTIVITY

Self-assessment questions

1. Considering the increased dangers presented by the new mechanised working practices during the Industrial Revolution why did employers' liability develop so long after it was first needed?
2. What were the major defects in the early law?
3. Was the common law always hostile to employees?
4. What are the four main aspects of the duty owed by an employer to its employee?
5. To what extent is an employer responsible for the actions of practical jokers within the workforce?
6. Which is likely to be more important the common law or statute in relation to safe plant and equipment?
7. To what extent can an employer follow an established trade practice if it is dangerous?
8. What is the standard of care appropriate to maintaining safe premises?
9. What effect does causation have on the duty of an employer to its employee?
10. How easy is it for an employer to defend a case of breach of a common law duty?
11. How has the scope of an employer's duty of care expanded recently?
12. What difficulties confront an employee who is trying to bring a claim for a stress related injury?

KEY FACTS

The scope of the duty	Case/statute
The employer owes a non-delegable duty for the health and safety of the employee, so:	*Wilsons & Clyde Coal Co v English*
• must provide competent staff for duties undertaken	*General Cleaning Contractors v Christmas*
• must provide safe working colleagues	*Hudson v Ridge Manufacturing*
• must provide safe plant and equipment and properly maintain it (but now Employers' Liability (Defective Equipment) Act 1969 applies)	*Smith v Baker*
• must take reasonable steps to provide safe premises (which may extend to other premises)	*Latimer v AEC* *Wilson v Tyneside Cleaning Co*
• must provide a safe system of work	
• must create and implement safe system	
• and ensure system is carried out	*Bux v Slough Metals*
• and system must meet dangers	*General Cleaning Contractors v Christmas*
• cannot rely on unsafe system just because it is common practice	*Re Herald of Free Enterprise*
The character of the duty	**Case/statute**
The duty is non-delegable	*Wilsons & Clyde Coal Co v English*
And the employer only need take reasonable precautions	*Latimer v AEC* *Davidson v Handley Page Ltd*
The duty extends to reasonable and incidental activities	
Duty does not extend to employees properly	*Deyong v Shenburn*
Trade practices can only be relied upon if reasonable	*Cavanagh v Ulster Weaving Co*
The employer should consider the possible extent of injury	*Paris v Stepney BC*
And may consider practicality of any precautions	*Charlton v Forrest Printing Ink Co*
And must prevent only reasonably foreseeable accidents	*Doughty v Turner Manufacturing*

Defences	Case/statute
Volenti (consent), has limited use – the employee must fully appreciate and consent to the actual risk	*Smith v Baker*
• this is possible if the agreement is free from pressure	*ICI v Shatwell*
• and where the claimant is the sole cause of injury	*Ginty v Belmont Building Supplies Ltd*
• but it is not available for breach of a statutory duty	
Contributory negligence – this is a possible defence to any duty	
• it is covered by the provisions of the Law Reform (Contributory Negligence) Act 1945	
• damages may be reduced when the worker contributed to own injury	*Jones v Livox Quarries Ltd*
• and even 100 per cent reduction is possible	*Jayes v IMI (Kynoch) Ltd*

Developments in the duty	Case/statute
The duty now applies also to psychiatric health and well-being	*Walker v Northumberland CC*
The Court of Appeal has issued guidelines – must know of existing vulnerability, it must be foreseeable that the employment practices will lead to a stress related psychiatric injury and the employment practices must actually cause or worsen the psychiatric illness	*Sutherland v Hatton*
An employer may be vicariously liable under the Protection from Harassment Act 1997	*Majrowski v Guy's and St Thomas' NHS Trust*

16.4 Statutory and EU health and safety protections

16.4.1 The Health and Safety at Work Act 1974

Introduction

The sheer volume of work related injuries and illnesses indicated in the introduction at the start of Chapter 16 demonstrates the need for effective regulation of health and safety at work. As we have seen in Chapter 1.4.5 the common law was originally unhelpful in respect of the safety of employees. Indeed by the restrictions placed on the tort the then House of Lords may have missed a great opportunity in the case of *Rylands v Fletcher* [1868] LR 1 Exch 265, LR 3 HL 330 to develop a general duty concerning responsibility for dangers which might have been very beneficial to employees in the changed conditions brought about by industrialisation. As a result legislation was always significant in developing regulation of health and safety at work from the very first Act, Peel's Health and Morals of Apprentices Act 1802 through to the very extensive Factories Act 1961 and Offices, Shops and Railway Premises Act 1963.

However, the defects in the law developed by successive Parliaments were obvious by the late 1960s and the Labour government in 1969 set up the Robens Committee to review the whole area of industrial safety. The committee's Report was published in 1972. It identified a series of problems with the existing law:

- It was cumbersome and therefore complex being contained in numerous different statutes.
- It was made more complex because the various statutes often overlapped in their application.
- In general the law focused on premises rather than employees.

- As a result of this large numbers of workers were not covered by existing legislation.
- Responsibility for health and safety was divided between too many different ministries and government departments.
- The number of different inspectorates, seven, was excessive.

As a result the Committee suggested that there should be three separate levels of control of health and safety at work:

- a broadly based general legislative framework;
- made more specific through regulations and statutory codes of practice;
- with the addition of voluntary codes in individual establishments.

The Act – general points

The Act, apart from placing all of the general legal obligations in a single enactment and answering the first criticism of the previous law, also made some fundamental changes to the way that health and safety at work is regulated. It applies to workers not to premises, covering all employees except domestic workers. As a result of this seven million employees who had previously had no protection came within the statutory protection. Subsequent legislation has extended this to trainees on government training schemes, certain offshore workers and police officers, and the Act now also covers many people who while not strictly employees may be affected by activities in workplaces.

Like the common law the Act introduces a series of duties imposed on employers found in sections 2–9. Some duties are absolute; others depend on what is 'reasonably practicable'. In contrast to the common law the Act is based on criminal sanctions for breaches. Section 47 identifies that no civil proceedings arise from the Act. Although of course under the Civil Evidence Act 1968 criminal conviction could be used as evidence in a civil action.

However, it also looks for cooperation with employers through voluntary codes.

The duties under the Act

The basic duty is in section 2(1):

SECTION

's2(1)
"It shall be the duty of every employer to ensure, so far as is reasonably practicable, the health, safety and at work of all his employees"

This basic duty is supplemented and developed in section 2(2) to include:

(2) Without prejudice to the generality of an employer's duty under the preceding subsection, the matters to which that duty extends include in particular –

(a) the provision and maintenance of plant and systems of work that are, so far as is reasonably practicable, safe and without risks to health;

(b) arrangements for ensuring, so far as is reasonably practicable, safety and absence of risks to health in connection with the use, handling, storage and transport of articles and substances;

(c) the provision of such information, instruction, training and supervision as is necessary to ensure, so far as is reasonably practicable, the health and safety at work of his employees;

(d) so far as is reasonably practicable as regards any place of work under the employer's control, the maintenance of it in a condition that is safe and without risks to health and the provision and maintenance of means of access to and egress from it that are safe and without such risks;

(e) the provision and maintenance of a working environment for his employees that is, so far as is reasonably practicable, safe, without risks to health, and adequate as regards facilities and arrangements for their welfare at work.'

The duties all depend on what is 'reasonably practicable'. This mirrors common law where the standard of care is that of the reasonable employer who is not bound to go to extraordinary lengths to guarantee safety but only to do what is reasonable in the circumstances.

CASE EXAMPLE

West Bromwich Building Society Ltd v Townsend [1983] ICR 257

Health and Safety Inspectors issued an improvement notice under section 21 of the Act. This required the employer to install 'bandit screens'. These are designed to protect staff in banks and building societies during robberies. The building society appealed arguing that the risk of harm was quite low by contrast to the quite prohibitive cost of installing such equipment. The High Court balanced the risk with the cost and, since the employer was only obliged to do what was reasonable, granted the appeal.

Under section 2(3) the employer is bound to produce a written health and safety policy statement and to bring this to the attention of all employees. This must be updated as often as is needed for changes in the workplace. There is no statutory guidance on the contents of the statement so it is based on the individual needs of the workplace. Although there are some minimum contents, however, that a statement would need to cover and that could be gained from advice from the Health and Safety Executive. These would include:

- the employer's general health and safety policy;
- the form and frequency of health and safety inspections;
- the identity of persons responsible for health and safety and their individual responsibilities;
- procedures for raising and dealing with health and safety issues;
- procedures in the case of emergencies.

One major innovation of the Act appears in sections 2(4), 2(6) and 2(7). This is the duty to consult employees on health and safety matters and to appoint safety representatives for the purpose of consultation. Where there are recognised trade unions it would be common for the union to appoint or elect the representatives and the employer has a duty to consult with these safety representatives. Safety representatives will:

- make regular inspections;
- investigate health and safety risks and hazards;
- investigate employees' complaints and raise these with management;
- represent employees in consultation with management and with HSE inspectors.

Under section 2(7) if two or more employees request it the employer should set up a safety committee. The employer must consult with the committee when introducing any new equipment or machinery and should also give full information on any health and safety hazards. Health and safety representatives are entitled to reasonable time off work for training and to fulfil their role.

Under section 3 the employer's duty also extends to non-employees who may be affected by health and safety risks. This duty is also placed on the self-employed. This duty obviously covers any legitimate visitors to the employer's premises. It might also include sub-contractors working on the employer's premises.

CASE EXAMPLE

R v Associated Octel Co Ltd [1997] IRLR 123

An independent contractor was cleaning the inside of a tank on Associated Octel's premises. He was burnt when a light he was using smashed and ignited chemicals that he was using. On appeal against its conviction under section 3 the then House of Lords held that Octel was in overall control of its premises and therefore in breach of its duty although Octel had argued that it in fact had no control over the incident which resulted from the manner in which the independent contractor was working.

JUDGMENT

Lord Hoffmann stated: 'The employer must take reasonably practical steps to avoid risk to the contractors' servants which arise, not merely from the physical state of the premises but also from the inadequacy of the arrangements which the employer makes with the contractors for how they will do their work.'

Under section 4 there is a duty on anybody in control of premises, other than domestic premises, to ensure as far as is reasonably practicable against risks to health and safety in all access and exits to plant and premises to people who work on the premises.

Under section 6 there is a duty on manufacturers, designers, importers, and suppliers of articles or substances:

- to ensure as far as is reasonably practicable that they are free from risks to health and safety;

- to test such articles and substances and to provide necessary information on how they should be used.

Following on from these duties some further complimentary duties owed by the employer under the Employment Rights Act 1996 are worth noting:

- under section 44 ERA 1996 there is a duty on the employer not to cause an employee a detriment for involvement in a legitimate health and safety activity;

- under section 100 ERA 1996 there is a duty not to dismiss an employee for any reason associated with health and safety, which would rank as an automatically unfair dismissal.

The Act also places certain duties of employees and others:

- under section 7 every employee is under a duty while at work to take reasonable care for his own health and safety and of others who may be affected by his acts or omissions at work, and to cooperate fully with his employer on all HASAW issues;

- under section 8 all persons owe a duty not to intentionally or recklessly interfere with or misuse anything provided in the interest of health and safety at work.

These are important because the duty to take reasonable care for one's own safety include using all protective equipment and properly following all health and safety procedures. This helps to ensure that the working environment is in fact safe and mirrors the similar duty under common law.

Introduction of regulations under section 15 and Schedule 3 of the Act

The Act replaced the old system of individual statutes and so it gives the Secretary of State the power to introduce regulations by statutory instrument and also Codes of Practice to advance health and safety at work.

Three types of regulations are possible:

- those which lay down standards that apply generally to all employment;
- those which control specific hazards in particular industries;
- those which control specific hazards but ones which cross industries.

They are usually introduced in statutory instrument by Secretary of State following recommendations by the Health and Safety Executive (HSE).

Such regulations can as well as other things:

- repeal or amend existing provisions;
- grant authority to specific bodies to enforce statutory duties;
- identify parties who may be subject to criminal sanctions;
- grant exemptions.

Enforcement of the Act and related Regulations

The Act originally set up two separate bodies:

- the Health and Safety Commission (HSC) with the responsibility of administration;
- the Health and Safety Executive (HSE) with the responsibility of enforcing the law.

In practice the HSC commonly delegated its responsibilities to the HSE and in 2008 the two were merged into the HSE.

Enforcement of the duties in the Act is by Inspectors with wide powers.

- They may enter premises (and may do so with the support of the police if necessary, or indeed can be accompanied by other authorised persons).
- They may investigate health and safety risks, carry out examinations, take photographs, take samples, make recordings, seize documents, take custody and control of hazardous substances or situations.
- They may require relevant parties to answer questions.
- They may use any other power necessary to carry out their duties.

Under section 21 Inspectors may issue Improvement Notices where any health and safety provisions have been contravened. These notices identify the provision which has been breached, indicate the improvement that is required and the period within which the improvement must occur.

Under section 22 Inspectors can also issue Prohibition Notices where a breach of a provision involves a risk of personal injury. The notice prohibits that activity until the risk has been removed.

Employers can appeal against either type of notice.

A further power under section 25 gives inspectors the power to take whatever action is necessary in a situation of imminent danger. Under section 42 the courts can order an employer to take steps to eliminate risks and can also impose fines.

ACTIVITY

Self-assessment questions

1. What was wrong with statutory provision on health and safety at work prior to the 1974 Act?
2. What was the major difference in application of the law from the previous statutory provisions?
3. What is the basic duty under section 2(1)?
4. How similar are the further duties under section 2(2) to the common law duty?
5. What difficulties may arise from the use of the words 'as far as is reasonably practicable' in relation to the duties?
6. How important are the further rights of employees under sections 44 and 100 Employment Rights Act 1996 to ensuring health and safety in the workplace?
7. How do the duties under section 7 and section 8 help ensure health and safety in the workplace?
8. How wide are the powers of inspectors?

16.4.2 The 'six pack' of regulations

Introduction

The European Union is a major provider of HASAW law originally through Article 118A, which was inserted into the EC Treaty by the Single European Act 1986 and later became Article 137 following the Amsterdam Treaty. The Article gave power to issue Directives in furtherance of HASAW by a qualified majority voting system. This is now covered by Article 153 of the Treaty on the Functioning of the European Union (TFEU).

A number of directives have been issued. Probably the most significant is the so-called 'six-pack' introduced in 1992 but subsequently amended. One of the most significant aspects of the directives is the requirement for proactive steps to be taken, for example risk assessments, as well as provision of information and training. They have all been implemented in the UK through statutory instruments.

The Management of Health and Safety at Work Regulations 1999 (amended 2006)

The regulations introduced the basic requirement of risk assessment, that employers must make 'suitable and efficient assessments of the dangers facing their employees and anyone else likely to be affected by their work'. Risk assessment should cover everything in the work environment that is likely to cause harm. Procedures can then be put in place to deal with these risks and prevent harm. Risk assessments should be carried out regularly. Other than for small employers the results of risk assessments should be recorded in writing.

The regulations also require the appointment of safety officers and the establishment of emergency procedures. Employees should be fully aware of these procedures and be able to leave work and go to a place of safety in the event of an immediate danger in the workplace.

Employers must ensure that all employees are capable of doing the work safely and must provide the necessary training and information. Training should be carried out when an employee first joins but also at all points when the equipment or the work has changed.

Employees are under a duty to comply with all procedures and training given and to report to safety officers or the employer all dangers in the workplace and any failings in health and safety arrangements.

Workplace (Health, Safety and Welfare) Regulations 1992

These regulations develop duties already in place in the 1974 Act. They involve the environment in which employees work and seek not only to make this a safe and healthy environment but also to ensure the provision of adequate welfare facilities.

There are various aspects to this:

- There should be efficient maintenance, repair and cleaning of the work environment.
- There should be sufficient fresh or purified air.
- Temperatures should be reasonable and any source of heating premises should not produce any fumes that could be harmful to the employees.
- There should be adequate lighting which is suitable for the activities being carried out.
- There should be adequate floor space and all travel routes through the workplace should be adequate and suitable.
- If it is possible for the work to be carried out while seated then suitable seats should be provided.
- Doors, windows, gates, staircases, escalators etc. should all be safe.
- There should be provision of adequate sanitary arrangements including both toilet and washing facilities.
- There should be drinking water available.
- There should be provision for changing clothes where necessary.
- There should also be provision for rest breaks and eating and a designated suitable area for this.

Provision and Use of Work Equipment Regulations 1998

These regulations seek to ensure that all machinery and other work equipment is safe and also used safely. The regulations require that all such equipment must be suitable for its use, it must be properly maintained and kept in good repair, and it must conform to EU requirements.

Besides this effective steps must be taken to prevent access to dangerous parts of machinery. Controls, including starting and stopping controls as well as emergency stopping controls should be provided and clearly marked with adequate warnings, and there should be provision for immediate isolation from power sources. All maintenance of machinery must be carried out with the machine switched off.

As with all the regulations, employees must be given appropriate information and be adequately trained in the use of equipment.

Personal Protective Equipment at Work Regulations 1992

Personal Protection Equipment is defined in the regulations as: 'all equipment (including clothing affording protection against the weather) which is intended to be worn or held by a person at work, and which protects him against one or more risks to his health and safety'.

The regulations seek to ensure that all such equipment is indeed safe to use. On this basis all such equipment must conform to EU standards or it is considered unsuitable.

There are some fairly obvious examples including helmets, gloves, goggles, hard hats, harnesses, safety footwear, high visibility clothes.

The main provisions are:

- There should be an assessment of suitability of the equipment.
- All such equipment must be compatible with any other used.
- It should be kept in good repair, cleaned or replaced regularly as appropriate.
- Employees must be given full information regarding risks.
- Employees must be trained in the use of the equipment.
- The employer must ensure that it is used properly.

Manual Handling Operations Regulations 1992

These regulations cover any form of manual lifting in the workplace, including lifting objects, putting them down, pushing them, pulling them or any other form of carrying or movement by hand. The main obligation on the employer is, as far as is reasonably practicable, to avoid any form of manual lifting. The HSE identify that as many as one-third of back injuries lasting more than three days result from manual lifting.

If it is impossible to avoid manual lifting then a risk assessment should be carried out in order to do everything possible to minimise the risk of injury through manual lifting. In particular the employer should reduce the risk of injury by considering the size, shape and location of objects that require manual lifting.

Schedule 1 of the Regulations contains a lengthy list of questions that an employer should check in order to reduce the risk of injury.

The employer is also obliged to provide employees required to engage in manual lifting with full details of the risk.

Health & Safety (Display Screen Equipment) Regulations 1992

The regulations deal with work with computers and other display screens, which has become a big feature of many areas of work, quite apart from there being certain jobs such as data entry which are completely involved with using such screens. Inevitably there are many health problems such as eye strain and muscular strain that can result from using display screens for long periods. Health problems appear to arise from poor equipment, poor environment and poor posture, so the regulations seek to cover all of these.

Employers are obliged to analyse all workstations to assess HASAW risks to employees, and there is an inevitable duty on employers to reduce such risks.

The main provisions are:

- VDUs must not flicker, should be free from glare, and must swivel and tilt.
- Keyboards must tilt and must be free from glare and the workspace in front of keyboards must be sufficient for the employee to rest his arms comfortably.
- Desks must also be free from glare, and there must be enough space on desks to allow flexible arrangement of other equipment and documents.
- Seats must be adjustable in height, and the back in height and angle, and footrests should be available if requested.
- There must be appropriate contrast in lighting between the screen and its background, and windows should have blinds.
- Heat and humidity levels should be adequate and not uncomfortable.

- Radiation must be negligible.
- There should be regular breaks or changes of activity from working with the VDU.
- Employers must offer free eyesight testing at regular intervals and provide special glasses for screen work if necessary.
- Employees should be consulted about health and safety measures and should be trained in the use of equipment.

ACTIVITY

Quick quiz

Consider which of the six regulations is appropriate in the following circumstances:

1. Maurice works on construction of tall buildings. He is injured when a hammer is dropped by another worker who is on a higher level than Maurice. The hammer strikes Maurice and pierces his hard hat. On investigation the hard hat does not conform to EU standards.
2. Naomi works for an insurance company inputting customer information into a computer database. Naomi is suffering from severe eye strain. There is no anti-glare screen on her computer and she is obliged to spend all of her seven-and-a-half hour working day at her computer with no change of activity.
3. Owen is a machinist. He has been badly electrocuted when there was a short circuit in the machine he works on. There was no automatic emergency cut off of the electricity supply to the machine.
4. Paul has recently suffered painful dermatitis (a skin condition). Paul works in very dusty conditions in high temperatures and there is no facility at his place of work either for washing or for changing clothes.

16.4.3 The Working Time regulations

The regulations emanate from EU law and implement the provisions of the Working Time Directive 93/104 and the Young Workers Directive 94/33. They were only implemented after a change of government, and the previous government's failure in an action in the ECJ. It had argued that the directive was social policy for which the UK had an opt out. In fact the directive was introduced as health and safety law.

The directive was updated in the Working Time Directive 2003/88. As well as the basic protections, this provides special rules for working time in certain specific sectors such as doctors in training, offshore workers, sea fishing workers, workers in urban passenger transport and in other specific transport sectors. The EU Commission has in fact initiated a series of consultations reviewing how working time arrangements operate in different Member States and drafted a proposal in 2009 for further amendment to the directive. However, the Commission and the European Parliament could not agree on the proposal and so it has not progressed.

The directive introduced a set of minimum rules to protect the health and safety of workers in all Member States. Every worker is entitled to:

- a limit to weekly working time, which must not exceed forty-eight hours on average, including any overtime;
- a minimum daily rest period, of eleven consecutive hours in every twenty-four;
- a rest break during working time, if the worker is on duty for longer than six hours;
- a minimum weekly rest period of twenty-four uninterrupted hours for each seven day period, which is added to the eleven hours' daily rest;

- paid annual leave, of at least four weeks per year;
- extra protection in the case of night work (for example, average working hours must not exceed eight hours per twenty-four hour period; night workers must not perform heavy or dangerous work for longer than eight hours in any twenty-four hour period; there should be a right to free health assessments and in certain situations, to transfer to day work).

The Regulations make the following provisions:

Maximum weekly working time

Under Regulation 4 this must be no more than forty-eight hours per week averaged out over a seventeen-week period (although in certain circumstances the period can be longer). Under Regulation 5 the worker can also agree in writing to work longer than forty-eight hours. The average of forty-eight hours has to be calculated in a way which takes into account periods of leave, sickness and other periods which would normally occur. For example, a worker cannot be asked to work excess hours to make up for periods of holiday taken.

Working hours include any time when the worker is at the employer's disposal and is expected to carry out activities for the employer. So it can include:

- work related training is counted as part of the working week;
- being on call.

But it will not generally include:

- travel time to and from work;
- lunch breaks (except for working lunches).

Minimum rest periods

Under Regulation 10 the minimum daily rest period is an uninterrupted eleven consecutive hours for an adult worker and twelve for a young worker.

Under Regulation 12 the minimum daily rest break period is twenty minutes after six hours of work (although in special circumstances these periods can be accumulated) or thirty minutes for young workers. Rest breaks should be uninterrupted and spent away from the work station. There is also a provision for adequate rest breaks where the monotony of the work would put the worker's health at risk (although there is no definition of 'adequate').

Under Regulation 11 the minimum weekly rest period is an uninterrupted period of twenty-four hours in each seven day period (although this can be converted to two days off in each two week period and in special circumstances days off can be accumulated and taken off later). In the case of a young worker the period of interrupted rest is forty-eight hours in each seven-day period.

Paid annual leave

Under Regulation 13, as amended in the Working Time (Amendment) Regulations 2007, since April 2009 the minimum paid holiday leave entitlement is 5.6 weeks or twenty-eight days (worked out pro rata for part-time workers). It is not possible to replace holiday entitlement with payment in lieu except where service comes to an end. Nor can payment in lieu be made for any statutory holiday entitlement. It is also no longer possible to pay 'rolled up' holiday pay (in other words weekly pay which includes a payment for holiday pay). This is because holiday payment should be made at the time the holiday is taken. Workers are entitled to take leave from the commencement of their employment. Holiday entitlement should accrue on the basis of the number of working days in the year.

Night work

Under Regulation 6 night working is also regulated. Night work should not exceed eight hours in any twenty-four hour period aggregated over seventeen weeks. Night time for the purposes of the regulations is a period of seven hours including the period from midnight to 5.00 a.m. Night workers whose work includes special hazards e.g. steel workers should not exceed eight hours' work in any twenty-four hour period (although there are exemptions in healthcare work). Night workers are entitled to a health assessment before being asked to work nights. Sixteen- to eighteen-year-olds should not normally be expected to work nights.

A number of different classes of worker are excluded from the Regulations. These include under Regulation 18 people working on sea-going vessels who have their own provisions. It also under Regulation 19 includes domestic servants working in a private household. Regulation 20 covers people such as managing executives and people carrying out religious ceremonies where it would be difficult to measure times precisely. A variety of situations are also covered by Regulation 21 for instance where the employee's work and residence are distant from one another, where the work involves security or surveillance, or care, works at docks or airports, broadcasting, public utility services, research and development, and also work that cannot be interrupted for technical reasons. Besides this exclusion from the Regulations can also result from a collective agreement under Regulation 23.

KEY FACTS

HASAW 1974 – duties	Statute
Employer's duty is so far as is practicable to ensure HASAW and welfare of employees including: • provide and maintain safe plant and systems, premises, exits • remove risks in handling, storing, transport, of articles/substances • inform, instruct, train, supervise • provide safe working environment	S2(1)
Must have a HASAW policy statement	S2(3)
Must appoint safety representatives and consult on HASAW issues	S2(4),(6),(7)
Must not cause employee detriment	S4
Employer's HASAW duties extends to people other than employees	S3
Duty on manufacturers, designers, importers suppliers to ensure articles and substances are free from risks and tested	S6
Employee also has a duty to take care of self and others	S7
A dismissal for asserting any HASAW right is automatically unfair	S100 ERA 1996

HASAW 1974 – regulations and enforcement	
Three types of regulations possible	
• those laying down standards applying to all employment • those controlling specific hazards in particular industries • those controlling specific hazards which cross industries	
The Act set up two separate bodies	
• The Health and Safety Commission – to administrate the law • The Health and Safety Executive – to enforce the law • Now merged into HSE	

Inspectors have powers to		
• enter premises, investigate, make examinations, take photographs, take samples, make recordings, seize documents, take custody and control of hazardous substances • issue Improvement Notices and Prohibition Notices		
Regulations implementing EU directives		
Management of HASAW Regulations 1999 (amended 2006) • introduces risk assessment, health surveillance, safety officers, emergency procedures, training Workplace (HASAW) Regulations 1992 • requires efficient maintenance and repair, clean air, appropriate lighting, appropriate sanitation facilities, facilities for changing clothing, rest periods and designated areas for rest and eating Provision and Use of Work Equipment Regulations 1998 • requires suitable and efficient work equipment, proper controls on machines which conform to EU standards, preventing access to dangerous parts of machinery, emergency stop controls, effective training Personal Protective Equipment at Work Regulations 1992 • all PPE must be in good repair and conform to EU standards Manual Handling Operations Regulations 1992 • should reduce manual handling and avoid if possible and reduce risks Health & Safety (Display Screen Equipment) Regulations 1992 • provides controls on work stations, free eye tests, periodic change of activities where possible		
Working Time Regulations		
• Maximum forty-eight hour week averaged out • Eight hour night work limit • Eleven hour minimum daily rest period • Twenty-four hour minimum weekly rest period • Twenty minutes minimum break period after six hours' work • Four weeks' paid holiday annually • Provision of health checks		

	Employer's liability in tort	Statutory liability
Basis of action	The employer's personal non-delegable duty of care for the health, safety and welfare of the employee	Duties under the Health and Safety at Work Act 1974, and subordinate legislation
Cause of action	The employer has breached the duty of care by failing to protect the health, safety or welfare of the employee	The employer has breached a duty under HASAW or subordinate legislation, or has failed to comply with an improvement notice or a prohibition notice
Type of action	Civil action in the tort of negligence	A prosecution in the criminal courts
Consequence of action if breach proved	Employer will be bound to pay compensation to the employee	Employer will receive a penalty which will normally be a fine, which could be unlimited, but imprisonment is also possible

SAMPLE ESSAY QUESTION

ESSAY Discuss the extent to which health and safety law is too complex and difficult for employees to use because there are duties under common law, statute and deriving from EU law.

Explain that there are duties under common law, statute and EU Law

Explain the duty under common law

- To provide safe working colleagues.
- To provide safe plant and equipment.
- To provide a safe system of work.
- To provide safe premises.
- To protect the psychiatric health and general well being of the employee.

Explain the basic duties under statute (under the Health and Safety at Work Act 1974) and subordinate legislation

- So far as is practicable to ensure HASAW and welfare of employees including:
  - provide and maintain safe plant and systems, premises, exits;
  - remove risks in handling, storing, transport, of articles/substances;
  - inform, instruct, train, and supervise;
  - provide safe working environment;
  - must have a HASAW policy statement;
  - must appoint safety representatives and consult on HASAW issues;
  - must not cause employee detriment;
  - must not dismiss for a HASAW reason;
  - employer's HASAW duties extend to people other than employees;
  - duty on manufacturers, designers, importers and suppliers to ensure articles and substances are free from risks and tested.

Explain the basic duties arising from EU law

- Risk assessment, health surveillance, safety officers, emergency procedures, training.
- Efficient maintenance and repair, clean air, appropriate lighting, appropriate sanitation facilities, facilities for changing clothing, rest periods and designated areas for rest and eating.
- Suitable and efficient work equipment, proper controls on machines which conform to EU standards, preventing access to dangerous parts of machinery, emergency stop controls, effective training.
- All Personal Protection Equipment must be in good repair and conform to EU standards.
- Should reduce manual handling and avoid if possible and reduce risks.
- Should control work stations for VDU's, provide free eye tests, and periodic change of activities where possible.

Discuss the duties arising under common law

- Cover some major areas – working colleagues, plant and equipment, work systems, premises.
- And in many cases this overlaps with statutory provisions.
- And have developed to include psychiatric damage which statute and EU law does not.
- And is a personal duty so cannot be delegated.
- So good protection for employee.
- Is subject to the usual problems and constraints of actions in negligence.
- But does provide compensation on a successful claim so benefits the worker.

Discuss the duties arising by statute

- Basic duty is duty is that so far as is practicable to ensure HASAW and welfare of employees – so is limited by the same requirement of reasonableness as common law.
- Also requires HASAW policy statement, appointment of safety representatives and

consultation on HASAW issues and – must not cause employee detriment or dismiss on HASAW grounds.
- And employer's HASAW duties extend to people other than employees.
- And there is a duty on manufacturers, designers, importers suppliers to ensure articles and substances are free from risks and tested.
- And significant also that employee also has a duty to take care of self and others.
- So statutory duties quite wide and supported by effective enforcement procedures.
- But subject to criminal proceedings and penalties – so might create detriment but does not necessarily help employee.

Discuss the duties arising under EU law
- Creates some basic effective requirements such as risk assessment not covered by existing English law.
- Covers a wide range of specific issues such as clean air, proper controls on machines, effective rules on the use of VDU's etc.
- So has taken the law well beyond existing English law.

Consider whether the law is too complex and difficult for employees to use
- Consider that there is much overlap between common law, statute and law arising from EU law.
- Consider whether or not the law is mutually obstructive or indeed complements each other.
- Consider the contrasting context of common law and statute – common law looks towards civil remedies and statute imposes criminal sanctions.

REACH REASONED CONCLUSIONS

SUMMARY

- Regulation of health and safety at work is a significant area – the extent of work related injuries and illnesses indicated in HSE statistics indicate the need for effective regulation.
- HASAW law developed from three sources: common law duties owed by employers, statutory regulation, regulation developed from EU law.
- The common law duty is to provide safe working colleagues, safe plant and equipment, a safe working system and safe premises.
- This has subsequently been extended to cover welfare also – so there is now a duty to protect the psychiatric health and well-being of the employee – the Protection from Harassment Act 1997 has also been used in the context of workplace bullying.
- The main statutory provision is the Health and Safety at Work Act 1974.
- The basic duty is to ensure the health, safety and well-being of the employee.
- Other aspects of the duty include the appointment of safety officers and having a HASAW policy statement – it is also an automatically unfair dismissal to dismiss an employee for asserting a HASAW right.
- Regulations can be introduced under the Act of three types: those that lay down standards applying to all employment; those that control specific hazards in particular industries; and those that control specific hazards which cross industries.
- The Act set up two bodies: the Health and Safety Commission to administrate the law and the Health and Safety Executive to enforce the law.
- Inspectors have powers under the Act to enter premises, investigate, make examinations, take photographs, take samples, make recordings, seize documents, take custody and control of hazardous substances and to issue Improvement Notices and Prohibition Notices.
- A 'six pack' of regulations has been introduced to comply with EU directives: the Management of HASAW Regulations 1999 (amended 2006) introduces risk assessment, appointment of safety officers, emergency procedures and training; the Workplace (HASAW) Regulations 1992 require efficient maintenance and repair, clean air, appropriate lighting, appropriate sanitation facilities, facilities for changing clothing, rest periods and designated areas for rest and eating; the Provision and Use of Work Equipment Regulations 1998 require suitable and efficient work equipment, proper controls on machines which conform to EU standards, preventing access to dangerous parts of machinery, emergency stop controls, effectivetraining; the Personal Protective Equipment at Work Regulations 1992 require that all PPE must be in good repair and conform to EU standards; the Manual Handling Operations Regulations 1992 seek to reduce manual handling and avoid it if possible and reduce risks associated with manual handling; the Health & Safety (Display Screen Equipment) Regulations 1992 create controls on work stations, free eye tests and periodic change of activities where possible.

Further reading

Duddington, John, *Employment Law 2nd edition*. Pearson, 2007, Chapter 8.
Emir, Astra, *Selwyn's Law of Employment 17th edition*. Oxford University Press, 2012, Chapter 11.
Nairns, Janice, *Employment Law for Business Students 4th edition*, Longman, 2006, Chapter 9.
Willey, Brian, *Employment Law in Context 3rd edition*. Pearson, 2009, Chapters 10 and 12.

17

Grievances and discipline

AIMS AND OBJECTIVES

After reading this chapter you should be able to:

▓ Understand what is meant by a grievance

▓ Understand the procedures for bringing a grievance

▓ Understand the character of grievance procedure

▓ Understand the importance of the ACAS Code of Practice

▓ Understand the rules on bringing disciplinary proceedings

▓ Understand the character of disciplinary measures, disciplinary hearings and the use of warnings

▓ Understand the significance of the ACAS Code of Practice

▓ Critically analyse the area

▓ Apply the law to factual situations and reach conclusions

17.1 Grievance procedure

17.1.1 Causes of grievance

Employees spend around half of their waking day at work but have no control over who they work with. It is almost inevitable that some interpersonal relationships at work will be less than perfect. As a result it is also logical that employees may suffer grievances in their work. These need not only be to do with colleagues at whatever level. They could be to do with management decisions, relationships with other employees or personality clashes with management, or to do with management styles or from workload or from a variety of conditions at work or even from external factors.

They can arise as a result of simple misunderstandings or fundamental break-downs in communications. But they can also result from actual unfair treatment or perceptions that treatment is unfair. Where there are conflicts of interest this can often lead to grievance as can overly competitive behaviour and petty jealousies. Frustration and a sense of injustice can arise from poor performance in others or from excessive and undue discipline and a feeling of being devalued is probably more destructive than most other factors. Besides this of course a grievance can often arise from fundamental breaches of legal rights in the workplace such as all aspects of discrimination, unilateral variation in terms not being provided with appropriate remuneration or facilities even breaches of proper health and safety standards.

A demotivated employee is not a productive employee and therefore it is always important to take an employee's complaints seriously. This is why a proper formal grievance procedure properly applied is essential.

17.1.2 Formal procedure for hearing grievances

Grievance procedures produced by employers should conform to the ACAS Code of Practice on Grievance and Disciplinary Procedures.

The Code sets out the basic standards that should apply to a grievance procedure and this mirrors the standards that are also set out for disciplinary procedure. In short there are five aspects to a good procedure as identified in the Code:

▧ having raised a grievance the employee should first of all set out in writing the nature of the grievance;

▧ the employer should then hold a meeting with the employee to discuss the precise nature of the grievance;

▧ the employer must allow the employee to be accompanied at that meeting by a colleague or trade union representative – this is a statutory right provided by section 10 Employment Relations Act 1999;

▧ having considered the grievance the employer must decide on the appropriate action to be taken;

▧ finally the employer must allow the employee to take the grievance further through an appeal process if it cannot be resolved initially.

As with the disciplinary procedures, employees must make 'every effort' to attend meetings, although unlike the disciplinary procedures, the Code does not require employers to tell employees that they have the right to be accompanied at grievance meetings; however, such an obligation to tell employees should be implied. The Code states that employees must submit grievances 'formally' and in writing.

The grievance provisions do not apply to collective grievances raised on or behalf of two or more employees by a trade union or workplace representative under a collective grievance process. In such cases the collectively agreed processes should be followed. Further, where there are overlapping grievance and disciplinary cases, disciplinary cases may be suspended in order to deal with the grievance, or if both cases are related it may be appropriate to deal with the issues together.

Most formal procedures usually follow a similar pattern (see Figure 17.1).

While for the protection of all parties the process should be formal it must not have the character of a disciplinary hearing process but should be seeking to achieve alternative objectives. These would in essence be either of two:

▧ The internal procedure is able to identify that the grievance has some foundation in which case management should be seeking the most appropriate method of remedying it which may of course involve deploying disciplinary procedure against another employee, including managers where the grievance has been based on unfair treatment. Of course where the grievance has to do with interpersonal relationships between fellow employees then the appropriate means of resolving the issue may involve trying to reconcile the parties.

The employee is advised to try to settle the matter informally if possible

↓

Failing informal resolution a manager or supervisor will try to settle the matter

↓

Failing resolution in this manner a formal interview is arranged with a higher management body and the employee is usually accompanied for example by a trade union representative or a trusted colleague

↓

Failing any internal resolution of the grievance arbitration is a possibility

Figure 17.1 Common procedures in handling grievances

- The other possibility is that there is no real foundation for the grievance having been raised. For good working relations management should not merely then treat the grievance dismissively as the employee's sense of grievance will remain. The responsibility of those operating a sound procedure is to explain to the satisfaction of the employee why the grievance has no foundation and to persuade that employee that there is no cause to feel aggrieved.

Formal grievance hearings are usually inquisitorial in character and tend to follow a set pattern:

- The employee alleging the grievance is asked to outline and explain the cause of the grievance and will probably have been asked to do so already in writing for the benefit of the hearing panel.
- The panel will try to iron out any ambiguities or contradictions so that the issues are clear and can be examined and even investigated accurately.
- It is possible that other employees might be able to clarify matters and throw light on the subject of the grievance so these may be asked to attend the hearing as witnesses and interviewed by the panel.
- The panel may adjourn in order to consider the matter.
- If possible a remedy or a reasoned answer is given to the employee.

Formal procedures are necessary because it is rare that if an issue has reached a point where the employee has raised it with management that it can be simply and informally resolved. Apart from anything else by this stage the employee will usually have developed a stronger sense of grievance or injustice. Formal procedures do have both advantages and disadvantages:

Advantages:

- A formal procedure will inevitably operate according to a set time scale and have a well established and predictable procedure. An employer should be careful to ensure that the whole procedure is carried out in as short a time as possible – where a formal grievance procedure is drawn out and takes weeks or even months to be completed then this is only adding to the employee's sense of grievance and weakening his productivity.

- A formal procedure can be formulated and drafted by both management and representatives of employees – this is good employment strategy since it is inclusive and allows employees to have trust in the procedure.

- The procedure will be a constant in the organisation even though staff may change over time – of course it should also always be possible for the procedure to develop if necessary to reflect necessary changes.

- Everything in a formal procedure will be recorded so there is far less room for later misunderstanding – each meeting should be minuted and the minutes agreed by both sides.

- A formal procedure has different stages and therefore allows employees to take their grievance to the highest level if necessary.

Disadvantages:

- The fact that a formal procedure is already established may mean that there is some lack of flexibility in dealing with individual grievances and there may have developed set precedents for dealing with specific types of grievance.

- Management may also feel that the procedure allows the workforce to challenge management decisions.

- There is also the possibility of employees or groups of employees using the grievance procedure for ulterior 'political' aims.

- Failing to deal with grievances on the spot might in any case allow an employee's resentment to build up so that the issue is not in effect resolved.

- There is always the risk in any case that the procedure and the outcome of the grievance does not necessarily remove the cause of the grievance.

17.1.3 The right to be accompanied

The right to be accompanied by a representative at grievance (as well as disciplinary) hearings is now ensured by section 10 Employment Relations Act 1999.

SECTION

'10 Right to be accompanied
(1) This section applies where a worker –
  (a) is required or invited by his employer to attend a disciplinary or grievance hearing, and
  (b) reasonably requests to be accompanied at the hearing.
(2) Where this section applies the employer must permit the worker to be accompanied at the hearing by a single companion who –
  (a) is chosen by the worker and is within subsection (3),
  (b) is to be permitted to address the hearing (but not to answer questions on behalf of the worker), and
  (c) is to be permitted to confer with the worker during the hearing.
(3) A person is within this subsection if he is –
  (a) employed by a trade union of which he is an official within the meaning of sections 1 and 119 of the Trade Union and Labour Relations (Consolidation) Act 1992,
  (b) an official of a trade union (within that meaning) whom the union has reasonably certified in writing as having experience of, or as having received training in, acting as a worker's companion at disciplinary or grievance hearings, or
  (c) another of the employer's workers.'

So the choice of representative is limited to a fellow worker or a paid trade union official or a trade union member who is certified as being qualified in handling such procedures. One other significant aspect of the right is that if the chosen representative is not available then the hearing can be postponed for a reasonable time for the representative to attend. Nevertheless by virtue of the ACAS Code the procedure must still be held in good time.

The right to be accompanied is significant not only because there is another impartial witness to the proceedings but also because the person accompanying the employee is not personally involved and therefore will have a better chance of remembering what went on.

17.1.4 Breaches of procedure

Not providing a grievance procedure at all or not providing an adequate procedure or failing to follow the set procedure could all lead to a successful claim of constructive dismissal by the employee.

CASE EXAMPLE

W A Goold (Pearmak) Ltd v McConnell [1995] IRLR 516

Two sales representatives were employed on a salary and commission basis. A new managing director was appointed to the company when it was facing financial difficulties. He introduced a new payment system as a result of which the men's pay dropped significantly. They approached their manager but he refused to do anything about it and the new managing director was similarly disinterested in listening to their complaints. The men then left claiming a constructive dismissal and brought a claim for unfair dismissal. The court held that the failure by the company to provide any form of proper grievance procedure was a fundamental breach of the contract justifying a claim of constructive dismissal. Their claim for unfair dismissal succeeded.

JUDGMENT

Morison J explained: 'Parliament considered that good industrial relations requires employers to provide their employees with a method of dealing with grievances in a proper and [timely] manner ... the right to obtain redress against a grievance is fundamental.'

An employee who fails to use the complete procedure available to him may fail in a claim of constructive dismissal unless this has been justified by the employer's breach of duty.

ACTIVITY

Self-assessment questions

1. Why is it necessary to have a formal procedure for dealing with employees' grievances?
2. What essential elements of a grievance procedure are identified in the ACAS Code of Practice?
3. What are the consequences for an employer of not meeting the standard identified in the Code?
4. What is the purpose of a grievance hearing?
5. What should the panel be trying to achieve from the procedure?
6. Who can accompany the employee to the grievance hearing?
7. What benefits are gained by an employee having someone to accompany them to the hearing?

17.2 Disciplinary procedure

17.2.1 The ACAS Code of Practice

The starting point for any disciplinary procedure in the workplace is the ACAS Code of Practice on Disciplinary and Grievance Procedures. The Code as well as offering more detailed advice in paragraphs 19–25 on dealing with discipline, poor performance and absenteeism and misconduct and providing advice on warnings, also identifies the essential requirements of a sound procedure which employees should follow:

- Employers and employees should act consistently.
- Employers should carry out any necessary investigations, to establish the facts of the case.
- Employers should inform the employee of the problem and give them the opportunity to put their case in response before any decision is taken.
- In this respect employers should hold a meeting with the employee.
- At any formal meeting the employer should allow the employee to be accompanied (and this is in any case guaranteed by section 10 Employment Relations Act 1999).
- Employers should then decide on appropriate action.
- Finally employers should provide the employee with an opportunity to appeal against any formal decision that has been made as a result of the investigation and hearing.

The Code also suggests that 'Procedures should not be viewed primarily as a means of imposing sanctions. They should also be designed to emphasise and encourage improvements in individual conduct.'

'When drawing up rules the aim should be to specify clearly and concisely those necessary for the efficient and safe performance of work and for the maintenance of satisfactory relations within the workforce and between employees and management. Rules should not be so general as to be meaningless.'

Codes of practice have become increasingly important in modern employment law for the following reasons:

- the possibility of a claim of 'procedural unfairness' by an employee at a tribunal;
- the fact that tribunals are increasingly encouraged to consider 'good industrial relations practice' in their decision making;
- the fact that a lot of modern legislation refers to the use of Codes, even thought they may have no legal force.

The ACAS Code of Practice does in fact have no legal force and is not legally binding on either party to a dispute on discipline. However, following or not following the Code may be evidence in a tribunal of good or bad practice. A tribunal will always take the Code into account and look at any dispute involving discipline in the context of the Code. Where either party has failed to follow the Code this could affect their position.

On this basis most employers will have a disciplinary procedure in the contract of employment itself or more commonly in a separate booklet. A sensible employer will ensure that its disciplinary procedure meets all of the requirements of the ACAS Code. Inevitably a failure by an employer to follow its own procedure will be seen as a breach of contract. It is always a good idea for the procedure to be drafted after negotiation with the recognised trade union or other representatives of employees. It would then have both the understanding of and in general the support of the workforce.

Besides the general principles of fairness in the procedure indicated in the Code, there are a number of other points, that an employer should take note of:

- The Code only covers a specific range of disciplinary issues including misconduct and poor performance. It will in consequence cover disciplinary warnings and dismissals for misconduct and poor performance, but it does not cover dismissals for individual redundancies and the non-renewal of fixed-term contracts on their expiry. In these cases employers should still follow a fair procedure, as determined by other legislation and case law.

- In misconduct cases the Code identifies that, where practicable, the investigation and the disciplinary hearing should be carried out by different people.

- The Code also suggests that the notification of a disciplinary meeting must inform employees of their right to be accompanied.

- The Code also indicates that employees and those people who accompany them to hearings are obliged to make 'every effort' to attend the hearing.

- The Code also suggests that where an employee is persistently unable or unwilling to attend a disciplinary meeting without good cause, then the employer should be entitled to make a decision on the basis of the available evidence.

17.2.2 Disciplinary measures

A disciplinary procedure is only lawful if the employer has express or implied authority in the contract to use it. Without contractual authority it is possible that the employee may seek to have a decision arising from disciplinary proceedings overturned and if this is dismissal then unfair dismissal is a possibility.

ACAS Code of Practice states that a disciplinary procedure should:

- be in writing;
- specify to whom it applies;
- provide for matters to be dealt with quickly;
- indicate the disciplinary actions which may be taken and in what context;
- specify the levels of management who have the authority to take the various forms of disciplinary action (in general immediate superiors and line managers should not have the power to dismiss);
- provide for individual employees facing disciplinary proceedings to be informed of complaints that have been made against them, and to be given the opportunity to state their case before any decisions are reached;
- allow individuals the right to be accompanied by a TU representative or a fellow employee (a right that is in any case guaranteed by section 10 Employment Relations Act 1999 (see 17.2.3 below);
- ensure that, except in the case of gross misconduct, employees are not dismissed for a first breach of a disciplinary rule;
- ensure that no decisions are made and no action is taken without there having first been a full investigation;

■ ensure that individual employees are given full explanations of any penalty imposed;

■ provide a right of appeal together with specified procedures for appeal.

For a good procedure it could obviously also be added: follows the guidance given in the ACAS Code of Practice throughout the proceedings.

The employee must clearly be aware of all disciplinary rules. These may be in a separate handbook on discipline or in the works rules. Wherever they are contained they must be brought to the attention of each employee and in any case their whereabouts is information which is required to be identified in the statutory statement of particulars under section 1 Employment Rights Act 1996 (see Chapter 5.2.1). An employee who is unaware of the rules can hardly be said to be in a position of being able to observe them (see *Brooks & Son v Skinner* [1984] IRLR 379 in 17.2.7 below). As a result either the employees should have a copy of the disciplinary rules or the rules must be clearly accessible to employees at all times. So communicating by notices about disciplinary rules on notice boards was common in the past but is not now acceptable, particularly where breach of the rule results in dismissal. It follows that the rules should also be clear and easily comprehensible.

An employer is entitled to create a set of disciplinary rules which suit the particular employment. The rules can be used as a deterrent to bad behaviour or to ensure that employees do the job properly. They can clearly cover things such as performance and timekeeping. It is also possible to have rules that maintain standards such as dress codes which may be particularly significant when the employee meets the public.

CASE EXAMPLE

Schmidt v Austicks Bookshops Ltd [1977] IRLR 360

The claimant worked in retailing. The employer operated a dress code which was also a disciplinary rule and insisted that women were not able to wear trousers. The employee claimed that this was discrimination on the basis that men were allowed to wear trousers. In fact there was nothing discriminatory about the rule. Men were also subjected to a dress code and were not allowed to wear t-shirts. The rule was justified on the basis of presenting a reasonable image to customers.

Rules concerning the honesty of employees are clearly also very necessary and employers will easily be able to justify such rules. Such rules can be enforced even where the employee in question has not in fact been dishonest but is connected to a dishonest incident.

CASE EXAMPLE

Turner v Pleasurama Casinos Ltd [1976] IRLR 151

The claimant who was employed in a casino had the role of watching all of the gaming tables to ensure that there was no dishonesty amongst the croupiers. When it was found that a croupier and a customer had conspired to cheat and the claimant had failed to spot it he was dismissed following a thorough investigation. His claim for unfair dismissal failed because his role was significant to the employer and he had not matched up to the standard required.

In fact dishonesty is well recognised as possible gross misconduct which may justify summary dismissal.

CASE EXAMPLE

Sinclair v Neighbour [1967] 2 WLR 1

A betting shop manager borrowed £15 from the till and put an IOU in the till for the amount intending to repay the money next day. He was summarily dismissed. The County Court found that his actions were improper but not dishonest. In the employer's appeal the court held that the employee's conduct was incompatible with his duty and did justify dismissal (see Chapter 19.3.2).

Another common feature of any disciplinary rules is that any violent behaviour will not be tolerated and usually the works rules or the disciplinary code will also usually identify this as conduct justifying summary dismissal.

CASE EXAMPLE

Parsons & Co Ltd v McLoughlin [1978] IRLR 65

The claimant was dismissed following a thorough investigation of the incident after he had been involved in a fight with a fellow employee, who was also dismissed. The claimant argued that he had only defended himself and that his dismissal was unfair. The EAT held that it was a fundamental aspect of any contract of employment that any form of violence was unacceptable and so his dismissal was fair (see Chapter 22.4.2).

Employers should be careful to avoid treating different employees differently for the same disciplinary breaches. However, different treatment can be justified in certain circumstances. This could be for instance where there are different levels of blame attached to the different employees.

CASE EXAMPLE

Securicor Ltd v Smith [1989] IRLR 356 CA

Two security guards whose jobs involved collecting and delivering money were both dismissed after an investigation, an internal hearing and an internal appeal when they had breached strict guidelines. They were then allowed a further internal appeal which found that one employee was less blameworthy than the other and should not be dismissed. The other employee claimed unfair dismissal and the tribunal held that the second appeal had been unreasonable. The EAT confirmed this but the Court of Appeal held that the appeal panel had reached its decision following a thorough investigation which had revealed that the one employee was in fact more blameworthy than the other. It had not acted in a way that no reasonable employer would have done in the circumstances.

Another factor that could be taken into account by an employer in subjecting different employees to different treatment is their actual work histories and prior disciplinary records. In *London Borough of Harrow v Cunningham* [1996] IRLR 256 an employer's decision to dismiss one employee but only give a final warning to the other for the same disciplinary offence was held to be justified by the EAT. The employee dismissed had already been the subject of a final written warning while the other employee had a faultless disciplinary record before the offence in question.

The important question for the tribunal in all cases is how reasonably the employer has acted in reaching the decision and taking the action that he has.

Palmer v Vauxhall Motors Ltd [1977] ICR 24

The claimant was dismissed for returning to work late having spent some time after her proper break in a bar. The employer argued that this was gross misconduct according to the works rules although there was some ambiguity in the wording. The EAT held that the dismissal would only be unfair if it could be shown that no reasonable employer would have acted in the same way.

17.2.3 Disciplinary hearings

Hearings are not an absolute requirement of a disciplinary procedure but they are sound policy since the ACAS Code of Practice states that an employee should have the right to be informed of the allegations made against him and to be able to state his own case so this would be difficult without a hearing.

Generally any references to the nature of disciplinary hearings and the composition of such hearings and procedure to be used are found in the employer's disciplinary procedures. However, ad hoc hearings are possible particularly where an immediate supervisor needs to raise a minor issue and possibly make an informal caution.

There are two significant functions of a disciplinary hearing:

■ They are a means of ascertaining true facts of the incident or incidents which led to the requirement for any disciplinary sanction to be imposed – of course they may be preceded by thorough investigations of the issues.

■ They allow the employee to state his case in response or alternatively to introduce mitigating factors for the panel to consider.

The composition of a disciplinary hearing panel is ultimately for the employer to determine but it should be identified in the procedure. One significant issue is that the person who issues any disciplinary sanction should have the authority to do so and this also should be identified in the procedure. It may be appropriate for an immediate supervisor to issue informal warnings but more formal sanctions would logically be by a person with higher authority. In any case hearing panels should always comprise the appropriate persons and should certainly avoid any allegation of bias in case any resulting dismissal is held to be unfair.

CASE EXAMPLE

Westminster City Council v Cabaj [1996] IRLR 399

The claimant was dismissed and lodged an appeal which in his contract should have been before three members of the Council but in fact was heard by only two. The EAT held that for the appeal to be heard by only two members 'was so fundamental a defect in the dismissal process' that the only conclusion the tribunal could reach if the case was returned to it was that the dismissal was unfair. The Court of Appeal held that the EAT was right to regard the defect in the composition as a significant failure rather than merely a procedural error. However, it also found that the EAT was wrong to hold that the failure to observe the contractual appeals procedure meant that the decision to dismiss was automatically unfair and directed that the case should be sent back to the tribunal.

Hearings must be conducted according to fair practice and so in general they should follow the rules of natural justice:

- The employee should know the details of the allegations that have been made against him.

CASE EXAMPLE

Boyd v Renfrewshire Council [2008] SCLR 578

The appellant worked as a refuse collection driver. A new system had been introduced which meant that men had to work longer rather than the 'job and finish' system that they had formerly worked to. The appellant had been found without any other crew member and asked to attend a disciplinary meeting. His crew member had actually left his duty and gone for a drink and the appellant did not want to get him into trouble and he had also been threatened by other refuse workers who were on a work to rule. His union representative told him not to say much at the meeting and that he would only get a warning so he said nothing in his own defence and was dismissed. The Court of Session held that he had been unfairly dismissed since he had not been made fully aware of the allegations against him and had failed to provide any defence because he feared reprisals from his work colleagues who were on a work to rule.

- So the employee should always be able to prepare a case and have the opportunity to state his own case at any hearing.

CASE EXAMPLE

Fuller v Lloyds Bank plc [1991] IRLR 336

The claimant attacked a work colleague with a glass at a works party. Witness statements were taken for the disciplinary proceedings but were not shown to the claimant which should have been done according to the disciplinary policy. The claimant was then dismissed and claimed unfair dismissal claiming an unfair procedure. The tribunal held that the dismissal was not unfair since the employee knew the nature of the allegations against him. The EAT upheld the dismissal and held that the procedure was not so flawed that it made the outcome unfair. There was no absolute requirement for witness statements to be shown to the employee only if the basis of the case was in the statements (see 17.2.7 below).

- The employee should always have access to representation of his choice.

This is now guaranteed by section 10 Employment Relations Act 1999. The representative can be a fellow worker or an appropriate trade union representative. This representative accompanying the employee is able to take a full part but not answer on behalf of the employee. The right arises where there is a formal warning, or some other action, or confirmation of a warning issued by some other action. If the employer merges the investigation and the disciplinary hearing he is bound to allow representation or no further action is possible after any informal stage. Hearings should be postponed for a reasonable time to allow the representative to attend.

- The employee should always be informed that he has a right to an appeal which should be before a differently constituted panel. The person who has taken a decision to dismiss should not be involved in any appeal process or there is a clear danger of the rule against bias being offended.

17.2.4 Disciplinary warnings

Warnings are a common feature of modern disciplinary procedures. There is no fixed procedure required but the ACAS Code suggests that there should be:

- informal oral warnings usually given by immediate supervisors for minor infringements;
- verbal warnings for minor misconduct – a written note of the warning is kept on personnel files for a specified period and the employee is informed of the reason for the warning and given the chance of a hearing;
- written warnings for more serious misconduct or for repeated misconduct – again this is recorded and the employee has the chance of a hearing;
- final written warning for serious misconduct or for a failure to respond to previous warnings – this warning should identify the possibility of suspension or dismissal.

There is no need for any power in the contract to issue warnings but power to issue warnings is often contractual and would usually be identified in the works rules. The presence or absence of a warning system is obviously important in determining the fairness or otherwise of a dismissal. The employer should set any procedure in advance make it known to all employees and conform to it at all stages in the process.

Warnings should always be:

- given by a person with the appropriate authority;
- made in clear and precise form and in precise and firm language;
- made in writing if formal.

If there is a proper system of warnings then the system of warnings should be used in its correct sequence. However, it is sometimes possible to miss out stages where the seriousness of breach of discipline warrants it. In *Bendall v Paine & Betteridge* [1973] IRLR 44 an employee was dismissed after having been given a verbal warning only for smoking on the premises which was contrary to the rules. The court held that the failure to issue a written warning made the dismissal unfair.

It is vital in any case that the employer only issues a warning after a full investigation of the issue. The fact that a final written warning is issued rather than any other does not automatically make dismissal the next step. The tribunal should examine all of the circumstances leading up to the warning.

CASE EXAMPLE

Newalls Insulation Co Ltd v Blakeman [1976] IRLR 303

The employee was ultimately dismissed after two absences within fourteen days. The employee had received a final written warning and before that two verbal warnings. The EAT identified that a tribunal should consider the whole background leading up to the dismissal in deciding whether it was unfair. This would include the number of absences, the reasons for the absences and the employee's general employment history.

It is possible for the employer to use the warning system to deal with specific issues but also to deal with the employee's general conduct. In this way the employer is not forced to have separate regimes of warnings running at the same time for different types of misconduct but can consider the overall behaviour of the employer in reaching decisions over disciplinary action.

CASE EXAMPLE

Donald Cook v Carter [1977] IRLR 88

The employee received two warnings within a one year period for using bad language. He was also given a final warning for inefficiency in his work with the threat that he would either be dismissed or demoted and this was only two months later. He also received a final warning for leaving work early and was suspended and then dismissed. He claimed unfair dismissal and the tribunal held that it was unfair because he should have received a further final warning. However, the EAT held that this was unnecessary in the circumstances. It was not for a tribunal to judge the fairness of the type of warning used provided that the matter had been thoroughly investigated as it had been. The type of warning should only be challenged if it was manifestly inappropriate in the circumstances.

A system of warnings is usually also linked to distinct periods, for instance they may last for one year after which they lapse, but any further warning within the period may justify a higher level of warning. The period is for the employer to choose in the disciplinary policy. However, warnings lapse when the stated period expires and an employer cannot then take it into account as a determining factor in a dismissal of an employee for a misdemeanour after the expiry date.

CASE EXAMPLE

Bevan Ashford v Malin [1995] IRLR 360

The employee was given a final written warning which was to remain on his file for one year. He was later dismissed for an incident one year to the day after his warning was issued. The EAT held that the employer could not use this final written warning to justify the dismissal since it would have expired on midnight of the day before. The principle has also subsequently been applied by the Scottish Court of Session in *Doisynth Ltd v Thomson* [2006] IRLR 284. This involved an employee who ignored a health and safety requirement and received a final written warning to last twelve months. He then breached the same rule seventeen months later. His dismissal was unfair, even though his misconduct amounted to gross misconduct it was acknowledged that he would not have been dismissed but for taking into account the previous written warning.

Other sanctions

There are obviously other disciplinary sanctions that an employer might use. Suspension is a possibility and will usually be used during a thorough investigation. The most extreme disciplinary measure is dismissal. This will usually follow exhaustion of a system of warnings. It might also be summary where it is for gross misconduct. An employer should be careful that where summary dismissal is used the behaviour in question does in fact amount to gross misconduct. Common examples of gross misconduct include theft or fraud or other dishonesty, violence, gross insubordination, wilful damage to property, intoxication through alcohol or drugs, serious breaches of confidence, serious breaches of health and safety legislation and serious breaches of anti-discrimination legislation (see Chapter 19.3.2).

17.2.5 The right to be accompanied

Again as with grievance hearings the employee is entitled to be accompanied and again this right is guaranteed under section 10 Employment Relations Act 1999 (see 17.1.3 above). Again under section 10(3) the person accompanying the employee to the disciplinary hearing must be either a fellow worker or a paid trade union official or a trade union official who is certified as qualified in handling such procedures. Again another significant aspect of the right is that if the chosen representative is not available then the hearing can be postponed for a reasonable time for the representative to attend. Nevertheless by virtue of the ACAS Code the procedure must still be held in good time.

In general section 10 of the Employment Relations Act 1999 does not give any right to an employee to have legal representation during disciplinary hearings. However, under Article 6 of the European Convention on Human Rights everybody is entitled to a fair trial. This would mean that if the employee was potentially facing criminal charges then he is entitled to legal representation.

CASE EXAMPLE

Kulkarni v Milton Keynes Hospitals NHS Trust [2009] EWCA Civ 789

A doctor was accused of professional misconduct after it was alleged that he had engaged in an improper examination of a female patient. As a result he faced a disciplinary hearing. After enquiring whether he would be entitled to have legal representation at the disciplinary hearing he was told that that he would not. The procedure did not allow for legal representation and whoever might accompany the claimant 'must not be acting in a legal capacity'. The Court of Appeal later considered the issue of whether the doctor was entitled to legal representation. It stated *in obiter* that if the outcome of such proceedings was such that he may be prevented from working that in those circumstances Article 6 of the European Convention of Human Rights would require that he be allowed legal representation at the hearing.

JUDGMENT

Lady Justice Smith explained: 'there is nothing to stop a practitioner from asking the employer to permit him to be legally represented.... The employer faced with such a request is in some difficulty in that the line between cases in which Article 6 is and is not engaged (because of the potentially grave effect of an adverse finding on the doctor's ability to practise his profession) may be a difficult line to draw. If the employer refuses to grant representation in a case which does engage Article 6, his refusal will be unlawful. It may be that an employer who receives such a request would be well advised to give it fair consideration and when doing so to bear in mind the possibility that a denial of full rights of representation might be held to be a breach of Article 6.'

The mere fact that employment might be lost in these circumstances is not enough on its own to justify allowing legal representation.

CASE EXAMPLE

R v Governors of X School [2010] EWCA Civ 1

A school teacher was accused of inappropriate behaviour with a young person on work experience at the school and was taken through disciplinary procedure. If the complaint was established he might face not only dismissal by his employer but also being prohibited from working with young people and vulnerable adults following a hearing with the Independent Safeguarding Authority. The issue was whether he was entitled to legal representation. The Supreme Court held that, although the procedure was not the same as being subjected to criminal charges the gravity of the allegations and the potential consequences if they were proven meant that he was entitled to legal representation at the hearing of the Independent Safeguarding Authority which would decide whether he should be barred from being a teacher but not at the internal disciplinary hearing which would only deal with his employment.

If an employer denies an employee the right to be accompanied at the hearing by a fellow employee or trade union officer it can lead to a claim being made in a tribunal and possible compensation. Similarly a person who accompanies the employee to a disciplinary hearing has the right himself not to suffer any detriment as a consequence and a dismissal in such circumstances would be an automatically unfair dismissal.

17.2.6 Appeals

According to the ACAS Code of Practice an employer must have an appeals procedure available for employees who have gone through a disciplinary procedure, although no particular form is required. Appeals could be a complete rehearing of the evidence or they could merely be a review of the processes used in the original investigation and hearing. Whichever is used the whole proceedings should be fair and in any resulting dispute a tribunal should always consider the fairness of every stage of the procedure.

CASE EXAMPLE

Taylor v OCS Group Ltd [2006] EWCA Civ 702

The claimant, a profoundly deaf employee, who was classed as disabled for the purposes of the Disability Discrimination Act 1995, was asked by another member of staff to remedy problems she was experiencing with a database that he had created. He then forwarded e-mails to himself from her computer to his own. One was personal and the others contained confidential information including staff salary levels. This was a serious breach of the company's policy. He was reported to and suspended from duty by the intranet manager who then carried out an investigation and held a meeting with him. He mistakenly thought that she was representing him and when asked said that he did not wish to be accompanied. He admitted what he had done and a disciplinary meeting was held that afternoon by the Communications Manager. No interpreter was provided and the claimant did not fully understand what was happening during the meeting. The meeting concluded that the claimant was guilty of misconduct and he was told that he was dismissed, which was apparent from the notes of the meeting but the claimant later argued that he had not understood what had happened. He appealed, and the appeal hearing was conducted by a senior member of staff. An interpreter attended, although she was unable to stay throughout. The claimant was represented by his sister, a qualified teacher of the deaf. When the interpreter had to leave the sister took over as interpreter and representative. The decision to dismiss was affirmed and the claimant brought an action for unfair dismissal and disability discrimination. In the company's appeal against the decision of the EAT the Court of Appeal held that there was no disability related reason for the dismissal. It also identified that the tribunal should look at the whole proceedings from start to finish to establish whether there was any unfairness in the decision reached. If the early stages of the procedure were flawed in any way then it should look at the later stages with care to see if the early stages influenced the later stages making the whole proceedings unfair.

JUDGMENT

Lady Justice Smith explained: 'the ET [should] approach their task broadly as an industrial jury. That means that they should consider the procedural issues together with the reason for the dismissal, as they have found it to be. The two impact upon each other and the ET's task is to decide whether, in all the circumstances of the case, the employer acted reasonably in treating the reason they have found as a sufficient reason to dismiss. So for example, where the misconduct which founds the reason for the dismissal is serious, an ET might well decide (after considering equity and the substantial merits of the case) that, notwithstanding some procedural imperfections, the employer acted reasonably in treating the reason as a sufficient reason to dismiss the employee. Where the misconduct was of a less serious nature, so that the decision to dismiss was nearer to the borderline, the ET might well conclude that a procedural deficiency had such impact that the employer did not act reasonably in dismissing the employee.'

However, internal appeals procedures do not have to be excessively legalistic in character or follow court procedures.

CASE EXAMPLE

Rowe v Radio Rentals [1982] IRLR 177

In this case the issue was whether the employee had been subjected to bias because of the procedures which it was therefore argued were unfair. The claimant had been found guilty of gross misconduct and had been dismissed by the Area Manager who had conducted the hearing. He then had told the facts to the members of the appeal panel before the appeal hearing and had also been present throughout the appeal hearing. The court accepted that the rules of natural justice were an issue but it also considered that it may not always be practicable to expect a complete separation between the person dismissing and the person conducting the appeal because they might both be ordinary line managers. The issue was whether the internal procedure was fair.

17.2.7 Breaches of procedure

The conduct of an employer during disciplinary proceedings can be vital, particularly in the face of claims of unfair dismissal. For a while following the Employment Act 2002 employers were bound to follow a process identified in the Act known as Statutory Discipline and Dismissal Procedure. This has now been abandoned and there has been a return to the ACAS Code of Practice as a guideline and also the principle from the case of *Polkey v AE Dayton Services Ltd* [1988] AC 344 where the then House of Lords held a dismissal to be unfair because there was no way to determine what the outcome would have been if the employer had in fact adopted the correct procedure (see Chapter 22.5.2).

JUDGMENT

Lord Bridge identified that an employer cannot treat a dismissal as being fair: 'unless and until he has taken the steps, conveniently classified in most of the authorities as "procedural", which are necessary in the circumstances of the case to justify the action'.

Failures to follow procedure do not on their own form the basis of a claim but the tribunal will always take them into account in determining the fairness of the employer's actions.

So it may well amount to an unfair dismissal where the employee has simply flouted the proper procedures in order to gain an unfair advantage.

CASE EXAMPLE

Raspin v United News Shops Ltd [1999] IRLR 9

The employer following disciplinary procedures dismissed the employee but in fact failed to follow the agreed procedures. The employee claimed unfair dismissal and succeeded. The tribunal found that if the correct procedure had been followed the claimant would have remained in employment for a further three weeks which would then have enabled her to bring a claim for unfair dismissal. The dismissal as a result had no real foundation and the employee was entitled to a claim for damages.

A significant breach of procedure will also occur when the employee is not in fact aware of the disciplinary rule that he is breaching. In all cases employees should be made fully aware of all disciplinary rules. If the employee is unaware of the rule then how can he ensure that he observes it?

CASE EXAMPLE

Brooks & Son v Skinner [1984] IRLR 379

The employer had previously reached an agreement on disciplinary matters with the recognised trade union representatives that included a rule that employees who failed to return to work on the day after the works Christmas party would be dismissed. The claimant failed to return to work on the day after Christmas and was dismissed. He claimed unfair dismissal on the basis that he had never been told about the decision to dismiss in such circumstances. The EAT accepted that he could not be subject to rules, particularly those leading to dismissal, without those rules having been bought to his attention or at the very least being given a proper hearing.

Similarly an absolute essential of any proper procedure is a proper hearing of the issues in which the employee is able to state his own case.

CASE EXAMPLE

Jones v Lee and Guilding [1980] IRLR 67

A headmaster of a Catholic school was dismissed after he divorced his wife and then remarried. Under his contract before he could be dismissed he was entitled to a hearing in front of the local education authority and also to be represented at those proceedings. The procedure was not followed and the dismissed headmaster sought an injunction. The court of Appeal accepted that the injunction should be awarded. The school could not dismiss without following the correct procedure. It had not only failed to follow its contractual obligations but even without the contract a procedure which did not include a hearing at which the employee could state his own case would have been entirely flawed.

However, failures to follow procedural requirements or following flawed procedures will not always be to the employee's advantage. The absolute test is still whether in all the circumstances the employer acted fairly in the decision that he made.

CASE EXAMPLE

Fuller v Lloyds Bank plc [1991] IRLR 336

At the works Christmas party on Christmas Eve the claimant had attacked a fellow employee with a glass and injured that person's face. In the disciplinary proceedings that inevitably followed the employer took a number of statements from witnesses to the event but in fact failed to reveal them to the claimant which according to its disciplinary policy it should have done. Following the investigation and hearing the claimant was dismissed and claimed unfair dismissal arguing that he had been subjected to an unfair procedure. The tribunal held that the dismissal was not unfair since the employee knew the nature of the allegations against him. The EAT agreed and also added that the procedure was not so flawed that it made the outcome unfair. It held that there was no general principle that witness statements should be shown to an employee facing disciplinary proceedings but only if the essence of the case against him was contained in those statements.

Is there a disciplinary problem?

YES

Has the employer been able to resolve the issue through informal procedures?

NO

Has the employer taken appropriate formal action using an established procedure?
- the employer has made a thorough investigation and established the facts
- the employer has fully informed the employee of these findings
- the employer has held a hearing at which the employee has been allowed to state his own side and has been allowed to be accompanied by an appropriate representative
- the employer has decided on action appropriate to the findings and the type of disciplinary breach

YES

Is the action appropriate to the breach?
- no action taken (if no real breach of rules)
- verbal warning (minor breaches)
- written warning (more serious breaches or a series of breaches)
- final written warning (for serious misconduct or a failure to respond to earlier written warnings)
- dismissal (usually very serious misconduct)
- summary dismissal (for gross misconduct only)

YES

Has the employee been allowed to appeal the decision?

YES

Has the employer followed the ACAS Code of Practice throughout the proceedings?

Figure 17.2 Check list for an appropriate disciplinary procedure

ACTIVITY

Self-assessment questions

1. How does the ACAS Code of Practice affect disciplinary matters?
2. What does the Code suggest are the essential attributes of a sound disciplinary procedure?
3. What should the employee do to ensure that employees follow and are bound by the disciplinary procedure?
4. What types of rules can be in an employer's disciplinary code?
5. How should disciplinary hearings be conducted?
6. Why is it important to have a system of disciplinary warnings?
7. Who can accompany an employee to a disciplinary hearing?
8. What form should an internal appeal take?
9. What are the consequences if an employer fails to properly follow the procedure?

KEY FACTS

Grievances	Case/statute
Formal procedure	
<ul><li>employee should set out grievance in writing</li><li>employer should hold meeting with employee</li><li>employer must allow employee to be accompanied by a colleague or trade union representative</li><li>employer must decide on the appropriate action to be taken</li><li>employer must allow an appeal</li></ul>	ACAS Code of Practice
The right to be accompanied	
Breaches of procedure	
<ul><li>can lead to successful constructive dismissal claim</li></ul>	S10 Employment Relations Act 1999 W A Goold (Pearmak) Ltd v McConnell
The ACAS Code of Practice on disciplinary procedures	Case/statute
<ul><li>Employers and employees should act consistently.</li><li>Employers should carry out necessary investigations</li><li>Employers should inform employee of the problem and give him/her the opportunity to put his case</li><li>Employers should hold a meeting with the employee</li><li>At meeting the employer should allow the employee to be accompanied</li><li>Employers should then decide on appropriate action</li><li>Employers should provide an appeal</li></ul>	S10 Employment Relations Act 1999

Disciplinary measures	Case/statute
• All disciplinary codes and procedures should be identified in the contract	*ACAS Code of Practice*
• And they must be brought to the attention of the employee to be binding	*Brooks & Son v Skinner*
• Rules can involve maintaining standards	*Schmidt v Austicks Bookshops Ltd*
• And also competence in the work	*Turner v Pleasurama Casinos Ltd*
• And prohibit dishonesty	*Sinclair v Neighbour*
• And prohibit violent behaviour	*Parsons & Co Ltd v McLoughlin*
• Differential treatment of employees needs to be justified by e.g. one being more blameworthy	*Securicor Ltd v Smith*
• The important question is whether the employer has acted reasonably	*Palmer v Vauxhall Motors Ltd*

Disciplinary hearings	Case/statute
• Generally subject to formal procedures but can be ad hoc for informal cautions	*ACAS Code of Practice*
• Hearing panels should be authorised persons and avoid bias	*Westminster City Council v Cabaj*
• The employee should be made aware of the allegations	*Boyd v Renfrewshire Council*
• And have the opportunity to research and present his own case	*Fuller v Lloyds Bank plc*
• And has the right to be accompanied by a union official or work colleague	*S10 Employment Relations Act 1999*
• And should be told of his right to appeal before a differently constituted panel	

Disciplinary warnings	Case/statute
• Can be informal, verbal, written or final written	*ACAS Code of Practice*
• Should be given by a person with appropriate authority, be clear and precise and in firm language and made in writing if formal	*ACAS Code of Practice*
• Where warnings lead to dismissal tribunal must consider all of the circumstances	*Newalls Insulation Co Ltd v Blakeman*
• Can cover specific conduct or conduct in general	*Donald Cook v Carter*
• Cannot use a warning once it is lapsed	*Bevan Ashford v Malin*

The right to be accompanied	Case/statute
• There is a statutory right to be accompanied at disciplinary hearings	*S10 Employment Relations Act 1999*
• This can be an appropriate trade union official or a work colleague	*S10(3) Employment Relations Act 1999*
• Legal representation may be possible where the employee might face criminal charges	*Kulkarni v Milton Keynes Hospitals NHS Trust*
• But there is no absolute right to legal representation just because dismissal is a possibility	*R v Governors of X School*

Appeals	Case/statute
• Can be rehearing or review of procedure	
• Tribunal should consider fairness of every stage of the procedure	*Taylor v OCS Group Ltd*
• But need not follow court procedures	*Rowe v Radio Rentals*

Breaches of procedure	Case/statute
• Should follow ACAS Code of Practice • And dismissal not fair unless procedure followed • May be unfair dismissal where employer has ignored procedure to gain an unfair advantage • Breach of procedure also if employee not made aware of rules • And procedure unfair unless employee is able to state his own case • But the absolute test is whether the employer acted fairly in reaching his decision	*Polkey v AE Dayton Services Ltd* *Raspin v United News Shops Ltd* *Brooks & Son v Skinner* *Jones v Lee and Guilding* *Fuller v Lloyds Bank plc*

SAMPLE ESSAY QUESTION

ESSAY Critically analyse the significance of the ACAS Code of Practice on Grievance and Disciplinary Procedures.

Explain what ACAS is

- ACAS is the Arbitration Conciliation and Advisory Service.
- It is an independent body set up by government.
- It has the aim of improving organisations that employ staff and improving working life through better employment relations.

Explain the role of ACAS

- The promoting of good practice.
- Providing advice and information.
- Preventing and resolving disputes through collective conciliation and advisory mediation.
- Providing conciliation and arbitration in disputes brought before employment tribunals.

Explain what the ACAS Code of Practice on Grievance and Disciplinary Procedure is

- It provides basic practical guidance to employers, employees and their representatives and sets out principles for handling disciplinary and grievance situations in the workplace.

- The Code does not apply to dismissals due to redundancy or the non-renewal of fixed term contracts on their expiry.

Discuss what the Code says on Grievance Procedures

- Sets out an appropriate procedure.
- Employee should set out grievance in writing.
- Employer should hold meeting with employee.
- Employer must allow employee to be accompanied by a colleague or trade union representative.
- Employer must decide on the appropriate action to be taken.
- Employer must allow an appeal.

Discuss what the ACAS Code says on Disciplinary Procedure

- Sets out an appropriate procedure.
- Employers and employees should act consistently.
- Employers should carry out necessary investigations.
- Employers should inform employee of the problem and give them the opportunity to put their case.
- Employers should hold a meeting with the employee.
- At meeting the employer should allow the employee to be accompanied.
- Employers should then decide on appropriate action.
- Employers should provide an appeal.

Discuss the significance of the ACAS Code

- Employers should follow the ACAS Code of Practice.
- Because it is good practice.
- It is not legally enforceable.
- But it will be taken into account by a tribunal.
- So for example may be evidence of bad practice and could be unfair dismissal.

REACH REASONED CONCLUSIONS

SUMMARY

- The ACAS Code of Practice on Grievance and Disciplinary Procedures sets out proper procedure for carrying out a grievance.
- One essential is that the employee has a right to be accompanied.
- And a breach of procedure may lead to a successful constructive dismissal claim.
- The ACAS Code also sets out proper procedures for disciplinary procedures.
- Disciplinary codes and procedures need contractual authority and must be brought to the attention of the employee to be binding.
- Rules can be general or cover specific issues.
- Any differential treatment of employees should be justified.
- Disciplinary hearings can be formal or ad hoc for informal cautions.
- Hearing panels should be authorised persons and avoid bias.
- The employee should be made aware of the allegations and have the opportunity to research and present his own case and be accompanied by a union official or work colleague and be told of his right to appeal before a differently constituted panel.
- One sanction for an employer is a system of warnings which are set at higher levels depending on the nature of the misconduct.
- It is usual for warnings to be recorded even if they are verbal.
- An accumulation of warnings can obviously ultimately lead to dismissal.
- Again there is a right to be accompanied by an appropriate trade union representative or a work colleague.
- And where the employee may potentially face criminal charges he may also be entitled to legal representation.
- Where the correct procedure is not followed or the employee is unaware of the rules or prevented from stating his case then a successful claim of constructive dismissal is possible.

Further reading

Emir, Astra, *Selwyn's Law of Employment 17th edition*. Oxford University Press, 2012, Chapter 12.

Pitt, Gwyneth, *Cases and Materials on Employment Law 3rd edition*. Pearson, 2008, Chapter 8.

Sargeant, Malcolm and Lewis, David, *Employment Law 6th edition*. Pearson, 2012, Chapter 3.2.15.

18

TUPE transfers

AIMS AND OBJECTIVES

After reading this chapter you should be able to:

▦ Understand the background to the Acquired Rights Directive and its implementation in the Transfer of Undertakings (Protection of Employment) Regulations

▦ Understand to whom the regulations apply

▦ Understand the nature of a TUPE transfer

▦ Understand the effect of a TUPE transfer

▦ Understand the position on dismissal resulting from a TUPE transfer

▦ Understand the role of consultation in a transfer

▦ Critically analyse the area of TUPE transfers and the relationship between the Directive and the Regulations

▦ Apply the principles to factual situations

18.1 The origins and aims of law on transfer of undertakings

A transfer of an undertaking refers to the situation where one business is sold off or otherwise transferred to another business. The original common law position was that the contract ceased on the transfer of the business and so there was no contractual obligation on the party buying the business to the employees whose contracts in effect were terminated. This was obviously very unfair on employees.

The Transfer of Undertakings (Protection of Employment) Regulations 1981 were passed in order to implement the Acquired Rights Directive 77/187. Both have subsequently been amended. The Directive was amended in 1998 and now there is a new Acquired Rights Directive 2001/23 and the 1977 and 1998 directives were replaced. The 1981 regulations were also amended in 1993 and in 1999. Now English law is contained in the Transfer of Undertakings (Protection of Employment) Regulations 2006.

The Acquired Rights Directive generally tried to remove the unfairness and insecurity of an employee in a transfer and to transfer the obligations of the old employer who sold the business, known as the transferor, to the new employer who bought the business, known as the transferee. The aims of the Directive were:

- to ensure that employees affected by a transfer of the business are consulted with and kept informed;
- to ensure that the contracts of employment are also transferred with the business;
- to ensure the maintenance of collective agreements for at least one year after the transfer of the business;
- to ensure that the transfer itself should not be a ground for any dismissals even though there might be dismissals because of economic, technical or organisational reasons;
- the ensure that if an employee suffers dramatic changes in working conditions after the transfer of the business that this should count as a dismissal.

The Directive and the Regulations that implement it have caused significant controversy, not least during the 1980s and 1990s when the UK government was busy outsourcing large areas of public service work to private enterprise and there was a significant issue of whether the rules should apply in these situations. (It is interesting that the present UK government is keen to implement elements of a report by the venture capitalist Adrian Beecroft which the government commissioned and that one suggested reform is that employees whose jobs are outsourced should not retain their rights and should be outside the scope of the Regulations. Outsourcing was a contentious area where a number of contractors felt that the Regulations were in fact more generous than was in fact intended by the Directive so it is arguable whether such a move would put the government in conflict with its EU obligations once again.) The period in any case led to a number of cases in which UK law and EU law were in apparent conflict (see 18.2 below).

The House of Lords (now the Supreme Court) nevertheless has clearly identified that the Regulations should be interpreted purposively so that as far as possible employee's rights on TUPE transfers should be safeguarded because the Regulations represent EU law.

CASE EXAMPLE

Litster v Forth Dry Dock & Engineering Co Ltd [1990] 1 AC 546

An employee was dismissed one hour before a transfer of the business to new owners took place. The employee claimed that he had been unfairly dismissed. The claim would have been ineffective because the old employer had gone out of business. However, the House of Lords (now the Supreme Court) held that his rights had transferred to the new owner and that therefore his action could be pursued against the new owner. The court considered that if the employee is dismissed by redundancy because of the transfer but without any contractual basis then the dismissal is unfair. The court in effect implied a meaning into the earlier Regulation that is now included in the 2006 Regulations that the provisions apply also to: 'a person so employed immediately before the transfer, or who would have been so employed if he had not been dismissed'.

JUDGMENT

Lord Keith of Kinkel observed: 'it is the duty of the court to give to [the Regulation] a construction which accords with the decisions of the European Court upon the corresponding provisions of the Directive to which the regulation was intended by Parliament to give effect. The precedent established by *Pickstone v Freemans Plc*, indicates that this is to be done by implying the words necessary to achieve that result. So there must be implied in [the] regulation … words indicating that where a person has been unfairly dismissed in the circumstances described … he is to be deemed to have been employed in the undertaking immediately before the transfer or any of a series of transactions whereby it was effected.'

The decision broadened the scope of the regulations significantly. It was said that even if there is an economic, technical or organisational (ETO) reason for the dismissal the employer is still bound to act fairly. However, the problems of application of the regulations as well as conflicting application with ECJ decisions continued and eventually the Transfer of Undertakings (Protection of Employment) Regulations 2006 were introduced with the aim of removing earlier problems.

For the Regulations to apply a tribunal must in any case be certain of two key facts:

- that there was a relevant and sufficiently identifiable economic entity; and
- that there was a relevant transfer.

18.2 To whom the regulations apply

The Regulations apply to employees but the definition is wider than that in the Employment Rights Act 1996. The definition is provided in Regulation 2(1) which identifies that '"employee" means any individual who works for another person whether under a contract of service or apprenticeship or otherwise'.

So it is wide enough to include agency workers, and casual workers. However, 'it does not include anyone who provides services under a contract for services'. In *Cowell v Quilter Goodison Co Ltd* [1989] IRLR 392 the Court of Appeal held that an equity partner in a firm of stockbrokers and was then employed by the company that bought it out was not an employee within the meaning of TUPE. Since his position was that of a person who provides services under a contract for services such a situation was specifically excluded from the TUPE Regulations.

By Regulation 3(1) the Regulations apply to 'a transfer of an undertaking, business or part of an undertaking or business situated immediately before the transfer in the United Kingdom to another person where there is a transfer of an economic entity which retains its identity'. Under Regulation 3(2) an economic entity is defined as 'an organised grouping of resources which has the objective of pursuing an economic activity, whether or not that activity is central or ancillary'.

The ECJ at one point in fact appeared to have extended the Directive to include virtually all business transfers regardless of whether or not there was any actual transfer of tangible assets.

CASE EXAMPLE

Schmidt v Spar und Leihkasse der Fruheren Amter Bordesholm, Kiel und Cronshagen (C-392/92) [1995] 2 CMLR 331

The employee was the only cleaner in a branch of a bank. Cleaning duties were then transferred to a firm of contractors. The cleaner refused to accept the terms imposed by the contractors which were inferior to those under her former contract and she was dismissed. The ECJ held that (i) the mere fact that there was no transfer of tangible assets did not mean that the Acquired Rights Directive could not apply; (ii) whether the business retained its identity was a decisive factor; (iii) the Directive can cover activities (such as here) that are ancillary to the main activity; and (iv) the fact that the activity was only carried out by one person also does not necessarily matter. As such the words 'an organised grouping of employees' in the Directive can sometimes apply to one employee.

JUDGMENT

The ECJ held: 'Article 1(1) of Council Directive 77/187/EEC … is to be interpreted as covering a situation, such as that outlined … in which an undertaking entrusts by contract to another undertaking the responsibility for carrying out cleaning operations which it previously performed itself, even though, prior to the transfer, such work was carried out by a single employee.'

It has been identified that the business has to be transferred as a going concern so that there is no relevant transfer under the Regulations if there is merely a transfer of assets.

CASE EXAMPLE

Spijkers v Gebroeders Benedik Abattoir [1986] ECR 1119; [1986] 2 CMLR 296

The claimant had been the assistant manager of the abattoir. The owner then sold the abattoir including the premises and the land to another company. Before the sale had taken place the former owner had been forced to cease trading so that there was no real goodwill left in the business when it was taken over. When the new owner reopened the abattoir it employed all but two of the former employees, the claimant being one of these two. The new owner also did not take on any of the former clients of the business and the question was whether the Directive could apply when there was no economic entity at the time of the transfer. The ECJ held that the Directive should be interpreted so as to include where the business retained its identity. The court identified that this would be determined by considering whether, having regard to all the facts, the business was disposed of as a going concern, which could be shown by the new employer continuing with the same or similar activities.

The Court of Justice later listed the factors that should be taken into account in determining whether the business had or had not retained its identity.

CASE EXAMPLE

Watson Rask and Christiansen v ISS Kantineservice A/S [1992] ECR-1 5755; [1993] IRLR 133

A company contracted out its canteen service to ISS. Under the contract ISS received a fee from which ISS met the labour, management and administrative costs and the company provided the premises, equipment, refuse collection and cleaning products. ISS offered employment to former employees of the company but on reduced terms as a result of which two of the employees brought a complaint. ISS responded by arguing that there was no relevant transfer but merely a transfer of services to an outside contractor and that there was no transfer of assets and no customers involved since the canteen was for the company's staff. The ECJ rejected these arguments and held that a relevant transfer included one where the responsibility for carrying on the business changed hands and that it did not matter that ownership of the business changed hands or not. The court outlined the factors that should be considered:

- the type of undertaking involved;
- whether or not tangible assets of the business transferred;
- the value of the intangible assets at the time of the transfer;
- whether or not the majority of employees were transferred;
- whether or not any customers of the business were transferred;
- the degree of similarity between the activities carried out before and after the transfer;
- if any of those activities were suspended, the period for which they were suspended.

It had also been accepted that the undertaking did not have to be a profit making body in order for the Directive (and thus the Regulations) to apply.

CASE EXAMPLE

Dr Sophie Redmond Stichting v Bartol [1994] CMLR 265

This involved a non-profit making charitable foundation which provided help for drug addicts and was funded by a grant given by an authority. The grant was then taken away from the foundation and given to another charitable body which took over the work formerly done by the foundation, using the foundation's premises and with the same clients. It continued to employ some of the foundation's employees and the ECJ held that the Directive applied to protect their former rights.

Another aspect of the test which developed to determine whether or not there was an undertaking for the purposes of the Directive was whether the new owner carried on the essential business activity.

CASE EXAMPLE

Kenny v South Manchester College [1993] IRLR 265

A tendering exercise for the contract to provide teaching for young offenders at a young offenders institute resulted in the contract changing hands. The question was whether the contracts of employment and therefore the rights under them changed hands to the new contractor on the transfer. The court held that there was a relevant transfer because the teaching existed before the transfer occurred and afterwards and so was an entity.

Considerable confusion and controversy was caused by the decision of the ECJ in *Ayse Suzen v Zehnake Gebaudereinigung GmbH Kraankenhausservice* [1997] 1 CMLR 768 where it was held that a relevant transfer must be of an economic 'entity' and this would not include something that was simply an economic 'activity'.

CASE EXAMPLE

Süzen v Zehnacker Gebäudereinigung GmbH [1997] 1 CMLR 768

The claimant worked for contractors as a cleaner in a school. The contract for cleaning then came to an end and the school entered into a contract with another contractor to provide cleaning services but this contractor failed to employ the claimant. The issue for the ECJ was whether the transfer of workers employed under a school cleaning contract from one contract to another was covered by the directive so that the claimant enjoyed rights under the contract.

The ECJ held that the criteria from *Spijkers v Gebroeders Benedik Abattoir* [1986] ECR 1119; [1986] 2 CMLR 296 should be applied. Nevertheless, it went on to state that such an entity could not be reduced to the activity entrusted to it but must comprise persons, assets and other features facilitating an economic activity. In effect the decision meant that, in the absence of a transfer of the workforce, contracting out of the workforce in a labour intensive sector could not be covered by the Acquired Rights Directive (from which TUPE rights derive). The court did, however, recognise that 'in certain labour intensive sectors a group of workers engaged in a joint activity on a permanent basis may constitute an economic entity'.

JUDGMENT

The court stated: 'the mere fact that the service provided by the old and the new awardees of a contract is similar does not therefore support the conclusion that an economic entity has been transferred. An entity cannot be reduced to the activity entrusted to it.'

The case caused much confusion in the area of contracting out in English courts and tribunals.

CASE EXAMPLE

Betts v Brintel Helicopters Ltd and KLM ERA Helicopters (UK) Ltd [1997] IRLR 361

Following the transfer of a contract for the supply of North Sea helicopter services the new contractor refused to take over either the plant or the personnel of the previous contractor. This was at least partly in order to avoid being tied to the previous contractual arrangements. Initially it was accepted that the employees transferred also and the directive applied but, following *Suzen*, the Court of Appeal held that, even though there was an economic entity involved there was nevertheless no relevant transfer attracting TUPE protection for the employees.

In contrast in *ECM (Vehicle Delivery Services) Ltd v Cox* [1998] IRLR 416 the EAT held that it was not possible for an incoming contractor to cause the Transfer of Undertakings Regulations to be disapplied by refusing to take on the outgoing contractor's employees. The Court of Appeal in *ECM (Vehicle Delivery Service) Ltd v Cox* [1999] IRLR 559 then held that the tribunal was entitled to conclude that, even though a transferee contractor declined to take on any of the transferor contractor's employees, the identity of the economic entity operated by the transferor was retained in the hands of the transferee.

On occasions in fact courts have still followed the approach in *Schmidt v Spar und Leihkasse der Fruheren Amter Bordesholm, Kiel und Cronshagen* in preference to the very restrictive approach in *Süzen v Zehnacker Gebäudereinigung GmbH*.

CASE EXAMPLE

Argyll Training Ltd v Sinclair [2000] IRLR 630

A training contract was transferred from one provider to another after a re-tendering exercise. The new provider took over two-thirds of the trainees but no assets were transferred and the new provider did not employ any of the staff that had formerly been in charge of the trainees. One of those complained that there had been a TUPE dismissal. The tribunal initially followed *Suzen* and held that there was no relevant TUPE transfer. However, the Scottish EAT held that *Suzen* could not be relied upon to establish whether there was a relevant transfer or not and preferred to apply *Schmidt*.

Now Regulation 3(1)(b) Transfer of Undertakings Regulations 2006 identifies that there can also be a relevant transfer for the purpose of TUPE protections in the case of 'service provision change' and this includes outsourcing, contracting out and indeed bringing the services back in house.

REGULATION

'3 These Regulations apply to
(1)
    (b) a service provision change, that is a situation in which –
        (i) activities cease to be carried out by a person ("a client") on his own behalf and are carried out instead by another person on the client's behalf ("a contractor");
        (ii) activities cease to be carried out by a contractor on a client's behalf (whether or not those activities had previously been carried out by the client on his own behalf) and are carried out instead by another person ("a subsequent contractor") on the client's behalf; or
        (iii) activities cease to be carried out by a contractor or a subsequent contractor on a client's behalf (whether or not those activities had previously been carried out by the client on his own behalf) and are carried out instead by the client on his own behalf,

        ▓ The first involves an initial outsourcing of services where a contractor is hired to provide the in house service
        ▓ The second involves the situation where there is a fresh tendering exercise and the tender is won by a new contractor
        ▓ The third involves the services being brought back in house.'

The EAT has subsequently identified that in defining service provision for the purposes of determining whether the Regulations apply the wording of the 2006 Regulations should be viewed without reference to former interpretations which it considered to be unhelpful.

CASE EXAMPLE

Metropolitan Resources Ltd v Churchill Dulwich Ltd [2009] IRLR 700

Through an intermediary the Home Office had a contract with Churchill Dulwich Ltd under which it provided accommodation for asylum seekers. Before that contract expired a replacement contract was negotiated with Metropolitan Resources Centre Ltd for the same provision but at a different location. When the original contract expired Churchill Dulwich employees claimed that there had been a transfer of their employment under Regulation 3(1)(b) of TUPE 2006, a service provision change, to Metropolitan Resources Ltd. The EAT held that there was indeed a relevant transfer and that the particular situation was covered by Regulation 3(1)(b).

A problematic situation in deciding whether the Regulations apply arises where the employee works for two or more companies in the same group, for instance for a holding company and also for its subsidiary and then one is transferred.

CASE EXAMPLE

Sunley Turriff Holdings Ltd v Thomson [1995] IRLR 184

The claimant here was company secretary and chief accountant for two companies in a group. His contract was actually with the one company but he obviously did work also for the other. Both companies then went into administration and the second of the two was sold to Sunley Turriff Holdings Ltd. It was held that the claimant's contract still automatically transferred since he was a part of the undertaking that had been transferred.

Most government departments now have guidelines on the application of TUPE to contracting out cases. The effect is that TUPE rules should always apply unless there are 'exceptional, genuine reasons not do so'. The organisations should also make appropriate arrangements for pensions and for redundancy and severance.

18.3 The nature of a transfer for TUPE purposes

A relevant transfer can be a sale of a company, or indeed of a partnership or of a sole trader's business in each case to another business. It could also in fact be any other disposition or by operation of law. This could involve a merger of two or more businesses, a change of licensee, a change of a franchise or a change of the contractor in the case of contracted out services or even a return to the body paying for the services.

The significant feature of a TUPE transfer is that there must be a change in the identity of the employer. This does not even mean that there has to be a change in the ownership of the business.

CASE EXAMPLE

Young v Daniel Thwaites & Co Ltd [1977] ICR 187

A tenant, in a hotel, gave up his tenancy but the employee who had been employed by the tenant continued to work as normal when the owners of the hotel, which was the brewery that had been supplying the hotel with beer during the tenancy, continued the business that the tenant had been conducting in the hotel. The court held that there had been a relevant transfer of the business. (In fact the case obviously predates the first TUPE Regulations and it was the provisions of schedule 1 of the Contracts of Employment Act 1972 which had to be interpreted which provided that: '(2) If a trade or business or an undertaking ... is transferred from one person to another, the period of employment of an employee in the trade or business or undertaking at the time shall count as a period of employment with the transfer, and the transfer shall not break the continuity of the period of employment.')

The critical question on transfer is whether the business has retained its identity. In this way it is not vital that there is a contractual link between the transferor and the transferee.

CASE EXAMPLE

Dines v Initial Healthcare Services Ltd [1995] IRLR 336

The case involved a group of cleaners at a hospital who were employed by Initial Health Care Services. Their jobs were then affected when the contract for cleaning was put out to competitive tender and the tender was won by a different contractor, Pall Mall. The cleaners were then made redundant by Initial. Pall Mall then agreed to employ them on but on considerably less favourable conditions than they had enjoyed with Initial. As a result they claimed unfair dismissal. The Court of Appeal held that there was a relevant transfer (under what at the time was Regulation 8 of the 1981 TUPE Regulations) since the services were essentially the same. The transfer was in effect in two stages: first the contract was returned to the hospital which had contracted it out to Initial and then second it was transferred on to the new contractor, Pall Mall. As a result the cleaners should have transferred with the contract and their contractual rights should have been protected. The fact that this had not occurred meant that they had been unfairly dismissed.

18.4 The effect of TUPE transfers

The major effects of the Acquired Rights Directive are now found in Regulation 4 of the Transfer of Undertakings (Protection of Employment) Regulations 2006. This completely reverses the old common law position in *Nokes v Doncaster Amalgamated Collieries Ltd* [1940] AC 1014 which was that when a business changed hands the contracts of employment did not transfer and employees started anew if they were taken on by the transferee, or in effect the contracts of employment came to an end.

Now Regulation 4 details the effects:

REGULATION

'4 Effect of relevant transfer on contracts of employment

(1) ... a relevant transfer shall not operate so as to terminate the contract of employment of any person employed by the transferor and assigned to the organised grouping of resources or employees that is subject to the relevant transfer, which would otherwise be terminated by the transfer, but any such contract shall have effect after the transfer as if originally made between the person so employed and the transferee.

(2) Without prejudice to paragraph (1) ... on the completion of a relevant transfer –

   (a) all the transferor's rights, powers, duties and liabilities under or in connection with any such contract shall be transferred by virtue of this regulation to the transferee; and

   (b) any act or omission before the transfer is completed, of or in relation to the transferor in respect of that contract or a person assigned to that organised grouping of resources or employees, shall be deemed to have been an act or omission of or in relation to the transferee.'

So in consequence of Regulation 4(2) all of the employee's rights and benefits are transferred to the new employer and this could include rights relating to health and safety and therefore liability for industrial injuries that occurred prior to the transfer.

CASE EXAMPLE

Martin v Lancashire County Council; Bernadone v Pall Mall Service Group Ltd [2000] IRLR 487

In joined appeals both involved claims against the new employers for industrial injuries that had been suffered while in the service of the former employers who had transferred the businesses. The first involved a Refuse Department worker who claimed that he suffered progressive injury to his back and neck and a specific injury to his wrist as the result of the former employer's negligence. The second involved a catering assistant in a hospital who claimed that she hurt her hand in an accident at work which was the fault of her employer. The Court of Appeal held that the obligation of an employer to compensate an employee for a negligent breach of the duty of care arises 'in connection with' the employee's contract of employment and therefore transfers to the new employer. It also held that the Regulations also give the new employer an indemnity in respect of the claimant's claim under the insurance policy between the old employer and its insurance company, even though this was in fact a right under a contract between the old employer and a third party. In any case it is not a major problem and not unfair on the new employer since both employers would be required by law to hold compulsory employer's liability insurance. However, the court did identify that this would not necessarily apply to local authorities which may have exemption.

JUDGMENT

Peter Gibson LJ said: 'It is clear that [the purpose of the Directive] is to safeguard the rights of employees on a change of employer by a transfer of an undertaking. The economic entity carrying on the undertaking after the transfer will be the transferee, and in general the employees are more likely to be protected if the rights and obligations to be transferred are more rather than less comprehensive.'

As a result the effect is also that anything done in relation to the contract prior to the transfer is deemed to have been done by the new employer.

CASE EXAMPLE

DJM International Ltd v Nicholas [1996] IRLR 76

Nicholas had worked for the company for many years and was then forced to retire at age sixty in 1992. She was re-engaged on a part-time contract and two months later the business was transferred and she continued working for the new owner. Five months later she brought a claim for discrimination based on her effective dismissal at age sixty. Her claim would have been out of time but the tribunal extended the three month limit to include it. It was accepted by the court that rights such as maternity, equal pay and other rights not to be discriminated against also transfer.

It also of course logically follows that the new employer after a transfer is also able to benefit from and enforce the terms of the contract which have transferred.

CASE EXAMPLE

Morris Angel & Son Ltd v Hollande [1993] IRLR 400

A managing director had a provision within his service contract that he would not within one year of leaving solicit any business from any of the company's clients. The company was then sold to new owners and when the managing director left the new owners sought to enforce the provision against him. The Court of Appeal held that the regulations applied so that the new owners were in effect in the shoes of the former owners and all contractual provisions remained. The new owners were, however, only allowed to enforce the provision in respect of clients of the former owners and not in respect of any of their own existing client base.

It must be remembered that the provisions only apply if the claimant was employed 'immediately before the transfer'. This was the issue that was resolved by purposive interpretation of the Acquired Rights Directive in *Litster v Forth Dry Dock & Engineering Co. Ltd.* [1990] 1 AC 546 (see 18.1 above). The provisions of course also apply to a person who would have been employed immediately before the transfer if they had not been unfairly dismissed.

CASE EXAMPLE

G4s Justice Services (UK) Ltd v Anstey [2006] IRLR 588

Two employees were dismissed for gross misconduct and before any hearing of their appeal could be heard the business was transferred. The original employer then heard the appeals and reinstated them but the new employer refused to reinstate them arguing that they were not employed 'immediately before the transfer'. The EAT held that the successful appeal had overturned the dismissals so that they were employed immediately before the transfer occurred. Because of this the new employer was obliged to reinstate them.

Under Regulation 4(4) TUPE Regulations 2006 'any purported variation of the contract shall be void if the sole or principal reason for the variation is (a) the transfer itself; or (b) a reason connected with the transfer that is not an economic, technical or organisational reason entailing changes in the workforce'. This means that if the variation is not for a reason connected with the transfer that it will be valid. In *Norris v Brown & Root Ealing Technical Services* [2002] All ER (D) 413 a change in terms two years after the transfer was because of cash flow difficulties so that the Regulations did not apply.

The new employer in effect steps into the shoes of the previous employer and has all of the obligations to employees that the previous employee did. In the case of Regulation 5 of the TUPE Regulations this means that the new employer also takes over collective agreements that were in force at the time of the transfer. However, while the employer may be bound to provide conditions and benefits that resulted from collective agreements it is less clear whether the employer is also bound to give effect to changes that the collective agreement bring about after the transfer if the new employer was not a party to the original collective agreement.

CASE EXAMPLE

Parkwood Leisure v Alemo-Herron [2011] UKSC 26

The claimants had all formerly worked a local council in its leisure services department until the part in which they worked was transferred to a private sector employer and then transferred to Parkwood Leisure, also a private sector employer. Their terms and conditions obviously transferred with them. While they had worked for the council their terms had been determined by a collective agreement. Their contracts included a clause 'During your employment with the Council your terms and conditions of employment will be in accordance with collective agreements negotiated from time to time by the National Joint Council for Local Government Services.' After they transferred to new employers a new pay award was made by the National Joint Council for Local Government Services and the claimants wished to benefit from it. The Court of Appeal held that the employees were not entitled to the pay rise because the new employer had not been a party to the collective agreement. However, the House of Lords rejected the argument that allowing the employees to continue to benefit from the collective agreement was inconsistent with the directive. Lord Hope suggested that the matter of whether the Acquired Rights Directive (and as a result the TUPE Regulations) can only apply to protect static employment rights arising from collective agreement and which do not change or whether it can also apply to dynamic collective agreements where the rights continue to change as in the case here.

Under Regulation 8 in the case of a transfer which results from the insolvency of the former employer employees cannot claim against either employer but should claim from the statutory fund for arrears of wages redundancy and additional payments such as holiday pay. Under Regulation 9 it is also possible to vary contractual terms during insolvency proceedings if the transferor or transferee (or an insolvency practitioner) and appropriate representatives of the assigned employees agree to the variations. This is obviously with a view to saving the business if possible.

Under Regulation 10 pension rights do not automatically transfer and there is no obligation on the new employer to recognise employee's occupational pension schemes. However, under section 257 of the Pensions Act 2004 where employees were members of a pension scheme the new employer must ensure that they are eligible to join its pension scheme or a stakeholder arrangement.

18.5 Dismissals on transfer

The rules on dismissal are found in Regulation 7 and are reasonably straightforward.

REGULATION

'7 Dismissal of employee because of relevant transfer

(1) Where either before or after a relevant transfer, any employee of the transferor or transferee is dismissed, that employee shall be treated ... as unfairly dismissed if the sole or principal reason for his dismissal is
    (a) the transfer itself; or
    (b) a reason connected with the transfer that is not an economic, technical or organisational reason entailing changes in the workforce.'

So where a dismissal is directly because of the transfer or connected to the transfer but cannot be justified as an economic, technical or organisational (ETO) reason then the dismissal is automatically unfair (see Chapter 22.3). As we have already seen the courts take a purposive approach and it does not matter whether the dismissal occurs before or after the transfer.

CASE EXAMPLE

Litster v Forth Dry Dock & Engineering Co Ltd [1990] 1 AC 546

The liquidator of an insolvent business dismissed the workforce only one hour before he transferred the business to a new owner. The claimant argued that his dismissal was unfair but his claim would have been ineffective because the former employer had of course gone out of business. The then House of Lords held the dismissal to be unfair and that the liability to pay had also transferred on to the new owner. In this way the House of Lords in effect expanded the scope of the Regulations at that time (see 18.1 above).

Regulation 7(2) identifies that there is an exception to the dismissal being automatically unfair, which is where either employer is able to show that the dismissal was in fact for an economic, technical or organisational reason.

CASE EXAMPLE

Meikle v McPhail [1983] IRLR 351

Ownership of a public house was transferred and the new owner had promised the previous employer that he would retain most of the existing staff. This included two full-time barmaids, one part-time barmaid and a cleaner. However, having consulted his accountant, the new owner realised that major economic savings were essential and that, without making staff reductions, he would be unable to run the business profitably. As a result he dismissed all of the staff, except one full-time barmaid. An employee that had been in effect dismissed then brought a claim for unfair dismissal. The tribunal held that there had been an economic reason for the dismissal and so there was an ETO defence to the claim and the dismissal was fair for any other substantial reason.

However, if the real reason for the dismissal cannot in fact be shown to be either economic or technical or organisational then the defence under Regulation 7(2) will be unavailable and the dismissal is likely to be unfair.

CASE EXAMPLE

Manchester College v Hazel & Huggins [2012] UKEAT 0642/11/0907

Some six months after a TUPE transfer had taken place the new employer engaged in a cost saving exercise. This included a request for voluntary redundancies and also significant wage cuts. The claimants who were in fact assured that their jobs were safe were nevertheless not willing to sign new contracts which meant wage cuts of 18 per cent and were dismissed. They then agreed to new contracts and continued in employment and brought claims for unfair dismissal. The tribunal considered that the reason for the dismissals was in fact connected with the transfer and was for an ETO reason but that it did not require changes in the workforce and so the appropriate time for reducing staff numbers had passed by the time of the dismissals. It also found that the dismissals were unfair on procedural grounds and it awarded re-engagement, which it felt was practicable in the circumstances. In the employer's appeal the EAT agreed with the tribunal's findings.

Traditionally in the case of TUPE transfers the meaning of economic, technical and organisational reasons has been construed narrowly.

CASE EXAMPLE

Wheeler v Patel & Goulding Group [1987] IRLR 211

Here the current employer in an impending transfer of the business was trying to obtain a higher price for the business. After negotiations he then gave in to the demands of the potential buyer and dismissed the workforce in advance of the transfer. The court held that dismissing the workforce to make the purchase of the business more attractive to the potential buyer was not an economic, technical or organisational reason for the dismissals and so the dismissals were unfair.

However, the courts have also considered that creating a redundancy exercise to obtain a contract is not the same as dismissing in order to obtain a better price.

CASE EXAMPLE

Whitehouse v Charles Blatchford & Sons Ltd [1999] All ER (D) 414

At the end of a contract to provide services to a hospital a contractor who was tendering for the contract had agreed to keep the existing staff and was provisionally offered the contract but was informed by the hospital that it needed to reduce the staff by one. The claimant was the employee who was made redundant as a result of this and he argued that the dismissal was unfair. The tribunal held that there was an ETO reason for the dismissal and the redundant employee appealed. The EAT distinguished *Wheeler v Patel* and agreed that there was an ETO reason for the dismissal because the reduction in staff numbers had been at the insistence of the hospital and without complying the new employer would have been unable to gain the contract and this same reasoning was later accepted in a further appeal to the Court of Appeal. It does, however, seem difficult to find any real distinction between the cases.

Where an employee is dismissed in consequence of a TUPE transfer then any claim in respect of the dismissal will be against the new employer even if the dismissal occurred before the transfer.

CASE EXAMPLE

Stirling District Council v Allan and others [1995] IRLR 301

The claimant had been employed by the council's direct service department and was dismissed the day after the contract had been given to an outside contractor following a competitive tendering exercise and the day before that contractor took over. The claimant brought an action for unfair dismissal against the council and failed. In what was seen as a controversial ruling the EAT held that the transferor and transferee are jointly liable under the Transfer of Undertakings Regulations for transfer-related unfair dismissals which take place before the transfer. The Scottish Court of Session, overturning this, held that any action must be against the new employer since under the Regulations all rights and obligations transfer to him.

In deciding whether the dismissal was for a genuine ETO reason consideration should be given to the reasons why the employer made the decision to dismiss.

CASE EXAMPLE

Dynamex Friction Ltd v Amicus [2008] EWCA Civ 381

A company manufactured friction parts for car brakes and clutches. Originally it employed about 1,000 staff but following a downturn in fortunes redundancies reduced that to about 200. An American then acquired the business and proposed to restructure the business in order to improve productivity and running costs. Unions then balloted for strike action and the company dismissed eighty-six of the strikers. They brought claims in a tribunal which found that they had been unfairly dismissed. The compensation which would have become payable to the strikers was estimated to be approximately £3 million. The company went into administration and the administrator dismissed the employees since there was no money to pay them. He then sold the business back to the managing director, although there was no question of any collusion between them. The Court of Appeal held that the dismissals were for an ETO reason, so that the administrator could sell the business.

It is also possible under Regulation 4(7) for an employee to refuse to transfer to the new employer otherwise this would interfere with an employee's freedom to work for who he wants. The result is that the employment contract ceases and the employee has no right to claim unfair dismissal. Effectively he has dismissed himself. The exception would be where the transfer involves a substantial and detrimental change in the employee's terms and conditions of work in which case Regulation 4(9) allows the employee to consider that the contract has been terminated by the employer with notice.

CASE EXAMPLE

University of Oxford v Humphreys [2000] 1 All ER 996

The claimant had worked for the University of Oxford Delegacy of Local Examinations for ten years as a Deputy Administration Officer. Under his contract his employment would continue until retiring age subject only to resignation by himself with not less than three months' written notice, and by the University in event that he was found guilty of misconduct or wilful disobedience. The University then indicated that it intended to transfer his contract of employment upon a transfer of the business of the Delegacy to the AEB. He objected on the basis that his terms would have been substantially altered by the new employer and it was accepted that this would be the case. The Court of Appeal accepted that he was entitled to compensation.

JUDGMENT

Potter LJ identified: 'The right to terminate the contract will lead on to the right to compensation for the transferring employer's conduct in bringing an end to the contract of employment by transferring his business on such terms as will bring about a substantial and detrimental alteration in the employee's working conditions.'

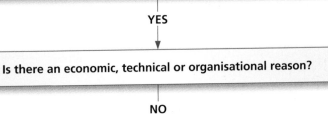

Does the claimant come under TUPE Regulations?
- The claimant is any individual who works for another person whether under a contract of service or apprenticeship or otherwise

YES

Has there been a relevant transfer?
- there has been a transfer of an undertaking, business or part of an undertaking or business situated immediately before the transfer in the United Kingdom to another person where there is a transfer of an economic entity which retains its identity
- this means that it is an organised grouping of resources which has the objective of pursuing an economic activity, whether or not that activity is central or ancillary
- and it can involve a service provision change – which is either an initial outsourcing of services where a contractor is hired to provide the in house service, or there is a fresh tendering exercise and the tender is won by a new contractor, or the services being brought back in house

YES

Has the claimant suffered changed conditions as a result of the transfer?
- the claimant has different terms and conditions as a result of the transfer
Or has the claimant been dismissed because of the transfer?
- the claimant has been dismissed by the transferor in advance of the transfer, or
- the claimant was dismissed by the transferee following the transfer

YES

Is there an economic, technical or organisational reason?

NO

The claimant may have a remedy under the TUPE Regulations

Figure 18.1 Diagram illustrating the operation of the Transfer of Undertakings (Protection of Employment) Regulations

18.6 Consultation

Under Regulation 11 the transferor must notify the transferee about any employee liability information of any person employed by him who is assigned to the organised grouping of resources or employees that is the subject of a relevant transfer. This must be done in writing or by making it available to him in a readily accessible form. The information that must be included is:

- the identity and age of the employee;
- all of the particulars of employment should be in the statutory statement under section 1 Employment Rights Act 1996;
- information of any disciplinary procedure taken against an employee; or any grievance procedure taken by an employee, within the previous two years;
- details of any court or tribunal case, claim or action brought by an employee against the transferor, within the previous two years; or that the transferor has reasonable grounds to believe that an employee may bring against the transferee, arising out of the employee's employment with the transferor;
- information of any collective agreement which will have effect after the transfer.

The information must be given at least two weeks before the transfer is completed. Under Regulation 12 a complaint can be made to a tribunal by the transferee if the Regulation has not been complied with and if the complaint is well founded the tribunal can award compensation that the tribunal considers to be just and equitable.

Under Regulation 13 long enough before a relevant transfer to enable the employer of any affected employees to consult the appropriate representatives of any affected employees, the employer shall inform those representatives of:

(a) the fact that the transfer is to take place, the date or proposed date of the transfer and the reasons for it;

(b) the legal, economic and social implications of the transfer for any affected employees;

(c) the measures which he envisages he will, in connection with the transfer, take in relation to any affected employees or, if he envisages that no measures will be so taken, that fact; and

(d) if the employer is the transferor, the measures, in connection with the transfer, which he envisages the transferee will take in relation to any affected employees who will become employees of the transferee after the transfer by virtue of Regulation 4 or, if he envisages that no measures will be so taken, that fact.

The requirement of consultation arises from the Collective Redundancies and Transfer of Undertakings (Protection of Employment) (Amendment) Regulations 1999. Appropriate representatives are usually the recognised trade union but could be other elected employee representatives and these must be given appropriate access to the affected employees.

ACTIVITY

Self-assessment questions

1. What exactly is a TUPE transfer?
2. What were the purposes of introducing the Acquired Rights Directive?
3. What potential problems did employees face before the Directive?

4. What was significant about the judgment in *Litster v Forth Dry Dock & Engineering Co. Ltd*?
5. What exactly is an 'economic entity'?
6. In what circumstances will a transfer of a business be a relevant transfer for the purpose of TUPE protections?
7. What rights and obligations transfer with the transfer of the business?
8. What potential difficulties for employees following a transfer did the case of *Süzen v Zehnacker Gebäudereinigung GmbH* present?
9. Why were transfers involving service provision such as outsourcing and contracting out cause a problem?
10. In what way has this been resolved in the 2006 Regulations?
11. How are dismissals connected to the transfer dealt with?
12. What duties of notification and consultation does the transferor have?

KEY FACTS

The origins and aims of TUPE	Case/statute
• Original common law position was that contract ceased on transfer of business so no obligation on transferee • EU law then dealt with situation requiring implementation in national law • Aims of Directive were: ensuring consultation with employees affected, ensuring transfer of rights, ensuring maintenance of collective agreements for one year, transfer not to be reason for dismissals, dramatic changes to count as dismissal • TUPE rights and obligations should be interpreted purposively – because they represent EU law • Two key facts – there was a sufficiently identifiable economic entity; and there was a relevant transfer	*Acquired Rights Directive 77/187; Transfer of Undertakings (Protection of Employment) Regulations 1981* *Litster v Forth Dry Dock & Engineering Co Ltd.*
To whom the Regulations apply	**Case/statute**
• Any individual who works for another person, whether under contract of service, apprenticeship or otherwise • Originally applied to all businesses regardless of whether there was a transfer of assets • Business must transfer as a going concern • Court should consider type of undertaking involved, whether or not tangible assets of the business transferred, value of intangible assets at time of transfer, whether or not majority of employees transferred, whether or not any customers transferred, degree of similarity between activities carried out before and after transfer, if any activities were suspended the period for which they were suspended	*Regulation 2(1)* *Schmidt v Spar und Leihkasse der Fruheren Amter Bordesholm, Kiel und Cronshagen* *Spijkers v Gebroeders Benedik Abattoir* *Watson Rask and Christiansen v ISS Kantineservice A/S*

	Case/statute
• Undertaking does not have to be profit making	*Dr Sophie Redmond Stichting v Bartol*
• There was controversy over whether economic entity meant economic activity	*Süzen v Zehnacker Gebäudereinigung GmbH*
• Some cases have followed *Süzen*	*Betts v Brintel Helicopters Ltd and KLM ERA Helicopters (UK) Ltd*
• And some have followed *Schmidt*	*Argyll Training Ltd v Sinclair*
• Service provision is covered and includes: initial outsourcing, a fresh tendering where the tender is won by a new contractor, services being brought back in house	*Regulation 3(1)(b) Transfer of Undertakings Regulations 2006* and *Metropolitan Resources Ltd v Churchill Dulwich Ltd*
• And the Regulations can cover a person who works for two parts of the same group	*Sunley Turriff Holdings Ltd v Thomson*

The nature of TUPE transfers	Case/statute
• Relevant transfer can be sale, or other disposition or by operation of law but identity of employer must change	*Young v Daniel Thwaites*
• Key question is whether the business has retained its identity	*Dines v Initial Health Care Services*

The effect of TUPE transfers	Case/statute
• Transfer does not terminate employment and all rights are transferred	*Regulation 4 TUPE Regulations 2006* *Regulation 4(2) TUPE Regulations 2006*
• On transfer transferor's rights, powers, duties and liabilities in employment contract transfer to transferee – e.g. tort claims	*Martin v Lancashire County Council; Bernadone v Pall Mall Service Group Ltd*
• Something done by the old employer is deemed to be the responsibility of the new employer	*DJM International Ltd v Nicholas*
• And the new employer is also able to benefit from contractual terms	*Morris Angel & Son Ltd v Hollande*
• The Regulations cover a person who would have been employed immediately before the transfer if they had not been unfairly dismissed	*G4s Justice Services (UK) Ltd v Anstey*
• The new employer is bound by rights arising from collective agreements but not to make changes after the transfer arising from a collective agreement to which he was not a party	*Parkwood Leisure v Alemo-Herron*

Dismissal on transfers	Case/statute
• A dismissal of an employee because of the transfer is automatically unfair	*Regulation 7 TUPE Regulations 2006*
• And the Regulations should be interpreted purposively	*Litster v Forth Dry Dock & Engineering Co Ltd*
• But this is not so if the dismissal is for an economic, technical or organisational (ETO) reason	*Regulation 7(2) TUPE Regulations 2006* *Meikle v McPhail*
• And ETO reasons are construed narrowly	*Wheeler v Patel & Goulding Group*
• But a redundancy exercise to obtain a contract is different to dismissals to gain a better price for the business	*Whitehouse v Charles Blatchford & Sons Ltd*
• All claims for unfair dismissal are against the new employer	*Stirling District Council v Allan*
• The tribunal should examine all of the reasons for the dismissal	*Dynamex Friction Ltd v Amicus*

• An employee can refuse to transfer but then there is no right to an unfair dismissal claim • Unless the changed conditions were significantly to the employee's detriment	*Regulation 4(7) TUPE Regulations 2006* *Regulation 4(9) TUPE Regulations 2006* *University of Oxford v Humphreys*
Consultation	**Case/statute**
• Old employer should notify new employer of any employee liability including identity and age of employee, particulars of employment, information of any disciplinary or grievance procedure taken by employee within previous two years, details of any court or tribunal case, claim or action brought by an employee within previous two years, or reasonable grounds to believe employee may bring action, information of collective agreements which will have effect after the transfer	*Regulation 11 TUPE Regulations 2006*
• Old employer must inform affected employees representatives of fact of, date of and reasons for transfer; legal, social and economic implications of transfer; likely effect of transfer on employees; any measures that the new employer might take	*Regulation 13 TUPE Regulations 2006*

SAMPLE ESSAY QUESTION

ESSAY Discuss the extent to which the EU has provided effective rights for employees who are affected by the transfer of the organisation for which they work into different hands.

Explain the original position

• Position was basic common law freedom of contract.
• So the contract ceased on the transfer of the business.
• So there was no obligation on a new employer.
• And employees lost rights – which could even mean losing their jobs with no remedy.

Explain how the EU changed this position

- The EU introduced the Acquired Rights Directive 77/187.
- Its aims were to ensure consultation with employees affected by a transfer, to ensure that employees' contractual rights also transferred, to ensure the maintenance of any collective agreements for one year after the transfer, and that the transfer should not result in dismissals, it also identified that dramatic changes in conditions would count as a dismissal.

Explain how the directive became law in the UK

- The UK government passed the Transfer of Undertakings (Protection of Employment) Regulations 1981.

Discuss the application of the Regulations (and the Directive)

- Applies to employees who are any individual who works for another person, whether under contract of service, apprenticeship, or otherwise.
- There must be a relevant transfer.
- There must be a transfer of a recognisable economic entity.

Discuss the fact that there has been controversy over what is an economic entity

- Originally applied to all businesses regardless of whether there was a transfer of assets.
- But then suggested economic entity meant economic activity.
- But does now cover service provision e.g. outsourcing.

Discuss the effects of the Regulations (and the Directive)

- All rights are transferred.
- So can be no dismissal because of a transfer.
- Something done by the old employer is deemed to be the responsibility of the new employer.
- And covers a person who would have been unfairly dismissed if employed immediately before the transfer.

Discuss how the law has improved the position on dismissals arising from a transfer of the business

- A dismissal because of the transfer is automatically unfair.
- Unless it is for an economic technical or organisational (ETO) reason.
- And any remedy is against the new employer.

REACH REASONED CONCLUSIONS

SUMMARY

- Originally a new employer had no obligations to existing employees when the business was transferred so the EU introduced law through a Directive to ensure that contractual rights transferred with the transfer of the business – notification and consultation were also required.
- The UK implemented the EU Directive as the TUPE Regulations which protected employees' rights where there was a transfer of a sufficiently identifiable economic entity and there was a relevant transfer.
- The Regulations protect 'any individual who works for another person, whether under contract of service, apprenticeship, or otherwise' and originally applied to all businesses even where there was no transfer of assets as long as it was transferred as a going concern and it does not have to be profit making.
- But there has been controversy over the meaning of economic entity.
- Service provision is also covered and includes: initial outsourcing, a fresh tendering where the tender is won by a new contractor, services being brought back in house.

- A relevant transfer will not terminate the contract of employment and all rights under the contract transfer to the new owner which means the new employer can also benefit from those contractual terms

- Dismissals that result from the transfer are automatically unfair unless they are for an economic, technical or organisational (ETO) reason.

- There is also an obligation to fully inform employees of the transfer.

Further reading

Emir, Astra, *Selwyn's Law of Employment 17th edition*. Oxford University Press, 2012, Chapter 9.
Pitt, Gwyneth, *Cases and Materials on Employment Law 3rd edition*. Pearson, 2008, Chapter 9.
Sargeant, Malcolm and Lewis, David, *Employment Law 6th edition*. Pearson, 2012, Chapter 9.6.

19

Termination of employment (1) continuity, notice and dismissal

AIMS AND OBJECTIVES

After reading this chapter you should be able to:

▨ Understand the significance of continuity of employment

▨ Understand how continuous employment is calculated for unfair dismissal purposes

▨ Understand the significance of notice periods

▨ Understand the statutory notice period in the absence of contractual notice

▨ Understand the meaning of dismissal

▨ Understand the three ways in which a contract of employment can be terminated by dismissal

▨ Understand what is meant by a constructive dismissal

▨ Understand the criteria for claiming constructive dismissal

▨ Critically analyse the concepts of continuity of employment, notice and dismissal

▨ Apply the rules on continuity of employment, notice and dismissal to factual situations

19.1 Continuity of employment

Nearly all employment protection rights depend on the employee having attained specific periods of continuous service. For unfair dismissal claims this has ranged from six months, one year and two years. While the last Labour government reduced the period to one year, since April 2012 it has been returned to two years by the present government (see Chapter 22.1).

Continuity is defined in section 212 Employment Rights Act 1996 and will not be affected by changes of conditions.

SECTION

'212 weeks counting in computing period.

(1) Any week during the whole or part of which an employee's relations with his employer are governed by a contract of employment counts in computing the employee's period of employment.'

Continuity of employment is significant to statutory rights such as qualifying for redundancy or being able to claim unfair dismissal. In this way private agreements may be reached with employers extending continuous employment but this will not alter statutory rights.

CASE EXAMPLE

Secretary of State for Employment v Globe Elastic Thread Co Ltd [1980] AC 506

The claimant had worked for the same company for twenty-two years when he was transferred to another company. He did so on the basis that he had been promised that his employment with both companies would be continuous. In fact he was then made redundant after a further five years and obviously felt that he was entitled to full redundancy rights. The then House of Lords thought that his continuous employment only started from the time he joined the different company.

Continuous employment begins with the contractual date of continuous employment rather than necessarily the actual date on which employment started which could be different.

CASE EXAMPLE

The General of the Salvation Army v Dewsbury [1984] IRLR 222

A part-time teacher changed over to a full-time contract commencing from 1 May: 3 May happened to be a bank holiday so she did not actually commence work on either the first of third days of her new contract. She was then dismissed a year later with effect from 1 May and the question for the court was whether she had completed one year's continuous employment or not. The EAT held that the date of commencement is that which is stated in the contract and that this may not be the date on which the employee actually first works.

Continuous employment is counted in complete weeks although length of continuous service is then counted in months and years.

CASE EXAMPLE

Sweeney v J & S Henderson [1999] IRLR 306

The claimant resigned on a Saturday and then left to start his new employment. He then regretted his decision and returned to his old employer on the following Friday. It was later necessary to determine whether that period was a break in the employee's continuous service or not. The court held that a break in continuous service does not occur unless there is a complete week in which the employee is not employed. Thus the week counted towards continuous service even though there was a short gap in his employment.

Continuous employment ends with the 'effective date of termination' (EDT). However, the length of continuous service needed depends on the right being claimed. For unfair dismissal claims this is now two years again (see Chapter 22.1). Interestingly there was a point at which there was a possibility of any qualifying period of continuous employment being considered unlawful.

CASE EXAMPLE

R v Secretary of State for Employment ex p Seymour-Smith and Perez (No 2)
[2000] IRLR 263

At the time of the case the qualifying period of continuous employment for unfair dismissal was two years. Two women wished to claim unfair dismissal but they lacked the necessary two years' continuous service. In a novel action they argued that they were being discriminated against by the law requiring two years' continuous service. They did so on the basis that they believed that the number of women who could comply with the requirement was significantly lower than the number of men who could, obviously because of career breaks for pregnancy and child care. The House of Lords (now the Supreme Court) referred the case to the European Court of Justice under the Article 177 (now Article 267 TFEU) procedure. Included in the questions that the House wished clarification on were whether the issue fell within the scope of Article 119 (now Article 157 TFEU), and whether on that basis the women were entitled to compensation. The ECJ held that it could indeed fall under Article 119 (now Article 157 TFEU) if the qualifying period had a disproportionate effect on women. It also identified:

1. that the alleged discriminatory rule was a legitimate aim of the UK's social policy;

2. that this aim was unrelated to any discrimination based on sex;

3. that the means chosen were suitable for achieving the aim.

The House of Lords did find that there was a disparity in the order of ten women to nine men but in effect that this was insufficient to represent real discrimination.

Certain situations do not break continuous employment. These are identified in section 212(3) Employment Rights Act 1996.

SECTION

'212(3) Subject to subsection (4), any week (not within subsection (1)) during the whole or part of which an employee is –
    (a) incapable of work in consequence of sickness or injury,
    (b) absent from work on account of a temporary cessation of work,
    (c) absent from work in circumstances such that, by arrangement or custom, he is regarded as continuing in the employment of his employer for any purpose counts in computing the employee's period of employment.
  (4) Not more than twenty-six weeks count under subsection (3)(a) ... between any periods falling under subsection (1).'

So the three types of absences which will not break continuous service are:

- periods of legitimate illness or injury;
- temporary cessation of work;
- arranged or customary absences.

As can be seen from section 212(4) above a sickness absence of more than twenty-six weeks could in effect break continuous service. If the employee leaves his job because he is incapable of work because of sickness and is reemployed within twenty-six weeks his service is then deemed to be continuous.

CASE EXAMPLE

Donnelly v Kelvin International Services [1992] IRLR 496

The claimant resigned his position and moved to another employer under advice from his doctor to get lighter work. He then returned to his employer after only five weeks. At a later point he was dismissed and wished to claim unfair dismissal counting all of his service with the employer. The tribunal rejected this argument since it held that he had not been incapable of work having moved to another job. The EAT, however, suggested that being incapable of work does not mean incapable of work of any kind since he may have taken light work in any case hoping to return to his original work when fit to do so.

Temporary cessation of work refers to those situations where there are lay-offs within the industry but also other temporary breaks in employment.

CASE EXAMPLE

Hussain v Acorn Independent College Ltd [2011] IRLR 463

The claimant was employed as a teacher to cover the illness of another teacher from April until the summer exams, the contract ending on 8 July. The teacher who had been on sickness leave then resigned and the claimant started a permanent job with the employer in September of that year. He was then dismissed in the following June. In the claim for unfair dismissal the employer argued that the claimant did not have one year's continuous employment (as required at that time). The EAT held that the correct approach is to look at the reason for the termination of the first contract and the length of the breaks in service.

JUDGMENT

McMullen J explained: 'There were the two contracts in sequence. The interval was short and temporary. There had been a cessation of the work at the end of the first contract and so all of the ingredients for the purposes of section 212(3)(b) were in place.'

Continuity of employment by custom has at times been prevalent in certain industries. In *Gray v Burntisland Shipbuilding Co* [1967] 2 ITR 253 such a custom was enforced whereby laid off workers in the shipbuilding industry returned when more work was available without a break in service. Arrangements to maintain continuity of employment can also be made between employer and employee for a variety of reasons.

CASE EXAMPLE

Lloyds Bank Ltd v Secretary of State for Employment [1979] IRLR 41

The employee had worked on the basis of one week in two for a period of five years. She then became pregnant and the employer paid her statutory maternity pay (SMP) and sought to claim this back from the government as is customary (see Chapter 8.4.4). The employer was held to be entitled to claim since the claimant's employment was continuous, the breaks between weeks of work being by a mutual arrangement.

However, there are situations that do break continuity of service and will be deducted from the overall period of employment:

- working abroad
- taking part in strikes
- illegality.

Under section 215(1) Employment Rights Act 1996 employees who work outside the UK are generally excluded from employment rights and protections. Weeks spent working abroad where the employee is not an employed earner in the UK for the purpose of paying National Insurance contributions will not usually count towards continuity of employment.

Under section 216 Employment Rights Act 1996 where an employee is on strike the period that he is absent from work will not count towards his period of continuous employment but will not break continuity. Where continuous employment later has to be calculated the number of days lost through strike will be deducted in calculating continuous employment.

Continuous employment only counts legal employment so that an employee should be careful not to allow the contract of employment to become tainted with illegality or engage in a contract which is for an illegal purpose or employment rights may be lost as a result.

CASE EXAMPLE

Hyland v JH Barker (North West) Ltd [1985] IRLR 403

The employee had in fact been employed since 1967 but in 1982 was given a tax free lodging allowance for four weeks while he was commuting in an arrangement with his employer. This was enough to taint the contract with illegality to the extent that it prevented the employee from gaining sufficient continuous service to qualify to make a claim for unfair dismissal when he was later dismissed (see 5.1.5 above).

ACTIVITY

Self-assessment questions

1. Why is continuity of employment important to an employee?
2. When does continuous employment start?
3. When does continuous employment end?
4. How is a period of continuous employment calculated?
5. Which types of absence or apparent breaks do not break continuous employment?
6. Which types of absence from work will not count towards continuous employment?

19.2 Notice and statutory notice periods

At common law the employer is bound to give reasonable notice. A contract of employment is a contract of continuous obligations so that the only way that it could logically end is if one party gives the other notice. The common law requirement merely refers back to the implied duty of mutual trust and respect. The period of notice required by either side in common law then is whatever is determined in the contract itself provided that it is reasonable. This is identified as information that must be in the statutory statement of particulars under section 1(4)(e) Employment Rights Act 1996. Courts may determine what amounts to a reasonable notice period in the circumstances.

CASE EXAMPLE

Hill v CA Parsons & Co Ltd [1972] Ch 305

The employer reached a 'closed shop' agreement (one where all employees have to belong to the union) with a recognised trade union. The claimant refused to join the union and the employer gave him one month's notice of his dismissal. The claimant was a senior engineer who had thirty-five years' service and he sought an injunction to gain a longer period of notice. The Court of Appeal granted the injunction and extended his notice period to six months which it felt was a reasonable period. The employer in fact had no real issue with the claimant but was merely acting under pressure from the trade union. The court was actually eager to grant the injunction because by the end of the changed notice period the Industrial Relations Act would be in force and this would make the closed shop agreement unlawful and mean that any dismissal of the claimant was unfair.

If there is no express term on notice in the contract then the notice period will be determined by statute and in any case statute lays down minimum notice periods. These are identified in section 86(1) Employment Rights Act 1996.

SECTION

'86 Rights of employer and employee to minimum notice

(1) The notice required to be given by an employer to terminate the contract of employment of a person who has been continuously employed for one month or more

   (a) is not less than one week's notice if his period of continuous employment is less than two years,

   (b) is not less than one week's notice for each year of continuous employment if his period of continuous employment is two years or more but less than twelve years, and

   (c) is not less than twelve weeks' notice if his period of continuous employment is twelve years or more.

(2) The notice required to be given by an employee who has been continuously employed for one month or more to terminate his contract of employment is not less than one week.'

So the statutory minimum notice periods are:

- one week for at least one month and less than two years' continuous service;
- one week extra for each year's continuous service up to a maximum of twelve weeks for twelve years' service.

And the minimum statutory notice required of an employee is:

- one week for an employee who has been employed for one month or more.

If the notice periods in the contract are greater than the statutory minimums then the contract notice periods will be followed and enforced by the courts. If the contract is less generous than the statutory minimums then the statutory periods from the Employment Rights Act 1996 will be followed. This latter point can actually prove critical for an employee who is being dismissed before qualifying periods for redundancy or unfair dismissal is reached.

In general once notice is given by either side it cannot be unilaterally withdrawn. However, it has been identified in *Mowlem Northern Ltd v Watson* [1990] IRLR 500 that employees who have been given notice can mutually agree with their employers to extend the notice period.

A payment in lieu of notice will also terminate the contract if the contract provides for that and if the payment properly reflects the required notice period. In *Delaney v Staples t/a De Montfort Recruitment* [1990] IRLR 86 where the claimant was summarily dismissed and given a cheque as payment in lieu Lord Browne-Wilkinson listed four circumstances where a lieu payment would be appropriate (see Chapter 8.1.2):

- the employer gives the appropriate notice but does not require work from the employee (garden leave);
- under the contract the employer is entitled to terminate the contract with notice or summarily on payment of a sum of money in lieu of notice;
- an agreement between employer and employee to terminate the contract for an agreed payment;
- the employer dismisses the employee summarily with a lieu payment.

The actual date of termination of the contract, the effective date of termination (EDT) is the date that the notice expires or the date of the lieu payment.

ACTIVITY

Self-assessment questions
1. What is notice?
2. What is the difference between contractual notice and statutory notice?
3. What happens if the contractual notice period and the minimum statutory notice period are different?
4. Is it possible to vary the notice period once notice has been given by either side?
5. In what circumstances is a payment in lieu of notice possible?

19.3 Dismissal

19.3.1 The statutory definition of dismissal

One of the first requirements in bringing a claim for unfair dismissal is to show that the contract of employment was terminated by a dismissal rather than as a result of another process such as frustration, a resignation by the employee or a mutual agreement between the parties (see Chapter 20). Dismissal is defined by statute in section 95 Employment Rights Act 1996.

SECTION

'95 Circumstances in which an employee is dismissed.
(1) For the purposes of this Part an employee is dismissed by his employer if (and, subject to subsection (2) only if) –
   (a) the contract under which he is employed is terminated by the employer (whether with or without notice),
   (b) he is employed under a limited-term contract and that contract terminates by virtue of the limiting event without being renewed under the same contract, or
   (c) the employee terminates the contract under which he is employed (with or without notice) in circumstances in which he is entitled to terminate it without notice by reason of the employer's conduct.'

So there are effectively only four ways in which a dismissal can occur:

- The employer dismisses the employee giving him notice – the question here would be whether the appropriate notice has been given (see 19.2 above) and also of course whether the dismissal is fair.

- The employer dismisses the employee without giving the appropriate notice – this generally would be summary dismissal and the question is whether the conduct of the employee is sufficient to warrant summary dismissal.

- A fixed-term or limited-term contract comes to an end without renewal – the question is whether it is fair not to renew the contract.

- The employee resigns and claims constructive dismissal – the question here is whether the employer's conduct amounts to a significant breach of the contract.

19.3.2 Summary dismissal

A summary dismissal is essentially an instant dismissal which has immediate effect ignoring contractual or statutory rights of notice. It follows that summary dismissal can be justified only in quite exceptional circumstances.

The only circumstances in which a summary dismissal can be justified is where there is gross misconduct by the employee. An employer might identify examples of gross misconduct in the contract of employment or in a booklet of disciplinary rules. However, for a summary dismissal to be justified the court would still need to accept that the particular behaviour did in fact amount to gross misconduct.

CASE EXAMPLE

Dunn & Another v AAH Ltd [2010] IRLR 709

A clause in two directors' contract of employment identified that they could be summarily dismissed for wilful neglect. Under his contract the finance director was also required to report any potential business risks to the parent company. When he failed to report that the actions of a supplier to the company might expose the company to legal action he was dismissed. He challenged whether his failure did in fact amount to gross misconduct. Only the finance director appealed and the Court of Appeal accepted that summary dismissal was appropriate in the circumstances.

JUDGMENT

Rix LJ explained: 'In the terms of the modern formulation of gross misconduct, Mr Davidson must be regarded as so undermining the trust and confidence which is at the heart of a contract of employment that the employer should no longer be required to retain the employee in his employment, but should be entitled to accept that the contract for employment had been repudiated in its essence, permitting him to terminate it.'

Serious negligence on the part of the employee, particularly if this causes damage, could be an example of gross misconduct. A failure to follow instructions leading to damage was held to be gross misconduct in *Howe v Gloucester and Severnside Co-operative Society* [1975] IRLR 17. Usually negligence would only amount to gross misconduct where it was continuing conduct. However, it was also accepted in *Taylor v Alidair Ltd* [1978] IRLR 82 a single act of negligence where the potential consequences were sufficiently serious could also amount to gross misconduct (see Chapter 22.4.1).

Traditionally it has been accepted that gross insubordination or a failure to follow lawful and reasonable orders could be classified as gross misconduct justifying summary dismissal.

CASE EXAMPLE

Pepper v Webb [1969] 1 WLR 514

A gardener not only swore at his employer but also made it clear that he was refusing to follow his employer's instructions. He said 'I couldn't care less about your bloody greenhouse or your sodding garden.' He was summarily dismissed and argued that this was a wrongful dismissal. The court held that the dismissal was justified since the refusal to follow reasonable instructions amounted to gross misconduct. The swearing at the employer also showed disrespect and obviously aggravated the situation.

What is socially acceptable, however, including swearing, changes over time so it is important to judge each case on its merits in the context of current standards to determine whether or not particular conduct justifies summary dismissal. As a result, although there is a duty of mutual trust and respect (see Chapter 7.2.5) swearing on its own may be insufficient to justify summary dismissal.

CASE EXAMPLE

Wilson v Racher [1974] IRLR 114

The claimant was employed as head gardener on a large estate. From the start he had a complete conflict of personality with his employer. On one day when he was trimming a new yew hedge with an electric cutter it rained so heavily that he could not continue because there was danger of him being electrocuted. A few days later his employer shouted at him for not finishing the work and was very aggressive. The claimant explained that he had only stopped because it would have been dangerous to continue but also said: 'If you remember it was pissing with rain on Friday. Do you expect me to get fucking wet?' Although the employer's wife and children were present it was accepted that they did not hear this. A few days later the employer was telling the claimant off again about a piece of string having been left in the garden to which the claimant replied 'Get stuffed', and 'Go and shit yourself.' The claimant subsequently apologised for his bad language. The employer then dismissed the claimant in a letter which also indicated that the claimant could not remain in employment when he chose to swear in front of the employer's wife and children. The claimant brought an action for wrongful dismissal and the employer at first argued that the dismissal was for incompetence and misconduct, although he later withdrew the first of these. The court accepted that in the circumstances it was a wrongful dismissal and, unlike *Pepper v Webb*, there was no background of insolence or inefficiency. The claimant was a very good employee who had lost his temper and used bad language but otherwise he had done nothing which could be regarded as blame-worthy by any reasonable employer and the issue could have been resolved with a warning that such behaviour would not be tolerated in the future.

JUDGMENT

Edmund-Davies passed quite significant comment on the issue: 'Many of the decisions which are customarily cited … may be wholly out of accord with current social conditions. What would today be regarded as almost an attitude of Czar-serf, which is to be found in some of the older cases where a dismissed employee failed to recover damages, would, I venture to think, be decided differently today. We have by now come to realise that a contract of service imposes upon the parties a duty of mutual respect.'

Certain types of misconduct breach commonly accepted standards of behaviour and will almost inevitably be classed as gross misconduct. A typical example is dishonesty at work or even out of work where it is relevant to the employment, which it will be in most cases.

CASE EXAMPLE

Sinclair v Neighbour [1967] 2 WLR 1

The manager of a betting shop took £15 from his employer's till and put an IOU in the till for the amount and repaid the money next day knowing that his employer would not have allowed him to do so. He was then summarily dismissed. In the County Court his actions were held to be improper but not dishonest and so not justifying dismissal. The employer appealed successfully. It was held that the employee's conduct was incompatible with his duty.

JUDGMENT

Sellers LJ explained: 'The whole question is whether that conduct was of such a type that it was inconsistent, in a grave way – incompatible – with the employment in which he had been engaged as a manager.' Sachs LJ explained that it was: 'well established law that a servant can be instantly dismissed when his conduct is such that it not only amounts to a wrongful act inconsistent with his duty towards his master but is also inconsistent with the continuance of confidence between them'.

Violence at work as well as drunkenness at work are also likely to amount to misconduct that justifies dismissal, although in general an employer is likely to investigate before dismissing (see Chapter 22.4.2). Any conduct which is likely to adversely affect the mutual trust and confidence between employer and employee is likely to be classed as gross misconduct and justify summary dismissal. A breach of confidentiality is a classic example of this.

CASE EXAMPLE

Denco Ltd v Joinson [1991] IRLR 63

The claimant was employed as temporary supervisor on night shift and was a shop steward. He was summarily dismissed when his employer realised that he had accessed the company computer system and gained access to confidential information to which he had no authorisation, including customer lists and salary accounts. He challenged the dismissal but the court held that it was lawful because the claimant had deliberately used an unauthorised password to access the system and knew that it was confidential. This amounted to a breach of trust and gross misconduct.

On the other hand the employee's behaviour must be sufficiently serious to amount to gross misconduct. If it could be dealt with through usual disciplinary procedures then a summary dismissal may not be lawful.

CASE EXAMPLE

Laws v London Chronicle Ltd [1959] 1 WLR 698

The claimant was employed as assistant to an advertising manager. She had only worked for the newspaper for three weeks when she was summarily dismissed. She had attended an editorial meeting with her manager and had followed him when he walked out, despite being ordered to stay by the managing director. She was dismissed without notice for her act of disobedience. The Court of Appeal held that her behaviour was neither wilful nor sufficiently serious to amount to a breach of a fundamental term of her contract and was therefore not gross misconduct (see Chapter 21.2).

19.3.3 Failure to renew a fixed-term or limited-term contract

A fixed-term contract is one that lasts for a specific duration. A limited-term contract is one that lasts until performance of a specific task is completed or until an occurrence of a specific event. In either case if the contract is not renewed then this amounts to a dismissal under section 95 Employment Rights Act 1996.

While the contract is not intended to be permanent, it may still need to be tested whether the failure to renew is fair in the circumstances. In this way it is important to be able to show that there is a genuine need for the contract only to be temporary or only for a specific task. The employer should not use a fixed-term contract as a disguise to deprive the employee of statutory rights

Now under the Fixed Term Employees (Prevention of Less Favourable Treatment) Regulations 2002 where an employee is employed for four years or more under a single fixed term or successive fixed terms then the contract is deemed to be one of indefinite duration unless there is objective justification for the contrary.

19.3.4 Constructive dismissal

A constructive dismissal occurs in situations where the employee effectively resigns but in circumstances where he is entitled to do so because the employer's conduct amounts to a significant breach of the contract and therefore an unlawful repudiation of the contract. The employee first of all needs to make it clear that he considers it a constructive dismissal or he may lose his chance of a remedy.

The starting point for showing that there is indeed a constructive dismissal is Lord Denning's judgment in *Western Excavating v Sharp* [1978] QB 761 which explains what conduct by the employer entitles the employee to feel that there is a repudiatory breach.

CASE EXAMPLE

Western Excavating v Sharp [1978] QB 761

The claimant was suspended from work without pay during disciplinary proceedings. He was short of money so he asked his employer for an advance on wages that would be due to him when he returned to work. His employer refused and the claimant resigned as a result and claimed constructive dismissal. It was held that the refusal was not so serious as to amount to a breach of contract and certainly not a serious breach of contract. His claim for unfair dismissal failed.

JUDGMENT

Lord Denning explained the test for determining whether a constructive dismissal amounts to a breach: 'If the employer is guilty of conduct which is a significant breach going to the root of the contract of employment or which shows that the employer no longer intends to be bound by one or more of the essential terms of the contract; then the employee is entitled to treat himself as discharged from any further performance. If he does so, then he terminates the contract by reason of the employer's conduct. He is constructively dismissed.'

What amounts to a significant breach is for the tribunal to determine and it will only be a constructive dismissal where there is no alternative to the employee's resignation in the circumstances because the employer's breach is a significant one going to the root of the contract rather than as was once thought merely unreasonable behaviour by the employer.

CASE EXAMPLE

Weathersfield v Sargent [1999] IRLR 94

The claimant who worked for a car rental company was given instructions to discriminate against ethnic minority customers by telling them that there were no cars available. She was so upset that she phoned her employer and resigned but she did not give a reason at that time. In her claim for constructive dismissal the employer argued that her failure to give a reason at the time of her resignation amounted to a failure to accept the repudiatory breach. The Court of Appeal disagreed and considered that it was obvious why she resigned in the circumstances.

JUDGMENT

Pill LJ explained: 'For many employees, the more outrageous or embarrassing are the instructions given to them, or suggestions made to them, the less likely they may be to argue the point there and then. They may reasonably wish to remove themselves at the first opportunity and with a minimum of discussion. Leaving the employment without notifying the reason does not preclude a finding of constructive dismissal, though it will usually make it more difficult to obtain such a finding.'

Obviously it is also not merely the actions of the employer that give rise to a repudiatory breach justifying a claim of constructive dismissal. The tribunal needs to consider the full circumstances in which the event caused the employee to resign.

CASE EXAMPLE

Futty v D & D Brekkes Ltd [1974] IRLR 130

The claimant was a fish filleter and on one occasion his supervisor used a four letter word and in effect told him where to go. The claimant left and found himself another job and then claimed unfair dismissal. The tribunal accepted evidence that abusive language was a common feature of the workplace where the claimant worked and was used by everyone as part of their everyday banter. On this basis it was held that the claimant had in fact resigned rather than be dismissed. He could not complain that the abusive language was a significantly serious breach of contract in the circumstances to amount to a constructive dismissal.

It also does not need to be the employer's conduct that amounts to the breach. It could result from the conduct of another employee where the employer is responsible for the behaviour of the other employee.

CASE EXAMPLE

Hilton International Hotels (UK) Ltd v Protopapa [1990] IRLR 136

The claimant who was also a supervisor was reprimanded excessively in front of fellow employees by her immediate superior, conduct which would inevitably undermine her position. She resigned and claimed constructive dismissal on the basis of a breach of the implied term of mutual trust and confidence. The employer tried to argue that there was no repudiatory breach because the immediate superior would have had no authority to dismiss the claimant. The court held that there was indeed a breach of the implied term and so there was also a constructive dismissal.

It is quite common for the constructive dismissal to result from unilateral changes in central express terms of the contract such as pay, hours and duties.

CASE EXAMPLE

Alcan Extrusions v Yates [1996] IRLR 327

The employer had unilaterally made quite dramatic changes to the working conditions including working hours, changed shifts and weekend and bank holiday working, and to shift payment. Employees worked under the changed conditions under protest, and arguing that they retained their rights to redundancy and unfair dismissal claims. Eventually some did claim unfair dismissal. Both the tribunal and the EAT agreed that there was a dismissal, an essential feature of unfair dismissal claims. The EAT rejected the employer's argument that unilateral variations of the contract are only a potentially repudiatory breach giving the employee the right only to resign and claim constructive dismissal. It held that significant changes to the original contract made unilaterally can amount to a breach of contract in their own right.

Another act by the employer which undermines the employee's position and could amount to a repudiatory breach justifying a claim of constructive dismissal is demotion of the employee.

CASE EXAMPLE

BBC v Beckett [1983] IRLR 43

The claimant had been employed by the corporation for fourteen years as a scenic carpenter, obviously a skilled position. Following a single act of negligence he was then demoted to general maintenance work and this involved a significant reduction in both salary and status. He resigned and claimed constructive dismissal. The EAT held that the demotion and the consequential effect on the claimant's pay and standing were out of all proportion to the conduct in question, particularly given the claimant's lengthy and exemplary service.

It is also clearly possible for the constructive dismissal to result from the employer breaching one of the implied terms if this amounts to a significant breach. This is more straightforward where the duty is practical in nature.

CASE EXAMPLE

British Aircraft Corporation v Austin [1978] IRLR 332

The employer in this case breached the implied term to take reasonable care for the employee's safety and welfare. The employer had failed to properly investigate a complaint by the employee that protective spectacles that had been supplied were in fact inadequate. As a result of this the employee had been placed at risk which then amounted to a significant breach.

An employee does not necessarily have to leave immediately to claim constructive dismissal as long as the breach was significantly serious and it was still the actual cause of the resignation although there is of course always a risk that the tribunal might consider that the employee has accepted the situation.

CASE EXAMPLE

Waltons & Morse v Dorrington [1997] IRLR 488

The case predates legislation prohibiting smoking in public including in the workplace. The claimant had fought for a smoke free working environment arguing that this was part of the employer's duty to ensure her health and safety in the workplace. The employer failed to deal with her grievance so she eventually left when she had found work and claimed constructive dismissal. The employer argued that the delay in leaving meant that she had accepted the situation and there could be no constructive dismissal. The EAT rejected this argument and accepted that she needed to earn money and left as soon as she had suitable alternative employment.

ACTIVITY

Self-assessment questions

1. What are the only three circumstances in which a termination of the contract of employment will be a dismissal?
2. What is the only conduct which will be accepted as justifying a summary dismissal?
3. In what types of different situations could this conduct occur?
4. Is it important that the employer identifies such conduct in the contract of employment?
5. What additional protections have the Fixed Term Employees (Prevention of Less Favourable Treatment) Regulations 2002 given to employees on fixed-term contracts?
6. When will a constructive dismissal occur?
7. What will an employee claiming constructive dismissal have to show about the employer's behaviour?
8. Is it possible for the employer to avoid resigning immediately so that he has time to find other work?

KEY FACTS

Continuity of employment	Case/statute
• Defined as any week during the whole or part of which an employee's relations with his employer are governed by a contract of employment counts in computing the employee's period of employment	S212 Employment Rights Act 1996
• Continuity is important for statutory rights and private rights will not interfere • There may be a difference between the actual start date and the start of continuous employment • Only complete weeks are counted but continuity is measured in months and years	Secretary of State for Employment v Globe Elastic Thread Co Ltd The General of the Salvation Army v Dewsbury Sweeney v J & S Henderson
• Certain things do not break continuity – including • periods of legitimate illness • lay-offs or temporary breaks • arranged or customary absence • Working abroad does not count towards continuity • nor do strikes • and illegality breaks continuity	S212(3) Employment Rights Act 1996. Donnelly v Kelvin International Services Hussain v Acorn Independent College Ltd Lloyds Bank Ltd v Secretary of State for Employment S215(1) Employment Rights Act 1996 S216 Employment Rights Act 1996 Hyland v JH Barker (North West) Ltd
Notice periods	**Case/statute**
• Can be contractual and courts can determine what is reasonable notice	Hill v CA Parsons & Co Ltd
• Or can be statutory – which gives minimum periods – from employer one week for at least one month and less than two years' continuous service and one week extra for each year's continuous service up to a maximum of twelve weeks for twelve years' service – from the employee one week for an employee who has been employed for one month or more	S86(1) Employment Rights Act 1996
• A payment in lieu of notice is possible in four circumstances: the employer gives the appropriate notice but does not require work from the employee (garden leave); under the contract the employer is entitled to terminate the contract with notice or summarily on payment of a sum of money in lieu of notice; an agreement between employer and employee to terminate the contract for an agreed payment; the employer dismisses the employee summarily with a lieu payment	Delaney v Staples t/a De Montfort Recruitment
The statutory definition of dismissal	**Case/statute**
There are only four types of dismissal • the employer dismisses the employee with notice • the employer dismisses the employee without notice – summary dismissal • a fixed-term or limited-term contract comes to an end without renewal • the employee resigns and claims constructive dismissal	S95 Employment Rights Act 1996

Summary dismissal	Case/statute
• Only available for gross misconduct • Which can include gross insubordination • But must be judged in context • And can also include dishonesty • And can also include a breach of confidentiality • But must involve a serious breach of contract	*Dunn & Another v AAH Ltd* *Pepper v Webb* *Wilson v Racher* *Sinclair v Neighbour* *Denco Ltd v Joinson* *Laws v London Chronicle Ltd*
Failure to renew a fixed-term contract	**Case/statute**
• Must be fair not to renew or can be unfair dismissal • If fixed term or series of fixed terms continues for four years then deemed a permanent contract	*Fixed Term Employees (Prevention of Less Favourable Treatment) Regulations 2002*
Constructive dismissal	**Case/statute**
• Must be a breach of contract by the employer that goes to the root of the contract and entitles the employee to consider the contract repudiated	*Western Excavating v Sharp*
• And breach must mean employee has no choice but to resign	*Weathersfield v Sargent*
• The tribunal must consider all the circumstances leading to the resignation	*Futty v D & D Brekkes Ltd*
• And the breach could result from the behaviour of other employees	*Hilton International Hotels (UK) Ltd v Protopapa*
• And could also result from unilateral changes in the terms of the contract	*Alcan Extrusions v Yates*
• Or any act by the employer which undermines the employee's position	*BBC v Beckett*
• Or could be a breach of an implied term if serious enough	*British Aircraft Corporation v Austin*
• The employee does not have to resign immediately but must work under protest	*Waltons & Morse v Dorrington*

SAMPLE ESSAY QUESTION

ESSAY Discuss the argument that as a remedy for a breach of contract by an employer constructive dismissal is far from being an effective remedy.

Explain what constructive dismissal is

• There must be a breach of the contract by the employer that goes to the root of the contract and entitles the employee to consider the contract repudiated by the employer.

- And the breach must be so fundamental to the continuation of the contract that the employee has no choice but than to resign in the circumstances.

Discuss the types of circumstances in which such a breach could occur

- Could result from unilateral changes in the terms of the contract.
- Particularly where these involve significant changes.
- Could result from any act of the employer which undermines the employee's position.
- So certainly could include discrimination.
- And could include breaches of statutory rights.
- But could also result from the behaviour of other employees for whom the employer is vicariously liable.
- Particularly where the employer has failed to address the issue.
- Could also involve a breach of an implied term if serious enough.
- Breach of the implied duty of mutual trust and respect being an obvious one.

Discuss what the employee has to do to gain a remedy for the breach

- Employee resigns and leaves.
- Must tell the employer why.
- Will generally bring a claim for unfair dismissal – although a wrongful dismissal claim is possible for an employee who is not eligible or for a highly paid employee.

Discuss the advantages to the employee of such a course of action

- Does not have to suffer the breach any longer.
- May get a financial remedy.
- Or possibly reinstatement or re-engagement.
- May possibly be healthier avoiding possible stress at work.

Discuss potential disadvantages or drawbacks in such a course of action

- The employee will not have a job or income.
- The employee then has to bring a claim which will probably require legal advice which could be costly.
- The quality of the remedy will depend on the type of breach – e.g. discrimination does not require continuous employment and awards include injury to feelings.
- The employee might not win the claim.
- The employee might win but not be able to have reinstatement or re-engagement as a remedy as the tribunal will say that the employment relationship has broken down.
- The employee will then have to explain why he left to future potential employers.
- An employee who has fought a claim in a tribunal might not prove attractive to potential employees.

Discuss whether it is an effective remedy

- Probably not.
- It shows the imbalance in the employment relationship.
- The employee is taking a risk on success.
- And also on future employment.

REACH REASONED CONCLUSIONS

SUMMARY

- Continuity of employment is important for establishing employment protections.
- For unfair dismissal the period is two years 'continuous employment.
- The period is calculated by establishing the date of commencement of continuous employment, the effective date of termination and working out periods that do not interfere with continuity such as maternity and periods that do such as days lost through industrial action.
- Contracts of employment are contracts of continuous obligation so they will generally be terminated by one party giving notice to the other.

- Notice periods can be contractual but there are statutory minimum notice periods and if the contractual notice is less than the statutory minimum the statutory notice period will be enforced.
- Payments in lieu of notice can be made where the employer puts the employee on garden leave and for summary dismissal.
- There are four types of dismissal – dismissal with notice, without notice which is summary dismissal, expiry of a fixed-term contract without renewal and constructive dismissal.
- A summary dismissal is only possible where the employee has been guilty of gross misconduct.
- Failure to renew a fixed-term contract could be unfair dismissal.
- Constructive dismissal involves a breach of contract by the employer which goes to the root of the contract and makes it impossible for the employee to continue working.

Further reading

Emir, Astra, *Selwyn's Law of Employment 17th edition*. Oxford University Press, 2012, Chapters 13, 15 and 17.

Pitt, Gwyneth, *Cases and Materials on Employment Law 3rd edition*. Pearson, 2008, Chapter 8.

Sargeant, Malcolm and Lewis, David, *Employment Law 6th edition*. Pearson, 2012, Chapter 4.3.

20

Termination of employment (2) termination other than by dismissal

AIMS AND OBJECTIVES

After reading this chapter you should be able to:

▨ Understand how a contract of employment may be terminated when the contract is frustrated

▨ Understand how a contract of employment may be terminated by the death of the employer

▨ Understand how a contract of employment may be terminated when the employee voluntarily resigns his position

▨ Understand how a contract of employment may be terminated where there is a mutual agreement between employer and employee

▨ Critically analyse the area

▨ Apply the law to factual situations and reach conclusions

Most employment protection rights on termination of a contract of employment are connected with dismissal and in particular unfair dismissal, redundancy and, on some occasions, wrongful dismissal. However, there are effectively four types of termination of a contract of employment which do not amount to or result from a dismissal. Although the contract comes to an end there is not a dismissal. These are:

▨ where the contract is frustrated by an event that is beyond the control of either party;

▨ where the employer has died;

▨ where the employee voluntarily resigns his position;

▨ where both the employer and the employee reach a mutual agreement to terminate the contract.

20.1 Frustration of the contract

Frustration is a common law doctrine of contract law by which both parties to the contract are excused further performance where the contract has become impossible to perform because the circumstances are radically different to those originally envisaged by the parties.

JUDGMENT

In *Davies Contractors Ltd v Fareham UDC* [1956] AC 696 Lord Radcliffe explained those factors that would justify the application of the doctrine: 'without default of either party, a contractual obligation has become incapable of being performed because the circumstances in which performance is called for would render it a thing radically different from that which was undertaken by the contract'.

The House of Lords identified in *Paal Wilson & Co v Partenreederei Hannah Blumenthal* [1983] 1 AC 854 that in the context of a contract of employment there are two essential features that would render the contract frustrated:

- there must be some unforeseen change in the outside circumstances and not provided for by the parties which prevents continued performance of the contract; and
- this unforeseen change was not the fault of either party.

The significance of frustration to a contract is that the parties are relieved from any further liability to perform the contract. So it is obviously useful to an employer when a contract has in effect come to an end and it need not face the inconvenience of a claim for unfair dismissal.

There are two common situations which could frustrate a contract of employment:

- long term sickness absence of the employee;
- imprisonment of the employee.

Long term absence of the employee through illness

In the case of illness a contract of employment is not automatically frustrated merely because of a lengthy sickness absence. In *Maxwell v Walter Howard Designs Ltd* [1975] IRLR 77 a two year period of absence through illness did not frustrate the contract. It was possible for the position to be filled by a temporary replacement rather than filling the post permanently so it was still possible for the employee to return without damaging the business.

It would clearly be unfair to expect an employer to hold a position open indefinitely. While it inevitably is difficult to determine the point at which the contract has in fact ended, that is precisely what courts will have to determine when there is a dispute. It is not surprising that guidelines have been developed.

CASE EXAMPLE

Egg Stores (Stamford Hill) Ltd v Leibovici [1977] IRLR 376

An employee with about fifteen years' service with his employer was absent from work for five months following a road accident. The employer paid sick pay for two months until January 1975. In April 1975 the employee asked if he could now return to work but the employer refused: it had taken on a replacement doing his job. The employee claimed unfair dismissal but the employer argued that the contract was frustrated.

JUDGMENT

In the Employment Appeal Tribunal Phillips J offered the following guidelines: 'There may be an event (e.g. a crippling accident) so dramatic and shattering that everyone concerned will realise immediately that to all intents and purposes the contract must be regarded as at an end. Or there may be an event, such as illness or accident, the course and outcome of which is uncertain. It may be a long process before one is able to say whether the event is such as to bring about the frustration of the contract. But there will have been frustration of the contract, even though at the time of the event the outcome was uncertain, if the time arrives when, looking back, one can say that at some point (even if it is not possible to say precisely when) matters had gone on for so long, and the prospects for the future were so poor, that it was no longer practical to regard the contract as still subsisting.'

Phillips J also provided a list of matters that should be taken into account:

1. the length of the previous employment;
2. how long it had been expected that the employment would continue;
3. the nature of the job;
4. the nature, length and effect of the illness or disabling event;
5. the need of the employer for the work to be done, and the need for a replacement to do it;
6. the risk to the employer of acquiring obligations in respect of redundancy payments or compensation for unfair dismissal to the replacement employee;
7. whether wages have continued to be paid;
8. the acts and statements of the employer in relation to the employment, including the dismissal of, or failure to dismiss, the employee;
9. whether in all the circumstances a reasonable employer could be expected to wait any longer.

It is clear also that the employer has obligations to the employee and should not be too quick to consider the contract frustrated. As a result frustration of the contract will only apply where there has been long term sickness and it is only in very serious situations that the employee's sickness frustrates the contract.

CASE EXAMPLE

Williams v Watsons Luxury Coaches [1990] IRLR 164

A part-time typist injured her leg in an accident in June 1986 and went on sick leave as a result. She continued to send doctors' notes to her employer. In December 1986 her note identified that she would not be fit to return to work until February 1987 at the earliest. When she wished to return to work in January 1988 the employer stated that there was no work for her and that the contract was frustrated. The Employment Appeal Tribunal, applying the *Egg Store* test declared that there was a dismissal not frustration of the contract. The employer had not considered the prospect of recovery.

The operation of the doctrine may also depend on the status of the employee and his importance to the business.

CASE EXAMPLE

Hart v AR Marshall & Sons (Bulwell) Ltd [1977] IRLR 51

The employee was a night service fitter. He was on long term sickness absence from April 1974 to January 1976, a period of twenty months. He had produced doctors' notes through-out the period, although his employer had employed a permanent replacement in August 1974. When he eventually returned to work and was told his job was no longer available he claimed unfair dismissal. The EAT held that the contract was frustrated. Despite the fact that the employee had sent in sick notes and the employer had not dismissed him prior to his return the EAT held was only indicative of the employer maintaining contact in case there was any prospect of return. It was the fact that the employee had been described as a 'key worker' that meant the contract was frustrated.

However, frustration cannot be claimed merely because an event may or even is likely to occur. In *Converform (Darwen) Ltd v Bell* [1981] IRLR 195 it was held that it could not be argued as frustration of a contract that an employee returning to work after suffering a heart attack might suffer another one.

One other factor that may need to be considered is whether the illness becomes a dis-ability covered now by the Equality Act 2010. Where the illness results in the death of the employee then clearly the contract is at an end. Long term sickness could also of course be an issue in an employer arguing capability as a fair head of dismissal (see Chapter 22.4.1).

Imprisonment of the employee

In the case of imprisonment of the employee, then in essence the contract is frustrated because of the incapacity for work.

One potential problem here is that a frustrating event is one that occurs through no fault of either party. Of course in the case of an employee being imprisoned it is his own conduct which has caused the problem and in general contract law self-induced frustration has no effect on the contract which continues. In this way the EAT in *Norris v Southampton City Council* [1982] IRLR 141 concluded that there was no frustration because the imprisonment was the cause of the employee's own misconduct. Instead it argued there was a repudia-tory breach of contract by the employee which could then be accepted by the employer by dismissing the employee. Even this presents problems since it is hard to argue that the employee commits an offence with the intention of breaching his contract of employment.

The appropriate approach to the problem was later settled by the Court of Appeal.

CASE EXAMPLE

FC Shepherd & Co Ltd v Jerrom [1986] 3 WLR 801, IRLR 358

An apprentice was convicted and detained in a young offenders' institution after taking part in a motorcycle gang fight. The court held that imprisonment could frustrate a contract of employment where the party alleging the frustration, the employer, was not at fault in any way for the impossibility of performance of the contract, and the other party, the employee, could not rely on his own misconduct to prevent the contract terminating.

In general it will be long terms of imprisonment that frustrate the contract. In *Hare v Murphy Brothers* [1974] IRLR 34R2 twelve months' imprisonment was sufficient to frus-trate the contract. It was accepted that twelve months was too long a time to expect the employer to cope with the inability of the employee to attend work.

In treating the contract as frustrated the employer obviously has to consider:

▨ when it was commercially necessary to make a decision;

▨ what a reasonable employer would consider to be an acceptable length of absence;

▨ whether it would be reasonable to hire a permanent rather than a temporary replacement.

As a result an employer needs to consider carefully at what point it should consider the contract to be frustrated.

CASE EXAMPLE

Four Seasons Healthcare Ltd v Maughan [2005] IRLR 324

The employee who worked as a registered nurse was suspended for eleven months without pay after his arrest for allegedly abusing a patient. Bail conditions had prevented him from entering his place of work. When he was then convicted the employee claimed back pay during his time suspended. The contract only allowed for seven days' pay during suspension. The EAT held that the contract only became frustrated on his conviction and imprisonment and as a result he was entitled to be paid.

Of course imprisonment also indicates criminal conduct. Where this occurs an employer may also be able to consider that a dismissal is potentially fair for misconduct (see Chapter 22.4.2).

There are other limited circumstances in which a contract of employment might be considered to be frustrated because of the unavailability of one party. A classic example occurs in the case of an outbreak of war.

Is there an event that is not the fault of either party to the contract that prevents the contract from being performed?
- the employee is absent through long term illness
- the employee is imprisoned

YES
↓

Does the event make performance impossible?
- even though at the time of the event the outcome was uncertain, if the time arrives when, looking back, one can say that at some point (even if it is not possible to say precisely when) matters had gone on for so long, and the prospects for the future were so poor, that it was no longer practical to regard the contract as still subsisting.

YES
↓

The contract is frustrated, all obligations end at this point

---

Figure 20.1 Diagram illustrating when a contract of employment will be considered frustrated

CASE EXAMPLE

Morgan v Manser [1948] 1 KB 184

An artiste had entered a ten-year contract with his manager starting in 1938. However, from 1940 until 1946 he was conscripted into the armed forces during the Second World War. He was obviously unavailable to meet commitments and both parties were excused performance.

ACTIVITY

Self-assessment questions

1. What are the essential characteristics of a frustrated contract of employment identified by the House of Lords in *Paal Wilson & Co v Partenreederei Hannah Blumenthal*?
2. In what circumstances would a contract of employment usually be frustrated?
3. What is it that frustrates the contract and what is the effect on the parties generally? What are the three main frustrating events in a contract of employment?
4. The EAT in *Egg Stores Ltd v Leibovici* identified the main circumstance in which the illness of the employee frustrates the contract and produced also an extended list of factors to be taken into account in deciding whether the contract is frustrated. What is it about the illness that frustrates the contract and what is the relevance of the individual factors?
5. How have the courts resolved the problem of it being an employee's own conduct that has caused the termination?

20.2 Death of the employer

Where either party dies then this inevitably terminates the contract. In the case of an employee (see 20.1 above) it is possible that the contract can be considered to be frustrated.

Where the employer dies ordinarily the business may still continue in another form. If it is a public company then the death of an executive will have little effect since new officers may be appointed. However, in a private company which may be run by one person or in the case of a sole trader who runs a business and employs workers in either case his death may bring the business to an end. However, there are a variety of rights that might still subsist according to section 207 Employment Rights Act 1996 which will be treated as though they accrued before the death of the employer. These might include:

- a claim for an itemised pay statement;
- a guarantee payment;
- payment for time off work;
- rights in dismissal, redundancy, payments for either and insolvency protection.

20.3 Resignation

We have seen in Chapter 6.2.1 that courts are not willing to allow an employer to make it impossible for an employee to leave. Very often an employee can only advance his own position and conditions by taking other employment. Therefore an employee must be free to move on and take up different employment opportunities without fearing that an employer can prevent him from doing so.

An employee can do so simply by the mechanism of resignation. That is by providing the employer with the appropriate notice of his intention to leave the employment. What is appropriate notice will depend on what has been agreed in the contract of employment. Alternatively statutory notice periods from section 86(1) Employment Rights Act 1996 will apply (see Chapter 19.2). If the employee fails to provide appropriate notice then this will amount to a breach of contract and the employer could sue for damages. The practical reality is that this will never happen unless a large sum of money was involved.

A resignation has to be an entirely voluntary act so it will be a dismissal rather than a resignation if the employee is subjected to pressure or coercion to resign.

CASE EXAMPLE

Essex County Council v Walker [1972] (Unreported)

After a disagreement with her employer the employee was told that she should resign. She did so but claimed a redundancy payment. She was refused on the basis that there had been no dismissal. The court held that wherever an employee is coerced into resigning then this amounts to a dismissal.

JUDGMENT

It was said: 'if an employee is … expressly invited to resign, a court of law is entitled to come to the conclusion that, as a matter of course, the employee was dismissed'.

The principle was clearly explained by the Employment Appeal Tribunal. If the employer is forced to resign then it is in fact a dismissal but if the resignation is induced by other factors then it is a resignation.

CASE EXAMPLE

Sheffield v Oxford Controls Co Ltd [1979] IRLR 133

The employee was a director and held shares in the defendant company, the majority of shares being held by his co-director and that director's wife. After a very heated and nasty dispute between the employee's wife and the other directors she was threatened with dismissal. The employee then threatened to resign if his wife was dismissed. An agreement was eventually reached to pay him £10,000 on his resignation but he was also told that if he did not go he would be dismissed. He then brought an action for unfair dismissal and argued that he had been forced to resign against his will.

JUDGMENT

Arnold J clearly explains the principle: 'where an employee resigns and that resignation is determined upon by him because he prefers to resign rather than to be dismissed (the alternative having been expressed to him by the employer in terms of the threat that if he does not resign he will be dismissed), the mechanics of the resignation do not cause that to be other than a dismissal'. However, in the context of the case itself, Arnold also goes on to consider the inducement and states: 'the finding that the employee had agreed to terms upon which he was prepared to terminate his employment with the employers – terms which were satisfactory to him – means that there is no room for the principle and that it is impossible to upset the conclusion of the tribunal that he was not dismissed'.

The principle was followed in *Jones v Mid-Glamorgan County Council* [1997] IRLR 685 where the employee had been threatened to resign or be fired. The Court of Appeal recognised the lack of voluntariness in the arrangement and observed that it is: 'a principle of the utmost flexibility which is willing … to recognise a dismissal when it sees it'.

However, in applying the principle all of the circumstances must be taken into account.

CASE EXAMPLE

Sandhu v Jan de Rijk Transport Ltd [2007] EWCA Civ 430, IRLR 519

The employee here had been summoned to a meeting at which, without warning, he was told that his contract was to be terminated. He then negotiated a settlement but later claimed unfair dismissal. The Court of Appeal held that the apparent agreement was in fact a dismissal because, unlike in *Sheffield v Oxford Controls Co Ltd*, the employee had no real chance to consider his position or to take independent advice.

However, in *International Computers Ltd v Kennedy* [1981] IRLR 28 in a redundancy situation, it was held that merely advising an employee that it would be a good idea to look for other work would not amount to coercion to resign and so would not be a dismissal.

A resignation must always be expressed in clear terms. If for example a resignation in writing is required then in general it must be in writing. Problems may arise where an employee indicates resignation in vague terms and the employer acts on it. In this case what matters is the events leading to the termination.

CASE EXAMPLE

Ely v YKK Fasteners [1993] IRLR 500

An employee informed his employer that he was contemplating emigrating to Australia and that he had in fact applied for work there. The employee later changed his mind and informed the employer about this but by that stage the employer had found a replacement for him and considered the contract at an end. The employee claimed unfair dismissal and the court had to decide whether there was voluntary resignation by the employee or whether the employer had indeed dismissed him. The Court of Appeal held that, because the employer had only informed his employer of his plans and not resigned formally it did amount to a dismissal. However, in the circumstances it was held to be a fair dismissal under other substantial reason under section 98(1)(b) Employment Rights Act 1996.

Another issue is whether resignations made in the heat of the moment can be enforced. In this case the court must base its decision on the precise words used and the circumstances in which they were used. In *Kwik Fit (GB) Ltd v Lineham* [1992] IRLR 156 the employee threw his keys on the counter and walked off saying 'I'm off.' In this circumstance there was no ambiguity in the employee's intentions. By contrast in *Barclay v City of Glasgow DC* [1983] IRLR 313 the employee had learning difficulties and so it was held that the employer should have taken account of these special circumstances and allowed a few days for cooling off.

Ultimately again the real test is what would a reasonable employer have done in the same circumstances.

ACTIVITY

Self-assessment questions

1. What contractual or statutory requirements will an employee have to meet before resigning?
2. Why would an employee usually wish to resign from his employment?
3. Why does the resignation have to be voluntary?
4. What are the consequences if the employee has been coerced into resigning against his will?
5. What was the principle in *Sheffield v Oxford Controls Co Ltd*? Why was it not applied in the case?
6. How does the court approach the situation where an employee has resigned in the heat of the moment?

20.4 Termination by mutual agreement

Where both parties to the contract agree unconditionally to terminate the contract then there is no dismissal and no statutory rights can be asserted. This follows basic contract law where if the parties are capable of forming a contract by agreement they must also be able to end that contract by agreement.

A common context for a mutual agreement to end the contract is in early retirement. Here the employer is seeking to reduce the workforce and uses a financial inducement. This is an agreement based on good consideration on either side and so there is no dismissal.

CASE EXAMPLE

Birch & Humber v The University of Liverpool [1985] IRLR 165

The university sent out a circular to its lecturing staff in which it asked for volunteers for an early retirement scheme which would involve enhanced retirement payments. Two employees who were both lecturers volunteered for the scheme. A package and agreed leaving dates were both negotiated. After leaving their posts they then argued that they had been dismissed and, since they had not been replaced, that they should be entitled to redundancy payments. The Court of Appeal held that any dismissal could only be when they received their notification of their leaving dates. However, there had to be a genuine agreement in order for the early retirement to take place and the lecturers to gain their enhanced payment. On this basis their termination was by mutual agreement and was not a dismissal.

JUDGMENT

As Purchas LJ identified: 'dismissal … is not consistent with free, mutual consent, bringing a contract of employment to an end'.

Again the important issue to determine is whether the parties really did reach a mutual agreement to terminate the contract or whether the employee was in fact coerced into the agreement.

CASE EXAMPLE

Igbo v Johnson Matthey Chemicals Ltd [1986] IRLR 215

The employee had been required to sign her contract of employment in which there was a clause stating that a failure to return on the due date following extended leave would automatically terminate the contract. In this case the employee failed to return on the due date because she was actually ill at the time and had sent in appropriate doctors' certificates. The employer argued that the clause in the contract meant that the termination was by mutual agreement and not dismissal. The Court of Appeal held that there was no mutual agreement to terminate and there was a dismissal. It identified that to do otherwise would have conflicted with the employee's statutory unfair dismissal rights under the Employment Rights Act 1996. The decision overruled the previous case of *British Leyland (UK) v Ashraf* [1978] IRLR 330 which had held such clauses in employment contracts legitimate.

Igbo in effect is restricted to those agreements to terminate that are based on the occurrence of a particular event which is proscribed for in the contract of employment. It is still of course possible for employers and employees to negotiate an agreement that is satisfactory to both parties. A context for such an agreement which may not give rise to a finding of a dismissal is during disciplinary proceedings.

CASE EXAMPLE

Logan Salton v Durham County Council [1989] IRLR 99

The employee was the subject of disciplinary proceedings and it was likely that he would be dismissed summarily. His trade union representative then negotiated on his behalf a termination under which he would also be let off paying an outstanding car loan of £2,750 and both parties signed this. He then claimed that he had been placed under duress and in effect dismissed. The Employment Appeal Tribunal distinguished from *Igbo*. Here the agreement was not part of the existing contract of employment but a completely separate contract. He had entered the arrangement willingly following advice and had benefitted from it. There was no duress and no dismissal.

Method of termination	How the contract ends	Consequences	When will be a dismissal
Frustration	By operation of law	All obligations end	If employer acts at wrong time
Death of the employer	By employer dying	Some rights might subsist	–
Voluntary resignation	By employee's voluntary conduct	Employee free to take up other employment after serving notice	If there is coercion
Mutual agreement	By agreement by both parties	Depends on reason e.g. employee may get financial inducement to retire early	If there is coercion

Figure 20.2 Diagram illustrating the differences between different types of termination without dismissal

ACTIVITY

Self-assessment questions

1. When will a contract of employment be said to be terminated by a mutual agreement between employer and employee?
2. In what circumstances will such agreements commonly arise?
3. Why would the court not accept that there was a mutual agreement in *Igbo v Johnson Matthey Chemicals Ltd*?
4. How was the case distinguished in *Logan Salton v Durham County Council*?

ACTIVITY

Legal problem solving

Identify which type of terminating event is appropriate to the following. Consider also whether it may alternatively be held to be a dismissal.

1. Archie, a car assembly worker, has been convicted of grievous bodily harm and has been sentenced to five years' imprisonment.
2. Brenda attends a disciplinary meeting and is told that she will probably be dismissed following the hearing. She agrees that she will resign instantly in return for not getting a disciplinary record.
3. Calum has been on long term sick leave for more than nine months with severe, non-work related, depression. Although his contract only provides for six months' payment of full salary and six months' half salary, he has been paid full salary throughout his illness. It is possible for Calum's work to be carried out by a temporary replacement. Calum informs his employer that he will return to work next week but his manager has told him that he has been replaced and not to return.
4. Denis agrees a package to take early retirement at age sixty-three. This includes a lump sum payment and an enhanced pension for two years. The day Denis is due to leave he states that he wishes to change his mind.

KEY FACTS

Frustration	Case/statute
• Basic common law doctrine – obligations end on the frustrating event	*Davies Contractors Ltd v Fareham UDC*
• Two basic causes – long term illness or imprisonment	*Egg Stores Ltd v Leibovici*
• In the case of illness frustration occurs when – even though at the time of the event the outcome was uncertain, time has come where the situation has gone on for so long and the prospects of return so low that no longer practical for contract to continue	
• So only in very serious situations that the employee's sickness frustrates the contract	*Williams v Watsons Luxury Coaches*
• The operation of the doctrine may also depend on the status of the employee and his importance to the business	*Hart v AR Marshall & Sons (Bulwell) Ltd*
• With imprisonment in essence the contract is frustrated because of the incapacity for work	

• The approach is that the employer is not at fault and the employee cannot use his own misconduct to avoid the termination	*F C Shepherd & Co Ltd v Jerrom*
• The employer needs to consider carefully at what point it should consider the contract to be frustrated	*Four Seasons Healthcare Ltd v Maughan*
Death of the employer	**Case/statute**
• Some rights might still subsist which will be treated as though they accrued before the death of the employer, including: a claim for an itemised pay statement; a guarantee payment; payment for time off work; rights in dismissal, redundancy, payments for either and insolvency protection	S207 Employment Rights Act 1996
Voluntary resignation	**Case/statute**
• Resignation has to be entirely voluntary act	*Essex County Council v Walker*
• So it will be a dismissal rather than a resignation if the employee is subjected to pressure or coercion to resign	*Sheffield v Oxford Controls Co Ltd*
• The resignation must be expressed in clear terms	*Ely v YKK Fasteners*
• With resignations made in the heat of the moment court should look at the precise words	*Kwik Fit (GB) Ltd v Lineham*
• And any special circumstances	*Barclay v City of Glasgow DC*
Mutual agreement to terminate	**Case/statute**
• An agreement must be based on good consideration on either side	*Birch and Humber v University of Liverpool*
• Must determine whether the parties really did reach a mutual agreement to terminate or whether there was coercion	*Igbo v Johnson Matthey Chemicals Ltd*
• Negotiated terms during disciplinary proceedings are an agreed termination not dismissal	*Logan Salton v Durham CC*

SAMPLE ESSAY QUESTION

ESSAY Discuss the situations in which an employment contract may be terminated without a dismissal and the extent to which these benefit both parties and avoid disputes in tribunals.

Explain that there are four possible situations in which termination without dismissal may occur

- Frustration of the contract.
- The death of the employer.
- A voluntary resignation by the employee.
- A mutual agreement between both parties.

Explain the basis of frustration

- Frustration is an event not the fault of either party which ends the obligations on both sides.
- Can be caused through long term illness (and death) or imprisonment of the employee.
- With illness it must be that the time has come where the prospects of return are low and not practical to continue.
- With imprisonment the employee is not able to carry out his work.

Discuss whether frustration benefits both parties and avoids disputes

- It clearly does not benefit the employee who then has no job.
- But the employer should not have to wait indefinitely for an employee to return.
- Clearly in the case of illness the employee may not be able to return to work at all and the employer should not have to face an action for unfair dismissal.
- In the case of imprisonment it is the employee's misconduct that is the cause – the problem would be that this would be the employee's fault so courts have dealt with this that the employer is blameless and the employee cannot use his own misconduct to challenge frustration.
- There is still a close link between illness and capability and imprisonment and conduct – both potentially fair heads of dismissal – so an employee might still argue for unfair dismissal.

Discuss the situation when an employer dies

- Again it may not benefit the employee if he has no job.
- But a variety of rights subsist including rights to a redundancy payment.
- If the employer's estate fails to honour these rights there could still be a dispute.

Explain the basis of voluntary resignation

- Will usually be to take up other work – so preserves the idea of freedom of contract.
- Is only bound to give notice agreed in the contract or statutory notice period from section 86(1) Employment Rights Act 1996.

Discuss whether resignation benefits both parties and avoids disputes

- It benefits the employee who wants to move on and preserves freedom of contract.
- Problems can arise when the resignation results from coercion by the employer – in which case it may be a dismissal and there could be an unfair dismissal claim.
- All the circumstances will have to be taken into account.
- Another problem can arise when an employee has resigned in the heat of the moment – this again could lead to an unfair dismissal claim.

Explain the context for mutual agreements to terminate

- Could be for schemes such as early retirement.
- Or could follow disciplinary hearings and be an alternative to disciplinary action.

Discuss whether mutual agreements to terminate benefit both parties and avoid disputes

- A problem again is whether there is coercion – in which case there could be a dispute and unfair dismissal claimed.
- The other problem could be whether the arrangement is in fact mutually beneficial.

REACH ANY SENSIBLE CONCLUSION

SUMMARY

- In many cases an employment contract ends with a dismissal.
- But there are situations where termination of the contract is not a dismissal.
- These are: where the contract is frustrated, where the employer dies, where the employee resigns and where there is a mutual agreement.
- Frustration involves an event beyond the control and not the fault of either party.
- This can be long term sickness or imprisonment of the employee – because it would not be fair to expect the employer to hold the job open indefinitely and it may need a permanent replacement.
- Where the employer dies there may still exist rights that accrued before the contract terminated.
- A resignation must be voluntary and not result from coercion: resign or be fired.
- Courts look at the actual circumstances when employees resign in the heat of the moment.
- A mutual agreement will often result from a financial inducement by the employer.
- Again the important issue is that there is no coercion.

Further reading

Emir, Astra, *Selwyn's Law of Employment 17th edition*. Oxford University Press, 2012, Chapter 17, pp. 453–459.

Sargeant, Malcolm and Lewis, David, *Employment Law 6th edition*. Pearson, 2012, Chapter 4.2.

21

Termination of employment (3) wrongful dismissal

AIMS AND OBJECTIVES

After reading this chapter you should be able to:

- Understand the nature of wrongful dismissal
- Understand the circumstances in which an action for wrongful dismissal is likely to be brought
- Understand the context in which wrongful dismissal claims are still relevant
- Understand the process for masking wrongful dismissal claims
- Understand the available remedies for a successful claim of wrongful dismissal
- Critically analyse the concept of wrongful dismissal
- Apply the rules on wrongful dismissal to factual situations

21.1 Introduction

Before 1971 an employer could, with few exceptions, in effect dismiss an employee for any reason or indeed for no reason. The law on dismissals at that time reflected the old 'master and servant' rules (see Chapter 1.4.1) and a court could not enquire into the fairness of a dismissal.

At that time one of the only issues on which the employee could challenge the dismissal was on whether the employer had dismissed the employee and prevented the employee from serving the appropriate notice under the contract or the remainder of a fixed-term contract. The action would be a simple breach of contract and the remedy represented the money that the employee should have been able to earn during the period of notice or the remainder of the fixed term. This was the action traditionally known as an action for wrongful dismissal.

The Industrial Relations Act 1971 (since repealed), although it was actually enacted more for the purpose of the statutory regulation of industrial relations, also created an action for unfair dismissal. This was also inserted in later Acts, most notably the Employment Protection (Consolidation) Act 1978, which has been replaced by the Employment Rights Act 1996 (as amended). An action for unfair dismissal is obviously now the most common course for employees to take to challenge a dismissal (see Chapter 22) and in many ways the pre-1971 law could be said to be of historical interest only. However, there are still some circumstances in which an action for unfair dismissal would be impossible or where an employee could gain a better remedy by using the old common law breach of contract action, and therefore wrongful dismissal remains a significant aspect of the law on dismissal in these limited circumstances.

21.2 The nature of wrongful dismissal

Traditionally there were three main situations in which a common law action for damages arising from a breach of contract might occur:

- An employee was dismissed without the appropriate notice period being given (in effect this is a summary dismissal that cannot be justified).
- An employee was employed under a fixed-term contract which was terminated before the expiry of the fixed term.
- An employee was employed under a contract which stipulated the only circumstances under which a dismissal could occur and the employer dismissed the employee for some other reason.

CASE EXAMPLE

McClelland v Northern Ireland General Health Services [1957] 2 All ER 129

The claimant worked as a senior clerk for five years. She was dismissed and given six months' notice after a rule was introduced that female officers would be required to resign on getting married. She argued that this was a wrongful dismissal because her contract stipulated that the grounds for dismissal were gross misconduct and inefficiency. The health service argued that it was not wrongful because her contract could also be terminated on reasonable notice. The then House of Lords held that it was wrongful because the express conditions in her contract excluded any implied power to terminate on giving reasonable notice.

So wrongful dismissal is an action for breach of contract and is concerned only with the form or manner of the dismissal and not in any way with the relative merits or fairness of the dismissal. This is of course quite different to unfair dismissal where there are a range of dismissals which are classed as automatically unfair and even where the dismissal falls into a category which is identified as potentially fair it is precisely the merits or fairness of the situation which are the critical elements in determining the outcome of the case.

Since the action is for damages which is restricted to damage stemming from the breach, in essence the notice period or remainder of a fixed term, there are likely to be few employees who would benefit from such a claim. For most employees the remedy is likely to be ineffective since their periods of notice would usually be so short that any damages payable would be minimal.

As a result an action for wrongful dismissal is likely to be significant for only three specific groups of workers:

- Those on fixed-term contracts who have been dismissed before the end of the fixed term of employment.
- Very highly paid employees such as executive directors where the statutory maximum for unfair dismissal may mean that they have more to gain from a breach of contract claim for wrongful dismissal – since 1 February 2013, the basic rate of compensation is £450 times the appropriate amount of service (see Chapter 22.7) and

the 'maximum compensatory amount' is £74,200 – so the employee's wages during the notice period would have to exceed this to make a wrongful dismissal claim worthwhile. It is apparent from news broadcasts that this could certainly be the case for example with chief executives of leading companies who are said to earn 145 times the average wage. It can also result from a very long notice period. In *Clark v BET plc* [1997] IRLR 348 for instance the notice period was three years.

- Employees excluded from unfair dismissal claims – at the other end of the scale an employee who had insufficient continuous employment to claim unfair dismissal or who was ineligible might bring a wrongful dismissal claim although the damages are likely to be low, although better than nothing.

CASE EXAMPLE

Laws v London Chronicle [1959] 1WLR 698

An assistant to an advertising manager for a newspaper had only worked for the newspaper for three weeks when she was summarily dismissed. She had attended an editorial meeting with her manager and had followed him when he walked out, despite being ordered to stay by the managing director. She was dismissed without notice for her act of disobedience. She did not qualify for unfair dismissal rights but argued that the dismissal was a wrongful dismissal. The court held that her actions were neither wilful nor sufficiently serious to amount to a breach of a fundamental term of her contract to obey lawful and reasonable orders. As a result she had been wrongfully dismissed and was entitled to claim for damage.

Wrongful dismissal is of course inconsistent with the basic rules of contract law. The employee has been dismissed so has no choice but than to accept the unlawful repudiation of the contract by the employer and try to claim compensation equivalent to the notice period.

JUDGMENT

This was identified by Shaw LJ in *Gunton v London Borough of Richmond* [1980] IRLR 321 where he described the repudiatory breach in wrongful dismissal as: 'a total repudiation which is at once destructive of the contractual relationship'.

In contrast in pure contract law a repudiatory breach of a condition would entitle the victim of breach the choice of what to do. He could either accept the breach and sue for damages or consider his own contractual obligations to be discharged in which case he can sue for damages but cannot be sued for failing to carry out his own obligations or he could continue with the contract if it was to his advantage. This could be the case with a unilateral variation of the contract by the employer where the employee continues to work but raises objections to the variation and makes it clear that he has not accepted the repudiatory breach (see Chapter 5.6.2). As usual the cards are in favour of employers contradicting the contractual base of a voluntary arrangement between two parties.

21.3 Bringing an action for wrongful dismissal

Up until July 1994 an action for wrongful dismissal had to be brought in a County Court or in the High Court. Before then tribunals had no jurisdiction to hear claims for a breach of a contract of employment. However, in July 1994 section 131 of the Employment Protection (Consolidation) Act 1978 (now section 3 of the Employment Tribunals Act 1996) was brought into force by the Employment Tribunals Extension of Jurisdiction (England and Wales) Order 1994, as a result of which a claim for damages for breach of contract by failing to give the required notice can now be brought before an employment tribunal. Now a claimant would have a choice of whichever was the more advantageous.

The employee must bring the claim within three months of the dismissal if the claim is to a tribunal. If the claim is brought in court then, because it is a breach of contract action, the claimant has six years in which to bring the claim.

21.4 Remedies for wrongful dismissal

Unlike unfair dismissal (see 22.7 below) there are no remedies of reinstatement or re-engagement in wrongful dismissal since it is essentially a breach of contract action. Because of the reluctance of the courts to use other contractual remedies in contracts of personal service the main remedy is damages.

Damages

The amount of damages payable in a claim for wrongful dismissal is generally restricted to the amount of pay which would have been earned during the notice period the employee was entitled to or if it involves a fixed-term contract then this will be the pay for the remainder of the fixed term unless the contract allowed the parties to terminate before the end of the fixed term. In this case damages will be limited to whatever notice period was identified in the contract.

Sums that may also be included are any commission and overtime payments that would have been contractually due to be earned during the notice period. Loss of pension rights can also be calculated because a pension counts as wages.

CASE EXAMPLE

Silvey v Pendragon plc [2001] EWCA Civ 784; [2001] IRLR 685

The claimant following a transfer of the business was made redundant with immediate effect and paid redundancy pay and twelve weeks' pay in lieu of notice. He became fifty-five only twelve days after the date of the redundancy letter and if he had still been in employment until then, he would have been entitled to accrued pension rights which would have amounted to £5,788.57 more than he actually received. He made a number of claims in the tribunal including a breach of contract claim for his lost pension entitlement. The tribunal acknowledged that there was a breach of contract but did not accept the claim for pension rights. The Court of Appeal held that the defendant had indeed breached its contract and that the lost pension rights were a loss that was recoverable.

JUDGMENT

Clarke LJ explained: 'the letter of 6th November 1997 was a repudiatory breach of the contract because the respondent was not entitled to bring the appellant's contract of employment to an end without giving him 12 weeks' notice'. He also concluded: 'it was indeed not unlikely that, if a breach such as occurred here did occur, the appellant employee would lose significant pension rights as a result of the contract of employment terminating before his 55th birthday. The type or kind of loss was well within the reasonable contemplation of the parties, namely loss of pension rights … this loss was not too remote in law to be recoverable.'

The value of fringe benefits such as the use of a company car for private purposes can be claimed to the extent that these relate to the notice period which should have been given.

The claim also can include the value of any rights to which the employee would have become entitled if the termination had been delayed until the end of a notice period. Subsidised mortgages, share options, private medical insurance can all be quantified and form part of the award of damages.

It is also possible in limited circumstances that the contract envisages a greater reward than basic salary by way of publicity and damages can reflect this with an award for loss of reputation arising from the breach of contract.

CASE EXAMPLE

Marbe v George Edwards (Daly's Theatres) Ltd [1928] 1 KB 269

An American actress was contracted to perform in a play in London with the promise of full publicity for her role. When she was wrongfully prevented from taking part in the play she claimed wrongful dismissal. The court awarded damages which not only included her salary for the period of her contract but also an amount for loss of reputation. The Court of Appeal also took the same view.

JUDGMENT

Bankes LJ explained why: 'In my opinion it is sufficiently established that where there has been a breach of a contract to employ an actress, whose reputation depends on the continued and successful practice of her art, and where the engagement is accompanied by promises of widespread publicity and advertisement which will probably lead to future opportunities following on successful performance, the Court recognizes that the damages for that breach may properly include such a sum as a jury may award to compensate the plaintiff for the loss of the reputation which would have been acquired, or damage to reputation already acquired, or, to use another expression, for loss of publicity.'

The same principle applied in *Herbert Clayton & Jack Waller Ltd v Oliver* [1930] AC 209 (see Chapter 7.2.2) where an actor who had been given a leading role was then placed in a minor role in the production. The employer was held to have breached the contract because of the potential impact on the actor's reputation and future chances of work and the actor was awarded damages for the loss of opportunity that would result from his lowered reputation. It is unlikely, however, that this would occur other than in entertainment.

However, the courts will not award any damages in respect of the manner of the dismissal. So for instance there can be no general claim for injured reputation beyond the limited circumstances above.

CASE EXAMPLE

Addis v Gramophone Co Ltd [1909] AC 488

A manager was dismissed from his post and his employer had replaced him with a new manager even before he left. He claimed for wrongful dismissal and also sought damages for the humiliation and distress caused by the manner of his exit from the business. The House of Lords accepted his claim for wrongful dismissal but refused his claim for damages for injury to his reputation caused by the improper dismissal and also for the mental distress caused by the humiliating manner of his dismissal. The court held that he could recover only for the loss of salary and commission owed.

JUDGMENT

Lord Loreburn LC commented: 'If there be a dismissal without notice the employer must pay an indemnity; but that indemnity cannot include compensation either for the injured feelings of the servant, or for the loss he may sustain from the fact that his having been dismissed of itself makes it more difficult for him to obtain fresh employment.' Lord Atkinson added: 'In many other cases of breach of contract there may be circumstances of malice, fraud, defamation, or violence, which would sustain an action of tort as an alternative remedy to an action for breach of contract. If one should select the former mode of redress, he may, no doubt, recover exemplary damages, or what is sometimes styled vindictive damages; but if he should choose to seek redress in the form of an action for breach of contract, he lets in all the consequences of that form of action.... One of these consequences is ... that he is to be paid adequate compensation in money for the loss of that which he would have received had his contract been kept, and no more.'

As a development of this it has also been established that unfairness in the manner of the dismissal cannot form the basis of an action in either contract or tort.

CASE EXAMPLE

Johnson v Unisys Ltd [2001] UKHL 13; [2001] IRLR 279

The claimant was a director who had been employed by the company for twenty years and over a period of time suffered stress. He was summarily dismissed in breach of the company's disciplinary procedure following some vague allegations of misconduct and developed a severe psychiatric illness as a result. He claimed unfair dismissal and a breach of the implied term of mutual trust and confidence. The issue was whether he should be awarded in excess of the then limit for unfair dismissal claims of £11,000 since the claimant was arguing that the unfair manner of his dismissal had caused him financial loss. The House of Lords (now the Supreme Court) accepted his claim for unfair dismissal but held that to create a parallel right to damages in excess of the limit would be to go against Parliament's clear intentions.

However, a somewhat different view has subsequently been taken.

CASE EXAMPLE

Eastwood v Magnox Electric plc; McCabe v Cornwall CC [2004] IRLR 733

This involved joined appeals where both appellants had been dismissed following lengthy but flawed disciplinary procedures. Eastwood had successfully claimed unfair dismissal resulting from a grudge against him by his manager, the procedure leading up to the dismissal having taken an astonishing ten months. McCabe was a teacher who had been accused of improper behaviour with young female pupils. In this case the disciplinary process leading to dismissal even more astonishingly had taken more than two years to complete. Both claimants also claimed damages for breach of contract and negligence. The then House of Lords held that Eastwood's appeal succeeded but that McCabe's was dismissed. The House held that the cause of action in common law accrued before any dismissals occurred and suggested that *Johnson v Unisys* should be reconsidered.

As with any contractual claim for damages an employee bringing an action for wrongful dismissal has a duty to take reasonable steps to mitigate his loss. In this case that will involve taking reasonable steps to find comparable work. This does not necessarily mean that the employee must accept any work regardless of how suitable or comparable. Although after a reasonable time the employee may have to be less selective. A refusal by the employee to accept other work may be unreasonable in the circumstances. In *Brace v Calder* [1895] 2 QB 253 following changes in the organisation of a partnership one of the partners was dismissed but then asked back by the new partners. When he refused he was only then entitled to nominal damages since he had failed to mitigate his loss. In contrast in *Yetton v Eastwood Froy Ltd* [1967] 1 WLR 104 a managing director was offered the position of assistant manager following his dismissal and it was held that this was a significant demotion so that his refusal to accept was not unreasonable.

The award of damages takes into account the tax and other contributions that the employee would have paid but under sections 401–404 Income Tax (Earnings and Pensions) Act 2003 the damages are not taxed unless they are more than £30,000.

Injunctions

The courts are reluctant to directly or indirectly enforce a contract of employment, sometimes referred to as the 'rule against enforcement', as the relationship is a highly personal one.

CASE EXAMPLE

De Francesco v Barnum [1890] 45 Ch D 430

A contract of apprenticeship was very disadvantageous to a young dancer who was contractually bound by it. She got no payment under the contract and one clause prevented her from taking up any paid employment without express approval of the apprentice master. The girl then gained other work and the claimant's action to prevent it failed. The provisions of the apprenticeship deed were held to be unfair and unenforceable against her.

There are, however, some exceptions to the rule against enforcement:

- It is possible for a negative restraint clause to be included in a contract which a court will enforce where the employee has promised under the contract not to do certain things.

CASE EXAMPLE

Lumley v Wagner [1852] 42 ER 687

An opera singer had entered into a contract that contained an express stipulation that during the three months that the contract was to run she would not take up work with any other theatre. She did then in fact enter another contract which was to run simultaneously with her existing contract. She was successfully restrained from doing so by grant of the injunction. The court was content that given the brief duration of the contract it in no way interfered with her general ability to earn a living and as such was a reasonable and enforceable covenant in all the circumstances.

- It is also possible that an injunction may be granted in circumstances where damages are an inadequate remedy following to the rule in *Hill v Parsons*.

CASE EXAMPLE

Hill v CA Parsons & Co Ltd [1972] Ch 305

The claimant's employer had reached a 'closed shop' agreement with a recognised trade union (where all employees must belong to the union). The employer then wrote to the claimant, who refused to join the union, and gave him one month's notice of his dismissal. The claimant had thirty-five years' service as a senior engineer. He also had only two years left until his retirement and the dismissal would have an inevitable detrimental effect on his pension rights so he sought an injunction to lengthen the period of notice. The Court of Appeal allowed the injunction and extended the notice period to six months which it felt was a reasonable period. It also identified that the rule against enforcement was a rule of fact not of law. As a result it could be subject to exceptions for example where damages was an inadequate remedy as it was in the present case.

> The remedy is of course equitable and therefore is the discretion of the court. One of the problems that judges have to consider in allowing injunctions in employment matters is that they are similar in effect to specific performance.

CASE EXAMPLE

Anderson v Pringle Of Scotland Ltd [1998] IRLR 64

The contract of employment as a result of a collective agreement indicated that in any redundancy exercise the employer would operate a last in first out (LIFO) criteria for selection. The employer was trying to implement different criteria and the employee complained. The court granted an injunction to restrain the employer from using different criteria to those in the contract.

Is the employee of a type likely to claim wrongful dismissal?
- The employee was on a fixed term contract and was dismissed before the end of the fixed term of employment;
- The employee was very highly paid so that damages may exceed the maximum award for unfair dismissal
- The employee is excluded from claiming unfair dismissal

YES

Is the dismissal a breach of contract giving rise to a claim for damages?
- the employee was dismissed without the appropriate notice period being given (in effect this is a summary dismissal that cannot be justified)
- the employee was employed under a fixed-term contract which was terminated before the expiry of the fixed term
- the employee was employed under a contract which stipulated the only circumstances under which a dismissal could occur and the employer dismissed the employee for some other reason.

YES

A CLAIM FOR WRONGFUL DISMISSAL MAY BE POSSIBLE

Figure 21.1 Flow chart illustrating the necessary elements for a claim for wrongful dismissal

ACTIVITY

Self-assessment questions

1. Why was an action for wrongful dismissal significant before 1971?
2. What type of action is wrongful dismissal?
3. What are the only circumstances in which a claim for wrongful dismissal can be made?
4. What types of employees might benefit from such a claim?
5. For what is an employee entitled to claim following a successful claim of wrongful dismissal?
6. In what ways should an employee mitigate his loss?
7. Why was *Addis v The Gramophone Company* decided as it was?
8. Why are injunctions rarely granted?

KEY FACTS

The nature of wrongful dismissal	Case/statute
A common law action arising only if • the employer terminates the contract without notice or without the appropriate notice • the employee works under a fixed-term contract which is terminated before the end of the term • the employee works under a contract which stipulates the only grounds for dismissal and the employer dismisses him for another reason The claim is for breach of contract only so the claim is for damages only other remedies are not available or damages that are not restricted to the breach It is now possible to claim wrongful dismissal in a tribunal since Such a claim is only really useful to three groups • those on a fixed-term contract who are dismissed within the term – and who can claim the wages for the remaining time • highly paid employees e.g. executive directors – whose claim would exceed the maximum compensatory award for unfair dismissal • those excluded from claiming unfair dismissal or without sufficient continuous employment – who would be unable to bring a claim for unfair dismissal	*Addis v The Gramophone Company* *Employment Tribunals Extension of Jurisdiction Order 1994*
Bringing an action for wrongful dismissal	Case/statute
• A claim for damages for breach of contract by failing to give the required notice or for terminating a fixed-term contract before the end of the term can now be brought before an employment tribunal • Unlike the basic principle in contract law where the party who is the victim of a repudiatory breach can choose to continue with the contract with wrongful dismissal an employee who suffers a repudiatory breach has no choice but than to accept the breach and sue for damages	*Employment Tribunals Extension of Jurisdiction (England and Wales) Order 1994* *De Francesco v Barnum*

Remedies for wrongful dismissal	Case/statute
Damages:	
<ul><li>could be for any sum that is contractually due</li><li>if greater reward envisaged in contract then will cover that too</li><li>but damages are generally not recoverable for loss of reputation</li><li>and it has been held that the manner of the dismissal cannot form an action in contract or tort</li><li>as with all contract claims the employee is bound to mitigate his loss</li><li>award of damages takes into account the tax and other contributions</li></ul>	*Silvey v Pendragon plc* *Marbe v George Edwards (Daly's Theatres) Ltd* *Addis v Gramophone Co Ltd* *Johnson v Unisys Ltd* *Brace v Calder* *SS401–404 Income Tax (Earnings and Pensions) Act 2003*
Injunctions	
<ul><li>the rule against enforcement usually applies – the court will not directly or indirectly enforce a contract of employment</li></ul>	*De Francesco v Barnum*
Exceptions to the rule are	
<ul><li>a negative restraint – where the court can restrain the employee from doing something he is contractually bound not to do</li><li>where damages are an inadequate remedy</li><li>the remedy is at the discretion of the court</li></ul>	*Lumley v Wagner* *Hill v CA Parsons & Co Ltd* *Anderson v Pringle Of Scotland Ltd*

SAMPLE ESSAY QUESTION

ESSAY Discuss the extent to which an action for wrongful dismissal is still relevant after the introduction of unfair dismissal.

Explain what wrongful dismissal is

- A common law action.
- Where the employer has dismissed the employee with insufficient notice.

Explain the circumstances in which a wrongful dismissal may arise

- The employer terminates the contract without notice or without the appropriate notice.

- The employee works under a fixed term contract which is terminated before the end of the term.
- The employee works under a contract which stipulates the only grounds for dismissal and the employer dismisses him for another reason.

Discuss the limitations of the action

- The claim is for breach of contract only so the claim is for damages only.
- Other remedies are not available.
- Nor are damages that are not restricted to the breach.
- Injunctions rarely possible.
- Unlike contract law generally the employee who is the victim of a repudiatory breach cannot choose to continue with the contract but has no choice but than to accept the breach and sue for damages.

Discuss who is likely to benefit from a claim for wrongful dismissal

- Those on a fixed term contract who are dismissed within the term – and who can claim the wages for the remaining time.
- Highly paid employees e.g. executive directors – whose claim would exceed the maximum compensatory award for unfair dismissal.
- Those excluded from claiming unfair dismissal or without sufficient continuous employment – which would be unable to bring a claim for unfair dismissal.

Consider whether the action is still relevant since it applies to so few people

- May be useful to those on fixed term contracts but possibly have better protection now under statute.
- Would provide a limited remedy to those not eligible for unfair dismissal.
- So most relevant to high paid employees.

REACH ANY SENSIBLE CONCLUSION

SUMMARY

■ Wrongful dismissal is a common law action for breach of contract.

■ It occurs when an employer terminates the contract without notice or without the appropriate notice; or where he terminates a fixed-term contract before the end of the term; or where the contract stipulates the only grounds for dismissal and the employer dismisses for another reason.

■ Unlike the normal contractual rule on repudiatory breach the employee has no choice but than to accept the breach and claim for damages.

■ The action is only really useful to three groups of employees: those on a fixed-term contract who are dismissed within the term, and who can claim the wages for the remainder of the term; highly paid employees such as executive directors, whose claim would exceed the maximum compensatory award for unfair dismissal; those excluded from claiming unfair dismissal or without sufficient continuous employment, who otherwise would have no claim.

■ Such a claim is for what is due for the notice period or the remainder of a fixed-term contract and unlike with normal contract law principles an employee who suffers a repudiatory breach by wrongful dismissal has no choice but than to accept the breach and sue for damages.

■ Damages is for any sum that is contractually due or a greater reward if envisaged in the contract but damages are generally not recoverable for loss of reputation and an employee is bound to mitigate his loss and an award of damages takes into account tax and other contributions.

■ Injunctions are rarely granted because they would in effect enforce the contract but they may be granted where a negative restraint prevents the employee from breaking a promise and where damages would be an inadequate remedy.

Further reading

Emir, Astra, *Selwyn's Law of Employment 17th edition*. Oxford University Press, 2012, Chapter 16.

Pitt, Gwyneth, *Cases and Materials on Employment Law 3rd edition*. Pearson, 2008, Chapter 8, pp. 339–360.

Sargeant, Malcolm and Lewis, David, *Employment Law 6th edition*. Pearson, 2012, Chapter 4.3.

22

Termination of employment (4) unfair dismissal

AIMS AND OBJECTIVES

After reading this chapter you should be able to:

- Understand the basis behind unfair dismissal
- Understand who will be eligible for unfair dismissal purposes and who is excluded
- Understand the situations when a dismissal is automatically unfair
- Understand the potentially fair reasons for dismissing an employee
- Understand what is meant by and the significance of the term 'the band of reasonable responses'
- Understand the significance of the ACAS Code and the requirements of compliance with procedural guidelines
- Understand how the remedy afforded to a successful applicant will be determined
- Understand the considerations that determine the amount of any compensation awarded and in what circumstances a tribunal may choose to limit or reduce the basic or compensatory award made to a successful applicant
- Understand what the time limit is for submitting a claim and when that time limit will be relaxed
- Critically analyse the area of unfair dismissal
- Apply the unfair dismissal checklist to factual situations in order to determine whether a claim for unfair dismissal may succeed

22.1 The origins, aims and character of unfair dismissal law

Prior to 1971 the only real course to an employee who had been dismissed if he wished to challenge it was through the old common law action of wrongful dismissal (see Chapter 21). In effect the employer could dismiss an employee for no reason. The law on dismissals at that time reflected the old 'master and servant' rules (see Chapter 1.4.1) and the action for wrongful dismissal provided no possibility of enquiring into the fairness of the dismissal. Wrongful dismissal was based purely on form rather than fairness, whether the employer had dismissed the employee without giving the appropriate notice under the contract or by dismissing him he had prevented him from completing the remainder of a fixed-term contract. Inevitably the remedy for wrongful dismissal was very limited also since it only related to the breach of contract so damages would be restricted to the amount that should have been paid during the notice period. For most employees this would be a small sum only.

Unfair dismissal is a concept that was created in the Industrial Relations Act 1971. This Act was later repealed since it had more to do with the statutory regulation of industrial relations, and had its own court for enforcement. However, the provisions on unfair dismissal were later also inserted in the Employment Protection (Consolidation) Act 1978, and later still in the Employment Rights Act 1996 (as amended).

The original purpose of the rules on unfair dismissal was to detail in statutory form the situations in which a dismissal could be classed as unfair and therefore meriting a remedy, and in turn to discourage unfair dismissals.

There are a number of key aspects to a claim for unfair dismissal which must be demonstrated:

- The person claiming unfair dismissal must be an employee.
- There must have been a dismissal (which is defined in the Act).
- The person claiming must be eligible (which includes the appropriate period of continuous employment – although there are exceptions where continuity is not required).
- It must be decided whether the dismissal is one which is identified as an automatically unfair dismissal.
- If not it must be decided if the dismissal is of a class which is considered potentially fair.
- If the dismissal is for a potentially fair reason then it must be established that it was fair in fact according to the reasonable range of responses test.
- It must then be considered whether the dismissal was carried out according to fair procedures following the ACAS Code.
- Finally the appropriate remedy should be decided – if this is damages then the amount of the award should be calculated.

If employment status is a concern, the tests for establishing employee status are those that have been covered in Chapter 4.3.

As we have seen in Chapter 19.3.1 the only circumstances in which an employee is entitled to consider that he has been dismissed are the three identified in section 95(1) Employment Rights Act 1996.

SECTION

'95 Circumstances in which an employee is dismissed.

(1) For the purposes of this Part an employee is dismissed by his employer if (and, subject to subsection (2) only if) –

    (a) the contract under which he is employed is terminated by the employer (whether with or without notice),

    (b) he is employed under a limited-term contract and that contract terminates by virtue of the limiting event without being renewed under the same contract, or

    (c) the employee terminates the contract under which he is employed (with or without notice) in circumstances in which he is entitled to terminate it without notice by reason of the employer's conduct.'

These have been considered separately in Chapter 19 and a dismissal is clearly one of three things:

■ The employer actually dismisses the employee whether he gives him notice or not.

■ The employer fails to renew a contract that is limited.

■ The employee claims constructive dismissal – that is the employee actually resigns but because the employer has breached a fundamental term of the contract.

If there is a dismissal of an employee the next step is to establish that he is eligible to claim.

22.2 Eligibility

The basic right to a claim for unfair dismissal arises from the fundamental right in section 94 Employment Rights Act 1996.

SECTION

> '94 The right.
> (1) An employee has the right not to be unfairly dismissed by his employer.'

The section refers to any employee so in order to bring a claim a person must first be able to class himself as an employee (see Chapter 4.3). However, there are also a number of classes of employee who are excluded from the provisions and therefore ineligible to make such a claim. These include:

■ share fishermen (these are the crew of fishing ships who take pay as a share of the profits from the catch);

■ members of the police force (by section 200 Employment Rights Act 1996);

■ agreed exemptions authorised by the Secretary of State, e.g. in collective agreements with trade unions operating in substitution of the statutory scheme;

■ where there is an agreement to place the dispute under arbitration instead of under a scheme prepared by ACAS;

■ employees engaged in industrial action, providing that all of the workers are dismissed and none is taken back within three months;

■ employees working under an illegal contract – the general rule is that the courts will not enforce an illegal contract. The issue is what effect this may have on a claim for unfair dismissal. In some situations the courts are prepared to overlook the illegality.

CASE EXAMPLE

Hewcastle Catering Ltd v Ahmed and Elkamah [1991] IRLR 473

A number of employees cooperated with HMRC in relation to fraudulent VAT receipts on customers' bills. The employer was then prosecuted and the employees were dismissed. They had participated in the fraud but only the employer had benefited from it. The Court of Appeal felt that it would be wrong to allow the employer to use the argument of illegality which would then have meant that the unfair dismissal claim would fail.

A similar position is taken where the illegality is not causally connected to the claim.

CASE EXAMPLE

Hall v Woolston Hall Leisure Ltd [2001] 1 WLR 225

The dismissal was because of pregnancy so the claimant brought her action under the Sex Discrimination Act 1975. The contract was tainted with illegality because she knew that after she had been promoted part of her salary was paid without proper deductions for tax and NI. The Court of Appeal held that her acquiescence over the illegality was not fatal to her claim since it was not causally linked to the sex discrimination so it did not prevent her from gaining compensation.

- Traditionally employees reaching their normal retirement age under the contract of employment, or sixty-five if none exists, were also excluded from claiming (except where this would be discriminatory) – but from 1 October 2006 following the Employment Equality (Age) Regulations there are no such age limits to a claim.

Continuous service

There is also a limitation based on the employee having more than two years' continuous service at the time of the dismissal without which an employee is not eligible to claim. This qualifying period has been variously as little as six months and as much as two years. The current government returned the period to two years from April 2012.

The previous Labour government had returned the qualifying period from two years to one year. It seems therefore that there is a possible political motivation to the qualifying period of continuous service. It would in any case be possible to argue that it is both unnecessary for employers and unfair to employees. An employer already has very broad grounds for dismissing an employee fairly (see Chapter 22.4). This includes the very broad 'any other substantial reason' which will often be an economic, technical or organisational reason. There seems to be little justification for the employer to have an extra period of two years where the employee can be dismissed with no reason. When considered against the relative insecurity of the employee who may have left a secure job and then has two years with no job security unless he is dismissed for an automatically unfair reason seems to make unfair dismissal a very limited employment protection.

It is interesting to note that if the decision in *R v Secretary of State for Employment ex parte Seymour-Smith and Perez* [2000] IRLR 263 had been different then the qualifying period would have had to be abandoned entirely. Women had complained that the period, which was two years at the time, discriminated against them because more women than men would fall within the period because of child care. The ECJ held that it was potentially discriminatory. The House of Lords accepted that the statistics showed a greater proportion of women would fall within the period but insufficient to amount to actual discrimination.

In the following instances the two year qualification period does not apply:

- The dismissal is for legitimate trade union activities, for acting as an employee representative, or for membership or non-membership of a trade union.
- The dismissal is for asserting any Health and Safety provision.
- The dismissal is related to pregnancy, childbirth, maternity, maternity leave, parental leave or dependant care leave.
- The dismissal is discriminatory.
- The dismissal is of a protected shop worker or betting office worker refusing to work on a Sunday.
- The dismissal is for a refusal to work hours in excess of those required under the Working Time Regulations.
- The dismissal relates to performing functions as a trustee of a pension scheme.

- The dismissal relates to making a protected disclosure ('whistle blowing') under the Public Interest Disclosure Act 1998.
- The dismissal is for exercising a right under the National Minimum Wage Act 1998.
- The dismissal is for exercising a right under the EU Works Council Directive.
- The dismissal is for exercising a right under the Part-time Workers (Prevention of Less Favourable Treatment) Regulations 2000 or the Fixed-term Employees (Prevention of Less Favourable Treatment) Regulations 2002.
- The dismissal relates to spent offences – where disclosure is not required after the prescribed period under the Rehabilitation of Offenders Act 1974 (although there are exceptions in sensitive occupations).
- Dismissals following TUPE transfers (under the Transfer of Undertakings (Protection of Employment) Regulations 2006 – which developed out of the original EU Acquired Rights Directive).
- The dismissal relates to a demand for flexible working.
- The dismissal amounts to an unfair selection for redundancy for any of the above reasons – guided by extensive rules.
- The dismissal is on medical grounds (here the qualifying period is only one month – s108(2) ERA 1996).
- The dismissal is for asserting a statutory right.

22.3 Dismissals classed as automatically unfair

Certain dismissals will always be regarded as unfair: these are referred to as automatically unfair dismissals. Generally if an employer dismisses an employee for asserting or trying to exercise one of their statutory employment rights then it will be regarded as an automatically unfairly dismissal.

Employees enjoy a variety of statutory rights which include:

- The right to a written statement of employment particulars (the s1 statement or statutory statement (see Chapter 5).
- The right to an itemised pay statement.
- The right not to be subjected to unlawful deductions from wages.
- The right to guarantee payments when work is not available.
- The right to a minimum notice period if the contract is silent.
- Rights to maternity, paternity or adoption leave, time off for antenatal care, parental leave and dependant care leave, as well as the right to request flexible working arrangements and for the request to be considered.
- The right not to be discriminated against because of gender, race, disability, religion or belief, sexual orientation or age.
- The right to time off for public duties (e.g. jury service).
- The right to remuneration during suspension on medical grounds.
- The right in shop or betting work not to have to work on a Sunday.
- The right to 'whistle blow' (make a public interest disclosure).

A worker is allowed to assert all of these rights.

There are a number of situations where a dismissal will be regarded as automatically unfair.

A dismissal relating to trade union membership, non-membership or activities

Under section 152 of the Trade Union and Labour Relations (Consolidation) Act 1992 a dismissal for legitimate trade union membership, non-membership or activities is automatically unfair. Trade union membership and non-membership is a protectable right so an employee cannot be dismissed for membership of a union. In *Discount Tobacco & Confectionary Ltd v Armitage* [1995] ICR 431 a woman sought help from her union during a dispute over pay and conditions and was dismissed as a result. It was held that the reason for her dismissal was her trade union membership and so the dismissal was unfair automatically. It could include legitimate activities such as accompanying an employee at a disciplinary or grievance hearing. However, this would not include unofficial activities.

Dismissal during an industrial dispute

Under section 238A Trade Union and Labour Relations (Consolidation) Act 1992 certain industrial action is protected and a dismissal could be automatically unfair. A dismissal for taking part in unlawful industrial action could be fair as long as the employer treats all employees engaged in the industrial action the same. Otherwise where there is unequal treatment under sections 237–239 Trade Union and Labour Relations (Consolidation) Act 1992 the dismissal would be automatically unfair.

A dismissal in connection with the statutory recognition or derecognition of a trade union

This is also under the Trade Union and Labour Relations (Consolidation) Act 1992.

Unfair selection for redundancy

Under section 105 Employment Rights Act 1996 an unfair selection for redundancy is an automatically unfair dismissal.

A dismissal on a Transfer of Undertakings

Where an employee is protected under TUPE (see Chapter 18) and is dismissed by either the old or the new employer because of the transfer, or a reason connected with it, then the dismissal will be automatically unfair. In *Litster v Forth Dry Dock & Engineering Co Ltd* [1990] 1 AC 546 the liquidator of an insolvent business dismissed the workforce one hour before he sold it. The dismissals were held to be unfair and the liability to pay incurred by the liquidator was passed on to the new owner. The only exception to this would be if either employer could show that the dismissal was for an economic, technical or organisational reason. In *Meikle v McPhail* [1983] IRLR 351 a pub was taken over and the new owner decided that major economic savings were essential and dismissed a barmaid. The dismissal was held to be an ETO reason and necessary and fair in the circumstances so the dismissal was fair.

Dismissal on the grounds of pregnancy or maternity or parental rights

Under section 98 Employment Rights Act 1996 a dismissal for any reason connected to pregnancy is automatically unfair. This could include any reason connected with the employee's pregnancy, a dismissal during the ordinary or additional maternity leave, because the employee has taken, or wants to take, ordinary or additional maternity leave, or dismissal resulting from a suspension from work because of health and safety, or if the employee returned back to work late from maternity leave because the employer did not properly tell the employee when the leave ended, or gave the employee less than twenty-eight days' notice of the end date of the maternity leave and it was not practical for the employee to return to work.

Also covered is adoption leave, parental leave, paternity leave, time off to look after dependants. These are all under separate Regulations (see Chapter 8.5).

A dismissal in connection with a request for a flexible working arrangement

This falls under section 104C Employment Rights Act 1996.

A dismissal for any Health and Safety at Work related reason

Under Section 100 Employment Rights Act 1996 any dismissal for a reason related to health and safety is automatically unfair. This could include:

- carrying out activities in the role of health and safety representative to reduce risks to health and safety;
- performing or trying to perform duties as an official or employer-recognised health and safety representative or committee member;
- bringing a concern about health or safety in the workplace to the employer's attention;
- leaving, proposing to leave or refusing to return to the workplace (or any dangerous part of it) where there is a serious and imminent danger which cannot be prevented;
- the employee taking or trying to take the appropriate steps to protect himself or other people from a serious and imminent danger;
- it also includes where the employee has refused an order that would put himself, fellow workers and other persons at risk.

CASE EXAMPLE

Masiak v City Restaurants (UK) Ltd (1999) IRLR 780

The claimant was a chef who refused to cook a chicken which he believed was not thoroughly enough defrosted and therefore constituted a potential health hazard to the restaurant's customers. He successfully claimed unfair dismissal under the provision in section 100. Reversing the tribunal decision the EAT held that 'Other people' in the section could include customers of the employer.

A dismissal for exercising a right under the Public Interest Disclosure Act 1998

This is sometimes referred to as 'whistle blowing' and a dismissal because of this would be automatically unfair under section 103A Employment Rights Act 1996.

A dismissal that is discriminatory

This includes discrimination on gender, race, disability and more recently on sexual orientation, gender reassignment, religion or belief and age.

A dismissal of certain protected shop workers for refusal to work on Sundays

This falls under section 101 Employment Rights Act 1996.

A dismissal following the exercise of a right under the National Minimum Wage Act 1998

This falls under section 104A Employment Rights Act 1996. It could cover:

- a dismissal because the employee is qualifying, or is about to qualify, to be paid the National Minimum Wage;
- a dismissal because the employee is insisting on the right to be paid at least the National Minimum Wage;
- a dismissal because the employee reports the employer for not paying the National Minimum Wage.

A dismissal relating to the Working Time Regulations

This falls under section 101A Employment Rights Act 1996. The dismissal might result from the employee refusing to break his working time rights, or refusing to give up a working time right, or refusing to sign a workforce agreement that impacts upon working time rights.

A dismissal because the employee performs duties as a trustee of an occupational pension fund

An employee who is an occupational pension fund trustee has the right to reasonable paid time off for those duties. Dismissal for being a trustee of an occupational pension scheme is automatically unfair under section 102 Employment Rights Act 1996.

Dismissal relating to activities as an employee representative

Dismissal for being an employee representative falls under section 103 Employment Rights Act. An employee representative cannot be fairly dismissed for being an employee representative, or for carrying out duties as a European Works Council representative, or a member of a special negotiating body, or an information and consultation representative, or for consulting with the employer about redundancies or business transfers.

A dismissal for exercising rights under the Part-time Workers (Prevention of Less Favourable Treatment) Regulations 2000

A part-time worker should not be treated less favourably than a full-time employee. So the part-time employee should have the same or equivalent employment rights and benefits. Under the Regulations being dismissed for being part time, making a complaint about being treated less favourably than a full-time employee or giving evidence in another part-time employee's claim is automatically unfair.

A dismissal for exercising rights under the Fixed-term Employees (Prevention of Less Favourable Treatment) Regulations 2002

A fixed-term employee should not be treated less favourably than a permanent employee. So the fixed-term employee should have the same or equivalent employment rights and benefits. Under the Regulations being dismissed for being part time, making a complaint about being treated less favourably than a permanent employee or giving evidence in another fixed-term employee's claim is automatically unfair.

A dismissal relating to tax credits

Under section 104B Employment Rights Act 1996 a dismissal for taking action in respect of a tax credit is automatically unfair.

A dismissal in connection with disciplinary or grievance hearings

Under the Employment Relations Act 1999 an employee has the right to be accompanied by a trade union representative or a colleague to a disciplinary or grievance meeting. The employee could also reasonably postpone the hearing if the representative is unable to attend. A dismissal for trying to exercise these rights or for accompanying a colleague is automatically unfair.

A dismissal for asserting a statutory right

This falls under section 104 Employment Rights Act 1996.

22.4 Dismissals classed as potentially fair

The law sensibly recognises that an employer must have the right to dismiss employees in appropriate circumstances. Two points need to be made:

- There are only a limited number of recognised reasons where the law accepts that an employer may need to dismiss employees and these are identified as potentially fair reasons for dismissal.

- However, the fact that the dismissal can be categorised as potentially fair does not make it automatically fair, it has to be fair in fact so the employer will still need to justify the dismissal in law when a claim is made.

Once the employee has proved that the termination of the contract amounted to a dismissal and that he is eligible to pursue a claim the burden then shifts and it is for the employer to show:

- what the actual reason for the dismissal was;

- that the reason for the dismissal is one that the Employment Rights Act 1996 accepts as potentially fair, in other words it is a reason which is prima facie fair;

- that it was fair in fact.

The potentially fair reasons for dismissal are all identified in section 98 Employment Rights Act 1996.

SECTION

'98.

(1) In determining for the purposes of this Part of the statute, entitled "Unfair Dismissal" whether the dismissal of an employee was fair or unfair, it shall be for the employer to show –
  (a) the reason (or, if there was more than one, the principal reason) for the dismissal, and
  (b) that it is either a reason falling within subsection (2) or some other substantial reason of a kind such as to justify the dismissal of an employee holding the position which that employee held.

(2) A reason falls within this subsection if it –
  (a) relates to the capability or qualifications of the employee for performing work of the kind which he was employed by the employer to do, or
  (b) relates to the conduct of the employee, or
  (c) is that the employee was redundant, or
  (d) is that the employee could not continue to work in the position which he held without contravention (either on his part or on that of his employer) of a duty or restriction imposed by or under an enactment.'

So there are in effect five reasons, although even within the broad categories they can be broken down into other sub-categories.

- capability and qualifications;
- misconduct;
- a fair selection under a genuine redundancy scheme;
- a dismissal because of a statutory restriction;
- any other substantial reason (this is obviously the one which gives employers most flexibility to dismiss).

22.4.1 Capability and qualifications

Both capability and qualifications under section 98(2)(a) are defined later in section 98(3).

SECTION

'98.
(3) In subsection (2)(a) –
   (a) "capability", in relation to an employee, means capability assessed by reference to skill, aptitude, health or any other physical or mental quality, and
   (b) "qualifications", in relation to an employee, means any degree, diploma or other academic, technical or professional qualification relevant to the position which he held.'

Capability

So capability falls into two main aspects:

- skill and aptitude;
- absence through ill health or other persistent absence.

Skill and aptitude itself could divide into incompetence and neglect or poor performance. It is perfectly possible to dismiss on the basis of incompetence which would usually result from a series of incidents or poor performance. However, it could even involve summary dismissal for a single incident if the consequences of the incompetence are sufficiently serious.

CASE EXAMPLE

Taylor v Alidair Ltd [1978] IRLR 82

A pilot through his incompetence landed a plane very dangerously causing a risk to the lives of the passengers who in any case were caused great distress. He was subsequently dismissed after an investigation on lack of capability and he claimed unfair dismissal. The Court of Appeal held that even a small departure from expected high standards might justify dismissal in certain cases because of the potential consequences of not dismissing.

What the employer should clearly do where there is an issue of incompetence or poor performance is to support the employee to improve performance and the employee should of course be aware that their performance is lacking. It is also difficult to successfully argue that an employee is incompetent if the employee has not been adequately trained how to do the work.

CASE EXAMPLE

Davison v Kent Meters Ltd [1975] IRLR 145

An assembly worker was dismissed for lack of capability having wrongly assembled 500 components. She argued that she had been unfairly dismissed because she had only followed the process shown her by her supervisor. In countering this claim the supervisor stated that he had in fact never shown the claimant how to assemble the components. The court held that in the circumstances the dismissal was unfair. The evidence of the supervisor indicated that in reality the employee had never received proper instruction or training in assembling the components and she could not be held to be incapable without adequate instruction.

In reaching a decision to dismiss for lack of capability the employer should also have identified the employee's incompetence and carried through every necessary procedural step. This could of course include warnings about performance. The ultimate question here is whether warnings did or would have made any difference to the employee's performance. In *Lowndes v Specialist Heavy Engineering Ltd* [1976] IRLR 246 the employee was dismissed after making five very serious and very costly errors in his work. No warnings were given but the court still held that the dismissal was fair because it was felt that warnings would have made no difference in the circumstances.

The employer should obviously consider whether there are any alternatives to a dismissal. Ultimately, however, the employer is entitled to consider his business needs. Whether the dismissal is fair or unfair will depend on the individual circumstances in each case.

CASE EXAMPLE

Bevan Harris Ltd v Gair [1981] IRLR 520

A foreman who had given eleven years' service was eventually dismissed after consistently poor performance and four warnings. He claimed unfair dismissal. The tribunal initially upheld his claim on the basis that the employer should have considered reasonable alternatives before dismissing and one possible option would have been to demote the employee to a less responsible role. However, the EAT overturned this decision on appeal. It accepted that the employer had in fact considered demotion but had decided against it because it was a small business and there was a loss of confidence in the employee. As such the dismissal fell within the reasonable range of responses test.

Ill health and absenteeism

Capability might also concern the health of the employee if that results in a continued inability to work. An employee is entitled to some sympathy and support from the employer during long term or regular sickness. However, it would be unfair on the employer to be expected to wait indefinitely for an employee to return from sickness absence. Lack of capability through illness is obviously closely connected with a termination of the contract for frustration (see Chapter 20.1). For a dismissal to be fair the employer obviously needs to consider all of the circumstances and the possible alternatives before dismissing.

CASE EXAMPLE

Coulson v Felixstowe Dock & Railway Co Ltd [1975] IRLR 11

The employee suffered sickness absences over a long period and was eventually put on lighter work. He was also informed that he would be given six months in which to show that he was fit. When he suffered further illness and sickness absence he was dismissed and claimed unfair dismissal. The court held that the dismissal was fair since the employer had made reasonable steps to allow the employee to continue and to accommodate his illnesses. However, there has to come a time when in fairness to the employer and the necessities of the business that a constantly ill employee can be dismissed.

While it is more likely to be seen as a fair dismissal where the employer has tried to support the employee and come up with alternatives, in *Merseyside and North Wales Electricity Board v Taylor* [1975] IRLR 60, however, it was held that there is no requirement on an employer to create a special job for an employee who has suffered sickness absence.

It is also of course not for the employer to presume that the employee is unfit to return to work by speculating on the possible risk of further illness.

CASE EXAMPLE

Converform (Darwen) Ltd v Bell [1981] IRLR 195

A director suffered from a heart attack and had time off work. When he had recovered his employer refused to let him back to work arguing that he was at risk of another heart attack. The director claimed unfair dismissal. It was held that the risk of another heart attack alone could not be a fair ground for dismissal under capability. It would only be relevant if the risk made it unsafe for the employee in his work.

In the case of persistent sickness absence the employer needs to ensure that the employee is aware of the need to improve the attendance record. For the dismissal to be fair the employer should carry out a proper system of warnings.

CASE EXAMPLE

International Sport Ltd v Thompson [1980] IRLR 340

The claimant had sickness absences of approximately one week every month. These were all supported by doctors' notes and related to numerous illnesses including bronchitis, cystitis, arthritis in her knee, anxiety and dizzy spells, and dyspepsia. She was told on numerous occasions that her attendance needed to improve and was given several warnings. She was given a final written warning and when the attendance did not improve she was dismissed. She claimed unfair dismissal. The employer had consulted its medical adviser who felt that there was no point in further examination since there was no connection between the various illnesses. The EAT held that the dismissal was fair. The employer had done everything possible in the circumstances including numerous warnings with no result.

Qualifications

Qualification refers to any academic, technical or professional qualification relevant to the position held. This could relate to a formal qualification required in order to do the work.

CASE EXAMPLE

Mathieson v W J Noble [1972] IRLR 76

A travelling salesman who was obviously required to drive as part of his work was then disqualified from driving. He made his own arrangements to be able to continue his work, and was prepared to pay the cost of a chauffeur to drive him. His employer, however, did not accept this and dismissed him. Ordinarily where something like a clean driving licence is a necessary requirement of employment then a dismissal in circumstances such as these would be fair. Here, however, the dismissal was accepted as unfair since the employer had not acted reasonably in failing to see whether the arrangement proved satisfactory.

Even though the qualification in question is not a formal contractual requirement it may still be seen as essential to the continued employment of the employee.

CASE EXAMPLE

Tayside Regional Council v McIntosh [1982] IRLR 272

In the advertisement for a post of vehicle mechanic it was a condition of the employment that the successful applicant should possess a clean current driving licence, although there was no mention of this in the written contract. The employee had a clean driving licence at the time of his appointment but three years later he lost his licence. It was held that the requirement was substantially connected with his ability to do his job and there was no other suitable employment for him so his dismissal was fair.

It is also possible that the qualification referred to is a specific aptitude requirement that is necessary for the work while not relating to a formal qualification. If the employee lacks the necessary aptitude and is dismissed as a result then the dismissal may be fair.

CASE EXAMPLE

Blackman v The Post Office [1974] IRLR

A telegraph officer required to pass an aptitude test. In fact he failed the test three times and was then dismissed. There was a maximum number of times that he could sit the test and it was necessary for the work so the dismissal was fair.

However, the qualification must represent a real need of the business. If it is not really related or a useful addition that the employer might like but is not necessary then the dismissal may well be unfair. In *Woods v Olympic Aluminium Co* [1975] IRLR 356 the employee was dismissed because he lacked management potential. His actual job was not dependent on this so the dismissal was unfair.

The employer must also be acting fairly in the dismissal. Even if the employee lacks the necessary qualification but there are other alternatives to dismissal then the employer should consider them.

CASE EXAMPLE

Sutcliffe & Eaton Ltd v Pinney [1977] IRLR 349

A trainee hearing aid designer failed the exams that were a necessary qualification for the work and was dismissed as a result. The court accepted the claim for unfair dismissal. The employer could have provided an extension to the traineeship for the employee to have another chance at the exams.

22.4.2 Misconduct

Misconduct is a legitimate reason for dismissal but the employers must follow their own disciplinary procedures or a dismissal may be unfair. Misconduct can arise as an issue both in terms of the employee's misconduct during the employment but also from misconduct that occurs outside the employment if it is sufficiently serious to be relevant to the continued employment of the employee.

In the case of misconduct there may be a summary dismissal if there is sufficiently serious misconduct. Even where the misconduct is less serious for a dismissal to be fair it is vital that the employer has and follows its disciplinary procedures.

CASE EXAMPLE

British Home Stores Ltd v Burchell [1980] ICR 303

Here the EAT developed the reasonable range of responses test (see 22.5.1 below) and held that for the dismissal to be fair the employer must genuinely believe that the employee has committed an act of misconduct, the employer had reasonable grounds for that belief and also carried out a proper investigation. In this case the employee was dismissed as part of a group that had allegedly been making dishonest staff purchases. The employer began an investigation and the claimant was implicated by a colleague. In the EAT the employee argued that the employer had not proved her dishonesty. The EAT held that it was sufficient that it had a reasonable belief and had investigated.

There are numerous reasons when misconduct might justify a dismissal. These can include refusal to obey lawful and reasonable orders, dishonesty, violent behaviour at work, intoxication at work. To dismiss fairly for misconduct then an employer must follow the correct procedure, their own procedure and must investigate fully and make full use of any system of warnings before dismissal.

CASE EXAMPLE

Trusthouse Forte Hotels Ltd v Murphy [1977] IRLR 186

The employee was dismissed for a shortage of stock that he was responsible for. He was a night porter and was allowed to keep a supply of alcoholic drinks for hotel guests but the employer identified a stock shortage when it was checked. He admitted that he took some for himself and was dismissed. The EAT held that, although the value of the stock in question was low this did not mean that the employer had not made a reasonable decision when dismissing.

Stock losses were also the cause of a dismissal in *Whitbread & Co v Thomas* [1988] IRLR 43. Here stock losses in an off-licence were recurring. This could have been either incompetence in failing to control the stock or could have raised questions about the honesty of the employee. Honesty is an essential aspect of much employment where the employee deals with the employer's money or property. It can obviously lead to a fair dismissal.

CASE EXAMPLE

British Railways Board v Jackson [1994] IRLR 235

The employee was a buffet supervisor on trains. He was dismissed because his employer had reason to believe that he was intending to take his own goods on board to sell to customers on the train thus depriving the employer of the sales. Trains did not carry tills or anything that could monitor what the employee was doing in this respect so that the employer was absolutely dependent on the honesty of the employee. It was held that it could be a fair dismissal where the employer had good reason to believe that the misconduct was occurring and the employer was able to take into account the prevalence of the particular type of dishonesty amongst employees.

Where a dismissal is for dishonesty then the employer must follow a proper investigation. The investigation should be measured against the proper legal test for dishonesty. Inevitably in different contexts what one employer concludes is dishonest may differ to another employer.

CASE EXAMPLE

John Lewis plc v Coyne [2001] IRLR 139

The claimant had been employed by the company for nearly fourteen years and had an exemplary work record. She was dismissed when it was found that she had made 111 personal telephone calls on the works telephone in works time contrary to the disciplinary code during the previous twelve months. She was actually dismissed without any meaningful investigation. Because of the absence of a proper disciplinary investigation the dismissal did not follow the procedural requirements in the ACAS Code. It was an unfair dismissal despite being for a potentially fair head of dismissal, conduct. The EAT concluded that there should be a two stage process in determining whether the employee had in fact been dishonest. First it should be determined that according to the standards of ordinary reasonable and honest people what the employee did was dishonest. Second it should be considered whether the employee must have realised that the acts were dishonest. This in essence follows the criminal test for dishonesty.

Any serious infringement of an employer's disciplinary code might justify dismissal. It follows that if the employer is seeking to dismiss for gross misconduct then the disciplinary code should include the precise misconduct that the employer is intending to dismiss the employee for. In *Dietman v London Borough of Brent* [1988] IRLR 146 a clause in a contract defined gross misconduct for which summary dismissal was available. After an inquiry the employee was found to be grossly negligent in her duties. The court of appeal held that gross negligence did not fall under the employer's contractual definition of gross misconduct so it concluded that the employee had been unfairly dismissed.

Violent behaviour is always likely to be misconduct that justifies dismissal. Indeed it is often included by employers in their works rules or disciplinary procedures as conduct justifying summary dismissal.

CASE EXAMPLE

Parsons & Co Ltd v McLoughlin [1978] IRLR 65

Two employees were caught fighting and were then dismissed after proper enquiry. One employee complained that he had only defended himself and therefore his dismissal was unfair. However, the EAT held that it was a fundamental aspect of any contract of employment not to fight so the dismissal was fair.

In *Hussain v Elonex* [1999] IRLR 420 an allegation of head butting a colleague was investigated and resulted in dismissal and this was held to be a fair dismissal. *Fuller v Lloyds Bank plc* [1991] involved an employee smashing a glass into a colleague's face at the Christmas party. This was fully investigated by the employer before dismissing the employee and was held to be a fair dismissal.

A further issue is whether the employer is entitled to dismiss for misconduct that occurs outside work. In *Lovie Ltd v Anderson* [1999] IRLR 164 the employee was charged with indecent exposure. It was identified that the employer should still carry out a full investigation and allow the employee to state their case before any dismissal.

Dismissal for misconduct out of work probably depends on how much the misconduct could impact on the employment in question so it is very much an issue of context as the following cases show.

CASE EXAMPLE

Mathewson v RB Wilson Dental Laboratories Ltd [1988] IRLR 512

The employee a dental technician was arrested and charged with being in possession of cannabis. Despite the offence not having anything to do with his work the dismissal was held to be fair. The justification given was that it was accepted that it was inappropriate to have a highly skilled employee using drugs. Besides this it was felt that it could have an adverse effect on younger employees.

CASE EXAMPLE

Moore v C & A Modes [1981] IRLR 71

A section leader in a retail clothes store was dismissed after she had been caught shoplifting from another shop. The EAT held that her dismissal was fair because honesty was an absolute requirement of her job.

CASE EXAMPLE

P v Nottinghamshire County Council [1992] IRLR 362

An assistant groundsman in a school admitted a charge of a sexual offence with his daughter. The employer dismissed him and the decision was held to be fair because of the potential risk to the children in the school. The employer had been dismissed without any formal investigation but the Court of Appeal still held the dismissal was fair.

In contrast with the above cases the following cases were found differently.

CASE EXAMPLE

Bradshaw v Rugby Portland Cement Co Ltd [1972] IRLR 46

A quarryman was convicted of incest with his daughter and placed on probation rather than any more severe sentence. The employer dismissed him. The court held that the dismissal was unfair because his misconduct had no actual bearing on his work and there was in fact no deterioration in his relationship with his fellow employees.

CASE EXAMPLE

Securicor Guarding Ltd v R [1994] IRLR 633

The employee had been charged with sex offences against children which he had denied. His employer dismissed him after a disciplinary hearing. The employer's reasoning was the effect that this would have on important clients. The dismissal was held to be unfair because the employer had failed to consider alternatives such as moving him to non-client facing work.

CASE EXAMPLE

Norfolk County Council v Bernard [1979] IRLR 220

A drama teacher in a college was dismissed after a conviction for possession of cannabis. The EAT held that it was not related to his work so the dismissal was unfair.

22.4.3 Genuine redundancy

A genuine redundancy is also a prima facie fair reason for a dismissal. However, to be a fair dismissal it must also be a genuine redundancy situation. In *Sanders v Ernest A. Neale Ltd* [1974] IRLR 236 while there was a redundancy situation this was not the cause of the dismissal of the employees in question. In fact it was their refusal to work normally that had led to the redundancies.

It must also conform to all of the necessary procedural requirements – in *Williams v Compare Maxim Ltd* [1982] ICR 156 a test was established by the EAT: the selection criteria must be objectively justified and applied fairly, there must be proper individual and collective consultation, and the employer must have tried to find suitable alternative work for the redundant employees.

There must be objective criteria for selection and the person must be fairly selected according to that criteria. It is also vital that the employer should consult with the individuals affected and their representatives, although ultimately the employer should be looking for alternative ways of dealing with the problem. If a redundancy does not conform to these standards then it may well be unfair. There are extensive rules on redundancy in the Trade Union and Labour Relations (Consolidation) Act 1992 (see Chapter 23).

22.4.4 A dismissal because of a statutory restriction

A dismissal because of a statutory restriction could arise because the business is prevented from operating by statute or other regulation for example in the case of a farm during a foot-and-mouth outbreak. It could also relate to the employment of people who are subject to immigration controls and have not been granted the right to remain under the Immigration, Asylum and Nationality Act 2006.

Another way in which a statutory restriction might justify a dismissal would be where the employee originally did but now does not meet the statutory requirement. In *Mathieson v W J Noble* [1972] IRLR 76 (see 22.4.1 above) the dismissal was unfair because the employee was prepared to make his own arrangements during his driving ban at his own cost and the employer had not acted reasonably in failing to see whether the arrangement was satisfactory. In contrast in *Appleyard v Smith (Hull) Ltd* [1972] the dismissal of a mechanic required to have a clean current driving licence and who was banned from driving was fair. The employer's business was small, the employee needed to test drive vehicles that he had repaired and so had to be replaced. There was no alternative employment.

In each case the fact that there is a statutory restriction does not automatically make the dismissal fair. It still has to be fair in fact so the employer needs to take the appropriate steps to find suitable alternatives.

22.4.5 Other substantial reason

Dismissing for some other substantial reason is a kind of catch all category which gives the employer most flexibility to dismiss an employee.

JUDGMENT

In *RS Components Ltd v RE Irwin* [1973] IRLR 239 the court held: 'there are not only legal but also practical objections to a narrow construction of some other substantial reason. Parliament … can hardly have hoped to produce an exhaustive catalogue of all the circumstances in which a company would be justified in terminating the contract the services of an employee.'

CASE EXAMPLE

RS Components Ltd v RE Irwin [1973] IRLR 239

The employer's business was failing and this was due to sales staff leaving and going to work for competing businesses. The employer, acting on advice, imposed restrictive covenants on the remaining staff unilaterally without negotiating the variation to their contracts with them. The claimant was dismissed for refusing to agree to the change to his contract. The dismissal was held to be fair and for a substantial reason despite the unilateral variation to the contract.

In many instances a dismissal for some other substantial reason will in fact be as a result of the business needs of the employer. This is often referred to as an economic, technical or organisational (ETO) reason.

CASE EXAMPLE

Hollister v National Farmers Union [1979] IRLR 238

The National Farmers Union operates an insurance business and was in the process of reorganising it which involved changes to the contracts of employment of the staff. One insurance salesman would not accept the changes to his contract and was dismissed as a result and claimed unfair dismissal. The NFU argued that the dismissal was fair because the changes to the contract were necessary for the improvements in the running of the business. The Court of Appeal held that the changes to the contracts were essential to the business and represented a sufficiently substantial reason for the dismissal which was fair.

A lack of funding may well require a reduction in the conditions of employees and a refusal to accept this could lead to a fair dismissal under the category of some other substantial reason.

CASE EXAMPLE

John of God (Care Services) Ltd v Brook [1992] IRLR 546

The case involved a charity-run hospital where NHS funding had been significantly reduced. As a result the hospital faced possible closure and proposed to make cuts in the pay and conditions of the staff in order to make the necessary savings that would avoid it going out of business. These changes were accepted by 140 of the 170 employees and four of those refusing were eventually dismissed. The EAT held that the dismissals were fair for any other substantial reason, in this case an economic, technical or organisational reason. This was because the other employees had accepted the changes and the firm ran the risk of collapse without the changes.

It is also possible that a dismissal for some other substantial reason could be where pressure is put on the employer to dismiss the employee. The pressure could come from important clients. In this instance the employer is not going to risk the business and so provided alternatives are considered the dismissal may be fair.

CASE EXAMPLE

Dobie v Burns International Security Services (UK) Ltd [1995] IRLR 329

The employee was a security officer and was based at Liverpool Airport where his employer had the contract to provide security services. There were two breaches of security at the airport and, although the employee was not to blame for them, the airport refused to have him work there. As a result the employer offered him alternative work but which was at a lower rate of pay. The employee refused to accept the work and claimed unfair dismissal. The Court of Appeal held that the dismissal was fair and was for some other substantial reason. The employer had been put under pressure from its customer and had done everything it could to provide a suitable alternative.

CASE EXAMPLE

Henderson v Connect (South Tyneside) Ltd [2010] IRLR 466

The claimant was a minibus driver taking disabled children to school for a charity which provided transport services to community and voluntary groups. The charity operated under a contract with South Tyneside Metropolitan Borough Council which had an absolute right to veto the employment of particular individuals. The employee had initially received a clean CRB check but was then the subject of allegations about an abusive relationship with his two young nieces. No charges were ever brought against him but the council told the employer that he was not suitable to work with children. The employer did try to persuade the council otherwise but, when it had no other role to offer the employee he was dismissed. The EAT held that the dismissal was fair.

JUDGMENT

Underhill J explained: 'The Tribunal was plainly very conscious that the Appellant was being dismissed because of concerns based on allegations of misconduct which he had had no chance to rebut and for which he had never been charged: it referred explicitly to the representations to this effect which [the employer] made on his behalf. But it found that the Respondent had done "all it could reasonably be expected to do to assist the Claimant and prevent him from losing his employment". That conclusion ... was an answer which was open to it on the facts, if not indeed inevitable.'

Where the employer dismisses because of pressure this could also be the result of pressure from fellow employees of the employee who is dismissed. Again if it is reasonable in the circumstances then it may be a fair dismissal for some other substantial reason.

CASE EXAMPLE

Tregannowan v Robert Knee & Co Ltd [1975] IRLR 247

The claimant upset her fellow employees by continually boasting about and giving details about her affair with a younger man. Eventually the employees complained to management and refused to work with her. The employer dismissed the woman and it was held that it was a fair dismissal for some other substantial reason.

However, there are equally situations in which courts will reject an employer's submission that a dismissal was for some other substantial reason.

CASE EXAMPLE

Wadley v Eager Electrical Ltd [1986] IRLR 93

The claimant had worked for the employer for seventeen years and was well respected. He was dismissed after his wife, who was also employed by the same employer, was dismissed for theft. The employer felt that the claimant's continued employment would be detrimental to its customers and that it had no choice but to dismiss him. The EAT did not accept that the dismissal was fair in the circumstances or that it was for a substantial reason.

ACTIVITY

Quick quiz

Explain which type of potentially fair head of dismissal is appropriate in each of the following situations:

1. A Nigerian employee has been dismissed when her immigration officials pointed out to her employer that she had no permit to remain in the UK.
2. Brett has recently been dismissed along with five colleagues when their employer shut the branch of its business where they worked because of falling sales.
3. Callum, a law lecturer, has been dismissed after being convicted for being in possession of cannabis.
4. Daphne works in a private school and has been dismissed for refusing to sign a new contract. The school has a falling roll of pupils and had asked staff to take some reduced pay and conditions in order to avoid the school closing. All of the other staff had signed the new contract.
5. Euan, a forklift truck driver has been dismissed after crashing the forklift truck into racks of stock ten times in the last two months. His employer had given him three warnings before he dismissed Euan.

22.5 Determining whether the dismissal is fair

22.5.1 The reasonable range of responses test

Once it has been established that the dismissal came under one of the potentially fair heads of dismissal identified in section 98 Employment Rights Act 1996 then a tribunal must also determine whether the dismissal was fair in fact.

A tribunal can consider numerous factors in determining the fairness of a dismissal:

- duty to consult the employee at all stages;
- the existence and effect of any express or implied terms in the contract;
- breaches of mutual trust and confidence;
- introductions of new rules or procedures;
- procedural faults;
- instances of gross misconduct;
- blanket dismissals;
- selection criteria in redundancy;
- breaches of the duty of fidelity;
- internal hearings and appeals procedure;
- the nature of sickness;
- natural justice.

In essence the tribunal will use a statutory test to determine whether the dismissal is fair taking into account:

- the circumstances of the case;
- the behaviour of the employee;
- the proper use of disciplinary and/or grievance procedures;
- the consistency of treatment.

The test in section 98(4) Employment Rights Act 1996 is as follows:

SECTION

'Section 98

(4) Where the employer has fulfilled the requirements of subsection (1), the determination of the question whether the dismissal was fair or unfair (having regard to the reason shown by the employer)

(a) depends on whether in the circumstances (including the size and resources of the employer's undertaking) the employer acted reasonably or unreasonably in treating it as a sufficient reason for dismissing the employee, and

(b) shall be determined in accordance with the equity and substantial merits of the case.'

Above all the employer should act reasonably in dismissing the employee. This principle derived originally from the case *British Home Stores v Burchell* [1980] ICR 303 which concluded that an employer should base a decision to dismiss on a genuine belief, based on reasonable grounds and following a reasonable investigation that there were grounds to justify the dismissal. This has become known as 'the range of reasonable responses test'.

CASE EXAMPLE

British Home Stores Ltd v Burchell [1980] ICR 303

Burchell had been dismissed as one of a group of employees who had allegedly made dishonest staff purchases. The company had investigated and Burchell had been implicated by a fellow employee. Burchell argued that the employer had not in fact proved any dishonesty on her part and that, as a result, the dismissal was unfair. The Employment Appeal Tribunal held that it was sufficient that the employer had a reasonable belief in her misconduct and that it had investigated the allegations. The EAT also identified the bases of a test (to become known as the reasonable range of responses test):

- The employer must hold a genuine belief in the grounds for the dismissal.
- This belief must be based on reasonable grounds.
- The employer must have carried out a reasonable investigation.
- This must have resulted in there being found reasonable grounds to dismiss.

The test was later approved and explained in greater detail by the Employment Appeal Tribunal.

CASE EXTRACT

In the case extract below a significant section of the judgment has been reproduced in the left hand column. Individual points arising from the judgment are briefly explained in the right hand column. Read the extract including the commentary in the right hand column and complete the exercise that follows.

Extract adapted from the judgment in Iceland Frozen Foods Ltd v Jones [1983] ICR 17	
<u>Facts</u> A foreman on a night shift was dismissed when he had carelessly forgotten to lock up the premises at the end of the shift. The employer had also considered that he had been responsible for poor levels of production on the shift in question. He then claimed unfair dismissal. The tribunal had in fact failed to apply the test in [what would now be section 98(4) Employment Rights Act 1996] as a result of which the EAT held that the dismissal was unfair.	*Facts* *Tribunal had not applied statutory criteria*
<u>Judgment</u> BROWNE-WILKINSON J . . . it may be convenient if we should seek to summarise the present law. We consider that the authorities establish that in law the correct approach for the industrial tribunal to adopt in answering the question posed by [section 98(4)] is as follows.	*(1) to (5) below are the stages in the reasonable range of responses test*
(1) the starting point should always be the words of section [98(4)] themselves;	*Start with s98(4)*
(2) in applying the section an industrial tribunal must consider the reasonableness of the employer's conduct, not simply whether they (the members of the industrial tribunal) consider the dismissal to be fair;	*Identify whether employer was reasonable not whether tribunal thinks dismissal fair* *Must not substitute its own views*

(3) in judging the reasonableness of the employer's conduct an Industrial tribunal must not substitute its decision as to what was the right course to adopt for that of the employer;

(4) in many (though not all) cases there is a 'band of reasonable responses to the employee's conduct within which one employer might reasonably take one view, another quite reasonably take another';

Band of possible responses where different views could be taken

(5) the function of the industrial tribunal, as an industrial jury, is to determine whether in the particular circumstances of each case the decision to dismiss the employee fell within the band of reasonable responses which a reasonable employer might have adopted. If the dismissal falls within the band the dismissal is fair: if the dismissal falls outside the band it is unfair.

Tribunal's role to see whether employer's actions fell within that band

… The question in each case is whether the industrial tribunal considers the employer's conduct to fall within the band of reasonable responses and industrial tribunals would be well advised to follow the formulation of the principle …

Repeats role of tribunal – to see whether employer's actions fell within that band

Reverting now to the facts of this case, it is suggested that notwithstanding the misdirection, we can uphold the decision of the Industrial tribunal on the ground that on any footing it was manifestly unreasonable for the employers to dismiss in the circumstances of this case. The industrial tribunal obviously regarded the faults of Mr. Jones as minor ones. We cannot accede to the view that notwithstanding the misdirection we can substitute our own decision in this case. Take for example, the failure to lock the office and to set the alarm. The industrial tribunal took the view that the offence was comparatively trivial; it does not necessarily follow that all reasonable employers would share their view on the matter. It may well be that the misdirection on this point is fundamental to the decision of the case. We do not know enough of the circumstances of the employers' business to decide whether the importance which they obviously attached to the breach of security was such that a reasonable employer might take the view that the risk of repetition of the breach of security was too great to allow the risk to continue. We express no view on the point one way or the other. We simply cannot decide the matter ourselves on the material we have before us.

EAT feels that dismissal was manifestly unreasonable

Tribunal felt misconduct was minor

Recognises that different employers might act differently

As to the alternative ground relied on by the industrial tribunal, namely, procedural unfairness, as we have said we do not think it the Correct approach to deal separately with the reasonableness of the substantive decision to dismiss, and the reasonableness of the procedure Adopted. The correct approach is to consider together all the circumstances of the case, both substantive and procedural, and reach a conclusion in all the circumstances. Moreover, it has been demonstrated to us from the notes of evidence that on an important issue on procedure the industrial tribunal apparently misdirected itself.

Should consider fairness of decision and fairness of procedure used together

The industrial tribunal took the view that Mr. Boyland at the short interview did not give Mr. Jones an opportunity to state his case as to the reason for the go-slow. The notes of evidence disclose that both Mr. Boyland and Mr. Jones himself gave evidence that at that interview Mr. Jones did put forward his explanation of the go-slow by the night shift. In the circumstances, it cannot be safe for us to uphold the decision of the industrial tribunal on the grounds of procedural unfairness alone.

Procedural unfairness is not sufficient on its own

We therefore allow the appeal and remit the case to a differently constituted industrial tribunal to consider the matter afresh. It will be for the new industrial tribunal to consider whether in all the circumstances of the case the nature of Mr. Jones's shortcomings were such that a reasonable employer carrying on the company's business would have regarded the dismissal as being a reasonable response and whether, in the circumstances of the case, the dismissal was carried out in a fair way. As we say, that is a matter entirely for the new industrial tribunal. But we do point out that whatever the merits of the substantive decision in this case, the procedure by which the dismissal was carried out has to be carefully considered and taken into account. It may not have been fair, and we say no more than that, to have dismissed Mr. Jones with the haste which was shown in this case without giving him an opportunity to have a representative there. But that will be a matter for the tribunal to weigh together with all the other circumstances of the case.

EAT thinks facts should be heard again with new tribunal properly applying the reasonable range of responses test

Procedure should also be taken into account

Key Points from the case of *Iceland Frozen Foods Ltd v Jones* [1983] ICR 17 above:
Checklist for applying the reasonable range of responses test

(i) the tribunal should begin with the words of section 98(4) – whether the employer acted reasonably, determined in accordance with equity and the substantial merits of the case;

(ii) the tribunal must consider whether the employer acted reasonably – not whether or not the tribunal thinks that the dismissal was fair;

(iii) the tribunal must not substitute its own decision as to what the right course was for the employer to adopt;

(iv) there is a band of reasonable responses to employee's conduct in which different employers might take different views;

(v) the function of the tribunal is to determine whether the dismissal fell within the reasonable range of responses that a reasonable employer might take.

Other key points in judgment

▨ The test is vital because different employers may react differently – it is whether the decision to dismiss falls within the range where a reasonable employer could have reacted the same.

▨ Tribunals should always consider the fairness of the decision and the fairness of the procedure together.

▨ An unfair procedure on its own is insufficient to identify the dismissal as unfair.

ACTIVITY

Quick quiz

Consider the three scenarios below and applying the steps in the reasonable range of responses test above identify which scenario involves conduct that any reasonable employer would dismiss the employee for, which scenario that no reasonable employer would dismiss the employer for and which scenario a tribunal would accept falls within the reasonable range of responses so that different employers might reach a different decision but the dismissal would be fair.

1. Andy was dismissed after he was late for work last week when he had to take his mother to the cancer clinic. Andy had changed his shift so that he started at 2.00 p.m. but unfortunately he did not get back to work until 2.15 p.m.
2. Brendan is a maths teacher in a university. The university dismisses Brendan after he was convicted of possession of a small amount of cannabis at a rock festival during the summer holidays. The university justifies the dismissal on the basis that it sets a bad example to students.
3. Colin was dismissed after having been caught by CCTV footage stealing £500 from his employer's till. Colin admitted to the theft and also to other thefts worth over £20,000 from his employer during the past year.

Following on from *Iceland Frozen Foods Ltd v Jones* in *Haddon v Van den Bergh Foods Ltd* [1999] IRLR 672 the EAT, however, later suggested that there is nothing intrinsically wrong in the tribunal substituting its own view for that of the employer, although this of course would be in effect to ignore the 'range of reasonable responses test'.

CASE EXAMPLE

Haddon v Van den Bergh Foods Ltd [1999] IRLR 672

The employee had been invited to a drinks party to celebrate his fifteen years' service with his employer. Having become drunk he then failed to return for the remaining one-and-a-half hours of his shift and was subsequently dismissed. The tribunal had upheld the dismissal as fair. The EAT could simply have reversed the decision but chose to ignore and not apply the established test thus leaving the law in some confusion.

However, in *HSBC v Madden* [2000] IRLR 827 the EAT suggested that no court short of the Court of Appeal can discard the range of reasonable responses test, although accepting that the *Burchell* test might simply go to the reason for the dismissal rather than its reasonableness. In the subsequent joined appeals *Foley v Post Office; HSBC v Madden* [2001] All ER 550 the Court of Appeal clarified the position:

- the band of reasonable responses approach to the test of reasonableness in section 98(4) Employment Rights Act 1996 remains intact;
- the test of Browne-Wilkinson in *Iceland Frozen Foods* is approved;
- the three part test in *Burchell* is approved;
- so the ultimate test is whether, by the standard of a reasonable employer, the employer acted reasonably in treating the shown reason for the dismissal as a sufficient reason for dismissal.

22.5.2 Procedural fairness and the ACAS Code of Practice

Another aspect to a fair dismissal is procedural fairness. The Arbitration, Conciliation and Advisory Service (ACAS) produces a Code which was first introduced in 1977. Under section 199 Trade Union and Labour Relations (Consolidation) Act 1992 the Code can be updated regularly to take account of developments in statute. The Code is not, in itself, legally enforceable; however, employment tribunals will take its provisions into account when considering whether a dismissal is fair.

The Code does not cover dismissals for redundancy or for the non-renewal of a fixed-term contract. However, the case below does illustrate the attitude of the courts to procedural fairness and the significance of the Code.

CASE EXAMPLE

Polkey v AE Dayton Services Ltd [1988] AC 344

The claimant was made redundant following a reorganisation within the company for whom he worked. He complained that he had not been consulted but had been called into the manager's office and dismissed and sent home. In his unfair dismissal claim he argued that the code of practice in operation at the time had not been followed. The tribunal held that the dismissal was fair on the basis that the failure to consult would not have made any difference to his selection for redundancy. The House of Lords (now the Supreme Court) held that the dismissal was unfair since there was no way of ascertaining what the result would have been if the employer had adopted the correct procedure.

JUDGMENT

Lord Bridge identified: 'an employer having prima facie grounds to dismiss for [a potentially fair reason] will in the great majority of cases not act reasonably in treating the reason as a sufficient reason for dismissal unless and until he has taken the steps, conveniently classified in most of the authorities as "procedural", which are necessary in the circumstances of the case to justify the action'.

The Code is primarily aimed at misconduct issues, poor performance and grievances. In the context of dismissal it covers disciplinary warnings and dismissals for misconduct and poor performance but not dismissals for individual redundancies or for the non-renewal of fixed-term contracts on their expiry. However, it is important in all cases for employers to follow a fair procedure, as determined by other legislation and case law.

The code identifies fairness in the following:

- raising and dealing with issues promptly and avoiding unreasonable delays;
- consistency from both sides;
- carrying out necessary investigations;
- giving employees full information and allowing them to state their case (in this respect section 10 of the Employment Relations Act 1999 is also important in allowing the right to be accompanied at all hearings – and an employee should be advised of their right to be accompanied);
- the provision of appeals;
- keeping proper records.

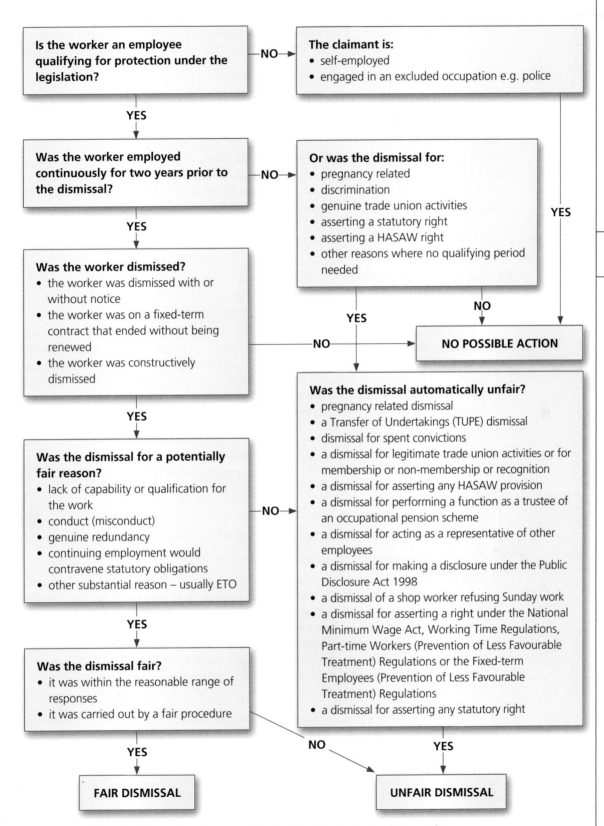

Figure 22.1 Flow chart illustrating the process for deciding if a dismissal is fair or unfair

In addition to these general principles of fairness and procedure, in misconduct cases the Code provides that where practicable, different people should carry out the investigation and the disciplinary hearing.

22.6 Pursuing a claim for unfair dismissal

A claim for unfair dismissal must usually be made to the employment tribunal within three months of the date of the effective date of termination of the contract (EDT). An exception to this is under sections 238 and 238A of the Trade Union and Labour Relations (Consolidation) Act 1992 where dismissals following protected industrial action are concerned. Under section 111(4) a claim can be made to the tribunal before the EDT if it has been lodged with the tribunal after notice has been given, which could occur in constructive dismissal claims.

If the claimant is out of time then the tribunal has no jurisdiction to hear the case.

CASE EXAMPLE

Glennie v Independent Magazines Ltd [1999] IRLR 719

The claimant alleged unfair dismissal from February 1997 but his ET1 (at that time IT1) was not received by the tribunal within the three months' time limit because it was put upside down in the solicitor's FAX machine. The tribunal said that it had no jurisdiction to hear the case. The claimant then appealed saying that the effective date of termination was March 1997 so it was still in time but the tribunal would not hear the claim. The Court of Appeal held that the tribunal was correct. The plea date could only be changed if fresh evidence was introduced.

Under section 111(2)(b) Employment Rights Act 1996, however, the tribunal may hear claims out of time where it is satisfied that it was not reasonably practicable to present the claim in time. The meaning of reasonably practicable has been considered by the courts.

CASE EXAMPLE

Cavaciuti v London Borough of Hammersmith & Fulham [1991] EAT 246/91

The claimant was dismissed on 4 July 1990 but a letter dated 6 July 1990 stated that he would be paid during his notice period but did not have to work. He then received numerous letters. The final one on 19 July 1990 stated that he would be paid up to and including 22 August 1990. The question was which date was the actual EDT. The tribunal said that the dismissal was not a summary dismissal with payment in lieu because the final payment included deductions like an employee would have. As a result the tribunal held that the EDT was 22 August 1990. The EAT held that if the EDT was ambiguous then the tribunal should use the date that was most favourable to the employee.

It will not necessarily be possible for the tribunal to extend the limit where the claimant argues that he has been misled by his legal advisers about the appropriate time limit. In *Royal Bank of Scotland plc v Theobald* [2007] UKEAT 0444 06 1001 the claimant was summarily dismissed for gross misconduct. He argued that his claim was submitted to the tribunal late only because he was erroneously advised by an adviser from a Citizens Advice Bureau that he had to complete his employer's internal appeal procedure before he submitted his claim. The EAT held that there was nothing to suggest that it was not reasonably practicable to submit the claim on time.

When there is an internal appeal time runs according to whether on proper construction of the contract the employee is suspended pending the outcome of the appeal or not.

CASE EXAMPLE

Drage v Governors of Greenford High School [2000] IRLR 314

The employee was dismissed and his dismissal was upheld by the internal appeal. The court was required to determine what the EDT date was, the actual dismissal date or the date of the appeal decision. The Court of Appeal held that the appropriate means of establishing the EDT is to look at the contract and whether it grants such an appeal to see whether the employee is employed between notification of dismissal and appeal but suspended pending the outcome of the appeal, or dismissal at date of notice subject to a possible reinstatement if the appeal is successful.

ACAS arbitration

ACAS arbitration schemes in unfair dismissals were initially set up by section 212A of the Trade Union and Labour Relations (Consolidation) Act 1992. An employee can submit his claim for arbitration rather to the tribunal. Both parties must agree to go to arbitration. The scheme is for straightforward claims and the arbitrator cannot deal with jurisdictional issues such as whether there is a dismissal or whether there is sufficient continuity of employment. Evidence is heard at the arbitration hearing and the arbitrator is able to make the same awards as the tribunal.

The current government is planning to adopt suggestions from a report which it commissioned produced by the venture capitalist Adrian Beecroft. Under these plans employers would be allowed to reach settlements with employees whom they wish to dismiss which if the employee accepts would then mean that no further claim would be possible. As part of the same changes the government also plans to introduce a system of fees before a claim could be brought and also to allow judges to filter out claims that they consider vexatious before they ever reach a tribunal. The changes are clearly aimed at making it much harder for employees to enforce the rights that other legislation offers them and can only be described as a retrograde step from the perspective of employment protection.

22.7 Remedies

There are three available remedies that a tribunal might award for an unfair dismissal:

- reinstatement
- re-engagement
- a compensatory award.

In reality the first two of these would rarely be granted because of the difficulty of enforcing and overseeing them and also because almost by definition the employment relationship will have broken down.

Reinstatement

The meaning of an order for reinstatement is in section 114 Employment Rights Act 1996.

SECTION

....

'114 Order for reinstatement.

(1) An order for reinstatement is an order that the employer shall treat the complainant in all respects as if he had not been dismissed.

(2) On making an order for reinstatement the tribunal shall specify –

(a) any amount payable by the employer in respect of any benefit which the complainant might reasonably be expected to have had but for the dismissal (including arrears of pay) for the period between the date of termination of employment and the date of reinstatement,

(b) any rights and privileges (including seniority and pension rights) which must be restored to the employee, and

(c) the date by which the order must be complied with.'

The effect of an order of reinstatement then is as follows:

- it means that the employer must take the employee back in the same job;
- the effect of the order is as if the employee has not been dismissed;
- as a result continuity of employment is protected;
- and the employee will be eligible for all back pay, and any improvement in terms that he would have received if he had remained in work.

Re-engagement

The meaning of an order for re-engagement is in section 115 Employment Rights Act 1996.

SECTION

....

'115 Order for re-engagement.

(1) An order for re-engagement is an order, on such terms as the tribunal may decide, that the complainant be engaged by the employer, or by a successor of the employer or by an associated employer, in employment comparable to that from which he was dismissed or other suitable employment.

(2) On making an order for re-engagement the tribunal shall specify the terms on which re-engagement is to take place, including –

(a) the identity of the employer,

(b) the nature of the employment,

(c) the remuneration for the employment,

(d) any amount payable by the employer in respect of any benefit which the complainant might reasonably be expected to have had but for the dismissal (including arrears of pay) for the period between the date of termination of employment and the date of re-engagement,

(e) any rights and privileges (including seniority and pension rights) which must be restored to the employee, and

(f) the date by which the order must be complied with.'

The effect of an order of re-engagement then is as follows:

- it means that the employee must be taken back on by the employer or an associated employer on terms that are comparable with those that he enjoyed when he was dismissed;

- again the employee should be entitled to back pay and any improvement in terms that he would have received if he had remained in work;
- and continuity of employment is again protected.

In deciding whether to make such an order the tribunal has discretion. It will take into account the claimant's wishes, the justice of the case and also the practicability of making the order.

CASE EXAMPLE

Wood Group Heavy Industrial Turbines Ltd v Crossan [1998] IRLR 680

The employee had been dismissed after investigation by the employer who held a genuine belief in the guilt of the employee who was suspected of various offences including supplying drugs. Because of procedural defects in the dismissal the tribunal found that the dismissal was unfair. Reinstatement was impossible because the claimant's job had gone. However, because the claimant had sixteen years' service the tribunal ordered that he be re-engaged on the same wages. The EAT reversed this decision since it was established that the employer no longer trusted the claimant and the employment relationship had irreversibly broken down.

Compensatory award

Section 118 Employment Rights Act 1996 identifies that there are two aspects to an award of compensation:

- a basic award
- a compensatory award.

The nature of the basic award is identified in section 119.

SECTION

'119 Basic award.
(1) Subject to the provisions of this section, sections 120 to 122 and section 126, the amount of the basic award shall be calculated by –
  (a) determining the period, ending with the effective date of termination, during which the employee has been continuously employed,
  (b) reckoning backwards from the end of that period the number of years of employment falling within that period, and
  (c) allowing the appropriate amount for each of those years of employment.
(2) In subsection (1)(c) "the appropriate amount" means –
  (a) one and a half weeks' pay for a year of employment in which the employee was not below the age of forty-one,
  (b) one week's pay for a year of employment (not within paragraph (a)) in which he was not below the age of twenty-two, and
  (c) half a week's pay for a year of employment not within paragraph (a) or (b).
(3) Where twenty years of employment have been reckoned under subsection (1), no account shall be taken under that subsection of any year of employment earlier than those twenty years.'

The basic award then is very similar to the calculation of the statutory maximums for redundancy (see Chapter 23.5). The multiplier rose in February 2013 to £450 and rises each year. The maximum basic award in 2012 then would be $20 \times 1\frac{1}{2}(30) \times £450 = £13,500$.

The compensatory award is identified and explained in section 123 Employment Rights Act 1996.

SECTION

'123 Compensatory award.

(1) Subject to the provisions of this section ... the amount of the compensatory award shall be such amount as the tribunal considers just and equitable in all the circumstances having regard to the loss sustained by the complainant in consequence of the dismissal in so far as that loss is attributable to action taken by the employer.'

As can be seen from section 123 the compensatory award is not worked out to a fixed formula but depends on what the tribunal believes is just and equitable in the circumstances subject to a statutory maximum which in 2013 stands at £74,200. In reaching a judgment on the compensatory award the tribunal takes into account:

- the immediate loss of earnings – from the time of the dismissal to the award;
- the future loss of earnings – a discretionary amount taking into account how long the dismissed employee may be without work;
- loss of statutory rights – which is a nominal figure;
- loss of pension rights;
- expenses – incurred in looking for a new job.

An additional award may also be made when an employer has unreasonably refused to comply with an order for reinstatement or re-engagement. This is under section 117 Employment Rights Act 1996.

In fact the current government plans to implement various aspects of the report that it commissioned by venture capitalist Adrian Beecroft. Amongst his suggestions which the government plans to implement is a cap on unfair dismissal compensation which is likely to be set at twelve months' wages but with a maximum below the current ceiling.

ACTIVITY

Self-assessment questions

1. What makes various classes of employee ineligible for an unfair dismissal claim?
2. How is dismissal defined?
3. What is a constructive dismissal?
4. In what circumstances will an employee be able to successfully claim constructive dismissal?
5. What are the justifications for classifying certain dismissals as automatically unfair?
6. What do the different classes of automatically unfair dismissals have in common?
7. What is 'asserting a statutory right'?
8. What would an employee have to do to be dismissed for lack of capability?
9. When will illness justify a dismissal?
10. What must an employer do to be sure of a fair dismissal on grounds of misconduct in employment?
11. Is misconduct out of employment ever a justification for dismissal?
12. When would a dismissal for a statutory restriction be justified?
13. How broad a category is 'any other substantial reason'?

14. What is the range of reasonable responses test?
15. What problem did the case of *Haddon* create?
16. What is the difference between 'reinstatement' and re-engagement?
17. Why are reinstatement and re-engagement rarely awarded as remedies?
18. Why is a dismissal which is discriminatory advantageous in relation to a compensatory award?

KEY FACTS

Origins, aims and character of unfair dismissal law	Case/statute
To detail in statutory form the situations in which a dismissal could be classed as unfair and therefore meriting a remedy, and in turn to discourage unfair dismissals	*Industrial Relations Act 1971*

Eligibility	Case/statute
Basic right: an employee has the right not to be unfairly dismissed by his employer Those ineligible are: • share fishermen • members of the police force • agreed exemptions authorised by the Secretary of State • where there is an agreement to place the dispute under arbitration instead of under a scheme prepared by ACAS • employees engaged in industrial action, providing that all of the workers are dismissed and none is taken back within three months • employees working under an illegal contract those without two years' continuous service except: • dismissal for legitimate trade union activities, or for membership or non-membership of a trade union • dismissal is for asserting any Health and Safety provision • dismissal related to pregnancy, childbirth, maternity, maternity leave, parental leave or dependant care leave • discriminatory dismissal • dismissal of a protected shop worker or betting office worker refusing to work on a Sunday • dismissal for a refusal to work hours in excess of those required under the Working Time Regulations • dismissal relates to performing functions as a trustee of a pension scheme • dismissal relates to making a protected disclosure • dismissal for exercising a right under the National Minimum Wage Act 1998 • dismissal for exercising a right under the EU Works Council Directive • dismissal for exercising a right under the Part-time Workers (Prevention of Less Favourable Treatment) Regulations 2000 or the Fixed-term Employees (Prevention of Less Favourable Treatment) Regulations 2002 • dismissal relates to spent offences – under the Rehabilitation of Offenders Act 1974 • dismissal following TUPE transfers	*S94(1) Employment Rights Act 1996* *S200 ERA 1996*

- dismissal relates to a demand for flexible working
- dismissal amounts to an unfair selection for redundancy
- dismissal is on medical grounds (qualifying period one month)
- the dismissal is for asserting a statutory right

Dismissals classed as automatically unfair	Case/statute
A dismissal relating to trade union membership, non-membership or activities	S152 Trade Union & Labour Relations (Consolidation) Act 1992
Dismissal during an industrial dispute	S238A TU&LR(C)A 1992
A dismissal in connection with statutory recognition or derecognition of a trade union	TU&LR(C)A 1992
Unfair selection for redundancy	S105 ERA 1996
A dismissal on a Transfer of Undertakings	
Dismissal on the grounds of pregnancy or maternity or parental rights	S98 ERA 1996
A dismissal in connection with a request for flexible working	S104C ERA 1996
A dismissal for any Health and Safety at Work related reason	S100 ERA 1996
A dismissal for exercising a right to a protected disclosure	S103 ERA 1996
A discriminatory dismissal	
A dismissal of protected shop workers for refusal to work on Sundays	S101 ERA 1996
A dismissal following the exercise of a right under the National Minimum Wage Act 1998	S104 ERA 1996
A dismissal relating to the Working Time Regulations	S101A ERA 1996
A dismissal because the employee performs duties as a trustee of an occupational pension fund	S102 ERA 1996
Dismissal relating to activities as an employee representative	S103 ERA 1996
A dismissal for exercising rights under the Part-time Workers (Prevention of Less Favourable Treatment) Regulations 2000	
A dismissal for exercising rights under the Fixed-term Employees (Prevention of Less Favourable Treatment) Regulations 2002	
A dismissal relating to tax credits	
A dismissal in connection with disciplinary or grievance hearings	S104B ERA 1996 Employment Relations Act 1999
A dismissal for asserting a statutory right	S104 ERA 1999

Dismissals classed as potentially fair	Case/statute
Capability and qualification	

- could result from serious incompetence - employer should consider alternatives - could be long term sickness but again employer should consider alternatives - but not for employer to presume employee unfit to return - and should go through proper procedures - could involve formal qualifications or aptitude - but employer should act fairly	Taylor v Alidair Ltd Bevan Harris Ltd v Gair Coulson v Felixstowe Dock & Railway Co Ltd Converform (Darwen) Ltd v Bell International Sport Ltd v Thompson Blackman v The Post Office Sutcliffe & Eaton Ltd v Pinney

Misconduct	
- employer must have reasonable belief in the misconduct and act reasonably	British Home Stores Ltd v Burchell

• and must follow procedures	*Trusthouse Forte Hotels Ltd v Murphy*
• must apply proper test in case of dishonesty • violent behaviour generally justifies dismissal • dismissal for misconduct out of work needs connection to the employment	*John Lewis plc v Coyne* *Parsons & Co Ltd v McLoughlin* *Moore v C & A Modes*

Genuine redundancy	
• must be genuine reason for dismissal	*Sanders v Ernest A. Neale Ltd*
• must conform to procedural requirements	*Williams v Compare Maxim Ltd* and *TU&LR(C)A 1992*

Statutory restriction	
• fair if employee no longer meets statutory requirement and there is no alternative work	*Appleyard v Smith (Hull) Ltd*
• unfair if employee makes alternative arrangements at own cost	*Mathieson v W J Noble*
Other substantial reason • is construed widely by the courts	*RS Components Ltd v RE Irwin*
• could be because of the business needs of the employer	*Hollister v National Farmers' Union*
• or because of pressure put on the employer by a third party	*Henderson v Connect (South Tyneside) Ltd*

Determining whether the dismissal is fair	Case/statute

Whether dismissal is fair or unfair in fact	
(a) depends on whether in the circumstances (including the size and resources of the employer's undertaking) the employer acted reasonably or unreasonably in treating it as a sufficient reason for dismissing the employee, and (b) shall be determined in accordance with the equity and substantial merits of the case	S98(4) ERA 1996

Reasonable range of responses test	
• employer holds genuine belief in grounds for the dismissal • belief must be based on reasonable grounds • employer must have carried out a reasonable investigation • this must have resulted in there being found reasonable grounds to dismiss	*British Home Stores Ltd v Burchell*

Developed to five part test	
'1. starting point is words of s98(4) ERA 1996; 2. tribunal must consider reasonableness of employer's conduct, not simply whether tribunal considers dismissal to be fair; 3. tribunal must not substitute its decision as to what the right course to adopt for that of the employer; 4. in many, (not all) cases there is a band of reasonable responses to the employee's conduct within which one employer might reasonably take one view, another quite reasonably take another;	*Iceland Frozen Foods Ltd v Jones*

5. function of tribunal is to determine whether in the particular circumstances of each case the decision to dismiss the employee fell within the band of reasonable responses which a reasonable employer might have adopted. If within the band dismissal is fair; if outside the band it is unfair.' At one point it was felt test could be ignored But test reaffirmed as correct approach	*Haddon v Van den Bergh's Foods Ltd* *Foley v Post Office; HSBC v Madden*

Procedural fairness	
ACAS Code – not legally binding but taken into account by tribunal Requires • raising and dealing with issues promptly and avoiding unreasonable delays • consistency from both sides • carrying out necessary investigations • giving employees full information and allowing them to state their case (in this respect section 10 of the Employment Relations Act 1999 is also important in allowing the right to be accompanied at all hearings – and an employee should be advised of their right to be accompanied) • the provision of appeals • keeping proper records	*Polkey v AE Dayton Services Ltd*

Pursuing a claim for unfair dismissal	Case/statute
Dismissed employee must submit claim to tribunal within three months of EDT Tribunal may hear claims out of time where it is satisfied that it was not reasonably practicable to present the claim in time The meaning of reasonably practicable has been considered by the courts Arbitration is also possible with an ACAS arbitrator	*S111 (2)(b) ERA 1996* *Cavaciuti v London Borough of Hammersmith & Fulham*

Remedies	Case/statute
Reinstatement	

• employer must take employee back in the same job • effect of order is as if employee had not been dismissed • continuity of employment is protected • and employee eligible for all back pay, and any improvement in terms that he would have had if he had remained in work	*S114 ERA 1996*

Re-engagement	

• employee must be taken back on by the employer or an associated employer on terms that are comparable with those that he enjoyed when he was dismissed • continuity of employment is protected • again employee entitled to back pay and any improvement in terms that he would have received if he had remained in work	*S115 ERA 1996*

Compensatory – has two components	
Basic award	

• similar to redundancy based on age and length of service times a set figure which is revised each year	*S118 ERA 1996*

Compensatory award	
• a figure that the tribunal thinks is just and equitable in the circumstances – which takes into account immediate loss of earnings, future loss of earnings, loss of statutory rights, loss of pension rights and expenses	*S123 ERA 1996*

SAMPLE ESSAY QUESTION

ESSAY Discuss the extent to which the law in relation to potentially fair heads of dismissal ensures that the dismissal is indeed fair.

Briefly explain the nature of an unfair dismissal claim

- There must be a dismissal under s95 Employment Rights Act 1996.
- The employee is not from an excluded group and has two years continuous service.
- If there is no automatically unfair dismissal the appropriate category of potentially fair dismissal should be identified.
- It should be considered whether the dismissal falls within the reasonable range of responses test and whether it is procedurally fair.
- If not a remedy is awarded.

Explain the five potentially fair heads of dismissal

Capability and qualifications
- Could be for incompetence, long term sickness, lack of qualification or aptitude.

Conduct
- Could involve breaches of rules or serious misconduct such as dishonesty or violence or could involve misconduct out of work.

Genuine redundancy
- Only if a genuine redundancy and all procedural requirements followed.

Statutory restriction
- Employer is bound to comply with the statutory requirement.

Other substantial reasons
• Wide construction by courts.
• Will often be for an economic, technical or organisational (ETO) reason.

Discuss whether these apply fairly

Capability and qualifications
• Would be unfair for employer to have to accept incompetence or keep a job open indefinitely for a sick employee and it is only fair that the employee should meet the necessary qualifications or aptitude.
• But the employer should do everything possible to ensure that the employee is capable e.g. training and should follow proper procedures and should not presume a sick employee is not fit to return.

Conduct
• Clearly employer should not have to accept misconduct and particularly where this is gross misconduct.
• The important thing is to follow procedure so the dismissal is fair.
• Could be unfair to employee when dismissed for misconduct outside of work.
• But generally justified if the misconduct relates to the work.

Genuine redundancy
• There are obviously justifiable circumstances where the employee needs to reduce the workforce.
• But an objective selection criteria and objective application of the criteria is essential or it could lead to abuses.

Statutory restriction
• Often this is where the employee no longer meets a statutory requirement.
• Likely to be fair unless the employee has taken steps to avoid the problem at his own cost and is still dismissed.

Other substantial reason
• Probably the most contentious because of the wide construction by courts.
• Possibly fair when based on a genuine business need.
• But seems less fair when it involves pressure from a third party.

Explain the reasonable range of responses test

- Start with s98(4) ERA 1996 – determined by equity and merits of case.
- Tribunal must consider reasonableness of employer's conduct, not whether fair.
- Must not substitute its own decision.
- Band of reasonable responses where one employer might reasonably take one view, another quite reasonably takes another.
- Did dismissal fall within the band of reasonable responses?

Explain procedural fairness

Based on ACAS Code – not legally binding but taken into account by tribunal.

- Should raise and deal with issues promptly and avoid unreasonable delays.
- Needs consistency from both sides.
- Should carry out necessary investigations.
- Should give employee full information and allowing them to state their case and be accompanied and have appeal process.
- Should keep proper records.

Discuss whether the tests apply fairly

- Takes into account employer's specific circumstances.
- And tribunal decision based on equity and substantial merits of each case.
- But is the band of reasonable responses too broad.
- Is it ultimately employer focused?
- Should ACAS Code be obligatory?

REACH REASONED CONCLUSIONS

SUMMARY

- Every employee has the right not to be unfairly dismissed so a person claiming must be an employee.

- There must be a dismissal rather than a termination of the contract by other means – so there must be a dismissal with or without notice or an expiry of a fixed-term contract without renewal or a constructive dismissal, one where the employee resigns but claims that this results from the employer's fundamental breach of the contract.

- Continuity of employment is important for establishing employment protections.

- For unfair dismissal the period is two years' continuous employment – although there are a large number of situations where no period of continuous employment is required such as discrimination claims but also many that have arisen because of statute such as whistle blowing or people asserting rights under the Working Time Regulations.

- The period is calculated by establishing the date of commencement of continuous employment, the effective date of termination and working out periods that do not interfere with continuity such as maternity and periods that do such as days lost through industrial action (strikes).

- There are also a number of employees who are ineligible for such claims such as share fishermen and police officers.

- There are numerous situations which give rise to automatically unfair dismissals – most of these arise from statute and include those that also require no qualifying period of continuous employment and which also include dismissals for asserting health and safety at work rights and dismissals on grounds of pregnancy and maternity.

- There are only five potentially fair heads of dismissal – dismissals for capability or qualification, for misconduct which can include in some circumstances criminal convictions outside employment, genuine redundancies, for a statutory restriction where the employer has no choice but than to dismiss and for any other substantial reason which generally will be an economic, technical or organisational (ETO) reason.

- Besides the dismissal being potentially fair it has to be fair in fact so it will have to fall within the reasonable range of responses test in which a reasonable employer might dismiss the employee in the same circumstances, and it must also be procedurally fair within the guidance of the ACAS Code of Practice.

- The remedies available for an unfair dismissal are an award of compensation, reinstatement where the employee gets his own job back on the same terms and re-engagement where the employee can return to another job on broadly similar terms.

Further reading

Emir, Astra, *Selwyn's Law of Employment 17th edition*. Oxford University Press, 2012, Chapter 17.

Pitt, Gwyneth, *Cases and Materials on Employment Law 3rd edition*. Pearson, 2008, Chapter 8, pp. 361–438.

Sargeant, Malcolm and Lewis, David, *Employment Law 6th edition*. Pearson, 2012, Chapter 4.4.

23

Termination of employment (5) redundancy

AIMS AND OBJECTIVES

After reading this chapter you should be able to:

▨ Understand the original aims of redundancy law

▨ Understand who is and who is not eligible for redundancy

▨ Understand the only three situations in which a redundancy can occur

▨ Understand the proper procedure for redundancy

▨ Understand what is suitable alternative employment

▨ Understand the significance of consultation

▨ Understand how a redundancy payment is calculated

▨ Understand what is meant by a lay-off and by short time

▨ Understand the consequences of either lay-off or short time

▨ Critically analyse the area of redundancy

▨ Apply the redundancy checklist to factual situations in order to determine whether there is a genuine redundancy

23.1 The origins and aims of redundancy law

The concept of redundancy was first introduced in the Redundancy Payments Act 1965. The Act had a number of basic purposes.

▨ to make employers conscious of the need for security in employment;

▨ to make employers conscious of the need to consider alternatives to dismissal;

▨ to provide a system for compensating employees who had lost their job – this is graded according to service so it is also a means of rewarding loyalty;

▨ to encourage mobility of labour and rationalisation of resources – although of course the role of the tribunal is merely to apply the statutory tests not to seek to look beyond the facts and assess the rights and wrongs of the employer's decision to carry out a redundancy.

Prior to the Act one common concern of trade unionists was that in any down turn of fortunes in a business it was always the workforce that was hit rather than any attempt to become more efficient and drive down costs by other means. In the light of the current lengthy economic recession it is questionable whether most of these aims are realised.

Compensation in the form of the redundancy payment was to be based on an uncomplicated method of calculation. The payment was to represent the loss suffered rather than being a tide over payment which would more appropriately come in the form of a benefit. As a result the payment is made even though the employee finds another job to go to. Originally it was not taxable. Now the first £30,000 is free of tax. It also did not disqualify the person from making a claim for benefit, which now would be job seeker's allowance.

Now redundancy is covered by Part XI of the Employment Rights Act 1996 and, in the case of rules on collective redundancies, also by the Trade Union and Labour Relations (Consolidation) Act 1992.

There are really four areas for consideration in relation to redundancy:

- eligibility for redundancy;
- what constitutes a dismissal for reasons of redundancy;
- redundancy procedure including the effects of offers of suitable alternative employment;
- how a redundancy payment is calculated.

The critical issue for an employer is that it follows the procedure.

23.2 Eligibility for redundancy

Certain people are not eligible for a redundancy payment. First and foremost the provisions only apply to employees, so anyone who is not classed as an employee will not be eligible (see Chapter 4). In the same way as unfair dismissal eligibility for a redundancy payment depends on the employee having completed two years' continuous service (see Chapter 19.1). Employees working under a fixed-term contract of two years or more which expires and is not renewed because of redundancy are also eligible for a redundancy payment. However, this only applies to agreements made since July 2002. In agreements made before that time an employee under a fixed-term contract could agree in writing to exclude his right to a redundancy payment.

Classes of employee who are ineligible for a redundancy payment include the following:

- share fishermen (those who take a share of the profit from the catch in remuneration);
- certain crown employees under section 159 Employment Rights Act 1996;
- those employed by the government of an overseas territory under section 160;
- those employed as a domestic servant in a household by a relative under section 161;
- those covered by a collective agreement between an employers' organisation and a trade union and approved by the Secretary of State where certain conditions under section 157 are met;
- employees in a redundancy situation who have unreasonably refused an offer of suitable alternative employment under section 141.

23.3 Dismissals for reasons of redundancy

There is a statutory presumption that a dismissal is for reasons of redundancy in section 163(2) Employment Rights Act 1996 unless the contrary is proved. An employer can challenge that there is a genuine redundancy or even that there is a dismissal at all. However, it will be for the employer then to show what the other reason for dismissal is or why there is no dismissal.

CASE EXAMPLE

Sanders v Ernest A. Neale Ltd [1974] IRLR 236

A company engaged in bookbinding decided to close down one of its departments because of loss of orders following a slump in the sale of hardback books and it was necessary to make some staff redundant as a result. After consultation with the unions two men were made redundant. The union thought that only one redundancy was necessary and so engaged in industrial action which included a work to rule, a refusal to do overtime and a refusal to do any of the work that had been carried out by the two men made redundant. The employer then wrote to the employees asking them to return to normal working or their contracts would be terminated which was what then happened. Eventually the business failed and closed down. The claimants argued that they should be entitled to a redundancy payment. The court held that they had been dismissed because of their refusal to work normally not because of redundancy. It was the industrial action which had caused the company to close down.

JUDGMENT

Sir John Donaldson explained: 'In the present appeals there was indeed a redundancy situation, but the tribunal found that it in no way caused the dismissals. The converse was true. It was the dismissals which caused the redundancy. The appellants were dismissed because they persistently refused to work normally. Their claim fails not because the redundancy was self-induced, but because it did not cause their dismissal.'

One other significant fact to consider (which can be seen from section 139 Employment Rights Act 1996 below) is that it is the job that is made redundant or that ceases to exist, not the employee. The consequence for the employee in a genuine redundancy will be a redundancy payment. If there is not a redundancy then there is no entitlement to a payment.

CASE EXAMPLE

Johnson v Nottinghamshire Combined Police Authority [1974] ICR 170

Two employees working as clerks for the Police Authority worked shifts from 9.30 a.m. until 5.30 p.m. A new split shift system was introduced which they were required to change to with shifts from 8.00 a.m. until 3.00 p.m. and 1.00 a.m. until 8.00 a.m. They were dismissed after they refused to work under the new shift system and claimed that instead they had been made redundant because of the significant change in the shift patterns. The court held that there was not a redundancy situation. In a genuine redundancy it is the job not the employee that is made redundant. In this case the Authority still had the same requirement for two clerical workers they merely needed them to work at different times.

There are only a limited number of circumstances in which a genuine redundancy actually occurs and these are identified in section 139 Employment Rights Act 1996.

SECTION

'139 Redundancy.

(1) For the purposes of this Act an employee who is dismissed shall be taken to be dismissed by reason of redundancy if the dismissal is wholly or mainly attributable to –

  (a) the fact that his employer has ceased or intends to cease –

    (i) to carry on the business for the purposes of which the employee was employed by him, or

    (ii) to carry on that business in the place where the employee was so employed, or

  (b) the fact that the requirements of that business –

    (i) for employees to carry out work of a particular kind, or

    (ii) for employees to carry out work of a particular kind in the place where the employee was employed by the employer, have ceased or diminished or are expected to cease or diminish.'

There are three different situations of a genuine redundancy that can be identified in the section:

- The employer has ceased business.
- The employer has ceased business at the place where the employee in question was employed.
- There has been a diminution in work.

The employer has ceased business

In general where an employer ceases to operate so that the entire workforce is redundant then this is a relatively straightforward situation and is unlikely to lead to questioning whether there is in fact a genuine redundancy. In *Moon v Homeworthy Furniture (Northern) Ltd* [1977] IRLR 298 the EAT identified that the role of the tribunal is merely to establish that the business has in fact been shut down not to inquire into the employer's reasons for dismissing the entire workforce.

JUDGMENT

The EAT concluded: 'the decision of the.... Tribunal was right and there could not and cannot be any investigation into the rights and wrongs of the declared redundancy'.

Cessation of business could also include a temporary cessation. The effect would still be that the whole workforce is made redundant. It was accepted in *Gemmell v Darngavil Brickworks Ltd* [1967] 2 ITR 20 that a dismissal of the workforce for thirteen weeks was a genuine redundancy.

The employer has ceased business at the place where the employee in question was employed

Cessation of the business at the place where the employee is employed can be straightforward but it can also involve a number of issues. In all cases it is a question of fact rather than of the contract. Originally in *United Kingdom Atomic Energy Authority v Claydon* [1974] IRLR 6 'the place where the employee was so employed' was held to mean the place where the employee could be required to work under his contract.

The consequence of this approach was that employers might rely on mobility clauses in the contract of employment and move employees freely to work elsewhere. If the employee then refused to move his place of work he could not claim that he was redundant.

CASE EXAMPLE

Rank Xerox Ltd v Churchill [1988] IRLR 280

The claimant worked at her employer's London headquarters. Her contract included a mobility clause in the following terms 'the company may require you to transfer to another location'. The company did then move its headquarters out of London. Churchill refused to move and argued that, since her place of work no longer existed, she was in fact redundant and entitled to a redundancy payment. The EAT held that, for the purposes of redundancy, place of work means place of work as required by the contract rather than the actual place of work where the employee has worked. In consequence her place of work had only moved and not ceased to exist and she could not claim entitlement to a redundancy payment.

Even if the courts at that time accepted express mobility clause an employer would not be able to argue that a mobility clause was implied in the contract.

CASE EXAMPLE

O'Brien v Associated Fire Alarms Ltd [1968] 1 WLR 1916

The claimants had worked for the company in the Liverpool area for many years. When there was a shortage of work they were told that they had to work in Barrow, a distance of 150 miles from Liverpool, despite there being no mobility clause in their contracts. The changed place of work made it impossible for them to see their families except at weekends. As a result they resigned and claimed that they were redundant. The employer argued that the court should imply a mobility clause into the contracts. It was held that no such clause could be implied. Since the men had worked around the Liverpool area for many years and there had never formerly been any question of the men relocating they were indeed redundant and entitled to a redundancy payment.

JUDGMENT

Salmon J in the Court of Appeal explained: 'Whether a term should be implied into a contract is a question of law. Whether the implication should be made in law ... depends on the facts ... there were no facts proved in evidence ... that it was a term of the men's employment that they could be asked to work anywhere within ... the area controlled from the company's Liverpool office.'

The courts subsequently rejected the contractual approach in favour of a factual approach. As a result an employer cannot rely absolutely on a mobility clause to avoid a dismissal being identified as a genuine redundancy situation.

CASE EXAMPLE

Bass Leisure Ltd v Thomas [1994] IRLR 104

The employee worked at a depot in Coventry and her contract included a mobility clause. The employer then decided to close that depot and transfer it to Birmingham, a distance of twenty miles and she was asked to transfer to that depot. She refused and claimed that she had in effect been made redundant. The EAT agreed that it was in fact a redundancy. It held that the true test should be a geographical test rather than a contractual one. On this basis the additional daily travel meant that operation of the clause was unreasonable and she was entitled to a redundancy payment.

JUDGMENT

The EAT identified: 'the question "Where is X employed?" is on the face of it a factual question. Indeed where there is no contractual term – express or implied – requiring mobility, we do not see how it can be answered other than factually; that is to say as being equivalent to "Where does X work?" '

This was later approved and the contractual approach rejected by the Court of Appeal.

CASE EXAMPLE

High Table Ltd v Horst [1998] ICR 409

Three employees had worked as 'silver service waitresses' for several years for a catering firm. Following a reduction in the need for catering service at the place where they worked they were made redundant by their employer. The women argued that, since there was an express mobility clause in their contracts, they had been unfairly selected for redundancy since they need only to have been redeployed to another place of work. The Court of Appeal rejected their argument and held that the mere existence of a mobility clause does not prevent a dismissal being for reasons of redundancy.

JUDGMENT

Peter Gibson LJ observed: 'The question ... where was the employee employed ... is one to be answered primarily by a consideration of the factual circumstances.... If an employee has worked in only one location under his contract ... it defies common sense to widen the extent of the place where he was so employed, merely because of the existence of a mobility clause ... the contract of employment may be helpful to determine the extent of the place where the employee was employed. But it cannot be right to let the contract be the sole determinant, regardless of where the employee actually worked.'

There has been a diminution in work

A redundancy because of a diminution in the need for the work is the area which is most volatile and subject to most controversy because it is inevitably where the claim that there has been an unfair selection for redundancy is most likely.

There are many situations that could result in the employer requiring fewer people to do the same work or fewer people because there is less work. The critical question for a tribunal in a dispute is whether the employer has a need for fewer employees to carry out the work.

A diminution could involve a decline in the particular type of work. In *Hindle v Percival Boats Ltd* [1969] 1 WLR 174 the employee repaired wooden boats. The work declined because fibre glass boats became more popular. The employee was too slow to adapt to the changed work and was dismissed for economic reasons. The court of Appeal accepted that there was no redundancy in the circumstances.

In a similar way if the dismissal in fact results from technological developments meaning that the requirements of the job are different then this could result in a genuine redundancy based on a diminution for the type of work.

CASE EXAMPLE

Murphy v Epsom College [1985] ICR 80

The claimant had been employed as a general plumber for which he was qualified. When the college changed to an electronically controlled heating system the claimant was made redundant because the new system required a qualified heating technician to run it. The Court of Appeal accepted that this was a genuine redundancy.

However, a mere failure to adapt to new conditions will not necessarily give rise to a genuine redundancy situation. In *North Riding Garages Ltd v Butterwick* [1967] 2 QB 56 the manager of a repair workshop was dismissed for inefficiency. His claim that he was entitled to a redundancy payment failed since the dismissal was simply because he could not adapt to the new business system. There was no diminution in the need for his role.

A dramatic change in the conditions of work may justify a claim that there is a redundancy. This was the case in *Macfisheries Ltd v Findlay* [1985] ICR 160. However, a change in time of work will not always give rise to a redundancy as in *Johnson v Nottinghamshire Combined Police Authority* [1974] ICR 170 above. Similarly a reorganisation for efficiency from a long day shift plus overtime to a double day shift in *Lesney Products & Co Ltd v Nolan* [1977] IRLR 77 was not a redundancy. The move to less earnings was irrelevant since the same number of employees was required.

Traditionally there was a concentration on the work that the employee actually did but courts have now established that the correct approach is to focus on the work not on the employee. The EAT in *Safeway Stores plc v Burrell* [1997] IRLR 200 identified a three stage process for determining whether there is a genuine redundancy:

JUDGMENT

'(a) even if a redundancy situation arises ... if that does not cause the dismissal, the employee has not been dismissed by reason of redundancy

(b) if the requirement for employees to perform the work ... diminishes, so that one employee can do both jobs, the dismissed employee is dismissed by reason of redundancy

(c) conversely, if the requirement for employees to do work of a particular kind remains the same, there can be no dismissal by reason of redundancy, notwithstanding any unilateral variation to their contracts of employment.'

The then House of Lords later approved this approach and identified that if the dismissal was attributable to a diminution then the contractual obligations are irrelevant.

CASE EXAMPLE

Murray v Foyle Meats Ltd [1999] ICR 827

Two men were employed in an abattoir as 'meat plant operatives'. There were two halls and a loading bay but the men always worked in one hall. Their line was closed down and they were made redundant following a decline in orders. The men tried to rely on a flexibility clause in their contract. This required them to do any job in the abattoir, so they argued that their dismissal was not a genuine redundancy but an unfair selection since they could have merely been moved elsewhere in the abattoir. The redundancy was based on diminution of the need for the work, the question concerned the selection. The House of Lords (now the Supreme Court) explained that the key issue for tribunals to consider is whether or not the dismissal is attributable to a diminution. If so then there is no need to consider what is in the contract.

JUDGMENT

Lord Irvine of Lairg explained the position: 'The key word in the statute is "attributable" and there is no reason in law why the dismissal of an employee should not be attributable to a diminution in the employer's need for employees irrespective of the terms of his contract or the function which he performed. Of course the dismissal of an employee who could perfectly well have been redeployed or who was doing work unaffected by the fall in demand may require some explanation to establish the necessary causal connection. But this is a question of fact, not law.'

ACTIVITY

Quick quiz

Consider which type of redundancy, if any, is appropriate in the following situations:

1. Mark teaches French and Spanish at a university. He is dismissed when the university fails to recruit any students for any modern language subjects. Because of the increase in student fees fewer students have applied for other subjects and there are no available teaching positions for which Mark could retrain.
2. Naomi works as a salesperson for an estate agent which has suffered an almost total stagnation in business during the past two years. Naomi's employer telephones her on Sunday night to tell her not to come into work on Monday as the business is being wound up.
3. Owen works as a recruitment consultant in the Birmingham office for an employment agency with offices throughout the Midlands. A clause in his contract identifies that he can be required to work at any of the company's offices. Owen is told that because of the downturn in employment opportunities the Birmingham office is to shut and he must move to the Shrewsbury office which is forty-five miles away.

23.4 Redundancy procedures

If a selection for redundancy is not fair then it can be a ground for a successful claim of unfair dismissal (see Chapter 22.4 and 22.5). On this basis an employer needs to ensure that it has followed a correct procedure. A fair dismissal for redundancy is one where:

- the employer has engaged in adequate consultation with the employee and his recognised trade union or other representative; and
- the system for selection was objectively fair; and
- there was no suitable alternative employment to offer the employee.

A failure in any of these areas might result in a successful claim for unfair dismissal.

The EAT has set out extensive guidelines to illustrate good industrial practice in redundancy situations:

CASE EXAMPLE

Williams v Compare Maxim Ltd [1982] ICR 156

The company was in financial difficulties and decided on a redundancy scheme in order to survive. It told the trade union representatives that there would be redundancies but no actual consultation with either the union or the staff occurred on either the criteria to be used or the identity of staff at risk. Williams was one of the staff who was dismissed without any warning.

The EAT laid down guidelines on the correct approach and held that the dismissal was unfair because the manner in which it had been carried out offended all commonly accepted standards of fairness.

JUDGMENT

Browne-Wilkinson J stated: 'The basic approach is that, in the unfortunate circumstances that necessarily attend redundancies, as much as is reasonably possible should be done to mitigate the impact of the work force and to satisfy them that the selection has been made fairly and not on the basis of personal whim.' He also identified the following good practice:

1. The employer will seek to give as much warning as possible of impending redundancies so as to enable the union and employees who may be affected to take early steps to inform themselves of the relevant facts, consider possible alternative solutions and, if necessary, find alternative employment in the undertaking or elsewhere.
2. The employer will consult the union as to the best means by which the desired management result can be achieved fairly and with as little hardship to the employees as possible. In particular, the employer will seek to agree with the union the criteria to be applied in selecting the employees to be made redundant. When a selection has been made, the employer will consider with the union whether the selection has been made in accordance with those criteria.
3. Whether or not an agreement as to the criteria to be adopted has been agreed with the union, the employer will seek to establish criteria for selection which so far as possible do not depend solely upon the opinion of the person making the selection but can be objectively checked against such things as attendance record, efficiency at the job, experience, or length of service.
4. The employer will seek to ensure that the selection is made fairly in accordance with these criteria and will consider any representations the union may make as to such selection.
5. The employer will seek to see whether instead of dismissing an employee he could offer him alternative employment.

This in effect creates three areas of consideration for the employer:

- proper consultation and advance warning;
- fair selection procedure and objective application of the selection procedure;
- reasonable consideration given to alternative courses of action and to offer suitable alternative employment.

Proper consultation and advance warning

The employer should give adequate warning of redundancy and engage in a proper consultation procedure. Consultation should be both individual with the employee and where there are collective redundancies with trade unions or representatives also. A failure to properly consult or warn may lead to unfair dismissal claim. In *Heron v Citylink Nottingham* [1993] IRLR 372 because it needed to make serious economic savings the employer dismissed the employee but without warning. It was said that if the employer fails to consult with the employee then it must be able to justify this, without justification it is unfair dismissal.

The duty to consult applies even when only one employee is selected for redundancy. The consultation should occur before the employee is given the notice of dismissal.

CASE EXAMPLE

Polkey v A E Dayton Services [1987] 3 WLR 1153

The employer needed to reduce its overheads and so decided to make some of its van drivers redundant. They had three male van drivers and one female van driver. It was decided to replace the four with two van salesmen. The manager decided that none of the three male van drivers was capable of van sales as well as driving but that the female van driver was so the three men were made redundant. The first that the claimant knew was when he was called into the office and dismissed. The tribunal felt that the lack of consultation and warning would have meant no difference to the end result. The House of Lords held that this was irrelevant and that there was still a duty to consult.

JUDGMENT

Lord Bridge explained: 'in the case of redundancy, the employer will not normally act reasonably unless he warns and consults any employees affected or their representatives, adopts a fair basis on which to select for redundancy and takes such steps as may be reasonable to avoid or minimise redundancy by redeployment within his own organisation. If an employer has failed to take the appropriate procedural steps ... the one question the ... tribunal is not permitted to ask in applying the test of reasonableness [in section 98(4) ERA 1996] is the hypothetical question whether it would have made any difference to the outcome.'

The fact that an employer has consulted with unions or representatives does not excuse it from the duty to consult also with the individual employee.

CASE EXAMPLE

Mugford v Midland Bank plc [1997] IRLR 208

The bank was restructuring and planned to make 3,000 staff including 858 managers redundant. The bank consulted with the union and the claimant's area manager was briefed on the criteria for selection. He then selected the claimant on the basis of performance reviews that identified that the claimant lacked some of the necessary skills. The claimant was then sent a letter informing him that he was at risk of redundancy and he was later made redundant. While the EAT dismissed the claimant's appeal it provided some guidance on lack of warning or consultation.

JUDGMENT

'(1) where no consultation about redundancy has taken place with either the trade union or the employee the dismissal will normally be unfair, unless the Industrial Tribunal finds that a reasonable employer would have concluded that consultation would be an utterly futile exercise in the particular circumstances of the case.

(2) consultation with the trade union over selection criteria does not of itself release the employer from considering with the employee individually his being identified for redundancy.

(3) it will be a question of fact and degree for the.... Tribunal to consider whether consultation with the individual and/or his union was so inadequate as to render the dismissal unfair. A lack of consultation in any particular respect will not automatically lead to that result. The overall picture must be viewed by the tribunal up to the date of termination to ascertain whether the employer has or has not acted reasonably in dismissing the employee on the grounds of redundancy.'

Fair selection procedure and objective application of the selection procedure

A tribunal is entitled to examine the employer's selection criteria and procedures to ensure that both have been carried out fairly, and an unfair selection for redundancy is an unfair dismissal.

The employer is bound to create genuine objective criteria for selection of redundant employees. If there is a pre-arranged criteria in place then the employer must follow it. In the past a common approach, which proved generally acceptable to trade unions, was known as last in first out or LIFO. This may have been appropriate in the past but with common employment practices it is more likely that an employer will wish to retain those elements of the workforce that are most useful and most productive. In any case LIFO may well offend age discrimination laws since it inevitably affects young workers most. However, if there is no agreed procedure then it was identified in *Selbe and Tesse v Plessey Co Ltd* [1972] IRLR 36 the employer should take into account superior capability and experience.

More recent criteria could be based on points systems which take into account not only capability and good qualities such as attendance and punctuality but poorer characteristics such as lateness and absences. As long as the criteria are objective and objectively applied then the selection for redundancy will generally be seen as fair. In *Clyde Pipeworks v Foster* [1978] IRLR 313 the employer applied a points criteria based on lateness, absence, quality of work and conduct which had been agreed with the trade union. The union was not consulted about the implementation of the scheme but the scheme was held to be fair and only needs to be fair in general terms, although it is good practice to consult unions.

The ultimate test for the tribunal is whether the employer acted reasonably in the selection. It is not relevant that the tribunal would have selected a different employee. This is what happened in *Grundy (Teddlington) Ltd v Willis* [1976] IRLR 118 where the tribunal differed with the selection but it was reversed by the EAT.

There is a wide range of situations where if an employee is selected for redundancy it will amount to an automatically unfair dismissal if other employees holding similar jobs are not selected. These include:

- dismissal on any discriminatory basis;

- pregnancy and maternity under section 94 Employment Rights Act 1996;

- maternity leave, parental leave, dependant care leave, adoption leave;

- any reason relating to a health and safety at work rights under section 100;

- in the case of protected shop workers who refuse to work on Sundays under section 101 Employment Rights Act 1996;

- acting as a trustee of an occupational pension scheme under section 102 Employment Rights Act 1996;

- in the case of trade union membership or non-membership, or trade union activities under Trade Union Labour Relations (Consolidation) Act 1992 section 153;

- acting as an employee representative;

- refusing to comply which is in breach of the Working Time Regulations under section 101A Employment Rights Act 1996;

- asserting any right under the National Minimum Wage Act under section 104A Employment Rights Act 1996;

- making a protected disclosure under section 103A Employment Rights Act 1996;

- taking action under the Part-time Workers (Prevention of Less Favourable Treatment) Regulations 2000;

- taking action under the Fixed-term Employees (Prevention of Less Favourable Treatment) Regulations 2002;

- exercising any statutory right under section 104 Employment Rights Act 1996.

There is no requirement of two years' continuous service for these.

Reasonable consideration given to alternative courses of action and to offer suitable alternative employment

A reasonable employer will be prepared to listen to and consider all reasonable alternatives to the redundancy. This could include a variety of alternatives including restricting recruitment, cutting overtime, introducing job sharing even retraining.

CASE EXAMPLE

Allwood v William Hill Ltd [1974] IRLR 258

The employer closed a number of shops and made staff redundant without warning. The employer should have seen redundancy as the last resort and considered alternatives. In the industry at the time there was a high wastage of staff so they could have been redeployed even if only on a temporary basis or even retrained.

An employer should also consider, if possible, an offer of suitable alternative employment. The offer should be on terms which are no less favourable and the employer must take into account the nature of the work, the working hours, the pay and conditions, qualifications and experience as well as status. So whether the alternative is suitable is a question of fact in each case and the tribunal has wide discretion in deciding whether it is suitable.

CASE EXAMPLE

Taylor v Kent CC [1969] 2 QB 560

A headmaster of a school was made redundant and offered alternative work as a supply teacher, although his salary and other benefits were to remain the same. He rejected the offer of alternative work and argued for a redundancy payment. The school in turn argued that his unreasonable refusal to accept the work meant that he was ineligible for a redundancy payment. The court accepted the argument that the offer of work was not a suitable alternative since it meant a significant reduction in status. As such the headmaster was entitled to a redundancy payment.

Section 138 identifies that if the employee is offered reinstatement or re-engagement before the end of his old contract and this occurs within four weeks of the old contract ending then it is not a dismissal. Inevitably the employee is entitled to a trial period of four weeks in order to retrain or assess the suitability of the post.

In making an offer of alternative employment the employer should obviously provide the redundant employee with all the information necessary for the employee to make an informed decision whether to accept or not.

Under section 141 a right to a redundancy payment is lost if the employee unreasonably refuses the offer of suitable alternative employment.

SECTION

'141

(4) The employee is not entitled to a redundancy payment if –

(a) his contract of employment is renewed, or he is re-engaged under a new contract of employment, in pursuance of the offer,

(b) the provisions of the contract as renewed or new contract as to the capacity or place in which he is employed or the other terms and conditions of his employment differ (wholly or in part) from the corresponding provisions of the previous contract,

(c) the employment is suitable in relation to him, and

(d) during the trial period he unreasonably terminates the contract, or unreasonably gives notice to terminate it and it is in consequence terminated.'

It follows that any refusal to take up the offer of suitable alternative employment must be reasonable or the employee will lose the right to a redundancy payment.

CASE EXAMPLE

Fuller v Stephanie Bowman (Sales) Ltd [1977] IRLR 87

The employer moved its premises in London from Mayfair to Soho. The employee, a secretary, objected to the move because the new premises were above a sex shop and she claimed that she had been made redundant. The tribunal disagreed and identified that the refusal to work in the new premises was based on oversensitivity and was therefore an unreasonable refusal.

The tribunal should take into account the possible impact on the employee of the alternative employment in the circumstances in assessing whether a refusal to accept it is reasonable or not.

CASE EXAMPLE

Paton, Calvert & Co v Waterside [1979] IRLR 108

The employee had been advised that he was to be made redundant and he found another job while he was working his notice. His employer then received a temporary employment subsidy from the government and offered him his job back. This would have only been until the subsidy ended so he rejected the offer. The employer then argued that his refusal was unreasonable and as a result he was not entitled to a redundancy payment. The EAT held that his refusal was reasonable in the circumstances. He was aged sixty-one and if the temporary position ended he would have difficulty finding another job.

The tribunal obviously has to assess the degree of suitability of the alternative employment in reaching a decision about a refusal to accept it. The greater the suitability as an alternative the more likely it is that the refusal is unreasonable. However, if the alternative employment is only marginally suitable then it is more likely that the refusal is reasonable.

CASE EXAMPLE

Commission for Healthcare Audit & Inspection v Ward [2008] UKEAT 0579 07

The claimant was the Head of Resources for the Commission. Following a restructure of the organisation her job had ceased to exist. She was offered alternative employment on three occasions and indeed asked for further information on the post on several occasions but eventually rejected the post claiming that it was not a suitable alternative. She argued instead that she was entitled to a redundancy payment. The EAT agreed with the findings of the tribunal that, while there was no reduction in status, there were a number of material differences between the two posts and, although it could be argued to be marginally suitable, it could not be classed as an ideal replacement for her old job. In the circumstances, it was reasonable for her to reject it.

JUDGMENT

The EAT identified: 'In an appropriate case where the offer of alternative work is overwhelmingly suitable it may be easier for the employer to show that a refusal by the employee is unreasonable. It is part of the balancing act which the Tribunal is charged to carry out.'

Procedure for collective redundancies

The rules on collective redundancies are contained in sections 188–192 of the Trade Union and Labour Relations (Consolidation) Act 1992. The sections have been amended on a number of occasions to reflect EU law.

There is also a provision in section 193 detailing circumstances where the employer has a duty to notify the Secretary of State in the case of mass redundancies.

The basic duty to consult is in section 188 TULR(C)A 1992.

SECTION

'188 duty of employer to consult representatives
(1)   Where an employer is proposing to dismiss as redundant 20 or more employees at one establishment within a period of 90 days or less, the employer shall consult about the dismissals all the persons who are appropriate representatives of any of the employees who may be affected by the proposed dismissals or may be affected by measures taken in connection with those dismissals.

(1A) The consultation shall begin in good time and in any event –
- (a) where the employer is proposing to dismiss 100 or more employees as mentioned in subsection (1), at least 90 days, and
- (b) otherwise, at least 30 days, before the first of the dismissals takes effect.'

There has been some debate on the subject of what amounts to 'in good time'. In *Burns v Scotch Premier Meats Ltd* [2000] IRLR 639 it was suggested that consultation should begin as soon as the employer decides that it will be making employees redundant. In *Junk v Wolfgang Kuhnel* [2005] (C-188/03) the ECJ said that consultation should be completed before any redundancy notice is given to an employee.

In *United States of America v Nolan* [2010] EWCA Civ 1223 the Court of Appeal referred the following question to the ECJ: 'Does the employer's obligation to consult about collective redundancies, pursuant to Directive 98/59 EC, arise (i) when the employer is proposing, but has not yet made, a strategic business or operational decision that will foreseeably or inevitably lead to collective redundancies; or (ii) only when that decision has actually been made and he is then proposing consequential redundancies?' On 12 March 2012 in *United States of America v Nolan* C-583/10 the Advocate General in his opinion stated that the obligation to consult arises when a strategic or commercial decision is taken that compels the employer to contemplate or plan collective redundancies. Neither of the alternatives contemplated in the question referred was to be preferred; consultation would be premature if the formulation at (i) was preferred and would be too late if the formulation at (ii) was preferred. Given the matters that must be consulted about in accordance with the Directive (ways of avoiding redundancies, reducing the numbers, and mitigating the consequences of dismissal) … the obligation to consult must arise at a time when there is still a possibility of preserving the effectiveness of such consultations.

The term 'establishment' is not defined in the Act. In *Clarks of Hove Ltd v Bakers' Union* [1978] IRLR 366 a bakery and twenty-eight shops were held to be an establishment. In *Barratt Developments (Bradford) Ltd v UCATT* [1978] ICR 319 a company headquarters together with fourteen separate building sites were held to be an establishment. In *Rockfon A/S v Specialarbejderforbundet I Danmark* [1996] ICR 673 establishment was held to mean the unit in which the workers are to be made redundant carry out their duties.

Section 188(1B) identifies with whom the consultation should be.

SECTION

'188
(1B) For the purposes of this section the appropriate representatives of any affected employees are:
- (a) if the employees are of a description in respect of which an independent trade union is recognised by their employer, representatives of the trade union, or
- (b) in any other case, whichever of the following employee representatives the employer chooses:
  - (i) employee representatives appointed or elected by the affected employees otherwise than for the purposes of this section, who (having regard to the purposes for and the method by which they were appointed or elected) have authority from those employees to receive information and to be consulted about the proposed dismissals on their behalf;
  - (ii) employee representatives elected by the affected employees, for the purposes of this section, in an election satisfying the requirements of section 188A(1).'

Section 188(2) goes on to identify what the consultation should be trying to achieve.

SECTION

'188

(2) The consultation shall include consultation about ways of –
   (a) avoiding the dismissals,
   (b) reducing the numbers of employees to be dismissed, and
   (c) mitigating the consequences of the dismissals,
       and shall be undertaken by the employer with a view to reaching agreement with the appropriate representatives.'

So there are two critical aspects to the process identified in this section:

- first that one major purpose of the consultation is to try to avoid the redundancies if possible;

- second that decisions should be reached by trying to reach agreement with the representatives.

In this way the consultation has to be a genuine process and treated with an open mind not prejudiced from the start.

CASE EXAMPLE

Middlesbrough Borough Council v TGWU [2002] IRLR 332

The Council had a large budget deficit and decided that it had to make a sizeable number of staff redundant. Trade unions heard rumours that there were to be large redundancies and were later given the numbers but they argued too little time to consult and consider alternatives. The EAT considered that the consultation process was a sham because the decisions on the number to be made redundant had already been decided.

JUDGMENT

The EAT identified: 'the decision to carry out redundancy dismissals was pre-determined by CMT before the Committee meeting held on 2 July, the outcome of which was known in advance because the Managing Director's briefing to all employees, referring to the Committee's decision and dated 3 July had been printed before the meeting took place. The CMT plan to deal with the budget deficit had been "squared" politically with the leader of the Council. There could be only one outcome. That, in our view, amounts to a clear finding that consultation over avoiding redundancies up to the service of dismissal notices on 3 July was a sham. It was not genuine consultation.'

Inevitably for consultation to be meaningful they should be conducted at an early stage while representatives have a chance to consider the situation and think of viable alternatives, should be provided with full information, and should be given adequate time to respond.

Section 188(4) goes on to detail what information the employer should provide during the consultation.

'188

(4) For the purposes of the consultation the employer shall disclose in writing to the appropriate representatives –

(a) the reasons for his proposals,

(b) the numbers and descriptions of employees whom it is proposed to dismiss as redundant,

(c) the total number of employees of any such description employed by the employer at the establishment in question,

(d) the proposed method of selecting the employees who may be dismissed,

(e) the proposed method of carrying out the dismissals, with due regard to any agreed procedure, including the period over which the dismissals are to take effect and

(f) the proposed method of calculating the amount of any redundancy payments to be made (otherwise than in compliance with an obligation imposed by or by virtue of any enactment) to employees who may be dismissed.'

Section 188(5) identifies the obligation on the employer to give representatives proper access to the employees affected by the redundancy.

Section 189(5) also introduces the idea of a protected award. The award is designed to compensate employees where there has been a lack of consultation. If such an award is made then it entitles the employee to one week's pay for every week of a protected period. The maximum period is ninety days. The decision is at the tribunal's discretion and it will make the award on the basis of what is just and equitable in the circumstances. The calculation of a week's pay is the same as for the basic award.

Section 189(6) identifies that there may be special circumstances which prevented the employer from carrying out proper consultation. The employer must show why it was not reasonably practicable for him to comply with the duty to consult. If this is shown then the employer may avoid liability for the lack of consultation.

There is no statutory definition of 'special circumstances' but in *Clarks of Hove Ltd v Bakers' Union* [1978] IRLR 366 the court suggested that it should be something exceptional or out of the ordinary or uncommon.

CASE EXAMPLE

Clarks of Hove Ltd v Bakers' Union [1978] IRLR 366

The employer was in dire financial difficulties and was no longer able to pay the staff their wages. It had in fact been aware of its perilous financial state for some time but had not engaged in any consultation and the workforce was told of the closure of the business two hours before it occurred. The court rejected the employer's argument that there were special circumstances.

Where an employer is proposing to make mass redundancies under section 193 of the Trade Union and Labour Relations (Consolidation) Act 1992 the Secretary of State must be informed. This would be where the proposal is to make 100 or more redundant in ninety days or twenty or more in thirty days. A copy of the notice must also be given to the appropriate employee representatives. Failure to do so can result in prosecution.

Time off to look for work

One final aspect of fair procedure is the obligation to allow the employee reasonable time off during his redundancy notice period to look for alternative work. This is in section 52 Employment Rights Act 1996.

SECTION

....

'52 Right to time off to look for work or arrange training
(1) An employee who is given notice of dismissal by reason of redundancy is entitled to be permitted by his employer to take reasonable time off during the employee's working hours before the end of his notice in order to –
   (a) look for new employment, or
   (b) make arrangements for training for future employment.'

The employee is also entitled to his normal pay while looking for work. The employee is not bound to give the employer details of interviews or appointments.

23.5 Calculating redundancy payments

A redundancy payment is calculated in a fairly similar way to an unfair dismissal basic award. First of all the employee must have two years' continuous service at the time of the dismissal.

The requirements and the method for calculating a redundancy payment are identified in section 162 Employment Rights Act 1996.

SECTION

....

'162 Amount of a redundancy payment.
(1) The amount of a redundancy payment shall be calculated by –
   (a) determining the period, ending with the relevant date, during which the employee has been continuously employed,
   (b) reckoning backwards from the end of that period the number of years of employment falling within that period, and
   (c) allowing the appropriate amount for each of those years of employment.
(2) In subsection (1)(c) "the appropriate amount" means –
   (a) one and a half weeks' pay for a year of employment in which the employee was not below the age of forty-one,
   (b) one week's pay for a year of employment (not within paragraph (a)) in which he was not below the age of twenty-two, and
   (c) half a week's pay for each year of employment not within paragraph (a) or (b).
(3) Where twenty years of employment have been reckoned under subsection (1), no account shall be taken under that subsection of any year of employment earlier than those twenty years.'

The calculation

There are a number of aspects to making the calculation:

- determining the relevant start and finish dates of employment for the purpose of calculating the continuous period of employment (the start date will be the first day of continuous employment and the finish date will in most instances be the last day of the notice period, the date when the employment ended);

- determining the number of complete years of the employee's continuous service (as identified in section 162 this is also up to a maximum of twenty years);

- the age of the employee (as can be seen in section 162 the statutory rate of pay is calculated at

- half a week's pay for each year of service between eighteen and twenty-two,
- one week's pay for each year of service between twenty-two and forty-one,
- one-and-a-half week's pay for each year of service over forty-one;
- the amount of pay (which will either be the employee's actual pay or the statutory maximum – in February 2013 this rose to £450 and rises each year).

Examples

The maximum redundancy payment would be for an employee that has twenty years' continuous service after the age of forty-one:

$$20 \times 1\frac{1}{2} (30) \times £450 = £13,500$$

The minimum redundancy payment would be for an employee under the age of twenty-two with two years' continuous service:

$$2 \times \frac{1}{2} (1) \times £450 = £450$$

In between an employee could receive a redundancy payment which is calculated with some years as half a week's pay and some as one week's pay and some as one-and-a-half week's pay. For an employee aged forty-five with fifteen years' continuous service the calculation would work as follows:

$$1\frac{1}{2} \times 4 (6) \times £450 = \mathbf{£2,700} \text{ (for the years over forty-one), plus}$$
$$1 \times 11 (11) \times £450 = \mathbf{£4,950} \text{ (for the years between twenty-two and forty-one)}$$
$$\text{Total} = \mathbf{£7,650}$$

Redundancy pay under £30,000 is not taxable. Employers are bound to provide a full written statement outlining how the redundancy payment was calculated and can be fined if they do not.

The calculations above are based on the statutory scheme and the statutory maximums. It is possible in some instances where an employer has agreed a redundancy scheme, usually with recognised trade unions, that a redundant employee will receive a payment that is more than the statutory maximum. One example is where employees earning more than the statutory maximum (currently £450) are paid at the rate of their actual weekly wage for each year of service.

Payments other than by the employer

As can be seen from 20.3 above section 139 identifies an area of genuine redundancy as the employer ceases trading. In the event of the employer's insolvency an employee is unlikely to get an immediate payment from the employer, although he would rank as a preferential creditor in the solvency when the assets are sold. However, there may still be insufficient funds. In this instance an employee can make application to the Secretary of State for a redundancy payment. This will be paid by the Insolvency Service under section 166 Employment Rights Act 1996. Payments that can be made are:

- up to eight weeks' wages;
- minimum pay during notice;
- up to six weeks' holiday pay;
- reimbursements of fees paid for apprenticeships.

All of these are subject to the statutory maximum.

■ The basic award made by the tribunal.

Voluntary redundancy

Voluntary redundancy is another possibility. This is when an employer offers employees a financial incentive to leave voluntarily, in order to avoid having to select people for redundancy. According to the Employment Rights Act 1996 a voluntary redundancy is still a dismissal and all the same rules apply as in a compulsory redundancy. Such schemes usually offer higher levels of redundancy payments to act as an incentive.

Employees who are invited to apply for voluntary redundancy should still be consulted on an individual basis and provided with all relevant information, such as notice periods. During compulsory redundancies, the consultation process is often tense as it will probably affect employees who do not wish to leave. The process is usually more straightforward in a voluntary redundancy. In voluntary redundancy it is also possible for an employee to put their name forward without being invited to. There is no obligation on the employer to accept this request since voluntary redundancy is usually a restructuring.

ACTIVITY

Quick quiz

Anthony has been employed by his employer since 1 April 1987. He is being made redundant on 22 May 2013. He will be fifty years old on 7 November 2013. Calculate his redundancy entitlement.

ACTIVITY

Self-assessment questions

1. What were the original purposes of introducing the concept of redundancy?
2. What is the prima facie difference between a genuine redundancy situation and an unfair dismissal?
3. What are the essential aspects of eligibility?
4. Are there any workers who are unfairly treated?
5. What are the circumstances in which an employee is the subject of a genuine redundancy?
6. Who and in what circumstances will show that a dismissal is not for reasons of redundancy?
7. Explain what a diminution in work is.
8. What difficulties, if any, does this present?
9. When and why will an employee be classed as redundant through failing to transfer place of work if requested?
10. How dramatic a change in working conditions is necessary to warrant a claim of redundancy?
11. What are the major considerations that an employer should give when contemplating a redundancy scheme?
12. When will a refusal to accept an offer of suitable alternative employment be unreasonable?
13. How important is the actual selection criteria?
14. With whom and for what purposes must an employer consult?

23.6 Lay-offs and short-time working

A lay-off is defined in section 147 Employment Rights Act 1996 as a week when an employee receives no pay due to him/her under the contract of employment. Short time is defined in section 147 Employment Rights Act 1996 as a week when an employee receives less than half the pay entitled under the contract.

Is the person eligible for redundancy?
He is an employee with two years' continuous employment with the employer
He is not ineligible:
- share fishermen
- certain crown employees under s159 ERA 1996
- employed by government of an overseas territory s160
- employed as a domestic servant in a household by a relative s161
- covered by a collective agreement between employers' organisation trade union and approved by the Secretary of State s157
- have unreasonably refused an offer of suitable alternative employment s141

YES

Has there been a dismissal under section 95 Employment Rights Act 1996?
- contract terminated with or without notice); or
- employed under a limited-term contract which is terminated without being renewed, or
- the employee terminates the contract in circumstances in which he is entitled to terminate it without notice by reason of the employer's conduct

YES

Has the dismissal been for reasons of redundancy under section 139 Employment Rights Act 1996?
- the employer has ceased business
- the employer has ceased business at the place where the employee in question was employed
- there has been a diminution in work

YES

Has the employer followed the correct procedure if appropriate?
- the employer has engaged in adequate consultation with the employee and his recognised trade union or other representative; and
- the system for selection was objectively fair and applied fairly; and
- there was no suitable alternative employment to offer the employee
- the employer has consulted with the appropriate representatives in a collective redundancy

Figure 23.1 Diagram illustrating the factors for consideration in a redundancy situation

'147 Meaning of "lay-off" and "short-time"
(1) For the purposes of this Part an employee shall be taken to be laid off for a week if –
  (a) he is employed under a contract on terms and conditions such that his remuneration under the contract depends on his being provided by the employer with work of the kind which he is employed to do, but
  (b) he is not entitled to any remuneration under the contract in respect of the week because the employer does not provide such work for him.
(2) For the purposes of this Part an employee shall be taken to be kept on short-time for a week if by reason of a diminution in the work provided for the employee by his employer (being work of a kind which under his contract the employee is employed to do) the employee's remuneration for the week is less than half a week's pay.'

Both lay-offs and short time may occur because of lack of orders, down turn in business and recession. Both have been common in the past in the construction industry, and longer ago in shipbuilding. In either case this is unsatisfactory uncertainty for the employee and as a result may eventually lead to the employee being able to make a claim to a redundancy payment if the conditions in section 148 Employment Rights Act are met.

SECTION

'148 Eligibility by reason of lay-off or short-time
(1) ... an employee is eligible for a redundancy payment by reason of being laid off or kept on short-time if –
  (a) he gives notice in writing to his employer indicating (in whatever terms) his intention to claim a redundancy payment in respect of lay-off or short-time ... and
  (b) before the service of the notice he has been laid off or kept on short-time in circumstances in which subsection (2) applies.
(2) This subsection applies if the employee has been laid off or kept on short-time –
  (a) for four or more consecutive weeks of which the last before the service of the notice ended on, or not more than four weeks before, the date of service of the notice, or
  (b) for a series of six or more weeks (of which not more than three were consecutive) within a period of thirteen weeks, where the last week of the series before the service of the notice ended on, or not more than four weeks before, the date of service of the notice.'

The employee must clearly give notice in writing to his employer that he intends to make a claim for redundancy arising from the length of the lay-off or short time, either at least four consecutive weeks or six or more weeks out of thirteen where more than three of the six were consecutive. He must also give the required period of notice.

The employer has two choices. It can decide that there is no or only limited prospect of work returning to normal and make a redundancy payment to the employee. Alternatively it can choose to make a counter notice. The conditions for a counter notice are in section 149 Employment Rights Act 1996.

SECTION

'149 Counter-notices

Where an employee gives to his employer notice of intention to claim but –

(a) the employer gives to the employee, within seven days after the service of that notice, notice in writing ... that he will contest any liability to pay to the employee a redundancy payment in pursuance of the employee's notice, and

(b) the employer does not withdraw the counter-notice by a subsequent notice in writing, the employee is not entitled to a redundancy payment in pursuance of his notice of intention to claim except in accordance with a decision of an employment tribunal.'

The employer may make a successful counterclaim if it can show the tribunal that proof exists of a reasonable prospect of normal working patterns returning for at least thirteen weeks, if it cannot then the employee will be entitled to a redundancy payment.

Both lay-offs and short time require express authority in the contract of employment. The uncertainty of the common law approach to lay-offs and short time as well as the obvious need for employees to maintain a regular and sustained income also led to the development of guarantee payments under statute. These were originally developed in the Employment Protection Act 1975 but are now in sections 28–35 of the Employment Rights Act 1996 (see Chapter 8.2). These were designed to encourage employers to act responsibly so any contractual payments are set off against a statutory scheme and employers can gain exemption.

KEY FACTS

The origins and aims of redundancy law	Case/statute
Introduced with aims	
• highlight employees' needs for job security • make employer consider alternatives to dismissal • provide compensation for loss of work • encourage mobility and rationalisation of resources	*Redundancy Payments Act 1965* Now in *Part XI ERA 1996, and for collective TULR[C]A 1992*
Eligibility for redundancy	Case/statute
Must be an employee with two years' continuous service or under a fixed-term contract of two years or more which expires and is not renewed because of redundancy (agreements made since July 2002)	
Ineligible for redundancy includes:	
• share fishermen • certain crown employees • those employed by the government of an overseas territory • those employed as a domestic servant in a household by a relative • those covered by a collective agreement between an employers' organisation and a trade union and approved by the Secretary of State • employees in a redundancy situation who have unreasonably refused an offer of suitable alternative employment	*S159 Employment Rights Act 1996* *S160* *S161* *S157* *S141*

Dismissals for reasons of redundancy	Case/statute
Statutory presumption of redundancy unless the contrary is proved • so the employer has the burden to show another reason Redundancy only occurs if • the employer ceases business • the employer ceases business at the employee's place of work • the need for work diminishes Cessation of business could be temporary	S163(2) Employment Rights Act 1996 Sanders v Ernest Neale S139 Employment Rights Act 1996. Gemmell v Darngavil Brickworks Ltd
Cessation at employee's place of work may be subject to mobility clause • but a factual rather than contractual test should be used Diminution follows reorganisation or change in work patterns e.g. • decline in work • change in character of work • dramatic changes in condition • but not mere changes in time of work Whether there is a diminution is measured factually	O'Brien v Associated Fire Alarms Co Bass Leisure Ltd v Thomas Hindle v Percival Boats Murphy v Epsom College Macfisheries v Findlay Johnson v Nottinghamshire Combined Police Authority Murray v Foyle Meats Ltd
Redundancy procedures	**Case/statute**
There should be:	
• proper consultation and advance warning • a fair selection procedure and objective application of the selection procedure • reasonable consideration given to alternative courses of action and to offer suitable alternative employment	Williams v Compare Maxim Ltd
An employer should consult with the individual employee as well as his union or representatives or it may be an unfair dismissal	
• the consultation should occur before the employee is given the notice of dismissal. • the fact that an employer has consulted with unions or representatives does not excuse it from the duty to consult also with the individual employee	Heron v Citylink Nottingham Polkey v A E Dayton Services Mugford v Midland Bank plc
A fair selection will be based on objective criteria objectively applied	
• only needs to be fair in general terms • the question is whether the employer acted reasonably not whether the tribunal agrees with the selection So should consider consideration e.g. redeployment, restricting recruitment, cutting overtime, job sharing, retraining	Clyde Pipeworks v Foster Grundy (Teddlington) Ltd v Willis Allwood v William Hill Ltd Taylor v Kent CC
And suitable alternative employment – which should be on terms which are no less favourable Right to a redundancy payment is lost if employee is offered new contract, on similar terms, which is suitable in relation to him, and he unreasonably terminates the contract, or unreasonably gives notice to terminate it and it is in consequence terminated • so refusal must be unreasonable	S141 Employment Rights Act 1996 Fuller v Stephanie Bowman (Sales) Ltd

• tribunal must consider employee's position • and assess the degree of suitability of the alternative employment offered	*Paton, Calvert & Co v Waterside Commission for Healthcare Audit & Inspection v Ward*
Where there are collective redundancies of twenty or more employees at one establishment within a period of ninety days or less the representatives should be consulted	*S188 Trade Union and Labour Relations (Consolidation) Act 1992*
• the consultation should be in good time	*S188(1A) Trade Union and Labour Relations (Consolidation) Act 1992*
• consultation should be completed before any redundancy notice is given to an employee	*Junk v Wolfgang Kuhnel*
• establishment means the unit in which the workers are to be made redundant carry out their duties	*Rockfon A/S v Specialarbejderforbundet I Danmark*
• representatives are trade union representatives or elected representatives	*S188(1B) Trade Union and Labour Relations (Consolidation) Act 1992*
• the purpose of consultation is to avoid the dismissals, reduce the numbers to be dismissed and mitigate the consequences of the dismissals	*S188(2) Trade Union and Labour Relations (Consolidation) Act 1992*
• so the consultation must be genuine and not prejudiced	*Middlesbrough Borough Council v TGWU*
• employer should reveal the reasons for his proposals, the numbers and descriptions of employees made redundant, the total number of employees of any such description, proposed method of selection, the employees who may be dismissed, proposed method of carrying out the dismissals, proposed method of calculating redundancy payments	*S188(4) Trade Union and Labour Relations (Consolidation) Act 1992*
• should give representatives proper access to affected employees	*S188(5) Trade Union and Labour Relations (Consolidation) Act 1992* *S188(5) Trade Union and Labour Relations (Consolidation) Act 1992*
• protected award is possible if employer fails to consult • special circumstances possible where impracticable for employer to consult • but must be exceptional circumstances • mass redundancies – over 100 in ninety days or over twenty in thirty days must inform Secretary of State • should give reasonable time off to look for work	*S188(6) Trade Union and Labour Relations (Consolidation) Act 1992* *Clarks of Hove Ltd v Bakers' Union* *S193 Trade Union and Labour Relations (Consolidation) Act 1992* *S52 Employment Rights Act 1996*

Calculating redundancy payments	Case/statute
Calculated on:	
• half a week's pay for each year of service between eighteen and twenty-two • one week's pay for each year of service between twenty-two and forty-one • one-and-a-half week's pay for each year of service over forty-one Up to a maximum of twenty years And maximum £430 (April 2012)	*S162 Employment Rights Act 1996*

Lay-offs and short-time working	Case/statute
An employee is laid off for a week if his pay depends on being in work but he gets no pay because the employer gives him no work	*S147 Employment Rights Act 1996*

An employee is on short-time for a week if because of diminution in the work provided his pay for the week is less than half a week's pay	
The employee can claim a redundancy payment if laid off or kept on short time for four or more consecutive weeks or for six or more weeks in thirteen where no more than three were consecutive	*S148 Employment Rights Act 1996*
The employee must serve notice in writing to the employer that he is claiming a redundancy payment	
But the employer can serve a counter notice if there is a reasonable prospect of work returning to normal	*S149 Employment Rights Act 1996*

SAMPLE ESSAY QUESTION

ESSAY Discuss the extent to which the rules on redundancy actually achieve the original aims.

Explain the original aims of redundancy
- To highlight employees' need for job security.
- To make the employer consider alternatives to dismissal.
- To provide compensation for loss of work.
- To encourage mobility and rationalisation of resources.

Explain the rules on eligibility
- Certain classes of employee e.g. share fishermen, domestic servants working for a relative and employees in a redundancy situation who have unreasonably refused an offer of suitable alternative employment are ineligible.
- Those without two years continuous employment are ineligible.

Discuss whether the rules on eligibility meet the original aims
- Not much job security for ineligible employees.
- So employer can look to dismiss these first.
- And will not have to provide compensation.
- But does help rationalisation of resources.

Discuss the reasons for redundancy

- Employer ceases trading.
- Employer ceases trading at the place where the employee in question works.
- There is a diminution of business.

Discuss whether the types of redundancy meet the original aims

- Not much job security where the employer goes out of business although employees can still get a payment from the government and the employer probably did not have the opportunity to consider alternatives.
- Ceasing trading at one place may make it difficult to rationalise sensibly and may seem unfair to particular employees.
- Diminution is probably the most contentious – usually follows a decline in business but can be used to disguise other motives for dismissal.

Explain the proper procedures for redundancy

- Should have proper consultation and give advance warning.
- Should have a fair selection procedure and objective application of the selection procedure.
- Reasonable consideration given to alternative courses of action and to offer suitable alternative employment.
- In collective redundancies there are extensive rules on consultation and informing the secretary of state.

Discuss whether the procedural rules meet the original aims

- Should consider e.g. redeployment, restricting recruitment, cutting overtime, job sharing, retraining and offering suitable alternative employment – which should be on terms which are no less favourable – so does make employer consider job security and alternatives and gives opportunity for rationalisation.
- Selection criteria where reason for redundancy is diminution must be fair and applied objectively – but could give wide scope for having another motive for dismissing.
- But using sick record, disciplinary record, performance etc does give employer better chance of effective rationalisation.

REACH REASONED CONCLUSIONS

SUMMARY

- Originally introduced to highlight the employees' needs for job security; to make the employer consider alternatives to dismissal; to provide compensation for loss of work; and to encourage mobility and rationalisation of resources.

- Eligibility is based on two years' continuous service and there are a number of exceptions who cannot receive redundancy payment such as share fishermen.

- There are only three circumstances in which a redundancy can occur – where the employer has ceased trading, where the employer has ceased trading at the employee's place of work and where there is a diminution in the need for the work to be done – the latter being the most common.

- Diminution can in fact involve reorganisation or a change in work patterns or follow a decline in work or orders or result from a change in the character of the work or result from dramatic changes in conditions but it should not merely be changes in the time of work – in any case whether there is a diminution is measured factually.

- For as proper procedure there should always be proper consultation and advance warning, a fair selection procedure and objective application of the selection procedure, and reasonable consideration given to alternative courses of action and to offer suitable alternative employment.

- A fair selection must always be based on objective criteria objectively applied.

- The right to a redundancy payment is lost if the employee is offered a new contract, on similar terms, which is suitable in relation to him, and he unreasonably terminates the contract, or unreasonably gives notice to terminate it.

- Where there are collective redundancies of twenty or more employees at one establishment within a period of ninety days or less the representatives should be consulted.

- The consultation should be meaningful.

- Redundancy pay is calculated on the basis of a week's pay or the statutory maximum payment for each year's service up to a maximum number of years.

- Lay-offs are when an employee's pay depends on him being at work but he gets no pay because the employer gives him no work.

- Short time is when because of a diminution in the work provided the employee's pay for the week is less than half a week's pay.

Further reading

Emir, Astra, *Selwyn's Law of Employment 17th edition*. Oxford University Press, 2012, Chapter 18.
Pitt, Gwyneth, *Cases and Materials on Employment Law 3rd edition*. Pearson, 2008, Chapter 9.
Sargeant, Malcolm and Lewis, David, *Employment Law 5th edition*. Pearson, 2010, Chapter 4.5.

24

Employment rights related to trade union membership and non-membership

AIMS AND OBJECTIVES

After reading this chapter you should be able to:

▨ Understand the basic right to trade union membership or non-membership

▨ Understand the rules related to recognition of trade unions

▨ Understand the circumstances in which time off for trade union related activities is allowed

▨ Understand the process of collective bargaining

▨ Understand the circumstances in which participation in a trade dispute gains statutory protection

▨ Understand the rules regarding dismissal for trade union membership, non-membership or trade union activity

▨ Critically analyse the area

▨ Apply the law to factual situations and reach conclusions

24.1 Introduction: the origins of modern trade union law

Trade unions really begin with the medieval guild system which regulated trade and apprenticeships. Modern trade unionism really begins with collective action by members of traditional crafts in the wake of developing mechanisation and industrialisation in the eighteenth century (see Chapter 1.1.2). The Industrial Revolution created enormous wealth but it was also characterised by great poverty and also mass unemployment amongst the adult male workforce from the traditional skills such as hand loom weaving in the woollen industry.

The use of child labour in the emerging cotton industry and the fact that poor relief at the time was the responsibility of the parish meant that there was a plentiful supply of cheap labour and enabled employers in the new industries to keep wages low. The Napoleonic wars at the start of the nineteenth century depressed exports and created more unemployment. The Corn Laws artificially increased the price of grain and worsened the effects of poverty. The widened use of mechanised industry led to an even bigger increase in child and female labour.

This was a time of great change and there were many factors that would cause distress to working people. Following the loss of a significant colony in the American War of Independence and with an eye on the recent so-called 'reign of terror' following the French Revolution the ruling class was wary of collective action by workers and fearful of mass social unrest of the kind seen in France. The result was the Combination Act 1799 and the Combination Act 1800. The Acts provided that any combination aimed at securing the advancement of wages or the reducing of hours or of improving the conditions of work were unlawful and subject to a period of three months' imprisonment or two months' hard labour. The Acts were significant because it was the first legislative repression of workers as a class.

Some workers responded by what the establishment identified as 'bread riots' where stocks of grain were taken and sold on at 'reasonable' prices. In specific areas such as Nottinghamshire where the woollen trade had been replaced by a mechanised cotton industry and there was large scale unemployment amongst traditional skilled workers the Luddite movement grew up which was characterised by the wrecking of the new machinery. With the suspension of habeas corpus such localised movements gradually developed into a wider movement for political reform led by leading radicals of the time such as Cobbett and Hunt. However, calls for reform came at a heavy price such as the so-called 'Peterloo Massacre' in Manchester in 1819 where at a peaceful demonstration magistrates ordered a cavalry charge through unarmed defenceless people with swords drawn. There were sixteen deaths and more than 600 injured.

Working people experienced a very mixed economic and social climate during the early nineteenth century. In fact while industrial and agricultural workers experienced completely different conditions this could also be said of the landowners and industrialists of the time. A partial repeal of the Combination Acts did in fact occur in 1824 which in a very limited way legitimised some trade union membership and even more limited industrial action. Nevertheless, this involved the most cynical strategy on the part of the ruling class who had clearly reached the conclusion that illegal combinations always posed a greater threat of sedition and revolution than legal ones that it was felt would quickly disappear. In any case the point became largely academic in 1825 when an amending Act (the Combination of Workmen Act 1825), whilst retaining the legality of membership of trade unions, nevertheless made illegal any form of industrial action thus rendering trade unions ineffective in law.

The benefits to working people of political reform as an answer at that time are shown by the impact of the so-called Great Reform Act 1832 which only extended the electorate from 220,000 to 670,000 out of a population of over fourteen million. As a result there was an upsurge of trade union activity in 1834 and the shift towards the idea of a national trade union. This eventually resulted in the formation of the Grand National Consolidated Trade Union which grew rapidly to a membership of half a million and coincided with a surge of militant action.

The case of *R v Loveless and Others* [1834] (the so-called Tolpuddle Martyrs) six Dorset farm labourers combined to form a union and swore the oath of the Grand National. They then tried to recruit other men from a neighbouring village. Local magistrates, who feared unrest if unionism spread, sought advice from the Law Officers in London and were advised to prosecute the men under the Mutiny Act 1797 for swearing unlawful oaths, although the section actually concerned oaths of silence made by serving soldiers and sailors during acts of mutiny. The actual date of the offences charged was also different to the date when the oaths had been made. Nevertheless, the men were transported to Australia (at that time a penal colony) for seven years in essence for membership of a legal trade union.

The volume of strikes in a short period caused the decline and collapse of the Grand National which had neither the organisational capability to organise widespread action nor the physical resources to support it.

Later in the century new model unions were created which concentrated on specific trades. The Amalgamated Society of Engineers is a classic example. The leaders of some of those unions coordinated their activities and were able to exert some moderate influence becoming known briefly as 'the junta'. A significant legal decision at the time which caused unions great distress and alarm was *Hornby v Close* [1867] 2 LRQB 153 in which it was deemed not to be unlawful for a branch treasurer who had embezzled the union to abscond with the funds of the union. Legislation in 1867 also prevented unions from being registered under the Friendly Societies Act 1793 because of the practice of paying strike pay to employees who otherwise would have no means of support. A subsequent Royal Commission which divided into two camps producing different reports nevertheless remedied the situation by passing the Trade Union Funds Protection Act 1869.

The government under pressure also later passed the Trade union Act 1871 which produced a major advance for trade unionists in section 2:

SECTION

'2 ... the purposes of any trade union shall not, by reason merely that they are in restraint of trade, be deemed to be unlawful so as to render any member of such trade union liable to a criminal prosecution for conspiracy or otherwise.'

The Act also permitted trade union property to be held by trustees so that it could be protected in law. However, it did not permit unions to gain the corporate personality enjoyed by business. The Criminal Law Amendment Act 1871 repealed the 1825 Combination of Workmen Act and thus legitimised the activities of unions in trade disputes except for molestation and obstruction. However, any benefits were short lived with the court in *R v Bunn* [1872] 12 Cox, CC 316; 14 Digest 116 where gas workers striking against the dismissal of a fellow worker were held guilty of common law conspiracy. The judge condemned the Criminal Law Amendment Act 1871 and held that molestation was 'any unjustifiable annoyance and interference with the masters in the conduct of their business' in effect reversing the immunities granted in the Act.

There were also a significant number of successful actions for breach of contract following strikes despite statutory modifications to the master and servant rules. In fact greater union militancy, a refusal to cooperate with the Royal Commission and the new strategy of unions of putting forward their own candidates in parliamentary elections which resulted in the election of two officials, all persuaded Disraeli, the Prime Minister, to repeal the remaining master and servant rules in the Employers and Workmen Act 1875. The immunities from the 1871 Act which the judges had rendered ineffective were replaced with more specific immunities in the Conspiracy and Protection of Property Act 1875. This provided in section 2 that the doing or procuring of an act in furtherance of a trade dispute was not actionable as a conspiracy unless the act itself was actionable. So it removed the ambiguity surrounding molestation, specifically overruled *R v Bunn* and meant that trade unions were legal both in terms of their membership and their activities in furtherance of trade disputes.

Despite this apparent statutory protection, unions still on occasions suffered harshly at the hands of the judiciary. Picketing was expressly illegalised in *Lyons v Wilkins* [1899] 1 Ch 255. Procuring a breach of contract was held to be illegal in *Bowen v Hall* [1881] 6 QBD 333. Inducing a party not to enter into a contract was declared illegal in *Temperton v Russell* [1893] 1 QB 715 which might appear acceptable if it was not for the fact that the court held the opposite in the case of a business in *Mogul Steamship Co v McGregor, Gow & Co* [1892] AC 25. Some cases did go the unions' way as in *Curran v Treleaven* [1891] 2 QB 545 where the court would not accept boycotting as intimidation under the 1875 Act and *Allen v Flood* [1898] AC 1 which held that an inducement to breach a contract was not illegal unless the means used to secure it were also illegal. In this latter case Lord Chancellor Halsbury tried to obtain the opposite result by packing the court with his own supporters but was in fact defeated by the influence of Lord Herschell, himself a former Lord Chancellor.

Nevertheless, the court in *Quinn v Leatham* [1901] AC 495 (see 24.6.1 below) accepted that a conspiracy to induce breaches of contract injurious to the employer was unlawful. The judicial dispute was between illegal means and illegal motive so many commentators have suggested that *Allen v Flood* was the safer decision. Only a few days prior to *Quinn v Leatham* the so-called Taff Vale case *Taff Vale Railway Co v Amalgamated Society of Railway Servants* [1901] UKHL 1 allowed that a union registered under the 1871 and 1876 Acts was able to be sued allowing the employer recovery of £23,000 from union funds. The result of these cases was almost express reversal of statutory provisions which threatened not just unions but the friendly societies also.

The unions had enjoyed twenty years of progress, had grown steadily in membership, had begun to coordinate their activities under the umbrella of a Trade Union Congress. In parallel with this there had been renewed interest in parliamentary representation through the Social Democratic Federation, the Independent Labour Party and the Labour Party. Candidates stood in the 1900 elections with no success but following the judicial interference with statutory rights in the 1906 elections, besides the government being routed for the first time, twenty-nine Labour Party MPs were elected to Parliament. Following this the new Liberal government introduced the Trade Disputes Act 1906. The Act removed certain illegal conspiracies, restated the former statutory immunities and identified in section 1 that 'an act if done in contemplation or furtherance of a trade dispute, shall not be actionable unless the act, if done without any such agreement or combination, would be actionable'. It also in section 2 legalised some picketing and in section 4 prevented tortious actions against union members. The Act had legal force for much of the twentieth century until the Thatcher government of the 1980s.

24.2 Trade union membership and non-membership

There are a number of rights which an individual enjoys in relation to membership and non-membership of a trade union. These are mostly contained in the Trade Union and Labour Relations (Consolidation) Act 1992 but some rights are also identified in the Employment Rights Act 1996. The rights are quite diverse in character and cover access to employment, time off for legitimate activities engaged in at appropriate times, industrial action, discipline and dismissal.

The basic right is to belong to a trade union or indeed not to belong to a trade union. The employee should have complete freedom to do either. In terms of access to employment the basic right not to be denied access to employment because of membership or non-membership of a trade union is found in section 137 Trade Union and Labour Relations (Consolidation) Act 1992.

SECTION

> '137 Refusal of employment on grounds related to union membership.
> (1) It is unlawful to refuse a person employment –
>   (a) because he is, or is not, a member of a trade union, or
>   (b) because he is unwilling to accept a requirement –
>   (i) to take steps to become or cease to be, or to remain or not to become, a member of a trade union, or
>   (ii) to make payments or suffer deductions in the event of his not being a member of a trade union.'

Denial of access to employment on these grounds covers:

- refusing or deliberately omitting to consider the application or enquiry; or
- causing the applicant to withdraw or cease to pursue the application or enquiry; or
- refusing or deliberately omitting to offer the applicant employment of that description; or
- making the applicant an offer of such employment the terms of which are such as no reasonable employer who wished to fill the post would offer and which is not accepted; or
- making him an offer of such employment but withdrawing it or causing the applicant not to accept it.

Different approaches have been taken to the application of section 137. It was traditionally accepted for instance that a refusal to employ a person for past trade union activities was legitimate.

CASE EXAMPLE

Birmingham District Council v Beyer [1978] 1 All ER 910

The claimant was refused employment because of his previous trade union activities. He argued that this was an unlawful refusal. However, the claimant was a well-known militant and the EAT accepted that the refusal was not specifically because of his trade union membership but because of his disruptive record in employment.

However, this contrasts with the position where the claimant is being dismissed for past trade union activities which has been held to be contrary to section 146 Trade Union and Labour Relations (Consolidation) Act 1992 in *Fitzpatrick v British Railways Board* [1992] ICR 221 (see Chapter 24.8.1).

Each case has to be judged on its individual circumstances but it is also clear that there is a significant overlap between membership and activity.

CASE EXAMPLE

Harrison v Kent County Council [1995] ICR 434

The employee was also a trade union representative and had formerly led a lengthy industrial dispute in his employment which became quite hostile and bitter at times. He left that employment and applied for another position unsuccessfully. He claimed that the decision not to appoint him was because of his trade union membership and therefore was contrary to section 137. The EAT accepted that there was a significant overlap between trade union membership and trade union activity and therefore not being given the position could have been based on his trade union membership.

However, a distinction has been drawn between the purpose of refusing the person employment and the effect of refusing them employment and this is something that the court also needs to consider. This was the position of the then House of Lords in *Associated British Ports v Palmer* [1995] IRLR 399 where the employer had replaced a collective agreement to which it was a party with redrafted individual contracts. This was challenged as unlawful and, while the Court of Appeal stated that this discriminated against trade union rights, the House of Lords overruled and held that the purpose was in fact flexibility and it was therefore lawful. It is likely that this latter view conflicts with the position taken by the European Court of Human Rights in *Wilson, National Union of Journalists and Others v the United Kingdom* [2002] IRLR 568 ECHR which also concerned discrimination against trade union rights during employment (see Chapter 24.7). It may be then that the position is different before employment and during employment.

Under section 137(3) a job advertisement that indicates in any way that employment is only open to applicants who are a member of a particular trade union or who are not a member of a trade union will straightforwardly create a presumption that employment has been refused because of trade union membership or non-membership or past activities and so is contrary to section 137. On this basis it would be best practice for an employer to remove any mention of trade unions at all in job advertisements.

Section 138 extends the provisions to employment agencies. However, there are a number of exclusions from the operation of section 137:

- self-employed;
- members of the armed forces;
- police officers;
- share fishermen;
- employees who ordinarily work outside the UK;
- seamen working on ships that are not registered in the UK;
- exemptions made by the Secretary of State for national security reasons.

Remedies are under sections 139–142. Complaints should be made to the tribunal within three months of the act complained of. If the claimant succeeds in the claim then the court may make a declaration, award compensation and may make recommendations for remedial action by the employer.

ACTIVITY

Self-assessment questions

1. What is the basic protection in section 137 TULR(C)A?
2. In what different ways will access to employment for trade union related reasons be unlawfully denied?
3. When will job advertisements be unlawful and what is the sensible way to avoid this?
4. What groups of people are excluded from the protections?

24.3 Trade union recognition

Recognition of a trade union by an employer is important for all sorts of reasons but in particular it enables the two to engage in collective bargaining and allows the union to have disclosure of information which is essential to collective bargaining (see 24.5 below) and also it means that the union must be consulted where there are collective redundancies (see Chapter 23.4) and on transfer of undertakings (see Chapter 18.6).

Recognition is defined in section 178(3) Trade Union and Labour Relations (Consolidation) Act 1992 as 'recognition by an employer, or two or more associated employers ... for the purposes of collective bargaining'.

Recognition can be of two types:

- voluntary
- statutory.

Voluntary recognition

Where recognition of a trade union by an employer is voluntary this is unremarkable and as the term voluntary suggests the employer will have reached an agreement with a particular trade union or unions by which the employer is prepared to engage in collective bargaining. This is actually useful for the employer since it potentially reduces the number of parties with whom the employer has to negotiate and therefore the amount of time taken up by negotiations. It is also the case that a trade union may be more prepared to compromise and reach an agreement than many individual employees. Furthermore if the contract is expressly made subject to collective agreements made periodically with the recognised trade union employees are bound.

Statutory recognition

Following the Employment Relations Act 1999 Schedule 1.1 a new Schedule A1 was inserted in the Trade Union and Labour Relations (Consolidation) Act 1992 setting out rules for statutory recognition of trade unions.

The rules are complex but in order to gain recognition a trade union must make a request under Schedule A1 paragraph 4 Trade Union and Labour Relations (Consolidation) Act 1992 to an employer which employs more than twenty-one employees for recognition for the purposes of collective bargaining. The request should be in writing and state that the request is being made under the provisions of the Act.

There is then a ten-day period for the employer and the trade union to negotiate on recognition. If the negotiations are unsuccessful then there is a further twenty-day period for the parties to try to agree on the bargaining unit. During this time the parties can seek the assistance of ACAS.

If the negotiations have still not resolved the issue then the union may apply to the Central Arbitration Committee which will need to determine whether:

- the proposed bargaining unit is appropriate;
- the union has the support of the majority of the workforce.

At least 10 per cent of the proposed bargaining unit must be members of the trade union. If there are less then the Central Arbitration Committee will not proceed further. However, if more than 50 per cent are union members then automatic recognition applies and a declaration to that effect is made.

In some instances a secret ballot is carried out. Under Schedule A1 paragraph 22(4) Trade Union and Labour Relations (Consolidation) Act 1992 this is where:

- The ballot would be in the interests of good industrial relations.
- There is evidence of a significant number of members who do not wish to be represented in collective bargaining.
- There is evidence of a significant number of members who do not wish to be represented by the union or unions.

Once recognition is obtained it is effective for three years.

ACTIVITY

Self-assessment questions

1. How is trade union recognition defined?
2. What are the main purposes of seeking recognition of a trade union with a particular employer?
3. What is voluntary recognition?
4. What is statutory recognition?
5. What is the role of the Central Arbitration Committee in statutory recognition?

24.4 Trade union related time off

There would be little point in guaranteeing rights of membership of trade unions if members were not then able to engage in legitimate activities. In similar fashion an official or representative of a trade union would be rendered functionless if they were not able to carry out their duties to their members. For these reasons there are also rules relating to time off to carry out trade union duties and time off to engage in trade union activities.

24.4.1 Time off for trade union duties

Under section 168 Trade Union and Labour Relations (Consolidation) Act 1992 an employer must permit an official of a recognised trade union time off during working hours to carry out his official duties in respect of:

- negotiations with the employer connected with collective bargaining; or
- the performance on behalf of employees of the employer of functions related to or connected with matters falling within collective bargaining which the employer has agreed may be so performed by the trade union; or
- the receipt of information from the employer and consultation by the employer in connection with collective redundancies or transfer of undertakings; or
- receiving training in industrial relations relevant to carrying out the duties for which recognition is given and which is approved by the TUC and the specific trade union.

Under section 168(3) the amount of time off which an employee who is an official of the trade union can take off for these purposes is that which is reasonable in all the circumstances having regard to any relevant provisions of a Code of Practice issued by ACAS and the employee will be paid as normal.

If the employer fails to allow the employee the appropriate time off for the purposes of section 168 or fails to pay the employee then the employee can make a complaint to the tribunal. However, it is not reasonable to expect the employer to pay for duties carried out in the employee's own time.

CASE EXAMPLE

Hairsine v Kingston-Upon-Hull City Council [1992] IRLR 211

The claimant was a swimming pool attendant who worked on a shift system. The employee was also shop steward and was allowed time off work with pay to attend some training appropriate to his trade union position. Some of the training was in work time and was paid but the employer would not pay the employee for time spent on the training course that was not in work time. The EAT held that there was no obligation on the employer to allow the employee either extra time off or pay in lieu of the union training which was done outside normal working hours.

24.4.2 Time off for trade union activities

Time off for taking part in trade union activities is covered in section 170 Trade Union and Labour Relations (Consolidation) Act 1992 which is fairly clearly stated.

SECTION

'170 Time off for trade union activities.
(1) An employer shall permit an employee of his who is a member of an independent trade union recognised by the employer in respect of that description of employee to take time off during his working hours for the purpose of taking part in –
(a) any activities of the union, and
(b) any activities in relation to which the employee is acting as a representative of the union.'

Again as with time off for carrying out trade union duties time can only be taken that is reasonable in the circumstances having regard to the ACAS Code of Practice and under section 170 there is no right to pay.

CASE EXAMPLE

Wignall v British Gas Corporation [1984] IRLR 493

An employee asked for ten days off to prepare a trade union magazine. This might have been considered reasonable in isolation. However, the employee already enjoyed twelve weeks' leave a year partly paid and partly unpaid, although this was in fact unconnected to her trade union membership. The EAT held that such requests should be judged on all the circumstances.

Obviously again if a request for time off to engage in trade union activities is unreasonably refused then the employee may make a complaint to a tribunal.

One further qualification of the right is in section 170(2) which identifies that the right does not extend to activities which are in fact industrial action, whether or not these are in contemplation or furtherance of a trade dispute.

ACTIVITY

Self-assessment questions

1. What are the differences between trade union duties and trade union activities?
2. Why is it important that there should be rights to time off for trade union duties and activities?
3. What trade union duties is a trade union official able to have time off to undertake?
4. What amount of time off is the official able to take and how is this measured?
5. What activities is a member of a trade union able to take time off for?
6. What is the key difference between time off to engage in trade union duties and time off to engage in trade union activities?

24.5 Collective bargaining

Collective bargaining refers to the process whereby the officers of trade unions negotiate with employers for the furtherance of their members' interests. The matters that can be the subject of these negotiations are identified in section 178(2) Trade Union and Labour Relations (Consolidation) Act 1992 and these are:

- terms and conditions of employment, or the physical conditions in which any workers are required to work;
- engagement or non-engagement, or termination or suspension of one or more of the employees;
- allocation of work or of the duties of employment between workers or groups of workers;
- disciplinary matters;
- membership or non-membership of a trade union;
- facilities for officials of trade unions;
- machinery for negotiation or consultation, and other procedures, relating to any of the above matters, including the recognition by employers or employers' associations of the right of a trade union to represent workers in such negotiation or consultation or in the carrying out of such procedures.

Under Schedule A1 in fact the scope of collective bargaining is more restrictive but where there is an existing voluntary arrangement all of the matters identified in section 178(2) are covered whereas when statutory recognition is awarded under Part 1 of Schedule A1 then the matters covered by a collective agreement are limited to the core issues of pay, hours and holidays.

There is a requirement under section 181 Trade Union and Labour Relations (Consolidation) Act 1992 that on request from a representative of a recognised trade union the employer will disclose such information which is relevant to collective bargaining and without which the trade union representative would be prevented from bargaining effectively. However, the employer is entitled to withhold certain information:

- information which if disclosed would be against the interests of national security;
- information which if disclosed would involve breaking the law;
- information which if disclosed would cause substantial damage to the employer's business;
- information which relates specifically to one employee;
- information which the employer received in confidence;
- information which was obtained by the employer for the purpose of bringing or defending legal proceedings.

Under sections 183–184 if the employer is not covered by one of these exceptions and fails to disclose the information that has been requested then the officers of the trade union can make a complaint to the Central Arbitration Committee. This can either deal with the complaint itself or pass it on to ACAS. If the complaint is well founded then a declaration is given which in effect gives the employer one week to disclose the information.

The significance of a regime of collective bargaining between employer and recognised trade union is that agreements reached during the process may be incorporated into the contract of employment of the employees either expressly or by implication (see Chapter 5.4).

ACTIVITY

Self-assessment questions

1. What is collective bargaining and which parties take part?
2. What is the only lawful subject matter of collective bargaining?

3. What is an employer obliged to disclose to the officers of a recognised trade union in advance of collective bargaining?
4. Why is the employer obliged to disclose this information?
5. What information is exempt from disclosure?

24.6 Statutory protection during trade disputes

24.6.1 Tortious liability in trade disputes

The classic example of industrial action of course is the strike where workers absent themselves from work that they are contractually bound to do in furtherance of whatever dispute. Quite straightforwardly a strike is a breach of contract. There are also a variety of torts that have developed in relation to industrial action.

Inducing or procuring a breach of contract or otherwise interfering with a contract

This occurs where the trade union instructs its members to take action which would amount to a breach of contract. The tort was first developed in *Lumley v Gye* [1853] 2 E & B 216 where a theatre owner succeeded in his action against another theatre owner who had induced an opera singer to perform at his theatre in breach of her contract to perform at the claimant's theatre.

However, the tort is wide enough in its scope to include an inducement to any breach of an employment contract.

CASE EXAMPLE

D C Thompson & Co v Deakin [1952] 2 All ER 361

A trade union engaged in a dispute induced employees of a bulk paper supplier to refuse to deliver supplies to a printer with whom it was in dispute. The printer had operated a policy of insisting that its employees did not belong to a trade union. At the time of the dispute a number of employees had joined the National Society of Operative Printers and Assistants (NATSOPA) and one had recently been dismissed. The claimant successfully sought an injunction to restrain the trade union from pursuing this course. Jenkins LJ identified the categories of interference with a contract by a third party that were actionable:

- direct persuasion or procurement or inducement by the third party knowing of the existence of the contract and intending to bring about its breach;
- dealings by the third party with the party who breaches the contract which he knows are inconsistent with the contract;
- an act done by the third party knowing of the existence of the contract which if done by one of the parties to the contract would amount to a breach;
- an imposition by the third party with knowledge of the existence of the contract of a restraint upon a party to the contract making it impossible to perform.

He also then identified that there were four necessary conditions to show that there was an actionable tortious interference:

- The person interfering with the contract knew of the existence of the contract and intended to procure a breach of the contract.
- That person induced or persuaded employees to breach their contracts.
- Those employees then did breach their contracts.
- Because of this breach the employer was unable to fulfil a contract.

To this could also be added that damages are nominal and there is no justification.

The above all involve direct inducements but it is also possible for inducements that are made indirectly to be actionable.

CASE EXAMPLE

Middlebrook Mushrooms Ltd v TGWU [1993] IRLR 232

Some employees who had been dismissed by their employer handed out leaflets outside a supermarket. The idea of the leaflets was to persuade shoppers not to buy their ex-employer's products. This was held to be an indirect inducement to a breach of the contract between the supermarket and the supplier which had formerly been the employee's employer. However, there would still need to be evidence of knowledge of the existence of the contract and intent to induce a breach of the contract and here it could not be established that there would have been a contract between the supermarket and the supplier.

A similar approach was taken in *Mainstream Properties Ltd v Young* [2007] IRLR 608 where two employees of a property company, in breach of their contracts, diverted a development opportunity to a joint venture in which they were interested. The defendant, mistakenly thinking that they would not be in breach, provided finance which allowed the acquisition to occur. The property company then brought an action for wrongfully inducing a breach of contract. The House of Lords held that it could not be in the circumstances.

JUDGMENT

Lord Hoffmann explained: 'An honest belief by the defendant that the outcome sought by him will not involve a breach of contract is inconsistent with him intending to induce a breach of contract. He is not to be held responsible for the third party's breach of contract in such a case.'

The tort also includes procuring the breach of a commercial contract.

CASE EXAMPLE

Torquay Hotel Co Ltd v Cousins [1969] 2 Ch 106

A trade union was in dispute with a hotel and instructed members who worked for a company that supplied the hotel with oil not to deliver to the hotel. The hotel brought an action and the Court of Appeal held that it was unlawful to cause the fuel supplier to breach its contract with the hotel. An injunction was granted to the hotel restraining the trade union official from giving the instructions to the members in question.

The tort could also of course include any wrongful interference with a contract. In *Time-plan Education Group v National Union of Teachers* [1997] IRLR 457 a trade union was attempting to interfere with advertising for recruits by a teacher supply agency. The Court of Appeal identified the essential elements of a wrongful interference with a contract:

- The third party persuaded or procured or induced a party to a contract to breach the contract.

- The third party knew of the existence of the contract.
- The third party intended to procure or to induce a breach of contract.
- The claimant suffered more than nominal damage.
- If the third party claimed that there was a justification for the actions the claimant was able to successfully rebut that justification.

Intimidation

The tort of intimidation involves the making of an unlawful threat to the claimant with the intention of causing a loss to the claimant. The tort was in fact little used before the case of *Rookes v Barnard* [1964] AC 1129 where the then House of Lords made it almost impossible to threaten strike action and effectively removed the statutory immunity gained in the Trade Disputes Act 1906 (see 24.6.2 below).

CASE EXAMPLE

Rookes v Barnard [1964] AC 1129

An employee at Heathrow Airport had left that trade union to which he was a member. At the time of the case it was lawful to have what was known as a 'closed shop', meaning that it was a contractual requirement in particular employment that an employee was a member of a recognised trade union. Shop stewards at Heathrow then threatened to call a strike unless the employee was dismissed which the employer did and the sacked man then brought action against the trade union. The House of Lords, taking a very political view, held that the threat of a strike was no different to any unlawful threat, for example the threat of violence. As such the House held that the threat of strike amounted to unlawful and actionable intimidation.

Intimidation could also result from action taken in furtherance or because of the unlawful threats.

CASE EXAMPLE

Newsgroup Newspapers Ltd v Society of Graphical and Allied Trades 1982 (SOGAT 82) [1986] IRLR 227

A trade union of print workers in the newspaper industry was in dispute with an employer over a proposed move away from Fleet Street to new headquarters in Wapping where the employer proposed to use what at the time were completely new methods of printing newspapers and to use only non-union labour. The trade union called its members out on strike and the employer immediately dismissed them all and replaced them. There was then mass picketing, rallies and demonstrations outside the new premises and the owner brought an action. The High Court held that there were sufficient threats of violence to amount to unlawful intimidation and the newspaper owner was granted an injunction restraining the action by the members of the union.

Conspiracy

A conspiracy is where two or more people combine together to do an unlawful act or to do an act in an unlawful manner. In the context of trade union action this would mean combining to induce customers, clients, suppliers or employees of a company to breach their contracts with it.

CASE EXAMPLE

Quinn v Leatham [1901] AC 495

Leatham was a butcher who employed some non-union workers. A trade union tried to coerce him to dismiss his non-union workers but he refused to do so but offered instead to pay any arrears on their subscriptions if the men joined the union. However, the trade union wished to make an example of these men and threatened to call a strike of the employees of Leatham's major supplier unless the supplier ceased supplying Leatham. The union officials had exceeded their legitimate trade union objectives and as a result in the ensuing legal action the court held that the officials had unlawfully conspired to harm Leatham's business.

The significant point about a conspiracy then is that the purpose of the combination is without justification. In other words it is not in furtherance of a legitimate trade dispute but is for the purpose of causing damage to the claimant.

CASE EXAMPLE

Huntley v Thornton [1957] 1 WLR 321

A member of a trade union failed to go on strike when a strike was called by the union. Officials of the union then circulated information about this to trade union officials at other places of employment with the aim of preventing the man from getting work elsewhere. He succeeded in his action for conspiracy since there was no justification for the action of the trade union officials, they were merely trying to cause the man harm.

However, if the combination is actually pursuing a purpose which is for the furtherance of a legitimate trade dispute then there is no actionable conspiracy.

CASE EXAMPLE

Crofter Hand Woven Harris Tweed Co Ltd v Veitch [1942] AC 435

Most Harris Tweed cloth produced in the island of Lewis was made in mechanised mills from local yarn. The claimant brought in cheap yarn and used several crofters to produce cheaper cloth. The mills were mostly union labour whereas the crofters were not. The trade union was trying to improve wages overall and placed an embargo on the export of the cloth made by the crofters as it also had members who were dockers. The claimant brought an action for conspiracy but the then House of Lords held that it was not a conspiracy because the purpose of the combination was furthering the interests of the union members and not specifically to harm the claimant.

JUDGMENT

The Lord Chancellor explained: 'in my opinion, . . . the predominant object of the respondents in getting the embargo imposed was to benefit their trade union members by preventing under-cutting and unregulated competition, and so helping to secure the economic stability of the island industry. The result they aimed at achieving was to create a better basis for collective bargaining, and thus directly to improve wage prospects. A combination with such an object is not unlawful, because the object is the legitimate promotion of the interests of the combiners, and because the damage necessarily inflicted on the Appellants is not inflicted by criminal or tortious means and is not "the real purpose" of the combination.'

Similarly in *Scala Ballroom (Wolverhampton) Ltd v Ratcliffe* [1958] 1 WLR 1057 the operation of a colour bar by the ballroom management led to the musicians' union placing a boycott on the venue to its members. This was not an actionable conspiracy as it was for the furtherance of the members' interests.

Economic duress

In contract law a doctrine of economic duress developed which usually occurs in a commercial context but has also been applied in the case of trade union activity.

CASE EXAMPLE

Universe Tankships Incorporated of Monrovia v International Transport Workers Federation [1983] 1 AC 366 (The *Universal Sentinel*)

This was one of a number of cases involving a campaign by the International Transport Workers Federation (ITWF) to improve the conditions of crew members on ships 'flying flags of convenience'. (Flags of convenience means where ships are registered with countries that do not operate according to established working conditions, pay very low wages and cut corners in working practices, and therefore are more profitable but undermine reputable shipping companies.) The ship in question was blacked by the union and forced to pay towards the ITWF welfare fund to secure the ship's release. The court considered that this amounted to economic duress, the pressure being illegitimate, and was sufficient to vitiate the contract. However, the court was undecided on the difference between legitimate pressure and pressure which was not.

There are inevitable arguments as to what amounts to legitimate industrial action and what goes beyond the law and amounts to economic duress allowing a party to avoid an agreement that they have made under pressure.

CASE EXAMPLE

Dimskal Shipping Co SA v International Transport Workers Federation [1992] 2 AC 152 (The *Evia Luck*)

The ITWF had conducted a long campaign against ships sailing under 'flags of convenience' in an attempt to improve the conditions of workers at sea and to improve safety standards in sailing. When the *Evia Luck*, one such ship, was in port in Sweden the agents of the ITWF boarded the vessel and informed the master of the ship that it would be 'blacked' (this means that sailors would be asked to avoid enlisting for service on it or dockers asked to avoid loading or unloading it). He was also warned that it would not be loaded or allowed to leave port till the company that owned it and was sailing it under a Panamanian flag agreed to a number of demands in respect of extra payment for the crew and improved conditions of service. When the owners initially refused the ship was in fact 'blacked' and so they gave in to the pressure and agreed to the demands. They later successfully claimed economic duress. The court held that the pressure applied was unlawful coercion vitiating the agreement by which they were not then bound.

24.6.2 Immunity from legal action

Some protection against liability for collective action by the members of trade unions was originally provided by the Trade Union Act 1871 and then by the Conspiracy and Protection of Property Act 1875. Following many judicial decisions which appeared to disregard or remove this immunity from legal action the Trades Disputes Act 1906 was passed which effectively provided protection for certain trade union activity right up to the Industrial Relations Act 1971. This introduced a complete new legal framework for industrial relations. However, it failed ultimately because the trade unions would not cooperate and the government was unable to enforce it and this ultimately led to a change of government. The Trade Union and Labour Relations Acts of 1974 and 1976 returned the law to the previous position. Following a further change of government the Employment Act 1980, the Employment Act 1982, the Trade Union Act 1984, the Employment Act 1988 and the Employment Act 1990 all placed significant limitations on the immunity.

The law is now found in section 219 Trade Union and Labour Relations (Consolidation) Act 1992.

SECTION

'219 Protection from certain tort liabilities

(1) An act done by a person in contemplation or furtherance of a trade dispute is not actionable in tort on the ground only –

 (a) that it induces another person to break a contract or interferes or induces another person to interfere with its performance, or

 (b) that it consists in his threatening that a contract (whether one to which he is a party or not) will be broken or its performance interfered with, or that he will induce another person to break a contract or interfere with its performance.'

There are three issues arising from the section:

- The meaning of 'in contemplation of';
- The meaning of 'in furtherance of';
- The meaning of 'trade dispute'.

In contemplation of

This means that the act is done before the trade dispute. The trade dispute must actually therefore be imminent and is actually going to occur.

CASE EXAMPLE

Bents Brewery Co Ltd v Hogan [1945] 2 All ER 570

A trade union official asked the employer to provide information about the performance of the business and the terms and conditions of its employees. In giving this information the employer was then in breach of its contractual obligations not to reveal confidential information. The trade union official as a result had induced a breach of contract. He was not immune from subsequent legal action on this tort because, while there was a possibility of a trade dispute in the future it was not imminent and it was therefore not 'in contemplation of' a trade dispute.

In furtherance of

The action must be in furtherance of the trade dispute. It must therefore be for the legitimate objectives of the trade union in relation to the particular dispute in question. If the action is for any other purpose then it is not 'in furtherance of' a trade dispute and there will be no immunity from legal action.

CASE EXAMPLE

Conway v Wade [1909] AC 506

A trade union official informed the employer that there would be a strike if a specific employee was not dismissed. In fact the employee had been a former member of the union but had been expelled for not paying a fine. The official was actually trying to put pressure on so that the employee would pay the fine and although the official might have considered the possibility of a strike at a later date there was no trade dispute imminent and so no immunity from legal action for the official.

JUDGMENT

Lord Loreburn LC stated: 'an act done in furtherance or contemplation of a trade dispute ... mean[s] that either a dispute is imminent and the act is done in expectation of and with a view to it, or that the dispute is already existing and the act is done in support of one side to it. In either case the act must be genuinely done as described and the dispute must be as real thing imminent or existing.'

Trade dispute

Trade dispute is defined in section 244 Trade Union and Labour Relations (Consolidation) Act 1992.

SECTION

'244 Meaning of "trade dispute" in Part V
(1) In this Part a "trade dispute" means a dispute between workers and their employer which relates wholly or mainly to one or more of the following –
  (a) terms and conditions of employment, or the physical conditions in which any workers are required to work;
  (b) engagement or non-engagement, or termination or suspension of employment or the duties of employment, of one or more workers;
  (c) allocation of work or the duties of employment between workers or groups of workers;
  (d) matters of discipline;
  (e) a worker's membership or non-membership of a trade union;
  (f) facilities for officials of trade unions; and
  (g) machinery for negotiation or consultation, and other procedures, relating to any of the above matters, including the recognition by employers or employers' associations of the right of a trade union to represent workers in such negotiation or consultation or in the carrying out of such procedures.'

Worker is then defined in section 244(5) Trade Union and Labour Relations (Consolidation) Act 1992 as a person who is employed by the employer; or a person who is no longer employed by the employer if his employment was terminated in connection with the dispute or if the termination of his employment was one of the circumstances giving rise to the dispute.

The dispute must be between existing workers and their current employer within the definition in section 244(5). As a result there is no immunity under section 219 Trade Union and Labour Relations (Consolidation) Act 1992 if the dispute concerns the contracts of future employees.

CASE EXAMPLE

University College London Hospitals NHS Trust v UNISON [1999] IRLR 31

The trust contracted with a consortium to build and run a new hospital. The trade union was opposed to the scheme and tried to persuade the employer to reach a contractual agreement with the consortium that the terms and conditions of employment of employees transferred to the new hospital would be the same as those who did not transfer. When the employer refused the trade union called a strike after balloting its members. The employer successfully sought an injunction to restrain the union. The Court of Appeal held that the dispute concerned a future employer and future employees and was not therefore between 'workers and their employer'. The court identified that there were three essential elements to a trade dispute:

▓ It must be a dispute between workers and their employer.

▓ The dispute must relate wholly or mainly to one of those activities in section 244 Trade Union and Labour Relations (Consolidation) Act 1992.

▓ The act must be carried out in contemplation or furtherance of a trade dispute.

So a dispute that relates wholly or mainly to terms or conditions of employment or any of the other factors in section 244 can be classed as a trade dispute and attracts the immunity of section 219.

CASE EXAMPLE

Wandsworth London Borough Council v National Association of Schoolmasters Union of Women Teachers [1994] ICR 81

At the time when the government first introduced the national curriculum for schools the union was opposed to the move and proposed to ballot its members to take action in protest against the massively increased workload that the new assessment requirements involved. A local authority sought an injunction to restrain the union arguing that the dispute was with government policy rather than being about terms and conditions as required for it to be a trade dispute attracting immunity. The Court of Appeal held that the dispute was in fact a trade dispute gaining protection under section 219 because it was about the increased workload and so was wholly or mainly to do with one of the factors identified in section 244.

However, by definition if the dispute is in reality with government policy and in fact has little if anything to do with terms and conditions of work then it will not be classed as a trade dispute for the purposes of immunity under section 219.

CASE EXAMPLE

Mercury Communications Ltd v Scott Garner [1984] Ch 37; [1984] ICR 74

The government of the time pursued a policy of increasing privatisation and widening competition. It planned to privatise British Telecommunications which at the time was part of the state run General Post Office. It then granted a licence to the claimant to run a telecommunications network. The whole policy was opposed by the Post Office Engineering Union which then instructed its members not to carry out work that would allow the claimant to operate. The claimant successfully applied for an injunction to restrain the union. The Court of Appeal held that there was no trade dispute merely a campaign of protest against the government's policy of privatisation and competition.

It follows that any dispute where the principal purpose is political in character is not wholly or mainly for the purpose of one of the factors identified in section 244 and therefore is not a trade dispute and will not gain the protection of section 219.

CASE EXAMPLE

British Broadcasting Corporation v D A Hearn [1977] IRLR 273

A trade union threatened to prevent the broadcasting of the FA Cup Final of that year via satellite. This was to prevent it being seen in South Africa although it would obviously affect other countries as well. The purpose of the action was to protest against the racist policies of the South African government which existed at the time. The Court of Appeal held that there was no trade dispute and granted the BBC restraining the union from its action.

24.6.3 Loss of immunity

There are a number of situations in which any immunity gained by the trade union through the operation of section 219 Trade Union and Labour Relations (Consolidation) Act 1992 is lost:

- where the law relating to the holding of secret ballots has not been followed;
- where there is unlawful secondary action;
- where there is pressure to impose union recognition, union membership or to retain a closed shop;
- where the action is to persuade an employer to reinstate unofficial strikers who have been dismissed.

Secret ballots before industrial action

There was an unsuccessful attempt to introduce a requirement for ballots prior to industrial action in the Industrial Relations Act 1971. The view at the time was that strikes were often not the real wishes of the majority of trade union members and that the practice of voting by a show of hands at mass meetings was intimidating.

The requirement for ballots was first introduced in the Trade Union Act 1974. The rules are now in sections 226–234 Trade Union and Labour Relations (Consolidation) Act 1992 as amended. There is also now a Code of Practice on Industrial Action Ballots and Notice to Employers.

There is no legal requirement to hold a ballot but if official industrial action is taken without a ballot having been held then the union will lose its immunity under section 219 and the affected employer will be able to sue. Section 226 Trade Union and Labour Relations (Consolidation) Act 1992 (as amended by the Employment Relations Act 2004) identifies that a trade union that induces an employee to take part in industrial action will have no immunity under section 219 unless there has been a proper secret ballot. There is also a variety of other requirements.

Under section 226A(2) the union must take reasonable steps to notify the employer of the ballot. The notice must be in writing and must include:

- that the union intends to hold a ballot calling for industrial action;
- the date on which the union reasonably believes the ballot will take place;
- a list of all the employees concerned – so this must include the categories of the employees to which the employees concerned belong, a list of the workplaces affected, the total number of employees, the number of employees at each workplace and an explanation of how the figures were arrived at.

A sample voting paper must also be sent to the employer at least three days before the ballot is to take place.

The union must also appoint an appropriate scrutineer before the ballot occurs. Appropriate person is defined in section 226(B) but is basically a person approved by the Secretary of State for the purpose, and includes bodies such as the Electoral Reform Service. The role of the scrutineer is to prepare a report on the ballot identifying whether it was satisfactory and offering a copy to the employer. The report must be made not later than four weeks after the ballot.

Under section 227(1) all of those members of the union whom it is reasonable for the union to believe at the time of the ballot will be induced to take part in the industrial action are entitled to vote but no others. The general rule in section 228(3) is that there should be a separate ballot for each workplace. However, there are exceptions in section 228A where the union wishes to call a ballot of a 'genuine bargaining unit' and the ballot is limited to all the members of the union who according to the union's reasonable belief have an occupation of a particular kind or have any of a number of particular kinds of occupation, and are employed by a particular employer, or by any of a number of particular employers, with whom the union is in dispute.

CASE EXAMPLE

University of Central England v NALGO [1993] IRLR 81

The industrial action concerned conditions of work in several educational facilities where the union had members and concerned conditions of work which would affect all because there was national negotiating machinery between the union and an employer's association. On this basis it was held that there was no requirement for separate workplace ballots since all of the union members entitled to vote would be affected.

A voting paper should be sent to the home address of each separate union member who is entitled to vote where it is reasonably practicable to do so. Under section 230(2) each member entitled to vote must also be given a reasonable opportunity to vote by post.

Under section 229(1) the voting paper must state the name of the independent scrutineer and clearly identify the address to which the voting paper is sent and by what date. The voting paper must ask one of two questions, or if the union wishes to have authority for both forms of action then both questions should be asked on the voting paper. The one question is whether the member wishes to take part in strike action and the other question is whether the member wishes to take part in industrial action short of strike action. The questions should also be phrased so that only the responses yes or no are possible. It must also identify who has authority to call industrial action in event of a yes vote. Finally, under section 229(4) it must also explain that taking industrial action is a breach of contract and the circumstances in which a dismissal for strike action will be unfair dismissal.

There are also strict rules governing the ballot itself. Voting should be secret and each person entitled to vote should be able to do so without interference from any trade union official. Votes should also be fairly counted.

As soon as is reasonably practicable after the ballot the union must inform both the members and the employer of the result.

The union will lose its immunity under section 219 if there was either no ballot or there was a ballot but it was not carried out according to all of the rules above.

Unlawful secondary action

Secondary action is defined in section 224(2) Trade Union and Labour Relations (Consolidation) Act 1992. It will occur when a person:

- induces another to break a contract of employment; or

- interferes or induces another to interfere with its performance; or

- threatens that a contract of employment under which he or another is employed will be broken or its performance interfered with; or

- that he will induce another to break a contract of employment or to interfere with its performance;

and the employer under the contract of employment is not the employer party to the dispute.

In all cases secondary action is unlawful and so does not gain the protection of section 219 and can be an actionable tort leading to liability. At one time use of 'flying pickets' (ones who were not linked to the dispute but sympathised with it) gained some notoriety but also some success (for instance when members of the National Union of Mineworkers picketed Saltley Coke Depot in 1972 to prevent supplies of coal from being delivered). However, the courts were generally unsympathetic to such action even before statute outlawed the practice.

CASE EXAMPLE

Express Newspapers v McShane [1980] ICR 42

Journalists working for various publications were dismissed and so a call was made for a national strike. Unions aimed at preventing their members from working so that newspapers had no stories and could not print. In fact this action was prevented from succeeding because the Press Association gave stories to the newspapers involved so that they were unharmed and under no pressure from the industrial action. The unions then called on employees of national newspapers to boycott the association and the then House of Lords held that there was no immunity from civil action because this secondary action was not in furtherance of a trade dispute.

Pressure to impose union recognition, union membership or to retain a closed shop

Under section 222 Trade Union and Labour Relations (Consolidation) Act 1992 there is no immunity from civil action where industrial action is for the purpose of enforcing membership of a trade union or retaining a closed shop where employees must belong to a specific union.

Under section 225 Trade Union and Labour Relations (Consolidation) Act 1992 any potential immunity from civil action is lost where the industrial action is carried out in order to impose a recognition of a trade union for the purposes of negotiating on members behalf.

Action to persuade an employer to reinstate dismissed unofficial strikers

Where a person is engaged in unofficial industrial action a dismissal is fair since there is a clear breach of contract with no statutory immunity (see 24.8.2 below). In consequence section 223 Trade Union and Labour Relations (Consolidation) Act 1992 removes statutory immunity available under section 219 where industrial action is taken in support of an employee or employees who have been dismissed for unofficial industrial action.

Picketing

As well as the torts identified above there are a variety of other torts that could be involved where union members during an industrial dispute engage in the process of picketing. Picketing generally involves members of the union standing outside the employer's premises protesting and trying to persuade other employees to take part in the action or to show sympathy or possibly even suppliers to refuse to supply or customers to take their business elsewhere. Other torts arising out of this activity then could include trespass to the employer's land and private or public nuisance.

There is no immunity from liability for picketing except in the limited conditions identified in section 220 Trade Union and Labour Relations (Consolidation) Act 1992 which identifies that picketing may be lawful if the union member in contemplation or furtherance of a trade dispute attends at or near his own place of work or, if he is an official of a trade union, at or near the place of work of a member of that union whom he is accompanying and whom he represents. In all other circumstances picketing is unlawful.

ACTIVITY

Self-assessment questions

1. What different types of tortious behaviour might a trade union engage in in connection with a trade dispute?
2. According to the judgment in *D C Thompson & Co v Deakin* what are the different types of actionable interference with a contract and what are the conditions that are required to show that there is an actionable interference?
3. How is the tort of intimidation committed?
4. What are the necessary requirements for an action of conspiracy in the context of trade disputes?
5. In respect of immunity from civil action how is 'in contemplation of' defined by the courts?
6. In respect of immunity from civil action what does 'in furtherance of' mean?
7. What are the three essential elements of a 'trade dispute'?
8. What are the only matters which a trade dispute can be about?
9. What is the position if the dispute is really political in character?
10. Why was the idea of secret ballots prior to industrial action introduced and what was felt to be wrong with the previous method or methods by which union members decided to take industrial action?
11. What does the union need to inform an employer of before the ballot takes place?
12. What is the role of the scrutineer?
13. What is a 'workplace ballot' and in what circumstances will a union be able to hold a ballot that is not a workplace ballot?
14. What information should be provided on the voting paper and how should the questions be phrased?
15. What is the meaning of secondary action?
16. In what other circumstances is immunity for industrial action lost?
17. What is picketing?
18. In what circumstances is picketing a lawful activity?

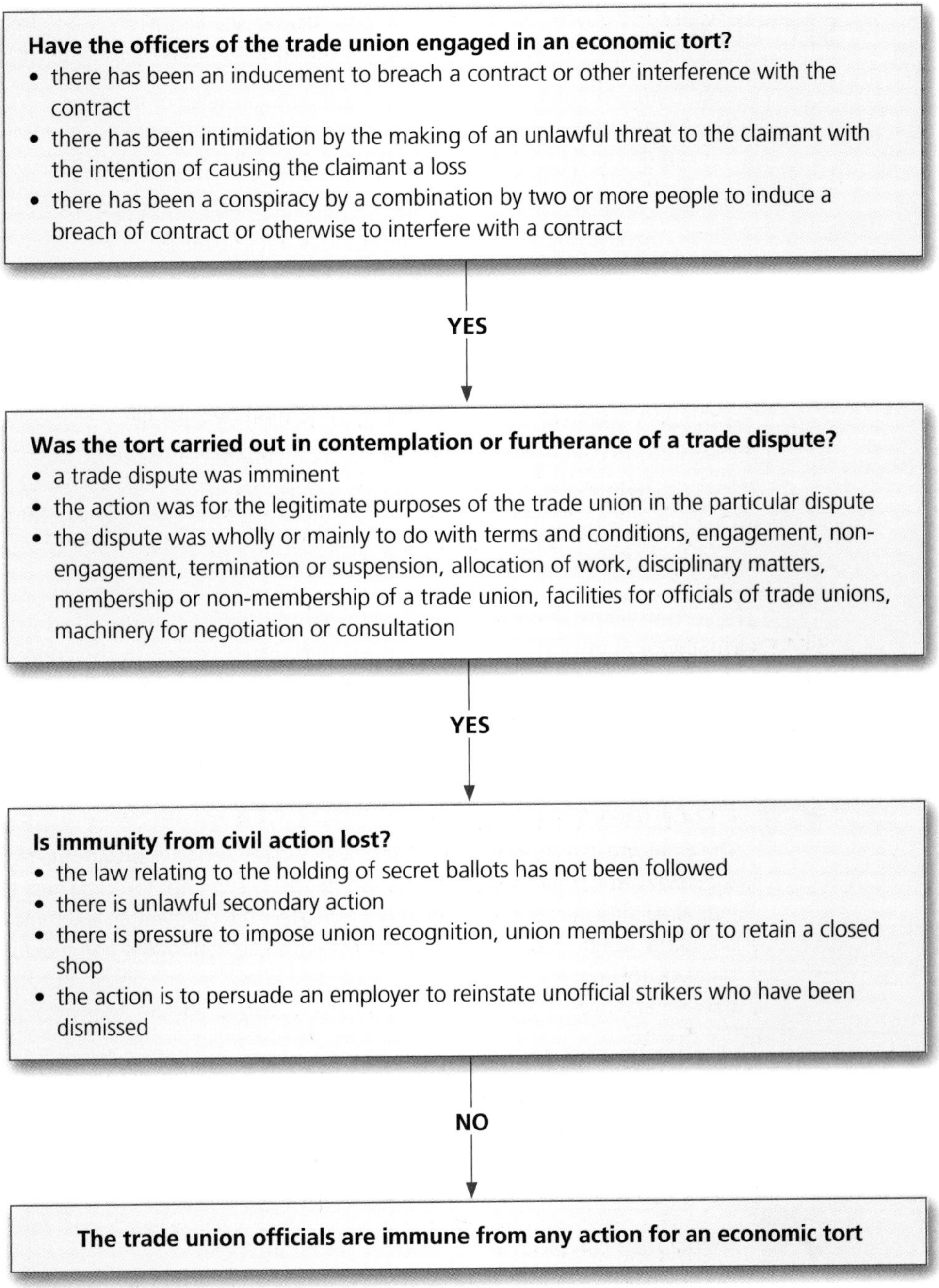

Have the officers of the trade union engaged in an economic tort?
- there has been an inducement to breach a contract or other interference with the contract
- there has been intimidation by the making of an unlawful threat to the claimant with the intention of causing the claimant a loss
- there has been a conspiracy by a combination by two or more people to induce a breach of contract or otherwise to interfere with a contract

YES

Was the tort carried out in contemplation or furtherance of a trade dispute?
- a trade dispute was imminent
- the action was for the legitimate purposes of the trade union in the particular dispute
- the dispute was wholly or mainly to do with terms and conditions, engagement, non-engagement, termination or suspension, allocation of work, disciplinary matters, membership or non-membership of a trade union, facilities for officials of trade unions, machinery for negotiation or consultation

YES

Is immunity from civil action lost?
- the law relating to the holding of secret ballots has not been followed
- there is unlawful secondary action
- there is pressure to impose union recognition, union membership or to retain a closed shop
- the action is to persuade an employer to reinstate unofficial strikers who have been dismissed

NO

The trade union officials are immune from any action for an economic tort

Figure 24.1 Diagram illustrating the immunity of trade union officials from actions in tort

24.7 Discipline short of dismissal

An employee who is also a member of a trade union has a right not to suffer a detriment which falls short of dismissal because of his membership of a trade union or because of involvement in trade union activities. The right is in section 146 Trade Union and Labour Relations (Consolidation) Act 1992 as amended.

SECTION

'146 Detriment] on grounds related to union membership or activities
(1) A worker has the right not to be subjected to any detriment as an individual by any act, or any deliberate failure to act, by his employer if the act or failure takes place for the sole or main purpose of –
   (a) preventing or deterring him from being or seeking to become a member of an independent trade union, or penalising him for doing so
   (b) preventing or deterring him from taking part in the activities of an independent trade union at an appropriate time, or penalising him for doing so
   (c) preventing or deterring him from making use of trade union services at an appropriate time, or penalising him for doing so, or
   (d) compelling him to be or become a member of any trade union or of a particular trade union or of one of a number of particular trade unions.'

So section 146 covers being subjected to a detriment because of:

- membership or non-membership of a trade union;
- taking part in trade union activities;
- taking advantage of trade union services.

The section refers also to the fact that the employee must suffer the detriment as an individual so it is important to know what individual means in the context of the section. Inevitably it affects trade union officials adversely.

CASE EXAMPLE

F W Farnsworth Ltd v McCoid [1999] IRLR 626

The employer derecognised the trade union and refused to deal with the claimant who was a shop steward. The employer argued that this action was not taken against the claimant as an individual, but against the union. It did not affect the claimant as an employee, but rather as an official of the trade union. The EAT rejected the employer's argument and held that the claimant was not merely a victim of a general attack on the union, but that the action was directed at him as an individual.

The claimant must also show that the reason for the action taken against him was to prevent or deter him from taking part in union activities or to penalise him for doing so, which in effect means that the action is denying the employee his statutory rights.

CASE EXAMPLE

Associated Newspapers v Wilson [1995] IRLR 258

The employer ceased negotiating with a trade union and insisted instead on entering into individual negotiations with employees towards individual contracts. Employees were promised that if they signed the new contract by a specific date they would receive a significant pay rise. Those that objected like the claimant received less pay than those that had signed away their rights to be represented by the trade union. The then House of Lords held that the inducement and the different terms was not for the purpose of deterring employees from being members of a trade union, taking part in activities or taking advantage of services but was aimed merely at ending the process of collective bargaining with the union that had previously occurred. The House felt that this did not prevent employees from gaining other benefits from their trade union membership and that collective bargaining was not an essential part of trade union related rights.

The issue was later appealed in joined appeals to the European Court of Human Rights in *Wilson, National Union of Journalists and Others v the United Kingdom* [2002] IRLR 568 ECHR where the European Court of Human Rights held that the employer's conduct amounted to disincentive to employees exercising their legitimate trade union rights and was even a restraint.

JUDGMENT

The Court explained: 'it must be possible for a trade union which is not recognised by an employer to take steps including, if necessary, organising industrial action, with a view to persuading the employer to enter into collective bargaining with it on those issues which the union believes are important for its members' interests. . . . It is the role of the State to ensure that trade union members are not prevented or restrained from using their union to represent them in attempts to regulate their relations with their employers . . . United Kingdom law permitted employers to treat less favourably employees who were not prepared to renounce a freedom that was an essential feature of union membership. . . . Under United Kingdom law . . . it was, therefore, possible for an employer effectively to undermine or frustrate a trade union's ability to strive for the protection of its members' interests.'

The test is in fact a difficult one for a trade union official to prove because he must show the purpose of the employer's actions as well as the effect.

CASE EXAMPLE

Gallacher v Department of Transport [1994] IRLR 231

The claimant was a civil servant who was also an officer of the trade union. He in fact spent virtually all of his time at work carrying out duties for the trade union. He then applied for a promotion and was turned down on the basis that he had insufficient managerial experience and skills. When he challenged this he was told that he should take a line job and get more experience so that he would be in a position to apply more successfully in future. This would mean him reducing his trade union activities so he complained to a tribunal which initially found in his favour. However, both the EAT and the Court of Appeal identified that, while the effect of the advice and the decision on his application might appear to be subjecting him to a detriment because of his role within the trade union, in fact the only purpose of the decision was ensure that only people with sufficient experience and expertise should be successful in applications for promotion.

It will of course also depend on the nature of the action taken by the employer which is detrimental to the employee. In *Carlson v The Post Office* [1981] IRLR 158 the deliberate failure to act was not providing a car parking permit to an employee who belonged to a trade union with small membership because allocation of parking spaces was determined in an agreement between the employer and the recognised trade union.

The section also identifies that the employer should not subject the employee to a detriment where the trade union activities or using trade union services are being carried out at an appropriate time. In this respect it is important to know what an appropriate time is.

CASE EXAMPLE

Robb v Leon Motor Services [1978] IRLR 26

The claimant was employed as a long distance coach driver. He was then also appointed as shop steward inevitably resulting in him having a lot of trade union duties to attend to. The employer then transferred him on to alternative driving duties because of the interference with his work and this was at a lower rate of pay. He claimed that he was being prevented or deterred from carrying out his legitimate trade union activities. The court held that there was no arrangement with the employer that these trade union activities should occur during work time and therefore he was not being prevented from engaging in trade union activity at an appropriate time. The court felt that there was no reason why he should not carry out his trade union duties in his own time which is an appropriate time.

It is of course possible that work time could be an appropriate time but only where there is agreement with the employer that this should be so. In *Brennan & Ging v Ellward (Lancs) Ltd* [1974] IRLR 153 employees wished to consult their shop steward but this involved going off site during works time. They were warned that they would be dismissed if they did so and it was held that without the agreement of the employer during work time is not an appropriate time.

Now under section 12 Employment Relations Act 1999 an employee has the right not to suffer any detriment for instance any disciplinary measure where the employee is exercising his right under section 10 Employment Relations Act 1999 either to be accompanied at hearing by an appropriate trade union official or work colleague or as an appropriate union representative or work colleague accompanying another employee.

ACTIVITY

Self-assessment questions

1. What are the grounds for action short of a dismissal that are unlawful?
2. What detriments short of dismissal is an employee protected against when the reason for them is trade union related?
3. What does suffering a detriment as an individual mean?
4. What is the significance of the ECHR ruling in *Wilson, National Union of Journalists and Others v the United Kingdom* and how does the position of the court differ to the previous stance of English courts?
5. What is meant by the employee having to show the purpose of the employee's actions as well as their effect?
6. How have the courts defined what is an appropriate time to engage in trade union activities or to make use of trade union services?

24.8 Dismissal

24.8.1 Trade union related dismissal

Trade union related dismissals are governed by section 152 Trade Union and Labour Relations (Consolidation) Act 1992. Under this it will be unfair to dismiss an employee where the principal reason for the dismissal is either:

■ the employee was a member or proposed to become a member of a trade union;

■ the employee had taken part or proposed to take part in the activities of a trade union or to take advantage of the services offered by the trade union at an appropriate time (what is an appropriate time is out of working hours or within working hours but with the express or implied consent of the employer);

- the employee was not a member of a trade union or refused to become a member of a trade union;

- the employee failed to accept an offer in contravention of section 145A or 145B Trade Union and Labour Relations (Consolidation) Act 1992 (in relation to giving up trade union rights).

A dismissal for any of these reasons will be automatically unfair see (Chapter 22.3). However, if it is for taking part in legitimate union activities then the activity would have to be legitimate in fact and be carried out at an appropriate time.

CASE EXAMPLE

Burgess v Bass Taverns Ltd [1995] EWCA Civ 40

The claimant was employed as a manager of a public house. He also acted as a trainer for the brewery giving presentations at a six week induction course for trainee managers and practical training at the premises he managed, for which he received an additional fee. He was also a shop steward of a relevant trade union and was allowed to make presentations on the union in the training sessions. During one training session he was critical of the brewery and suggested that it only cared about its profits, not about the welfare of its managers. Saying 'You will get threatened and if you get hurt it will be the union who will fight for you, not the company. At the end of the day the company is concerned with profits and this comes before everything else.' The brewery objected to this and withdrew his post as a trainer, which resulted in a loss of salary also. He claimed constructive dismissal and argued that this was because of his legitimate trade union activities. The tribunal found that he had been unfairly dismissed on this basis. However, both the EAT and the Court of Appeal held that there was an implied term that the presentation would not be used to criticise the employer so that it could not fall within the definition of trade union activities at an appropriate time.

On this basis the only times that are appropriate in respect of trade union activities are either the employee's own time or in work time only where there is express or implied agreement with the employer.

CASE EXAMPLE

Marley Tile Co Ltd v Shaw [1980] IRLR 75

The claimant had become shop steward for a group of fellow employees although he had only been with the company for two months. When he raised an issue with management he was informed that he was not recognised because of his short service. The claimant then called his district official and held a meeting during works time as a result of which he was dismissed. He then brought a claim for unfair dismissal arguing that the dismissal was due to legitimate trade union activities. The Court of Appeal held that there was no implied term in the contract of employment that employees could be called to a meeting during works time so the dismissal was lawful and not unfair.

An interesting question on what is an appropriate time arose in the case of *Zucker v Astrid Jewels Ltd* [1978] ICR 1088 EAT where the employee tried to persuade colleagues to join the trade union at all opportunities. The tribunal held that she was not carrying out trade union activities at an appropriate time. However, the EAT held that the employer was not in a position to dictate the topics of conversation while employees worked and so the specific activity was at an appropriate time.

JUDGMENT

Phillips J explained: 'if ... employees while working are permitted to converse upon anything ... there seems to be no reason why they should not, amongst other things, converse upon trade union activities; and if they were to do so, and if such conversation were generally allowed, to the extent that it did not interfere with the proper completion of the work ... there seems no reason why an employment tribunal ... could not come to the conclusion that ... there was implied consent'.

The section of course also covers those situations where an employee has been dismissed when his employer has discovered that he engaged in trade union activities while working for a former employer.

CASE EXAMPLE

Fitzpatrick v British Railways Board [1992] ICR 221

The claimant was dismissed from the post that she had occupied for about nine months when her employer discovered that she had been a union activist in her previous job and also had ultra-left Trotskyite views. She had in fact only been in this job briefly and had not mentioned this job in her application. Although it was clear that the employer feared that she was a potential trouble maker, the justification given for the dismissal was the deceit in not revealing her previous employment. The tribunal felt that while the dismissal was because of her trade union activities she did not fall within the protection of section 152. The Court of Appeal disagreed and held that the dismissal was unfair.

JUDGMENT

Woolf LJ explained: 'If an employer, having learnt of an employee's previous trade union activities, decides ... to dismiss that employee, that is likely to be a situation where almost inevitably the employer is dismissing the employee because he feels that the employee will indulge in industrial activities of trade union nature in his current employment. There is no reason for a rational and reasonable employer to object to the previous activities of an employee except in so far as they will impinge upon the employer's current employment.'

A dismissal for taking advantage of trade union services will also be an unfair dismissal if that is the sole reason or the principal reason for the dismissal.

CASE EXAMPLE

Discount Tobacco and Confectionary Ltd v Armitage [1990] IRLR 14

The claimant sought the help of her trade union representative in order to obtain a written contract from her employer. She then wanted to iron out some differences between terms in the written contract and the terms that the employer had originally offered her. The employer dismissed her. The EAT confirmed that the dismissal was for using the services of a trade union which fell within section 152 so that the dismissal was unfair.

Under section 153 Trade Union and Labour Relations (Consolidation) Act 1992 it is also an unfair dismissal to select an employee for redundancy where the main reason for the selection is because of his membership or non-membership, his trade union activities or one of the other elements of section 152. Section 153 also identifies that the circumstances constituting the redundancy must have applied equally to other employees in positions similar to the claimant but who have not been selected for redundancy.

CASE EXAMPLE

O'Dea v ISC Chemicals Ltd [1996] IRLR 599

The claimant was paid as a technical services operator but in fact only worked as a packaging operator and then for only half of his hours. This was because the claimant was also a shop steward and spent the other half of his work time on trade union duties. He was later made redundant although two technical service operators were not. He argued that this was unfair selection for redundancy and therefore unfair dismissal. In fact the Court of Appeal held that the selection was not unfair and neither was his dismissal. The court identified that he did not in fact work as a technical services operator so it would not be appropriate for him to compare himself with the other technical services operators.

24.8.2 Dismissal for taking part in industrial action

The rules on dismissal for taking part in industrial action are relatively complex since there are a number of possible situations:

- where a dismissal follows a lock-out by the employer;
- where there is a dismissal following an unofficial strike by trade union members and non-trade unionists;
- where there is a dismissal following a strike of employees none of whom are members of a trade union – this will always be an unofficial strike;
- where there is a dismissal following strike action which is not protected under section 219 Trade Union and Labour Relations (Consolidation) Act 1992 because either there has been no ballot held to approve industrial action or there has been secondary action taken;
- protected official action which is fully covered by the immunity in section 219.

Lock-out by the employer

In the case of lock-out by an employer this is regulated by section 238(1)(a) Trade Union and Labour Relations (Consolidation) Act 1992. A lock-out is a situation where the employer is suspending work, refusing to allow his employees to work generally in order to make the employees accept conditions of work that they otherwise would not be prepared to.

Any lock-out amounts to a breach of contract by the employer. If an employee is dismissed because of the lock-out the tribunal has to assess that an employee has been dismissed because of the lock-out, that some were re-engaged by the employer within three months but not the claimant and that the claimant had an interest in the dispute. If these are shown then the dismissal will be unfair.

CASE EXAMPLE

Express and Star Ltd v Bunday [1987] ICR 58

The employer produced provincial newspapers. It wanted to install new technology which meant that a representative of the newspaper who received an order for advertising could copy this directly into the plate from which the newspaper was to be printed. The trade union was opposed to this innovation. The employer had tried for a long time to persuade the union to accept it, but without success. The union then instructed its members not to accept the new technology and the employer responded by closing its premises with managers directing employees who arrived for work to a meeting. This was done so that each employee would be seen by management and it would also avoid industrial action taking place inside rather than outside. At the meeting employees were asked whether they were prepared to work under their contract of employment without restriction and to handle work however processed when asked to do so and told that if they answered no then they could be dismissed and were in any case immediately suspended without pay. The Court of Appeal held that these circumstances amounted to a lock-out by the employer as a result of which the dismissals were unfair.

Unofficial strike involving union members and non-members

Where there is an unofficial strike which involves both members of trade unions and non-members then there is no fundamental right to claim unfair dismissal since the action is fundamentally a breach of contract.

This is covered by section 237 Trade Union and Labour Relations (Consolidation) Act 1992 and a strike is unofficial unless the striking employee:

- is a member of a trade union and the strike was authorised by the trade union to which he belongs; or
- he is not a member of the trade union but other employees taking part in the strike are members of the union which authorised the strike.

Problems can arise of course where the employer tries to resolve the issue by dismissing all employees but there are in fact employees who have not taken part in the industrial action.

CASE EXAMPLE

Sehmi v Gate Gourmet London Ltd [2009] IRLR 807

The employer prepared food at Heathow Airport. There was widespread discontent amongst employees about the engagement of a large number of seasonal staff. A large number of employees stopped work on one particular day and gathered in a canteen. They were told that they were dismissed and the employer later sent out dismissal letters to every member of the particular shift amounting to around 600. After investigation a number of employees were re-engaged. Twenty-two employees claimed unfair dismissal for different reasons. Some were not at work on the day and claimed that their absence was for other reasons and some were trade union officials who claimed that they had gone to see the employees in the canteen as union leaders but were not participating in the action but had been sent home by management. After the tribunal dismissed a number of claims and upheld others as unfair six claimants appealed to the EAT. Sehmi who was a shop steward had been in India at a funeral when the unofficial action occurred but had been dismissed by the same letter that was sent to several other employees but was allowed to appeal because he had not been on the premises on the day. On his return he had received a letter asking him to confirm that he did not take part in industrial action. He had in fact not received either letter because he had moved house without notifying his employer of his change of address. On his return to work he claimed that he was turned away by management and he did not attend work after that time. He did attend a picket line at the workplace on several occasions. The EAT held that his dismissal, while it was unfortunate for Sehmi that he did not initially receive the letters that would have fully explained the situation and could not properly have been dismissed on the original date since he was in India, he nevertheless took part in unofficial industrial action on his return and therefore was beyond the protection of section 237.

Unofficial action by non-unionists

In situations where none of the employees taking part in a strike or other industrial action are members of a trade union then the situation cannot be described as either official or unofficial action because there is no trade union involved so it can merely be described as industrial action.

Dismissals in such circumstances are generally fair unless they fall under section 238 Trade Union and Labour Relations (Consolidation) Act 1992 where:

▨ some of the employees are not dismissed but the claimant is not one of these;

▨ some of the employees are dismissed but are re-engaged within three months of the industrial dispute and the claimant is not one of these.

If either of these apply then the dismissals are unfair. However, if the employer dismisses all of the strikers or re-engages some but only after three months have passed, then an employee who has been dismissed in such circumstances will have no claim to unfair dismissal. The important date is the date of the dismissal.

CASE EXAMPLE

McCormick v Horsepower [1981] IRLR 217

An employee who was taking part in industrial action was then made redundant after all of the other strikers had been dismissed but before any tribunal hearing. It was held that because all of the strikers had been dismissed including the one that was made redundant the employer had immunity and the tribunal had no jurisdiction to hear claims of the other strikers.

The employer is free to re-engage employees who were dismissed for being on strike after three months. However, the employer loses the protection of section 238 if he dismisses employees before any industrial action is in fact taken.

CASE EXAMPLE

Midlands Plastic Ltd v Till [1983] IRLR 9

Management was informed by the trade union that unless certain demands were met the employees would be on strike from a particular time. Before the strike was due to begin the managing director dismissed four employees who confirmed when asked that they would take part in the industrial action. The employer was not able to rely on section 238 and the dismissals were unfair.

Similarly there will be no protection from section 238 for an employer who dismisses employees who have returned to work after the strike in an act of retribution.

CASE EXAMPLE

Heath v Longman (Meat Salesmen) Ltd [1973] IRLR 214

There had been a strike and the employees had decided to return to work and one of the strikers had informed the employer that the strike was over. Nevertheless, the employer dismissed the employees and it was an unfair dismissal since there was no longer any industrial action.

Where an employee has been legitimately dismissed under section 238 for taking part in industrial action then he is not entitled to a redundancy payment when it is later identified that a redundancy situation exists.

CASE EXAMPLE

Baxter v Limb Group of Companies [1994] IRLR 572

Dockers had refused to work overtime during a dispute over rates of pay. The employer dismissed them and then ceased to employ labour directly but contracted the work out to contractors. The dismissed employees argued that there was in fact a redundancy situation since their roles had been done away with and a different system put in place. They also argued that the employer had simply engineered the strike so that he could dismiss them. The Court of Appeal held that in reality the dismissal was for industrial action and section 238 applied to protect the employer.

JUDGMENT

Waite LJ identified: 'The industrial action which the appellants took in support of their views on the short hand working bonus generated both the dismissal of the appellants and the decision to use contract labour and not any further direct labour. Both were consequences of the industrial action, and the "redundancy situation" was not the cause, or reason for, the dismissal of the appellants.'

Unprotected official action

This covers situations where a union has called its members out on strike in contemplation or furtherance of a trade dispute but has lost the protection of section 219 Trade Union and Labour Relations (Consolidation) Act 1992. The dismissals of employees in these circumstances would not then be unlawful.

This is commonly because the balloting requirements under sections 226–234 Trade Union and Labour Relations (Consolidation) Act 1992 were not complied with or the appropriate notice was not given to the employer as required by section 234A. However, it could be because secondary action was taken contrary to section 224 or the strike was called in order to impose trade union recognition on the employer contrary to section 225, or to enforce trade union membership contrary to section 222. It could also result from action over the dismissal of an unofficial striker contrary to section 223.

Protected official action

Protected industrial action is that action which attracts the immunity for the trade union found in section 219 Trade Union and Labour Relations (Consolidation) Act 1992. In the case of employees engaged in protected industrial action they have protection under section 238A and any dismissal will be automatically unfair if the date of the dismissal is:

■ within the protected period – this is twelve weeks beginning with the first day of protected industrial action – and any extension if there is an employer lock-out; or

- after the protected period is over and the employee has ceased to take part in the industrial action before the end of that period; or
- after the protected period is over but the employer has failed to take reasonable procedural steps necessary to end the dispute such as resuming negotiations or using a conciliator.

Section 238A(6) identifies the reasonable steps that the employer should take:

- whether the employer or a union had complied with procedures established by any applicable collective or other agreement;
- whether the employer or a union offered or agreed to commence or resume negotiations after the start of the protected industrial action;
- whether the employer or a union unreasonably refused, after the start of the protected industrial action, a request that conciliation services be used;
- whether the employer or a union unreasonably refused, after the start of the protected industrial action, a request that mediation services be used in relation to procedures to be adopted for the purposes of resolving the dispute.

24.8.3 Dismissal because of industrial pressure

There are also times when an employer might be forced to dismiss an employee not because of anything wrong with the employee but because the employer has been subjected to unfair pressure by other employees, most commonly where there is a threat of industrial action of some kind. This is now covered by section 107 Employment Rights Act 1996 which in effect means that such a dismissal could be unfair.

The section identifies that in determining whether the employer acted reasonably in dismissing the employee no account will be taken of any pressure placed on the employer through strike or other industrial action or the threat of it.

CASE EXAMPLE

Hazell Offsets v Luckett [1977] IRLR 430

The claimant was employed as manager. He was dismissed when representatives of a trade union indicated that they were not prepared to work with him. The only reason for the dismissal was the unfair pressure and so it was unfair.

In circumstances where the dismissal following unfair pressure results from the claimant not being a member of the trade union then the trade union can be joined as a party to the proceedings and an award of compensation can be made against it rather than the employer.

ACTIVITY

Self-assessment questions

1. What are the situations in which a dismissal for trade union related issues might occur?
2. What is the effect of a dismissal for taking part in a legitimate activity at an appropriate time?
3. How is appropriate time defined?
4. What is interesting about the approach taken by the court in *Zucker v Astrid Jewels Ltd*?
5. What is the effect of a dismissal for trade union activities carried out during a previous employment?

6. What are the consequences of a dismissal during a lock-out?
7. What is unofficial industrial action?
8. What is official industrial action?
9. What is the difference between how dismissals for official industrial action and unofficial industrial action are treated by the courts?
10. When will official industrial action not be protected?
11. When can a dismissal for protected official action be automatically unfair?
12. What is the basic position on dismissals where the employer has been put under unfair pressure to dismiss?

KEY FACTS

Trade union membership and non-membership	Case/statute
• Employees have freedom to join or not to join a trade union • So cannot be refused employment because of membership, non-membership, or refusing to give up or take up membership or to make payments	S137 Trade Union and Labour Relations (Consolidation) Act 1992
• It may be legitimate to refuse employment because of past trade union activities • And there is a significant overlap between membership and activities • Human Rights law identifies that deterring trade union activities is denying rights	Birmingham District Council v Beyer Harrison v Kent County Council Wilson, National Union of Journalists and Others v the United Kingdom
• Job advertisements that stipulate membership or non-membership are unlawful	S137(3) TULR(C)A1992
• There are various exclusions including self-employed, share fishermen, police, armed forces, overseas workers, seamen on non-UK registered ships	S138 TULR(C)A1992
• Remedies include declaration, compensation, recommendation	S139–142 TULR(C)A1992

Trade union recognition	Case/statute
• Defined as recognition by an employer, or two or more associated employers for the purposes of collective bargaining	S178(3) TULR(C)A1992
• Voluntary recognition is always possible following agreement between the employer and the trade union • Statutory recognition is now possible subject to a complex set of rules involving the Central Arbitration Committee – which must decide whether there is an appropriate bargaining unit which has the support of the majority of employees	Schedule A1 TULR(C)A1992

Time off for trade union duties and activities	Case/statute
Time off for trade union duties	
• An official of a recognised trade union is entitled to have paid time for negotiations with the employer connected with collective bargaining; or other functions connected to collective bargaining or receiving information from the employer and consultation with the employer in connection with collective redundancies or transfer of undertakings; or receiving training in industrial relations relevant to carrying out the duties	S168 TULR(C)A1992

• Time off is what is reasonable in the circumstances taking the ACAS Code into account	*S168(3) TULR(C)A1992*
• It is not reasonable to expect the employer to pay for duties carried out in the employee's own time	*Hairsine v Kingston-Upon-Hull City Council*

Time off for trade union activities

• The employer must allow an employee who is a member of a recognised trade union time off for any activities of the union and any activities in relation to which the employee is acting as a representative of the union	*S170 TULR(C)A1992*
• Again it is only time off that is reasonable in all the circumstances	*Wignall v British Gas Corporation*
• And the right does not cover industrial action	*S170(2) TULR(C)A1992*

Collective bargaining | Case/statute

There are a number of employment issues that can be the subject of collective bargaining between an employer and a recognised trade union	*S178(2) TULR(C)A1992*
• terms and conditions of employment, or physical conditions of work	
• engagement, non-engagement, termination suspension	
• allocation of work or duties	
• disciplinary matters	
• membership or non-membership of a trade union	
• facilities for officials of trade unions	
• machinery for negotiation or consultation, relating to any of the above matters	*Part 1 Sch A1 TULR(C)A1992*
Core issues are pay, hours and holidays	*S181 TULR(C)A1992*
An employer has a duty to disclose information necessary to make collective bargaining effective – but can withhold information which if disclosed:	
• is against the interests of national security	
• would involve breaking the law	
• would cause damage to the employer's business	
• which relates specifically to one employee	
• which the employer received in confidence	
• which was obtained by the employer for the purpose of bringing or defending legal proceedings	*SS183–184 TULR(C)A1992*
If the employer fails to disclose a complaint can be made to the Central Arbitration Committee	

Industrial action, immunity and loss of immunity | Case/statute

Tortious liability in trade disputes

• any inducement to breach a contract is unlawful	*D C Thompson & Co v Deakin*
• which could include by indirect means	*Middlebrook Mushrooms Ltd v TGWU*
• and also procuring a breach of a commercial contract	*Torquay Hotel Co Ltd v Cousins*
• or any other wrongful interference with a contract	*Timeplan Education Group v National Union of Teachers*
• any threat of intimidation is also an actionable tort	*Rookes v Barnard*
• which could also include action taken because of or in furtherance of the wrongful threats	*Newsgroup Newspapers Ltd v Society of Graphical and Allied Trades 1982*
• a conspiracy is combining together to induce other parties to breach a contract	*Quinn v Leatham*

• an unlawful conspiracy only aims to damage the employer • but a combination for the furtherance of a trade dispute is not an actionable conspiracy • economic duress is also actionable	*Huntley v Thornton* *Crofter Hand Woven Harris Tweed Co Ltd v Veitch* *Universe Tankships Incorporated of Monrovia v ITWF*
Immunity from legal action	
• an act done in contemplation or furtherance of a trade dispute is not actionable only because it induces another to breach a contract or otherwise interferes with performance of a contract	*S219 TULR(C)A1992*
• in contemplation of means the dispute must be imminent • in furtherance means it must be for the legitimate objectives of the trade union in relation to the particular dispute in question	*Bents Brewery Co Ltd v Hogan* *Conway v Wade*
• a trade dispute is one between employer and employees which relates wholly or mainly to terms and conditions, engagement, non-engagement, termination suspension, allocation of work, disciplinary matters, membership or non-membership of a trade union, facilities for officials of trade unions, machinery for negotiation or consultation – but nothing else	*S244 TULR(C)A1992* *Wandsworth London Borough Council v NASUWT*
• the dispute must be between the existing employer and existing employees • and an objection to government policy is not a trade dispute • nor is an objection to the policies of other governments	*University College London Hospitals NHS Trust v UNISON* *Mercury Communications Ltd v Scott Garner* *British Broadcasting Corporation v D A Hearn*
Loss of immunity	
• there is no immunity for industrial action which is not authorised by a secret ballot	*S226 TULR(C)A1992*
• the union must inform the employer of the ballot when it will occur and what categories of employees are involved	*S226A(2) TULR(C)A1992*
• an appropriate scrutineer must be appointed	*S226B TULR(C)A1992*
• all members whom it is reasonable for the union to believe at the time of the ballot will be induced to take part in the industrial action are entitled to vote but no others	*S227(1) TULR(C)A 1992*
• there should usually be separate workplace ballots	*S228(3) TULR(C)A 1992*
• except where the dispute involves a wider group of workers because negotiating machinery is national and the dispute involves all of them	*S228A TULR(C)A 1992*
• various information should be on the voting paper which should also phrase the questions whether a strike or action short of a strike should be taken so that they are answered yes or no	*S229(1) TULR(C)A 1992*
• the union loses immunity if there is no ballot or the ballot does not conform to the rules	
• there is no immunity from civil action where there is secondary action which induces another to break a contract of employment, or interferes or induces another to interfere with its performance, or threatens that a contract of employment under which he or another is employed will be broken or its performance interfered with, or that he will induce another to break a contract of employment or to interfere with its performance	*S224(2) TULR(C)A1992*

• nor where industrial action is for the purpose of enforcing membership of a trade union	S222 TULR(C)A1992
• nor where industrial action is taken in support of employees who have been dismissed for unofficial industrial action	S223 TULR(C)A1992
• and there is no immunity for picketing except where it involves a union member who is acting in contemplation or furtherance of a trade dispute and attends at or near his own place of work or, a union official at or near the place of work of a union member whom he is accompanying and whom he represents	S220 TULR(C)A1992

Discipline short of dismissal	Case/statute
An employer should not subject an employer to any detriment because of membership or non-membership of a trade union, taking part in trade union activities or taking advantage of trade union services	S146 TULR(C)A1992
• the detriment must affect the employee as an individual	F W Farnsworth Ltd v McCoid
• and the action taken by the employer must be to prevent the employee from exercising his statutory rights as a member of a trade union	Wilson, National Union of Journalists and Others v the United Kingdom
• it has been held that the employee must show the employer's purpose as well as the effect of the action	Gallacher v Department of Transport
• the trade union activities must be being carried out at an appropriate time which is either in own time or in work time if expressly or impliedly agreed to by the employer	Robb v Leon Motor Services
• an employee also has the right not to suffer a detriment because of being accompanied by a representative at a hearing or accompanying an employee at a hearing	S12 Employment Relations Act 1999

Dismissal for trade union reasons	Case/statute
Trade union related dismissal	
• an employee should not be dismissed for being or not being a member of a trade union, or refusing to join a trade union, or taking part in trade union activities or using trade union services or refusing to be induced into giving up trade union rights	S152 TULR(C)A1992
• activity must be legitimate and carried out at an appropriate time	Burgess v Bass Taverns Ltd
• appropriate time is in the employee's own time or in works time with the employer's agreement	Marley Tile Co Ltd v Shaw
• and an employer cannot dismiss an employee for taking part in trade union activities in previous employment	Fitzpatrick v British Railways Board
• a dismissal for using trade union services is unlawful if that is the sole reason for the dismissal	Discount Tobacco and Confectionary Ltd v Armitage
• selection for redundancy is also unfair dismissal if it is related to the employee's trade unionism	S153 TULR(C)A1992
• and there must be other employees similar to the claimant who were not selected	O'Dea v ISC Chemicals Ltd

Dismissal for taking part in industrial action	
• in the case of a lock-out by the employer this amounts to a breach of contract by the employer	S238(1)(a) TULR(C)A1992
• if employees are dismissed because of the lock-out and some are re-engaged within three months but not the claimant then the dismissal is unfair	Express and Star Ltd v Bunday

• a strike involving union members and non-members is unofficial and there is no claim to unfair dismissal unless the claimant is a member of a union which called official action or is not a member but other employees taking action are	*S237 TULR(C)A1992*
• dismissal for action taken by employees who are all non-members is fair unless some of the employees are not dismissed but the claimant is not one of these or some of the employees are dismissed but are re-engaged within three months of the industrial dispute and the claimant is not one of these	*S238 TULR(C)A1992*
• a dismissal before any industrial action is taken is unfair	*Midlands Plastic Ltd v Till*
• as is a dismissal after strikers return to work	*Heath v Longman (Meat Salesmen) Ltd*
• a dismissal for unofficial action – which can be for a failure to ballot properly, or appropriate notice was not given to the employer, or secondary action was taken, or the strike was called in order to impose trade union recognition on the employer, or to enforce trade union membership or action over the dismissal of an unofficial striker	*SS226–234 TULR(C)A1992* *S234A TULR(C)A1992* *S224 TULR(C)A1992* *S225 TULR(C)A1992* *S222 TULR(C)A1992* *S223 TULR(C)A1992*
• a dismissal where there is protected industrial action is unfair if it is in the protected period or after the protected period but the employee has stopped taking part before the end of the period or the employer has failed to take reasonable steps to end the dispute	*S238A TULR(C)A1992*

Dismissal because of industrial pressure

• a dismissal because industrial pressure is put on the employer through industrial action or the threat of it is unfair	*S107 Employment Rights Act 1996*

SAMPLE ESSAY QUESTION

ESSAY Discuss the extent to which the rules on dismissals of employees for trade union reasons are fair to both employees and employers.

Explain the rules on trade union related dismissals

• Employee should not be dismissed for being or not being a member of a trade union, or refusing to join a trade union, or taking part in trade union activities or using trade union services or refusing to be induced into giving up trade union rights.
• Activity must be legitimate and carried out at an appropriate time.
• Appropriate time is in the employee's own time or in works time with the employer's agreement.

- And an employer cannot dismiss an employee for taking part in trade union activities in previous employment.
- A dismissal for using trade union services is unlawful if that is the sole reason for the dismissal.
- Selection for redundancy is also unfair dismissal if it is related to the employee's trade unionism.
- And there must be other employees similar to the claimant who were not selected.

Discuss whether the rules on trade union related dismissals are fair to both employer and employees

- Fair to employee as basic right to trade union membership is guaranteed.
- Also protects right to engage in activities and take advantage of services that the trade union offers.
- Fair also to employer because only has to accept legitimate activities and use of services carried out at an appropriate time.
- And appropriate time is limited to out of work unless employer agrees – fair to employer but could limit ability of union to be effective for its members and limit benefits members can gain.
- Provision on union activities in past employment is fair to employees but employers may feel that they should be entitled to get rid of known militants.
- Selection for redundancy can also not be used as a disguise to get rid of activists.

Explain the rules on dismissal for taking part in industrial action

- A dismissal during a lock-out by the employer is a breach of contract and if some re-engaged within three months but not the claimant then dismissal is unfair.
- A strike involving union members and non-members is unofficial so no claim for unfair dismissal unless the claimant is a member of a union which called official action or is not a member but other employees taking action are.

- Action all by non-members is unofficial so dismissal is fair unless some are not dismissed but the claimant is not one of these or some of the employees are dismissed but are re-engaged within three months and the claimant is not one.
- Dismissal before industrial action is unfair.
- As is a dismissal after strikers return to work.
- A dismissal for unofficial action – which can be for a failure to ballot properly; or appropriate notice not given to employer; or secondary action taken; or strike called to impose trade union recognition; or to enforce trade union membership; or action over the dismissal of an unofficial striker; or unlawful picketing is fair.
- A dismissal for protected industrial action is unfair if it is in the protected period or after the protected period but the employee has stopped taking part before the end of the period or the employer has failed to take reasonable steps to end the dispute.

Discuss whether the rules on dismissal for taking part in industrial action are fair to both employer and employees

- A lock-out is an unfair reaction by an employer to an industrial dispute so the rule redresses the imbalance and is fair to both sides.
- Unofficial strikes by members and non-members have not been based on the proscribed methods so are unfair to employers and so dismissals in such circumstances are fair when all strikers are treated the same when individuals are treated differently this is unfair to them so the rules are fair and avoid discrimination.
- When strike action is taken by non-unionists then this is always unofficial so dismissals are fair to the employer – however it is possible that employees in a particular industry are not well represented or have not been able to gain recognition for a union so could in fact be unfair.
- Dismissing employees because they are threatening industrial action is intimidation and dismissing employees who have taken industrial action is revenge – both are therefore unfair to the employees and the rules are fair.

- Where proper procedures have not been taken in official action this is careless and silly so the rules are fair.
- Where the dismissal is fair and proper procedures are taken dismissal is an unfair reaction so the rules are fair.

Explain the rules on dismissal because of industrial pressure and discuss whether they are fair

- A dismissal because industrial pressure is put on the employer through industrial action or the threat of it is generally unfair.
- So it is a fair protection for the individual employee who is the subject of the pressure.
- But it depends on the strength of the union and of the pressure whether it can be absolutely said to be fair to the employer who may feel that he has no options in the circumstances.

REACH REASONED CONCLUSIONS

SUMMARY

- There is a basic right to be a member or indeed not to be a member of a trade union so that an employer cannot refuse to employ a person because of their membership or indeed non-membership of a trade union.
- It may be possible to refuse to employ because of past trade union activities where they are uncooperative.
- There are various exclusions from the right including the usual share fishermen, armed forces and police.
- There are three possible remedies: a declaration, compensation and a recommendation to alter practice.
- A trade union can only engage in collective bargaining with an employer if it is a recognised trade union – recognition can be voluntary between the employer and the trade union but there is now also a complex process for achieving statutory recognition.
- A trade union official of a union recognised by the employer is entitled to use work time where this is reasonable in the circumstances and should be paid at the normal rate – but the employer is not bound to pay for duties carried out in the employee's own time.

- An employer is also bound to allow reasonable time off for an employee who is a member of a recognised trade union to engage in trade union activities or activities that involve the employee as a representative – however, the right does not extend to industrial action.

- Collective bargaining is the process whereby an employer and representatives of a recognised trade union negotiate on terms and conditions of employment, engagement, non-engagement, termination or suspension of employees, allocation of work, disciplinary matters, membership or non-membership of a trade union, facilities for officials of trade unions and the machinery for negotiation or consultation.

- An employer is also under a duty to disclose the information that would make the process ineffective if not revealed but is not bound to disclose certain information such as that which would endanger national security if disclosed or damage the employer's business.

- Industrial action is obviously aimed at applying pressure on the employer but could be tortious in a number of ways including inducing a breach of contract or otherwise wrongfully interfering with a contract, intimidation and conspiracy – in contract law there is also economic duress which is applying unlawful coercion in circumstances where economic necessity means that the coercion will work.

- Tortious or other actions done in contemplation or furtherance of a trade dispute are immune from action as long as they concern conditions of employment, engagement, non-engagement, termination or suspension of employees, allocation of work, disciplinary matters, membership or non-membership of a trade union, facilities for officials of trade unions, and the machinery for negotiation or consultation and the dispute is imminent.

- Immunity of the trade union from civil action is lost if the law relating to the holding of secret ballots has not been followed, there is unlawful secondary action, there is pressure to impose union recognition, union membership or to retain a closed shop, or if the action is to persuade an employer to reinstate unofficial strikers who have been dismissed.

- Employees should not be dismissed for being or not being a member of a trade union, or refusing to join a trade union, or taking part in trade union activities, or using trade union services or refusing to be induced into giving up their trade union rights and to do so would be an unfair dismissal.

- Dismissals for taking part in industrial action are either fair or unfair depending on the nature of the industrial action – generally if the action is unofficial then the dismissal resulting from it is fair, it could still be fair where the action is official but balloting requirements have not been met, proper notice of the action is not given, there is secondary action, or the action was to impose union recognition or to enforce membership or to support an unofficial striker.

- Generally dismissals where unfair pressure has been put on the employer are still unfair.

Further reading

Emir, Astra, *Selwyn's Law of Employment 17th edition*. Oxford University Press, 2012, Chapters 21 and 23.

Pitt, Gwyneth, *Cases and Materials on Employment Law 3rd edition*. Pearson, 2008, Chapters 11, 12 and 13.

Sargeant, Malcolm and Lewis, David, *Employment Law 6th edition*. Pearson, 2012, Chapters 10 and 11.

Appendix 1

Activity: Essay writing

Below is a sample essay title and a guide on how to prepare to answer it

Discuss the extent to which EU discrimination law which is clearly binding on the UK has moved from a limited economic protection of women in the original EC Treaty to a much broader social agenda now, which has been reflected in the UK by the Equality Act 2010.

Answering the question

There are usually two key elements to answering essays in law:

- first you are required to reproduce a certain factual information on a particular area of law and this is usually identified for you in the question;

- second you are required to answer the specific question set, which usually is in the form of some sort of critical element, i.e. you are likely to see the words discuss, or analyse, or comment on, or critically consider, or even compare and contrast if two areas are involved.

Students for the most part seem quite capable of doing the first, and also generally seem less skilled at the second. The important points in any case are to ensure that you only deal with relevant legal material in your answer and that you do answer the question set, rather than one you have made up yourself, or the one that was on last year's paper.

For instance, in the case of the first, in this essay you are likely to provide detail on the following: Article 157 TFEU (originally Article 119 EC Treaty) which introduced the concept of men and women receiving equal pay for equal work, the development of more specific detail in Directive 75/117, the extension to conditions as well as pay in Directive 76/207, the Equal Pay Act 1970 and Sex Discrimination Act 1975 and subsequent amendments, the Recast Directive 2006/54, the Framework Directive on Equal Treatment 2000/78 and the Race Directive 2000/43, the various Regulations giving force to provisions from those directives and then the Equality Act 2010 creating a broad single framework for discrimination law. So there is quite a broad base of knowledge required.

In the case of the second the essay asks you to discuss the extent to which there is a development from a purely economic protection to a broad social agenda and also how this development has influenced the UK. So you must discuss the limitations of the original Treaty Article and the developments that have been made in EU law and how they have been implemented into UK law and the extent to which this involves a move from a limited economic protection to a wide social agenda and you must also reach a conclusion based on your discussion.

Relevant law

The appropriate law appears to be:

- that discrimination law was created by the EC Treaty, the basic right in Article 157 TFEU (originally Article 119 EC Treaty) that men and women should receive equal pay for equal work;

- that the provision is directly effective both vertically and horizontally *Defrenne v SABENA*;

- that there is a broad definition of comparator to include the person who has formerly done the job *MacArthys' v Smith* (in contrast to the original view of the English courts);

- that the definition of pay is broad and includes e.g. perks *Garland v BREL*; sick pay *Rinner Kuhn*; training *Botel*; non-contributory occupational pension schemes *Bilka Kaufhaus*; redundancy payments *ex p EOC*; most importantly contracted out schemes *Barber v Guardian Royal Exchange*;

- that the equal pay directive 75/117 (now part of the Recast Directive 2006/54) includes work of equal value as well as like work (where UK law did not *61/81 Commission v UK* and *Hayward v Cammell Laird Shipbuilders*), and explain the significance of job evaluation studies, and that the claimant can only achieve equal not fair pay *Murphy v An Bord Telecom Eireann*, and explain the criteria for such schemes in *Rummler*;

- the importance of the *Bilka Kaufhaus* criteria for justifying pay differentials;

- the position on back pay in equal pay claims *Preston v Wolverhampton NHS Trust*;

- that there was an early extension away from pay into conditions in directive 76/207 the original equal access directive (now see Directive 2006/54);

- the importance of direct effect *Marshall*;

- (possibly could also consider the extension into social security matters – directive 79/7 and self-employment – Directive 86/613);

- that there is a new social agenda in the EU treaties – and anti-discrimination is now covered in the broadest terms through the Race Directive 2000/43 and the Framework Directive 2000/78 which extended discrimination law to cover age, disability, gender reassignment, sexual orientation, religion and belief – and introduced a new definition of indirect discrimination which favours claimants;

- that the UK introduced various Regulations to cover these areas e.g. the Employment Equality (Sexual Orientation) Regulations 2003 and the Employment Equality (Religion or Belief) Regulations 2003;

- that subsequently the UK has passed the Equality Act which includes eight protected characteristics – age, disability, gender reassignment, marriage and civil partnership, pregnancy and maternity, race, religion or belief, sex and sexual orientation';

- that the Act also introduces prohibited conduct, the areas of discrimination, which are direct, indirect, harassment and victimisation and there are some more specific ones that operate in relation to specific protected characteristics – and also covers discrimination in employment in recruitment and selection, during employment and on dismissal.

Evaluation

- Consider the original incongruity of the basic right in Article 157. It was not really part of the free market aims – so there was some economic context but it always looked like a social provision.

- But consider that it was part of the economic agenda.

- Consider the 'dual objectives' and the reasons for them – the economic objective (to ensure that there is no distortion of competition based on unfair advantage caused by differential wage policies for men and women) – the social objective (to improve the living and working conditions of people in the Community generally.

- Consider how the ECJ expanded the scope of the Article in the case law on the meaning of pay, on the definition and nature of comparator and in various other ways.
- Consider the problems associated with differential conditions of e.g. part-time workers.
- Consider the tension between the EU and Member States in terms of direct effect.
- Consider the expansion and amplification into Directive 75/117 and with other directives on e.g. pensions.
- Consider the problems associated with work of equal value.
- Discuss the problems associated with the UK failure to provide an action for work of equal value.
- Discuss the expansion into conditions in Directive 76/207.
- Discuss the problems that this caused for the UK in relation to differential retirement ages.
- Discuss how EU moved away from a purely economic agenda and how there is now a much broader social agenda which runs well beyond pure parity of pay.
- Discuss how this broader social agenda now includes rules on discrimination in race, age, disability, sexual orientation, religion and belief.
- Discuss how the EU in any case developed and defined e.g. principles of harassment and contrast with the lack of any real definition in UK law and the only action being for 'suffering any other detriment'.
- Discuss the effect of equality legislation – that it regulates more internally within Member States than on an intra-EU basis.
- Discuss also the new Recast Directive – replacing earlier directives and drawing together decisions of the ECJ in legislative form.
- Discuss the impact of the Framework Directive and Race Directive on UK discrimination law and consider whether the Equality Act now moves UK discrimination law more into a social agenda improving conditions generally rather than a pure economic protection which the original Equal Pay Act may have been seen as.
- Reach any sensible conclusion in relation to the quote.

Appendix 2

Activity: Applying the law

Below is a reasonably straightforward problem question and a guide on how to prepare to answer it

There are always four essential ingredients to answering problem questions:

- First you must be able to identify which are the key facts in the problem, the ones on which any resolution of the problem will depend.

- Second you will need to identify which is the appropriate law which applies to the particular situation in the problem.

- The third task is to apply the law to the facts.

- Finally you will need to reach conclusions of some sort. If the question asks you to advise then that is what you need to do. On the other hand if the problem says 'Discuss the legal consequences of...' then you know that you can be less positive in your conclusions.

Problem

Alan has been employed as a delivery driver for Prontocouriers for seventeen years. In the works rules is a clause requiring that drivers must reach delivery points by set times and failure to do so is subject to disciplinary proceedings. Alan was dismissed last week with immediate effect. He was told that this was because he had arrived twenty minutes late at a delivery. He received no disciplinary warning of any sort, nor was he allowed to appeal the decision. Alan is aware that two other delivery drivers regularly arrive late at deliveries but that no action has ever been taken against them.

The facts

It is important to have a clear idea of what the principal facts are, particularly here where there are a number of significant aspects to the question. We are told that Alan is an employee so we do not have to consider that, continuity also looks not to be an issue and it looks unlikely that there is an automatically unfair dismissal; however, we can still mention both. We do need to consider what potentially fair head of dismissal is likely in the circumstances and whether the dismissal is fair in fact. The main facts seem to be:

- Alan has been employed for seventeen years by Prontocouriers.

- He is contractually bound to reach his delivery points on time or face disciplinary proceedings.

- He arrived at a destination twenty minutes late.

- He was summarily dismissed as result.

- He was given no warning or allowed to appeal the decision to dismiss him.

- Alan is aware that two other delivery drivers regularly arrive late at deliveries but have never been disciplined.

The appropriate law

It is very important when answering problem questions that you use only the law that is relevant to the precise facts, if for no other reason that you are not getting any marks for using law that is irrelevant, and so you are wasting valuable writing time. By looking at the various facts we can say that the following law may be relevant in our problem here

▦ Under s94 ERA an employee is entitled not to be unfairly dismissed.

▦ Under s95 there must be a dismissal – which can be with or without notice.

▦ There are a number of exclusions not able to bring claims.

▦ There is a qualifying period of two years' continuous employment – but this does not apply in certain circumstances.

▦ There a number of areas of automatically unfair dismissal.

▦ There are five categories of potentially fair dismissals – including capability and qualifications, and conduct (misconduct).

▦ Capability it might involve incompetence that would justify dismissal *Woods v Olympic Aluminium Co* (1975), but not if the employee was properly instructed *Davison v Kent Meters Ltd* (1975), and proper disciplinary procedure should be carried through *Lowndes v Specialist Heavy Engineering Ltd*, but the longer an employee's service the more difficult it is to prove.

▦ Explain that a dismissal for conduct may be appropriate where disciplinary standards are infringed sufficiently seriously *Parsons v McLoughlin*.

▦ Explain that for a dismissal to be fair the employer must genuinely believe that the employee has committed an act of misconduct, had reasonable grounds for that belief and carried out a proper investigation *British Home Stores Ltd v Burchill* (1980).

▦ Explain that a test, in five stages, was outlined in detail by Browne-Wilkinson J in *Iceland Frozen Foods v Jones* [1983]:

⬤ The tribunal should begin with the words of s98(4) ERA 1996 – whether the employer acted reasonably, determined in accordance with equity and the substantial merits of the case.

⬤ The tribunal must consider whether the employer acted reasonably – not whether or not they think the dismissal was fair.

⬤ The tribunal must not substitute its own decision as to what the right course was for the employer to adopt.

⬤ There is a band of reasonable responses to employee's conduct in which different employers might take different views.

▦ Explain that the function of the tribunal is to determine whether the dismissal fell within that band.

▦ Explain that there must also be procedural fairness measured against the ACAS code which identifies fairness in the following:

⬤ raising and dealing with issues promptly and avoiding unreasonable delays;

⬤ consistency from both sides;

⬤ carrying out necessary investigations;

⬤ giving employees full information and allowing them to state their case (in this respect s10 Employment Relations Act 1999 is also important in allowing the right to be accompanied at all hearings);

⬤ the provision of appeals;

⬤ keeping proper records.

▦ Explain that summary dismissal is only available for gross misconduct.

Applying the law to the facts

■ It looks unlikely that Alan will not have sufficient continuous employment to claim.

■ Alan has been dismissed according to s95 ERA 1996 – he has been dismissed without notice.

■ There is no apparent issue of ineligibility for a claim or an automatically unfair dismissal.

■ The possible heads of potentially fair dismissal appear to be either capability or conduct.

■ It seems unlikely that Prontocouriers would be able to claim incompetence after such a long period of employment – seventeen years.

■ The more likely reason for the dismissal is conduct because not reaching the delivery point on time is identified as subject to disciplinary proceedings in the works rules.

■ Using the reasonable range of responses test – there is no real indication of a full investigation – the question is whether the dismissal could be considered reasonable such that other employers may have reached the same decision – it seems quite harsh in the circumstances – other disciplinary action may have been more appropriate.

■ It is questionable whether Prontocouriers has acted procedurally fairly since there is no appeal available.

■ There is inconsistency of treatment between different workers – although this will not always make the employer's action unfair.

■ The dismissal is in effect summary and could only be justified for gross misconduct – it is unlikely that Alan's behaviour amounts to gross misconduct.

Conclusions

The dismissal is likely to be considered unfair.

Glossary

agency worker

a worker whose services are hired through a third party, the agent – a common feature of modern employment practices is employment agencies that have a data base of workers with different skills that they will then provide assignments with employers who want workers with these skills on a temporary basis

antenatal care

appointments with health professionals during pregnancy

apprentice

a person learning a trade

arbitration

a means of resolving a legal dispute without going to court where the parties agree to be bound by the arbitrator's decision

artificer

a craftsman

belief

any religious or philosophical belief including lack of belief

benefits in kind

forms of remuneration which are other than wages and which are generally not in a cash form – an example could be a company car

blue-pencilling

severing parts of restraint of trade clauses that are not reasonable to save ones that are – this can only be done if the clause still makes sense after severing the offending part

burden of proof

the person in a legal action who must prove the case – the general rule in English law is that he who accuses must prove – so in an employment context this will generally mean the employee

casual worker

a worker who works as and when required or irregularly

civil partnership

a legal relationship between two people of the same sex

codes of practice

usually introduced under authority granted by Parliament – they are not legally binding but are an indication of good practice so will be taken into account by tribunals

collective agreement

an agreement that is made between one or more trade unions and one or more employers following collective bargaining which may then be incorporated into the contract of employment

collective bargaining

a process of negotiation between an employer and a recognised trade union usually about conditions of work

combination

a group of workers collecting together for a common purpose usually to try to persuade their employers to improve their conditions

comparator

in discrimination the person with whom the person with a protected characteristic is comparing themselves for instance to identify that there is less favourable treatment or in equal pay a person of the opposite sex who is getting more money for doing the same work or work of equal value

common employment

a rule in the nineteenth century that where an employee was injured by the negligence of a fellow employee the employer would avoid liability

condition precedent

a formal requirement that must be complied with before the contract is in fact legally formed – in a contract of employment this could be as simple as the production of the results of a medical examination or the receipt of a satisfactory reference

conciliation

a process where an independent party tries to help the parties in a dispute to reach an agreement

constructive dismissal

there is no actual dismissal but the employee resigns and claims that it was impossible to continue because of a significant breach of the contract by the employer which in law may be classed as a dismissal

consultation
a process where the employer provides necessary information to employees or their representatives which may or may not involve responses from the employees – common in the case of transfer of undertakings and collective redundancies

continuity of employment
the period of continuous service in employment from the day that continuous service commences (which need not be the first day at work) until the effective date of termination (EDT) (which can be the date that notice expires or the date a lieu payment is made) – continuity is required as a qualification for many employment protections for instance a period of two years to bring a claim for unfair dismissal

contract for services
a contract between the hirer of services and a self-employed person who provides them

contract of service
the contract that exists between an employer and an employee

contributory negligence
a defence where the claimant fails to take care of himself and is therefore partly responsible for the injury or damage that he suffers

custom and practice
the process by which something is considered to be a term of the contract because of long acceptance but only where it is reasonable certain and notorious

damages
a remedy which involves the payment of a sum of money in compensation for the wrong done

declaration
a possible action of a tribunal or court in which the tribunal or court may for instance declare what the employee's rights are in the situation

dependant care leave
time legally allowed to be absent from work in circumstances where a dependant falls ill or in other ways needs care or the employee needs to make arrangements for care or on the death of a dependant

detriment
any form of harm or wrong or less favourable or unfavourable treatment suffered by an employee because of an employer's wrongful acts or omissions

direct applicability
EU law which applies throughout the EU

direct discrimination
occurs when a person is treated less favourably because of their protected characteristic than a person not sharing that protected characteristic would be treated

direct effect
enforceability of EU law

directive
a type of EU legislative provision which has to be implemented by Member States within a set time

disability
a physical or mental impairment which has a substantial and long term adverse effect on a person's ability to carry out normal day-to-day activities

disciplinary procedure
a formal procedure to deal with disciplinary issues involving staff – should include a process whereby employees know of the complaint against them, have the opportunity to state their own case, be accompanied at any hearing, have a reasoned decision based on a thorough investigation of the facts and the availability of an appeal

discrimination
where a person is subjected to some form of unfavourable treatment because of a protected characteristic – protected characteristics are age, disability, gender reassignment, marriage and civil partnership, pregnancy and maternity, race, religion or belief, sex and sexual orientation – discrimination can be direct, indirect, harassment or victimisation

dismissal
a specific type of termination of the contract of employment either where the employer terminates the contract with or without giving the employee notice, or where a fixed-term contract ends without being renewed, or where the employee resigns and claims that it is a constructive dismissal

duty
a legal obligation on the employer to carry out some process for example to consult in collective redundancies

duty of care
the duty owed by the employer to take care of the employee's health, safety, welfare and well-being

economic entity

in a TUPE transfer an organised grouping of resources which has the objective of pursuing an economic activity, whether or not that activity is central or ancillary

economic torts

wrongful actions that harm the employer's business – they include inducing a breach of contract or any other wrongful interference with the contract, intimidation and conspiracy

emanation of the state

in EU law a body which is like the state in that it provides a public service, is subject to state control and has powers over and above those that would be enjoyed by a private body

employee

a person who according to statute is employed under a contract of employment or is identified as an employee under one of the tests of employment status

equality clause

a principle of equal pay law whereby if a term in a woman's contract is less favourable than a corresponding term in a man's contract then the woman's contract is modified so as not to be less favourable

ETO reason

an economic, technical or organisational reason usually for a dismissal

express terms

terms in the contract of employment that are agreed by the parties – the reality is that they will almost always be what the employer decides

fellow servant rule

another way of identifying common employment – a rule in the nineteenth century that where an employee's injuries were caused by the negligence of a 'fellow servant' then the employer was not liable

fidelity

the duty that an employee should give faithful service to the employer – he should therefore not do anything that would harm the employer's business

fixed-term contract

an employment contract that is limited to a particular time scale, or until the occurrence of a particular event, or until completion of a particular task

fixed-term worker

an employee who works under a fixed-term contract

frustration

where the contract terminates because of an unforeseen change in the outside circumstances which was not provided for by the parties and which prevents continued performance of the contract and which was not the fault of either party

garden leave

where an employer pays the employee during the notice period but requires that the employee does no work and does not work either for any competitor

gender reassignment

where a person is proposing to undergo, is undergoing or has undergone a process (or part of a process) for the purpose of reassigning that person's sex by changing physiological or other attributes of sex

grievance procedure

a formal procedure for hearing complaints from employees on things that have upset them in their work or where they feel badly treated – could be actions by fellow employees or by management or could relate to conditions of work

gross misconduct

misconduct which it is accepted is so bad that it destroys the basis of the contract and therefore justifies summary dismissal

guarantee payments

statutory payments that are made to employees who are laid off or who work short time and therefore are receiving no pay or much less pay than they would normally be entitled to

immunity

a trade union is protected against civil actions for economic torts where they occur in contemplation of furtherance of a trade dispute

implied terms

terms in a contract that have not been expressly inserted in the contract by the parties themselves but which are implied by process of law which may include common law duties but also a great many implied by statute

indirect discrimination

occurs where a person is subjected to a provision, criterion or practice that is universally applied but is likely to disadvantage a person who has a particular protected characteristic more and is not a proportional means of achieving a legitimate aim

industrial action

action taken by employees and usually organised by trade unions in connection with trade disputes – can be official where it is called by a trade which has followed the correct procedure in terms of balloting or unofficial where either correct procedures have not been followed or the action is taken by employees who are not union members – action can involve strikes (withdrawing labour) or action less than a strike for example overtime bans

injunction

a type of equitable remedy – will usually be prohibitory (preventing a person from doing something) rather than mandatory (insisting that a person does something) because the latter is very difficult for a court to oversee or enforce

lay-offs

any week when an employee receives no pay due to him under his contract of employment

LIFO (last in first out)

a selection criterion for redundancy – used to be common for employers in a redundancy exercise selecting the employees with the least service – now employers are more likely to use more sophisticated criteria in order to retain the best employees

like work

work done by a woman which is the same or broadly similar to that done by a man

limitation

set time limits within which a person must bring their claim otherwise they are out of time

lock out

in an industrial dispute where the employer suspends work and refuses to allow his employees to work generally in order to make the employees accept conditions of work that they otherwise would not be prepared to

manual handling

lifting anything unaided and without the support of any device or machine

maternity

the period during pregnancy and after giving birth during which a woman is entitled to certain paid leave from work as well as paid suspension from work in certain circumstances and also the right to attend antenatal care

maternity leave

leave during maternity which is of three types – compulsory (the first two weeks after giving birth), ordinary (twenty-six weeks surrounding the birth), additional (a further twenty-six weeks)

medical suspension

a situation where an employer has to suspend an employee on pay because of a number of possible statutory requirements for example where a health risk occurs because they are exposed to certain hazardous substances

minor

a person under the age of eighteen

National Minimum Wage

a scale of minimum hourly payments which an employer is bound by law to make to employees – the rates vary between apprentices, those sixteen and seventeen, those between eighteen and twenty, and those that are over twenty-one

negligence

where a duty of care is owed (for example the duty of care owed by the employer to protect the employee's health and safety) and is breached by falling below the standard that is appropriate to the duty owed and this breach of duty causes foreseeable harm to the person the duty is owed to

night work

any work done in the period between midnight and 5.00 a.m.

non-delegable duty of care

a duty that cannot be avoided by delegating it to another party for example to an employee in a managerial role

non-standard employment situations

the hiring of labour in non-standard ways so that the employment relationship is not obvious – typical examples include outwork, casual work and agency work

notice

the period between the employee being made aware of a dismissal and the date of leaving or the date between the employee notifying the employer that he is resigning and the date of leaving – notice can be contractual but there also statutory minimum periods of notice

occupational requirement

a requirement that may on the face of it discriminate because a person with a particular protected characteristic cannot meet it but which is justified as it is necessary

officious bystander test
a test devised by the courts to determine whether a term is implied into a contract – it will be so where it was something that the parties obviously intended to include but for some reason failed to

outsourcing
in a TUPE transfer an undertaking transferring part of the operations of the undertaking to an outside body

outworker
a worker who works from home

parental leave
an entitlement that can be shared between both parents

part-time work
employment that is for less than a standard working week – a thirty-seven-and-a-half hour week is fairly common in the UK so it could involve a working week that is anything under that

paternity
male parental rights including leave and pay

pension rights
rights to a regular payment following retirement from employment

personal protective equipment
any equipment that an employee might use for personal protection against health and safety risks – so could include things like hard hats, safety goggles and steel-toe-capped boots

picketing
in the context of industrial action where employees engaged in industrial action are at or near the premises where they are employed trying to persuade other employees to join the industrial action or to persuade clients of the business from entering with or dealing with the business

prohibited conduct
in discrimination law acts which are discrimination and therefore unlawful – these include direct discrimination, indirect discrimination, harassment and victimisation

qualifying period
a set amount of time which an employee needs to have served to qualify for certain employment protections for example two years' continuous service for either a

redundancy payment or to be able to bring an unfair dismissal claim

recognition
the process by which a trade union gains a formal relationship with an employer for the purpose of collective bargaining

recommendation
another order or remedy of a court or tribunal for instance that the employee should cease discriminating against the employee

red circling
protecting the pay of an employee which is then at a higher rate than others doing the same work

redundancy
a type of dismissal where either the employer has ceased trading or has ceased trading at the place where the employee works or there is a diminution in work requiring objective selection criteria to be produced – the employee in a redundancy situation is also entitled to a redundancy payment

regulation (EU)
a type of EU legislative provision which automatically becomes law in member states once passed

regulation (UK)
a legislative provision of English law introduced through statutory instrument

resignation
a voluntary termination of the contract of employment by the employee giving the employer the required notice

res ipsa loquitur
a means of reversing the burden of proof where the damage has obviously been caused by negligence but the claimant is unable to supply precise details of the negligence

restraint of trade
a practice designed to prevent genuine competition – could be a clause in a contract of employment preventing the employee from carrying on particular roles on leaving the employment – but will be void unless it only protects a legitimate business interest and is reasonable

RIDDOR
Reporting of Injuries, Diseases and Dangerous Occurrences under the Reporting of Injuries, Diseases and Dangerous Occurrences Regulations 1995

risk assessment
a process whereby an employer identifies the specific risks to an employee's health, safety, welfare or well-being at work and as a result can put in place measures that would avoid the risk

safety representatives
sometimes called safety officers – these are employee representatives given statutory authority to represent employees' interests in respect of health and safety at work

secondary action
in the context of industrial disputes action that is taken by third parties to a dispute

self-certification
a process whereby an employee certifies that he is unfit to attend work during the first seven days of an illness after which the employee must see a doctor

service provision change
in a TUPE transfer a situation in which activities cease to be carried out by the undertaking on its own behalf and are carried out instead by a contractor or activities cease to be carried out by a contractor on the undertaking's behalf (whether or not those activities had previously been carried out by the undertaking) and are carried out instead by a subsequent contractor for the undertaking; or activities cease to be carried out by a contractor or a subsequent contractor on the undertaking's behalf (whether or not those activities had previously been carried out by the undertaking) and are carried out instead by the undertaking

share fishermen
a class of trawlermen who take a share of the profits from the sale of the fish that they catch rather than being paid a wage – as such these workers have few if any employment protections

short time
any week when an employee receives less than half the pay that he is entitled to under his contract of employment

sick leave
any absence from work which is explained by the genuine illness of the employee

Statutory Maternity Pay (SMP)
a government scheme which guarantees that pregnant employees get some form of pay during maternity leave

Statutory Sick Pay (SSP)
a government scheme which guarantees that employees get some form of pay during periods of sickness regardless of whether they are entitled to pay during sickness absence contractually – the employer pays SSP but recovers it by deducting the figure from National Insurance payments made to the government

statutory statement of particulars (section 1 statement)
sometimes referred to as the section 1 statement because it is required by section 1 Employment Rights Act 1996 – it is a written statement of a proscribed list of terms in the contract such as the address of the employer, the frequency and manner of pay, holiday entitlement, arrangements on sickness and many others

summary dismissal
a dismissal without notice and with immediate effect which can only be for gross misconduct – in practice most employers would suspend the employee first and only then dismiss after a thorough investigation

supranational
above national – so superior to national provisions

trade dispute
a dispute between employees and their employer often through a trade union about conditions of work, engagement, non-engagement, termination suspension; allocation of work, disciplinary matters; membership or non-membership of a trade union; facilities for officials of trade unions; machinery for negotiation or consultation – but nothing else

trade secret
must be secret information or a secret process which is specific to the employer and the revealing of which may damage the employer – so can be protected in a restraint of trade clause but the employee cannot prevent the employee on leaving from merely using the expertise and knowledge that is generic to the type of work

trade union
an organisation of employees for the purposes of collective bargaining and collective action for the protection of employees and to advance their working conditions

transfer of undertakings
a sale or other disposition of a business

transferee

the employer who has received the business or organisation from another party the transferor

transferor

the employer who has transferred the business or organisation to another party the transferee

transsexual

a person who has undergone or who is undergoing gender reassignment

truck

a method of paying wages other than by cash, for instance with tokens to be spent in a shop owned by the employer, common during the Industrial Revolution and abolished in 1831

unfair dismissal

a dismissal which is one of a list of circumstances in which the dismissal is automatically unfair or a dismissal where though the reason for the dismissal falls within a list of reasons which is identified in statute as potentially fair is nevertheless not fair in fact

unilateral variation

changes to the terms of the employment contract by the employer without any consultation with or agreement by the employees

variation of contract

where changes are made to the contract – this could be to reflect changes in the way in which the work is done but also changes in conditions of work – can be bilateral where both the employer and employee agree to the variation or can be unilateral where the employer makes a change without consultation with or the agreement of the workforce which in general is a breach of contract by the employer

vicarious liability

liability for the tortious acts or omission of another person – in most cases of an employer for the wrongs of an employee

victimisation

a type of prohibited conduct in discrimination law which is where the employer subjects the employee to some detriment for example dismissal because the employee has asserted his rights not to be discriminated against for instance by seeking advice or bringing action in a tribunal

visual display units (VDUs)

monitors or other televisual devices – in a work context will commonly be computer monitors

volenti non fit injuria

a defence meaning 'voluntary assumption of a risk' – only applies if the claimant understands the precise risk and is able to exercise free will in accepting it

wages

the form of remuneration received by employees for the work that they do

work equipment

any machinery tools or other equipment at work

work of equal value

work done by a woman which is of the same value to the employer as that done by named men even though the work is not the same work

worker

a wider definition than employee and involves persons who have some employment protections but not the full range available to employees

works rules

rules on how the employee does his work or the circumstances in which the work is done – can involve a variety of things but are generally not contractual in nature so give the employer greater freedom to vary them

wrongful dismissal

a common law remedy involving a breach of contract by the employer who fails to give the proper notice of dismissal or where the contract identifies the only circumstances in which a dismissal can occur and the employer dismisses for a different reason

Index